T0189079

Lecture Notes in Artificial Intelligence 12414

Subseries of Lecture Notes in Computer Science

Series Editors

Randy Goebel
University of Alberta, Edmonton, Canada
Yuzuru Tanaka
Hokkaido University, Sapporo, Japan
Wolfgang Wahlster
DFKI and Saarland University, Saarbrücken, Germany

Founding Editor

Jörg Siekmann
DFKI and Saarland University, Saarbrücken, Germany

More information about this subseries at http://www.springer.com/series/1244

Matteo Baldoni · Stefania Bandini (Eds.)

AIxIA 2020 – Advances in Artificial Intelligence

XIXth International Conference
of the Italian Association for Artificial Intelligence
Virtual Event, November 25–27, 2020
Revised Selected Papers

 Springer

Editors
Matteo Baldoni 🆔
Università degli Studi di Torino
Turin, Italy

Stefania Bandini 🆔
Department of Informatics, Systems and C
University of Milano-Bicocca
Milan, Italy

ISSN 0302-9743   ISSN 1611-3349   (electronic)
Lecture Notes in Artificial Intelligence
ISBN 978-3-030-77090-7   ISBN 978-3-030-77091-4   (eBook)
https://doi.org/10.1007/978-3-030-77091-4

LNCS Sublibrary: SL7 – Artificial Intelligence

This Springer imprint is published by the registered company Springer Nature Switzerland AG
The registered company address is: Gewerbestrasse 11, 6330 Cham, Switzerland

Preface

The 19th International Conference of the Italian Association for Artificial Intelligence, AIxIA 2020 (reboot), was organized by the Associazione Italiana per l'Intelligenza Artificiale, which is a non-profit scientific society founded in 1998 devoted to the promotion of Artificial Intelligence. The society aims at increasing the public awareness of Artificial Intelligence, encouraging teaching and promoting research in the field.

AIxIA 2020 (reboot) focused on the communities working on the various research areas of the field; it hosted 10 workshops with submission deadlines set for the late summer of 2020. Keynote speakers, open events, and award events completed the conference. AIxIA 2020 (reboot) was held virtually during November 25–27, 2020, "anywhere" in the world, rather than in a single physical place: the event was open to all members of the organizing association and its program was (and still is) accessible on the internet (https://aixia2020.di.unito.it/).

The conference covered broadly the many aspects of theoretical and applied Artificial Intelligence through a series of workshops dedicated to specific topics:

- 9th Italian Workshop on Machine Learning and Data Mining, MLDM.it 2020, organized by Alessio Micheli and Claudio Gallicchio;
- Italian Workshop on Explainable Artificial Intelligence, XAI.it 2020, organized by Daniele Magazzeni, Cataldo Musto, Salvatore Ruggieri, and Giovanni Semeraro;
- Workshop on Evolutionary and Population-based Optimization, WEPO 2020, organized by Andrea De Lorenzo and Luca Manzoni;
- 4th Workshop on Advances In Argumentation In Artificial Intelligence, AI^3 2020, organized by Bettina Fazzinga, Filippo Furfaro, and Francesco Parisi;
- 8th Italian Workshop on Planning and Scheduling, IPS 2020, organized by Riccardo De Benedictis, Enrico Scala, Ivan Serina, Andrea Micheli, and Alessandro Umbrico;
- 7th Italian Workshop on Artificial Intelligence and Robotics, AIRO 2020, organized by Salvatore Anzalone, Luca Buoncompagni, Alberto Castellini, and Alberto Finzi;
- 4th Workshop on Natural Language for Artificial Intelligence, NL4AI 2020, organized by Pierpaolo Basile, Valerio Basile, Elena Cabrio, and Danilo Croce;
- 27th RCRA International Workshop on Experimental Evaluation of Algorithms for Solving Problems with Combinatorial Explosion, RCRA 2020, organized by Marco Maratea and Mauro Vallati;
- Italian Workshop on Artificial Intelligence for an Ageing Society, AIxAS 2020, organized by Filippo Palumbo, Francesa Gasparini, and Francesca Fracasso;
- AIxIA 2020 Discussion Papers, AIxIA 2020 DP, organized by Andrea Orlandini, Matteo Palmonari, and Giuseppe Vizzari.

Apart from MLDM.it 2020, which was based on invitations, overall the workshops received 89 submissions. Each submission was carefully reviewed by at least three members of the workshop Program Committee. The workshop organizers selected 26 of the best submissions and invited the authors to submit revised and extended versions of their papers, after a second review phase, for inclusion in the post-proceedings volume. The winner of the "Pietro Torasso" award, Popularize Artificial Intelligence (PAI 2020), organized by Matteo Baldoni, Daniela Briola, and Fabio Stella, was also invited to submit an extended version of the paper submitted for the award. In total, 27 papers are included in this post-proceedings.

The conference also included three keynote talks:

- "Responsible Artificial Intelligence", by Carles Sierra, Artificial Intelligence Research Institute (IIIA-CSIC), Spain;
- "No ontology without Ontology: the role of formal ontological analysis in AI (and beyond)", by Nicola Guarino, Consiglio Nazionale delle Ricerche, Trento, Italy;
- "Thinking Fast and Slow in AI", by Francesca Rossi, IBM Research, USA.

The conference hosted three open events:

- "Questioni di Genere in Intelligenza Artificiale", on gender issues in AI, organized by Francesca Alessandra Lisi. The event hosted Sveva Avveduto, emeritus research director at the Consiglio Nazionale delle Ricerche for Research on Population and Social Policies (IRPPS-CNR), and president of "Associazione Donne e Scienza", Giulia Baccarin, entrepreneur, and founder of "MIPU Predictive Hub", Silvana Badaloni, former professor at the Università di Padova, Alessandro Fusacchia, politician and member of the Italian Parliament, Pietro Greco, journalist and writer at "Il Bo Live" from the Università di Padova, Isadora Pei, director of the performing arts collective "AjaRiot", and Francesca Romana Recchia Luciani, a philosopher from the Università degli Studi Bari "Aldo Moro";
- "Insegnamento dell'Intelligenza Artificiale in Italia, dibattito aperto per una didattica di qualità", organized by Matteo Baldoni and Francesco Ricca. The event hosted Giovanni Adorni, president of AICA, Stefano Bistarelli, member of "Commissione didattica GRIN`", Giuseppe De Giacomo, Università La Sapienza, CLAIRE, and the CINI AIIS Lab, Maurizio Gabbrielli, chair of "Consiglio di Studi in Intelligenza Artificiale" from the Università di Bologna, Enrico Nardelli, president of Informatics Europe, and Piero Poccianti, president of AIxIA;
- "Etica dell'Intelligenza Artificiale o Etica Umana? Voce AI ragazzi", organized by Piero Poccianti. The event hosted Emanuela Girardi, founder of "Pop Ai" and AI expert at MiSE, Dino Pedreschi, from the Università di Pisa and member of the GPAI Global Partnership on AI, Anna Pettini, from the Università degli Studi di Firenze, Don Luca Peyron, director of the "Apostolato Digitale di Torino", Piero Poccianti, president of AIxIA, Cristina Pozzi, cofounder and CEO of Impactscool and Young Global Leader of WEF, and Francesca Rossi, the AI ethics global leader at IBM Research. The panel were interviewed by students from ISIS Gobetti-Volta and members of Progetto RApP along with undergraduate students selected by Impactscool.

Finally, the conference hosted the "Marco Cadoli" Ph.D. Thesis Award and the "Leonardo Lesmo" M.Sc. Thesis Award, organized by Stefania Costantini and Viviana Mascardi. The winner of the "Marco Cadoli" Ph.D. Thesis Award, Giuseppe Marra, and of the "Leonardo Lesmo" M.Sc. Thesis Award, Emanuele Albini, gave a talk at the conference.

We would like to thank all individuals, institutions, and sponsors that supported AIxIA 2020 (reboot), in particular the Artificial Intelligence Journal for the "Funding Opportunities for Promoting AI Research" program, the Università degli Studi di Torino for offering the web conference tool, and the Dipartimento di Informatica of the Università degli Studi di Torino for the website hosting. We thank the authors for submitting high-quality research papers. We are indebted to the workshop program committees members and additional reviewers for spending their valuable time by providing careful reviews and recommendations on the submissions, the workshop organizers, the respective research communities (that were the soul of this conference edition), and all the members of the organizations involved in the conference. Finally, a special thanks to Piero Poccianti, the president of the Associazione Italiana per l'Intelligenza Artificiale.

March 2021

Matteo Baldoni
Stefania Bandini

Organization

General Chairs

Matteo Baldoni — Università degli Studi di Torino, Italy
Stefania Bandini — Università degli Studi di Milano-Bicocca, Italy
Piero Poccianti — Associazione Italiana per l'Intelligenza Artificiale, Italy

Workshop Chairs

Davide Ciucci — Università degli Studi di Milano-Bicocca, Italy
Gabriella Cortellessa — Consiglio Nazionale delle Ricerche, Roma, Italy
Rafael Peñaloza — Università degli Studi di Milano-Bicocca, Italy

Open Events Chairs

Matteo Baldoni — Università degli Studi di Torino, Italy
Francesca Alessandra Lisi — Università degli Studi di Bari "Aldo Moro", Italy
Piero Poccianti — Associazione Italiana per l'Intelligenza Artificiale, Italy
Francesco Ricca — Università della Calabria, Italy

Awards Chairs

Daniela Briola — Università degli Studi di Milano-Bicocca, Italy
Stefania Costantini — Università degli Studi dell'Aquila, Italy
Viviana Mascardi — Università degli Studi di Genova, Italy
Fabio Stella — Università degli Studi di Milano-Bicocca, Italy

Organization Chair

Matteo Baldoni — Università degli Studi di Torino, Italy

Financial and Sponsorship Chairs

Roberto Micalizio — Università degli Studi di Torino, Italy
Stefano Ferilli — Università degli Studi di Bari "Aldo Moro", Italy

Web Chair

Stefano Tedeschi — Università degli Studi di Torino, Italy

9th Italian Workshop on Machine Learning and Data Mining (MLDM.it 2020) – Organizers

Alessio Micheli	Università di Pisa, Italy
Claudio Gallicchio	Università di Pisa, Italy

Italian Workshop on Explainable Artificial Intelligence (XAI.it 2020) – Organizers

Daniele Magazzeni	J. P. Morgan AI Research, UK
Cataldo Musto	Università degli Studi di Bari "Aldo Moro", Italy
Salvatore Ruggieri	Università di Pisa, Italy
Giovanni Semeraro	Università degli Studi di Bari "Aldo Moro", Italy

Workshop on Evolutionary and Population-Based Optimization (WEPO 2020) – Organizers

Andrea De Lorenzo	Università degli Studi di Trieste, Italy
Luca Manzoni	Università degli Studi di Trieste, Italy

4th Workshop on Advances In Argumentation In Artificial Intelligence (AI^3 2020) – Organizers

Bettina Fazzinga	Consiglio Nazionale delle Ricerche, Rende, Italy
Filippo Furfaro	Università della Calabria, Italy
Francesco Parisi	Università della Calabria, Italy

8th Italian Workshop on Planning and Scheduling (IPS 2020) – Organizers

Riccardo De Benedictis	Consiglio Nazionale delle Ricerche, Roma, Italy
Enrico Scala	Università degli Studi di Brescia, Italy
Ivan Serina	Università degli Studi di Brescia, Italy
Andrea Micheli	Fondazione Bruno Kessler, Italy
Alessandro Umbrico	Consiglio Nazionale delle Ricerche, Roma, Italy

7th Italian Workshop on Artificial Intelligence and Robotics (AIRO 2020) – Organizers

Salvatore Anzalone	Université Paris 8, France
Luca Buoncompagni	Università degli Studi di Genova, Italy
Alberto Castellini	Università di Verona, Italy
Alberto Finzi	Università di Napoli "Federico II", Italy

4th Workshop on Natural Language for Artificial Intelligence (NL4AI-2020) – Organizers

Pierpaolo Basile — Università degli Studi di Bari "Aldo Moro", Italy
Valerio Basile — Università degli Studi di Torino, Italy
Elena Cabrio — Universite Cote d'Azur, France
Danilo Croce — Università degli Studi di Roma "Tor Vergata", Italy

27th RCRA International Workshop on Experimental Evaluation of Algorithms for Solving Problems with Combinatorial Explosion (RCRA 2020) – Organizers

Marco Maratea — Università degli Studi di Genova, Italy
Mauro Vallati — University of Huddersfield, UK

Italian Workshop on Artificial Intelligence for an Ageing Society (AIxAS 2020) – Organizers

Filippo Palumbo — Consiglio Nazionale delle Ricerche, Pisa, Italy
Francesa Gasparini — Università degli Studi di Milano-Bicocca, Italy
Francesca Fracasso — Consiglio Nazionale delle Ricerche, Roma, Italy

AIxIA 2020 Discussion Papers (AIxIA 2020 DP) – Organizers

Andrea Orlandini — Consiglio Nazionale delle Ricerche, Roma, Italy
Matteo Palmonari — Università degli Studi di Milano-Bicocca, Italy
Giuseppe Vizzari — Università degli Studi di Milano-Bicocca, Italy

Popularize Artificial Intelligence – "Pietro Torasso" Award (PAI 2020) – Organizers

Matteo Baldoni — Università degli Studi di Torino, Italy
Daniela Briola — Università degli Studi di Milano-Bicocca, Italy
Fabio Stella — Università degli Studi di Milano-Bicocca, Italy

AIxIA Steering Committee

Davide Bacciu — Università di Pisa, Italy
Matteo Baldoni — Università degli Studi di Torino, Italy
Roberto Basili — Università degli Studi di Roma "Tor Vergata", Italy
Amedeo Cesta — Consiglio Nazionale delle Ricerche, Roma, Italy
Federico Chesani — Alma Mater Studiorum – Università di Bologna, Italy
Stefania Costantini — Università degli Studi dell'Aquila, Italy
Stefano Ferilli — Università degli Studi di Bari "Aldo Moro", Italy
Nicola Gatti — Politecnico di Milano, Italy

Chiara Ghidini	Fondazione Bruno Kessler, Italy
Manuela Girardi	Pop Ai, Italy
Francesca Alessandra Lisi	Università degli Studi di Bari "Aldo Moro", Italy
Marco Maratea	Università degli Studi di Genova, Italy
Piero Poccianti	Associazione Italiana per l'Intelligenza Artificiale, Italy
Francesco Ricca	Università della Calabria, Italy
Fabrizio Riguzzi	Università degli Studi di Ferrara, Italy
Francesco Ulivi	Consorzio Operativo Gruppo MPS, Italy

Reviewers

Aiello, Luca Maria
Alfano, Gianvincenzo
Attardi, Giuseppe
Attaullah, Buriro
Atutxa, Aitziber
Bacciu, Davide
Baioletti, Marco
Baldoni, Matteo
Barbulescu, Laura
Baroni, Pietro
Barsocchi, Paolo
Barták, Roman
Basile, Pierpaolo
Basile, Valerio
Basili, Roberto
Bianchi, Federico
Bianco, Simone
Bistarelli, Stefano
Bodria, Francesco
Boratto, Ludovico
Borghese, Alberto
Bosco, Cristina
Brunato, Dominique
Cabalar, Pedro
Cacace, Jonathan
Caccavale, Riccardo
Cagnoni, Stefano
Calegari, Roberta
Calimeri, Francesco
Casiddu, Niccolò
Castelli, Mauro
Cavallo, Filippo
Cena, Federica
Cerutti, Federico

Cesta, Amedeo
Conati, Cristina
Confalonieri, Roberto
Correa da Silva, Flavio S.
Cortellessa, Gabriella
Cosentino, Sarah
Costantini, Stefania
Cremonesi, Paolo
Cutugno, Francesco
D'Agostino, Marcello
Daini, Roberta
De Benedictis, Riccardo
De Carolis, Berardina Nadja
Dell'Orletta, Felice
Della Penna, Giuseppe
Dodaro, Carmine
Dovier, Agostino
Dragoni, Mauro
Fandinno, Jorge
Farinelli, Alessandro
Ferilli, Stefano
Fersini, Elisabetta
Flesca, Sergio
Formisano, Andrea
Fratini, Simone
Gadducci, Fabio
Gasparetti, Fabio
Gavanelli, Marco
Geffner, Hector
Giacomin, Massimiliano
Gigante, Nicola
Giltri, Marta
Giuliani, Alessandro
Giunchiglia, Enrico

Grasso, Floriana
Greco, Sergio
Grossi, Davide
Guidotti, Riccardo
Guzmán, César
Iovine, Andrea
Kalimeri, Kyriaki
Kudo, Hiroko
Lanza, Francesco
Lenci, Alessandro
Leone, Alessandro
Lieto, Antonio
Lippi, Marco
Lisi, Francesca Alessandra
Macagno, Fabrizio
Mancini, Toni
Maratea, Marco
Marelli, Marco
Mariot, Luca
Marques-Silva, Joao
Mayer, Tobias
Mazzei, Alessandro
McCluskey, Lee
McGillivray, Barbara
Medvet, Eric
Mensa, Enrico
Mercorio, Fabio
Mitrović, Jelena
Monreale, Anna
Montani, Stefania
Monti, Johanna
Nardi, Daniele
Nissim, Malvina
Nobile, Marco S.
Nozza, Debora
Oddi, Angelo
Omicini, Andrea
Orlandini, Andrea
Parkinson, Simon
Passerini, Andrea
Percassi, Francesco

Pilato, Giovanni
Pirrone, Roberto
Policella, Nicola
Polignano, Marco
Pozzato, Gianluca
Proietti, Carlo
Pulina, Luca
Radicioni, Daniele P.
Rapp, Amon
Rasconi, Riccardo
Refanidis, Ioannis
Restocchi, Valerio
Ricca, Francesco
Rossiello, Gaetano
Saetti, Alessandro
Saibene, Aurora
Sansonetti, Giuseppe
Santini, Francesco
Santucci, Valentino
Sartor, Gabriele
Scala, Enrico
Schaerf, Andrea
Serina, Ivan
Setzu, Mattia
Silva, Sara
Spano, Lucio Davide
Stella, Fabio
Taticchi, Carlo
Teso, Stefano
Toniolo, Alice
Trujillo, Leonardo
Vallati, Mauro
Vanneschi, Leonardo
Vargiu, Eloisa
Varni, Giovanna
Venable, Kristen Brent
Villata, Serena
Virgolin, Marco
Wallner, Johannes
Woltran, Stefan
Zanzotto, Fabio Massimo

Contents

Explainable Artificial Intelligence

Exploring Contextual Importance and Utility in Explaining Affect Detection

Nazanin Fouladgar[1]([✉]), Marjan Alirezaie[2], and Kary Främling[1,3]

[1] Department of Computing Science, Umeå University, Umeå, Sweden
nazanin@cs.umu.se, kary.framling@umu.se
[2] Center for Applied Autonomous Sensor Systems, Örebro University,
Örebro, Sweden
marjan.alirezaie@oru.se
[3] School of Science and Technology, Aalto University, Espoo, Finland

Abstract. By the ubiquitous usage of machine learning models with their inherent black-box nature, the necessity of explaining the decisions made by these models has become crucial. Although outcome explanation has been recently taken into account as a solution to the transparency issue in many areas, affect computing is one of the domains with the least dedicated effort on the practice of explainable AI, particularly over different machine learning models. The aim of this work is to evaluate the outcome explanations of two black-box models, namely neural network (NN) and linear discriminant analysis (LDA), to understand individuals affective states measured by wearable sensors. Emphasizing on context-aware decision explanations of these models, the two concepts of Contextual Importance (CI) and Contextual Utility (CU) are employed as a model-agnostic outcome explanation approach. We conduct our experiments on the two multimodal affect computing datasets, namely WESAD and MAHNOB-HCI. The results of applying a neural-based model on the first dataset reveal that the electrodermal activity, respiration as well as accelerometer sensors contribute significantly in the detection of "meditation" state for a particular participant. However, the respiration sensor does not intervene in the LDA decision of the same state. On the course of second dataset and the neural network model, the importance and utility of electrocardiogram and respiration sensors are shown as the dominant features in the detection of an individual "surprised" state, while the LDA model does not rely on the respiration sensor to detect this mental state.

Keywords: Explainable AI · Affect detection · Black-Box decision · Contextual importance and utility

1 Introduction

The rapid growth of producing wearable sensors in health-related applications and the success of machine learning (ML) methods in analysing the sensors data

© Springer Nature Switzerland AG 2021
M. Baldoni and S. Bandini (Eds.): AIxIA 2020, LNAI 12414, pp. 3–18, 2021.
https://doi.org/10.1007/978-3-030-73065-9_1

are incontrovertible. These facilities have revolutionized the doctor-patients relationships [17] and provided continuous monitoring of patients to a considerable degree [2]. In some situations, an individual could also follow his/her well-being status independent of a third-party interventions. Nevertheless, the extent of trust to such models is questionable as the advanced artificial intelligence (AI) methods lack transparency intrinsically. Therefore, relying solely on such methods is not recommended, particularly in critical decision-making processes [16]. From the view of health practitioners, their decisions could be finalized more confidently if they are provided with a concrete outcome explanation of AI models. Moreover, from the end-users perspective, explainable AI (XAI) can influence their own follow-up schedule.

Capitalizing these advantages, XAI has recently appealed a great attention among research communities as well as industries [4,11]. Some scholars have theoretically scrutinized the XAI potentiality [16,26] on the lens of multidisciplinary fields, while others made efforts to unveil the practical aspects of XAI [5,12]. Moreover, in a very recent work [8], XAI in theory and practice has been reconciled and reviewed briefly. As mentioned before, the main concern of both aspects lies on the ground of intelligent systems transparency and thereby appealing the experts or end-users trust. Addressing the aforementioned issues, the XAI applicability is pinpointed in a vast body of works such as tutoring [21], fault diagnosis [3] as well as healthcare [19].

Despite the research efforts in equipping ML models of different domains with XAI techniques, the intersection of XAI and affect computing is still immature and there are open rooms for researchers of this area. In an extension to our previous work [7], we study the outcome explanations of two machine learning models, namely neural network (NN) and linear discriminant analysis (LDA), designed to classify human state-of-mind. We employ two datasets including WESAD [23], and MAHNOB-HCI [25], as publicly and academically available datasets respectively, in the realm of multi-modal affect computing (see Sect. 4). Our main focus is on signal-level explanations, relying on the two concepts of Contextual Importance (CI) and Contextual Utility (CU) proposed by Främling [10]. Applying (CI) and (CU), we represent how important and favorable different sensors (features) are for the decision of each examined model. Both CI and CU present numerical values applicable in textual and visual representations and thereby understandable to professionals and end-users.

The rest of paper is organized as follows: a brief review of the recent corpus of black-box outcome explanation in health-related works is given in Sect. 2. We investigate the CI and CU concepts in Sect. 3. After introducing the datasets and their specification in Sect. 4, we present the results in Sect. 5 which is followed by the conclusion and discussion about the future works in Sect. 6.

2   Background

Contribution of AI in healthcare is mainly about certain practices including diagnosis upon medical imaging or tabular data samples. These diagnosis are expected to be transparent and explainable to its users such as physicians, other medical practitioners and ideally the patients. Singh et al. [24] have categorized different methods addressing the explainability upon medical image analysis process, into attribution and non-attribution based methods.

Attribution-based methods are able to determine the contribution of an input feature to a target output neuron (of the correct class) in a classification process accomplished by a convolutional neural network (CNN). Due to their ease of use, such methods are employed upon brain imaging in Alzheimer classification task [6], retinal imaging to assist diabetic retinopathy [22] and also breast imaging in estrogen receptor classification task [20].

Unlike the attribution-based methods, in non-attribution based or post-model, another methodology than the original model is utilized on the given problem, mainly independent of the latter model attributes [24]. As some examples of non-attribution based methods used for the purpose of output explanation, we can refer to concept vectors and also textual justification [24]. Testing Concept Activation Vectors (TCAV) [27] is a concept vector method, capable of explaining the features learned by different layers to the domain experts by taking the directional derivative of the network in the concept space. In the context of text justification, these models generate linguistic outputs that justify the classifier's output in an understanding way for both the expert users and patients. Lee. et al. [14] applied a justification model to generate textual explanation associated with a heat-map for breast classification task.

Apart from explanations in medical imaging, some studies in the literature have focused on the explainability of AI methods prediction upon tabular physiological and clinical data. The work in [18] examined three interpretable models, mainly Generalized Linear Model, Decision Tree and Random Forest, on electro-cardiogram data (ECG) for the purpose of heart beat classification. Under the magnitude of early clinical prediction, Lauritsen et al. [13] utilized a post-model explanation module, decomposing the outputs of a temporal convolutional network into clinical parameters. Deep Taylor Decomposition (DTD) was the main tool of this module, providing the relevance explanation of prediction in a Layer-wise Relevance Propagation (LRP) manner. Among few works addressing the output explanation of human affect detection with tabular physiological data, the authors in [15] suggested two explanation components in signal- and sensor-level. The signal-level explanation was achieved by removing one of the signals iteratively from the prediction process while the sensor-level explanation was provided by applying entropy criterion to calculate the feature importance of two chest- and wrist-worn sensors. Similar to our work, the applied dataset was relied on WESAD. However, different from ours, this work could not provide the importance extent of the chest-worn signals in a specific context.

3   Contextual Importance and Contextual Utility

One of the earliest work in the realm of black-box outcome explanation was proposed by Främling [10] in 1996. He argued that expert systems had the main contribution to explain any decisions. He added, however these systems were mainly rule-based and any changes in the input values result in firing a set of rules in a discrete manner. The gap of representing the outcomes of continuous real-valued functions was the reason to go beyond symbolic reasoning models.

The notions of *Contextual Importance* (*CI*) and *Contextual Utility* (*CU*) were proposed to explain the neural networks output in the context of Multiple Criteria Decision Making (MCDM). In MCDM, decisions are established on a consensus between different stakeholders preferences [9]. The stakeholders often consist of a group of people and/or an abstract entity (e.g. economy), whose preferences are highly subjective and more likely form a non-linear and continuous function. To provide a convenient explanation of these functions in MCDM, it was reasonable to explore how important each criterion was and to what extent it was favorable in a specific context. These were the main reasons pushing the two concepts of *CI* and *CU* forward. The concepts are formulated as following:

$$CI = \frac{Cmax_x(C_i) - Cmin_x(C_i)}{absmax - absmin} \tag{1}$$

$$CU = \frac{y_{ij} - Cmin_x(C_i)}{Cmax_x(C_i) - Cmin_x(C_i)} \tag{2}$$

Where C_i is the ith context (specific input of black-box referring as 'Case' in Sect. 5), y_{ij} is the value of jth output (class probability) with respect to the context C_i, $Cmax_x(C_i)$ and $Cmin_x(C_i)$ are the maximum and minimum values indicating the range of output values observed by varying each attribute x of context C_i, $absmax = 1$ and $absmin = 0$ are also the maximum and minimum values indicating the range of jth output (the class probability value).

We highlight that *CI* and *CU* return numerical values which allow us to represent the explanations to the end-users in the form of visual (e.g., in the form of graphs) or textual outputs.

4   Dataset Description and Preprocessing

We have tried two different datasets in order to evaluate our results. The first data set is WESAD which is publicly available and applicable for the purpose of multi-modal sensory analysis as well as detecting multiple affective states [23]. According to the dataset's protocol, there are three main affective states in addition to the *baseline* state, including *stress*, *amusement* and *meditation*. These states have been examined on 15 different subjects, wearing RespiBAN Professional device on the chest and Empatica E4 device on the wrist. The former encompasses of data collected from eight different signals, namely electrocardiogram (ECG), electromyogram (EMG), electrodermal activity (EDA), temperature (TEMP), respiration (RESP) and three-axes accelerometer (ACC0, ACC1, ACC2), while the latter fetches blood volume pulse (BVP), EDA, TEMP, and accelerometer signals data. All RespiBAN data are sampled under 700 HZ, however the sampling rates are different among Empatica E4 signals. BVP, EDA and

TEMP data have been recorded 64 Hz, 4 Hz, 32 Hz respectively. Validating the study protocols, a supplementary of five self-reports in terms of questionnaire were also provided for each subject.

The WESAD dataset consists of around 4 million instances for each subject and in total 60 million samples for all the 15 subjects. Due to the time complexity of processing such a large dataset, we only extract the chest-worn signals of one participant to detect the four aforementioned affective states. After down-sampling the signals into 10 HZ we end up with 29350 data instances for the selected participant. One of the major properties of WESAD is that it is highly imbalanced. The highest number of samples belongs to the baseline state while the lowest amount refers to the amusement state. More specifically, the data includes the following ranges: [0–11400] labeled as baseline state, [11400–17800] labeled as stress state, [17800–21550] labeled as amusement state and the rest refers to the meditation state of our selected participant.

The second dataset is MAHNOB-HCI [25], only available to academia community with the aim of emotion recognition and multimedia tagging studies. The dataset consists of two trials collecting multimodal physiological sensor data as well as facial expression, audio signals and eye gaze data of 27 participants. The physiological signals refer to 32 electroencephalogram (EEG) channels, two ECG electrodes attached to the chest upper right (ECG1) and left (ECG2) corners below the clavicle bones as well as one ECG electrode placed at abdomn below the last rib (ECG3), two galvanic skin response (GSR) positioning on the distal phalanges of the middle (GSR1) and index fingers (GSR2), a RESP belt around the abdomen and a skin temperature (TEMP) placed at little finger. All signals except EEG are accessible to the end-user in 256 HZ sampling rate. To gather this data, 20 video clips were used to stimulate the participants' emotions in the first trial while 28 images and 14 video fragments were shown to partici-pants, tagged by either correct or incorrect words in the second trial. Moreover, the participants feedback were collected after each stimuli to provide the videos annotations as well as agreement or disagreements of tags. In the first trial, 9 emotional labels such as *amusement, happiness* and *surprised* were under focus while in the second trial only two modes of tag correctness or incorrectness were under consideration. Due to the large size of the dataset, we only extracted ECG1, ECG2, ECG3, GSR1, GSR2, RESP and TEMP data of one participant. Moreover, we focused only on the first trial of this dataset with three emotional states, mainly amusement, happiness and surprised for the purpose of classifica-tion task. The accordant data accounts for 1920 instances after downsampling the signals to 10 HZ sampling rate.

5   Outcome Explanations

One of our examined black-box models to classify human affective states is a neu-ral network, consisting of one hidden layer with 100 units. The basic idea behind the neural-based networks is their capability of approximating non-linear but differentiable variations. This capability makes local gradients meaningful and thereby the importance of each input feature explainable. Linear discriminant analysis is appointed as the second black-box model of this study, profound in considering the statistical properties of data in the classification process. After training these models on the data of specific participant in WESAD, the average accuracies of 0.92 and 0.91 are achieved in the neural network and LDA models, respectively. Following the same procedure on the second dataset, the neural network and LDA showed a performance of 0.99 and 1.0 respectively, in terms of accuracy.

In order to provide local outcome explanations of these models, we randomly choose an input instance (referring to 'Case' in this study) of an individual data in each dataset. Assuming the following 'Case' in WESAD: 0.898 (ACC0), -0.003(ACC1), -0.179 (ACC2), -0.003 (ECG), 7.078 (EDA), 0.001 (EMG), 32.97 (TEMP), -0.865 (RESP), the trained neural network and LDA models result in "meditation" state (class) as the classification output. The following class probabilities are achieved for each model respectively: meditation class 97% and 99%, baseline class 0.5% and 0%, stress class 0.1% and 0%, and amusement class 1% and 0%. The same procedure could verify the state of 'Case' in MAHNOB-HCI dataset. Here, the 'Case' is randomly chosen as: -849000 (ECG1), -544000 (ECG2), -777000 (ECG3), 2900000 (GSR1), 90 (GSR2), -1560000 (RESP), 26078 (TEMP) from an individual data. The classification output of both models on this specific instance yields to "surprised" state with the highest probability (100%), and to amusement and happiness states with the lowest probability (0%) in both models.

According to the CI and CU formulas, the values of $Cmax_x$ and $Cmin_x$ are required to examine the explanations. However, estimating $Cmax_x$ and $Cmin_x$ is not a trivial process. To simplify the process, we have applied Monte-Carlo simulation and generated 100 random samples for each feature. This process provides varying in each feature of context ('Case') every time and allows to find out how considerable the output has been changed. The samples are uniformly distributed within the range of minimum and maximum values of each sensor data in the training set. To calculate the numerical values of $Cmin_x$ and $Cmax_x$ and later CI and CU, we follow an iterative process. Each time, we modify the values of one sensor data by one of the 100 generated samples while keeping the data of other sensors unchanged. Later, we calculate the class probability of each sample by our neural network and LDA models separately. Therefore, the knowledge about the minimum and maximum class probability within each sensor is obtained, implying for $Cmin_x$ and $Cmax_x$ in the context of our specific instance. Accordingly, the values of CI and CU could be calculated. The process is repeated eight times to extract the appropriate values for all the eight signals of our problem space in the first dataset. In other words, eight different $Cmin_x$, $Cmax_x$, CI and CU values are generated in total with respect to each model. The same procedure is dominated on the second dataset, yet generating seven $Cmin_x$, $Cmax_x$, CI and CU values in accordance with seven sensors of MAHNOB-HCI dataset for each model. In all the iterations, the *absmin* and *absmax* values in Eq. 1 are set to 0 and 1 respectively, indicating all possible values for the class probability (output). Moreover, CI and CU values range between [0–1]. To be more readable, the values of CI and CU are then converted to the percentage scale.

5.1   Generated Explanation on WESAD

Table 1 demonstrates the numerical results of aforementioned iterative process in WESAD for both the neural network and LDA models. In addition, Fig. 1 shows visual representations of how important and favorable the sensors are in the detection of "meditation", the predicted class of our 'Case' by both models.

The results of neural network reveal that ACC1, ACC2, EDA and RESP are highly important and favorable sensors contributing in the outcome class, while the other sensors data except TEMP could be ignored within the decision making process (see Figs. 1(a) and 1(b)). In theory, the former sensors produce CI and CU values approximately to 100%, whereas the latter ones provide CI values around zero in spite of (highly) favorable utilities. In practice, the importance of EDA, TEMP and RESP sensors could be justified as the meditation state had been designed to de-excite participants after exciting them in the stress and amusement states. This situation results in either lower average conductance changes at the skin surface or lower variation in temperature and breathing. Similar argument could be true for ACC1 and ACC2 to differentiate the baseline state from meditation since the participants in general were allowed to sit and stand in baseline while only to sit in a comfortable position in the meditation state.

We also observe that ACC1, ACC2 and EDA intervene significantly in the detection of "meditation" state by the LDA model, similar to the results of neural network. These sensors show both the CI and CU values of 100% (see Fig. 1(c) and 1(d)). The values indicate the high change of outcome w.r.t. these sensors and the high contribution extent of these features of "Case" w.r.t. the change. However, despite the high/rather high contributions of RESP and TEMP sensors in the outcome of neural network, they exclude their intervention in case of LDA model. That is because LDA employs the global structure information of the total training data to determine the linear discriminant vectors [1], and thereby the model shows powerless when the statistical patterns of different classes are fairly similar. Clarifying this argument, we depicted the distribution of TEMP data, as an example, in the state of stress and meditation in Fig. 2. Assuming the training set consists of these two states, LDA fails to produce a linear discriminant vector separating the classes. On the other hand, such LDA characteristic leads to the contribution of ACC0 in the model outcome.

In a more granular level, Figs. 3 and 4 illustrate the sensors probability variations within the "meditation" class, in the neural network and LDA models respectively. The red dot point in all subfigures stands for the 'Case' sample. The 'Case' should be located somewhere between the $Cmin_x$ and $Cmax_x$, comparable with synthetically generated samples. Such location preserves the relative nature of CU concept. The closer the 'Case' to $Cmax_x$, the higher utility the sensor has, and in contrary, the farther the 'Case' from $Cmax_x$ (closer to

Table 1. Numerical results of models outcome explanation related to WESAD

		ACC0	ACC1	ACC2	ECG	EDA	EMG	TEMP	RESP
Sample		0.898	−0.003	−0.179	−0.003	7.078	0.001	32.97	−0.865
NN	Cmin	0.933	0.0	0.0	0.975	0.0	0.823	0.0	0.0
	Cmax	0.999	0.978	0.975	0.985	0.999	0.990	0.565	0.994
	CI%	7%	98%	98%	1%	100%	17%	57%	99%
	CU%	71%	100%	100%	56%	98%	94%	100%	99%
LDA	Cmin	0.0	0.0	0.0	0.998	0.0	0.997	0.0	0.993
	Cmax	0.999	0.999	0.999	0.999	0.999	0.999	0.999	0.999
	CI%	100%	100%	100%	0%	100%	0.1%	0%	0.6%
	CU%	100%	100%	100%	54%	100%	89%	100%	88%

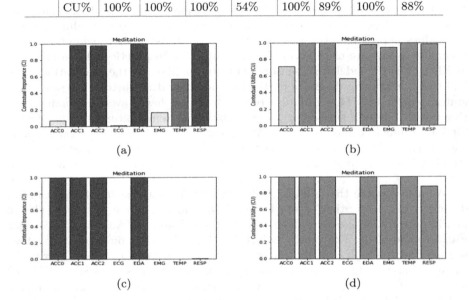

Fig. 1. (a) CI and (b) CU values of all sensors in meditation state, detected by neural network in WESAD, and (c) CI and (d) CU values of all sensors in meditation state, detected by LDA in WESAD

$Cmin_x$), the lower value for CU. Nevertheless, inferring from Figs. 3(g) and 3(c) as well as Fig. 4(g), the 'Case' probability exceeds $Cmax_x$ in ACC2 and TEMP sensors, basically contradicting our previous argument. To solve this problem, we consider the 'Case' probability equal to $Cmax_x$, however one could define CU with a constraint $y_{ij} < Cmax_x(C_i)$. Moreover, when 'Case' has a lower value than $Cmin_x$, a constraint of $y_{ij} > Cmin_x(C_i)$ enforces the process to produce a random data with at least the same value as the 'Case' probability. Therefore, we reformulate the Eq. 2 as follows:

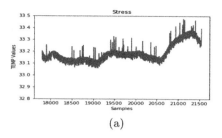 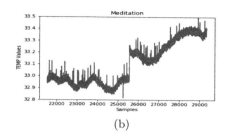

(a)   (b)

Fig. 2. The data distribution of TEMP sensor in (a) stress and (b) meditation states in WESAD

$$CU = \frac{y_{ij} - Cmin_x(C_i)}{Cmax_x(C_i) - Cmin_x(C_i)}$$

(3)

$$\text{s.t.} \quad Cmin_x(C_i) < y_{ij} < Cmax_x(C_i)$$

5.2 Generated Explanation on MAHNOB-HCI

For the second dataset, we followed the same procedure of generating random samples on each sensor. Table 2 shows the importance and utility of sensors in the decision of "surprised" class, based on the CI and CU values calculated using Eqs. 1 and 2. For better clarification, Fig. 5 also visually illustrates the results for each sensor.

In the context of "Case", the values of ECG2 and RESP sensors are highly contributing in the neural network outcome. As shown in Table 2 and correspondingly Figs. 5(a) and 5(b), CI and CU values are 100%. However, other physiological responses do not represent their relative contribution in the decision of "surprised" class, as their CI and CU values are dropped to 0%). We also found that the data samples of "surprised" class are overlapped completely or partially with the samples of other class (es) in all sensors except ECG2 and RESP (see Fig. 6). Therefore, distinguishing this class from the "amusement" and "happiness" class is a challenging task for a neural network, relying on ECG1, ECG3, GSR1, GSR2 in comparison with ECG2 and RESP sensors. Although TEMP sensor seems to influence the model outcome, due to its fairly non-overlapping class samples, the values of CI and CU could not represent a descent explanation for such case.

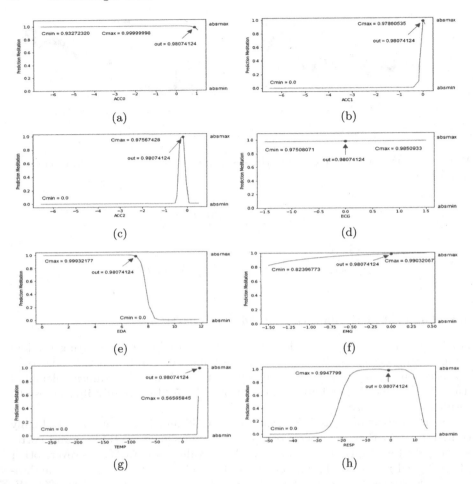

Fig. 3. *Cmin* and *Cmax* values for input variations in (a) ACC0 (b) ACC1 (c) ACC2 (d) ECG (e) EDA (f) EMG (g) TEMP (h) RESP signals with neural network in WESAD

Applying LDA for making decision about the "Case" in MAHNOB-HCI, the provided explanation only relies on the intervention of ECG2 sensor. In other word, the *CI* and *CU* values of this sensor indicate a high importance and utility of 100%. This result is inconsistent with the neural network outcome explanation, as in the latter model, RESP sensor shows a high contribution in the model outcome. This inconsistency partly refers to the intrinsic algorithmic structure of LDA which is sensitive to the outliers [1]. In case of other sensors non-intervention, the same arguments as in the neural network apply well in the LDA as well.

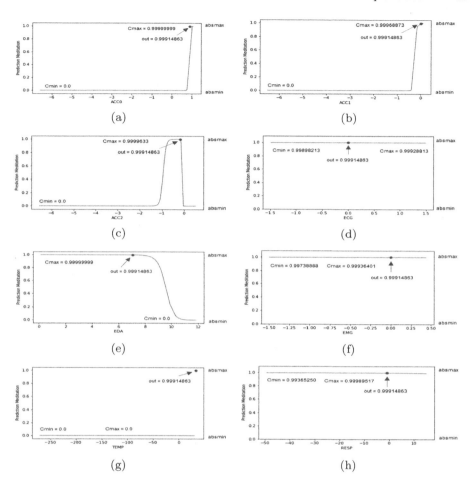

Fig. 4. $Cmin$ and $Cmax$ values for input variations in (a) ACC0 (b) ACC1 (c) ACC2 (d) ECG (e) EDA (f) EMG (g) TEMP (h) RESP signals with LDA in WESAD

Complementary Comments on Experiments:

- To better understand the intensity of CI and CU values, we have used different colors in Figs. 1 and 5. The higher the CI and CU values, the darker the colors become.
- Figures 7(a) and 7(b) represent the textual explanation of CI and CU values for all sensors of WESAD and MAHNOB-HCI datasets respectively, in the neural network model. This representation is based on a conversion (see Table 3) from numerical values to linguistic texts [7].
- We have examined other instances of the same class as "Case" in both datasets and ended up with quite similar results shown in the Tables 1 and 2.

Table 2. Numerical results of models outcome explanation related to MAHNOB-HCI

		ECG1	ECG2	ECG3	GSR1	GSR2	RESP	TEMP
Sample		−849000	−544000	−777000	2900000	90	−1560000	26078
NN	Cmin	1.0	0.0	1.0	1.0	1.0	0.0	1.0
	Cmax	1.0	1.0	1.0	1.0	1.0	1.0	1.0
	CI%	0%	100%	0%	0%	0%	100%	0%
	CU%	0%	100%	0%	0%	0%	100%	0%
LDA	Cmin	1.0	0.0	1.0	1.0	1.0	1.0	1.0
	Cmax	1.0	1.0	1.0	1.0	1.0	1.0	1.0
	CI%	0%	100%	0%	0%	0%	0%	0%
	CU%	0%	100%	0%	0%	0%	0%	0%

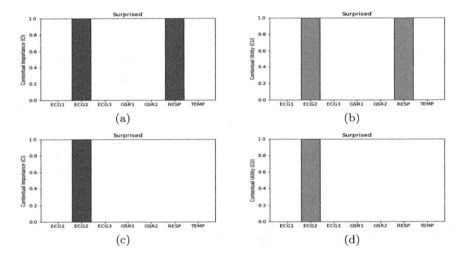

Fig. 5. (a) CI and (b) CU values of all signals in surprised state, detected by neural network in MAHNOB-HCI, and (c) CI and (d) CU values of all signals in surprised state, detected by LDA in MAHNOB-HCI

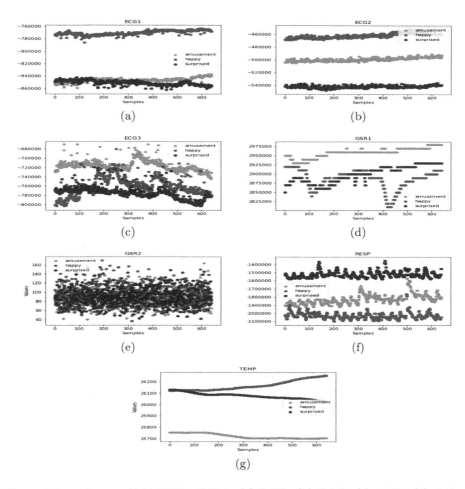

Fig. 6. Three classes of MAHNOB-HCI in (a) ECG1 (b) ECG2 (c) ECG3 (d) GSR1 (e) GSR2 (f) RESP (g) TEMP signals

Table 3. Symbolic representation of the CI and CU values

Degree (d)	Contextual Importance	Contextual Utility
$0 < d \leq 0.25$	Not important	Not favorable
$0.25 < d \leq 0.5$	Important	Unlikely
$0.5 < d \leq 0.75$	Rather important	Favorable
$0.75 < d \leq 1.0$	Highly important	Highly favorable

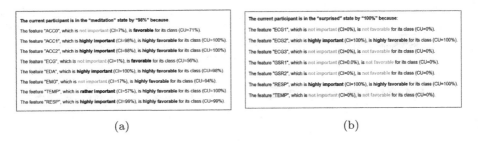

(a)   (b)

Fig. 7. Textual explanation of neural network prediction for each signal in (a) WESAD (b) MAHNOB-HCI

6   Conclusion and Future Works

We examined one of the earliest concepts in the realm of black-box outcome explanation, namely Contextual Importance (CI) and Contextual Utility (CU). Since these concepts are realized as a model-agnostic explanation approach, we steered our experiments on two black-box models including neural network (NN) and linear discriminant analysis (LDA). The aim was to explain recognition of human mental states and explore the extent of difference in the generated outcome explanation of applied models. We conducted our experiments on WESAD and MAHNOB-HCI, as publicly and academically available benchmarks in the domain of multimodal affective computation. Different sensor data were experimented in the process of personalized decision making in the first and second datasets. The results revealed that the outputs of electrodermal activity, respiration as well as accelorometer sensors, significantly influence the neural network decision in recognition of "meditation" state in the first dataset. Given LDA, the respiration sensor, however, was excluded. In the second dataset, the electrocardiogram and respiration sensors provided interventions in the "surprised" outcome of neural network, while the importance and utility of solely electrocardiogram sensor was demonstrated by LDA. According to these results, we found that not necessarily the same sensors intervened in the detection of the same class by our examined models, although the models accuracy were tightly close to each other. Another interesting finding of explainability referred to the fact that not only the sensors types, but also their position on the body affects the expression of mental states. For instance, in the first dataset only ACC1 and ACC2 and in the second dataset only ECG2 proved their contribution in the decision making of neural network. In conclusion, this work opened a new room of XAI in affective computation by critically examining different classification models.

Some directions of future works are as follow: although CI and CU concepts provided explanations to both expert and non-expert users in terms of visual and textual representations, yet such explanations alone do not meet the requirements of real-world applications. Augmenting these concepts with further clarifications of users type and their current affective states provides more realistic explanation. We will also focus on improving the CI and CU formulations to explain the prediction of more complex models such as deep neural networks, considering additive information from the hidden layers.

References

1. Arunasakthi, K., KamatchiPriya, L.: A review on linear and non-linear dimensionality reduction techniques. Mach. Learn. Appl.: Int. J. **1**(1), 65–76 (2014)
2. Chakraborty, S., Aich, S., Joo, M.I., Sain, M., Kim, H.C.: A multichannel convolutional neural network architecture for the detection of the state of mind using physiological signals from wearable devices. J Healthc Eng. (2019)
3. Chen, H., Lee, C.: Vibration signals analysis by explainable artificial intelligence (XAI) approach: Application on bearing faults diagnosis. IEEE Access **8** (2020)
4. Dragoni, M., Donadello, I., Eccher, C.: Explainable AI meets persuasiveness: translating reasoning results into behavioral change advice. Artif. Intell. Med. **105** (2020)
5. Du, M., Liu, N., Hu, X.: Techniques for interpretable machine learning. Commun. ACM **63**(1), 68–77 (2019)
6. Eitel, F., Ritter, K.: Testing the robustness of attribution methods for convolutional neural networks in MRI-based Alzheimer's disease classification. In: Suzuki, K., et al. (eds.) ML-CDS/IMIMIC -2019. LNCS, vol. 11797, pp. 3–11. Springer, Cham (2019). https://doi.org/10.1007/978-3-030-33850-3_1
7. Fouladgar, N., Alirezaie, M., Främling, K.: Decision explanation: applying contextual importance and contextual utility in affect detection. In: Proceedings of the Italian Workshop on Explainable Artificial Intelligence, XAI.it 2020. AI*IA SERIES, vol. 2742, pp. 1–13 (2020)
8. Fouladgar, N., Främling, K.: XAI-P-T: a brief review of explainable artificial intelligence from practice to theory. arXiv:2012.09636 (2020)
9. Främling, K.: Decision theory meets explainable AI. In: Calvaresi, D., Najjar, A., Winikoff, M., Främling, K. (eds.) EXTRAAMAS 2020. LNCS (LNAI), vol. 12175, pp. 57–74. Springer, Cham (2020). https://doi.org/10.1007/978-3-030-51924-7_4
10. Främling, K.: Explaining results of neural networks by contextual importance and utility. In: The AISB 1996 conf. Citeseer (1996)
11. Grath, R.M., et al.: Interpretable credit application predictions with counterfactual explanations. CoRR abs/1811.05245 (2018)
12. Guidotti, R., Monreale, A., Ruggieri, S., Turini, F., Giannotti, F., Pedreschi, D.: A survey of methods for explaining black box models. ACM Comp. Sur. **51**(5) (2018)
13. Lauritsen, S.M., et al.: Explainable artificial intelligence model to predict acute critical illness from electronic health records. ArXiv abs/1912.01266 (2019)
14. Lee, H., Kim, S.T., Ro, Y.M.: Generation of multimodal justification using visual word constraint model for explainable computer-aided diagnosis. In: Interpretability of Machine Intelligence in Medical Image Computing and Multimodal Learning for Clinical Decision Support. pp. 21–29. Springer (2019)
15. Lin, J., Pan, S., Lee, C.S., Oviatt, S.: An explainable deep fusion network for affect recognition using physiological signals. In: Proceedings of the 28th ACM International Conference on Information and Knowledge Management, CIKM 2019, pp. 2069–2072. ACM (2019)
16. Miller, T.: Explanation in artificial intelligence: insights from the social sciences. Artif. Intell. **267**, 1–38 (2019)

17. Mukhopadhyay, S.C.: Wearable sensors for human activity monitoring: a review. IEEE Sens. J. **15**(3), 1321–1330 (2015)
18. Nisha, P., Pawar, U., O'Reilly, R.: Interpretable machine learning models for assisting clinicians in the analysis of physiological data. In: Proceedings for the 27th AIAI Irish Conference on Artificial Intelligence and Cognitive Science, Galway, Ireland, 5–6 December 2019. CEUR, vol. 2563, pp. 434–445. CEUR-WS.org (2019)
19. Panigutti, C., Perotti, A., Pedreschi, D.: Doctor XAI: an ontology-based approach to black-box sequential data classification explanations. In: Proceedings of the 2020 Conference on Fairness, Accountability, and Transparency, FAT* 2020, pp. 629–639. ACM (2020)
20. Papanastasopoulos, Z., et al.: Explainable AI for medical imaging: deep-learning cnn ensemble for classification of estrogen receptor status from breast MRI. In: Medical Imaging 2020: Computer-Aided Diagnosis, vol. 11314, pp. 228–235. International Society for Optics and Photonics, SPIE (2020)
21. Putnam, V., Conati, C.: Exploring the need for explainable artificial intelligence (XAI) in intelligent tutoring systems (ITS). In: IUI Workshops (2019)
22. Sayres, R., et al.: Using a deep learning algorithm and integrated gradients explanation to assist grading for diabetic retinopathy. Ophthalmology **126**(4), 552–564 (2019)
23. Schmidt, P., Reiss, A., Duerichen, R., Marberger, C., Van Laerhoven, K.: Introducing wesad, a multimodal dataset for wearable stress and affect detection. In: Proceedings the 20th ACM International Conference on Multimodal Interaction, pp. 400–408. ACM (2018)
24. Singh, A., Sengupta, S., Lakshminarayanan, V.: Explainable deep learning models in medical image analysis. J. Imaging **6**(6), 52 (2020)
25. Soleymani, M., Lichtenauer, J., Pun, T., Pantic, M.: A multimodal database for affect recognition and implicit tagging. IEEE Trans. Affective Comput. **3**(1), 42–55 (2012)
26. Wang, D., Yang, Q., Abdul, A., Lim, B.Y.: Designing theory-driven user-centric explainable AI. In: Proceedings of the 2019 CHI Conference on Human Factors in Computing Systems, CHI 2019, pp. 1–15. ACM (2019)
27. Zhang, Z., Xie, Y., Xing, F., McGough, M., Yang, L.: MDNet: a semantically and visually interpretable medical image diagnosis network. In: IEEE Conference on Computer Vision and Pattern Recognition (CVPR), pp. 3549–3557 (2017)

Explainable and Ethical AI: A Perspective on Argumentation and Logic Programming

Roberta Calegari[1]([✉])[iD], Andrea Omicini[2][iD], and Giovanni Sartor[1][iD]

[1] Alma AI – Alma Mater Research Institute for Human-Centered Artificial Intelligence, Alma Mater Studiorum—Università di Bologna, Bologna, Italy
roberta.calegari@unibo.it
[2] Dipartimento di Informatica – Scienza e Ingegneria (DISI), Alma Mater Studiorum—Università di Bologna, Cesena, Italy

Abstract. In this paper we sketch a vision of explainability of intelligent systems as a logic approach suitable to be injected into and exploited by the system actors once integrated with sub-symbolic techniques.

In particular, we show how argumentation could be combined with different extensions of logic programming – namely, abduction, inductive logic programming, and probabilistic logic programming – to address the issues of explainable AI as well as some ethical concerns about AI.

Keywords: Explainable AI · Ethical AI · Argumentation · Logic programming · Abduction · Probabilistic LP · Inductive LP

1 Introduction

In the new artificial intelligence (AI) era, intelligent systems are increasingly relying on sub-symbolic techniques such as deep learning [2,7]. Since opaqueness of most sub-symbolic techniques engenders fear and distrust, the behaviour of intelligent systems should be observable, explainable, and accountable—which is the goal of the eXplainable Artificial Intelligence (XAI) field [2,8].

In this paper we focus on logic-based approaches and discuss their potential to address XAI issues especially in pervasive scenarios that can be designed as open multi-agent systems (MAS)—the reference for the design of intelligent systems [7,44,45]. In particular, this paper proposes an architecture for delivering (ubiquitous) symbolic intelligence to achieve explainability in pervasive contexts based on two assumptions: *(i) ubiquitous symbolic intelligence* is the key to making the environment truly smart and self-explainable, *(ii) declarativeness* and *transparency* can lead to the injection of ethical behaviours—see e.g. [34].

Roberta Calegari and Giovanni Sartor have been supported by the H2020 ERC Project "CompuLaw" (G.A. 833647). Andrea Omicini has been supported by the H2020 Project "AI4EU" (G.A. 825619).

M. Baldoni and S. Bandini (Eds.): AIxIA 2020, LNAI 12414, pp. 19–36, 2021.
https://doi.org/10.1007/978-3-030-77091-4_2

The architecture enables on-demand symbolic intelligence injection only *where* and *when* required. Sub-symbolic techniques – e.g., deep networks algorithms – are therefore part of our vision and can coexist in the system even in case they are not fully explainable. One of the main requirements of any system is then to identify which parts need to be explained – for ethical or legal purposes, responsibility issues, etc. – and which ones can instead remain opaque.

Logic-based approaches already play a well-understood role in the engineering of intelligent (multi-agent) systems; declarative, logic-based approaches have the potential to represent an alternative way of delivering symbolic intelligence, complementary to the one pursued by sub-symbolic approaches [7]. Logic-based technologies address opaqueness issues, and, once suitably integrated with argumentation capabilities, can provide for features like interpretability, observability, accountability, and explainability. In our vision, explainability depends on a system's capability of conversing and debating about situations and choices, providing reports and insights into what is happening. An explanation can be seen as a sort of *conversation* among the person asking for clarification and the system actors – agents, environment, and (e-)institution. As far as ethics is concerned, LP has recently been deeply studied by the research community, precisely in relation to the implementation of ethical machines and systems [40].

Argumentation is the spearhead of the proposed approach, yet – in order to tackle the AI requirements for ubiquitous intelligence – it should be strongly intertwined with logic programming and its extensions. In particular, our vision of symbolic intelligence leverages argumentation, abduction, inductive logic programming, and probabilistic logic programming, along the line of some recent research works—e.g., [22, 26, 31].

2   Explanation: Meaning and Roles

The first issue to be clarified when it comes to explainability is the acceptation of the term. Since explainability has become one of the hottest research topics in AI, the very notion of explainability has become the subject of scientific debate, also aimed at defining related concepts and terms such as explanation, interpretability, and understandability. Yet, there is still no widely-shared definition, also due to the pervasiveness of terms from the common language [32].

Formally defining those terms is not the goal of this paper. Instead, in the following, we point out some issues to consider when dealing with explainability and discuss how they affect the design of the proposed architecture.

Explanation vs Interpretation. The terms "interpretability" and "explainability" are often used carelessly and interchanged in the context of XAI [16]. Although the two terms are closely related and both contributing to the ultimate goal of understandability, they should be kept well distinct. Accordingly, here we borrow the definition of *interpretation* from logic, where the word essentially describes the operation of binding objects to their actual meaning in some context—thus, the goal of interpretability is to convey to humans the meaning of data [15]. Then, we conceive *explanation* can be seen as an activity of symbolic representation and transformation by the *explanator*, aimed at making the subjective activity of interpretation by the *explainee* easier [16, 32].

Once this distinction has been made, two general remarks are useful: *(i)* most XAI approaches proposed in the recent literature mostly focus on interpretability, *(ii)* to reach explainability, a mechanism for unwinding a reasoning and a corresponding conversation enabler is somehow required. This mechanism allows distinct actors' roles to be taken into account in the explanation process. Also, conversations can be used to clarify non-understandable explanations.

Explanation Actors and Kind of Explanation. Who are the explanators, and who the explainees? Can we proceed beyond the simplistic hypothesis that software systems/agents are the explanators, and explainees are just humans? In the literature [1, 24, 39] explanators are typically software components (i.e., agents in multi-agent systems), explainees are intended to be humans.

Instead, every possible direction that explanation could follow in AI systems should be explored [32]: human-agent, agent-human, agent-agent. Accordingly, tools and methods for explainability should be light-weight, easy integrable in existing technologies, embeddable in different AI techniques, and easily usable by software developers and engineers. For the same reasons, interoperability is one of the main requirements we take into account in the design of the architecture.

Furthermore, the sort of explanation that a system can provide is relevant, indeed. An explanation for a human is not necessarily useful for an agent, and viceversa. So, for instance, a logic-based tool generating an effective explanation for agents may not necessarily be immediately useful for humans; yet, once integrated with the appropriate AI techniques – such as tools for translation into natural language – it could become effective for humans, too.

3 Logic Techniques for XAI

3.1 Why Logic?

Our driving question here is: "What is or can be the added value of logic programming for implementing machine ethics and explainable AI?" The main answer lies in the three main features of LP: *(i)* being a declarative paradigm, *(ii)* working as a tool for knowledge representation, and *(iii)* allowing for different forms of reasoning and inference. These features lead to some properties for intelligent systems that can be critical in the design of ubiquitous intelligence.

Provability. By relying on LP, the models can provide for well-founded semantics ensuring some fundamental computational properties – such as correctness and completeness. Moreover, extensions can be formalised, well-founded as well, based on recognised theorems—like for instance, correctness of transitive closure, strongly equivalent transformation, modularity, and splitting set theorem. Provability is a key feature in the case of trusted and safe systems.

Explainability. The explainability feature is somehow intrinsic in LP techniques. Formal methods for argumentation-, justification-, and counterfactual-based methods are often based on a logic programming approach [21,35,40]. These techniques make the system capable to engage in dialogues with other actors to communicate its reasoning, explain its choices, or to coordinate in the pursuit of a common goal. So, the explanation can be a dialogue showing insights on reasoning or, again, the explanation can be the unraveling of causal reasoning based on counterfactual. Counterfactuals are the base for hypothetical reasoning, a necessary feature both for explanation and machine ethics. Furthermore, other logical forms of explanation can be envisaged via non-monotonic reasoning and argumentation, through a direct extension of the semantics of LP.

Expressivity and Situatedness. As far as the knowledge representation is concerned, the logical paradigm brings non-obvious advantages—beyond the fact of being human-readable. First of all, a logical framework makes it possible to grasp different nuances according to the extensions considered—e.g., nondeterminism, constraints, aggregates [20]. Also, assumptions and exceptions can be made explicit, as well as preferences—e.g., weighted weak constraints [4]. Finally, extensions targeting the Internet of Things can allow knowledge to be situated in order to be able to capture the specificities of the context in which it is located [12]. Expressive, flexible, and situated frameworks are needed to cover various problems and reasoning tasks closely related to each other.

Hybridization. One of the strengths of computational logic is to make it possible the integration of diverse techniques [11,42]—e.g., logic programming paradigms, database technologies, knowledge representation, non-monotonic reasoning, constraint programming, mathematical programming, etc. This makes it possible to represent the heterogeneity of the contexts of intelligent systems – also in relation to the application domains – and to customise as needed the symbolic intelligence that is provided while remaining within a well-founded formal framework.

3.2   User Requirements for XAI

Before we move into the discussion of the main extensions that a symbolic intelligence engine needs to have in order to inject explainability, let us define what we should expect from an explainable system and what kind of intelligence the system is supposed to deal with.

R$_1$ First of all, the system should be able to answer *what* questions, i.e., it should provide query answering and activity planning in order to achieve a user-specified goal.

R$_2$ The system should be able to answer *why* questions, i.e., it should provide explanation generation (in the form of text, images, narration, conversation) and diagnostic reasoning.

R$_3$ The system should be able to answer *what if* questions, i.e., it should provide counterfactual reasoning and predictions about what would happen under certain conditions and given certain choices.

R$_4$ The system should be able to answer *which* questions, i.e., it should be able to choose which scenarios to implement, once plausible scenarios have been identified as in the previous point. The choice should result from the system's preferences, which could possibly be user-defined or related to the context.

R$_5$ The system should be able to provide *suggestions*, i.e., to indicate what to do given the current state of affairs, exploiting hypothetical reasoning.

R$_6$ The system should be able to support two types of intelligence and therefore reasoning, i.e., *reactive reasoning* – related to the data and the current situation – and *deliberative reasoning*—related more to consciousness, knowledge, and moral, normative principles.

Even if only **R$_2$** is strictly and explicitly related to the explainability feature, also the other requirements can help to understand and interpret the system model, so all the above-mentioned requirements can be identified as mandatory for reaching ethical features such as interpretability, explainability, and trustworthiness. According to the requirements, in the following we discuss what logical approach should be part of an engine that enables symbolic intelligence to be injected in contexts demanding the aforementioned properties.

3.3   Logic Approaches and Technologies Involved for XAI

In our vision, logic programming is the foundation upon which the architecture for a symbolic intelligence engine can be built, enabling an intelligent system to meet the **R$_1$** requirement. Clearly, enabling different forms of inference and reasoning – e.g., non-monotonic reasoning – paves the way for the possibility to get different answers (appropriate to the context) to the *what* questions. Furthermore, the techniques of inference and reasoning grafted into the symbolic engine make it possible to reason about preferences by meeting requirement **R$_4$**.

However, LP needs to be extended in order to address explainability in different AI technologies and applications, and to be able to reconcile the two aspects of intelligence present in today's AI systems—namely, *reactive* and *deliberative* reasoning. In particular, in the following we show how argumentation, abduction, induction, and probabilistic LP can be fundamental ingredients to shape explainable and ethical AI.

Argumentation. In this vision, argumentation is the enabler to meet requirement **R$_2$**. Argumentation is a required feature of the envisioned symbolic intelligence engine to enable system actors to talk and discuss in order to explain and justify judgments and choices, and reach agreements.

Several existing works set the maturity of argumentation models as a key enabler of our vision [25,30]. In spite of the long history of research in argumentation and the many fundamental results achieved, much effort is still needed to effectively exploit argumentation in our envisioned framework. First, research on formal argumentation has mostly been theoretical: practical applications to real-world scenarios have only recently gained attention, and are not yet reified in a ready-to-use technology [10]. Second, many open issues of existing argumentation frameworks concern their integration with contingency situations and situated reasoning to achieve a blended integration of reactive and deliberative reasoning. Finally, the argumentation architecture should be designed in order to be highly scalable, distributed, open, and dynamic, and hybrid approaches should be investigated.

Abduction. Abduction is the enabling technique to meet $\mathbf{R_3}$. Abduction, in fact, allows plausible scenarios to be generated under certain conditions, and enables hypothetical reasoning, including the consideration of counterfactual scenarios about the past. Counterfactual reasoning suggests thoughts about what might have been, what might have happened if any event had been different in the past. What if I have to do it today? What have I learned from the past? It gives hints about the future by allowing for the comparison of different alternatives inferred from the changes in the past. It supports a justification of why different alternatives would have been worse or not better. After excluding those abducibles that have been ruled out a priori by integrity constraints, the consequences of the considered abducibles have first to be evaluated to determine what solution affords the greater good. Thus, reasoning over preferences becomes possible. Counterfactual reasoning is increasingly used in a variety of AI applications, and especially in XAI [23].

Probabilistic Logic Programming. Probabilistic logic programming (PLP) allows symbolic reasoning to be enriched with degrees of uncertainty. Uncertainty can be related to facts, events, scenarios, arguments, opinions, and so on. On the one side, PLP allows abduction to take scenario uncertainty measures into account [37]. On the other side, probabilistic argumentation can account for diverse types of uncertainty, in particular uncertainty on the credibility of the premises, uncertainty about which arguments to consider, and uncertainty on the acceptance status of arguments or statements [38]. Reasoning by taking into account probability is one of the key factors that allow a system to fully meet $\mathbf{R_4}$ and $\mathbf{R_5}$, managing to formulate well-founded reasoning on which scenario to prefer and which suggestions to provide as outcomes.

Inductive Logic Programming. Inductive logic programming (ILP) can help us bridging the gap between the symbolic and the sub-symbolic models—by inserting data and context into the reasoning. As already expressed by $\mathbf{R_6}$, data, context, and reactive reasoning are key features to take into account when designing intelligence. ILP makes it possible to learn from data enabling inductive construction of first-order clausal theories from examples and background knowledge. ILP is a good candidate to meet $\mathbf{R_6}$ and preliminary studies show ILP can be the glue between symbolic techniques and sub-symbolic ones such as numerical/statistical machine learning (ML) and deep learning [3].

All these techniques should be suitably integrated into a unique consistent framework, in order to be used appropriately when needed: they should be involved in the engineering of systems and services for XAI.

4   System Architecture

Figure 1 summarises our vision by highlighting the main roles involved in the system as well as the main activity flows. The grey boxes represent the technologies involved in the vision, while arrows represent the expected provided functionalities. The symbolic reasoner embodies the unique framework integrating the aforementioned logic approaches.

On one side, knowledge is collected from various sources – e.g., domain-specific knowledge, ontologies, sensors raw data – and is then exploited by agents that live in a normative environment. Note that we mean to exploit already existing techniques to convert ML knowledge into logic KB [9] and to explore other possibilities – always related to the exploitation of the aforementioned LP approaches – to explain (part of) deep knowledge.

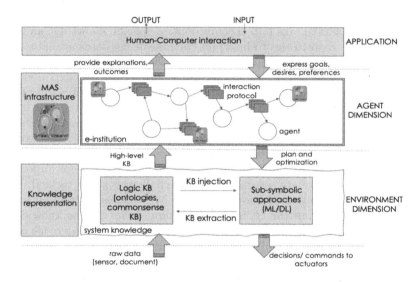

Fig. 1. Main architecture components and techniques in the vision.

The cognitive ability of the system is expanded with the concept of symbolic (micro-)intelligence which provides the techniques of symbolic reasoning discussed in Sect. 3 and tailored to LP. The multi-agent system, also thanks to its rational reasoning and argumentation capabilities, can provide outcomes to the users as well as explanations for their behaviours. On the other side, humans can insert input into the system – like desires, preferences, or goals to achieve – and these are transposed into agents' goals, corresponding activity planning, and lower-level commands for actuators.

Our vision stems from two basic premises: *(i)* knowledge is locally scattered in a distributed environment, hence its situated nature; *(ii)* symbolic capabilities are available over this knowledge, with the goal of extending local knowledge through argumentation, induction, deduction, abduction, and probabilistic reasoning and therefore pave the way towards explanations generation; *(iii)* distributed knowledge can be considered as compartmentalised in distinct knowledge modules and can be used by itself, or by referring to other modules for specific questions (according to the model of modular LP).

4.1   Main Enabling Technologies

The architecture described so far is rooted in a well-founded integration of different AI approaches and techniques. In the following, we describe the main ones – as well as open challenges and issues – well aware that a methodology for their integration is far from being already defined.

Knowledge Representation and Sharing. Knowledge representation and related techniques are some of the main ingredients of the envisioned distributed system, to enable conversation, argumentation, and reasoning. The system knowledge has to take into account domain-specific knowledge and large-scale ontologies as repositories to interpret the knowledge bases available to the agents and to reason and argument over it. Knowledge could be continuously modified, adapted, and refined by the agents, according to their experience and perception of the environment or to learning from experience. Accordingly, the knowledge base is plausible that is assembled by two main sources: on the one hand, ontologies and hand-crafted rules, on the other hand, rules learned from big data. Advances in machine learning will allow extracting knowledge from this data and merging it with the former. Hybrid approaches dealing with the integration of symbolic and sub-symbolic approaches become of paramount importance.

In this context, there are several issues and challenges to be tackled, to cite a few, automatic extraction of knowledge from ML models, extraction of commonsense knowledge from the context, integration of the diverse knowledge in an appropriate logical language that allows argumentation and inference process to be performed. Several research fields are already facing these issues, but the general problem is far from being solved. For sure, we believe that a suitable integration of symbolic and sub-symbolic approaches can help in the achievement of the construction of proper system knowledge. In addition, agents' mental state, including cultural features and commonsense knowledge, is necessary to deal with humans and be on par with their knowledge of real-world concepts. Moreover, their emotional state, including the support of trust and the capability to entertain the user in a believable way is fundamental. To this end, possibly new forms of knowledge representation should be envisioned and synergistically integrated enabling argumentation and semantic reasoning over it.

Finally, it is worth emphasising that the sharing of knowledge, therefore the possibility of making it explicit – and so explainable –, is one of the main purposes of XAI, as well as of human beings.

Machine Learning. In our vision, a fundamental role is played by machine learning involved in different phases—namely, data processing & rule learning, and planning.

Data Processing and Rule Learning. At the most straightforward level, machine learning techniques are clearly involved in raw input data elaboration, coming from sensors and/or documents, into more complex, high-level, structured information. Moreover, agents should be able to learn policies from past experience, by adapting both to the changing environment, and to the continuous progress of the society. Data aggregation, feature extraction, clustering, classification, data, and pattern mining techniques are typically employed today to reach these objectives. We believe that hybrid approaches could provide promising solutions to these tasks, by merging logic with probabilistic models and statistical learning, so to efficiently handle advantages of both symbolic and sub-symbolic approaches and moving towards explainable systems [9]. As highlighted above, the ML knowledge should somehow be translated into logical knowledge and properly merged with logical knowledge coming from ontologies or domain-expert norm translation or similar.

Planning. Distributed problem solving, planning, reinforcement learning, and cooperation [41] are some of the well-known ML techniques exploited in MAS. Our framework adds the challenge of integrating these techniques in the argumentation setting so that the planning and cooperation derive from a continuous, natural interaction between agents with the environment. Once the user has specified his desires, the agent must be able to achieve them, interacting and coordinating with other individuals and with the e-institution to define the actions to perform and consequently defining appropriate plans to reify the decisions.

Symbolic Reasoning Engine. The symbolic reasoning engine is the cornerstone of the proposed approach. Each of the symbolic techniques described in Sect. 3 allows one of the XAI requirements to be achieved. Accordingly, the foundation of our vision is to have a symbolic reasoning engine – which carries out the techniques discussed above – to be injectable on-demand into the various system's components—agents and/or environment and/or institutions. Symbolic (micro-)intelligence architecture [5,33] is exploited to deliver symbolic intelligence according to the new paradigms of AI. The architecture of symbolic (micro-)intelligence should enable – only where and when necessary – actions at the micro-level, to respond to local and specific needs [6]. Symbolic (micro-)intelligence complements agents' cognitive processes because it augments the cognitive capabilities of agents, by embodying situated knowledge about the local environment along with the relative inference processes, based on argumentation, abduction, ILP, and PLP. Beyond the open issues that belong to each of the logical fields considered, the main open issue to be tackled is their integration within the desired framework—i.e., a well-founded integration methodology. The methodology should employ a multidisciplinary approach that combines expertise in the fields of software engineering, natural language processing, argumentation, logic, ontologies, and of course distributed and autonomous systems.

MAS and Normative MAS: Middleware. From a more implementation-oriented perspective, given that conversations are a new means of orchestrating the activities of distributed agents, an open research question – and a key one, too – is to understand which services should a middleware provide in order to support such distributed conversations [13].

The multi-agent infrastructure needs not only to enable coordination among system actors but also include the possibility of customisable and reactive artefacts, capable of incorporating regulation and norms and micro-intelligence. Moreover, the middleware should provide support for discussions via an open and shared discussion space, enabling dialogue among components that do not necessarily know each other in advance, and also providing services and or techniques for sharing knowledge, e.g., a tuple space [28]. However, unlike traditional tuple space models, the evolution of the conversation, the argumentation process, and the reached consensus should be taken into account, also to be exploited in similar situations and/or to provide explanations. The best way to build such shared dialogue spaces – also taking into account different sources of knowledge (e.g., commonsense kb) and different artefacts acting as both law enforcers and intelligence promoters – is a fertile ground for research.

Human-Computer Interaction. Knowledge sharing, also in terms of explanation, requires a form of conversation among agents and humans, but also agents and agents, and conversation requires mind-reading – in terms of ability to understand motivations, beliefs, goals of others –, or, more generally, a theory of mind [43]. Accordingly, for human interaction, techniques coming from natural language processing, computer vision speech recognition become essential components of our vision.

The challenge here is twofold. On the one hand, the challenge is always related to the distributed issues, i.e., making commands possibly understandable to a multitude of agents and vice-versa. Existing algorithms should, therefore, be adapted for dealing with distributed and pervasive environments. On the other hand, existing techniques should be enhanced to understand hidden emotions possibly based on human culture, tone of voice and so on.

5   Preliminary Investigation: Examples

To ground our proposal, let us discuss a preliminary example from a case study in the area of traffic management, considering the near future of self-driving cars. In that scenario, cars are capable of communicating with each other and with the road infrastructure while cities and roads are suitably enriched with sensors and virtual traffic signs able to dynamically interact with cars to provide for information and supervision.

Accordingly, self-driving cars need to *(i)* exhibit some degree of intelligence for taking autonomous decisions; they need to *(ii)* converse with the context that surrounds them, *(iii)* have humans in the loop, *(iv)* respond to the legal setting characterising the environment and the society, and *(v)* offer explanations when required—e.g., in case of accidents to determine causes and responsibilities. Figure 2 (left) contains a possible example of the logical knowledge that, despite its simplicity, highlights the main different sources of knowledge taken into account in such a scenario. First of all, knowledge includes data collected by vehicle sensors as well as the beliefs of vehicles—possibly related to the outcome of a joint discussion among other entities in the system. Then, commonsense rules enrich the system knowledge, for instance, linking perceptions to beliefs about the factual situations at stake. Also, commonsense rules can state general superiority relations, such as that sensors' perceptions must be considered prevailing over vehicles' beliefs. An additional source of knowledge is e-institution knowledge. Loosely speaking, e-institutions are computational realisations of traditional institutions that incarnate the global system norms as global, national, state, and local laws, regulations, and policies. For instance, the e-institution knowledge defined in Fig. 2 declares that the general speed limit – according to German federal government – is 100 km/h outside built-up areas (no highways). In addition, a general norm is stated by the e-institution declaring that the overtake is permitted only if it is not raining. Another possible source of knowledge is situated knowledge collected by the surrounding context (infrastructure) that can include specific local rules stating exceptions to the general e-institutions rules. For instance, in the example, situated knowledge states that in the road being represented the general speed limit only applies if it does not rain, otherwise vehicles must slow down to 60 km/h. Note that in the example we list all the different kinds of knowledge in a unique file, but a suitable technology that embodies the envisioned architecture needs to manage different modules and to combine them—depending on the situation.

Figure 2 (right) shows some system outcomes, depending on the situation. All examples have been implemented and tested on the preliminary implementation of the system—namely, Arg-tuProlog (Arg2P in short) [36][1]. Arg2P – designed according to the vision discussed in this paper – is a lightweight modular argumentation tool that fruitfully combines modular logic programming and legal reasoning according to an argumentation labelling semantics where any statement (and argument) is associated with one label that is IN, OUT, UND, respectively meaning that the argument is accepted, rejected, or undecided. Example 1 is run without taking into account the superiority relation of perceptions over beliefs. In this situation, beliefs and perceptions are in conflict and no decision can be taken by the system, i.e., vehicles can base their decision only by taking into account the e-institution obligation and cannot be sure on the permission of overtaking. Example 2, instead, takes superiority relation into account, and according to the fact that sensor perception imposes a speed limit of 60 km/h and negate permission to overtake. The argumentation process among the system actors makes them meet the conclusion that it rains, so both vehicles, despite their beliefs, will set the maximum speed to 60 km/h. Conversely, Example 3 is run by negating rain perception. The system then recognises that it is not raining, so vehicle speed can be set to 100 km/h, and overtakes are allowed.

---

[1] http://arg2p.apice.unibo.it.

```
%******** SYSTEM KB ********************    %**** Example 1 ****
%******** ************* ***************    IN(accepted) =======>
                                            [obl, [max_speed(100)]]
%** PERCEPTIONS and BELIEFS **              [neg, belief(agent2, rain)]
pr1:[] => perception(rain).                 [belief(agent1, rain)]
                                            [perception(rain)]
b1: [] => belief(agent1, rain).             UND(undecided) ====>
b2: [] => -belief(agent2, rain).            [fact(rain)] [fact(rain)]
                                            [neg, fact(rain)][speed(60)]
                                            [speed(100)] [speed(60)]
%** GENERAL-COMMONSENSE KB **               [perm, [overtaking]]
% perceptions/beliefs translation
r1: perception(X) => fact(X).               %**** Example 2 ****
r2: -perception(X) => -fact(X).             IN(accepted) =======>
                                            [speed(60)][speed(60)]
r3: belief(A, X) => fact(X).                [obl, [max_speed(100)]]
r4: -belief(A, X) => -fact(X).              [fact(rain)][fact(rain)]
                                            [neg, belief(agent2, rain)]
%** GENERAL-COMMONSENSE KB **               [belief(agent1, rain)]
% perceptions are superior to beliefs       [perception(rain)]
sup(r1,r3).                                 OUT (rejected) ======>
sup(r1,r4).                                 [speed(100)][neg, fact(rain)]
sup(r2,r3).                                 [perm, [overtaking]]
sup(r2,r4).
                                            %**** Example 3 ****
                                            IN(accepted) =======>
                                            [speed(100)][speed(100)]
%** e-INSTITUTION RULES **                  [perm, [overtaking]]
% permissions and obligations               [obl, [max_speed(100)]]
o1: [] => o(max_speed(100)).                [neg, fact(rain)][neg, fact(rain)]
p1: -fact(rain) => p(overtaking).           [neg, belief(agent2, rain)]
                                            [belief(agent1, rain)]
%** SITUATED LOCAL KB **                    [neg, perception(rain)]
% specific road obligation                  [perm, [overtaking]]
% if rains max speed 60 km/h                OUT (rejected) ======>
r5: fact(rain) => speed(60).                [speed(60)][fact(rain)]
r6:-fact(rain),o(max_speed(X))=>speed(X).
```

Fig. 2. Example of system knowledge in the self-driving cars scenario, implemented in Arg2P (left). Arg2P system outcomes in three discussed examples (right).

The autonomous cars example, despite its simplicity, points out one of the key aspects discussed in Sect. 2: in fact, it is clear that the conversation, aimed at explaining and reaching an agreement necessarily has to involve also agent-to-agent communication with no necessarily humans in the loop. In the example, the two vehicles have an opposite perception of the surrounding environment – one thinks that it rains and one does not – so, they must converse and argue to understand what is the most possible matter of facts and then stick to that.

The examples discussed are just a simplification of the scenario but already illustrate the potential of rooting explanation in LP and argumentation. A first explanation is provided by the argumentation labelling which allows correlating arguments (and statements) accepted as plausible to a graph of attacks, superiority and non-defeasible rules, detailing the system reasoning. If we think about how the scenario could be enriched through abducibles and counterfactuals enabling a what-if analysis of different scenarios, the possibilities of the system to be explainable become manifold. Furthermore, probabilistic concepts make it possible to stick weight on assumptions, rules and arguments, for instance, agents' beliefs can be weighted according to the social credibility of each of them—possibly measured on numbers of sanctions or whatever. Ethics behaviours can be computed as well – in a human-readable way – preferring, for instance, to minimise the number of deaths in case of accidents. Interesting discussions on the moral choices of the system can be introduced and compared exploiting what-if analysis.

6   Related Works and Discussion

Just as AI sub-symbolic techniques are gaining momentum, symbolic techniques rooted in logic approaches are getting more and more attention—mostly because symbolic approaches can more easily meet the requirements of intelligent systems in terms of ethical concerns, explainability, and understandability.

Several efforts have been made for the integration of symbolic and sub-symbolic techniques under the XAI perspective, as discussed in some existing survey [9]. However, most of the works focus on a single type of logic that can effectively address the specific needs of the application at hand; less attention is typically reserved to devise a comprehensive integrated framework.

Logic programming is already undergoing a re-interpretation from an ethical perspective, as discussed in the literature [34,35,40]. Despite that, neither a comprehensive architecture nor a general methodology for integrating sub-symbolic AI techniques and logic programming can be found in the literature.

Our work aims at igniting a discussion about the integration of different logic approaches and AI techniques to achieve the XAI objectives. However, the architecture proposed in this paper is just the starting point for the design and the implementation of the envisioned symbolic engine and its integration with other existing AI techniques. Many issues and research challenges are still open.

First of all, the model formalisation deserves attention. Argumentation, *per se*, has been seen as an effective means to facilitate many aspects of decision-making and decision-support systems especially when decisions recommended by such systems need to be explained. Several works show its effectiveness [14,19], in particular in the generation of an explanation that justifies the solution found by the black boxes of ML [17,46]. Some works exist in the most recent literature, that underline the possible synergies of integration of different logic approaches, especially when combined with statistical ML algorithms. For instance, [26] discuss abduction and argumentation as two principled forms for reasoning and fleshes out the fundamental role that they can play within ML surveying the main works in the area. More generally, abduction and argumentation have been combined in different ways in the literature, starting from Dung's foundational work [18] introducing the preferred extension semantics of abductive logic programs. Abduction and argumentation can both be seen as processes for generating explanations either for a given observation as in the case of abduction or for a conclusion (claim or decision) in the case of argumentation. Explanations under abduction are in terms of underlying (theoretical or non-observable) hypotheses, whereas explanations under argumentation are in terms of arguments (among a set of known ones) that provide justified reasons for a conclusion to hold. Once again, however, a reference model does not emerge and often theoretical formalisations are not reified into any working technology.

A model for the integration of abduction and PLP is discussed in [22]; other works deal with the integration of abduction and induction [31]. In spite of the number of research activities on the subject, most approaches are scattered, and ad-hoc to solve a specific application need, and a general, well-founded framework for the integration of these models is still missing today. As a result, we are still a long way from the reification into a powerful technology – or integration of several technologies – that would allow its effective use in intelligent systems.

Moreover, for a well-founded coherent integration of all the approaches mentioned in Sect. 4, knowledge extraction and injection techniques have to be explored. A first overview of the main existing techniques is provided by [9], but some challenges remain open—in particular, knowledge injection and extraction when dealing with neural networks are a huge problem *per se*, and it is not clear *how* and *where* to inject the symbolic knowledge in nets [27].

Finally, as mentioned in Sect. 2, one of the main problems in the XAI and ethical AI field is that of selecting a satisfactory explanation. As far as the explanation selection is concerned, cognitive limitations come into play. For instance, if the explanation is required by a human, due to humans' cognitive limitations, the explanation cannot be presented with the whole chain of causal connections explaining a given algorithmic decision, rather users demand a synthetic explanation going to the core of the causal chain. Therefore, depending on the explanation's receiver the techniques to be applied may be different and could require subsequent refinement to make them cognitively understandable. The individuation of the mechanisms behind such a selection is, however, far from trivial, and many cognitive techniques should be taken into account [29].

To sum up, logic and symbolic approaches in general, especially once well integrated, can certainly be the turning point in the design of explainable and ethical systems. Nevertheless, a lot of work has to be done to ensure a well-founded integration between logic and the other AI techniques.

7   Conclusion

The paper presents a vision of how explainability and ethical behaviours in AI systems can be linked to logical concepts that find their roots in logic programming, argumentation, abduction, probabilistic LP, and inductive LP. The proposed solution is based on a (micro-)engine for injecting symbolic intelligence where and when needed. A simple example is discussed in the scenario of the self-driving car, along with its reification on a (yet preliminary) technology— namely Arg2P. However, the discussion and the corresponding example already highlight the potential benefits of the approach, once it is fruitfully integrated with the sub-symbolic models and techniques exploited in the AI field. In particular, the analysis carried out in the paper points out the key requirements of explainable and ethical autonomous behaviour, and relates them to specific logic-based approaches. The results presented here represent just a preliminary exploration of the intersection between LP and explainability: yet we think they have the potential to work as a starting point for further research.

References

1. Anjomshoae, S., Najjar, A., Calvaresi, D., Främling, K.: Explainable agents and robots: results from a systematic literature review. In: 18th International Conference on Autonomous Agents and Multi-Agent Systems (AAMAS 2019), pp. 1078–1088. IFAAMAS, May 2019. https://dl.acm.org/doi/10.5555/3306127.3331806
2. Arrieta, A.B., et al.: Explainable Artificial Intelligence (XAI): concepts, taxonomies, opportunities and challenges toward responsible AI. Inf. Fusion **58**, 82–115 (2020). https://doi.org/10.1016/j.inffus.2019.12.012
3. Belle, V.: Symbolic logic meets machine learning: a brief survey in infinite domains. In: Davis, J., Tabia, K. (eds.) SUM 2020. LNCS (LNAI), vol. 12322, pp. 3–16. Springer, Cham (2020). https://doi.org/10.1007/978-3-030-58449-8_1
4. Borning, A., Maher, M.J., Martindale, A., Wilson, M.: Constraint hierarchies and logic programming. In: Levi, G., Martelli, M. (eds.) 6th International Conference on Logic Programming, vol. 89, pp. 149–164. MIT Press, Lisbon, Portugal (1989)
5. Calegari, R.: Micro-intelligence for the IoT: logic-based models and technologies. Ph.D. thesis, Alma Mater Studiorum-Università di Bologna, Bologna, Italy (2018). https://doi.org/10.6092/unibo/amsdottorato/8521
6. Calegari, R., Ciatto, G., Denti, E., Omicini, A.: Engineering micro-intelligence at the edge of CPCS: design guidelines. In: Montella, R., Ciaramella, A., Fortino, G., Guerrieri, A., Liotta, A. (eds.) IDCS 2019. LNCS, vol. 11874, pp. 260–270. Springer, Cham (2019). https://doi.org/10.1007/978-3-030-34914-1_25
7. Calegari, R., Ciatto, G., Denti, E., Omicini, A.: Logic-based technologies for intelligent systems: state of the art and perspectives. Information **11**(3), 1–29 (2020). https://doi.org/10.3390/info11030167
8. Calegari, R., Ciatto, G., Mascardi, V., Omicini, A.: Logic-based technologies for multi-agent systems: a systematic literature review. Auton. Agent. Multi-Agent Syst. **35**(1), 1–67 (2020). https://doi.org/10.1007/s10458-020-09478-3
9. Calegari, R., Ciatto, G., Omicini, A.: On the integration of symbolic and sub-symbolic techniques for XAI: a survey. Intelligenza Artificiale **14**(1), 7–32 (2020). https://doi.org/10.3233/IA-190036
10. Calegari, R., Contissa, G., Lagioia, F., Omicini, A., Sartor, G.: Defeasible systems in legal reasoning: a comparative assessment. In: Araszkiewicz, M., Rodríguez-Doncel, V. (eds.) Legal Knowledge and Information Systems. JURIX 2019: The Thirty-second Annual Conference, Frontiers in Artificial Intelligence and Applications, vol. 322, pp. 169–174. IOS Press, 11–13 December 2019. https://doi.org/10.3233/FAIA190320

11. Calegari, R., Denti, E., Dovier, A., Omicini, A.: Extending logic programming with labelled variables: model and semantics. Fund. Inform. **161**(1–2), 53–74 (2018). https://doi.org/10.3233/FI-2018-1695
12. Calegari, R., Denti, E., Mariani, S., Omicini, A.: Logic programming as a service. Theory Pract. Logic Program. **18**(3–4), 1–28 (2018). https://doi.org/10.1017/S1471068418000364
13. Calegari, R., Omicini, A., Sartor, G.: Computable law as argumentation-based MAS. In: Calegari, R., Ciatto, G., Denti, E., Omicini, A., Sartor, G. (eds.) WOA 2020–21st Workshop "From Objects to Agents". CEUR Workshop Proceedings, vol. 2706, pp. 54–68. Sun SITE Central Europe, RWTH Aachen University, Aachen, Germany, October 2020. http://ceur-ws.org/Vol-2706/paper10.pdf
14. Caminada, M.: Argumentation semantics as formal discussion. J. Appl. Logics **4**(8), 2457–2492 (2017)
15. Ciatto, G., Calegari, R., Omicini, A., Calvaresi, D.: Towards XMAS: eXplainability through Multi-Agent Systems. In: Savaglio, C., Fortino, G., Ciatto, G., Omicini, A. (eds.) AI&IoT 2019 - Artificial Intelligence and Internet of Things 2019, CEUR Workshop Proceedings, vol. 2502, pp. 40–53. Sun SITE Central Europe, RWTH Aachen University, November 2019. http://ceur-ws.org/Vol-2502/paper3.pdf
16. Ciatto, G., Schumacher, M.I., Omicini, A., Calvaresi, D.: Agent-based explanations in AI: towards an abstract framework. In: Calvaresi, D., Najjar, A., Winikoff, M., Främling, K. (eds.) Explainable, Transparent Autonomous Agents and Multi-Agent Systems. LNCS, vol. 12175, pp. 3–20. Springer, Cham (2020). https://doi.org/10.1007/978-3-030-51924-7_1
17. Cyras, K., Letsios, D., Misener, R., Toni, F.: Argumentation for explainable scheduling. In: Proceedings of the AAAI Conference on Artificial Intelligence, vol. 33, pp. 2752–2759 (2019). https://doi.org/10.1609/aaai.v33i01.33012752
18. Dung, P.M.: Negations as hypotheses: an abductive foundation for logic programming. In: International Conference on Logic Programming, vol. 91, pp. 3–17 (1991)
19. Dung, P.M., Mancarella, P., Toni, F.: Computing ideal sceptical argumentation. Artif. Intell. **171**(10–15), 642–674 (2007). https://doi.org/10.1016/j.artint.2007.05.003
20. Dyckhoff, Roy, Herre, Heinrich, Schroeder-Heister, Peter (eds.): ELP 1996. LNCS, vol. 1050. Springer, Heidelberg (1996). https://doi.org/10.1007/3-540-60983-0
21. Esposito, F., Fanizzi, N., Iannone, L., Palmisano, I., Semeraro, G.: A counterfactual-based learning algorithm for $\mathcal{ALC}$ description logic. In: Bandini, S., Manzoni, S. (eds.) AI*IA 2005. LNCS (LNAI), vol. 3673, pp. 406–417. Springer, Heidelberg (2005). https://doi.org/10.1007/11558590_41
22. Ferilli, S.: Extending expressivity and flexibility of abductive logic programming. J. Intell. Inf. Syst. **51**(3), 647–672 (2018). https://doi.org/10.1007/s10844-018-0531-6
23. Fernández, R.R., de Diego, I.M., Aceña, V., Fernández-Isabel, A., Moguerza, J.M.: Random forest explainability using counterfactual sets. Inf. Fusion **63**, 196–207 (2020). https://doi.org/10.1016/j.inffus.2020.07.001
24. Guidotti, R., Monreale, A., Turini, F., Pedreschi, D., Giannotti, F.: A survey of methods for explaining black box models. ACM Comput. Surv. **51**(5), 1–42 (2019). https://doi.org/10.1145/3236009
25. Hulstijn, J., van der Torre, L.W.: Combining goal generation and planning in an argumentation framework. In: Hunter, A. (ed.) International Workshop on Non-monotonic Reasoning (NMR 2004), pp. 212–218. Pacific Institute, Whistler, Canada, January 2004

26. Kakas, A., Michael, L.: Abduction and argumentation for explainable machine learning: A position survey. arXiv preprint arXiv:2010.12896 (2020)

27. Kemker, R., McClure, M., Abitino, A., Hayes, T., Kanan, C.: Measuring catastrophic forgetting in neural networks. In: McIlraith, S.A., Weinberger, K.Q. (eds.) AAAI Conference on Artificial Intelligence. pp. 3390–3398. AAAI Press (2018). https://www.aaai.org/ocs/index.php/AAAI/AAAI18/paper/view/16410

28. Mariani, S., Omicini, A.: Coordination in situated systems: engineering MAS environment in TuCSoN. In: Fortino, G., Di Fatta, G., Li, W., Ochoa, S., Cuzzocrea, A., Pathan, M. (eds.) IDCS 2014. LNCS, vol. 8729, pp. 99–110. Springer, Cham (2014). https://doi.org/10.1007/978-3-319-11692-1_9

29. Miller, T.: Explanation in artificial intelligence: insights from the social sciences. Artif. Intell. **267**, 1–38 (2019). https://doi.org/10.1016/j.artint.2018.07.007

30. Modgil, S., Caminada, M.: Proof theories and algorithms for abstract argumentation frameworks. In: Simari, G., Rahwan, I. (eds.) Argumentation in artificial intelligence, pp. 105–129. Springer, Boston (2009). https://doi.org/10.1007/978-0-387-98197-0_6

31. Mooney, R.J.: Integrating abduction and induction in machine learning. In: Flach, P.A., Kakas, A.C. (eds.) Abduction and Induction, pp. 181–191. Springer (2000). https://doi.org/10.1007/978-94-017-0606-3_12

32. Omicini, A.: Not just for humans: explanation for agent-to-agent communication. In: Vizzari, G., Palmonari, M., Orlandini, A. (eds.) AIxIA 2020 DP - AIxIA 2020 Discussion Papers Workshop. AI*IA Series, vol. 2776, pp. 1–11. Sun SITE Central Europe, RWTH Aachen University, Aachen, Germany, November 2020. http://ceur-ws.org/Vol-2776/paper-1.pdf

33. Omicini, A., Calegari, R.: Injecting (micro)intelligence in the IoT: logic-based approaches for (M)MAS. In: Lin, D., Ishida, T., Zambonelli, F., Noda, I. (eds.) MMAS 2018. LNCS (LNAI), vol. 11422, pp. 21–35. Springer, Cham (2019). https://doi.org/10.1007/978-3-030-20937-7_2

34. Pereira, L.M., Saptawijaya, A.: Programming Machine Ethics. SAPERE, vol. 26. Springer, Cham (2016). https://doi.org/10.1007/978-3-319-29354-7

35. Pereira, L.M., Saptawijaya, A.: Counterfactuals, logic programming and agent morality. In: Urbaniak, R., Payette, G. (eds.) Applications of Formal Philosophy. LAR, vol. 14, pp. 25–53. Springer, Cham (2017). https://doi.org/10.1007/978-3-319-58507-9_3

36. Pisano, G., Calegari, R., Omicini, A., Sartor, G.: Arg-tuProlog: a tuProlog-based argumentation framework. In: Calimeri, F., Perri, S., Zumpano, E. (eds.) CILC 2020 - Italian Conference on Computational Logic. Proceedings of the 35th Italian Conference on Computational Logic. CEUR Workshop Proceedings, vol. 2719, pp. 51–66. Sun SITE Central Europe, RWTH Aachen University, CEUR-WS, Aachen, Germany, 13–15 October 2020. http://ceur-ws.org/Vol-2710/paper4.pdf

37. Poole, D.: Logic programming, abduction and probability. N. Gener. Comput. **11**(3–4), 377 (1993). https://doi.org/10.1007/BF03037184

38. Riveret, R., Oren, N., Sartor, G.: A probabilistic deontic argumentation framework. Int. J. Approximate Reasoning **126**, 249–271 (2020). https://doi.org/10.1016/j.ijar.2020.08.012

39. Rosenfeld, A., Richardson, A.: Explainability in human–agent systems. Auton. Agent. Multi-Agent Syst. **33**(6), 673–705 (2019). https://doi.org/10.1007/s10458-019-09408-y

40. Saptawijaya, A., Pereira, L.M.: From logic programming to machine ethics. In: Bendel, O. (ed.) Handbuch Maschinenethik. LAR, pp. 209–227. Springer, Wiesbaden (2019). https://doi.org/10.1007/978-3-658-17483-5_14

41. Stone, P., Veloso, M.: Multiagent systems: a survey from a machine learning perspective. Auton. Robot. **8**(3), 345–383 (2000). https://doi.org/10.1023/A:1008942012299
42. Vranes, S., Stanojevic, M.: Integrating multiple paradigms within the blackboard framework. IEEE Trans. Softw. Eng. **21**(3), 244–262 (1995). https://doi.org/10.1109/32.372151
43. Wellman, H.M.: The Child's Theory of Mind. The MIT Press (1992)
44. Wooldridge, M.J., Jennings, N.R.: Intelligent agents: theory and practice. Knowl. Eng. Rev. **10**(2), 115–152 (1995). https://doi.org/10.1017/S0269888900008122
45. Xhafa, F., Patnaik, S., Tavana, M. (eds.): IISA 2019. AISC, vol. 1084. Springer, Cham (2020). https://doi.org/10.1007/978-3-030-34387-3
46. Zhong, Q., Fan, X., Luo, X., Toni, F.: An explainable multi-attribute decision model based on argumentation. Expert Syst. Appl. **117**, 42–61 (2019). https://doi.org/10.1016/j.eswa.2018.09.038

Understanding Automatic Pneumonia Classification Using Chest X-Ray Images

Pierangela Bruno$^{(\boxtimes)}$ ⓘ and Francesco Calimeri ⓘ

Department of Mathematics and Computer Science, University of Calabria,
Rende, Italy
{bruno,calimeri}@mat.unical.it

Abstract. Pneumonia has been recognized as a common and potentially lethal condition for nearly two centuries. The COVID-19 disease
caused by the SARS-CoV-2 virus first appeared in Wuhan, China, and is
considered a serious disease due to its high permeability, and contagious-
ness. Patients with COVID-19 may suffer from cough, fever, tiredness,
dyspnea, and other signs and symptoms similar to those of tuberculosis
(TB) and other respiratory infections disease. The similarity of COVID-
19 disease with other lung infections, along with its high spreading rate,
makes the diagnosis difficult.

Solutions based on machine learning techniques achieved relevant
results in identifying the correct disease and providing early diagnosis, and can hence provide significant clinical decision support; however,
such approaches suffer from the lack of proper means for interpreting the
choices made by the models, especially in case of deep learning ones.

With the aim to improve interpretability and explainability in the
process of making qualified decisions, we designed a system that allows
a partial opening of this black box by means of proper investigations on
the rationale behind the decisions. We tested our approach over artificial neural networks trained for multiple classifications based on Chest
X-ray images; our tool analyzed the internal processes performed by the
networks during the classification tasks to identify the most important
elements involved in the training process that influence the network's
decisions. We report the results of an experimental analysis aimed at
assessing the viability of the proposed approach.

Keywords: Convolutional Neural Networks · GradCAM · Chest
X-ray images · COVID-19 · Tuberculosis

1 Introduction

The Novel Coronavirus, that reportedly started to infect human individuals
at the end of 2019, rapidly caused a pandemic, as the infection can spread
quickly from individual to individual in the community [21]. Signs of infection
include respiratory symptoms, fever, cough and dyspnea. In more serious cases,
the infection can cause Pneumonia, severe acute respiratory syndrome, septic

© Springer Nature Switzerland AG 2021
M. Baldoni and S. Bandini (Eds.): AIxIA 2020, LNAI 12414, pp. 37–50, 2021.
https://doi.org/10.1007/978-3-030-77091-4_3

shock, multi-organ failure, and death [17,20]. These symptoms are similar to those caused by other respiratory infections diseases, such as tuberculosis (TB). TB is a chronic lung disease caused by bacterial infection, and is one of the top-10 leading causes of death [25]. Both TB and COVID-19 primarily attack the lungs, although with different incubation period from exposure to disease, and ill people show similar symptoms such as cough, fever and difficulty breathing [19]. In such scenarios, correct classification of the diseases is crucial for ensuring that patients get the right treatment. Early and automatic diagnoses can provide support to clinicians in such complex decisions as well as to control the epidemic, paving the way to timely referral of patients to quarantine, rapid intubation of serious cases in specialized hospitals, and monitoring of the spread of the disease. Since the disease heavily affects human lungs, analyzing Chest X-ray images of the lungs may prove to be a powerful tool for disease investigation. Several methods have been proposed in the literature in order to perform disease classification from Chest X-ray images, especially based on deep learning approaches [5,13,36]. Notably, in this context, solutions featuring interpretability and explainability approaches can significantly help at improving disease classification and providing context-aware assistance and understanding. Indeed, interpreting the decision-making processes of neural networks can be of great help at enhancing the diagnostic capabilities and providing direct patient- and process-specific support to diagnosis and surgical tool detection. However, interpretability and explainability represent critical points in approaches based on deep learning models, that achieved great results in disease classification.

In this work, we investigate the use of convolutional neural networks (CNNs) with the aim to perform multiple-disease classification from Chest X-ray images. Diseases that are a matter of concern for our experiments are COVID-19 and TB Pneumonia. Notably, although these diseases are characterized by pulmonary inflammation caused by different pathogens, TB Pneumonia has similar clinical symptoms to COVID-19 [19] that could affect a proper diagnosis and treatment plan. Moreover, we include in our experiments Healthy patients to learn how they differ from symptomatic patients.

We analyze the CNNs-based model to identify the mechanisms and the motivations steering neural networks decisions in classification task. In particular, we use gradient visualization techniques to produce coarse localization maps highlighting the image regions most likely to be referred to by the model when the classification decision is taken. The highlighted areas are then used to discover (i) patterns in Chest X-ray images related to a specific disease, and (ii) correlation between these areas and classification accuracy, by analyzing a possible performance worsening after their removal.

The remainder of the paper is structured as follows. We first briefly report on related work in Sect. 2; in Sect. 3 we then provide a detailed description of our approach, that has been assessed via a careful experimental activity, which is discussed in Sect. 4; we analyze and discuss results in Sect. 5, eventually drawing our conclusions in Sect. 6.

2   Related Work

In this section we present state-of-the-art methods used to (*i*) perform disease classification through Chest X-ray images and (*ii*) provide interpretability and explainability of the rationale behind the decisions performed.

Disease Classification. Deep learning-based models recently achieved promising results in image-based disease classification. These models, such as CNNs [8, 18,29,33], are proven to be appropriate and effective when compared to conventional methods; indeed, CNNs currently represent the most widely used method for image processing. Abbas et al. [1] proposed a deep learning approach (DeTraC) to perform disease classification using X-ray images. The approach was used to distinguish COVID-19 X-ray images from normal ones, achieving an accuracy of 95.12%. An improvement in terms of binary classification accuracy was presented by Ozturk et al. [22]. The authors proposed a deep learning model (DarkCovidNet) for automatic diagnosis of COVID-19 based on Chest X-ray images. They both performed a binary and multi-class classification, dealing with patients with COVID-19, no-findings and Pneumonia. The accuracy achieved is of 98.08% and 87.02%, respectively. Similarly, Wang et al. [31] proposed a deep learning-based approach (COVID-Net) to detect distinctive abnormalities in Chest X-ray images among patients with non-COVID-19 viral infections, bacterial infections, and healthy patients, achieving an overall accuracy of 92.6%. All the approaches showed limitations related to low number of image samples and imprecise localization on the chest region. More accurate localization of model's prediction was proposed by Mangal et al. [15] and Haghanifar et al. [9]. The authors proposed a deep learning-based approach to classify COVID-19 patients from others/normal ones. They also generated saliency maps to show the classification score obtained during the prediction and to validate the results.

Explainability of Deep Learning Model. In the last year, attempts at understanding neural networks decision-making have raised a lot of interest in the scientific community. Several approaches have been proposed to visualize the behavior of a CNN by sampling image patches that maximize the activation of hidden units [34], and by back-propagation to identify or generate salient image features [14]. Other researchers were trying to solve this problem by explaining neural network decisions by generating informative heatmaps such as Gradient-weighted Class Activation Mapping (GradCAM) [3,9,23,24,27,28], or through layer-wise relevance propagation [2]. However, these methods present some limitations; indeed, the generated heatmaps were basically qualitative, and not informative enough to specify which concepts have been detected. An improvement was provided using semantically explanation from visual representation [35] to decompose the evidence for a prediction for image classification into semantically interpretable components, each with an identified purpose, a heatmap, and a ranked contribution.

In this work, we propose the use of Deep Learning approach to perform multiple disease classification using Chest X-ray. Additionally, we take advantage of

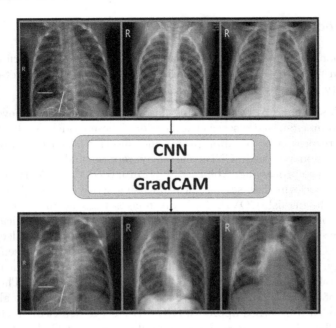

Fig. 1. Workflow of the proposed framework. Chest X-ray images are used to train the CNN. The last convolution layer of the CNN is used as input of the GradCAM approach to provide the corresponding visual explanations (i.e., the regions of input that are "important" for classification).

a novel technique for analyzing the internal processes and the decision performed by a neural network during the training phase.

3   Proposed Approach

In the following we illustrate the herein proposed approach: we first describe how the classification methods are designed and then how the choices are explained by properly highlighting regions that are considered discriminant for the classification.

3.1   Classification

Given that symptoms of COVID-19 pneumonia can be similar to those caused by other respiratory illnesses, including TB, distinguishing between them is extremely important, especially during a pandemic. Therefore, our purpose aims at providing methods for automatically identifying the "correct" condition of a given patient based on her Chest X-ray images, and also some details about the reasons for the resulting classifications.

The herein proposed approach, illustrated in Fig. 1, is based on: (*i*) Multiple-disease classification using CNNs (trained according to 2 similar-based symptoms

Table 1. Architecture of the networks DenseNet-121, DenseNet-169 and DenseNet-201 from [10]. More in detail, Conv stands for convolution, DB for Dense Block, TL for Transition Layer, CL for Classification Layer.

Layers	Output Size	DenseNet-121	DenseNet-169	DenseNet-201
Conv	112×112	7×7 conv, stride 2		
Pooling	56×56	3×3 max pool, stride 2		
DB (1)	56×56	$\begin{bmatrix} 1 \times 1 \text{ conv} \\ 3 \times 3 \text{ conv} \end{bmatrix} \times 6$	$\begin{bmatrix} 1 \times 1 \text{ conv} \\ 3 \times 3 \text{ conv} \end{bmatrix} \times 6$	$\begin{bmatrix} 1 \times 1 \text{ conv} \\ 3 \times 3 \text{ conv} \end{bmatrix} \times 6$
TL (1)	56×56	1×1 conv		
	28×28	2×2 average pool, stride 2		
DB (2)	28×28	$\begin{bmatrix} 1 \times 1 \text{ conv} \\ 3 \times 3 \text{ conv} \end{bmatrix} \times 12$	$\begin{bmatrix} 1 \times 1 \text{ conv} \\ 3 \times 3 \text{ conv} \end{bmatrix} \times 12$	$\begin{bmatrix} 1 \times 1 \text{ conv} \\ 3 \times 3 \text{ conv} \end{bmatrix} \times 12$
TL (2)	28×28	1×1 conv		
	14×14	2×2 average pool, stride 2		
DB (3)	14×14	$\begin{bmatrix} 1 \times 1 \text{ conv} \\ 3 \times 3 \text{ conv} \end{bmatrix} \times 24$	$\begin{bmatrix} 1 \times 1 \text{ conv} \\ 3 \times 3 \text{ conv} \end{bmatrix} \times 32$	$\begin{bmatrix} 1 \times 1 \text{ conv} \\ 3 \times 3 \text{ conv} \end{bmatrix} \times 48$
TL (3)	14×14	1×1 conv		
	7×7	2×2 average pool, stride 2		
DB (4)	7×7	$\begin{bmatrix} 1 \times 1 \text{ conv} \\ 3 \times 3 \text{ conv} \end{bmatrix} \times 16$	$\begin{bmatrix} 1 \times 1 \text{ conv} \\ 3 \times 3 \text{ conv} \end{bmatrix} \times 32$	$\begin{bmatrix} 1 \times 1 \text{ conv} \\ 3 \times 3 \text{ conv} \end{bmatrix} \times 32$
CL	4×1	7×7 global average pool		
		4D fully-connected, softmax		

diseases, namely COVID-19 and TB Pneumonia), and (*ii*) Visual Explanations using GradCAM to indicate the discriminative image regions used by the CNN.

To classify patients, we used and compared the results of three neural networks chosen on the basis of the good performance obtained on the *ImageNet* data set over several competitions [26]. In particular, we make use of DenseNet 121, DenseNet 169 and DenseNet 201.

DenseNet networks [10] are made of dense blocks, as shown in Table 1, where for each layer the inputs are the feature maps of all the previous layers with the aim to improve the information flow on 224×224 input images.

More in detail, for convolutional layers with kernel size 3×3, each side of the inputs is zero-padded by one pixel to keep the feature-map size fixed. The layers between two contiguous dense blocks are referred as transition layers for convolution and pooling, which contain 1×1 convolution and 2×2 average pooling. A 1×1 convolution is introduced as a bottleneck layer before each 3×3 convolution to reduce the number of input feature-maps, and thus to improve computational efficiency. At the end of the last dense block, a global average pooling and a softmax classifier are applied.

3.2 Visual Explanations

We used GradCAM to identify visual features in the input images that explain result process achieved during the multiple classification. The overall structure of GradCAM is showed in Fig. 2. In particular, it uses the gradient information

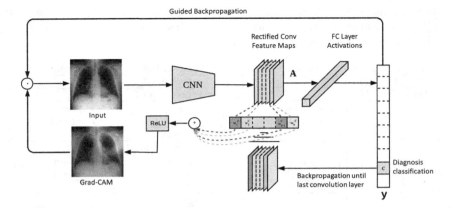

Fig. 2. An example of GradCAM structure. Given an image and a category ("Diagnosis c") as input, we forward-propagate the image through the model to obtain the raw class scores before softmax. The gradients are set to zero for all classes, except for desired class ("Diagnosis c"), which is set to 1. This signal is then back-propagated to the rectified convolutional feature map (A) of interest, where we can compute the coarse GradCAM localization (blue heatmap).

flowing into the last convolutional layer of the CNN to assign importance values to each neuron. GradCAM is applied to a trained neural network with fixed weights. Given a class of interest c, let y^c the raw output of the neural network, that is, the value obtained before the application of softmax used to transform the raw score into a probability. GradCAM performs the following three steps:

1. **Compute Gradient** of y_c w.r.t. feature maps activation A^k, for any arbitrary k, of a convolutional layer (i.e., $\frac{\delta y^c}{\delta A^k}$). This gradient value depends on the input image chosen; indeed, the input image determines both the feature maps A^k and the final class score y^c that is produced.
2. **Calculate Alphas by Averaging Gradients** over the width dimension (indexed by i) and the height dimension (indexed by j) to obtain neuron importance weights α_k^c, as follows:

$$\alpha_k^c = \frac{1}{Z} \overbrace{\sum_i \sum_j} \underbrace{\frac{\delta y^c}{\delta A_{i,j}^k}}_{\text{gradients via backprop}},$$

where Z is a constant (i.e., number of pixels in the activation map).
3. **Calculate Final GradCAM Heatmap** by performing a weighted combination of the feature map activations A^k as follows:

$$L_{GradCAM}^c = ReLU \left(\underbrace{\sum_k \alpha_k^c A^k}_{\text{linear combination}} \right),$$

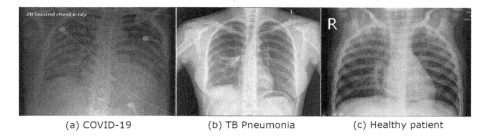

(a) COVID-19   (b) TB Pneumonia   (c) Healthy patient

Fig. 3. Example of frontal-view Chest X-ray images for the treated pathologies.

where α_k^c is a different weight for each k, and $ReLU$ is the Rectified Linear Unit operation used to emphasize only the positive values and to convert the negative values into 0.

4   Experimental Protocol

We describe next the setting of the experimental analysis performed in order to assess the viability of our approach.

4.1   Dataset Description

For the experimental analysis we used datasets provided by Cohen et al. [7], Kermany et al. [12] for COVID-19 and normal patients, respectively, and Jaeger et al. [11], Candemir et al. [6] and Wang et al. [32] for patients which suffer from TB. The datasets consist of several X-ray extracted from various online publications and websites. Examples of X-ray images are shown in Fig. 3.

In particular, we considered only 3 specific categories distributed as follows:

1. COVID-19 Pneumonia, counting 434 patients
2. Tuberculosis Pneumonia, counting 336 patients
3. Healthy patients, counting 1667 patients

In order to obtain a valid classification and avoid majority class selection, we properly made use of data augmentation techniques to over-sample imbalanced data an obtain an equal number of samples in abundant class. More specifically, we performed:

- Translating medical images: shift the region of interest with respect to the center of the training images;
- Rotating medical images: rotate the training images by a random amount of degrees;
- Flipping medical images: use randomized flipping, through which the image information is mirrored horizontally or vertically.

4.2   Training Phase

The dataset was split into training (80%) and testing (20%) sets. We performed 10-fold cross-validation in order to choose the data division that gives the lowest cross-validation average error; experiments were performed on the very same machine with the same configuration of the other approaches. We started relying on the work on [15]. We used CheXNet model [30] as pre-trained weights to improve the robustness of our approach and sigmoid classifier, as suggested by Mangal et al. [15].

All experiments have been performed on a machine equipped with a 12 x86 64 Intel(R) Core(TM) CPUs @3.50 GHz, running GNU/Linux Debian 7 and using CUDA compilation tools, release 7.5, V 7.5.17 NVIDIA Corporation GM 204 on GeForce GTX 970.

Fine-Tuning. For the training phase we performed hyperparameters optimization. DenseNets was trained with both optimizers Adam and SGD and for each optimizer 4 learning rate were tried. The best performance is obtained with the following configuration, trained for 200 epochs: SGD optimizer, learning rate 10^{-4}, batch size 4, and binary cross-entropy as loss function.

The configuration of networks was modified in terms of the number of nodes or levels to optimize the performance. We empirically changed the number of layers and we trimmed network size by pruning nodes to improve computational performance and identify those nodes which would not noticeably affect network performance. However, since we performed the experiments using well-know networks already optimized, we achieved the best performance using the standard configuration as originally proposed by respective authors.

4.3   Performance Metrics

We assessed the effectiveness of our approach by measuring Area Under the Curve (AUC) and Recall, especially focusing on the last one; indeed, in this context, the most important thing is to minimize False Negatives (i.e., disease is present but is not identified).

Let TP be a True Positive, TN a True Negative, FN a False Negative, and FP a False Positive, a ROC curve is a plot of true positive fractions ($S_e = \frac{TP}{TP+FN}$) versus false positive fractions ($S_p = 1 - \frac{TN}{TN+FP}$) by varying the threshold on the probability map. Closer a curve approaches the top left corner, then better is the performance of the system.

The Area Under the Curve (AUC), which is 1 for a perfect system, is a single measure to quantify this behavior [16].

Recall ($Rec = \frac{TP}{TP+FN}$) considers prediction accuracy among only actual positives and explain how correct our prediction is among all people.

Table 2. Validation Recall (and variance) for the 3 tested neural networks after 10-fold cross-validation for each dataset. Most significant results hare highlighted.

DATASET	DenseNet 121	DenseNet 169	DenseNet 201
COVID-19	0.94 (0.02)	**0.95** (0.01)	0.90 (0.02)
TB Pneumonia	0.79 (0.05)	**0.84** (0.04)	0.66 (0.06)
Healthy patients	**0.94** (0.02)	0.88 (0.04)	0.87 (0.04)

Table 3. AUC values for the 3 tested neural networks after 10-fold cross-validation for each dataset. Most significant results hare highlighted.

DATASET	DenseNet 121	DenseNet 169	DenseNet 201
COVID-19	0.96	**0.97**	0.92
TB Pneumonia	**0.95**	0.92	0.94
Healthy patients	0.95	**0.96**	0.93

5   Results and Discussion

In the following, we first discuss the quality of the classifications performed by our models, and then assess the visual explanations of the choices, as provided by GradCAM.

5.1   Classification Performance

Table 2 and Table 3 report classification results after 10-fold cross-validation for all datasets in terms of Recall and AUC, respectively. Each network is evaluated on a test set generated performing random data augmentation. Even though similar results are achieved in all DenseNet-based experiments, DenseNet 169 shows one of the most efficient architecture: if reports AUC mean value of 0.95 and Recall mean value of 0.89 over all the classes: hence, it was the one selected for the study.

The herein proposed approach achieves promisingly results; in particular, DenseNet 169 achieves the best performance on COVID-19 dataset (i.e., Recall mean value: 0.95 and AUC: 0.97), outperforming results on Healthy patients (i.e., Recall mean value of 0.88 and AUC: 0.96), and especially results in classifying TB Pneumonia (i.e., Recall mean value: 0.84 and AUC: 0.92).

A more thorough analysis shows that TB Pneumonia is often confused with COVID-19; this is not surprising, given the overlapping imaging characteristics that leads to a Recall mean value below 0.85 in all experiments performed. Furthermore, it is worth noting that, in general, the extraction of CT scan images from published articles, rather than from actual sources, might lessen image quality, thus affecting performance of the machine learning model.

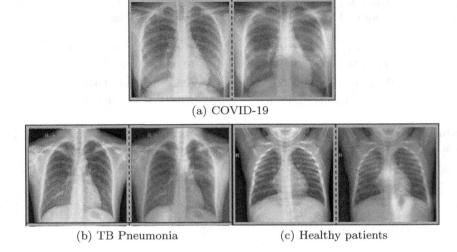

(a) COVID-19

(b) TB Pneumonia   (c) Healthy patients

Fig. 4. Visual example of achieved results. For each diagnostic class, we show raw Chest X-ray image (left) and GradCAM result (right). Images on the right sides highlight the most important areas involved in the classification process.

5.2   Assessing Explanations from GradCAM

As already mentioned, we make use of GradCAM for highlighting the most significant regions w.r.t. classification. A visual inspection of the GradCAM output confirms the quality of the model; indeed, it exhibits strong classification criteria in the Chest region (see Fig. 4). In particular, red areas refer to the parts where the attention is strong, while blue areas refer to weaker attention. In general, the warmer the color, the more important to the network are the highlighted features.

In order to confirm that the portions identified by GradCAM are actually significant, we performed both quantitative and qualitative analyses.

As for a quantitative assessment, we selected and removed, for each dataset, the 40% of highlighted elements as suggested in [4]. A substantial decrease of Recall (on average around 5%) is shown using COVID-19, TB Pneumonia and Healthy patients (i.e., p-value <0.05 for paired t-test computed before and after images cutting). This result suggests that GradCAM is actually able to identify the important elements involved in the training process and, consequently, responsibility for this diminishment is due to images cutting that removed some peculiar characteristic of the disease.

Furthermore, we took advantage from the TB dataset, that feature labels assigned by expert clinicians to the areas of the images they considered relevant for the classification. The current clinical practice consists in visually inspecting and evaluating Chest X-ray to identify abnormality of the lung and define the clinical condition of the patient. To the best of our knowledge no clinical evaluations are provided for COVID-19 patients: this is why this analysis is limited to

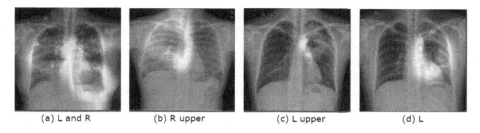

| (a) L and R | (b) R upper | (c) L upper | (d) L |

Fig. 5. Example of results obtained after GradCAM application. For each image, label assigned by clinicians is provided.

TB patients only. We wanted to assess the capability of GradCAM in identifying relevant elements involved in the training process and discovering potentially bio-markers able to suggests clinical condition, and also check to what extent the features identified by GradCAM overlap with those used by the clinicians.

Clinicians provided the evaluation of Chest X-ray of TB patients identifying the approximate location of the abnormality in lung; in particular, clinical categories are subdivided into individual lung (left, right) or bilateral lungs and, for each of these three categories, clinicians specified areas involved in TB disease (i.e., upper, lower, middle lung). As an example, Fig. 4b shows an image of the lungs of a patient suffering from pulmonary TB: clinicians assigned the label "L upper" starting from the image on the left, while the image on the right reports the highlighted region by GradCAM. A visual example of the preliminary results is shown in Fig. 5: they show that what GradCAM highlights in our approach based on DenseNet-169 coincides with at least 60% of the area suggested by clinicians, thus identifying a great number of suggested areas. However, the accuracy does not reach a considerably high value due to (i) the capability of our network in classifying TB patients, as discussed in Sect. 5.1, (ii) the way areas identified by clinicians are labelled, as labels are not defined at pixels level nor delimited, but rather by means of texts, thus resulting in non-precise delimitation. Furthermore, result suggest that there might be some cases in which the artificial networks and the human operators just focus on different features; this can be subject of future investigations.

6   Conclusion

In this work we exploit the use of CNNs and visual explanation techniques to estimate diagnosis using Chest X-ray and to analyze the internal processes performed by a neural network during the training phase with the aim of improving explainability in the process of making qualified decisions. Basically, we try to identify the most important regions that influence the network's decisions.

We fine-tuned the approach by means of accurate experimental activities; in particular, we classified three different datasets (i.e., two for ill and one for healthy patients), and three different CNNs for the classification.

Experimental results show that our proposal is robust and it is able to identify specific regions that are crucial in the neural network decision-making process, thus improving explainability. Indeed, classification accuracy is lower when highlighted regions are removed from the input images; this suggests the importance of these areas in disease classification and the possibility to consider the set of elements identified as potential disease markers. We also discussed the relationships between the highlighted visual features suggested by GradCAM and the abnormalities identified by clinicians on TB Chest X-ray.

In context where early and accurate medical diagnosis of specific pathologies are essential, our method proves that visual explanation method combined with machine learning techniques can be used to provide solid disease classifications and automatically discover new bio-markers by interpreting network decisions.

As future work is concerned, we aim to investigate misclassification errors and improve the generalization capability of the model. Our efforts will also focus on including clinical evaluations of COVID-19 Chest X-ray; we also plan to find medical expertise at pixels or coordinates level to judge and better assess the quality of the regions highlighted by explanation approach. With this respect, we also plan to explore explanations methods other than GradCAM.

References

1. Abbas, A., Abdelsamea, M.M., Gaber, M.M.: Classification of COVID-19 in chest X-ray images using detrac deep convolutional neural network. arXiv preprint arXiv:2003.13815 (2020)
2. Bach, S., Binder, A., Montavon, G., Klauschen, F., Müller, K.R., Samek, W.: On pixel-wise explanations for non-linear classifier decisions by layer-wise relevance propagation. PloS One **10**(7), e0130140 (2015)
3. Bruno, P., Calimeri, F., Kitanidis, A.S., De Momi, E.: Understanding automatic diagnosis and classification processes with data visualization. In: 2020 IEEE International Conference on Human-Machine Systems (ICHMS), pp. 1–6. IEEE (2020)
4. Bruno, P., Cinzia, M., Calimeri, F.: Understanding automatic COVID-19 classification using chest X-ray images (2020)
5. Bullock, J., Cuesta-Lázaro, C., Quera-Bofarull, A.: Xnet: a convolutional neural network (CNN) implementation for medical X-ray image segmentation suitable for small datasets. In: Medical Imaging 2019: Biomedical Applications in Molecular, Structural, and Functional Imaging, vol. 10953, p. 109531Z. International Society for Optics and Photonics (2019)
6. Candemir, S., et al.: Lung segmentation in chest radiographs using anatomical atlases with nonrigid registration. IEEE Trans. Med. Imaging **33**(2), 577–590 (2013)
7. Cohen, J.P., Morrison, P., Dao, L., Roth, K., Duong, T.Q., Ghassemi, M.: COVID-19 image data collection: prospective predictions are the future. arXiv preprint arXiv:2006.11988 (2020)
8. Colleoni, E., Moccia, S., Du, X., De Momi, E., Stoyanov, D.: Deep learning based robotic tool detection and articulation estimation with spatio-temporal layers. IEEE Robot. Autom. Lett. **4**(3), 2714–2721 (2019)

9. Haghanifar, A., Majdabadi, M.M., Ko, S.: COVID-CXNET: detecting COVID-19 in frontal chest X-ray images using deep learning. arXiv preprint arXiv:2006.13807 (2020)
10. Huang, G., Liu, Z., Van Der Maaten, L., Weinberger, K.Q.: Densely connected convolutional networks. In: Proceedings of the IEEE Conference on Computer Vision and Pattern Recognition, pp. 4700–4708 (2017)
11. Jaeger, S., et al.: Automatic tuberculosis screening using chest radiographs. IEEE Trans. Med. Imaging **33**(2), 233–245 (2013)
12. Kermany, D., Zhang, K., Goldbaum, M., et al.: Labeled optical coherence tomography (oct) and chest X-ray images for classification. Mendeley Data **2**(2) (2018)
13. Liu, H., Wang, L., Nan, Y., Jin, F., Wang, Q., Pu, J.: SDFN: segmentation-based deep fusion network for thoracic disease classification in chest x-ray images. Comput. Med. Imaging Graph. **75**, 66–73 (2019)
14. Mahendran, A., Vedaldi, A.: Understanding deep image representations by inverting them. In: Proceedings of the IEEE Conference on Computer Vision and Pattern Recognition, pp. 5188–5196 (2015)
15. Mangal, A., et al.: Covidaid: COVID-19 detection using chest X-ray. arXiv preprint arXiv:2004.09803 (2020)
16. Marín, D., Aquino, A., Gegúndez-Arias, M.E., Bravo, J.M.: A new supervised method for blood vessel segmentation in retinal images by using gray-level and moment invariants-based features. IEEE Trans. Med. Imaging **30**(1), 146–158 (2010)
17. McKeever, A.: Here's what coronavirus does to the body. National Geograph. (2020)
18. Moccia, S., et al.: Development and testing of a deep learning-based strategy for scar segmentation on CMR-LGE images. Magnet. Reson. Mater. Phys. Biol. Med. **32**(2), 187–195 (2019)
19. Motta, I., et al.: Tuberculosis, COVID-19 and migrants: preliminary analysis of deaths occurring in 69 patients from two cohorts. Pulmonology **26**(4), 233–240 (2020)
20. Organization, W.H., et al.: Health topics. coronavírus. Coronavirus: symptoms. World Health Organization, 2020a. Disponível em: https://www.who.int/healthtopics/coronavirus#tab=tab_3. Acesso em 7 (2020)
21. Öztürk, Ş., Özkaya, U., Barstuğan, M.: Classification of coronavirus (COVID-19) from X-ray and CT images using shrunken features. Int. J. Imaging Syst. Technol. **31**(1), 5–15 (2020)
22. Ozturk, T., Talo, M., Yildirim, E.A., Baloglu, U.B., Yildirim, O., Acharya, U.R.: Automated detection of COVID-19 cases using deep neural networks with X-ray images. Comput. Biol. Med. **121**, 103792 (2020)
23. Pandit, M.K., Banday, S.A., Naaz, R., Chishti, M.A.: Automatic detection of COVID-19 from chest radiographs using deep learning. Radiography **27**(2), 483–489 (2020)
24. Panwar, H., Gupta, P., Siddiqui, M.K., Morales-Menendez, R., Bhardwaj, P., Singh, V.: A deep learning and grad-CAM based color visualization approach for fast detection of COVID-19 cases using chest X-ray and CT-scan images. Chaos Solitons Fractals **140**, 110190 (2020)
25. Rahman, T., et al.: Reliable tuberculosis detection using chest X-ray with deep learning, segmentation and visualization. IEEE Access **8**, 191586–191601 (2020)
26. Rosebrock, A.: Imagenet: VGGNet, RESNet, inception, and xception with keras. Mars (2017)

27. Selvaraju, R.R., Cogswell, M., Das, A., Vedantam, R., Parikh, D., Batra, D.: Grad-CAM: visual explanations from deep networks via gradient-based localization. In: Proceedings of the IEEE International Conference on Computer Vision, pp. 618–626 (2017)

28. Singh, R.K., Pandey, R., Babu, R.N.: COVIDScreen: explainable deep learning framework for differential diagnosis of COVID-19 using chest X-rays. Neural Comput. Appl. 1–22 (2021). https://doi.org/10.1007/s00521-020-05636-6

29. Spadea, M.F., et al.: Deep convolution neural network (DCNN) multiplane approach to synthetic CT generation from MR images-application in brain proton therapy. Int. J. Radiat. Oncol. * Biol.* Phys. 105(3), 495–503 (2019)

30. Wang, H., Xia, Y.: Chestnet: a deep neural network for classification of thoracic diseases on chest radiography. arXiv preprint arXiv:1807.03058 (2018)

31. Wang, L., Wong, A.: COVID-net: a tailored deep convolutional neural network design for detection of COVID-19 cases from chest X-ray images. arXiv preprint arXiv:2003.09871 (2020)

32. Wang, X., Peng, Y., Lu, L., Lu, Z., Bagheri, M., Summers, R.M.: Chestx-ray8: hospital-scale chest X-ray database and benchmarks on weakly-supervised classification and localization of common thorax diseases. In: Proceedings of the IEEE Conference on Computer Vision and Pattern Recognition, pp. 2097–2106 (2017)

33. Zaffino, P., et al.: Fully automatic catheter segmentation in MRI with 3D convolutional neural networks: application to MRI-guided gynecologic brachytherapy. Phys. Med. Biol. 64(16), 165008 (2019)

34. Zeiler, M.D., Fergus, R.: Visualizing and understanding convolutional networks. In: Fleet, D., Pajdla, T., Schiele, B., Tuytelaars, T. (eds.) ECCV 2014. LNCS, vol. 8689, pp. 818–833. Springer, Cham (2014). https://doi.org/10.1007/978-3-319-10590-1_53

35. Zhou, B., Sun, Y., Bau, D., Torralba, A.: Interpretable basis decomposition for visual explanation. In: Proceedings of the European Conference on Computer Vision (ECCV), pp. 119–134 (2018)

36. Zotin, A., Hamad, Y., Simonov, K., Kurako, M.: Lung boundary detection for chest X-ray images classification based on GLCM and probabilistic neural networks. Proc. Comput. Sci. 159, 1439–1448 (2019)

SeXAI: A Semantic Explainable Artificial Intelligence Framework

Ivan Donadello[1](✉) ⬤ and Mauro Dragoni[2] ⬤

[1] KRDB Research Centre, Free University of Bozen-Bolzano, Bolzano, Italy
`ivan.donadello@unibz.it`
[2] Fondazione Bruno Kessler, Via Sommarive 18, 38123 Trento, Italy
`dragoni@fbk.eu`

Abstract. The interest in Explainable Artificial Intelligence (XAI) research is dramatically grown during the last few years. The main reason is the need of having systems that beyond being effective are also able to describe how a certain output has been obtained and to present such a description in a comprehensive manner with respect to the target users. A promising research direction making black boxes more transparent is the exploitation of semantic information. Such information can be exploited from different perspectives in order to provide a more comprehensive and interpretable representation of AI models. In this paper, we present the first version of SeXAI, a semantic-based explainable framework aiming to exploit semantic information for making black boxes more transparent. After a theoretical discussion, we show how this research direction is suitable and worthy of investigation by showing its application to a real-world use case.

Keywords: Explainable Artificial Intelligence · Ontologies · Knowledge bases · Artificial intelligence · Interpretability · Transparency

1 Introduction

Explainable Artificial Intelligence (XAI) aims at explaining the algorithmic decisions of AI solutions with non-technical terms in order to make these decisions trusted and easily comprehensible by humans [1]. If these AI solutions are based on learning algorithms and perceived as black boxes due to their complexity, XAI makes them more transparent and interpretable too. This is of great interest for both logical reasoning in rule engines and Machine Learning (ML) methods. The explanation of a reasoning process can be very difficult, especially when a system is based on a set of complex logical axioms whose logical inferences are performed with, for example, tableau algorithms [4]. Indeed, inconsistencies in logical axioms may be not well understood by users if the system limits to just report the violated axioms. Indeed, users are generally skilled to understand neither formal languages nor the behavior of a whole system. This is crucial for some

© Springer Nature Switzerland AG 2021
M. Baldoni and S. Bandini (Eds.): AIxIA 2020, LNAI 12414, pp. 51–66, 2021.
https://doi.org/10.1007/978-3-030-77091-4_4

applications, such as a power plant system where a warning message to the user must be clear and concise to avoid catastrophic consequences. On the other hand, ML methods are based on statistical models of the data where some explanatory variables (i.e., the features) of the data are leveraged in order to predict a dependent variable (i.e., a class or a numeric value). Many statistical methods (e.g., the principal component analysis) are able to detect what are the main involved features in a ML task. These involved features can be used to *explain* to user the reason of a particular decision. These features are usually handcrafted by human experts and consequently present a shared semantics. Modern Deep Neural Network (DNN) are able to learn these features with no need of human effort. However, the semantics of these learnt features is nor explicit or shareable with humans. Therefore, a human-comprehensible explanation about how and why an AI system took a decision is necessary.

A shared and agreed definition on explainability has not been reached in the AI community so far. Here we follow the definition of Adadi and Berrada [1] that argue for a distinction between interpretability and explainability. The former regards the study of a mathematical mapping between the inputs and the outputs of a black-box system. The latter regards a human comprehension of the logic and/or semantics of such a system. Doran et al. [15] refine the notion of explainability stating that an explainable (or comprehensible) system should provide a reason or justification about its output instead of focusing solely on the mathematical mapping. Moreover, they argue that *truly explainable systems* have to adopt reasoning engines that run on knowledge bases containing an explicit semantics in order to generate a human comprehensible explanation. In addition, the explainability power depends also on the background knowledge of the users.

To this extent, the logical reasoning associated to semantics is fundamental as it represents a bridge between the output machine and human concepts. This differs from other XAI works that try to analyze the activations of the hidden neurons (i.e., the learnt features) with respect to a given output without attaching a shared semantics. However, logical reasoning on the back-box output is not sufficient as it performs a post-hoc explanation of the black-box guided only by the axioms of a knowledge base. Indeed, no explicit link from the black-box learned features and the concepts in the knowledge base is used. The contribution of the paper addresses this issue.

We propose a novel semantic-based XAI (SeXAI) framework that generates explanations for a black-box output. Differently from Doran et al., such explanations are First-Order logic formulas whose predicates are semantic features connected to the classes of the black box output. Logic formulas are then easy to translate in natural language for a better human comprehension. Moreover, the semantic features are aligned with the neurons of the black box thus creating a neural-symbolic model. This allows reasoning between the output and the features and the improvement of both the knowledge base and the black box output. In addition, the semantics in the knowledge base is aligned with the annotation in the dataset. This is fundamental both for the neural-symbolic alignment and for the black box performance. The latter were tested with experiments on image classification showing that a semantic aligned with the training set outperforms a model whose semantics is deduced from the output with only logical reasoning. The rest of the paper follows with Sect. 2 that provides a state-of-the-art of techniques for generating explanations from logical formulas. Section 3 describes the main concepts of the SeXAI framework whereas Sect. 4 shows a first application and results of the framework in an image classification task. Section 5 concludes the paper.

2 Related Work

The research on XAI has been widely explored in the last years [19], but most of the contributions focused only on the analysis of how learning models (a.k.a. black boxes) work. This is a limited view of the topic since there is a school of thought arguing that an effective explainability of learning models cannot be achieved without the use of domain knowledge since data analysis alone is not enough for achieving a full-fledged explainable system [8]. This statement has been further discussed recently by asserting that the key for designing a completely explainable AI system is the integration of Semantic Web technologies [21,22,31]. Semantic Web technologies enabling the design of strategies for providing explanations in natural language [2,28] where explanations are provided through textual rule-like notation. NLG strategies have been designed also for generating natural language text from triples [38] and for translating SPARQL queries into a natural language form understandable by non-experts [17]. Here, we focused on the integration of semantic information as enabler for improving the comprehensiveness of XAI systems. Our aim is to generate natural language explanations as result of the synergies between neural models and logic inferences for supporting end-users in understanding the output provided by the systems.

One of the explanation of the logical reasoning in an ontology is implemented with two orthogonal approaches: *justifications* and *proofs*. The former computes the minimal subset of the ontology axioms that logically entails an axiom. The latter computes also all the inference steps [27].

One of the first user studies dealing with explanations for entailments of OWL ontologies was performed by [26]. The study investigated the effectiveness of different types of explanation for explaining unsatisfiable classes in OWL ontologies. The authors found that the subjects receiving full debugging support performed best (i.e., fastest) on the task, and that users approved of the debugging facilities. Similarly, [30] performed a user study to evaluate an explanation tool, but did not carry out any detailed analysis of the difficulty users had with understanding these explanations. While, [5] presents a user study evaluating a model-exploration based approach to explanation in OWL ontologies. The study revealed that the majority of participants could solve specific tasks with the help of the developed model-exploration tool, however, there was no detailed analysis of which aspects of the ontology the subjects struggled with and how they used the tool. The work [25] presents several algorithms for computing all the justifications of an entailment in a OWL-DL knowledge base. However, nor study or user evaluation is performed to assess the capability of the computed justifications of the logical entailments. The work in [20] focuses on the explanation, through justifications, of the disclosure of personal data to users (patients and staff) of hospitals. This is performed by translating SWRL rules inconsistencies into natural language utterances. Moreover, the SWRL rules translation is performed axiom by axiom, thus generating a quite long sentence. This could require too much time for reading and understanding. Whereas, our method returns only a single utterance summarizing the whole justification.

Formal proofs are the other form of explanation for logical reasoning. In [33] the authors present an approach to provide proof-based explanations for entailments of the CLASSIC system. The system omits intermediate steps and provides further filtering strategies in order to generate short and simple explanations. The work proposed in [7] first introduced a proof-based explanation system for knowledge bases in the Description Logic ALC [4]. The system generates sequent calculus style proofs using an extension of a tableaux reasoning algorithm, which are then enriched to create natural language explanations. However, there exists no user studies to explore the effectiveness of these proofs. In [29] the authors proposed several (tree, graphical, logical and hybrid) visualizations of defeasible logic proofs and present a user study in order to evaluate the impact of the different approaches. These representations are hard to understand for non-expert users. Indeed, the study is based on participants from a postgraduate course (who have attended a Semantic Web course) and from the research staff. In general, proof algorithms for Description Logic are based on Tableau techniques [4] whereas proof algorithms for other logics are studied in the field of Automated Reasoning [35].

This wide range of approaches to explanation of logical entailments is more focused on the development of efficient algorithms than on effective algorithms for common users. Indeed, all the computed explanations are sets of logical axioms understandable only by expert users. The aim of our work is to provide and effective representation to explanation for all users. This representation is based on the verbalization of the explanation in natural language. This verbalization can be performed by using methods that translate axioms of an OWL ontology in Attempto Controlled English [23,24] or in standard English [3] with the use of templates. This last work also presents some users' studies on the quality of the generated sentences. However, these works do not handle with the reasoning results (justifications or proofs), indeed, no strategy for selecting and rendering an explanation is studied.

3   The Framework

In the fields of Machine Learning and Pattern Recognition, a feature is a characteristic or a measurable property of an object/phenomenon under observation [6]. Features can be numeric or structured and they are crucial in tasks

such as pattern detection, classification or regression as they serve as explanatory variables. Indeed, informative and discriminating features are combined in
a simple or complex manner by the main ML algorithms. This also holds in our
everyday experience, a dish composed by pasta, bacon, eggs, pepper and aged
cheese (features) is recognized as pasta with Carbonara sauce (the class). Diseases are recognized according to the symptoms (features), or some features of a
person (e.g., age, high meat consumption, obesity and sedentary life) can be the
cause of a certain disease. The price of the houses is computed according to the
features of, e.g., location, square meters and years of the real estate. However,
with the rise of Deep Neural Networks (DNN), features are learnt by the system
from the raw data without the necessity of handcrafting from domain experts.
This has improved the performance of such systems with the drawback of loosing
comprehensibility from users. Indeed, DNNs embed the data in a vector space
in the most discriminating way without any link to a formal semantics. The
aim of SeXAI is to link a DNN with a formal semantics in order to provide a
comprehensible explanation of the DNN output to everyday users.

Following the definitions of Doran et al. [15], we ground the notion of explainable system into the concept of a *comprehensible system*, that is a system that
computes its output along with symbols that allow users to understand what
are the main *semantic features* in the data that triggered that particular output. Here, we refine the work of Doran et al. by introducing the concept of
semantic feature. These are features that can be expressed through predicates
of a First-Order Logic (FOL) language and represent the common and shared
attributes of an object/phenomenon that allow its recognition. Examples can
be $ContainsBacon(x)$ or $ContainsEggs(x)$ indicating the ingredients of a dish
in a picture. Semantic features in principle can be further explained by more
fine-grained semantic features. For example, the $ChoppedBacon(x)$ feature can
be explained by the $HasCubicShape(x)$ and $HasPinkColor(x)$ features. However, in a nutritional domain, these latter features do not add further comprehension to users and can represent an overload of information. Therefore, the
knowledge engineering and/or domain expert have to select the right granularity of the semantic features to present to users and therefore ensuring a sort
of atomic property of these features. Semantic features are different from the
learnt numeric (and not comprehensible) features of a DNN. The aim of a comprehensible system is to find an alignment between the learnt and the semantic
features.

The connection between a DNN output and its semantic features is formalized
through the definition of *comprehension axiom*.

Definition 1 (Comprehension axiom). *Given a FOL language with* $\mathcal{P} =$
$\{O\}_1^n \cup \{A\}_1^m$ *the set of its predicate symbols, a comprehension axiom is a formula of the form*

$$\bigwedge_{i=1}^{k} O_i(x) \leftrightarrow \bigwedge_{i=1}^{l} A_i(x)$$

with $\{O\}_1^n$ the set of output symbols of a DNN and $\{A\}_1^m$ the corresponding semantic features (or attributes).

A comprehension axiom formalizes the main tasks of a DNN:

Multiclass Classification: the predicate $O_i(x)$ represents a class (e.g., pasta with Carbonara sauce or sushi) for x and $k = 1$ as a softmax is applied in the last layer of the DNN. The semantic features represent, for example, ingredients contained in the recognized dish.

Multilabel Classification: $O_i(x)$ is part of a list of predicates being computed by the DNN (e.g., dinner and party) for x and $k > 1$ as a sigmoid is applied in the last layer of the DNN. The semantic features represent, for example, objects in the scene, such as, pizza, table, bottles, person and balloons.

Regression: $O_i(x)$ can be part of a list of predicates being computed by the DNN (e.g., the asked price and the real values of house) for x. Here $k \geq 1$ with a sigmoid applied in the last layer of the DNN. The semantic features are properties of interest for buying a house.

Once a set of comprehension axioms is returned by our comprehensible system, the former can be easily transformed into a graph representation where the nodes are the unary predicates O_i and A_i plus other information such as a possible neural network scores for these predicates. The edges are the logic relations between these predicates, such as implications and n-ary predicates with $n > 1$. A single comprehension axiom can be represented as a star-shape graph with O in the center, A_i at the end of the branches and the biimplications as edges. A graph representation can be easily rendered as an image or a natural language sentence used in a dialogue with the user. All these kinds of rendering can be performed with automatic tools. Moreover, the predicates A_i can be linked with other predicates through logical relations. This would make the explanation more structured with more information for the users. In addition, such a structured representation can be easily queried with languages such as SPARQL. Graph representations for explanations are proved to be effective for the users, that is, more comprehensible, in persuasion systems for healthcare [12]. In this case, explanations are attached to a user model in order to return a tailored explanation according to the user obstacles and capacities.

We present the SeXAI framework for comprehensible systems in Fig. 1. The knowledge base $\mathcal{KB}$ contains both the predicate symbols in $\mathcal{P}$ and the comprehension axioms for annotating the data. This annotation requires an effort that depends on both the classification task (annotating a picture with bounding boxes requires more effort than annotating the scene without bounding boxes) and on the complexity of $\mathcal{KB}$. Indeed, if the output is linked with many semantic features this would make the annotation challenging. However, this effort can be alleviate with the use of crowdsourcing and of emerging approaches and tools for annotating documents [34]. Among those, Prodigy[1] is one of the most promising and targeted at tasks typical for Artificial Intelligence, Machine Learning,

---

[1] https://prodi.gy/.

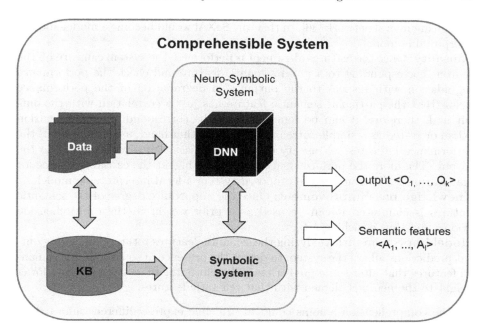

Fig. 1. In the SeXAI framework data are annotated with symbols of a knowledge base. A symbolic system is aligned with a DNN in order to provide an output and a set of semantic features consistent with the comprehension axioms in the knowledge base.

Natural Language Processing, and Computer Vision. Prodigy is also open to the customisation of annotation tags linked with concepts coming from a domain knowledge base. The comprehension axioms are passed to the symbolic system that is in charge of i) analyzing the output of the DNN and the associated semantic features; ii) reasoning about them according to the comprehension axioms; iii) returning a, possibly refined, output along with the related semantic features. This makes the proposed framework a local interpreter that provides a reason (the semantic features) for a given output. This architecture extends the one in [15], where a reasoner computes the explanation of the output, with a semantic module that enables several tasks that improve the comprehension and the transparency (i.e., the interpretation) of the DNN:

Output and semantic features refinement: The DNN is trained to return both the output and the semantic features. Then, with the use of fuzzy reasoning or neural-symbolic systems [9,11,13,14,32], both outputs can be refined according to the comprehension axioms and to the evidence coming from the scores of the DNN.

Feature Alignment: Once a DNN is trained, it is possible to analyze which are the most activated neurons of the last hidden layer [18] for each semantic feature. In this manner, we can align the high-level features of the DNN with the semantic features in $\mathcal{KB}$. Such an alignment can also be learnt with an additional supporting neural network [36]. In this way SeXAI would become a model-specific interpretable model.

Causality: Once the features alignment is performed, the system can turn off the neurons corresponding to a given semantic feature and check the performance degradation with respect to the output. No degradation of the performance means that the particular semantic feature has just a correlation with the output and, therefore, it can be removed from the corresponding comprehension axiom or stated as a simple correlation. On the other hand, a degradation of the performance indicates a causality of the semantic features with respect to the output. The more the performance degrades the higher the causality degree for that feature is. This makes the proposed system a local interpretable model.

Knowledge base improvement: Once the importance degree of the semantic features is computed it can be used as a prior weight in the comprehension axioms and thus enriching $\mathcal{KB}$.

Model improvement: Analyzing the semantic features returned by wrong output predictions allows the system to detect the presence of some common semantic features that alter some predictions. Therefore, the model can assign a lower weight to the neurons aligned with that semantic features.

The comprehension axioms could in principle express different information for an output O. For instance, in the pasta with Carbonara sauce recipe, some axioms in $\mathcal{KB}$ state the standard food categories but other axioms could state a slightly different version for Carbonara with different categories. This case can be addressed by assigning different weights to each comprehension axiom. These weights represent the trust of the system to each recipe and can be a-priori defined or learnt from the data. Neural-symbolic systems [9] are able to deal with these weighted axioms in order to return a reliable output along with the more probable involved semantic features.

The symbolic system in SeXAI extends the framework of Doran et al. [15] by computing the alignment of semantic and DNN features that enables the improvement of both $\mathcal{KB}$ and of the model. Differently, in [15] the reasoner module is able to only generate the output and the semantic features. In addition, our work makes a step forward a more structured definition of explanation by defining the explanation as a feature vector of semantic features. These can be further linked with other predicates in $\mathcal{KB}$ enabling a more structured (and richer in semantics) representation for the explanation.

4   SeXAI in Action

Section 3 provided the general description of the SeXAI framework that we proposed for increasing the overall comprehensiveness of AI models. In this Section, we show how the SeXAI framework can be instantiated within a real-world scenario. In particular, we applied the SeXAI framework to image classification with the aim of demonstrating how the integration of semantics into an AI-based classification systems triggers both the generation of explanations and, at the same time, an improvement of the overall effectiveness of the classification model.

As described in Sect. 3, the SeXAI framework is composed by different modules that, depending on the scenario in which the framework is deployed, can be instantiated or not. Let us consider a running example of food recognition from images. In this case, the output is the label of the food in the dish (e.g., pasta with Carbonara sauce) and the semantic features are the detected food categories (aged cheese, cold cuts, pasta and eggs) that have high classification scores. In this case a possible rendering of the system output and explanation in natural language would be: "I recognized a pasta with Carbonara sauce dish as I have a good confidence about its food categories: aged cheese, pasta, cold cuts and eggs". Information about food categories are particularly useful in scenario where physicians are supported by information systems concerning the diet monitoring of people affected by nutritional diseases (e.g., diabetes, hypertension, obesity, etc.). However, as very first evaluation of this framework, we focused on predicting only the semantic features in order to check whether the semantics posed at dataset annotation level is more effective than the semantics posed after a prediction applying simple logical rules. The aim of our experiments is to check the right place for the semantics. This setting does not lose generality as a multitasking neural network can be trained to jointly predict both the food image classification and its semantic features (the contained food categories). The performance of a multitasking setting are the same on the semantic features here presented (see Table 1) and good ones on the food image classification (more than 70% of mean average precision). The aim of our evaluation is expressed by the following research question:

RQ: Does the injection of knowledge at data-annotation level improve the explainability of the SeXAI framework?

This involves to check whether the annotation of the dataset with the comprehension axioms improve the quality of the semantic features and therefore the system explainability. We address the research question with a multi-label classification setting of the semantic features. Therefore, by starting from the SeXAI architecture shown in Fig. 1, we instantiated the modules as follows.

- The "Data" module contains our dataset of food images we used for training the classification model. A more detailed description of the dataset is provided in Sect. 4.1.
- The "Knowledge Base" contains, beyond a taxonomy of recipes and food categories, the composition of each recipe in terms of its food categories. Recipes compositions are described through object properties within the knowledge base. More specifically, in our scenario we adopted the HeLiS ontology [16] where we have the food category-based composition of more than 8,000 recipes[2]. Each food image is annotated with both the recipe label (pasta with Carbonara sauce) and the corresponding food categories (pasta, cold cuts, etc.).

---

[2] In the remaining of the paper, we will refer to some concepts defined within the HeLiS ontology. We leave to the reader the task of checking the meaning of each concept within the reference paper.

- As "Black-box model", we implemented a DNN trained with recipe/food images annotated with the list of related food categories. Given a food image x, the recipe/food label represents the $O(x)$ output neuron, while the food categories represent the semantic features $A(x)$ output neurons. As mentioned above, we decided to not include the $O(x)$ output neurons and to classify each image by its semantic features $A(x)$. Hence, each neuron of the DNN output layer indicates if one of the food categories contained in the dataset has been detected within the images or not.
- Finally, in our scenario the "Symbolic System" links together the "Knowledge Base" and the output of the DNN for generating natural language explanations of the classification results.

The evaluation of explanations quality is still an open topic within the AI research area [21]. Moreover, in our scenario, explanations aim to provide a comprehensive description of the output rather than being a vehicle for improving the model. Hence, the evaluation of their language content is not of interest. Instead, the SeXAI framework evaluation, provided in this work, focuses on the effectiveness of exploiting semantic features for both training and classification purposes. As baseline, we used a post-hoc semantic-based strategy where images used for training the DNN were annotated only with the corresponding recipe label. In our running example, the baseline would automatically retrieve the corresponding food categories from HeLiS once the DNN classified the input image with, e.g., pasta with Carbonara sauce. Here, the list of food categories has been extracted after the classification of each images by exploiting the predicted recipe label. Figure 2 shows the building blocks of the baseline. For readability, hereafter we will refer to the instantiation of the SeXAI framework as "multi-label classifier", while the baseline will be labeled as "single-label classifier".

4.1   Quantitative Evaluation

In the considered scenario, a good performance on recognizing food categories is important as the misclassification of images could trigger wrong behaviors of the systems in which the classifier is integrated. For example, if the framework would be integrated into a recommendation system, a misclassification of a food image would lead to the generation of wrong messages or even no message to the target user.

The Food and Food Categories (FFoCat) Dataset[3]. We leverage the food and food category concepts in HeLiS for the multi-label classification. However, current food image datasets are not built with these concepts as labels, so it was necessary to build a new dataset (named FFoCat) with these concepts. We start by sampling some of the most common recipes in *Recipe* and use them as food labels. The food categories are then automatically retrieved from *BasicFood* with a SPARQL query. Examples of food labels are *Pasta with Carbonara Sauce* and

---

[3] The dataset, its comparison and the code are available at https://bit.ly/2Y7zSWZ.

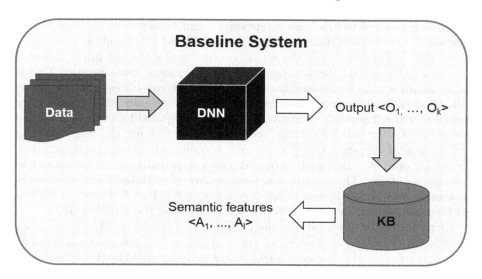

Fig. 2. The architecture of the baseline system we used for comparing the effectiveness of the SeXAI framework concerning the food images classification task.

Baked Sea Bream. Their associated food categories are *Pasta, AgedCheese, VegetalOils, Eggs, ColdCuts* and *FreshFish, VegetalOils,* respectively. We collect 156 labels for foods (*Recipe* concept) and 51 for food categories (*BasicFood* concept). We scrape the Web, using Google Images as search engine, to automatically download all the images related to the food labels. Then, we manually clean the dataset by checking if the images are compliant with the related labels. This results in 58,962 images with 47,108 images for the training set and 11,854 images for the test set (80–20 ratio of splitting). Then, we use the comprehension axioms to annotate the images with both the food label (the output O) and the corresponding food categories labels (that are our semantic features A_i). This has been obtained by leveraging HeLiS properties, we enrich the image annotations with the corresponding food category labels to perform multi-label classification. The dataset is affected by some natural imbalance, indeed the food categories present a long-tail distribution: only few food categories labels have the majority of the examples. On the contrary, many food categories labels have few examples. This makes the food classification challenging.

Experimental Settings and Metrics. For both multi and single-label classification we separately train the Inception-V3 network [37] from scratch on the FFoCat training set to find the best set of weights. The fine tuning using pre-trained ImageNet [10] weights did not perform sufficiently. This is probably due to the fact that the learnt low-level features of the first layers of the network belong to general domains and do not match properly with the specific Mediterranean food domain. Indeed, many food images in ImageNet belong to oriental food. For the multi-label classification, we use a sigmoid as activation function of the last fully-connected layer of the Inception-V3 and binary cross entropy as loss function. This is the standard setting for multi-label classification. Regarding the single-label classification, the activation function of the last fully-connected layer is a softmax and the loss function is a categorical cross entropy. This is the standard setting for multi-class classification. We run 100 epochs of training with batch size of 16 and a learning rate of 10^{-6}. At each epoch images are resized to 299×299 pixels to fit the input format required by Inception-V3 and are augmented by using rotations, width and height shifts, shearing, zooming and horizontal flipping. This results in a training set 100 times bigger than the initial one. We used early stopping (with a patience of 15 iterations) to prevent overfitting. The training has been performed with the Keras framework (TensorFlow as backend) on a PC equipped with a NVIDIA GeForce GTX 1080. All these details can be checked in the link pointing at the source code.

As performance metric we use the mean average precision (MAP) that summarizes the classifier precision-recall curve: $MAP = \sum_{i=1}^{n}(R_n - R_{n-1})P_n$, i.e., the weighted mean of precision P_n achieved at each threshold level n. The weight is the increase of the recall in the previous threshold: $R_n - R_{n-1}$. The macro AP is the average of the AP over the classes, the micro instead considers each entry of the predictions as a label. We preferred MAP instead of accuracy as the latter for sparse vectors can give misleading results: high results for output vectors with all zeros.

Results. Given an (set of) input image(s) x, the computing of the precision-recall curve requires the predicted vector(s) y of food category labels and a score associated to each label in y. In the multi-label method this score is directly returned by the Inception-V3 network (the final logits). In the single-label and inference method this score needs to be computed. We test two strategies: (i) we perform *exact inference* of the food categories from HeLiS and assign the value 1 to the scores of each $y_i \in y$; (ii) the food categories labels inherit the *uncertainty* returned the DNN: the score of each y_i is the logit value s_i returned by $DNN(x)$. Results are in Table 1. The direct multi-label has very good performance (both in micro and macro AP) in comparison with the single-label models. The micro-AP is always better than the macro-AP as it is sensible to the mentioned imbalance of the data. This means that errors in the single food classification propagate to the majority of the food categories the given food contains. That is, the inferred food categories will be wrong because the food classification is wrong. On the other hand, errors in the direct multi-label classification will affect only few food categories. We inspected in more detail some of the errors committed by the classifiers in order to have a better understanding of their behaviors. In some cases, the single-label method misclassified an image with *Backed Potatoes* as *Backed Pumpkin* thus missing the category of *FreshStarchyVegetables*. Another image contains a *Vegetable Pie* but the single-label method infers the wrong category of *PizzaBread*. In another image, this method mistakes *Pasta with Garlic, Oil and Chili Peppers* with *Pasta with Carbonara Sauce*, thus inferring wrong *Eggs* and *ColdCuts*. Here the multi-label method classifies all the categories correctly. Therefore, the multi-label method allows a more fine grained classification of the

Table 1. The multi-label classification of food categories outperforms in average precision (AP) the methods based on single-label classification and logical inference.

Method	Micro-AP (%)	Macro-AP (%)
Multi-label (SeXAI framework)	**76.24**	**50.12**
Single-class without uncertainty (baseline)	50.53	31.79
Single-class with uncertainty (baseline)	60.21	42.51

food categories with respect tto the single-label method. The latter has better results if the score returned by the DNN is propagated to the food categories labels withe respect to the exact inference.

4.2 Discussion

The experience of designing the SeXAI framework and the analysis of results obtained from a preliminary validation within a real-world use case highlighted two important directions towards the long-term goal of achieving a fully-explainable AI system.

First, the integration of semantic features with black-box models enabled the generation of comprehensive explanations. SeXAI can be considered a neuro-symbolic framework conjugating the effectiveness of black-box models (e.g., DNN) with the transparency of semantic knowledge that, where possible, can support the generation of explanations describing the behavior of AI systems. This aspect opens to a very interesting and innovative research direction centered on the content of the generated explanations. Indeed, the integration of semantic features for generating explanations can be exploited for refining the statistical model itself (as described in Sect. 3). For instance by analyzing correlations between the presence of specific semantic features within explanations and the performance of the black-box model. Future work will focus on strengthening this liaison within the SeXAI framework in order to validate if an inference process could improve the classification capability and, at the same time, to observe how inference results could be exploited for refining the black-box model.

Second, the integration of semantic features can lead to better classification performance. Results presented in Table 1 show that through the integration of semantic features, it is possible to improve the overall effectiveness of the black-box model. This is a very interesting finding since it confirms the importance of a by-design integration of semantic features. Future activities will further investigate this hypothesis within other scenarios with the aim of understanding which are the boundaries and if there exist some constraints in the application of this strategy. For instance, the granularity of semantic features with respect to the entities that have to be classified could play an important role. Hence, a trade-off has to be found in order to maintain the explainable capability of the system and, at the same time, an acceptable effectiveness of the classification model.

5   Conclusions

The aim of Explainable Artificial Intelligence is to provide black-box algorithms with strategies to produce a reason or justification for their outputs. This is fundamental to make these algorithms trusted and easily comprehensible by humans. A formal semantics, provided by knowledge bases, encoded in a logical language allows the connection between the numeric features of a black box and the human concepts. Indeed, a justification in a logical language format can be easily translated in natural language sentences in an automatic way.

In this paper, we presented the first version of SeXAI, a semantic-based explainable framework aiming at exploiting semantic information for making black boxes more comprehensible. SeXAI is a neural-symbolic system that analyses the output of a black box and creates a connection between the learnt features and the semantic concepts of a knowledge base in order to generate an explanation in a logical language. This allows reasoning on the black box and its explanation, the improvement of the knowledge base and of the black box output. The semantics in the knowledge base is aligned with the annotations in the dataset. This improves the performance of SeXAI on a task of multi-label image classification with respect to a system that performs solely logical reasoning on the black box output. Therefore, we satisfied our research question about the right place for the semantics: a semantics at data-annotation level improves the explainability of the system.

As future work, we will perform some experiments on the quality of the alignment between the learnt and the semantic features. In particular, we will evaluate the degree of causality of the semantic features with respect to the output and how the attention of a black box can be moved towards the semantic features in order to improve the model performance.

References

1. Adadi, A., Berrada, M.: Peeking inside the black-box: a survey on explainable artificial intelligence (XAI). IEEE Access **6**, 52138–52160 (2018)
2. Ai, Q., Azizi, V., Chen, X., Zhang, Y.: Learning heterogeneous knowledge base embeddings for explainable recommendation. Algorithms **11**(9), 137 (2018)
3. Androutsopoulos, I., Lampouras, G., Galanis, D.: Generating natural language descriptions from OWL ontologies: the NaturalOWL system. J. Artif. Intell. Res. **48**, 671–715 (2013)
4. Baader, F., Calvanese, D., McGuinness, D.L., Nardi, D., Patel-Schneider, P.F. (eds.): The Description Logic Handbook: Theory, Implementation, and Applications. Cambridge University Press, Cambridge (2003)
5. Bauer, J., Sattler, U., Parsia, B.: Explaining by example: model exploration for ontology comprehension. In: Description Logics. CEUR Workshop Proceedings, vol. 477. CEUR-WS.org (2009)
6. Bishop, C.M.: Pattern Recognition and Machine Learning. Information Science and Statistics, 5th edn. Springer, New York (2007)
7. Borgida, A., Franconi, E., Horrocks, I.: Explaining ALC subsumption. In: Horn, W. (ed.) ECAI 2000, Proceedings of the 14th European Conference on Artificial Intelligence, Berlin, Germany, 20–25 August 2000, pp. 209–213. IOS Press (2000)

8. Cherkassky, V., Dhar, S.: Interpretation of black-box predictive models. In: Vovk, V., Papadopoulos, H., Gammerman, A. (eds.) Measures of Complexity, pp. 267–286. Springer, Cham (2015). https://doi.org/10.1007/978-3-319-21852-6_19

9. Daniele, A., Serafini, L.: Neural networks enhancement through prior logical knowledge. CoRR abs/2009.06087 (2020)

10. Deng, J., Dong, W., Socher, R., Li, L.J., Li, K., Fei-Fei, L.: ImageNet: a large-scale hierarchical image database. In: CVPR 2009 (2009)

11. Diligenti, M., Gori, M., Saccà, C.: Semantic-based regularization for learning and inference. Artif. Intell. **244**, 143–165 (2017)

12. Donadello, I., Dragoni, M., Eccher, C.: Persuasive explanation of reasoning inferences on dietary data. In: SEMEX: 1st Workshop on Semantic Explainability, vol. 2465, pp. 46–61. CEUR-WS.org (2019)

13. Donadello, I., Serafini, L.: Mixing low-level and semantic features for image interpretation. In: Agapito, L., Bronstein, M.M., Rother, C. (eds.) ECCV 2014. LNCS, vol. 8926, pp. 283–298. Springer, Cham (2015). https://doi.org/10.1007/978-3-319-16181-5_20

14. Donadello, I., Serafini, L.: Compensating supervision incompleteness with prior knowledge in semantic image interpretation. In: IJCNN, pp. 1–8. IEEE (2019)

15. Doran, D., Schulz, S., Besold, T.R.: What does explainable AI really mean? A new conceptualization of perspectives. In: Besold, T.R., Kutz, O. (eds.) Proceedings of the First International Workshop on Comprehensibility and Explanation in AI and ML 2017 Co-Located with 16th International Conference of the Italian Association for Artificial Intelligence (AI*IA 2017). CEUR Workshop Proceedings, Bari, Italy, 16–17 November 2017, vol. 2071. CEUR-WS.org (2017)

16. Dragoni, M., Bailoni, T., Maimone, R., Eccher, C.: HeLiS: an ontology for supporting healthy lifestyles. In: Vrandečić, D., et al. (eds.) ISWC 2018. LNCS, vol. 11137, pp. 53–69. Springer, Cham (2018). https://doi.org/10.1007/978-3-030-00668-6_4

17. Ell, B., Harth, A., Simperl, E.: SPARQL query verbalization for explaining semantic search engine queries. In: Presutti, V., d'Amato, C., Gandon, F., d'Aquin, M., Staab, S., Tordai, A. (eds.) ESWC 2014. LNCS, vol. 8465, pp. 426–441. Springer, Cham (2014). https://doi.org/10.1007/978-3-319-07443-6_29

18. Erhan, D., Bengio, Y., Courville, A., Vincent, P.: Visualizing higher-layer features of a deep network. University of Montreal **1341**(3), 1 (2009)

19. Gilpin, L.H., Bau, D., Yuan, B.Z., Bajwa, A., Specter, M., Kagal, L.: Explaining explanations: an overview of interpretability of machine learning. In: Bonchi, F., Provost, F.J., Eliassi-Rad, T., Wang, W., Cattuto, C., Ghani, R. (eds.) 5th IEEE International Conference on Data Science and Advanced Analytics, DSAA 2018, Turin, Italy, 1–3 October 2018, pp. 80–89. IEEE (2018)

20. Hamed, R.G., Pandit, H.J., O'Sullivan, D., Conlan, O.: Explaining disclosure decisions over personal data. In: ISWC Satellites. CEUR Workshop Proceedings, vol. 2456, pp. 41–44. CEUR-WS.org (2019)

21. Holzinger, A., Biemann, C., Pattichis, C.S., Kell, D.B.: What do we need to build explainable AI systems for the medical domain? CoRR abs/1712.09923 (2017)

22. Holzinger, A., Kieseberg, P., Weippl, E., Tjoa, A.M.: Current advances, trends and challenges of machine learning and knowledge extraction: from machine learning to explainable AI. In: Holzinger, A., Kieseberg, P., Tjoa, A.M., Weippl, E. (eds.) CD-MAKE 2018. LNCS, vol. 11015, pp. 1–8. Springer, Cham (2018). https://doi.org/10.1007/978-3-319-99740-7_1

23. Kaljurand, K.: ACE view – an ontology and rule editor based on attempto controlled English. In: OWLED. CEUR Workshop Proceedings, vol. 432. CEUR-WS.org (2008)

24. Kaljurand, K., Fuchs, N.E.: Verbalizing OWL in attempto controlled English. In: OWLED. CEUR Workshop Proceedings, vol. 258. CEUR-WS.org (2007)
25. Kalyanpur, A., Parsia, B., Horridge, M., Sirin, E.: Finding all justifications of OWL DL entailments. In: Aberer, K., et al. (eds.) ASWC/ISWC -2007. LNCS, vol. 4825, pp. 267–280. Springer, Heidelberg (2007). https://doi.org/10.1007/978-3-540-76298-0_20
26. Kalyanpur, A., Parsia, B., Sirin, E., Hendler, J.A.: Debugging unsatisfiable classes in OWL ontologies. J. Web Semant. 3(4), 268–293 (2005)
27. Kazakov, Y., Klinov, P., Stupnikov, A.: Towards reusable explanation services in protege. In: Description Logics. CEUR Workshop Proceedings, vol. 1879. CEUR-WS.org (2017)
28. Khan, O.Z., Poupart, P., Black, J.P.: Explaining recommendations generated by MDPs. In: Roth-Berghofer, T., Schulz, S., Leake, D.B., Bahls, D. (eds.) Explanation-Aware Computing, Papers from the 2008 ECAI Workshop, Patras, Greece, 21–22 July 2008, pp. 13–24. University of Patras (2008)
29. Kontopoulos, E., Bassiliades, N., Antoniou, G.: Visualizing semantic web proofs of defeasible logic in the DR-DEVICE system. Knowl.-Based Syst. 24(3), 406–419 (2011)
30. Lam, J.S.C.: Methods for resolving inconsistencies in ontologies. Ph.D. thesis, University of Aberdeen, UK (2007)
31. Lécué, F.: On the role of knowledge graphs in explainable AI. Semant. Web 11(1), 41–51 (2020)
32. Mao, J., Gan, C., Kohli, P., Tenenbaum, J.B., Wu, J.: The neuro-symbolic concept learner: interpreting scenes, words, and sentences from natural supervision. In: ICLR. OpenReview.net (2019)
33. McGuinness, D.L., Borgida, A.: Explaining subsumption in description logics. In: IJCAI (1), pp. 816–821. Morgan Kaufmann (1995)
34. Neves, M., Ševa, J.: An extensive review of tools for manual annotation of documents. Briefings Bioinform. 22(1), 146–163 (2019)
35. Robinson, J.A., Voronkov, A. (eds.): Handbook of Automated Reasoning, vol. 2. Elsevier and MIT Press (2001)
36. Selvaraju, R.R.: Choose your neuron: incorporating domain knowledge through neuron-importance. In: Ferrari, V., Hebert, M., Sminchisescu, C., Weiss, Y. (eds.) ECCV 2018. LNCS, vol. 11217, pp. 540–556. Springer, Cham (2018). https://doi.org/10.1007/978-3-030-01261-8_32
37. Szegedy, C., Vanhoucke, V., Ioffe, S., Shlens, J., Wojna, Z.: Rethinking the inception architecture for computer vision. In: CVPR, pp. 2818–2826. IEEE Computer Society (2016)
38. Vougiouklis, P., et al.: Neural wikipedian: generating textual summaries from knowledge base triples. J. Web Semant. 52–53, 1–15 (2018)

Explainable Attentional Neural Recommendations for Personalized Social Learning

Luca Marconi[1,2(✉)] 📷, Ricardo Anibal Matamoros Aragon[1,2]📷, Italo Zoppis[1]📷, Sara Manzoni[1]📷, Giancarlo Mauri[1]📷, and Francesco Epifania[2]

[1] Department of Computer science, University of Milano Bicocca, Milano, Italy
{l.marconi3,r.matamorosaragon}@campus.unimib.it
{italo.zoppis,sara.manzoni,giancarlo.mauri}@unimib.it
[2] Social Things srl, Milano, Italy
{luca.marconi,ricardo.matamoros,francesco.epifania}@socialthingum.com

Abstract. Learning and training processes are starting to be affected by the diffusion of Artificial Intelligence (AI) techniques and methods. AI can be variously exploited for supporting education, though especially deep learning (DL) models are normally suffering from some degree of opacity and lack of interpretability. Explainable AI (XAI) is aimed at creating a set of new AI techniques able to improve their output or decisions with more transparency and interpretability. In the educational field it could be particularly significant and challenging to understand the reasons behind models outcomes, especially when it comes to suggestions to create, manage or evaluate courses or didactic resources. Deep attentional mechanisms proved to be particularly effective for identifying relevant communities and relationships in any given input network that can be exploited with the aim of improving useful information to interpret the suggested decision process. In this paper we provide the first stages of our ongoing research project, aimed at significantly empowering the recommender system of the educational platform "WhoTeach" by means of explainability, to help teachers or experts to create and manage high-quality courses for personalized learning.

The presented model is actually our first tentative to start to include explainability in the system. As shown, the model has strong potentialities to provide relevant recommendations. Moreover, it allows the possibility to implement effective techniques to completely reach explainability.

Keywords: Explainable AI · Personalized learning · WhoTeach · Social recommendations · Graph attention networks

1 Introduction

Nowadays, learning and training processes are starting to be affected by the diffusion of AI techniques and methods [1,2]. However, in order to effectively and

© Springer Nature Switzerland AG 2021
M. Baldoni and S. Bandini (Eds.): AIxIA 2020, LNAI 12414, pp. 67–79, 2021.
https://doi.org/10.1007/978-3-030-77091-4_5

significantly improve education, researchers, teachers or experts need to exploit their full potential. In the educational field it could be particularly significant to understand the reasons behind models outcomes, especially when it comes to suggestions to create, manage or evaluate courses or didactic resources. In order to address this issue, explainable AI (XAI) could be crucial and determining in education, as in many other fields [6], being aimed at creating a set of new AI techniques able to make their own decisions more transparent and interpretable.

In this context, explainable AI in the field of Recommender Systems (XRS) is aimed at providing intuitive explanations for the suggestions and recommendations given by the algorithms [10]. Basically the community tries to address the problem of why certain recommendations are suggested by the applied models.

At the same time, different attempts in current deep learning literature try to extend deep techniques to deal with social data, recommendations and explanations. In particular, dynamic explainable RS are recently gained specific attention in literature, due to the fact that users' preferences are usually affected by some dynamics. In [33], the approach proposed is based on recursive neural networks (RNN), which allows to dynamically analyse the users' preferences. This approach is specifically interesting thanks to its ability to jointly learns image and text representations, thus improving the way explanations are provided. Instead, in [34], dynamic explanations are generated based on the users' reviews and by the means of a gated recurrent unit (GRU), integrated with a convolutional neural network (CNN) to model their preferences. It also is important to notice that explainable recommender methods can be focused either on the use of reviews written by users or attribute information, which can also be integrated to provide high-quality explanations [35].

The "attentional mechanism" was introduced for the first time in the deep learning community in order to allow the model to detect the most relevant information due to the attention weights [22] and has recently been successful for the resolution of a series of objectives [11].

Specifically, in literature explainable attentional models have been used in domains ranging from medical care [24,25] to e-commerce and online purchase [26]. Nevertheless, there is still need to explore the way they could impact in the educational field, especially when it comes to supporting teachers, rather than learners, more generally considered [36].

It is worth to notice that attention weights can have a role in starting to fostering explainability [27]. The attention weights permit to capture and give a weight to the most relevant information associated to the evaluation of a specific resource by a given users. Indeed, they allow to detect the most relevant information related to the user's evaluation, so as to understand the reason why it was considered or not. This allows to start to strive to circumscribe the reason why a didactic resource has been considered or not. Besides the possibility to directly associate a weight to a significant piece of information, the attentional weights can also be linked to the resources keywords and metadata, in order to try to capture the semantics and similarity among resources, in addition to the single user's evaluations.

In this article, we provide the first stages of our ongoing research project, aimed at significantly empowering the RS of our educational platform "WhoTeach" [29] by the means of an explainable attention model (XAM). Specifically, we report our current positioning in the state of the art with the proposed model to extend the social engine of "WhoTeach" with a graph attentional mechanism aiming to provide social recommendations for the design of new didactic programs and courses. The presented model allows us to start to include explainability in the system.

2   WhoTeach

WhoTeach (WT) is a complete digital learning platform for supporting heterogenous learning ecosystems in their processes and activities, due to its numerous synchronous and asynchronous features and functionalities. WT is aimed at promoting the development of customized learning and training paths by aggregating and disseminating knowledge created and updated by experts. The platform is conceived as a Social Intelligent Learning Management System (SILMS) and it is structured around three components:

1. The Recommender System (RS), to help experts and teachers to quickly and effectively assemble high-quality contents into courses: thanks to an intelligent analysis of available material, it is aimed at suggesting teachers the best resources to include, in any format, according to teachers' needs or requirements.
2. The "Knowledge co-creation Social Platform", which is a technological infrastructure based on an integrated and highly interactive social network, endowed with many features to share information, thematic groups and discussion forums.
3. The content's repository where to upload contents from any course or training material, either proprietary or open. This serves as a basis for both the recommender system to elaborate materials and also users who want to create personalized courses.

The platform allows to represent users, with their own profile, as well as didactic resources provided by teachers. Specifically, users are represented by the means of their associated metadata: as users intend to register on WhoTeach, they have to provide their personal data, as mail and home address or educational level. On the other hand, resources are represented by the means of their precise features and it is possibile to have access to the specific resources users have interacted with. Thus, this possibility allows to have a complete overview of the information related to both users and resources, as well as to detect the most relevant topics for users.

3   Main Concepts and Definitions

A graph (annotated with $G = (V, E)$) is a theoretical object widely applied to model the complex set of relationships that typically characterize current networks. This object consists of a set of "entities" (vertices or nodes), V, and relationships between them, i.e. edges, E. In this paper, we use attributed graphs, i.e., particular graphs where each vertex $v \in V$ is labeled with a set of attribute values. Moreover, given a vertex $v \in V$, we indicate with $\mathcal{N}(v) = \{u : \{v, u\} \in E\}$ the neighborhood of the vertex v.

Given a graph G, we use the corresponding adjacency matrix A to indicate whether two vertices v_i, v_j of G are connected by an edge, i.e., $(A)_{i,j} = 1$, if $\{v_i, v_j\} \in E$.

In order to summarize the relationships between vertices and capture relevant information in a graph, embedding (i.e., objects transformation to lower dimensional spaces) is typically applied [23]. This approach allows to use a rich set of analytical methods, offering to deep neural networks the capability of providing different levels of representation. Embedding can be performed at different level: for example, at the node level, at the graph level, or even through different mathematical strategies. Typically, the embedding is realized by fitting the (deep) network's parameters using standard gradient-based optimization. In particular, the following definitions can be useful [11].

Definition 1. *Given a graph $G = (V, E)$ with V as the set of vertices and E the set of edges, the objective of node embedding is to learn a function $f : V \to \mathcal{R}^k$ such that each vertex $i \in V$ is mapped to a k-dimensional vector, $\vec{h}$.*

Definition 2. *Given a set of graphs, $\mathcal{G}$, the objective of graph embedding is to learn a function $f : \mathcal{G} \to \mathcal{R}^k$ that maps an input graph $G \in \mathcal{G}$ to a low dimensional embedding vector, $\vec{h}$.*

4   GAT Models

In our application, we use the attentional-based node embedding proposed in [12]. For a general definition of the notion of "attention", here we conveniently adapt the one reported in [11].

Definition 3. *Let A be an user/item relationship matrix, $G[A] = (V, E)$ the corresponding weighted graph, and $V = \{U, R\}$ the set of users U and items R, respectively. Given a pair of vertices $(u, r), u \in U, r \in R$, an attentional mechanism for G is a function $a : \mathcal{R}^n \times \mathcal{R}^n \to \mathcal{R}$ which computes coefficients $e_{u,r} = a(\vec{h}_u^{(l)}, \vec{h}_r^{(l)})$ across the pairs of vertices, u, r, based on their feature representation $\vec{h}_u^{(l)}, \vec{h}_r^{(l)}$ at level l.*

Coefficients $e_{u,r}$ are considered as the importance of the vertex r's features to (user) u.

Following [12], we define a as a feed-forward neural network with a learnable (weight) vector of parameters $\vec{a}$ and nonlinear $LeakyReLU$ activation function. In this way, we have

$$e_{u,r}^{(l)} = LeakyReLU\left(\vec{a}^{(l)^T} \left[\mathbf{W}^{(l)} \vec{h}_u^{(l)} || \mathbf{W}^{(l)} \vec{h}_r^{(l)} \right] \right). \qquad (1)$$

where $\mathbf{W}$ is a learnable parameter matrix and $\mathbf{W}^{(l)} \vec{h}_u^{(l)} || \mathbf{W}^{(l)} \vec{h}_r^{(l)}$ is the concatenation of the embedded representation for the vertices u, r.

The coefficients $e_{u,r}$ can be normalized using, e.g., the *softmax* function

$$\alpha_{u,r}^{(l)} = \frac{\exp(e_{u,r}^{(l)})}{\sum_{k \in \mathcal{N}(u)} \exp(e_{u,k}^{(l)})}.$$

The mechanisms parameters, $\vec{a}$, are then updated with the others network's parameters accordingly to typical optimization algorithms. When only resources (items) around u are considered, the normalized (attention) coefficients $\alpha_{u,r}$ can be used to compute a combination of the resources $\vec{h}_r^{(l)}$ in $\mathcal{N}(u)$ as follows

$$\vec{h}_u^{(l+1)} = \sigma \Big(\sum_{r \in \mathcal{N}(u), r \in R} \alpha_{u,r}^{(l)} \mathbf{W}^{(l)} \vec{h}_r^{(l)} \Big) \tag{2}$$

where σ is non linear vector-valued function (sigmoid). With this formulation, Eq. 2 provides the next level embedding for user u scaled by the attention scores which, in turn, can be interpreted as the relevance of the resources used by the user u. Similarly to Eq. 2, the following quantity can be interpreted as the user scores who applied, in particular, the resource r.

$$\vec{h}_r^{(l+1)} = \sigma \Big(\sum_{u \in \mathcal{N}(r), u \in U} \alpha_{u,r}^{(l)} \mathbf{W}^{(l)} \vec{h}_u^{(l)} \Big) \tag{3}$$

In this way, the "GAT layer" returns for each pair $(u, r) \in U \times R$ the embedded representation $(\vec{h}_u^{(l+1)}, \vec{h}_r^{(l+1)})$. In our experiments we will consider only one level of embedding, i.e., $l = 1$.

Therefore, as previously described in the Sect. 3, we introduce a novel kind of information representation $\vec{h}_u^{(l)}$ for users and $\vec{h}_r^{(l)}$ resources, allowing us to visualize either the user u or the resource r as the main element according to its neighborhood. Nevertheless, this representation is still not able to explain and justify the recommendations given to a specific user. Indeed, it provides the starting point to apply the attention mechanism, which introduces the possibility to give a weight $e_{u,r}^{(l)}$ to the most relevant information encoded in the embedded representation for both the user $\vec{h}_u^{(l+1)}$ and the resource $\vec{h}_r^{(l+1)}$. Then, the attention weights $e_{u,r}^{(l)}$ permit to improve the model performances, reducing the error for the recommendations.

Above all, they foster the possibility to explain why a given resource r is recommended to a specific user u. In literature, this approach for computing the attention weights $e_{u,r}^{(l)}$ is also applied in other works related to collaborative filtering RS [32]. Other works explore different display styles, as visual explanations [31].

Indeed, the attentional weights permit to assess the most relevant information associated to the evaluation provided by users. This information detection mechanism can be exploited to start to understand the reason why a specific resource was considered by a given user. Moreover, the attentional weights can also be used to identify similarity among resources based on their semantics, in addition to the specific users' evaluations.

More in detail, given the initial user-item matrix with the past users' evaluations, the attentional mechanism basically generates a new matrix filled by the new ones, computed by the application of the attentional weights. This allows to infer the missing evaluations in the initial matrix, so as to generate the model recommendations.

In addition, given each keyword associated to a single resource, we aim to compute the average value coming from the different attentional coefficient provided by the model. Thus, each keyword would be linked to an average value and we can recommend the one with higher average values. Then, we can compare the keywords associated to a single user's profile to the one recommended: we expect them to be similar to each other.

Therefore, in order to better justify and thus explain the recommendation provided by the model, we aim to also take in consideration the implicit semantic structure of the resources, in addition to the explicit user's evaluation coming by previous interactions with them.

In conclusion, the ability to highlight the most useful explicit and implicit information to realize the recommendations allows us to start to introduce explainability in the system.

5   Numerical Experiments

Here we report a short review of the numerical experiments described in [29].

The experiments use an homogeneous set of data whose characteristics combine well with the requirements of the WhoTeach platform. These data come from the "Goodbooks" data-set (https://www.kaggle.com/zygmunt/goodbooks-10k), a large collection reporting up to 10K books and 1000000 ratings (from "1" to "5") assigned by 53400 readers.

In particular, numerical ratings, ranging from "1" to "5", are given by users (readers) for each resource type, in this case, different sort of book. The experiments aim to evaluate the capability of the attentional-based models to reduce error (loss function) between the reported and predicted preference scores. To provide robust estimation, we sub-sampled the data using cross-validation.

The models was implemented using the Pytorch library (https://pytorch.org/), and then executed using different hyperparameters. At the present stage, the attention-based model with concatenation operator in the stacked layer (see Fig. 1) was compared with alternative models: dot product model, element-wise product model (Hadamard product model), concatenation model. Performances were averaged on the number of folds (10 cross-validation).

1. Dot product model.
   Input: Training set $\mathcal{T} = \{((u_i, r_j), s_{i,j}) : 1 \leq s_{i,j} \leq 5\}$ **Output:** score $\hat{s}_{i,j}$ recommended for user i and resource j.

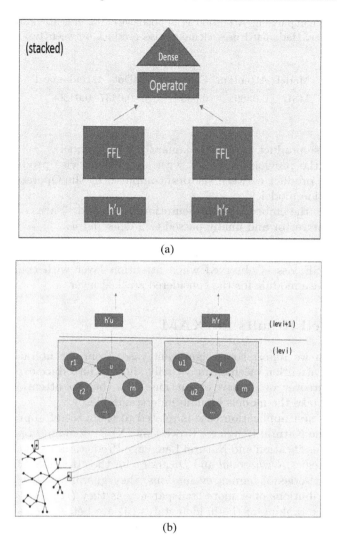

Fig. 1. System architecture. A feed-forward based network (module B) is stacked on the top of the GAT layer (module A). Users and items scores embedded representations (respectively, $\vec{h}_i^{(l+1)}$ and $\vec{h}_r^{(+1)}$) are passed and combined (operator layer in mod. B) with further embedding (FFL sub-modules) in order to provide through a sigmod-based activation (output of dense layer) the predicted final suggestion.

Loss function: MSE; **Optimizer**: SGD.

Architecture: similar to the stacked architecture (with no attention). A dot product operation is applied to "aggregate" the embedded representations of $\vec{u}_i$ and $\vec{r}_j$.

Table 1. MSE comparison: Attention is applied with the concatenation operator at the stacked layer. Hadamard uses element-wise product between two vectors at the operator layer.

Model	Attention	Concatenate	Dot	Hadamard
MSE	0.0389	0.0439	0.0437	0.0436

2. Element-wise product model (Hadamard product model).
   Similar to the previous case but with an element wise product operation (Hadamard product between vectors) computed by the Operator Layer.
3. Concatenation model.
   In this case, the embedded representations of $\vec{u}_i$ and $\vec{r}_j$ are concatenated in a new latent vector and finally passed to a dense layer.

Preliminary results are reported in Table 1. A general better tendency to reduce the MSE loss is observed when attention layer with concatenation is applied as a base module for the considered stacked layer.

6 Expected Results for XAM

In this section we report some significant cases from the literature, so as to show that the attention mechanism actually allow to introduce explainability in the model. Moreover, qualitative evaluations show that the attention mechanism also helps to make the models human-understandable.

In [27] the first application case is related to the a set of approaches aimed to deal with the Natural Language Processing (NLP) domain: in particular, the Binary Text classification and Natural Language Prediction. By the means of the proposed strategies, *Orthogonal* and *Diversity*, for the attentional LSTM model, and through a series of human evaluations, they guarantee that the resulting attention distributions offer more transparency as they (i) provide a more precise importance ranking of the hidden states (ii) are better indicative of words important for the model's predictions (iii) correlate better with gradient-based attribution methods. By the means a random sampling process of 200 data points on different datasets (in particular on Yelp, composed by user evaluations and reviews for different restaurants), several experiments were conducted on the test sets and human evaluators assessed the model explainability by the use of three criteria: *Overall, Completeness, Correctness*.

It is worth to notice that the evaluators for the test phase were chosen among domain experts in computer science. In our domain, we will need to choose expert teachers to evaluate the recommendations provided by the model, so as to infer the level of explaianability in our system. In [27] the performed tests and evaluations show that the model employing the strategy called *Diversity* allows to realize an attentional distribution by the means of the information-weighting process, improving the quality of the inferences in the NLP domain.

Specifically, the comparisons with other standard models used in this domain help to assess that the model employing the attentional mechanism is actually the one providing the best results.

In this paper, thus, the attentional mechanism was exploited to make inferences on the NLP domain: in our case, instead, we aim to make inferences for users' evaluation.

In [37], the authors present a model called *Dynamic Explainable Recommender* (DER), aiming to concretely match the explanation and the users' preferences. In this work, they report relevant results with high explaianability: it is thus definitely worth to notice that here there is no any significant trade-off between the model explaianbility and performances. Thus, in the case of [37] the authors have two different aims: first, to find significant correspondence between the explanations provided and the users' preferences; second, to empower the model transparency, thus improving the user's satisfaction and trust. Nevertheless, this does not affect the numerical results, which either remain stable or are even improved.

Therefore, the reported application cases and the evaluations performed show that the attentional mechanism actually allow to find a relevant trade-off between the system's accuracy and the recommendations explainability.

In conclusion, the proposed approaches will be definitely useful to further studies on evaluation methodologies involving domain experts as teachers (e.g. questionnaires), so to assess the expected level of explaianability in the system.

7   Conclusions and Future Works

In this work we have reported our work in progress for providing "WhoTeach" with an explainable recommender system, aimed to significantly empower its ability to help teachers or experts to create high-quality courses. At the present stage, we started to propose a model based on the attentional mechanisms, which allows to justify the chosen recommendations provided by the model by the means of the attention weights. This model is specifically focused on exploiting social information for educational services, thus extending the social engine of our educational platform "WhoTeach" to reinforce the AI engine.

It is totally clear that further improvements of the present XRS could significantly help users to better understand the reason why specific items are recommended.

In order to orient ourselves in the future steps of our work, we have started to define our positioning in the state-of-the-art according to three dimensions studied in the XAI literature [10,16]: the model itself, the display style of the explanations we aim to provide and the social aspects of our potential XRS. The first and the second dimension considered come from the literature, while the third one is the result of the importance of the social feature and data in WT.

In particular:

- **Display style:** in order to optimize the user experience we are working to define the way explanations will be provided, as the different possibilities in literature show [14,28], also when it comes to joint textual and visual fusion, like in [28]. We will definitely strive to exploit the information captured by the attention weights to design how effectively present the explaianble recommendations provided by the complete model, both from the semantic and explicit way, as described in the Sect. 4.
- **XRS model:** as described, the present attentional model shows the potentialities to actually include explainability in the RS. Thus, in the next stages of the project we are going to both improve the present model and empirically evaluate other possible models, so as to integrate them and effectively include explainability in the RS. In particular, we are actually developing a plugin aimed at favoring the semantic extraction process anticipated in the Sect. 4. In addition, we are going to train and effectively validate the model with respect to specific, *ad-hoc* empirical data coming from realistic domain situations, typically teachers evaluating didactical resources in real-life scenarios. We are also exploring the possibility to integrate the present attentional model with a symbolic approach, like decision-trees, as well as to exploit tools to help represent and understand the attention scores, like a Saliency heatmap. One of the most important further step will be the optimization of the computational complexity for the computation of the attention weights. Finally, we will put effort in improving the numerical results and their evaluations by the means of comparisons respect to some baseline to be chosen.
- **Social dimension:** by the means of the social data in the platform from users (e.g. teachers, students, experts) we are going to perform further experimentation to assess the present situation and understand the way to empirically evaluate other models.

To recap, we have reported our present and further positioning in the state of the art of XAI, showing the potentialities of the present model and the next steps in our work. From the study of the state of the art, we then strive to inscribe our current work and its future steps in the XRS literature, so as to define our present positioning and prepare for future work and stages towards explainability.

References

1. Holmes, R., Wayne, B., Author, M., Fadel, A.C.: Artificial intelligence in education. J (2019). Center for Curriculum Redesign, Boston. https://doi.org/10.1109/MIS. 2016.93
2. Timms, M.J.: Letting artificial intelligence in education out of the box: educational cobots and smart classrooms. Int. J. Artif. Intell. Educ. **26**(2), 701–712 (2016). https://doi.org/10.1007/s40593-016-0095-y

3. Dondi, R., Mauri, G., Zoppis, I.: Clique editing to support case versus control discrimination. In: Czarnowski, I., Caballero, A.M., Howlett, R.J., Jain, L.C. (eds.) Intelligent Decision Technologies 2016. SIST, vol. 56, pp. 27–36. Springer, Cham (2016). https://doi.org/10.1007/978-3-319-39630-9_3
4. Zoppis, I., Dondi, R., Coppetti, D., Beltramo, A., Mauri, G.: Distributed heuristics for optimizing cohesive groups: a support for clinical patient engagement in social network analysis. In: 2018 26th Euromicro International Conference on Parallel, Distributed and Network-based Processing (PDP) (2018). https://doi.org/10.1109/PDP44162.2018
5. Zoppis, I., Manzoni, S., Mauri, G.: A computational model for promoting targeted communication and supplying social explainable recommendations. In: 2019 IEEE 32nd International Symposium on Computer-Based Medical Systems (CBMS) (2019). https://doi.org/10.1109/CBMS.2019.00090
6. Fox, M., Long, D., Magazzeni, D.: Explainable planning (2017)
7. Bonhard, P., Sasse, M.A.: 'Knowing me, knowing you'-using profiles and social networking to improve recommender systems. BT Technol. J. (2006). https://doi.org/10.1007/s10550-006-0080-3
8. Gupta, P., Goel, A., Lin, J., Sharma, A., Wang, D., Zadeh, R.: WTF: the who to follow service at Twitter. In: Proceedings of the 22nd International Conference on World Wide Web (2013). https://doi.org/10.1145/2488388.2488433
9. Zhou, X., Xu, Y., Li, Y., Josang, A., Cox, C.: The state-of-the-art in personalized recommender systems for social networking. Artif. Intell. Rev. **37**, 119–132 (2012). https://doi.org/10.1007/s10462-011-9222-1
10. Zhang, Y., Chen, X.: Explainable recommendation: a survey and new perspectives (2018). https://doi.org/10.1561/1500000066
11. Boaz Lee, J., Rossi, R.A., Kim, S., Ahmed, N.K., Koh, E.: Attention models in graphs: a survey. arXiv preprint arXiv:1807.07984 (2018). https://doi.org/10.1145/3363574
12. Velickovic, P., Cucurull, G., Casanova, A., Romero, A., Lio, P., Bengio, Y.: Graph attention networks. arXiv preprint arXiv:1710.10903 (2017). https://doi.org/10.17863/CAM.48429
13. Sharma, A., Cosley, D.: Do social explanations work? Studying and modeling the effects of social explanations in recommender systems. In: Proceedings of the 22nd International Conference on World Wide Web (2013). https://doi.org/10.1145/2488388.2488487
14. Pedreschi, D., Giannotti, F., Guidotti, R., Monreale, A., Ruggieri, S., Turini, F.: Meaningful explanations of Black Box AI decision systems. In: Proceedings of the AAAI Conference on Artificial Intelligence (2019). https://doi.org/10.1609/aaai.v33i01.33018001
15. Adadi, A., Berrada, M.: Peeking inside the black-box: a survey on explainable artificial intelligence (XAI). IEEE Access **6**, 52138–52160 (2018). https://doi.org/10.1109/ACCESS.2018.2870052
16. Guidotti, R., Monreale, A., Ruggieri, S., Turini, F., Giannotti, F., Pedreschi, D.: A survey of methods for explaining black box models. ACM Comput. Surv. (2018). https://doi.org/10.1145/3236009
17. Apolloni, B., Bassis, S., Mesiti, M., Valtolina, S., Epifania, F.: A rule based recommender system. In: Bassis, S., Esposito, A., Morabito, F.C., Pasero, E. (eds.) Advances in Neural Networks. SIST, vol. 54, pp. 87–96. Springer, Cham (2016). https://doi.org/10.1007/978-3-319-33747-0_9
18. Park, H., Jeon, H., Kim, J., Ahn, B., Kang, U.: UniWalk: explainable and accurate recommendation for rating and network data (2017)

19. Gori, M., Monfardini, G., Scarselli, F.: A new model for learning in graph domains. In: Proceedings of the 2005 IEEE International Joint Conference on Neural Networks (2005). https://doi.org/10.1109/IJCNN.2005.1555942
20. Zoppis, I., Dondi, R., Manzoni, S., Mauri, G., Marconi, L., Epifania, F.: Optimized social explanation for educational platforms (2019). https://doi.org/10.5220/0007749500850091
21. Scarselli, F., Gori, M., Tsoi, A.C., Hagenbuchner, M., Monfardini, G.: The graph neural network model (2008). https://doi.org/10.1109/TNN.2008.2005605
22. Bahdanau, D., Cho, K., Bengio, Y.: Neural machine translation by jointly learning to align and translate. arXiv preprint arXiv 1409.0473 (2014)
23. Goyal, P., Ferrara, E.: Graph embedding techniques, applications, and performance: a survey. Knowl. Based Syst. (2018). https://doi.org/10.1016/j.knosys.2018.03.022
24. Mullenbach, J., Wiegreffe, S., Duke, J., Sun, J., Eisenstein, J.: Explainable prediction of medical codes from clinical text (2018)
25. Wang, N., Chen, M., Subbalakshmi, K.P.: Explainable CNN attention networks (C-attention network) for automated detection of Alzheimers disease (2020)
26. Chen, C., Zhang, M., Liu, Y., Ma, S.: Neural attentional rating regression with review-level explanations. In: International World Wide Web Conferences Steering Committee (2018). https://doi.org/10.1145/3178876.3186070
27. Mohankumar, A., Nema, P., Narasimhan, S., Khapra, M., Srinivasan, B., Ravindran, B.: Towards transparent and explainable attention models (2020). https://doi.org/10.18653/v1/2020.acl-main.387
28. Liu, P., Zhang, L., Gulla, J.A.: Dynamic attention-based explainable recommendation with textual and visual fusion. Inf. Process. Manag. (2019). https://doi.org/10.1016/j.ipm.2019.102099
29. Zoppis, I., Manzoni, S., Mauri, G., Aragon, R.A.M., Marconi, L., Epifania, F.: Attentional neural mechanisms for social recommendations in educational platforms. In: Proceedings of the 12th International Conference on Computer Supported Education - Volume 1 CSEDU (2020). https://doi.org/10.5220/0009568901110117
30. Dondi, R., Mauri, G., Zoppis, I.: On the tractability of finding disjoint clubs in a network. Theor. Comput. Sci. **777**, 243–251 (2019)
31. Chen, X., et al.: Personalized fashion recommendation with visual explanations based on multimodal attention network: towards visually explainable recommendation (2019). https://doi.org/10.1145/3331184.3331254
32. Chen, J., Zhuang, F., Hong, X., Ao, X., Xie, X., He, Q.: Attention-driven factor model for explainable personalized recommendation (2018). https://doi.org/10.1145/3209978.3210083
33. Liu, P., Zhang, L., Gulla, J.A.: Dynamic attention-based explainable recommendation with textual and visual fusion. Inf. Process. Manag. (2020). https://doi.org/10.1016/j.ipm.2019.102099
34. Chen, X., Zhang, Y., Qin, Z.: Dynamic explainable recommendation based on neural attentive models. In: Proceedings of the AAAI Conference on Artificial Intelligence (2019). https://doi.org/10.1609/aaai.v33i01.330153
35. Liu, Y.-Y., Yang, B., Pei, H.-B., Huang, J.: Neural explainable recommender model based on attributes and reviews. J. Comput. Sci. Technol. **35**(6), 1446–1460 (2020). https://doi.org/10.1007/s11390-020-0152-8

36. Zhang, H., Huang, T., Lv, Z., Liu, S., Yang, H.: MOOCRC: a highly accurate resource recommendation model for use in MOOC environments. Mob. Netw. Appl. **24**(1), 34–46 (2018). https://doi.org/10.1007/s11036-018-1131-y

37. Chen, X., Zhang, Y., Qin, Z.: Dynamic explainable recommendation based on neural attentive models. In: Proceedings of the AAAI Conference on Artificial Intelligence, vol. 33, no. 01, pp. 53–60 (2019). https://doi.org/10.1609/aaai.v33i01.330153

Evolutionary and Population-Based Optimization

Evolutionary Optimization of Graphs with GraphEA

Eric Medvet[(✉)] and Alberto Bartoli

Department of Engineering and Architecture, University of Trieste, Trieste, Italy
emedvet@units.it

Abstract. Many practically relevant computing artifacts are forms of graphs, as, e.g., neural networks, mathematical expressions, finite automata. This great generality of the graph abstraction makes it desirable a way for searching in the space of graphs able to work effectively regardless of the graph form and application. In this paper, we propose GraphEA, a modular evolutionary algorithm (EA) for evolving graphs. GraphEA is modular in the sense that it can be tailored to any graph optimization task by providing components for specifying how to vary edges and nodes, and how to check the validity of a graph. We designed GraphEA by building on previous EAs dealing with particular kinds of graphs and included a speciation mechanism for the preservation of structural innovations and one for the gradual complexification of the solutions structure. To validate the generality of GraphEA, we applied it to 3 radically different tasks (regressions, in two flavors, text extraction from examples, evolution of controllers for soft robots) and compared its effectiveness against less general approaches. The results are promising and indicate some directions for further improvement of GraphEA.

Keywords: Optimization · Symbolic regression · DFAs · Neuroevolution

1 Introduction and Related Works

The ever more ubiquitous neural networks, mathematical expressions that model in an interpretable way the dependency of one variable on other variables, finite automata constituting a broad model for computation, are all actionable forms of *graphs*. Graphs are thus an abstraction of great practical relevance. It would be hence desirable to leverage this generality for enabling the usage of a general optimization technique that, given a way for evaluating the quality of a graph, searches the space of graphs for the one with greatest quality. On the one hand, that optimization technique should be applicable to *all* kinds of graphs, i.e., regardless of the nature of their nodes and edges, without requiring the user to tune many parameters; on the other hand, it should be effective enough to be useful in practice.

© Springer Nature Switzerland AG 2021
M. Baldoni and S. Bandini (Eds.): AIxIA 2020, LNAI 12414, pp. 83–98, 2021.
https://doi.org/10.1007/978-3-030-77091-4_6

In this paper, we head towards the ambitious goal of designing that optimization technique by proposing an evolutionary algorithm (EA) and a representation for evolving graphs, that we called GraphEA. GraphEA works on any graph, directed or undirected, whose nodes are defined over a predefined set and edges are labeled with labels defined over another set. GraphEA is a form of evolutionary computation (EC). The optimization consists in evolving a fixed-size population of candidate solutions (here graphs) to a given problem by means of the reiterated applications of two steps: selection and variation. For variation in particular, GraphEA is modular: it provides a template scheme for variation of the solutions that has to be instantiated to a particular form of graphs by the user. For example, when using GraphEA for evolving neural networks, edges are labeled with real numbers (the weights of the corresponding connections) and one variation consists in perturbing those numbers with some noise.

While designing GraphEA, we took into account previous works in which EC has been applied to graphs and included in our EA (a) a mechanism for preserving the structural innovation introduced by variation operators (*speciation*) and (b) a mechanism for starting from an initial population of simple graphs that get more complex during the evolution (*complexification*).

We performed an experimental evaluation of GraphEA for validating the claim that it is general and sufficiently effective in the search. To this aim, we considered three radically different problems in which the graph abstraction is instantiated in different ways: *regression*, where we use graphs for representing networks of mathematical operators or of base univariate functions, *text extraction from examples*, where graphs represent discrete finite automata, and *neuroevolution of controllers for soft robots*, where graphs represent neural networks with free topology. We compared our proposed approach to challenging baseline methods specific to each problem and the results are highly promising. They show that GraphEA is competitive with other, more specific forms of optimization in two of the three problems, while it struggles in the neuroevolution problem. By digging in the results, we noticed that when GraphEA exhibits a gap with respect to the effectiveness of other optimization techniques, it often produces solutions which are remarkably simpler (and hence less expressive) than those of the counterpart. We interpret this finding as an opportunity to further improve GraphEA by adapting the complexification mechanism or the template variation operators.

The idea of applying EC for optimizing a graph is not new. Several applications have been proposed and some approaches exhibiting some degrees of generality exist, e.g., [21,27]. However, only recently researchers devoted their effort to design a general approach that can be applied to any kind of graphs, as we do in this paper: one of the most interesting proposals is likely the one by Atkinson et al. [1,2]. In their EGGP (Evolving Graphs by Graph Programming), the authors rely on rule-based graph programming to perform variation in an evolutionary optimization search. In a recent study [24], EGGP is experimentally compared against other representations and EAs suitable for evolving graphs: the authors conclude that there is not a single EA, nor a single representation, that systematically outperforms the other options in the considered problems. This result suggested that more research has to be done about general optimization techniques for graphs and hence somehow motivated us in designing GraphEA. For space constraints, we cannot present a direct comparison against EGGP: we reserve this activity for future work.

2 GraphEA

We consider the task of optimization in the set $\mathcal{G}_{\mathcal{N},\mathcal{E}}$ of *directed decorated graphs*, later simply graphs, defined over a set $\mathcal{N}$ of nodes and a set $\mathcal{E}$ of edge labels.

A graph $g \in \mathcal{G}$ is a pair (N, e) composed of a set $N \subseteq \mathcal{N}$ of nodes and a function $e \colon N \times N \to \mathcal{E} \cup \varnothing$. N is the set of nodes of g: for a given pair $n_1, n_2 \in N \times N$, an edge connecting n_1 to n_2 exists in g if and only if $e(n_1, n_2) \neq \varnothing$ and its label is $e(n_1, n_2) \in \mathcal{E}$. Note that, in general, $e(n_1, n_2) \neq e(n_2, n_1)$.

We assume that, for the purpose of optimization, a *validity predicate* $v \colon \mathcal{G}_{\mathcal{N},\mathcal{E}} \to \{\text{TRUE}, \text{FALSE}\}$ is available for delimiting a subset $\mathcal{G}'_{\mathcal{N},\mathcal{E}} \subseteq \mathcal{G}_{\mathcal{N},\mathcal{E}}$ in which performing the search: we say that a graph g is *valid* iff $v(g)$ is true, i.e., iff v belongs to $\mathcal{G}'_{\mathcal{N},\mathcal{E}}$. We denote by $f \colon \mathcal{G}'_{\mathcal{N},\mathcal{E}} \to \mathbb{R}$ the *fitness function* that measures the quality (or fitness) $f(g)$ of any valid graph g. Note that GraphEA does not require that the range of f is $\mathbb{R}$, but only that a total ordering is defined over the range: since all the problems that we considered in this study measures the solution quality as a number, for the sake of clarity we assume that fitness is defined in $\mathbb{R}$.

The task consists in finding a graph that maximizes (or minimizes) the fitness, i.e., the goal of the optimization is to find $g^\star$ such that $g^\star = \arg\min_{g \in \mathcal{G}'_{\mathcal{N},\mathcal{E}}} f(g)$ (or $\arg\max_{g \in \mathcal{G}'_{\mathcal{N},\mathcal{E}}} f(g)$).

2.1 Representation

When designing a representation for evolutionary optimization, and in particular the genetic operators, it is important to take into account one of the key principles of EC, the *variational inheritance* principle, that states that the offspring should be similar, but not identical, to the parents [9]. When operating on graphs, designing a crossover operator that adheres to this principle may be particularly tricky, due to the *competing conventions problem* [23], i.e., the fact that there may exist different ways of representing the same graph. In GraphEA, we circumvent this difficulty pragmatically by not designing a crossover operator, hence relying only on mutation operators. Despite there are some indications in the EC literature that the crossover operator is beneficial in specific cases (e.g., [8,11]), in a preliminary experimental evaluation we found that this operator does not significantly improve the optimization effectiveness and efficiency of GraphEA, while requiring a fair amount of additional complexity in the representation; we hence decided to not include it for the sake of simplicity and for circumventing the competing conventions problem.

GraphEA employs a direct representation, i.e., genetic operators operate directly on graphs. However, the representation is general, not tight to a specific kind of nodes or edge labels, i.e., specific $\mathcal{N}$ or $\mathcal{E}$ sets. Consistently, the genetic operators are agnostic with respect to the nature of nodes and edges, but assume that ways for building or modifying nodes and edges are available: we call *factory* a stochastic method for obtaining a node or edge label in, respectively, $\mathcal{N}$ or $\mathcal{E}$; we call mutation a stochastic method for modifying an edge label, i.e., a stochastic operator from $\mathcal{E}$ to $\mathcal{E}$. We denote by $n \sim f_{\mathcal{N}}$ ($e \sim f_{\mathcal{E}}$) a node (edge label) obtained from a node (edge label) factory $f_{\mathcal{N}}$. We denote by $e \sim m_{\mathcal{E}}(e')$ an edge label obtained by mutating an edge label e' with a mutation $m_{\mathcal{E}}$.

In Sect. 3, we present three cases of application of GraphEA to different domains, i.e., with different sets $\mathcal{N}, \mathcal{E}$ along with the corresponding factories and mutations.

In the following, we describe the three mutation operators $\mathcal{G}_{\mathcal{N},\mathcal{E}} \rightarrow \mathcal{G}_{\mathcal{N},\mathcal{E}}$ used in GraphEA (edge addition, edge modification, node addition). For all the operators, if, after the application of the operator on the parent the resulting graph is not valid, then the parent graph is returned, hence ensuring the closure property with respect to $\mathcal{G}'_{\mathcal{N},\mathcal{E}}$.

Edge Addition. Given an edge label factory $f_{\mathcal{E}}$, this operator builds the offspring graph $g_c = (N_c, e_c)$ from a parent graph $g_p = (N_p, e_p)$ as follows. First, N_c is set to N_p. Then, a random pair of nodes n_1, n_2 is chosen in N_c^2 such that $e_c(n_1, n_2) = \varnothing$, i.e., that they are not connected in the parent graph. Then e_c is set to behave as e_p with the exception of the input n_1, n_2 for which $e_c(n_1, n_2) = e \sim f_{\mathcal{E}}$.

In other words, the edge addition adds a new edge to the graph with an edge label obtained from $f_{\mathcal{E}}$.

Edge Modification. Given an edge label mutation $m_{\mathcal{E}} : \mathcal{E} \rightarrow \mathcal{E}$ and a mutation rate $p_{\text{mut}} \in [0, 1]$, this operator builds the offspring graph $g_c = (N_c, e_c)$ from a parent graph $g_p = (N_p, e_p)$ as follows. First, N_c is set to N_p. Then, for each pair of nodes $n_i, n_j \in N_c^2$ for which $e_p(n_i, n_j) \neq \varnothing$, $e_c(n_i, n_j)$ is set to $e_p(n_i, n_j)$ with probability $1 - p_{\text{mut}}$ or to $e \sim m_{\mathcal{E}}(e_p(n_i, n_j))$ with probability p_{mut}.

In other words, the edge modification modifies the labels of a fraction p_{mut} (on average) of existing edges using $m_{\mathcal{E}}$.

Node Addition. Given two edge label mutations $m_{\mathcal{E}}^{\text{src}}, m_{\mathcal{E}}^{\text{dst}}$ and a node factory $f_{\mathcal{N}}$, this operator builds the offspring graph $g_c = (N_c, e_c)$ from a parent graph $g_p = (N_p, e_p)$ as follows. First, a pair of nodes n_1, n_2 is chosen in N_c^2 such that $e_p(n_1, n_2) \neq \varnothing$. Second, a new node $n \sim f_{\mathcal{N}}$ is obtained from the node factory $f_{\mathcal{N}}$. Third, N_c is set to $N_p \cup \{n\}$. Finally, e_c is set to behave as e_p with the exceptions of the three input pairs (n_1, n_2), (n_1, n), (n, n_2), for which it holds $e_c(n_1, n_2) = \varnothing$, $e_c(n_1, n) = e_{\text{src}} \sim m_{\mathcal{E}}^{\text{src}}(e_p(n_1, n_2))$, and $e_c(n, n_2) = e_{\text{dst}} \sim m_{\mathcal{E}}^{\text{dst}}(e_p(n, n_2))$.

In other words, the node addition selects an existing edge, removes it, and adds a new node obtained from $f_{\mathcal{N}}$ in the middle of the two endpoints of the removed edge: the endpoint are then connected to the new node with edges whose labels are mutations of the removed edge.

2.2   Evolutionary Algorithm

Two of the three genetic operators described in the previous section can introduce structural modifications in a graph, i.e., the number of nodes of edges can change. In the context of the evolutionary optimization, those structural modifications are innovations that can be, on the long term, beneficial; yet, on the short term, they might affect negatively the fitness of a graph. In order to allow the structural modifications enough time to express their potential, if any, we employ in GraphEA an innovation protection mechanism.

In brief, the protection mechanism is a form of *speciation* based on fitness sharing [25] inspired by the similar mechanism employed in NEAT [27]. Individuals in the population are partitioned in species: all the individuals of the same species have the same chance of reproducing that depends on the fitness of one representative of the species; moreover, species larger than a predefined size have their best individuals moved in the next generation, as well as the global best (a form of *elitism*). Intuitively, an innovative individual resulting from a structural modification of a fit parent will likely belong to the same species of the parent and hence will not be penalized, in terms of chances of reproducing, if its fitness is lower. However, if it is fitter, the entire species will potentially benefit, having a higher chance to reproduce.

Beyond the speciation mechanism, the generational model of GraphEA is based on a fixed-size population that is updated iteratively without overlapping (i.e., the offspring replaces the parents) and with elitism. The offspring is built from the parents by applying, for each individual, one of the three mutation operators chosen with predefined probabilities.

Algorithm 1 shows the iterative algorithm of GraphEA. The most salient part is in the offspring generation part (lines 4–20). After the population P is partitioned in n species (line 5, explained below), the offspring P' is composed by first adding the best individuals (lines 6–12) and then reproducing the individuals in each species (lines 13–20). In the first step, the overall best and the best of each species with size $\geq s_{\min}$, a parameter of the algorithm, are added to P'.

In the second step, for generating the n'_{pop} offspring, one representative individual (the $g_{i,1}$ in line 4) is randomly chosen in each of the n species: the representatives are then sorted according to their fitness and their rank is stored in r. Then, a number o of offspring is reserved to each species depending on the rank of the corresponding representative, according to a rank-proportional scheme where $o = n'_{\text{pop}} \alpha^{r_i} \frac{1}{\sum_{i=1}^{i=n} \alpha^{r_i}}$ (line 15). $\alpha \in \,]0,1]$ is a parameter of the algorithm: the closer to 1, the less the preference to fittest species. Finally, the overall offspring for the next generation is completed by reproducing the individual of each species until a corresponding number o of new individuals are obtained. Since, in general, a species might get a reserved a number o larger than the current size, some individual of that species might reproduce more than one time ($c \bmod s_i$

```
 1  function evolve():
 2  |   P ← initialize(n_pop)
 3  |   foreach i ∈ {1, ..., n_gen} do
 4  |   |   P' ← ∅
 5  |   |   ({g_{1,1}, ..., g_{1,s_1}}, ..., {g_{n,1}, ..., g_{n,s_n}}) ← speciate(P, τ)
 6  |   |   P' ← P' ∪ {best(P)}
 7  |   |   foreach i ∈ {1, ..., n} do
 8  |   |   |   if s_i ≥ s_min then
 9  |   |   |   |   P' ← P' ∪ {best({g_{i,1}, ..., g_{i,s_1}})}
10  |   |   |   end
11  |   |   end
12  |   |   n'_pop ← n_pop − |P'|
13  |   |   r ← ranks(g_{1,1}, ..., g_{n,1})
14  |   |   foreach i ∈ {1, ..., n} do
15  |   |   |   o ← n'_pop α^{r_i} (1 / Σ_{i=1}^{i=n} α^{r_i})
16  |   |   |   foreach c ∈ {1, ..., o} do
17  |   |   |   |   P' ← P' ∪ {mutate(g_{i,c mod s_i})}
18  |   |   |   end
19  |   |   end
20  |   |   P ← P'
21  |   end
22  |   return best(P)
23  end
```

Algorithm 1: The GraphEA algorithm.

in line 17). Reproduction consists in the application of one of the three mutation operators presented above with probabilities $p_{\text{edge-add}}$, $p_{\text{edge-mod}}$, $p_{\text{node-add}}$ (summing to 1). The evolution terminates after n_{gen} iterations.

The actual partitioning of the population is performed in speciate() (line 5 in Algorithm 1), that takes a collection of graphs P and a threshold τ (a parameter of GraphEA) and returns a partition $(P_1, P_2, ...)$ of P, with $P = \bigcup_i P_i$. The partition is built iteratively in a bottom-up agglomerative fashion starting from the empty set of subsets of P, as follows. For each $g \in P$, if the partition is empty, a new subset $\{g\} = P_1$ is add to the partition; otherwise, the distances $d_1, d_2, ...$ between g and the representative of each subset P_i are computed—the representative being the first graph added in each subset. Then the shortest distance d_{i^*}, with $i^* = \arg\min_i d_i$ is compared against the threshold τ: if $d_{i^*} < \tau$, g is added to P_{i^*}; otherwise a new subset $\{g\}$ is added to the partition.

For computing the distance between graphs we use the Jaccard distance between the corresponding sets of nodes, i.e., 1 minus the (size of) intersection over union of the two sets. Despite more complex distances might be appropriate for specific kinds of graphs, we chose the Jaccard distance because it does not hamper the generality of GraphEA while still capturing the concept of structural similarity that we wanted to address in the speciation mechanism.

3   Experimental Evaluation

We performed three suites of experiments by applying GraphEA to three different domains: (symbolic) regression, text extraction, evolution of controllers of simulated soft robots.

The goals of the experiments were two: (a) demonstrate the general applicability of GraphEA to radically different domains and (b) verify that this generality does not come at the cost of unpractical search effectiveness. For the latter goal, we considered for each of the three cases at least one viable alternative based on a different representation, that we used as a baseline for the search effectiveness.

Non-goals of this experimental analysis were (c) find the best values for the three main hyper-parameters of GraphEA τ, $s_{\min}$, and α (or a way to set their values in a given application or domain), and (d) compare GraphEA to the state-of-the-art EA for each of the considered domains. We leave these investigations for future work.

For the hyper-parameters, we set their values after a very shallow exploratory analysis to $\tau = 0.25$, $s_{\min} = 5$, $\alpha = 0.75$ (and $p_{\text{edge-add}} = 0.6$, $p_{\text{edge-mod}} = 0.2$, and $p_{\text{node-add}} = 0.2$, unless otherwise indicated). As a consequence regarding goal (b), we cannot exclude that better effectiveness can be achieved by putting bigger effort in hyper-parameter tuning.

We performed all the experiments with a Java framework for evolutionary optimization (JGEA, publicly available at https://github.com/ericmedvet/jgea), that we augmented with a prototype implementation of GraphEA. For the experiments involving the simulated robots, we used 2D-VSR-Sim [19].

3.1   Regression

The goal of regression is to fit a model that accurately describes how an dependent numerical variable y depends on one or more independent numerical variables x, based on a learning set of observations $\{x_i, y_i\}_i$. If the space of the models is the space of mathematical expressions, this task is called *symbolic regression* (SR). Symbolic regression is one of the most crowded playfields in EC, the most prominent role being played by tree-based genetic programming (GP) [15]. Building on plain GP, many improvement are continuously proposed and evaluated on SR (e.g., [29]). At the same time, the ability of GP to solve practical SR problems has been exploited more and more in other research fields [10].

We applied GraphEA to SR in two ways. In the first case, the graphs evolved by GraphEA are a generalization of the abstract syntax trees of the common tree-based GP: nodes are either mathematical operators, variables (input or output), or constants; directed edges are not labeled—we denote this variant by OG-GraphEA, OG standing for operator-graph. In the second case, the graphs are networks of univariate basic functions, each one processing a weighted sums of incoming edges; this representation basically corresponds to compositional pattern producing networks (CPPNs) [26] and we denote it by CPPN-GraphEA. We remark that while a solution found by OG-GraphEA can be expressed as a mathematical expression in a closed form, a CPPN can not: in this sense, hence, OG-GraphEA can solve SR problems, whereas CPPN actually solve "just" regression problems.

As fitness function for regression, we use the Mean Squared Error (MSE) with linear scaling, that have been showed to be beneficial when tackling symbolic regression with GP [14]. Let $\{\hat{y}_i\}_i$ be the output of a candidate solution on the input $\{x_i\}_i$, its fitness is $\min_{a,b} \frac{1}{n} \sum_{i=1}^{i=n} (a\hat{y}_i + b - y_i)^2$, n being the number of input cases.

OG-GraphEA for SR. In this representation, graphs are directed and nodes are either independent variables $(x_1, x_2, \ldots$, the actual number depending on the specific problem), the dependent variable y, constants (0.1, 1, and 10), and mathematical operators (we experimented with $+$, $-$, $\times$, p$\div$, and plog). p$\div$ and plog are the protected versions of the division and the logarithm, with x p$\div$ $0 \triangleq 0, \forall x$ and $\text{plog}(x) \triangleq 0, \forall x \leq 0$. Edges are not actually labeled in OG-GraphEA: formally $\mathcal{E}$ is a singleton with a single placeholder element e_0. Since, by definition, the set of nodes N in a graph cannot contain duplicates, for allowing a graph to contain many nodes with the same mathematical operator, we formally set $\mathcal{N}$ to $\{x_1, x_2, \ldots\} \cup \{y\} \cup \{0.1, 1, 10\} \cup \{+, -, \times, \text{p}\div, \text{plog}\} \times \mathbb{N}$: in other words, operator nodes are decorated with an index that does not matter when using the graph for computing an y value out of a x.

The validity predicate for OG-GraphEA tests if a graph g meets all the following criteria: (i) g is acyclic, (ii) the node y has exactly 1 predecessor (i.e., another node n for which $e(n, y) = e_0$) and no successors, (iii) for each operator node, it has the proper number of predecessors (≥ 1 for $+$ and $\times$, 2 for $-$ and p$\div$, 1 for plog), (iv) for each constant node, it has no predecessors.

Concerning the genetic operators, the edge label factory used in the edge addition always returns e_0. The edge modification operator is disabled (i.e., $p_{\text{edge-mod}} = 0$), since it is not meaningful. In node addition, both edge label mutations are set to the identity (i.e., $m_{\mathcal{E}}^{\text{src}}(e_0) = m_{\mathcal{E}}^{\text{dst}}(e_0) = e_0$) and the node factory produces a randomly chosen mathematical operator indexed with a random integer (chosen in a sufficiently large range in order to rarely have two nodes with the same operator and index in the same graph).

Finally, concerning the initialization of the population, it builds valid graphs with all the variable and constant nodes and no operator nodes. As a direct consequence of the validity predicate, only one node (either a constant or a independent variable node) is connected to the output node y. This form of initialization resembles the complexification principle of NEAT: the evolution starts from simple solutions, hence benefiting from a smaller search space, and then makes them more complex, as needed, during the evolution. Differently than NEAT, where edges can be removed as an outcome of variation, we did not include in GraphEA a mechanism for simplifying solutions that are not minimally complex: we experimentally observed that this choice did not result in the detrimental explosion of the size of the solutions.

CPPN-GraphEA for Regression. In this representation, graphs are directed, nodes are either x_i, y, the constant 1, or base functions $\mathbb{R} \to \mathbb{R}$ (we experimented with the ReLu, the Gaussian, $1 \div x$, and x^2). Edge labels are real numbers (i.e., $\mathcal{E} = \mathbb{R}$). As for OG-GraphEA, in $\mathcal{N}$ the base functions are decorated with an index.

The validity predicate for CPPN-GraphEA tests if a graph g meets all the following criteria: (i) g is acyclic, (ii) the node y has exactly at least one predecessor and no successors, (iii) for each constant or x_i node, it has no predecessors.

The edge label factory in the edge addition genetic operator is the Gaussian distribution with 0 mean and unit variance ($f_{\mathcal{E}} = N(0, 1)$). The edge label mutation in the edge modification consists in perturbing the label with a Gaussian noise $N(0, 1)$. The edge label mutations in the node addition are the identity, for the source node, and a replacement with a new label chosen with $N(0, 1)$, for the target node; the node factory produces decorated base functions with uniform probability, as for OG-GraphEA.

For the population initialization, the same complexification principle of OG-GraphEA is followed. Graphs in the initial populations contains only x_i, y, and the constant and all the possible edges are present, labeled with a value chosen with $N(0, 1)$.

Procedure and Results. We considered a set of four "classical" symbolic regression problems, chosen according to the indications of [32]: Keijzer-6 ($\sum_{i=1}^{i=\lfloor x_1 \rfloor} \frac{1}{i}$), Nguyen-7 ($\log(x_1 + 1) + \log(x_1^2 + 1)$), Pagie-1 ($\frac{1}{1+x_1^{-4}} + \frac{1}{1+x_2^{-4}}$), and Poly4 ($x_1^4 + x_1^3 + x_1^2 + x_1$)—we refer the reader to [32] and our publicly available code for the details about the fitness cases for each problem.

As baselines, we considered a standard implementation of GP (with the same building blocks of OG-GraphEA) and a grammar-based version of GP (CFGGP [31], with a grammar specifying the same operators and constants of GP and OG-GraphEA) augmented with a diversity promotion strategy [3] that consists in attempting to avoid generating individuals whose genotype is already present in the population. For both GP and CFGGP we reproduce individuals using subtree-crossover for 0.8 of the offspring and subtree-mutation for the remaining 0.2; we used tournament selection with size 5 for reproduction and truncation selection for survival selection after merging the offspring with the parents at each generation (i.e., overlapping generational model); we built the initial population with the ramped half-and-half method [18]. For each of the four EAs, we set $n_{\text{pop}} = 100$ and stopped the evolution after 100 generations.

For each problem and each EA, we performed 20 independent runs with different random seeds. Table 1 summarizes the results in terms of the fitness of the best solution at the end of the evolution (median and standard deviation across the runs).

It can be seen that CPPN-GraphEA obtains the best fitness in 3 on 4 problems, while not performing well on Keijzer-6. On the other hand, OG-GraphEA struggles in all the problems, obtaining the last or second-last effectiveness. We interpret this finding as a consequence of the different expressiveness of the

Table 1. Fitness (median and standard deviation across 20 runs) of the best solution at the end of the evolution for the regression problems: fitness is MSE with linear scaling: the lower, the better.

EA	Keijzer-6	Nguyen-7	Pagie-1	Poly4
CFGGP	0.001 ± 0.004	0.028 ± 0.046	16.571 ± 15.305	0.499 ± 3.042
CPPN-GraphEA	0.242 ± 0.229	0.001 ± 0.003	2.169 ± 8.080	0.320 ± 0.925
OG-GraphEA	0.010 ± 0.060	0.149 ± 0.214	24.340 ± 25.211	3.807 ± 2.673
GP	0.002 ± 0.002	0.040 ± 0.067	22.642 ± 11.709	0.410 ± 2.334

two representations: where the required degree of composition between building blocks is larger, CPPN-GraphEA finds good solutions by approximation, whereas OG-GraphEA is not able to (within the 100 generations) build the required substructures in the graph. As a further confirmation of this interpretation, we looked at the size of the found solutions (number of nodes and edges for GraphEA, number of tree nodes in GP and CFGGP) and found that it was much lower for the former: it turns out, hence, that the complexification strategy is detrimental for OG-GraphEA. Interestingly, this observation is a consequence of the fact that with a unique EA, along with its general representation for graphs, we were able to approach the same class of problems from two radically different points of view.

3.2   Text Extraction

Syntax-based extraction of text portions based on examples is a key step in many practical workflows related to information extraction. Different approaches have been proposed for solving this problem, based, e.g., on classical machine learning [20], deep learning [30], or EC [4,7,17]. One of the most effective approaches, in which the outcome of the learning from the examples is a regular expression, is based on GP [5]: building blocks for the trees are regular expression constructs and constants (i.e., characters) and the regular expression is obtained by traversing the tree in a depth-first order.

Formally, the text extraction problem is defined as follows. An extractor is a function that takes in input a string s and outputs a (possibly empty) set S of substrings of s, each one identified by the start and end index in s. A problem of text extraction consists in, given a string s and a set S of substrings to be extracted from s, learning an extractor that, when applied to s, returns S. In practical settings, the learned extractor should also generalize beyond the examples represented by s, S and learn the underlying pattern of substrings of interest. This additional objective makes the task harder [6]: we here do not focus on the generalization ability and consider instead just the simpler version of the text extraction problem. The fitness of a candidate extractor is the char error rate measured on a pair s, S: each character is considered as a data point in a binary classification setting, i.e., it can be a positive, if it belongs to a string of S, or a negative, otherwise. The char error rate, measured on a pair s, S of an extractor extracting $\hat{S}$ from S, is the ratio of characters in s that are misclassified by the extractor, i.e., that "belong" to S but not to $\hat{S}$ or the opposite.

We here exploited the generality of GraphEA for exploring a radically different approach with respect to GP for regular expressions: we evolve deterministic finite automata (DFAs) in which transitions are set of characters. Indeed, the idea of evolving a DFA for binary strings have been already proposed in [17]. In terms of GraphEA, given a learning dataset s, S in which the positives characters form a set $\mathcal{A}$, $\mathcal{E}$ is the set of non-empty subsets of $\mathcal{A}$, i.e., $\mathcal{E} = \mathcal{P}(\mathcal{A}) \backslash \emptyset$, and $\mathcal{N} = \{\text{TRUE}, \text{FALSE}\} \times \mathbb{N}$, i.e., nodes can be accepting or not accepting and are decorated with an index (for the same reason of OG-GraphEA and CPPN-GraphEA). When applying the DFA to an input string, we consider the node with index 0 as the starting state.

The validity predicate for CPPN-GraphEA tests if a graph g (i) has exactly one node decorated with 0 and, (ii) for each node, the union of the labels (that are subsets of $\mathcal{A}$) of all outgoing edges is empty.

As edge label factory for the edge addition operator we use a random sampling of singletons in $\mathcal{P}(\mathcal{A})$. The edge label mutation for the edge mutation operator works as follows: given an edge label A, if $|A| = 1$, it adds a random element of $\mathcal{A}$ to A; otherwise, if $A = \mathcal{A}$, it removes a random element from A; otherwise, it applies one of the previous modifications with equal probability. For both the edge label mutations in the node addition operator, we use the identity; the node factory samples with uniform probability $\{\text{TRUE}, \text{FALSE}\} \times \mathbb{N}_0$, i.e., picks randomly among all possible nodes not decorated with 0.

For the population initialization, we apply again the complexification principle. Graph in the initial population are composed of only two nodes—one being decorated with 0, and hence being the starting state, the other being an accepting node—connected by an edge labeled with a randomly chosen singleton of $\mathcal{P}(\mathcal{A})$.

Procedure and Results. We defined a procedure for building synthetic datasets s, S for text extraction based on two parameters related to the problem hardness: the size $n_s \leq 10$ of the alphabet of s and the number of positive examples n_S. Regardless of the values of these parameters, the set S of substrings is always composed of the matches of the following three regular expressions: 000000, 111(00)?+(11)++, and (110110)++. Given the values for n_s, n_S, a random s composed of the characters corresponding to the first n_s digits is generated randomly and incrementally until it contains at least n_S matches for each of the three regular expressions. We experimented with values $n_s = 2, n_S = 5, 3, 5,$ 4, 8, and 4, 10.

As a comparison baseline, we experimented with the same variant of CFGGP described in Sect. 3.1, with the same parameters and with a grammar tailored for building regular expressions composed of the characters in $\mathcal{A}$ and the constructs $(?:r)$, $.$, and $r|r$, r being a placeholder for another regular expression. Again, for both the EAs, we set $n_{\text{pop}} = 100$ and stopped the evolution after 100 generations.

Table 2. Fitness (median and standard deviation across 20 runs) of the best solution at the end of the evolution for the text extraction problems: fitness is the char error rate: the lower, the better.

EA	$n_s = 2, n_S = 5$	$n_s = 3, n_S = 5$	$n_s = 4, n_S = 10$	$n_s = 4, n_S = 8$
CFGGP	0.160 ± 0.030	0.120 ± 0.050	0.092 ± 0.037	0.097 ± 0.044
GraphEA	0.169 ± 0.027	0.093 ± 0.035	0.045 ± 0.015	0.043 ± 0.008

For each problem and each EA, we performed 20 independent runs with different random seeds. Table 1 summarizes the results in terms of the fitness of the best solution at the end of the evolution (median and standard deviation across the runs).

The figures in Table 2 suggests that GraphEA outperforms CFGGP for all but the hardest problem ($n_s = 2, n_S = 5$), for which the difference is not neat. A representation based on graphs is perfectly suitable for learning DFAs (that are graphs) and DFAs are a natural choice for extractors, at least if a compact, human-readable representation of the extractor is required. As a result, GraphEA seems to be more capable of searching the space of solutions than CFGGP that, in this case, works on a less direct representation.

3.3 Robotic Controller Optimization

Robots composed of soft materials constitute a promising approach to many tasks for which rigid robots are not suitable. Due to their nature, they can interact with fragile or sensible objects or exhibit degrees of compliance to the environment that are not feasible with rigid counterparts. One category of soft robots that is of further interest is the one of voxel-based soft robots (VSRs), that are composed of many simple deformable blocks (the voxels) [13]. Beside being soft, VSRs are inherently modular and represent hence a stepping-stone towards the ambitious goal of auto-reproducing machines. Unfortunately, designing a VSRs is a complex task, because the nontrivial interactions among its many components are difficult to model. For this reason, VSR design has been tackled with optimization, often by means of EC [16,28]: many aspects of a VSR can be subjected to optimization, most notably the shape and the controller. We here focus on the latter and consider the same scenario of [28], that we briefly summarize here—we refer the reader to the cited paper for the full details.

Given a 2-D shape for a VSR in which each one of the voxel is equipped with zero or more sensors (i.e., a VSR body), a controller is a law according to which the actuation value (a signal in $[-1, 1]$ corresponding to expansion or contraction of the voxel) of each voxel is determined at each time step based on the numerical values read by the sensors. Formally, the controller is hence a function from $\mathbb{R}^m$ to $\mathbb{R}^n$, m being the number of sensor readings and n the number of voxels. The problem of robotic controller optimization consists in learning the controller function that results in the best degree of achievement of a given task with a given body. We here focus on locomotion, and the fitness that measures the degree of achievement is the distance traveled by the VSR in a simulation lasting 20 s (simulated time).

For this problem, we used GraphEA for directly representing a artificial neural network (ANN) without a predefined topology, very similarly to NEAT—i.e., we realized a form of neuroevolution. All the parameters for the representation ($\mathcal{E}$, $\mathcal{N}$, the genetic operators, and the population initialization) are the same of CPPN-GraphEA, with the exceptions of the available base functions for the nodes, for which here we used only the tanh, and the output nodes, which are $y_1, \ldots, y_n$.

Procedure and Results. We considered the task of locomotion and two bodies: a "worm" composed of 6×2 voxels and a "biped" composed of a 4×2 trunk and two 1×1 legs. In both cases, the voxels in the top row were equipped with sensors sensing the x- and y-rotated-velocity of the voxel (see [19]), the bottom row (i.e., the legs for the biped) voxels with touch sensors, and all the voxels with current area ratio sensors.

As a baseline, we used CMA-ES [12], a popular numerical optimization algorithm that proved to be particularly effective in many reinforcement learning settings, for optimizing the weights of a fixed-topology multilayer perceptron (MLP): following the findings of [28], we used a topology composed of a single hidden layer with $0.65(m + 1)$ nodes, $m + 1$ being the number of input nodes (one plus the bias). As an aside, the present experiment is, to the best of our knowledge, the first application of CMA-ES for optimizing the controller of a VSR; nevertheless, successful applications of CMA-ES has been proposed for other kinds of modular robots (e.g., [22]). We used the basic version of CMA-ES with an initial vector of means randomly extracted in $[-1, 1]^p$, p being the number of weights in the MLP. The two considered bodies corresponded to MLPs having $p \approx 400$ and $p \approx 800$ weights for the biped and the worm, respectively.

For each problem and each EA, we performed 20 independent runs with different random seeds. Since CMA-ES uses a population size that depends on the dimension p of the search space, we stopped the evolution, for both EAs, after 20 000 fitness evaluations, while still using $n_{\mathrm{pop}} = 100$ for GraphEA. Table 3 summarizes the results in terms of the fitness of the best solution at the end of the evolution (median and standard deviation across the runs).

Table 3. Fitness (median and standard deviation across 20 runs) of the best solution at the end of the evolution for the robotic controller optimization problem, for two bodies: fitness is the traveled distance: the greater, the better.

EA	Biped	Worm
GraphEA	65.0 ± 8.3	43.5 ± 5.2
CMA-ES	94.7 ± 9.9	104.0 ± 10.4

It can be seen that in this case GraphEA does not compare favorably with the baseline, the gap in the final fitness being consistently large across all the experiments. In an attempt to understand this experimental observation, we analyzed the size (number of nodes and edges) of the graphs generated by GraphEA and found that, despite it consistently grows over the evolution, it never reaches the (fixed) size of the MLPs optimized by CMA-ES. Interestingly, the gap was larger for the worm (on average ≈ 320 vs. ≈ 445) than for the biped (on average ≈ 500 vs. ≈ 920) and the performance gap was larger for the worm than for the biped. We did not investigate in detail if every weight in the MLPs optimized by CMA-ES was actually important (ANNs may be pruned without being hampered in effectiveness), we think that the performance gap of GraphEA is at least partly due to the longest time it takes to evolve a graph that is complex enough for the task at hand. This limitation may be a consequence of many design choices for GraphEA, the most prominent being the initialization procedure following the complexification principle.

4 Concluding Remarks

Our experimental evaluation of GraphEA on three radically different problems based on the graph abstraction shows that the proposed approach is indeed general and effective. Specifically, GraphEA is competitive with more specific forms of optimization tailored to regression and text extraction from examples, while it is clearly outperformed by a state-of-the-art technique in neuroevolution of soft robot controllers. While this outcome is in line with other recent findings [24], in the sense there is not a single EA, nor a single representation, that systematically outperforms the other options across different problems, by digging in the results we noticed that when GraphEA struggles in matching the effectiveness of other optimization techniques, it often produces solutions which are remarkably simpler (and hence likely less expressive) than those of the baseline counterpart. We interpret this finding as an opportunity to further improve GraphEA. We speculate that some form of self-tuning of the population initialization and variation operators, capable of adaptively driving the search to the exploration of the search space where solutions are more complex, could be beneficial not only to GraphEA, but also to similar approaches, as EGGP.

Acknowledgments. We thanks Luca Zanella for the CMA-ES implementation in JGEA. The experimental evaluation of this work has been done on CINECA HPC cluster within the CINECA-University of Trieste agreement.

References

1. Atkinson, T.: Evolving graphs by graph programming. Ph.D. thesis, University of York (2019)
2. Atkinson, T., Plump, D., Stepney, S.: Evolving graphs by graph programming. In: Castelli, M., Sekanina, L., Zhang, M., Cagnoni, S., García-Sánchez, P. (eds.) EuroGP 2018. LNCS, vol. 10781, pp. 35–51. Springer, Cham (2018). https://doi.org/10.1007/978-3-319-77553-1_3

3. Bartoli, A., De Lorenzo, A., Medvet, E., Squillero, G.: Multi-level diversity promotion strategies for grammar-guided genetic programming. Appl. Soft Comput. **83**, 105599 (2019)
4. Bartoli, A., De Lorenzo, A., Medvet, E., Tarlao, F.: Learning text patterns using separate-and-conquer genetic programming. In: Machado, P., et al. (eds.) EuroGP 2015. LNCS, vol. 9025, pp. 16–27. Springer, Cham (2015). https://doi.org/10.1007/978-3-319-16501-1_2
5. Bartoli, A., De Lorenzo, A., Medvet, E., Tarlao, F.: Can a machine replace humans in building regular expressions? A case study. IEEE Intell. Syst. **31**(6), 15–21 (2016)
6. Bartoli, A., De Lorenzo, A., Medvet, E., Tarlao, F.: Inference of regular expressions for text extraction from examples. IEEE Trans. Knowl. Data Eng. **28**(5), 1217–1230 (2016)
7. Bartoli, A., De Lorenzo, A., Medvet, E., Tarlao, F.: Active learning of predefined models for information extraction: selecting regular expressions from examples. In: 5th Conference on Fuzzy Systems and Data Mining, pp. 645–651. IOS Press (2019)
8. Corus, D., Oliveto, P.S.: Standard steady state genetic algorithms can hillclimb faster than mutation-only evolutionary algorithms. IEEE Trans. Evol. Comput. **22**(5), 720–732 (2017)
9. De Jong, K.A.: Evolutionary Computation: A Unified Approach. MIT Press, Cambridge (2006)
10. De Lorenzo, A., Bartoli, A., Castelli, M., Medvet, E., Xue, B.: Genetic programming in the twenty-first century: a bibliometric and content-based analysis from both sides of the fence. Genet. Program Evolvable Mach. **21**(1), 181–204 (2019). https://doi.org/10.1007/s10710-019-09363-3
11. Doerr, B., Happ, E., Klein, C.: Crossover can provably be useful in evolutionary computation. Theor. Comput. Sci. **425**, 17–33 (2012)
12. Hansen, N.: The CMA evolution strategy: a comparing review. In: Lozano, J.A., Larrañaga, P., Inza, I., Bengoetxea, E. (eds.) Towards a New Evolutionary Computation. STUDFUZZ, vol. 192, pp. 75–102. Springer, Heidelberg (2006). https://doi.org/10.1007/3-540-32494-1_4
13. Hiller, J., Lipson, H.: Automatic design and manufacture of soft robots. IEEE Trans. Robot. **28**(2), 457–466 (2012)
14. Keijzer, M.: Scaled symbolic regression. Genet. Program Evolvable Mach. **5**(3), 259–269 (2004). https://doi.org/10.1023/B:GENP.0000030195.77571.f9
15. Koza, J.R.: Genetic Programming: On the Programming of Computers by Means of Natural Selection, vol. 1. MIT Press, Cambridge (1992)
16. Kriegman, S., Blackiston, D., Levin, M., Bongard, J.: A scalable pipeline for designing reconfigurable organisms. Proc. Natl. Acad. Sci. **117**(4), 1853–1859 (2020)
17. Lucas, S.M., Reynolds, T.J.: Learning deterministic finite automata with a smart state labeling evolutionary algorithm. IEEE Trans. Pattern Anal. Mach. Intell. **27**(7), 1063–1074 (2005)
18. Luke, S.: Essentials of Metaheuristics, vol. 113. Lulu, Raleigh (2009)
19. Medvet, E., Bartoli, A., De Lorenzo, A., Seriani, S.: 2D-VSR-Sim: a simulation tool for the optimization of 2-D voxel-based soft robots. SoftwareX **12**, 100573 (2020)
20. Medvet, E., Bartoli, A., De Lorenzo, A., Tarlao, F.: Interactive example-based finding of text items. Expert Syst. Appl. **154**, 113403 (2020)
21. Miller, J.F., Harding, S.L.: Cartesian genetic programming. In: Proceedings of the 10th Annual Conference Companion on Genetic and Evolutionary Computation, pp. 2701–2726 (2008)

22. Miras, K., De Carlo, M., Akhatou, S., Eiben, A.E.: Evolving-controllers versus learning-controllers for morphologically evolvable robots. In: Castillo, P.A., Jiménez Laredo, J.L., Fernández de Vega, F. (eds.) EvoApplications 2020. LNCS, vol. 12104, pp. 86–99. Springer, Cham (2020). https://doi.org/10.1007/978-3-030-43722-0_6
23. Schaffer, J.D., Whitley, D., Eshelman, L.J.: Combinations of genetic algorithms and neural networks: a survey of the state of the art. In: Proceedings of the COGANN-1992: International Workshop on Combinations of Genetic Algorithms and Neural Networks, pp. 1–37. IEEE (1992)
24. Sotto, L.F.D., Kaufmann, P., Atkinson, T., Kalkreuth, R., Basgalupp, M.P.: A study on graph representations for genetic programming. In: Proceedings of the 2020 Genetic and Evolutionary Computation Conference, pp. 931–939 (2020)
25. Squillero, G., Tonda, A.: Divergence of character and premature convergence: a survey of methodologies for promoting diversity in evolutionary optimization. Inf. Sci. **329**, 782–799 (2016)
26. Stanley, K.O.: Compositional pattern producing networks: a novel abstraction of development. Genet. Program Evolvable Mach. 8(2), 131–162 (2007). https://doi.org/10.1007/s10710-007-9028-8
27. Stanley, K.O., Miikkulainen, R.: Evolving neural networks through augmenting topologies. Evol. Comput. **10**(2), 99–127 (2002)
28. Talamini, J., Medvet, E., Bartoli, A., De Lorenzo, A.: Evolutionary synthesis of sensing controllers for voxel-based soft robots. In: The 2018 Conference on Artificial Life: A Hybrid of the European Conference on Artificial Life (ECAL) and the International Conference on the Synthesis and Simulation of Living Systems (ALIFE), pp. 574–581. MIT Press (2019)
29. Virgolin, M., Alderliesten, T., Bosman, P.A.: Linear scaling with and within semantic backpropagation-based genetic programming for symbolic regression. In: Proceedings of the Genetic and Evolutionary Computation Conference, pp. 1084–1092 (2019)
30. Wei, Q., et al.: A study of deep learning approaches for medication and adverse drug event extraction from clinical text. J. Am. Med. Inform. Assoc. **27**(1), 13–21 (2020)
31. Whigham, P.: Inductive bias and genetic programming. In: First International Conference on Genetic Algorithms in Engineering Systems: Innovations and Applications, pp. 461–466. IET (1995)
32. White, D.R., et al.: Better GP benchmarks: community survey results and proposals. Genet. Program Evolvable Mach. **14**(1), 3–29 (2013). https://doi.org/10.1007/s10710-012-9177-2

Where the Local Search Affects Best in an Immune Algorithm

Rocco A. Scollo⬤, Vincenzo Cutello⬤, and Mario Pavone(✉)⬤

Department of Mathematics and Computer Science, University of Catania,
V.le A. Doria 6, 95125 Catania, Italy
rocco.scollo@phd.unict.it, {cutello,mario.pavone}@unict.it

Abstract. Hybrid algorithms are powerful search algorithms obtained by the combination of metaheuristics with other optimization techniques, although the most common hybridization is to apply a local solver method within evolutionary computation algorithms. In many published works in the literature, such local solver is run in different ways, sometimes acting on the perturbed elements and other on the best ones, and this raises the question of when it is best to run the local solver and on which elements it acts best in order to improve the reliability of the algorithm. Thus, three different ways of running local search in an immune algorithm have been investigated, and well-known community detection was considered as test-problem. The three methods analyzed have been assessed with respect their effect on the performances in term of quality solution found and information gained.

Keywords: Hybrid algorithms · Hybrid metaheuristics · Hybrid immune algorithms · Hybrid-IA · Community detection · Modularity optimization · Network science

1 Introduction

Evolutionary computation represents today a consolidated and established class of algorithmic methodologies able to tackle hard and complex optimization problems mainly thanks to their ability to be easily applied on new and unknown problems, and, in general, on all those problems whose knowledge about their features and structures are very limited. Among the evolutionary computation methodologies, the immune-inspired algorithms represent a powerful algorithmic class, which takes inspiration by the principles and dynamics of the biological immune system (IS). What makes the IS very interesting and source of inspiration from a computational perspective is its ability in learning, detecting, and recognizing foreign and dangerous entities [10].

However, although many methodologies inspired by biology and nature have been developed, applied effectively in many combinatorial optimization problems, it clearly emerges from the literature that just on these kinds of problems their hybridization, that is their combination with concepts and/or components

© Springer Nature Switzerland AG 2021
M. Baldoni and S. Bandini (Eds.): AIxIA 2020, LNAI 12414, pp. 99–114, 2021.
https://doi.org/10.1007/978-3-030-77091-4_7

of other optimization techniques (e.g., Local Search algorithms), turns out to be much more efficient and successful, thus proving to be very powerful search algorithms [1]. The basic idea of this combination is to exploit the strengths of one to overcome the weaknesses of the other: random-search performs an excellent exploration of the search space (thanks to its stochastic nature), whilst deterministic approach, for instance, is useful for refine and improve the current solutions found. There are many different ways to generate hybrid methods, but the most common and popular is combine evolutionary algorithms and local improver methods (such as Local Search, Hill-Climbing, etc.), which are applied one after another, using the output of the former as input for the latter. Furthermore, it is also common in this case that the revised and improved individual, by the local improver method, replaces the original one in the population.

In this paper we want to investigate on when is better to perform the Local Search (LS), and if, in the overall, replace the original solution with the revised one by LS is the best choice. In light of this, a *Hybrid Immune Algorithm*, called HYBRID-IA, has been taken into account in an attempt to answer these questions. HYBRID-IA has been considered as it was successful applied in several and various combinatorial optimization problems. [2–5]. Thus, the effect of the local search on the performances of HYBRID-IA has been investigated considering three different positions in the evolutionary cycle where to run the local improver method: (1) acting and refining the best solutions found so far (to be run just after selecting the best elements for the next generation); (2) acting on the perturbed elements and replacing them (to be run after the hypermutation operator, see Algorithm 1); and, finally, (3) acting always on the perturbed elements but producing a new population, whose individuals will compete to the selection of the new population for the next generation.

In order to analyse which among of the three methods best affects the performance of HYBRID-IA, the well-known *Community Detection* problem has been considered, which is considered one of the most important problems in Network Sciences and Graph Analysis. The study of community structures inspires intense research activities to visualize and understand the dynamics of a network at different scales [8,11,12]. The goal of this task is uncovering the inherent community structure of a network, which means to discover those groups of nodes sharing common properties. The *modularity* is certainly the evaluation metric most used to assess the quality of the uncovered communities in a network [19], based on the idea that a random graph is not expected to have a community structure, therefore the possible existence of communities can be revealed by the difference of density between vertices of the graph and vertices of a random graph with the same size and degree distribution. Given an undirected graph $G = (V, E)$, with V the set of vertices ($|V| = N$), and E the set of edges ($|E| = M$), the modularity of a community is defined as:

$$Q = \frac{1}{2M} \left[\sum_{i=1}^{N} \sum_{j=1}^{N} \left(A_{ij} - \frac{d_i d_j}{2M} \right) \delta(i,j) \right], \tag{1}$$

where A_{ij} is the adjacency matrix of G, d_i and d_j are the degrees of nodes i and j respectively, and $\delta(i,j) = 1$ if i, j belong to the same community, 0 otherwise.

Several artificial networks have been produced using the well-known *LFR* algorithm [16,17] in order to assess what proposed method affect best in term of solution quality found, and information gained. The use of artificial networks allows to inspect these three methods under different complexity scenarios. It is important to highlight that this investigation begins from consolidated and asserted outcomes in [2] (precisely method A), which prove that HYBRID-IA is competitive and comparable with the state-of-the-art.

Analysing all experimental results emerges that performing the local improver just after the hypermutation operator, that means to act directly on the elements produced by the random search, is the one to produce best efficiency and reliability on Hybrid-IA since it allows to perform a better and wide exploration of the search space and this is useful to jump out from local optima.

2 The Hybrid Immune Algorithm

Immune Algorithms (IA) are among the most used population-based metaheuristics, successfully applied in search and optimization tasks. They take inspiration from the dynamics of the immune system in performing its job of protecting living organisms. One of the features of the immune system that makes it a very good source of inspiration is its ability to detect, distinguish, learn, and remember all foreign entities discovered [10]. The presented Hybrid Immune Algorithm, called HYBRID-IA, belongs to the special class *Clonal Selection Algorithms* (CSA) [5,20], whose efficiency is due to the three main immune operators: (*i*) cloning, (*ii*) hypermutation, and (*iii*) aging. The overall scheme of HYBRID-IA, proposed in [2,5], is shown in Algorithm 1. It is based on two main concepts: antigen (Ag), which represents the problem to tackle, and B cell, or antibody (Ab) that represents a candidate solution ($\boldsymbol{x}$), i.e., a point in the solution space. At each time step t, the algorithm maintains a population of d candidate solutions to the problem tackled. The population is randomly initialized at the time step $t = 0$. Then, just after the initialization step, the fitness function, specific to the problem, is evaluated for each randomly generated element ($\boldsymbol{x} \in P^{(t)}$) by using the function ComputeFitness($P^{(t)}$). The algorithm ends its evolutionary cycle when the halting criterion is reached. For this work, it was fixed to a maximum number of generations ($MaxGen$).

The first immune operator to take place is the *Cloning Operator* (6*th* line in Algorithm 1). This operator simply copies *dup* times each B cell producing an intermediate population $P^{(clo)}$ of size $d \times dup$. We used a static cloning in order to avoid premature convergences. Indeed, if a number of clones proportional to the fitness value is produced instead, we could have a population of B cells very similar to each other, and we would, consequently, be unable to perform a proper exploration of the search space getting easily trapped in local optima. Once created the copies of any B cell, to each of those is assigned an age, which determines how long it can live in the population, from the assigned age until it reaches the maximum age allowed (τ_B). Specifically, a random age chosen in the range $[0 : \frac{2}{3}\tau_B]$ is assigned to each clone [20]; in this way, each clone is guaranteed to stay in the population for at least a fixed number of generations ($\frac{1}{3}\tau_B$ in the worst case). The age assignment and the aging operator play a crucial role on HYBRID-IA performances, and any evolutionary algorithm in general, because they are able to keep a right amount of diversity among the solutions, thus avoiding premature convergences [7,21].

Algorithm 1. Pseudo-code of HYBRID-IA.

1: **procedure** HYBRID-IA(d, dup, ρ, τ_B)
2:       $t \leftarrow 0$
3:       $P^{(t)} \leftarrow$ InitializePopulation(d)
4:       ComputeFitness($P^{(t)}$)
5:       **while** ¬StopCriterion **do**
6:            $P^{(clo)} \leftarrow$ Cloning($P^{(t)}, dup$)
7:            $P^{(hyp)} \leftarrow$ Hypermutation($P^{(clo)}, \rho$)
8:            ComputeFitness($P^{(hyp)}$)
9:            $(P_a^{(t)}, P_a^{(hyp)}) \leftarrow$ Aging($P^{(t)}, P^{(hyp)}, \tau_B$)
10:           $P^{(select)} \leftarrow (\mu + \lambda)-$Selection($P_a^{(t)}, P_a^{(hyp)}$)
11:           $P^{(t+1)} \leftarrow$ LocalSearch($P^{(select)}$)
12:           ComputeFitness($P^{(t+1)}$)
13:           $t \leftarrow t + 1$;
14:      **end while**
15: **end procedure**

The *Hypermutation Operator* has the main goal of exploring the neighbourhoods of solutions by evaluating how good each clone is ($7th$ line in Algorithm 1). The mutation rate is determined through an *inversely proportional* law to the fitness function value of the B cell considered, that is, the better the fitness value of the element is, the smaller the mutation rate will be. In particular, let x be a cloned B cell, the number of mutations is determined by $M = \lfloor (\alpha \times \ell) + 1 \rfloor$, with ℓ the length of the B cell (i.e. $\ell = |V|$), and α representing the *mutation rate* obtained as $\alpha = e^{-\rho \hat{f}(x)}$, where ρ determines the shape of the mutation rate, and $\hat{f}(x)$ is the fitness function normalized in the range $[0, 1]$. Naturally, the mutation operator that acts on a single element of the cloned B cell is problem-dependent.

The static *Aging Operator* in HYBRID-IA acts on each mutated B cells by removing older ones from the two populations $P^{(t)}$ and $P^{(hyp)}$ ($9th$ line in Algorithm 1). Basically, let τ_B be the maximum number of generations allowed for every B cell to stay in its population; then, once the age of a B cell exceeds τ_B (i.e., age $= \tau_B+1$), it will be removed independently from its fitness value. However, an exception is done in HYBRID-IA for the best current solution, which is kept into the population even if its age is older than τ_B. Such a variant of the aging operator is called *elitist aging operator*. In the overall, the main goal of this operator is to allow the algorithm to escape and jump out from local optima, assuring a proper turnover between the B cells in the population, and producing, consequently, high diversity among them.

After the aging operator, the best d survivors from both populations $P_a^{(t)}$ and $P_a^{(hyp)}$ are selected, in order to generate the temporary population $P^{(select)}$, on the local search will be performed (10th line in Algorithm 1). Such a selection is performed by the $(\mu + \lambda)$-*Selection Operator*, where $\mu = d$ and $\lambda = (d \times dup)$. The operator identifies the d best elements among the set of offspring and the old parent B cells, ensuring consequently monotonicity in the evolution dynamics.

The main idea behind the *Local Search* operator is to refine and improve in deterministic way the solutions produced by the stochastic mutation operator. In this study the affect and impact of the position where to run the local search within Hybrid-IA is inspected (see Algorithm 1). Specifically, three approaches have been taken into account:

- **Method A:** applying the local search operator just after the selection operator, acting, consequently, on the individuals already selected to produce the new population for the next generation. In this way, the local search is always applied to the best solutions, intensifying the exploration in their relative neighbourhood.
- **Method B:** applying LS to the population generated by the hypermutation operator, where each revised individual replaces the hypermutated one, maintaining the same population. In this way, it is applied to a wider set of solutions generated from the current ones through mutation allowing a better exploration of the search space. Of course, the computational complexity is higher than in the previous case because it is applied to a population of $d \times dup$.
- **Method C:** applying LS to the hypermutated individuals, as in the previous method, but producing a new temporary population, which will compete with the other populations to the selection for the next generation. In this way, the algorithm keeps memory of the discoveries made via random search, which generates diversity in the population, and, at the same time, it carries out a careful exploration of their neighbourhood via local search. Computational complexity is the same as the previous method.

2.1   Hybrid-IA for the Community Detection

Once described the structure and features of Hybrid-IA in general, in this section all details on the operators and local search developed specifically for the community detection problem are reported. Any B cell in the population is represented as subdivision of the vertices of the graph $G = (V, E)$ in communities. A solution $\boldsymbol{x}$ is a sequence of $N = |V|$ elements in the range $[1, N]$ such that $x_i = j$ indicates that the node i belongs to the cluster j. In the initialization phase $(t = 0)$, each element of the population is randomly generated assigning each vertex i to a group j, with $j \in [1, N]$. The aim of the designed hypermutation operator is to explore the search space in order to create new communities by moving a nodes variable percentage from existing communities. For each B cell, it chooses randomly two communities c_i and c_j $(c_i \neq c_j)$ among all existing ones, and, with a probability given by α, all vertices in c_i are moved to c_j. The α *mutation rate* is, then, defined as the probability to move a node from one community to another one.

The designed Local Search, introduced in [2], allows to speed up the convergence of the algorithm and intensify the search in the neighbourhood of each solution. The idea is to deterministically improve a solution using the *Move Vertex* operator [14]. This operator moves a node from its community to another one within its neighbours, taking into account the gain of modularity, that can be defined as the variation in modularity produced when a node is moved from a community to another. The modularity Q, defined in Eq. (1), can be rewritten as:

$$Q(c) = \sum_{i=1}^{k} \left[\frac{\ell_i}{M} - \left(\frac{d_i}{2M} \right)^2 \right], \tag{2}$$

where k is the number of communities identified; $c = \{c_1, \ldots, c_i, \ldots c_k\}$ is a partition of V; ℓ_i and d_i are, respectively, the number of links inside the community i, and the sum of the degrees of vertices belonging to the i community. The gain of modularity of a vertex $u \in c_i$ is the modularity variation produced by moving u from c_i to c_j, that is:

$$\Delta Q_u(c_i, c_j) = \frac{l_{c_j}(u) - l_{c_i}(u)}{M} + d_V(u) \left[\frac{d_{c_i} - d_V(u) - d_{c_j}}{2M^2} \right], \tag{3}$$

where $l_{c_i}(u)$ and $l_{c_j}(u)$ are the number of links from u to nodes in c_i and c_j respectively, and $d_V(u)$ is the degree of u when considering all the vertices V. If the gain is greater than 0, then moving node u from c_i to c_j produces an improvement in modularity. Consequently, the goal of the move vertex operator is to find a node u to move to an adjacent community in order to maximize the gain of modularity. The local search, for each solution, works sorting the communities in increasing order with respect the ratio of internal links and degree of the community; in this way, it tries to repair the solutions starting from poorly formed communities, which are produced by the hypermutation operator (random search).

3   Experimental Results

In this section all experiments performed are presented in order to inspect what is the best position where to run the local search within the evolutionary cycle of HYBRID-IA. For this study, the community detection has been considered as the test problem, and, specifically, several artificial networks have been taken into account as benchmark instances. These networks were generated by *LFR* algorithm, proposed in [16,17], and have been used because they allow us to perform our study on different complexity scenarios thanks their diverse features. Note that the validity of this benchmark is given by faithfully reproducing the keys features of real graphs communities. In particular, networks with number of nodes 300, 500, 1000, and 5000 have been generated, with average degree 15, 20, and 25, and maximum degree 50. Further, for all $|V|$ values, the exponent of the degrees distribution was set to $\tau_1 = 2$, whilst the distribution of community sizes to $\tau_2 = 1$. Minimum and maximum of the communities' size for such artificial networks were considered, respectively, $min_c = 10$ and $max_c = 50$. The mixing parameter μ_t, which identifies the relationship between the node's external and internal degree with respect to its community, was instead set to 0.5: greater is the value of μ_t, greater is number of edges that a node shares with nodes outside of its communities. For each network parameters configuration 5 random instances have been generated. For all experiments performed on all tested networks the following parameters setting have been used for HYBRID-IA: B cells population size $d = 100$; number of generated clones $dup = 2$; ρ and τ_B, respectively, to 1.0 and 5. All these parameters have been identified both from the knowledge learned by previous works [2,5,20], and from preliminary experiments carried out. Maximum number of generations has been considered as stopping criterion and was set to $MaxGen = 100$. 50 independent runs were also performed. In order to assess which of the three method is the most efficient and reliable, in addition to the convergence behaviour analysis and solution (modularity) quality obtained by each method, also the Information Gain as been considered as evaluation metric. This entropic function measures the quantity of information the system discovers during the learning phase (see [3,15]).

For all network instances the convergence analysis was carried out for the three methods. Due to the space limit only the most significant ones are reported. In Figs. 1 and 2 are shown the convergence plots for the LFR instances with 1000 nodes and average degree k of 15 and 20 respectively. From these plots can be noted that method A reaches high modularity values in the first 10 generations, afterwards improves very slowly. The same trend is also visible in the average fitness of the population, with a peak in the first generations and a slow growth for the rest of the run. Methods B and C, on the other hand, have a growth much more constant and linear, both in terms of the best solution and average of the population. The average fitness curve is very close to the best solution one, indicating then a population composed of solutions with values of modularity very similar to each other and consequently very homogeneous. This is also supported by the information gain curve, in which the peak is reached in the earliest generations, after that it stays in a steady-state for the rest of the execution (Figs. 1c and 2c), while method A needs more generations to converge to the same value reached by the other two methods.

The same situation is obtained in the networks with 5000 nodes and average degree k equal to 20 and 25 (Figs. 3 and 4). Also in these plots, method A has a much slower convergence than the other two methods and maintains a certain degree of diversity within the population, demonstrated by the distance between the two curves: best solution, and average fitness of the population. In this case, in both methods B and C, the two curves have a higher slope, which suggests that with more generations they could achieve better solutions.

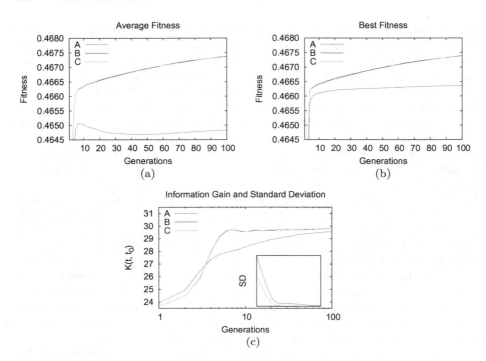

Fig. 1. Convergence behavior of the three methods on LFR(1000,15,0.5) graph. (a) Average and (b) best fitness value of the population versus generations. (c) Information gain and standard deviation.

The greater diversity introduced by methods B and C, allows to better explore the search space and to find solutions with a higher modularity value. The Table 1 shows the results of the experiments of the three methods carried out on benchmark instances. In particular, in the table are reported the maximum value of modularity (Q), average number of communities (K) and computational time, all averaged over 5 random instances. From these results, can be noted that on the networks with 300 nodes, all three methods reach what is most likely the maximum modularity value, detecting the same number of communities. On the other hands, for the instances with 500 nodes, only for $k = 20$ method A reaches the same modularity value of methods B and C, while for $k = 15$ reaches a slightly lower modularity value, about 1.79×10^{-4}, which leads to a different number of communities detected (17.6 for method A versus 16.8 for both method B and C). The difference in modularity becomes greater as the number of nodes increases. For the instances with 1000 nodes, method A reaches a lower modularity value than the other two methods (about 10^{-3} on average for both instances), as observed in the respectively convergence plots. The other two methods, B and C, reach the best modularity value for $k = 20$ and $k = 15$ respectively, with a minimum difference between each other.

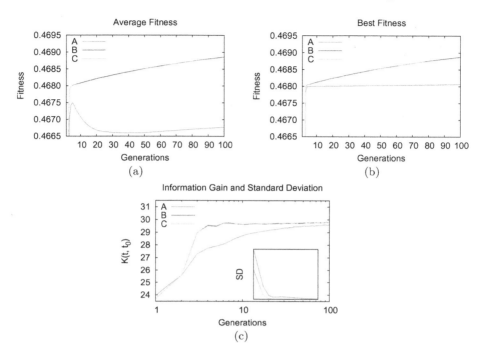

Fig. 2. Convergence behavior of the three methods on `LFR(1000,20,0.5)` graph. (a) Average and (b) best fitness value of the population versus generations. (c) Information gain and standard deviation.

The same results can be observed for the network with 5000 nodes, where method A is behind the other two methods in terms of modularity, although with a lower gap with respect the instances with 1000 nodes (about 4×10^{-4}), while methods B and C achieve the best modularity value for $k = 25$ and $k = 20$ respectively. Moreover, unlike smaller instances (300, and 500 nodes), on the networks with 1000 and 5000 nodes the number of communities found by methods B and C is different. Finally, from the computational time point of view, methods B and C, as expected, take about 90% more time than method A, but, nevertheless, they allow a better exploration of the search space, and then obtaining solutions with higher modularity values.

In order to consolidate the outcomes obtained so far and make them more reliable an extended further analysis has been performed at the varying of the mixing parameter (μ_t), on all three methods, whose outcomes are reported in Tables 2 and 3. As described above, the mixing parameter μ_t identifies the relationships between the communities, that is the ratio between the node's degree internal to the community, and the external one. In this way, it is possible to carry out a comparison analysis in different scenarios, each of which was designed as realistic as possible ($\mu_t = \{0.1, 0.2, \ldots, 0.8\}$). Table 2 reports the experimental results obtained by the three methods on networks with 300 and 500 vertices.

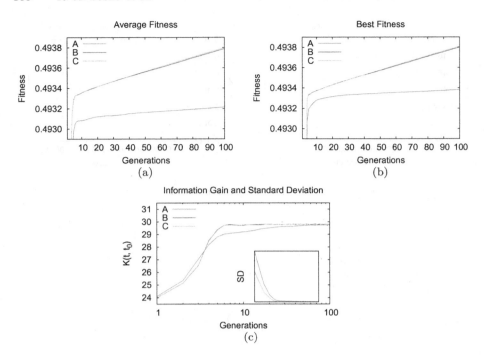

Fig. 3. Convergence behavior of the three methods on LFR(5000,20,0.5) graph. (a) Average and (b) best fitness value of the population versus generations. (c) Information gain and standard deviation.

Table 1. Results of the three methods on *LFR Benchmarks*. The results are averaged on 5 random instances and calculated over 100 independent runs.

Instance	A			B			C		
	K	Q	Time	K	Q	Time	K	Q	Time
$(300, 15, 0.5)$	11.6	**0.392061**	8.3	11.6	**0.392061**	14.5	11.6	**0.392061**	15.5
$(300, 20, 0.5)$	11.2	**0.386560**	9.4	11.2	**0.386560**	16.9	11.2	**0.386560**	17.9
$(500, 15, 0.5)$	17.6	0.436989	13.7	16.8	**0.437168**	24.6	16.8	**0.437168**	26.1
$(500, 20, 0.5)$	17.0	**0.430526**	16.3	17.0	**0.430526**	29.7	17.0	**0.430526**	31.3
$(1000, 15, 0.5)$	34.4	0.467073	28.0	30.0	0.468122	51.2	30.4	**0.468205**	53.9
$(1000, 20, 0.5)$	37.0	0.468532	33.8	33.0	**0.469451**	62.6	32.2	0.469442	65.2
$(5000, 20, 0.5)$	196.4	0.493532	182.4	190.2	0.493985	346.0	189.4	**0.493994**	353.5
$(5000, 25, 0.5)$	193.0	0.493379	228.8	185.4	**0.493741**	438.1	184.6	0.493740	427.1

Focusing on the first one, that is the network with 300 nodes, it is possible to note how the three methods are equivalent on all those instances where the external links are below, or around, the threshold of 50% ($\mu_t \leq 0.5$). By increasing this threshold, instead, methods B and C significantly improve method A, both in

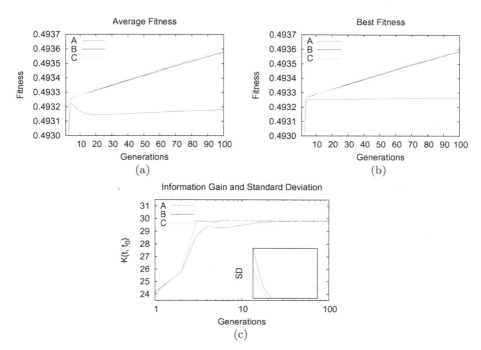

Fig. 4. Convergence behavior of the three methods on `LFR(5000,25,0.5)` graph. (a) Average and (b) best fitness value of the population versus generations. (c) Information gain and standard deviation.

terms of the modularity values and number of communities discovered. A similar behavior can be observed also on the network with 500 nodes, although the threshold, where the three methods are equivalent, decreases to $\mu_t \leq 0.4$ when the average degree k of the nodes is 15. What is more interesting to note is that the method C considerably outperforms not only the method A, which is to be expected based on the previous results, but also the method B, especially when the average degree is $k = 20$ and the external links grow ($\mu_t \geq 0.6$). This is due to the fact that as the nodes average degree and, primarily, the number of external links increase, the problem becomes harder and, consequently, to have two different populations competing with each other (the ones produced by the random search and by the refinement one) produce more heterogeneity and therefore higher diversity in the population, which helps the algorithm to carry out a better exploration in the search space, avoiding thus being trapped in local optima.

From Table 3, where are showed the experimental results on the networks with 1000 and 5000 nodes, appears even more obvious how the method A achieves worst performances than the other two, in all instances considered. On the other hand, analyzing the results obtained with the two methods B and C, it is possible to note that the improvements of one over the other are minimal, except in some

Table 2. Results of the three methods at the mixing parameter varying (μ_t), on networks with 300 and 500 nodes.

Instance	A			B			C		
	K	Q	Time	K	Q	Time	K	Q	Time
$\|V\| = 300$									
$(300, 15, 0.1)$	10.2	**0.766602**	3.8	10.2	**0.766602**	6.5	10.2	**0.766602**	7.4
$(300, 15, 0.2)$	12.0	**0.673573**	4.5	12.0	**0.673573**	7.9	12.0	**0.673573**	8.7
$(300, 15, 0.3)$	13.0	**0.583192**	5.3	13.0	**0.583192**	9.3	13.0	**0.583192**	10.1
$(300, 15, 0.4)$	11.2	**0.484404**	5.9	11.2	**0.484404**	10.5	11.2	**0.484404**	11.3
$(300, 15, 0.5)$	11.6	**0.392061**	8.3	11.6	**0.392061**	14.5	11.6	**0.392061**	15.5
$(300, 15, 0.6)$	11.0	0.305655	6.9	10.6	**0.306509**	12.4	10.6	**0.306509**	13.2
$(300, 15, 0.7)$	8.0	0.241728	7.1	6.6	0.247123	12.8	6.8	**0.247811**	13.5
$(300, 15, 0.8)$	7.8	0.232779	7.0	6.8	**0.240292**	12.7	6.8	0.239547	13.4
$(300, 20, 0.1)$	8.6	**0.754457**	4.5	8.6	**0.754457**	7.8	8.6	**0.754457**	8.7
$(300, 20, 0.2)$	11.8	**0.670396**	5.2	11.8	**0.670396**	9.3	11.8	**0.670396**	10.1
$(300, 20, 0.3)$	12.0	**0.577310**	6.1	12.0	**0.577310**	11.0	12.0	**0.577310**	11.8
$(300, 20, 0.4)$	12.6	**0.496497**	7.0	12.6	**0.496497**	12.7	12.6	**0.496497**	13.5
$(300, 20, 0.5)$	11.2	**0.386560**	9.4	11.2	**0.386560**	16.9	11.2	**0.386560**	17.9
$(300, 20, 0.6)$	11.0	0.288503	8.4	10.8	**0.288713**	15.4	10.8	**0.288713**	16.2
$(300, 20, 0.7)$	8.6	0.223786	8.5	7.8	0.227081	15.5	7.6	**0.227327**	16.2
$(300, 20, 0.8)$	7.6	0.202636	8.7	6.2	**0.207970**	15.8	6.4	0.207610	16.5
$\|V\| = 500$									
$(500, 15, 0.1)$	18.6	**0.820874**	6.1	18.6	**0.820874**	10.4	18.6	**0.820874**	11.6
$(500, 15, 0.2)$	20.4	**0.724672**	7.4	20.4	**0.724672**	13.0	20.4	**0.724672**	14.2
$(500, 15, 0.3)$	18.6	0.626449	8.7	18.4	**0.626457**	15.5	18.4	**0.626457**	16.7
$(500, 15, 0.4)$	17.0	**0.529800**	9.9	17.0	**0.529800**	18.0	17.0	**0.529800**	19.2
$(500, 15, 0.5)$	17.6	0.436989	13.7	16.8	**0.437168**	24.6	16.8	**0.437168**	26.1
$(500, 15, 0.6)$	16.6	0.336580	12.0	14.6	**0.337333**	22.0	14.8	0.337325	23.2
$(500, 15, 0.7)$	11.0	0.248666	12.1	8.8	0.256057	22.2	8.2	**0.256795**	23.3
$(500, 15, 0.8)$	10.2	0.237794	11.9	8.0	0.245876	21.8	7.6	**0.246542**	22.8
$(500, 20, 0.1)$	19.2	**0.817709**	7.1	19.2	**0.817709**	12.6	19.2	**0.817709**	13.8
$(500, 20, 0.2)$	17.6	**0.721416**	8.8	17.6	**0.721416**	15.9	17.6	**0.721416**	17.1
$(500, 20, 0.3)$	19.2	**0.629277**	10.4	19.2	**0.629277**	19.0	19.2	**0.629277**	20.2
$(500, 20, 0.4)$	18.6	0.533117	11.9	18.4	**0.533150**	22.1	18.4	**0.533150**	23.3
$(500, 20, 0.5)$	17.0	**0.430526**	16.3	17.0	**0.430526**	29.7	17.0	**0.430526**	31.3
$(500, 20, 0.6)$	17.4	0.338484	14.2	17.0	**0.338712**	26.5	17.0	**0.338712**	27.7
$(500, 20, 0.7)$	13.2	0.241751	15.0	11.2	0.245852	27.6	10.4	**0.246251**	28.6
$(500, 20, 0.8)$	9.0	0.211891	14.3	7.4	0.218448	26.3	7.0	**0.218741**	27.4

Table 3. Results of the three methods at the mixing parameter varying (μ_t), on networks with 1000 and 5000 nodes.

Instance	A			B			C		
	K	Q	Time	K	Q	Time	K	Q	Time
$|V| = 1000$									
$(1000, 15, 0.1)$	38.8	0.860777	12.3	38.0	**0.860833**	21.2	38.2	0.860826	23.4
$(1000, 15, 0.2)$	37.0	0.762139	15.1	35.8	0.762252	27.0	35.8	**0.762255**	29.2
$(1000, 15, 0.3)$	36.6	0.664539	17.6	35.2	0.664881	32.0	34.0	**0.664966**	34.2
$(1000, 15, 0.4)$	34.8	0.565415	20.6	33.0	**0.565756**	37.8	33.2	0.565726	40.0
$(1000, 15, 0.5)$	34.4	0.467073	28.0	30.0	0.468122	51.2	30.4	**0.468205**	53.9
$(1000, 15, 0.6)$	33.2	0.368714	25.1	28.2	0.370871	46.7	27.6	**0.370888**	48.9
$(1000, 15, 0.7)$	24.4	0.270108	25.3	16.8	**0.279350**	47.0	16.4	0.279087	49.1
$(1000, 15, 0.8)$	17.0	0.241944	23.9	9.0	0.249147	44.2	9.0	**0.250582**	46.2
$(1000, 20, 0.1)$	39.2	0.860630	14.2	37.8	**0.860694**	25.0	38.0	0.860692	27.3
$(1000, 20, 0.2)$	38.0	0.762173	17.9	36.2	**0.762229**	32.5	36.6	0.762228	34.8
$(1000, 20, 0.3)$	38.2	0.665545	21.2	36.0	**0.665768**	39.1	36.4	0.665732	41.5
$(1000, 20, 0.4)$	40.4	0.566834	24.3	35.6	**0.567383**	45.3	35.8	0.567336	47.6
$(1000, 20, 0.5)$	37.0	0.468532	33.8	33.0	**0.469451**	62.6	32.2	0.469442	65.2
$(1000, 20, 0.6)$	36.4	0.368643	30.1	29.4	**0.370331**	56.7	29.4	0.370210	59.0
$(1000, 20, 0.7)$	32.0	0.271142	31.6	26.2	**0.275290**	59.6	26.4	0.275260	62.0
$(1000, 20, 0.8)$	11.8	0.215022	29.4	8.2	**0.222399**	54.7	8.8	0.221720	56.8
$|V| = 5000$									
$(5000, 20, 0.1)$	199.8	0.892274	71.4	193.8	0.892360	129.3	193.0	**0.892371**	139.4
$(5000, 20, 0.2)$	200.4	0.792707	90.6	194.4	**0.792857**	167.7	194.4	0.792848	177.7
$(5000, 20, 0.3)$	191.0	0.692909	108.4	186.4	0.693102	203.3	185.2	**0.693111**	213.5
$(5000, 20, 0.4)$	190.4	0.593117	127.1	186.6	0.593357	240.5	184.0	**0.593378**	251.0
$(5000, 20, 0.5)$	196.4	0.493532	182.4	190.2	0.493985	346.0	189.4	**0.493994**	353.5
$(5000, 20, 0.6)$	196.6	0.393921	160.3	187.8	0.394428	306.1	186.0	**0.394455**	316.5
$(5000, 20, 0.7)$	203.8	0.292948	176.2	192.8	0.293851	337.3	191.0	**0.294002**	347.9
$(5000, 20, 0.8)$	87.2	0.209471	158.8	74.8	**0.212451**	299.5	73.6	0.212407	307.7
$(5000, 25, 0.1)$	173.8	0.892187	85.3	170.2	**0.892213**	156.9	170.2	0.892212	167.8
$(5000, 25, 0.2)$	184.6	0.792506	109.8	177.2	0.792600	205.6	176.6	**0.792608**	216.5
$(5000, 25, 0.3)$	190.2	0.692853	133.5	180.6	0.693021	252.5	179.8	**0.693028**	263.8
$(5000, 25, 0.4)$	203.6	0.593075	157.5	192.6	**0.593369**	300.6	191.0	0.593358	311.9
$(5000, 25, 0.5)$	193.0	0.493379	228.8	185.4	**0.493741**	438.1	184.6	0.493740	427.1
$(5000, 25, 0.6)$	195.6	0.393853	199.4	186.8	0.394274	383.5	184.2	**0.394325**	395.3
$(5000, 25, 0.7)$	198.4	0.293983	219.1	190.0	0.294451	421.9	186.6	**0.294483**	434.2
$(5000, 25, 0.8)$	136.8	0.187554	213.6	128.2	0.189877	409.5	121.0	**0.189884**	419.8

few instances, in which the difference in the results is more consistent, but in any case, there is no one method that outperforms the other.

Finally, at the conclusion of the analysis conducted, also on these experiments emerges that the methods B and C seem to be more suitable than method A

Table 4. Functional sensitivity analysis in community detection.

Instance	NMI			ARI			NVI		
	A	B	C	A	B	C	A	B	C
				$|V| = 1000$					
(1000, 15, 0.1)	**0.995076**	0.993003	0.993406	**0.987372**	0.981960	0.982767	**0.009774**	0.013864	0.013076
(1000, 15, 0.2)	**0.989911**	0.986152	0.986299	**0.972978**	0.961779	0.962704	**0.019958**	0.027290	0.026998
(1000, 15, 0.3)	**0.986682**	0.982557	0.978907	**0.959832**	0.947997	0.938800	**0.026279**	0.034215	0.041232
(1000, 15, 0.4)	**0.984039**	0.977067	0.978024	**0.951622**	0.928518	0.931673	**0.031354**	0.044819	0.042942
(1000, 15, 0.5)	**0.980926**	0.964332	0.966406	**0.929535**	0.880768	0.887543	**0.037157**	0.068856	0.064955
(1000, 15, 0.6)	**0.962855**	0.941986	0.938977	**0.878173**	0.810258	0.807698	**0.071483**	0.109514	0.114978
(1000, 15, 0.7)	0.566374	**0.570550**	0.561501	0.255813	**0.267680**	0.267179	0.602756	**0.598517**	0.607492
(1000, 15, 0.8)	**0.153777**	0.141303	0.133809	0.018578	**0.020726**	0.018665	**0.916663**	0.923923	0.928225
(1000, 20, 0.1)	**0.997058**	0.994186	0.994506	**0.992727**	0.986538	0.986870	**0.005859**	0.011530	0.010894
(1000, 20, 0.2)	**0.996428**	0.991117	0.992519	**0.991809**	0.977045	0.981142	**0.007108**	0.017577	0.014826
(1000, 20, 0.3)	**0.992238**	0.986079	0.987491	**0.975973**	0.960172	0.964767	**0.015342**	0.027357	0.024658
(1000, 20, 0.4)	**0.991002**	0.975938	0.976641	**0.969473**	0.924002	0.927008	**0.017786**	0.046974	0.045641
(1000, 20, 0.5)	**0.981394**	0.966023	0.963240	**0.938705**	0.887424	0.878358	**0.036511**	0.065719	0.070864
(1000, 20, 0.6)	**0.983971**	0.955068	0.956729	**0.938273**	0.844614	0.854032	**0.031441**	0.085971	0.082923
(1000, 20, 0.7)	**0.900786**	0.883085	0.889212	**0.697262**	0.647438	0.661896	**0.179480**	0.208653	0.198344
(1000, 20, 0.8)	**0.188565**	0.169013	0.178392	0.032102	0.030706	**0.032586**	**0.895656**	0.907590	0.901889
				$|V| = 5000$					
(5000, 20, 0.1)	**0.998699**	0.995858	0.995852	**0.993303**	0.979368	0.981182	**0.002598**	0.008249	0.008261
(5000, 20, 0.2)	**0.997220**	0.994302	0.994357	**0.985554**	0.970421	0.970917	**0.005540**	0.011330	0.011222
(5000, 20, 0.3)	**0.995626**	0.993126	0.992399	**0.978385**	0.963591	0.959471	**0.008707**	0.013653	0.015086
(5000, 20, 0.4)	**0.994701**	0.992059	0.990630	**0.971258**	0.953632	0.945201	**0.010541**	0.015756	0.018565
(5000, 20, 0.5)	**0.994329**	0.989973	0.989782	**0.965862**	0.935363	0.936114	**0.011278**	0.019852	0.020225
(5000, 20, 0.6)	**0.995598**	0.989923	0.989166	**0.967716**	0.932997	0.931082	**0.008751**	0.019952	0.021435
(5000, 20, 0.7)	**0.994403**	0.988913	0.990555	**0.962057**	0.914500	0.931269	**0.011110**	0.021893	0.018713
(5000, 20, 0.8)	**0.331168**	0.311846	0.285959	**0.017992**	0.017609	0.014301	**0.801519**	0.815065	0.832675
(5000, 25, 0.1)	**0.999453**	0.997549	0.997604	**0.997325**	0.988301	0.988875	**0.001094**	0.004889	0.004780
(5000, 25, 0.2)	**0.998614**	0.994864	0.994512	**0.992296**	0.974097	0.972542	**0.002767**	0.010219	0.010916
(5000, 25, 0.3)	**0.998593**	0.993634	0.993192	**0.991259**	0.966756	0.963601	**0.002809**	0.012650	0.013523
(5000, 25, 0.4)	**0.998201**	0.992714	0.991784	**0.988323**	0.959321	0.954605	**0.003589**	0.014465	0.016297
(5000, 25, 0.5)	**0.994865**	0.989942	0.989864	**0.970057**	0.937639	0.940216	**0.010211**	0.019912	0.020066
(5000, 25, 0.6)	**0.995162**	0.989456	0.987228	**0.967998**	0.930606	0.914103	**0.009626**	0.020867	0.025219
(5000, 25, 0.7)	**0.995383**	0.989142	0.988225	**0.967148**	0.922344	0.924432	**0.009187**	0.021477	0.023274
(5000, 25, 0.8)	**0.623561**	0.622423	0.602764	**0.080319**	0.078396	0.069817	**0.543574**	0.544915	0.565846

for solving this kind of task, dues to their feature of producing higher diversity in the population.

3.1   Functional Sensitivity Analysis

As last step of this work, in this subsection, the investigation on the sensitivity of the three community detection methods is reported from functional perspective. The main aim of this analysis is measuring the similarity between the detected communities and original ones. For doing this, commonly used community structure similarity metrics have been considered: (1) *Normalized Mutual Information* (*NMI*) [6], mostly used in community detection, which measures the amount of information correctly extracted, and allows for assessing how similar the detected communities are concerning to real ones; (2) *Adjusted Rand Index (ARI)* [13], which focuses on pairwise agreement: for each possible pair of elements it evaluates how similarly the two partitions treat them; and (3) *Normalized Variation of Information (NVI)* [18], expressed using the Shannon entropy, which measures the amount of information lost and gained in changing from one clustering to another one: sum of the information needed to describe C, given C', and the information needed to describe C' given C.

The results of the sensitivity analysis are displayed in Table 4 (only for 1000 and 5000 nodes). From this investigation, clearly appears how the method A outperforms the other two in almost all tests performed, uncovering, consequently, more similar communities to the target/real ones, in opposite to the outcomes obtained with respect the modularity evaluation metric. This is caused by the limitation in the modularity optimization which can fail to identify smaller communities; this limitation can depend on the degree of interconnectedness of the communities [9].

4   Conclusions

In this research paper, three different positions where run the local search within an immune algorithm, called HYBRID-IA, have been investigated in order to ascertain which of the three acts best on the algorithm's performance. Community detection problem has been considered for the analysis of this study, and the comparison between the three methods has been conducted with respect the solution quality found and learning process quality. Several artificial networks were generated ($|V| \in \{300, 500, 1000, 5000\}$) through which was possible to inspect the three methods in various complexity scenarios. The obtained outcomes highlight that running the local search just after the hypermutation operator is the best choice for this kind of optimization problem, because in this way higher diversity is produced that help the algorithm specially on larger and complex networks.

References

1. Blum, C., Raidl, G.R.: Hybrid Metaheuristics: Powerful Tools for Optimization. Artificial Intelligence: Foundations, Theory, and Algorithms. Springer, Heidelberg (2016). https://doi.org/10.1007/978-3-319-30883-8
2. Cutello, V., Fargetta, G., Pavone, M., Scollo, R.A.: Optimization algorithms for detection of social interactions. Algorithms **13**(6), 139 (2020). https://doi.org/10.3390/a13060139
3. Cutello, V., Nicosia, G., Pavone, M.: An immune algorithm with stochastic aging and kullback entropy for the chromatic number problem. J. Comb. Optim. **14**, 9–33 (2007). https://doi.org/10.1007/s10878-006-9036-2
4. Cutello, V., Oliva, M., Pavone, M., Scollo, R.A.: A hybrid immunological search for the weighted feedback vertex set problem. In: Matsatsinis, N.F., Marinakis, Y., Pardalos, P. (eds.) LION 2019. LNCS, vol. 11968, pp. 1–16. Springer, Cham (2020). https://doi.org/10.1007/978-3-030-38629-0_1

5. Cutello, V., Oliva, M., Pavone, M., Scollo, R.A.: An immune metaheuristics for large instances of the weighted feedback vertex set problem. In: 2019 IEEE Symposium Series on Computational Intelligence (SSCI), pp. 1928–1936, December 2019. https://doi.org/10.1109/SSCI44817.2019.9002988

6. Danon, L., Díaz-Guilera, A., Duch, J., Arenas, A.: Comparing community structure identification. J. Stat. Mech: Theory Exp. **2005**(09), P09008–P09008 (2005). https://doi.org/10.1088/1742-5468/2005/09/p09008

7. Di Stefano, A., Vitale, A., Cutello, V., Pavone, M.: How long should offspring lifespan be in order to obtain a proper exploration? In: 2016 IEEE Symposium Series on Computational Intelligence (SSCI), pp. 1–8, December 2016. https://doi.org/10.1109/SSCI.2016.7850270

8. Didimo, W., Montecchiani, F.: Fast layout computation of clustered networks: algorithmic advances and experimental analysis. Inf. Sci. **260**, 185–199 (2014). https://doi.org/10.1016/j.ins.2013.09.048

9. Fortunato, S., Barthélemy, M.: Resolution limit in community detection. Proc. Natl. Acad. Sci. **104**(1), 36–41 (2007). https://doi.org/10.1073/pnas.0605965104

10. Fouladvand, S., Osareh, A., Shadgar, B., Pavone, M., Sharafi, S.: DENSA: an effective negative selection algorithm with flexible boundaries for self-space and dynamic number of detectors. Eng. Appl. Artif. Intell. **62**, 359–372 (2017). https://doi.org/10.1016/j.engappai.2016.08.014

11. Girvan, M., Newman, M.E.J.: Community structure in social and biological networks. Proc. Natl. Acad. Sci. **99**(12), 7821–7826 (2002). https://doi.org/10.1073/pnas.122653799

12. Gulbahce, N., Lehmann, S.: The art of community detection. BioEssays **30**(10), 934–938 (2008). https://doi.org/10.1002/bies.20820

13. Hubert, L., Arabic, P.: Comparing partitions. J. Classif. **2**, 193–218 (1985). https://doi.org/10.1007/BF01908075

14. Kernighan, B.W., Lin, S.: An efficient heuristic procedure for partitioning graphs. Bell Syst. Tech. J. **49**(2), 291–307 (1970). https://doi.org/10.1002/j.1538-7305.1970.tb01770.x

15. Kullback, S.: Statistics and Information Theory. Wiley, Hoboken (1959)

16. Lancichinetti, A., Fortunato, S.: Benchmarks for testing community detection algorithms on directed and weighted graphs with overlapping communities. Phys. Rev. E **80** (2009). https://doi.org/10.1103/PhysRevE.80.016118

17. Lancichinetti, A., Fortunato, S., Radicchi, F.: Benchmark graphs for testing community detection algorithms. Phys. Rev. E **78** (2008). https://doi.org/10.1103/PhysRevE.78.046110

18. Meilă, M.: Comparing clusterings-an information based distance. J. Multivar. Anal. **98**, 873–895 (2007). https://doi.org/10.1016/j.jmva.2006.11.013

19. Newman, M.E.J., Girvan, M.: Finding and evaluating community structure in networks. Phys. Rev. E **69** (2004). https://doi.org/10.1103/PhysRevE.69.026113

20. Pavone, M., Narzisi, G., Nicosia, G.: Clonal selection: an immunological algorithm for global optimization over continuous spaces. J. Glob. Optim. **53**, 769–808 (2012). https://doi.org/10.1007/s10898-011-9736-8

21. Vitale, A., Di Stefano, A., Cutello, V., Pavone, M.: The influence of age assignments on the performance of immune algorithms. In: Lotfi, A., Bouchachia, H., Gegov, A., Langensiepen, C., McGinnity, M. (eds.) UKCI 2018. AISC, vol. 840, pp. 16–28. Springer, Cham (2019). https://doi.org/10.1007/978-3-319-97982-3_2

Advances in Argumentation in Artificial Intelligence

An Efficient Algorithm for Semi-stable Extensions

Federico Cerutti[1,3], Massimiliano Giacomin[1(✉)], Mauro Vallati[2], and Tobia Zanetti[1]

[1] University of Brescia, Brescia, Italy
massimiliano.giacomin@unibs.it
[2] University of Huddersfield, Huddersfield, UK
[3] Cardiff University, Cardiff, UK

Abstract. In this paper we introduce AASExts, an algorithm for computing semi–stable extensions. We improve techniques developed for other semantics, notably preferred semantics, as well as leverage recent advances in All-SAT community. We prove our proposed algorithm is sound and complete, we describe the experiments to select the most appropriate encoding to adopt, and we show empirically that our implementation significantly outperforms even sophisticated ASP-based and SAT-based reduction approaches on existing benchmarks.

Keywords: Abstract argumentation · Semi-stable semantics · Algorithm

1 Introduction

Research based on Dung's model of argumentation [13]—that considers only abstract arguments and attack relations between them—identified several *semantics*, viz. criteria for selecting *extensions*, i.e. sub-sets of arguments acceptable in some sense. Pivotal in Dung's theory is the notion of *admissible set*, i.e. conflict-free and defending itself against attacks. Building on top of such a notion, Dung [13] introduced the concept of grounded, stable, and preferred semantics, that can be equivalently expressed by means of the notion of labelling [5,7]. An interested reader is referred to Baroni *et al.* [2] for an introduction.

The notion of admissible argumentation stage extension was proposed by Verheij [28,29] to unify two lines of research in formal argumentation: admissibility-based extensions as suggested by Dung in his seminar paper, and the traditional approach based on dialectical evaluation of the defeat status of arguments, where the status of an argument—or of its conclusion—depends on the stage of the argumentation process, i.e. the process of supporting or opposing arguments [25]. The notion of admissible argumentation stage extension was later re-named as semi–stable extension and further investigated [6,7]. Semi-stable semantics has unique interesting properties, in particular it coincides with stable semantics

© Springer Nature Switzerland AG 2021
M. Baldoni and S. Bandini (Eds.): AIxIA 2020, LNAI 12414, pp. 117–135, 2021.
https://doi.org/10.1007/978-3-030-77091-4_8

in the case a stable extension exists, and each semi–stable extension is also a preferred extension.

Wallner *et al.* [30] proposed SSTMCS, an algorithm for computing semi–stable extensions exploiting algorithms for computing minimal correction sets (MCS) [20,21], i.e. subset-minimal sets of clauses of a formula. argmat-sat [24] re-implemented a very similar idea and scored first during the 2017 edition of the International Competition on Computational Models of Argumentation. An alternative system, Aspartix [16], exploits answer set programming [23] for computing argumentation semantics extensions, including semi–stable extensions[1].

In this paper, we improve recent advancements in exploiting SAT solvers as NP-oracles [9,11,14], and we propose AASExts, an algorithm for computing semi–stable extensions that reduces such a problem to a SAT problem[2]. Our extensive experimental analysis supports the claim that our proposal, despite its simplicity, performs better than some of the existing approaches looking at ASP-based and SAT-based reductions for computing semi–stable extensions. AASExts has been included in the version of the ArgSemSAT solver that took part in the 2017 edition of the ICCMA competition. The competition included a track focused on semi–stable extensions: ArgSemSAT achieved the second place of the track[3]. For a comparison with the other systems that participated in the 2017 edition, we refer the readers to [18]. We refrained from comparisons with the 2019 edition as we are aware—from personal communication—that the organisers are currently working on an extensive analysis also considering ArgSemSAT—that did not participate in the 2019 edition—as a baseline.

In order to adhere to the current terminological standards [2,26], hereafter we will consider the definitions provided in works from Caminada (*et al.*) [5–7], summarised in Sect. 2. In Sect. 3 we discuss the theoretical foundations of our proposal and introduce the proposed algorithm, AASExts, in Sect. 4 we illustrate the experimental analysis to select the encoding of complete labelling to adopt in AASExts, and in Sect. 5 we provide the outcomes of our experimentation analysis. Finally, in Sect. 6 we draw the conclusions and discuss future avenues of research.

2   Argumentation Framework and Complete Labelling Encodings

An argumentation framework [13] consists of a set of arguments[4] and a binary attack relation between them.

Definition 1. *An* argumentation framework *(AF) is a pair* $\Gamma = \langle \mathcal{A}, \mathcal{R} \rangle$ *where* $\mathcal{A}$ *is a set of arguments and* $\mathcal{R} \subseteq \mathcal{A} \times \mathcal{A}$. *We say that* b attacks a *iff* $\langle b, a \rangle \in \mathcal{R}$, *also denoted as* $b \rightarrow a$. *The set of attackers of an argument* a *is denoted as* $a^- \triangleq$

---

[1] http://www.dbai.tuwien.ac.at/research/project/argumentation/systempage/.

[2] Implementation available at https://github.com/federicocerutti/ArgSemSAT.

[3] http://argumentationcompetition.org/2017/index.html.

[4] In this paper we consider only *finite* sets of arguments: see Baroni *et al.* [3] for a discussion on infinite sets of arguments.

$\{b : b \to a\}$, the set of arguments attacked by a is denoted as $a^+ \triangleq \{b : a \to b\}$. These notations can be extended to sets of arguments, i.e. given $E, S \subseteq \mathcal{A}$, $E \to a$ iff $\exists b \in E$ s.t. $b \to a$; $a \to E$ iff $\exists b \in E$ s.t. $a \to b$; $E \to S$ iff $\exists b \in E, a \in S$ s.t. $b \to a$; $E^- \triangleq \{b \mid \exists a \in E, b \to a\}$ and $E^+ \triangleq \{b \mid \exists a \in E, a \to b\}$. The range of a set of arguments $S \subseteq \mathcal{A}$ is $S \cup S^+$.

The basic properties of conflict–freeness, acceptability, and admissibility of a set of arguments are fundamental for the definition of *argumentation semantics*.

Definition 2. *Given an AF $\Gamma = \langle \mathcal{A}, \mathcal{R} \rangle$:*

- *a set $S \subseteq \mathcal{A}$ is a* conflict–free *set of Γ if $\nexists$ $a, b \in S$ s.t. $a \to b$;*
- *an argument $a \in \mathcal{A}$ is* acceptable *with respect to a set $S \subseteq \mathcal{A}$ of Γ if $\forall b \in \mathcal{A}$ s.t. $b \to a$, $\exists$ $c \in S$ s.t. $c \to b$;*
- *the function $\mathcal{F}_\Gamma : 2^{\mathcal{A}} \to 2^{\mathcal{A}}$ such that $\mathcal{F}_\Gamma(S) = \{a \mid a$ is acceptable w.r.t. $S\}$ is called the* characteristic function *of Γ;*
- *a set $S \subseteq \mathcal{A}$ is an* admissible *set of Γ if S is a conflict–free set of Γ and every element of S is acceptable with respect to S, i.e. $S \subseteq \mathcal{F}_\Gamma(S)$.*

An argumentation semantics σ prescribes for any AF Γ a set of *extensions*, denoted as $\mathcal{E}_\sigma(\Gamma)$, namely a set of sets of arguments satisfying the conditions dictated by σ. Here we need to recall the definitions of complete (denoted as CO), stable (denoted as ST), preferred (denoted as PR), and semi–stable (denoted as SST) semantics.

Definition 3. *Given an AF $\Gamma = \langle \mathcal{A}, \mathcal{R} \rangle$:*

- *a set $S \subseteq \mathcal{A}$ is a* complete extension *of Γ iff S is a conflict-free set of Γ and $S = \mathcal{F}_\Gamma(S)$.*
- *a set $S \subseteq \mathcal{A}$ is a* stable extension *of Γ, i.e. $S \in \mathcal{E}_{ST}(\Gamma)$, iff S is a conflict-free set of Γ and $S \cup S^+ = \mathcal{A}$;*
- *a set $S \subseteq \mathcal{A}$ is a* preferred extension *of Γ, i.e. $S \in \mathcal{E}_{PR}(\Gamma)$, iff S is a maximal (w.r.t. set inclusion) admissible set of Γ;*
- *a set $S \subseteq \mathcal{A}$ is a* semi–stable extension *of Γ, i.e. $S \in \mathcal{E}_{SST}(\Gamma)$, iff S is an admissible set of Γ where $S \cup S^+$ (i.e. its range) is maximal (w.r.t. set inclusion).*

It is immediate to see from Definitions 2 and 3 that if a stable extension exists, the semi–stable extensions coincide with the stable extensions.

Proposition 1. *Given an AF $\Gamma = \langle \mathcal{A}, \mathcal{R} \rangle$, if $\mathcal{E}_{ST}(\Gamma) \neq \emptyset$, then $\mathcal{E}_{ST}(\Gamma) = \mathcal{E}_{SST}(\Gamma)$.*

Each extension S implicitly defines a three-valued *labelling* of arguments, or dialectical evaluation: an argument a is labelled **in** (*undefeated* [28]) iff $a \in S$; is labelled **out** (*defeated* [28]) iff $\exists$ $b \in S$ s.t. $b \to a$; is labelled **undec** if neither of the above conditions holds. In the light of this correspondence, argumentation semantics can be equivalently defined in terms of labellings rather than of extensions [2].

Definition 4. *Given a set of arguments S, a* labelling *of S is a total function $\mathcal{L}ab : S \mapsto \{\text{in}, \text{out}, \text{undec}\}$. The set of all* labellings *of S is denoted as $\mathfrak{L}_S$. Given an AF $\Gamma = \langle \mathcal{A}, \mathcal{R} \rangle$, a* labelling *of Γ is a labelling of $\mathcal{A}$. The set of all labellings of Γ is denoted as $\mathfrak{L}(\Gamma)$.*

Given a labelling $\mathcal{L}ab$, it is possible to write $\text{in}(\mathcal{L}ab)$ for $\{A | \mathcal{L}ab(A) = \text{in}\}$, $\text{out}(\mathcal{L}ab)$ for $\{A | \mathcal{L}ab(A) = \text{out}\}$ and $\text{undec}(\mathcal{L}ab)$ for $\{A | \mathcal{L}ab(A) = \text{undec}\}$. A labelling will sometimes be denoted as the triple $\langle \text{in}(\mathcal{L}ab), \text{out}(\mathcal{L}ab), \text{undec}(\mathcal{L}ab) \rangle$.

Complete labellings can be defined as follows.

Definition 5. *Let $\Gamma = \langle \mathcal{A}, \mathcal{R} \rangle$ be an argumentation framework. A labelling $\mathcal{L}ab \in \mathfrak{L}(\Gamma)$ is a* complete labelling *of Γ iff it satisfies the following conditions for any $a \in \mathcal{A}$:*

- $\mathcal{L}ab(a) = \text{in} \Leftrightarrow \forall b \in a^- \mathcal{L}ab(b) = \text{out};$
- $\mathcal{L}ab(a) = \text{out} \Leftrightarrow \exists b \in a^- : \mathcal{L}ab(b) = \text{in};$
- $\mathcal{L}ab(a) = \text{undec} \Leftrightarrow \forall b \in a^- \mathcal{L}ab(b) \neq \text{in} \land \exists c \in a^- : \mathcal{L}ab(c) = \text{undec}.$

The stable, preferred, and semi–stable labelling can then be defined on the basis of complete labellings.

Definition 6. *Let $\Gamma = \langle \mathcal{A}, \mathcal{R} \rangle$ be an argumentation framework. A labelling $\mathcal{L}ab \in \mathfrak{L}(\Gamma)$ is*

- *a* stable labelling *of Γ if it is a complete labelling of Γ and there is no argument labelled $\text{undec};$*
- *a* preferred labelling *of Γ if it is a complete labelling of Γ maximising the set of arguments labelled $\text{in};$*
- *a* semi–stable labelling *of Γ if it is a complete labelling of Γ minimising the set of arguments labelled $\text{undec};$*

For any semantics σ, the set of σ labellings of Γ is denoted as $\mathcal{L}_\sigma(\Gamma)$. The connection between extensions and labellings can be expressed by means of the function Ext2Lab [2] returning the labelling corresponding to a conflict–free set of arguments.

Definition 7. *Given an AF $\Gamma = \langle \mathcal{A}, \mathcal{R} \rangle$ and a conflict–free set $S \subseteq \mathcal{A}$, the corresponding labelling $\text{Ext2Lab}(S)$ is defined as $\text{Ext2Lab}(S) \equiv \mathcal{L}ab$, where*

- $\mathcal{L}ab(a) = \text{in} \Leftrightarrow a \in S$
- $\mathcal{L}ab(a) = \text{out} \Leftrightarrow \exists\ b \in S \text{ s.t. } b \to a$
- $\mathcal{L}ab(a) = \text{undec} \Leftrightarrow a \notin S \land \nexists\ b \in S \text{ s.t. } b \to a$

Caminada [5] shows that there is a bijective correspondence between the complete, stable, preferred, and semi–stable extensions and the complete, stable, preferred, and semi–stable labellings, respectively.

Proposition 2. *Given an AF $\Gamma = \langle \mathcal{A}, \mathcal{R} \rangle$, $\mathcal{L}ab$ is a complete (stable, preferred, semi–stable) labelling of Γ if and only if there is a complete (stable, preferred, semi–stable) extension S of Γ such that $\mathcal{L}ab = \text{Ext2Lab}(S)$.*

A propositional formula over a set of boolean variables is satisfiable iff there exists a truth assignment of the variables such that the formula evaluates to True. Checking whether such an assignment exists is the satisfiability (SAT) problem. Following Cerutti $et\ al.$ [9] where the case of preferred semantics is considered, given an $AF\ \Gamma = \langle \mathcal{A}, \mathcal{R} \rangle$ we derive a boolean formula, called $complete\ labelling\ formula$ and denoted as Π_Γ, such that each satisfying assignment of the formula corresponds to a complete labelling.

It is very important to underline that several syntactically different encodings can be devised which, despite being logically equivalent, can significantly affect the performance of the overall process of searching a satisfying assignment [8,11]. In particular, the requirements of Definition 5 can be expressed as a conjunction of 6 terms, i.e. $C_{\text{in}}^{\rightarrow} \wedge C_{\text{in}}^{\leftarrow} \wedge C_{\text{out}}^{\rightarrow} \wedge C_{\text{out}}^{\leftarrow} \wedge C_{\text{undec}}^{\rightarrow} \wedge C_{\text{undec}}^{\leftarrow}$ where:

- $C_{\text{in}}^{\rightarrow} \equiv (\mathcal{L}ab(A) = \text{in} \Rightarrow \forall B \in A^- \mathcal{L}ab(B) = \text{out})$;
- $C_{\text{in}}^{\leftarrow} \equiv (\mathcal{L}ab(A) = \text{in} \Leftarrow \forall B \in A^- \mathcal{L}ab(B) = \text{out})$;
- $C_{\text{out}}^{\rightarrow} \equiv (\mathcal{L}ab(A) = \text{out} \Rightarrow \exists B \in A^- : \mathcal{L}ab(B) = \text{in})$;
- $C_{\text{out}}^{\leftarrow} \equiv (\mathcal{L}ab(A) = \text{out} \Leftarrow \exists B \in A^- : \mathcal{L}ab(B) = \text{in})$;
- $C_{\text{undec}}^{\rightarrow} \equiv (\mathcal{L}ab(A) = \text{undec} \Rightarrow \forall B \in A^- \mathcal{L}ab(B) \neq \text{in} \wedge \exists C \in A^- : \mathcal{L}ab(C) = \text{undec})$;
- $C_{\text{undec}}^{\leftarrow} \equiv (\mathcal{L}ab(A) = \text{undec} \Leftarrow \forall B \in A^- \mathcal{L}ab(B) \neq \text{in} \wedge \exists C \in A^- : \mathcal{L}ab(C) = \text{undec})$.

The following shorthand notations will be adopted: $C_{\text{in}}^{\leftrightarrow} \equiv C_{\text{in}}^{\rightarrow} \wedge C_{\text{in}}^{\leftarrow}$, $C_{\text{out}}^{\leftrightarrow} \equiv C_{\text{out}}^{\rightarrow} \wedge C_{\text{out}}^{\leftarrow}$, $C_{\text{undec}}^{\leftrightarrow} \equiv C_{\text{undec}}^{\rightarrow} \wedge C_{\text{undec}}^{\leftarrow}$.

The complete labelling formula Π_Γ includes for each argument $\mathbf{a} \in \mathcal{A}$ three boolean variables, $I_{\mathbf{a}}, O_{\mathbf{a}}$, and $U_{\mathbf{a}}$, with the intended meaning that $I_{\mathbf{a}}$ is true when argument $\mathbf{a}$ is labelled in, false otherwise, and analogously $O_{\mathbf{a}}$ and $U_{\mathbf{a}}$ correspond to labels out and undec. Formally, given $\Gamma = \langle \mathcal{A}, \mathcal{R} \rangle$ we define the corresponding set of variables as $\mathcal{V}(\Gamma) \triangleq \bigcup_{\mathbf{a} \in \mathcal{A}} \{I_{\mathbf{a}}, O_{\mathbf{a}}, U_{\mathbf{a}}\}$. The constraints of Definition 5 can then be expressed in terms of the variables $\mathcal{V}(\Gamma)$ in conjunctive normal form (CNF), as usually required by SAT solvers. In particular, the $(C_{\text{in}}^{\leftrightarrow} \wedge C_{\text{out}}^{\leftrightarrow} \wedge C_{\text{undec}}^{\leftrightarrow})$ encoding is given by:

$$\bigwedge_{\mathbf{a} \in \mathcal{A}} \Big((I_{\mathbf{a}} \vee O_{\mathbf{a}} \vee U_{\mathbf{a}}) \wedge (\neg I_{\mathbf{a}} \vee \neg O_{\mathbf{a}}) \wedge (\neg I_{\mathbf{a}} \vee \neg U_{\mathbf{a}}) \wedge (\neg O_{\mathbf{a}} \vee \neg U_{\mathbf{a}}) \Big) \qquad (1)$$

$$\bigwedge_{\{\mathbf{a} | \mathbf{a}^- = \varnothing\}} (I_{\mathbf{a}} \wedge \neg O_{\mathbf{a}} \wedge \neg U_{\mathbf{a}}) \qquad (2)$$

$$\bigwedge_{\{\mathbf{a} | \mathbf{a}^- \neq \varnothing\}} \left(I_{\mathbf{a}} \vee \left(\bigvee_{\{\mathbf{b} | \mathbf{b} \rightarrow \mathbf{a}\}} (\neg O_{\mathbf{b}}) \right) \right) \qquad (3)$$

$$\bigwedge_{\{\mathbf{a} | \mathbf{a}^- \neq \varnothing\}} \left(\bigwedge_{\{\mathbf{b} | \mathbf{b} \rightarrow \mathbf{a}\}} \neg I_{\mathbf{a}} \vee O_{\mathbf{b}} \right) \qquad (4)$$

$$\bigwedge_{\{a|a^- \neq \varnothing\}} \left(\bigwedge_{\{b|b \to a\}} \neg I_b \vee O_a \right) \tag{5}$$

$$\bigwedge_{\{a|a^- \neq \varnothing\}} \left(\neg O_a \vee \left(\bigvee_{\{b|b \to a\}} I_b \right) \right) \tag{6}$$

$$\bigwedge_{\{a|a^- \neq \varnothing\}} \left(\bigwedge_{\{c|c \to a\}} \left(U_a \vee \neg U_c \vee \left(\bigvee_{\{b|b \to a\}} I_b \right) \right) \right) \tag{7}$$

$$\bigwedge_{\{a|a^- \neq \varnothing\}} \left(\left(\bigwedge_{\{b|b \to a\}} (\neg U_a \vee \neg I_b) \right) \wedge \left(\neg U_a \vee \left(\bigvee_{\{b|b \to a\}} U_b \right) \right) \right) \tag{8}$$

In particular, (1) enforces that for each argument exactly one of the variables is true, (2) represents an engineering improvement that constrains unattacked arguments to be labelled in, while (3), (4), (5), (6), (7) and (8) encode the constraints $C_{in}^{\leftarrow}$, $C_{in}^{\rightarrow}$, $C_{out}^{\leftarrow}$, $C_{out}^{\rightarrow}$, $C_{undec}^{\leftarrow}$ and $C_{undec}^{\rightarrow}$, respectively.

Following [8,11], we consider these logically equivalent encodings:

C_1: (1) ∧ (2) ∧ (3) ∧ (4) ∧ (5) ∧ (6) ∧ (7) ∧ (8) that corresponds to $C_{in}^{\leftrightarrow}$ ∧ $C_{out}^{\leftrightarrow}$ ∧ $C_{undec}^{\leftrightarrow}$;

C_1^a: (1) ∧ (2) ∧ (3) ∧ (4) ∧ (5) ∧ (6) that corresponds to $C_{in}^{\leftrightarrow}$ ∧ $C_{out}^{\leftrightarrow}$;

C_1^b: (1) ∧ (2) ∧ (5) ∧ (6) ∧ (7) ∧ (8) that corresponds to $C_{out}^{\leftrightarrow}$ ∧ $C_{undec}^{\leftrightarrow}$;

C_1^c: (1) ∧ (2) ∧ (3) ∧ (4) ∧ (7) ∧ (8) that corresponds to $C_{in}^{\leftrightarrow}$ ∧ $C_{undec}^{\leftrightarrow}$;

C_2: (1) ∧ (2) ∧ (4) ∧ (6) ∧ (8) that corresponds to $C_{in}^{\rightarrow}$ ∧ $C_{out}^{\rightarrow}$ ∧ $C_{undec}^{\rightarrow}$;

C_3: (1) ∧ (2) ∧ (3) ∧ (5) ∧ (7) that corresponds to $C_{in}^{\leftarrow}$ ∧ $C_{out}^{\leftarrow}$ ∧ $C_{undec}^{\leftarrow}$.

In the following Π_Γ represents any of the previous encodings for a given argumentation framework Γ. Given an assignment c of the variables in $\mathcal{V}(\Gamma)$ satisfying Π_Γ, we denote as $\mathcal{L}ab_c$ the corresponding labelling, i.e. $\mathcal{L}ab_c = \langle \{a : I_a \text{ is true}\}, \{b : O_b \text{ is true}\} \{c : U_c \text{ is true}\} \rangle$.

3   Overview of AASExts

In this section we introduce AASExts, our proposal for computing semi–stable extensions. To this aim, let us first consider the following intermediate theoretical results.

Firstly, to strictly expand the range of a complete extension—in order to minimise the set of undecided arguments given a complete labelling $\mathcal{L}ab$—it is necessary to transform a label from undec into in or out. However, no constraints should be imposed on the arguments labelled either in or out in $\mathcal{L}ab$. Those arguments are *free* to change their labels, provided that they do not become undec.

Lemma 1. *Let $\Gamma = \langle \mathcal{A}, \mathcal{R} \rangle$ be an argumentation framework and $\mathcal{L}ab \in \mathfrak{L}(\Gamma)$ a labelling. $\forall \mathcal{L}ab' \in \mathfrak{L}(\Gamma)$, $\mathrm{undec}(\mathcal{L}ab') \subsetneq \mathrm{undec}(\mathcal{L}ab)$ if and only if $\exists a \in \mathcal{A}$ such that $\mathcal{L}ab(a) = \mathrm{undec}$ and $\mathcal{L}ab'(a) = \{\mathrm{in}, \mathrm{out}\}$, and $\nexists b \in \mathcal{A}$ such that $\mathcal{L}ab(b) \neq \mathrm{undec}$ and $\mathcal{L}ab'(b) = \mathrm{undec}$.*

Proof. If $\mathrm{undec}(\mathcal{L}ab') \subsetneq \mathrm{undec}(\mathcal{L}ab)$, then there is an argument a which is undec in $\mathcal{L}ab$ and is not in $\mathcal{L}ab'$, and each argument that is undec in $\mathcal{L}ab'$ must also be undec in $\mathcal{L}ab$, entailing the two conditions of the Lemma. The other direction of the proof is immediate from the definition of the function $\mathrm{undec}()$.

Secondly, given the *freedom* of argument labelled in or out to swap their labels mentioned above, there might be multiple semi–stable labellings having the same set of undec arguments: they differ on the basis of the labels of the remaining arguments labelled either in or out.

Algorithm 1. STExts

    Input: $\Gamma = \langle \mathcal{A}, \mathcal{R} \rangle$
    Output: $\mathcal{E}_{st} = \mathcal{E}_{\mathsf{ST}}(\Gamma) \subseteq 2^{\mathcal{A}}$
1: $\mathcal{E}_{st} := \varnothing$
2: **for each** $st \in \mathsf{ALLSS}\left(\Pi_\Gamma \wedge \bigwedge_{a \in \mathcal{A}} \neg U_a \right)$ **do**
3:     $\mathcal{E}_{st} := \mathcal{E}_{st} \cup \{\mathsf{I\_A}(st)\}$
4: **end for**
5: **return** $\mathcal{E}_{st}$

Lemma 2. *Let $\Gamma = \langle \mathcal{A}, \mathcal{R} \rangle$ be an argumentation framework and $\mathcal{L}ab \in \mathfrak{L}(\Gamma)$ a semi–stable labelling. Then $\{\mathcal{L}ab' | \mathcal{L}ab'$ is semi–stable and $\mathrm{undec}(\mathcal{L}ab') = \mathrm{undec}(\mathcal{L}ab)\} = \{\mathcal{L}ab' | \mathcal{L}ab'$ is complete and $\mathrm{undec}(\mathcal{L}ab') = \mathrm{undec}(\mathcal{L}ab)\}$.*

Proof. First, semi–stable labellings are complete by Definition 6. On the other hand, given a complete labelling $\mathcal{L}ab'$ such that $\mathrm{undec}(\mathcal{L}ab') = \mathrm{undec}(\mathcal{L}ab)$, $\mathrm{undec}(\mathcal{L}ab')$ is minimal since $\mathcal{L}ab$ is semi–stable, thus $\mathcal{L}ab'$ is semi–stable.

AASExts resorts to several external functions: SS, I_A, U_A, ALLSS, and STExts.

SS is a SAT solver—in this paper we used MiniSAT [15]—able to prove unsatisfiability too: it accepts as input a CNF formula and returns a variable assignment satisfying the formula if it exists, ε otherwise. I_A (resp. U_A) accepts as input a variable assignment concerning $\mathcal{V}(\Gamma)$ and returns the corresponding set of arguments labelled as in (resp. undec).

ALLSS is a solver for the All-SAT problem: in this paper we used the proposal illustrated in [33]. The All-SAT problem [22] deals with determining all the satisfying assignments that exist for a given propositional logic formula. A typical All-SAT solver is based on iteratively computing satisfying assignments using a

Algorithm 2. AASExts

Input: $\Gamma = \langle \mathcal{A}, \mathcal{R} \rangle$

Output: $\mathcal{E}_{sem} = \mathcal{E}_{\mathsf{SST}}(\Gamma) \subseteq 2^{\mathcal{A}}$

1: $\mathcal{E}_{sem} := \mathsf{STExts}(\langle \mathcal{A}, \mathcal{R} \rangle)$

2: **if** $\mathcal{E}_{sem} \neq \varnothing$ **then**

3:     **return** $\mathcal{E}_{sem}$

4: **end if**

5: $ocnf := \Pi_\Gamma \wedge \bigvee_{\mathbf{a} \in \mathcal{A}} I_{\mathbf{a}}$

6: **repeat**

7:   $icnf := ocnf$

8:   $sstcand := \varnothing$

9:   **repeat**

10:     $compl := \mathsf{SS}(icnf)$

11:     **if** $compl \neq \varepsilon$ **then**

12:       $sstcand := compl$

13:       $icnf := icnf \wedge \bigwedge_{\mathbf{a} \notin \mathsf{U\_A}(compl)} (I_{\mathbf{a}} \vee O_{\mathbf{a}})$

14:       $icnf := icnf \wedge \bigvee_{\mathbf{a} \in \mathsf{U\_A}(compl)} \neg U_{\mathbf{a}}$

15:     **end if**

16:   **until** $(compl \neq \varepsilon)$

17:   **if** $sstcand \neq \varnothing$ **then**

18:     $\mathcal{E}_{sem} := \mathcal{E}_{sem} \cup \{\mathsf{I\_A}(sstcand)\}$

19:     $sU := \bigwedge_{\mathbf{a} \in \mathsf{U\_A}(sstcand)} U_{\mathbf{a}}$

20:     $sIO := \bigwedge_{\mathbf{a} \notin \mathsf{U\_A}(sstcand)} (I_{\mathbf{a}} \vee O_{\mathbf{a}})$

21:     **for each** $sst \in \mathsf{ALLSS}(ocnf \wedge sU \wedge sIO)$ **do**

22:       $\mathcal{E}_{sem} := \mathcal{E}_{sem} \cup \{\mathsf{I\_A}(sst)\}$

23:     **end for**

24:     $ocnf := ocnf \wedge \bigvee_{\mathbf{a} \in \mathsf{U\_A}(sstcand)} \neg U_{\mathbf{a}}$

25:   **end if**

26: **until** $(sstcand \neq \varnothing)$

27: **if** $\mathcal{E}_{sem} = \varnothing$ **then**

28:   $\mathcal{E}_{sem} = \{\varnothing\}$

29: **end if**

30: **return** $\mathcal{E}_{sem}$

---

traditional Boolean satisfiability (SAT) solver and adding blocking clauses which are the complement of the total/partial assignments.

STExts is an algorithm for computing stable extensions. For the sake of completeness, Algorithm 1 shows a straightforward implementation of STExts: all the complete labellings with no **undec** arguments are enumerated at line 2 and their **in** arguments form stable extensions, cf. Definitions 6 and 7, and Proposition 2.

AASExts is presented in Algorithm 2. At first it checks whether stable extensions exist (1. 1–4): in that case $\mathcal{E}_{ST}(\Gamma) = \mathcal{E}_{SST}(\Gamma)$ by Proposition 1. Otherwise, a CEGAR-like [14] approach to minimise the set of undec arguments is performed. In particular, a disjunctive clause to find at least one argument labelled in is enforced (1. 5) and then (1. 7–16) the algorithm starts the process to find a complete labelling with minimal set of undec arguments (see Lemma 1), i.e. a semi–stable labelling. Then it enumerates (1. 18–23) all the semi–stable labellings that share the same set of undec arguments (see Lemma 2) before searching for a new semi–stable labelling with a different set of undec arguments (1. 24).

To illustrate the algorithm, let us consider the following example evolving the one introduced by Verheij [29].

Example 1. Let $\Gamma_1 = \langle \mathcal{A}_1, \mathcal{R}_1 \rangle$ where $\mathcal{A}_1 = \{a, b, c, d, e, f\}$ and $\mathcal{R}_1 = \{\langle a, b \rangle, \langle b, a \rangle, \langle a, c \rangle, \langle c, d \rangle, \langle d, e \rangle, \langle e, c \rangle, \langle f, f \rangle\}$.

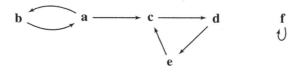

Fig. 1. Γ_1 as presented in Example 1

With reference to the argumentation framework $\langle \mathcal{A}_1, \mathcal{R}_1 \rangle$ depicted in Fig. 1, let us suppose that at 1. 10 of Algorithm 2 the labelling corresponding to the *compl* assignment is $\mathcal{L}ab_{compl} = \langle \text{in}(\mathcal{L}ab_{compl}), \text{out}(\mathcal{L}ab_{compl}), \text{undec}(\mathcal{L}ab_{compl}) \rangle = \langle \{b\}, \{a\}, \{c, d, e, f\} \rangle$. Then 1. 13 enforces the condition that arguments in $\text{in}(\mathcal{L}ab_{compl}) \cup \text{out}(\mathcal{L}ab_{compl}) = \{a, b\}$ can be labelled either in or out; and 1. 14 requires that at least one argument belonging to $\text{undec}(\mathcal{L}ab_{compl}) = \{c, d, e, f\}$ should be labelled either in or out. During the second execution of the loop (1. 9–16), at 1. 10 the only *compl'* assignment that satisfies the additional constraints is such that $\mathcal{L}ab_{compl'} = \langle \{a, d\}, \{b, c, e\}, \{f\} \rangle$. This assignment is then stored into *sstcand* (1. 12). Then, similarly as above, Algorithm 2 tries to label f either in or out, but at the third execution of the loop (1. 9–16) there is no further assignment able to satisfy such an additional constraint, therefore the loop is exited with *sstcand = compl'*, i.e. a variable assignment equivalent to a semi–stable labelling.

It is worth noticing that $\mathcal{E}_{ST}(\Gamma_1) = \varnothing$ because f is self-defeating and it is isolated from the rest of the framework, therefore in this case $\mathcal{E}_{SST}(\Gamma_1) \neq \mathcal{E}_{ST}(\Gamma_1)$. However, if we restrict Γ_1 to the set of arguments $\{a, b, c, d, e\}$, i.e. we *ignore* f and its self-defeating attack, then the stable and semi–stable extensions would coincide.

Finally, it also worth noticing that $\mathcal{E}_{\mathsf{SST}}(\varGamma_1) \neq \mathcal{E}_{\mathsf{PR}}(\varGamma_1)$. Indeed, there is another maximal admissible set of arguments, namely $\{\mathbf{b}\}$, i.e. a second preferred extension. However, its range—$\{\mathbf{b}, \mathbf{a}\}$—is not maximal.

The following theorem shows that AASExts is correct, i.e. it always terminates and returns the set of semi–stable extensions.

Theorem 1. *Let* $\varGamma = \langle \mathcal{A}, \mathcal{R} \rangle$ *be an argumentation framework. If AASExts is executed on* $\varGamma$ *then it terminates, and* AASExts$(\varGamma) = \mathcal{E}_{\mathsf{SST}}(\varGamma)$.

Proof. Let us first distinguish the following two cases. If $\mathcal{E}_{\mathsf{ST}}(\varGamma) \neq \varnothing$, *then* $\mathcal{E}_{\mathsf{SST}}(\varGamma) = \mathcal{E}_{\mathsf{ST}}(\varGamma)$ *by Proposition 1, and the algorithm correctly returns* $\mathcal{E}_{\mathsf{ST}}(\varGamma)$ *at l. 3. Otherwise, if* $\varGamma$ *has only one complete extension which is empty, then* $\mathcal{E}_{\mathsf{SST}}(\varGamma) = \{\varnothing\}$ *by Definition 6. In this case, ocnf has no satisfying assignments at l. 5, thus compl* $= \varepsilon$ *at l. 10 and the inner loop is directly exited at l. 16 with sstcand* $= \varnothing$. *It is then easy to see that* $\mathcal{E}_{sem} = \varnothing$ *at l. 27, and the algorithm correctly returns* $\{\varnothing\}$. *In the remainder of the proof we then assume that* $\mathcal{E}_{\mathsf{ST}}(\varGamma) = \varnothing$ *and there is a non empty complete extension, obviously entailing that there is a non empty semi–stable extension as well.*

We denote as $\mathcal{L}ab_{sem}$ *the set of labellings corresponding to the elements of* $\mathcal{E}_{sem}$, *i.e.* $\mathcal{L}ab_{sem} = \{\texttt{Ext2Lab}(S) \mid S \in \mathcal{E}_{sem}\}$, *and as* $\mathcal{L}ab_{ocnf}$ *the set of labellings corresponding to the assignments of ocnf, i.e.* $\mathcal{L}ab_{ocnf} = \{\mathcal{L}ab_c \mid c \text{ satisfies ocnf}\}$.

Let us first focus on l. 9–25 including the inner loop (l. 9–16). If $\mathcal{L}ab_{ocnf} = \varnothing$ *before an execution of the inner loop (l. 9), it is easy to see that the loop is immediately exited at l. 16 with sstcand* $= \varnothing$, *and no set is included into* $\mathcal{E}_{sem}$ *at l. 18 and l. 22. Otherwise, an assignment satisfying ocnf is selected in the first iteration of the inner loop (l. 10), and by Lemma 1 (see l. 13–14) at each iteration of the loop a labelling with a stricter set of undecided arguments is identified, and the corresponding assignment is stored into sstcand (l. 12). As a consequence the inner loop terminates, then at l. 18* $\texttt{in}(\mathcal{L}ab)$ *is added to* $\mathcal{E}_{sem}$ *where* $\mathcal{L}ab \in \mathcal{L}ab_{ocnf}$ *such that* $\texttt{undec}(\mathcal{L}ab)$ *is minimal. Then lines 19–23 add to* $\mathcal{E}_{sem}$ *all the sets corresponding to the labellings in* $\mathcal{L}ab_{ocnf}$ *sharing the same (minimal) set of undecided arguments.*

Let us turn to the outer loop (l. 6–26). We show inductively that at each iteration (l. 6) the following three conditions hold: (i) $\mathcal{L}ab_{sem} \subseteq \mathcal{L}_{\mathsf{SST}}(\varGamma)$; *(ii)* $\mathcal{L}_{\mathsf{SST}}(\varGamma) \backslash \mathcal{L}ab_{sem} \subseteq \mathcal{L}ab_{ocnf}$; *(iii)* $\forall \mathcal{L}ab \in \mathcal{L}ab_{sem}, \forall \mathcal{L}ab' \in \mathcal{L}ab_{ocnf}, \texttt{undec}(\mathcal{L}ab) \nsubseteq \texttt{undec}(\mathcal{L}ab')$. *The conditions obviously hold before the first iteration of the loop, since* $\mathcal{L}ab_{sem} = \varnothing$ *and* $\mathcal{L}ab_{ocnf}$ *includes all semi–stable labellings (see l. 5). Assuming that the conditions hold, let us prove that this is still the case after a further iteration. As to (i), we know from the above description that a labelling* $\mathcal{L}ab$ *in* $\mathcal{L}ab_{ocnf}$ *with* $\texttt{undec}(\mathcal{L}ab)$ *minimal is identified. Taking into account (iii) and (ii),* $\mathcal{L}ab$ *is a semi–stable labelling (otherwise there would be a semi–stable labelling in* $\mathcal{L}ab_{ocnf}$ *with a stricter set of undecided arguments, contradicting minimality), thus all sets included in* $\mathcal{E}_{sem}$ *(l. 18 and l. 22) are semi–stable extensions by Lemma 2. As to (ii), l. 24 only excludes from* $\mathcal{L}ab_{ocnf}$ *any labelling* $\mathcal{L}ab$ *with a greater set of undecided arguments w.r.t.*

that of the semi–stable labellings included in $\mathcal{L}ab_{sem}$, thus no other semi–stable labellings are excluded from $\mathcal{L}ab_{ocnf}$. For a similar reason also (iii) is satisfied.

We are now in a position to show termination and correctness. The first holds since at each iteration of the outer loop either at least a semi–stable extension is included in $\mathcal{E}_{sem}$, or sstcand $= \emptyset$ at l. 17, yielding termination. The result follows from the fact that Γ is finite, thus $\mathcal{E}_{\mathsf{SST}}(\Gamma)$ is finite too. As to correctness, the loop terminates with sstcand $= \emptyset$ and $\mathcal{L}ab_{ocnf} = \emptyset$. Taking into account condition (ii), this entails that $\mathcal{L}_{\mathsf{SST}}(\Gamma) \subseteq \mathcal{L}ab_{sem}$, which in turns entails $\mathcal{L}ab_{sem} = \mathcal{L}_{\mathsf{SST}}(\Gamma)$ by (i).

4 Experimental Assessment of Encodings

We performed a preliminary investigation to analyse the relative performance of the various propositional encodings introduced at the end of Sect. 2. To this purpose, we considered a small set of benchmarks[5] that we modified to ensure the non-existence of stable extensions by including a single isolated self-attacking argument.

Performance are measured in terms of IPC score and Penalised Average Runtime. The IPC score, borrowed from the planning community and exploited in recent editions of the International Planning Competition[6] [27], is defined as follows. For a solver S and an AF a, $score(S, a)$ is defined as:

$$ score(S, a) = \begin{cases} 0 & if\ a\ is\ not\ successfully\ analysed \\ \frac{1}{1+\log_{10}(\frac{T_a(S)}{T_a^*})} & otherwise \end{cases} $$

where $T_a(S)$ is the CPU time needed by a solver S to successfully analyse the AF a and T_a^* is the CPU-time needed by the best considered solver, otherwise. The total IPC score is the sum of the scores achieved on each considered AF. Runtimes below 1.0 sec get by default the maximal score of 1.

The Penalised Average Runtime (PAR score) is a real number calculated by counting (i) runs that fail to solve the considered problem as ten times the cutoff time (PAR10) and (ii) runs that succeed as the actual runtime. PAR scores are commonly used in automated algorithm configuration, algorithm selection, and portfolio construction [19], because using them allows runtime to be considered while still placing a strong emphasis on high instance set coverage.

---

[5] http://www.dbai.tuwien.ac.at/proj/argumentation/sat-based/.
[6] http://www.icaps-conference.org/index.php/Main/Competitions.

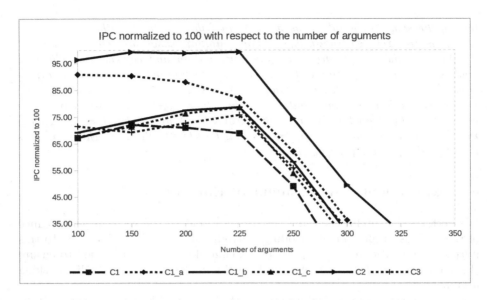

Fig. 2. IPC w.r.t $|Ar|$, comparing C_1, C_1^a, C_1^b, C_1^c, C_2 and C_3 encodings.

Figure 2 shows that the encoding C_2 is superior, considering the IPC score, compared to the alternatives. In addition, Fig. 3 shows that C_2 also covers— within a cut-off time of 900 s—the largest portion of frameworks in the dataset.

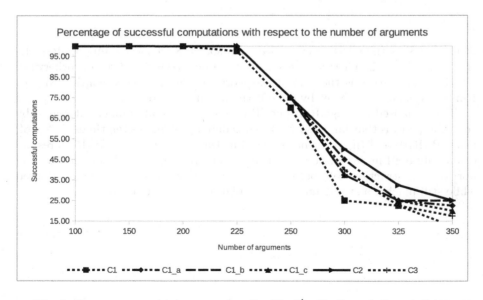

Fig. 3. Coverage w.r.t $|Ar|$, comparing C_1, C_1^a, C_1^b, C_1^c, C_2 and C_3 encodings.

Table 1. IPC and PAR10 comparing the various encodings. Best values in bold.

	C_1	C_1^a	C_1^b	C_1^c	C_2	C_3
PAR10	3164.17	2722.89	2769.77	2829.69	**2527.79**	2863.15
IPC	147.42	193.91	172.19	164.85	**228.55**	162.65

Table 1 summarises IPC and PAR10 for the various encodings. As C_2 outperforms the other options—as also shown in [11] for the case of preferred semantics—results in the following experimental evaluation are obtained by using it only.

5   Evaluation of **AASExts**

In this section, we present the result of a large experimental analysis comparing the performance of AASExts with respect to state-of-the-art approaches, on sets of differently-shaped AFs.

We implemented AASExts in C++. As per SS, we relied on MiniSAT [15], a small, complete, and efficient SAT-solver in the style of conflict-driven learning. Moreover, we considered the ALLSS developed by Yu *et al.* [33]. As mentioned above, a typical All-SAT solver is based on iteratively computing satisfying assignments using a traditional SAT solver and adding blocking clauses which are the complement of the total/partial assignments. Yu *et al.* [33] argue that such an algorithm is doing more work than needed and introduce more efficient algorithms: they also use MiniSAT as underlying SAT solver for their implementation.

5.1   Experimental Setup

We randomly generated 2,500 AFs based on five different graph models: Barabasi-Albert [1], Erdös-Rényi [17], Watts-Strogatz [31], graphs featuring a large number of stable extensions (hereinafter StableM), and a modified version of StableM (hereinafter SemiStableM) adding an artificial self-defeating attack detached from the rest of the graph—similarly to Example 1, cf. Fig. 1—thus ensuring that no stable extension exists.

Erdös-Rényi graphs [17] are generated by randomly selecting attacks between arguments according to a uniform distribution. While Erdös-Rényi was the predominant model used for randomly generated experiments, [4] investigated also other graph structures such as *scale-free* and *small-world* networks. As discussed by Barabasi and Albert [1], a common property of many large networks is that the node connectivities follow a *scale-free* power-law distribution. This is generally the case when: (i) networks expand continuously by the addition of new nodes, and (ii) new nodes attach preferentially to sites that are already well connected. Moreover, Watts and Strogatz [31] show that many biological, technological and social networks are neither completely regular nor completely random, but something in the between. They thus explored simple models of networks that can be tuned through this middle ground: regular networks *rewired* to introduce increasing amounts of disorder. These systems can be highly clustered, like regular lattices, yet have small characteristic path lengths, like random graphs, and they are named *small-world* networks by analogy with the small-world phenomenon.

The *AF*s belonging to the first three sets have been generated by AFBenchGen2 [10], submitted as a possible generator for the ICCMA 17. It is worth to emphasise that Watts-Strogatz and Barabasi-Albert produce undirected graphs: in this work, differently from Bistarelli *et al.* [4], each edge of the undirected graph is then associated with a direction following a probability distribution, that can be provided as input to AFBenchGen2. Such probability, provided as a parameter, varies between 0 and 1: if the parameter is 0, then the produced graph has unidirectional attacks only; if it is 1, each attack is mutual. The fourth set has been generated using the code provided in Probo [12] by the organisers of ICCMA-15 [26].[7] Finally, the SemiStableM set has been generated by adding to each *AF* of the StableM set and additional self-attacking argument.

In our experimental analysis we considered SSTMCS [30] and Aspartix [16]. All the considered benchmarks, and raw results, are available to download[8]. Experiments have been run on a cluster with computing nodes equipped with 2.5 Ghz Intel Core 2 Quad Processors, 4 GB of RAM and Linux operating system. A cutoff of 600 s was imposed to compute the extensions for each *AF* similarly to what chosen in ICCMA 17. For each solver we recorded the overall result: success (if it solved the considered problem), crashed, timed-out or ran out of memory. Unsuccessful runs—crashed, timed-out or out of memory—were assigned a runtime equal to the cutoff.

In the following we rely on the Wilcoxon Signed-Rank Test (WSRT) in order to identify significant subsets of data [32]. The Wilcoxon Signed-Rank test is used for comparing performance in terms of PAR10 of two solvers. From this perspective, "no correlation" between the observed results indicates that it is equally like that, given an *AF* from the considered set of benchmarks, one solver provides a solution faster than the second solver, than the vice-versa. For the purposes of this analysis, the Wilcoxon sign-rank test is appropriate because it does not require any knowledge about the sample distribution, and makes no assumption about the distribution. In our analysis we considered that the null-hypothesis, i.e. the performance of compared solvers is statistically similar, is accepted when *p-value* > 0.05. Otherwise, the null-hypothesis is rejected, and therefore the compared solvers performance is statistically different.

5.2   Experimental Results

Table 2 shows the performance, in terms of PAR10, coverage and IPC score, of the considered approaches on the different testing sets.

---

[7] http://argumentationcompetition.org/2015/results.html.

[8] https://helios.hud.ac.uk/scommv/storage/SemiStable2017.

Firstly, for each testing set, the performance of the solver that achieved the best PAR10 score are always statistically better than those of the other considered solvers.

Secondly, leaving aside the benchmarks of Barabasi—discussed in the following—AASExts shows outstanding performance. This is specially the case of Erdös-Rényi and Watts-Strogatz benchmarks, where the current state-of-the-art approaches often—if not always—fail to provide an answer in the given time. This seems consistent with some problems highlighted by Cerutti *et al.* [8] w.r.t. Aspartix in the case of preferred extensions.

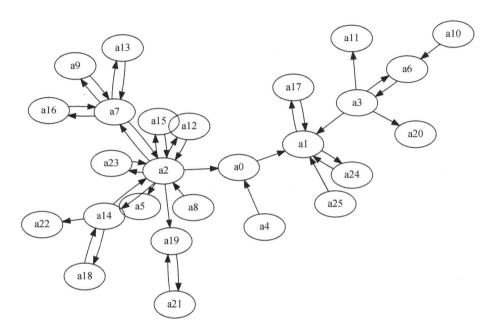

Fig. 4. A small example of an *AF* of the class Barabasi-Albert

The case of Barabasi-Albert benchmarks shows the main weakness of AASExts, namely the maximisation process where labels are left *free* to float between **in** and **out**. Figure 4 depicts a (small) example of an *AF* that would belong to the Barabasi-Albert benchmark—the actual benchmarks are composed of hundreds of arguments, Fig. 4 is for illustration purpose only. Given the large occurrence of cycles in such a structure, AASExts will spend a substantial amount of time within the inner loop (cf. Algorithm 2 l. 9–16) seeking for a maximal range, especially if the first assignment from SS (cf. Algorithm 2 l. 10) contains a large set of **undec** arguments. A way to mitigate this situation is to hack the MiniSAT code in order to prioritise a specific set of variables, i.e. *injecting* in MiniSAT the knowledge that it should search towards a maximal range. It is of little surprise that SSTMCS results to be the best solver in this case since it

Table 2. IPC score, PAR10 and coverage—percentage of *AF*s successfully analysed of the considered solvers—for solving the semi–stable enumeration problem on the complete testing set. Best results in **bold**.

Barabasi-Albert			
	IPC	PAR10	Coverage
Aspartix	1.1	5954.1	0.8
SSTMCS	**416.9**	**1012.6**	**84.3**
AASExts	157.8	3718.4	47.9

Erdös-Rényi			
	IPC	PAR10	Cov.
Aspartix	0.0	6000.0	0.0
SSTMCS	0.0	6000.0	0.0
AASExts	**263.0**	**2918.8**	**52.6**

SemiStableM			
	IPC	PAR10	Cov.
Aspartix	126.1	3273.0	48.8
SSTMCS	253.8	2568.1	58.2
AASExts	**312.8**	**2141.0**	**65.2**

StableM			
	IPC	PAR10	Cov.
Aspartix	116.3	3428.8	46.0
SSTMCS	242.6	2616.7	57.4
AASExts	**314.9**	**2147.8**	**65.0**

Watts-Strogatz			
	IPC	PAR10	Cov.
Aspartix	17.9	5429.0	11.0
SSTMCS	8.3	5789.9	4.6
AASExts	**395.0**	**1376.9**	**79.0**

exploits efficient techniques for computing minimal correction sets (MCS) [20,21] that are subset-minimal sets of clauses of a formula, thus solving the dual problem of maximising the range, namely to minimise the set of undec arguments.

Lastly, the similarities of the results between SemiStableM and StableM suggest that the introduction of the self-defeating argument for enforcing the absence of stable extensions—cf. Example 1 and Fig. 1—has no significant impact on solvers' performance. AASExts performs slightly better—according to the IPC metric—on the StableM domain no doubt because a large of benchmark instances (61%) have a stable extension, and thus it can fully exploit the All-SAT solver.

However, it is interesting to note that the coverage is slightly higher in the case of SemiStableM. If an *AF* in StableM has a stable extension, AASExts will compute the semi-stable extensions by using STExts. However, the *AF* in SemiStableM, derived from the previous one by adding a self-defeating argument, will not have a stable extension and thus AASExts cannot exploits STExts. In 0.2% of *AF*s in SemiStableM, the procedure in AASExts identifies semi-stable extensions before the cut-off time, while it fails when searching for stable extensions in the corresponding original *AF* in StableM. We will investigate further this behaviour to identify the reasons those relatively rare cases are potentially problematic for the All-SAT solver exploited by STExts.

6   Conclusion

In this paper we introduced AASExts, an efficient algorithm for computing semi–stable extensions in abstract argumentation. We proved its correctness and we demonstrated its performance against existing approaches in the literature, and overall this approach scored second at the ICCMA 2017 for the semi-stable semantics track. Moreover, to our knowledge, this is the first approach exploiting results from the All-SAT research to solve the considered problem in abstract argumentation.

The selection of the encoding of complete labellings to adopt in AASExts is pivotal in achieving algorithm performance. In this respect, an experimental analysis has been carried out to identify the best encoding among a set of equivalent ones.

An experimental analysis conducted on a large number of *AF*s based on five different graph models, has shown that: (i) AASExts is generally able to deliver better performance than existing state-of-the-art approaches; (ii) the main weakness of AASExts comes from its maximisation process, that can hardly cope with cases in which labels keep floating between in and out values, as in the Barabasi-Albert set, and (iii) the introduction of self-defeating arguments for enforcing the absence of stable extensions has no significant impact on considered solvers' performance.

As part of future work, we aim at deriving an efficient algorithm for computing (non-admissible) argumentation stage extensions, as well as for the skeptical/credulous acceptance of arguments. Moreover, we believe that it is the right time to start computing semantics evaluation considering the inner argument structure, therefore we will look at structured argumentation and how to identify semi–stable extensions, as well as other Dung's related extensions, possibly without the need of first deriving a Dung's argumentation framework as an intermediate system of representation.

References

1. Barabasi, A., Albert, R.: Emergence of scaling in random networks. Science **286**(5439), 509–512 (1999)
2. Baroni, P., Caminada, M., Giacomin, M.: An introduction to argumentation semantics. Knowl. Eng. Rev. **26**(4), 365–410 (2011)
3. Baroni, P., Cerutti, F., Dunne, P.E., Giacomin, M.: Automata for infinite argumentation structures. Artif. Intell. **203**, 104–150 (2013)
4. Bistarelli, S., Rossi, F., Santini, F.: Benchmarking hard problems in random abstract AFs: the stable semantics. In: Proceedings of COMMA, pp. 153–160 (2014)
5. Caminada, M.: On the issue of reinstatement in argumentation. In: Fisher, M., van der Hoek, W., Konev, B., Lisitsa, A. (eds.) JELIA 2006. LNCS (LNAI), vol. 4160, pp. 111–123. Springer, Heidelberg (2006). https://doi.org/10.1007/11853886_11
6. Caminada, M.: Semi-stable semantics. In: Proceedings of COMMA 2006, pp. 121–130 (2006)
7. Caminada, M., Gabbay, D.M.: A logical account of formal argumentation. Stud. Logica. **93**(2–3), 109–145 (2009). https://doi.org/10.1007/s11225-009-9218-x. (Special issue: new ideas in argumentation theory)
8. Cerutti, F., Dunne, P.E., Giacomin, M., Vallati, M.: A SAT-based approach for computing extensions in abstract argumentation. In: Second International Workshop on Theory and Applications of Formal Argumentation (TAFA-2013) (2013)
9. Cerutti, F., Dunne, P.E., Giacomin, M., Vallati, M.: Computing preferred extensions in abstract argumentation: a SAT-based approach. Technical report (2013). http://arxiv.org/abs/1310.4986
10. Cerutti, F., Giacomin, M., Vallati, M.: Generating structured argumentation frameworks: AFBenchGen2. In: Proceedings of COMMA, pp. 467–468 (2016)
11. Cerutti, F., Giacomin, M., Vallati, M.: How we designed winning algorithms for abstract argumentation and which insight we attained. Artif. Intell. **276**, 1–40 (2019). https://doi.org/10.1016/j.artint.2019.08.001
12. Cerutti, F., Oren, N., Strass, H., Thimm, M., Vallati, M.: A benchmark framework for a computational argumentation competition. In: Proceedings of the 5th International Conference on Computational Models of Argument, pp. 459–460 (2014)
13. Dung, P.M.: On the acceptability of arguments and its fundamental role in nonmonotonic reasoning, logic programming, and n-person games. Artif. Intell. **77**(2), 321–357 (1995)
14. Dvorák, W., Järvisalo, M., Wallner, J.P., Woltran, S.: Complexity-sensitive decision procedures for abstract argumentation. Artif. Intell. **206**, 53–78 (2014)
15. Eén, N., Sörensson, N.: An extensible SAT-solver. In: Giunchiglia, E., Tacchella, A. (eds.) SAT 2003. LNCS, vol. 2919, pp. 502–518. Springer, Heidelberg (2004). https://doi.org/10.1007/978-3-540-24605-3_37
16. Egly, U., Gaggl, S.A., Woltran, S.: Answer-set programming encodings for argumentation frameworks. Argument Comput. **1**(2), 147–177 (2010)
17. Erdös, P., Rényi, A.: On random graphs. I. Publ. Math. Debrecen **6**, 290–297 (1959)
18. Gaggl, S.A., Linsbichler, T., Maratea, M., Woltran, S.: Design and results of the second international competition on computational models of argumentation. Artif. Intell. **279**, 103193 (2020). https://doi.org/10.1016/j.artint.2019.103193
19. Hoos, H.H.: Automated algorithm configuration and parameter tuning. In: Hamadi, Y., Monfroy, E., Saubion, F. (eds.) Autonomous Search, pp. 37–71. Springer, Heidelberg (2011). https://doi.org/10.1007/978-3-642-21434-9_3

20. Liffiton, M.H., Sakallah, K.A.: Algorithms for computing minimal unsatisfiable subsets of constraints. J. Autom. Reason. **40**(1), 1–33 (2007). https://doi.org/10.1007/s10817-007-9084-z

21. Marques-Silva, J., Heras, F., Janota, M., Previti, A., Belov, A.: On computing minimal correction subsets. In: Proceedings of the Twenty-Third International Joint Conference on Artificial Intelligence, pp. 615–622. AAAI Press (2013)

22. McMillan, K.L.: Applying SAT methods in unbounded symbolic model checking. In: Brinksma, E., Larsen, K.G. (eds.) CAV 2002. LNCS, vol. 2404, pp. 250–264. Springer, Heidelberg (2002). https://doi.org/10.1007/3-540-45657-0_19

23. Niemelä, I.: Logic programs with stable model semantics as a constraint programming paradigm. Ann. Math. Artif. Intell. **25**, 241–273 (1999). https://doi.org/10.1023/A:1018930122475

24. Pu, F., Ya, H., Luo, G.: argmat-SAT: Applying SAT Solvers for Argumentation Problems Based on Boolean Matrix Algebra (2017). http://argumentationcompetition.org/2017/argmat-sat.pdf

25. Rescher, N.: Dialectics: A Controversy-Oriented Approach to the Theory of Knowledge. Suny Press, Albany (1977)

26. Thimm, M., Villata, S., Cerutti, F., Oren, N., Strass, H., Vallati, M.: Summary report of the first international competition on computational models of argumentation. AI Mag. **37**(1), 102 (2016)

27. Vallati, M., Chrpa, L., Grzes, M., McCluskey, T.L., Roberts, M., Sanner, S.: The 2014 international planning competition: progress and trends. AI Mag. **36**(3), 90–98 (2015)

28. Verheij, B.: The influence of defeated arguments in defeasible argumentation. In: WOCFAI, vol. 95, pp. 429–440. Citeseer (1995)

29. Verheij, B.: Two approaches to dialectical argumentation: admissible sets and argumentation stages. In: Meyer, J.J., van der Gaag, L.C. (eds.) Proceedings of the Eighth Dutch Conference on Artificial Intelligence (NAIC 1996), Utrecht, NL, pp. 357–368 (1996)

30. Wallner, J.P., Weissenbacher, G., Woltran, S.: Advanced SAT techniques for abstract argumentation. In: Leite, J., Son, T.C., Torroni, P., van der Torre, L., Woltran, S. (eds.) CLIMA 2013. LNCS (LNAI), vol. 8143, pp. 138–154. Springer, Heidelberg (2013). https://doi.org/10.1007/978-3-642-40624-9_9

31. Watts, D.J., Strogatz, S.H.: Collective dynamics of 'small-world' networks. Nature **393**(6684), 440–442 (1998)

32. Wilcoxon, F.: Individual comparisons by ranking methods. Biom. Bull. **1**(6), 80–83 (1945)

33. Yu, Y., Subramanyan, P., Tsiskaridze, N., Malik, S.: All-SAT using minimal blocking clauses. In: 2014 27th International Conference on VLSI Design and 2014 13th International Conference on Embedded Systems, pp. 86–91. IEEE, January 2014. https://doi.org/10.1109/VLSID.2014.22

Introducing General Argumentation Frameworks and Their Use

Stefano Ferilli(✉) 📵

Dipartimento di Informatica, Università di Bari, Bari, Italy
stefano.ferilli@uniba.it

Abstract. In its original definition, the Abstract Argumentation framework considers atomic claims and a binary attack relationship among them, based on which different semantics would select subsets of claims consistently supporting the same position in a dispute or debate. While attack is obviously the core relationship in this setting, in more complex (and in many real-world) situations additional information may help, or might even be crucial, in determining such positions, and especially those that are going to win the debate. Different kinds of additional features have often been considered separately in the literature, yielding disjoint models for argumentation frameworks. In this paper we propose a model, called General Argumentation Framework (or GAF), aimed at unifying the different perspectives, and at further extending them by allowing to express contextual information associated to the arguments, in addition to their relationships. We also show how to express a number of existing frameworks in the literature as GAFs.

Keywords: Abstract argumentation · Argumentation frameworks

1 Introduction

Argumentation is the inferential strategy for practical and uncertain reasoning aimed at coping with partial and inconsistent knowledge, in order to justify one of several contrasting positions in a discussion [17]. A typical case is a debate in which each participant tries to support one position with suitable claims (the *arguments*), also attacking the arguments put forward by others to support competing positions, and defending his position from the attacks of the others. Since different forms of disputes (or anyway situations with contrasting evidence) are ubiquitous in real life, the availability of automated techniques for carrying out argumentation would be extremely useful. Hence, the birth of a specific branch of Artificial Intelligence aimed at developing models, approaches, techniques and systems for dealing with different aspects of argumentative reasoning.

Abstract argumentation, in particular, focuses on the resolution of the dispute based only on 'external' information about the arguments (notably, the inter-relationships among them), neglecting their internal structure or interpretation. Traditional Abstract Argumentation Frameworks (AFs for short) can

© Springer Nature Switzerland AG 2021
M. Baldoni and S. Bandini (Eds.): AIxIA 2020, LNAI 12414, pp. 136–153, 2021.
https://doi.org/10.1007/978-3-030-77091-4_9

express only attacks among arguments. While already useful to tackle many cases (because the attack relationship is indeed the very core and driving feature in a debate), this is obviously a significant limitation in expressiveness. So, several lines of research tried to overcome such a limitation by introducing additional features to be considered in the argumentation frameworks. Most famous are the possibility of expressing supports between arguments (in addition to attacks), or the 'strength' of attacks (in the form of a number). These extensions were mainly developed independently of each other, so that they cannot be straightforwardly combined into a more powerful framework encompassing all of them.

This paper proposes a general framework that brings to a cooperation of the different features of the single frameworks, yielding a much more powerful model to carry out abstract argumentation. It can simulate any of those frameworks, and also provides for the additional possibility of assigning a degree of 'strength' also to the arguments, not just to their relationships. We call it *Generalized Argumentation Framework*, or GAF. Note that our aim is not proposing any evaluation strategy or computational procedure, but a model that can be specialized and tailored to different contexts and domains, and on which theoretical investigation can be carried out for defining semantics and evaluation strategies. We believe our proposal can be taken as a reference, both for porting solutions developed for previous partial extensions, and for developing new solutions that fully exploit its extended expressive power. Also, we show that our model can be easily expressed using matrix representations, which might bring significant improvements in efficiency in computing the argumentation outcomes thanks to the use of matrix operations.

The paper is organized as follows. After recalling basic concepts of abstract AFs and discussing related works in the next section, in Sect. 3 we will define the new generalized model and show how it maps onto existing AFs. Then, in Sect. 4 we show how some frameworks proposed in the literature can be expressed as GAFs. Before concluding the paper in Sect. 6, we suggest in Sect. 5 the possibility of expressing GAFs using matrix-based representations.

2   Basics and Related Work

The original (and now classical) Abstract Argumentation setting was proposed by Dung [7]. It can express only the attack relationship between pairs of arguments, as the core feature indicating inconsistency in the available information:

Definition 1. *An* argumentation framework *(AF for short) is a pair $F = \langle \mathcal{A}, \mathcal{R} \rangle$, where $\mathcal{A}$ is a finite set of arguments and $\mathcal{R} \subseteq \mathcal{A} \times \mathcal{A}$ is an attack relationship (meaning that, given $\alpha, \beta \in \mathcal{A}$, if $\alpha \mathcal{R} \beta$ then α attacks β).*

In this setting, no direct agreement between arguments can be expressed. Agreement can only indirectly be derived based on the attack relationship, yielding the notion of *defense*:

Definition 2. *Let $F = \langle \mathcal{A}, \mathcal{R} \rangle$ be an AF, and $S \subseteq \mathcal{A}$:*

- *$\alpha \in \mathcal{A}$ is defended by S if $\forall \beta \in \mathcal{A}$: $\beta \mathcal{R} \alpha \Rightarrow \exists \gamma \in S$ s.t. $\gamma \mathcal{R} \beta$;*
- *f_F: $2^{\mathcal{A}} \mapsto 2^{\mathcal{A}}$ s.t. $f_F(S) = \{\alpha \mid \alpha$ is defended by $S\}$ is the characteristic function of F.*

So, an argument may 'defend' other arguments by attacking their attacker (or, in other words, attacking an attacker amounts to a defense).

An argumentation *semantics* is the formal definition of a method ruling the argument evaluation process. In particular, extension-based semantics determine which subset(s) of arguments in an AF, called *extensions*, can stand together and possibly be considered as the 'winners' of the dispute expressed by the AF. On the other hand, ranking-based semantics [1] individually evaluate single arguments rather than sets of arguments, and, given an AF, determine a ranking of the available arguments in the form of a pre-order (reflexive and transitive relation). We will not delve further into semantics in the following, since the aim of this paper is providing a unified framework in which the existing semantics can be transposed, and new ones can be developed, leveraging its additional features.

Several works tried to overcome the limitations of the classical AFs by generalizing them in different ways. The most investigated limitations were the possibility of expressing only attacks between pairs of arguments, and the inability of distinguishing different degrees of 'strength' for the single attacks. Research on the former led to the so-called *Bipolar* AFs (or *BAFs*) [6], allowing two kinds of interactions between arguments, expressed respectively by the *attack* relation and the *support* relation. Research on the latter led to the so-called *Weighted* AFs (or *WAFs*) [8], allowing to specify a numeric weight for each attack between arguments, indicating its relative strength. BAFs and WAFs cannot be immediately combined, because the computational procedures for WAFs are specified only for attacks, and are not simply applicable to supports if no strategy for combining overall attack and support assessment is provided.

This was the reason behind some attempts to define extensions encompassing both possibilities. Specifically, [13] proposed a formal extension of the framework (named *Bipolar Weighted Argumentation Framework*, or BWAF) and a gradual evaluation strategy, while [4] extended their previous work on graph-based computational strategies for unipolar AFs. BWAFs embed the notions of attack and support into the weights, by considering negative weights for attacks and positive weights for supports.

Definition 3. *A BWAF is a triplet $F = \langle \mathcal{A}, \hat{\mathcal{R}}, w_{\hat{\mathcal{R}}} \rangle$, where $\mathcal{A}$ is a finite set of arguments, $\hat{\mathcal{R}} \subseteq \mathcal{A} \times \mathcal{A}$ and $w_{\hat{\mathcal{R}}}$: $\hat{\mathcal{R}} \mapsto [-1, 0[\cup]0, 1]$ assigns a weight to each relation instance. Within $\hat{\mathcal{R}}$, the attack sub-relation is defined as $\hat{\mathcal{R}}_{att} = \{\langle \alpha, \beta \rangle \in \hat{\mathcal{R}} \mid w_{\hat{\mathcal{R}}}(\langle \alpha, \beta \rangle) \in [-1, 0[\}$, while the support sub-relation is defined as $\hat{\mathcal{R}}_{sup} = \{\langle \alpha, \beta \rangle \in \hat{\mathcal{R}} \mid w_{\hat{\mathcal{R}}}(\langle \alpha, \beta \rangle) \in]0, 1] \}$.*

Weight 0 is not considered, since it would mean the absence of an attack or support relation. Note that this weighting scheme neatly distinguishes attacks from supports: a support is not considered as just the complement of an attack, but they are two distinct concepts, and only after determining the concept to be used (as the sign of the weight) the weight makes sense. This allows BWAFs to be consistent with previous bipolar approaches to Abstract Argumentation.

Some argumentation frameworks extend Dung's definition by introducing support requirements for arguments to be acceptable. We will summarize them taking their formalization in [16] as reference, and adapting notation. Evidential argumentation systems [11] are argumentation frameworks in which a special argument η (called *evidence* or *environment*) is present, such that all valid arguments (and attackers) need to trace back to η. This behavior is captured by the notions of e-support and e-supported attack.

Definition 4. *An* Evidential Argumentation System *(EAS) is a tuple* $\langle \mathcal{A}, \hat{\mathcal{R}}, \hat{\mathcal{E}} \rangle$ *where* $\mathcal{A}$ *is a set of arguments,* $\hat{\mathcal{R}} \subseteq (2^{\mathcal{A}} \backslash \emptyset) \times \mathcal{A}$ *is the attack relation, and* $\hat{\mathcal{E}} \subseteq (2^{\mathcal{A}} \backslash \emptyset) \times \mathcal{A}$ *is the support relation. We distinguish a special argument* $\eta \in \mathcal{A}$ *for which* $\nexists (X, y) \in \hat{\mathcal{R}}$ *s.t.* $\eta \in X$, *and* $\nexists X$ *s.t.* $(X, \eta) \in \hat{\mathcal{R}}$ *or* $(X, \eta) \in \hat{\mathcal{E}}$.

- *An argument* $a \in \mathcal{A}$ *has* evidential support *(e-support) from a set* $S \subseteq \mathcal{A}$ *iff* $a = \eta$ *or* $\exists S' \subseteq S, S' \neq \emptyset$ *such that* $S' \hat{\mathcal{E}} a$ *and* $\forall x \in S' : x$ *has evidential support from* $S \backslash \{a\}$.
- *Given a set of arguments* $X \subseteq \mathcal{A}$, *an* evidential sequence *for an argument* $a \in X$ *is a sequence* $\langle a_0, \ldots, a_n \rangle$ *of distinct elements of* X *s.t.* $a_n = a$, $a_0 = \eta$, *and* $n > 0 \Rightarrow \forall n_i = 1, \ldots, n : \exists T \subseteq \{a_0, \ldots, a_{i-1}\}, T \neq \emptyset$ *s.t.* $T \hat{\mathcal{E}} a_i$.

Necessary support [10] follows the intuition that if an argument supports another argument, then acceptance of the former is required for the acceptance of the latter.

Definition 5. *An* Abstract Argumentation framework with Necessities *(AFN) is a tuple* $\langle \mathcal{A}, \hat{\mathcal{R}}, \hat{\mathcal{N}} \rangle$ *where* $\mathcal{A}$ *is a set of arguments,* $\hat{\mathcal{R}} \subseteq \mathcal{A} \times \mathcal{A}$ *is the attack relation, and* $\hat{\mathcal{R}} \subseteq (2^{\mathcal{A}} \backslash \emptyset) \times \mathcal{A}$ *is the necessity relation.*

- *An argument* a *is* powerful *in* $S \subseteq \mathcal{A}$ *iff* $a \in S$ *and there is a sequence* $\langle a_0, \ldots, a_k \rangle$ *of elements of* S *such that:*
  - $a_k = a$
  - $\nexists E \subseteq \mathcal{A}$ *s.t.* $E \hat{\mathcal{N}} a_0$
  - $\forall 1 \leq i \leq k, \forall E \subseteq \mathcal{A} : E \hat{\mathcal{N}} a_i \Rightarrow E \cap \{a_0, \ldots, a_{i-1}\} \neq \emptyset$.
- *A set of arguments* $S \subseteq \mathcal{A}$ *is* coherent *iff each* $\alpha \in S$ *is powerful in* S.

So, while in EASs any acceptable argument must be traced back to the evidence η, in AFNs it must be traced back to an unsupported argument. In both cases, support cycles are insufficient to permit acceptance.

Some researchers pointed out that not only the relationships among arguments, but also the arguments themselves may have different degrees of 'strength' or 'reliability'. E.g., according to [2], the *intrinsic strength* of an argument may come from different sources: the certainty degree of its reason [3], the importance of the value it promotes if any [5], the reliability of its source [12]. In this line of thought, albeit there is no agreement in the literature about the possibility of using contextual information in an AF, [14] further extended the BWAF framework into the *Trust-affected Bipolar Weighted Argumentation Framework* (or T-BWAF), introducing the possibility of weighting also the arguments by determining their *intrinsic strength* as the result of several factors, internal to the argument (the authority of the source of the argument and its own confidence in the validity of the argument) or external to it (the trust of a community in the source of the argument[1]). This paper generalizes [14] so as to abstract away from the specific computational approaches.

[15] proposed a matrix representation for BWAFs, showing how to use it for computing some traditional semantics and defining a new semantics specifically associated to such a representation. We propose the use of matrix representations also for our extended framework.

3   The Generalized Argumentation Framework

Generalized Argumentation Frameworks extend traditional AFs with bipolarity, weights on both attacks and supports, and weights on the arguments. They come with no embedded solutions for the use of such components. Rather, they provide a flexible way for representing different possible interpretations and perspectives on them, and a basis to implement different evaluation procedures, including those proposed by previous works.

Definition 6. *A* Generalized Argumentation Framework *(**GAF**) is a tuple $F = \langle \mathcal{A}, \mathcal{S}, w_{\mathcal{A}}, w_{\mathcal{R}} \rangle$, where:*

- *$\mathcal{A}$ is a finite set of arguments,*
- *$\mathcal{S}$ is a system providing external information on the arguments[2] in $\mathcal{A}$,*
- *$w_{\mathcal{A}} \colon \mathcal{A} \mapsto [0,1]$ assigns a weight to each argument, to be considered as its intrinsic strength, also based on $\mathcal{S}$, and*
- *$w_{\mathcal{R}} \colon \mathcal{A} \times \mathcal{A} \mapsto [-1,1]$ assigns a weight to each pair of arguments, also based on $\mathcal{S}$.*

It is up to the knowledge engineer defining, case by case, what $\mathcal{S}$ is, and how it affects the assessment of the 'intrinsic' reliability of arguments or of their attack/support relationships. For those who are not comfortable with the use of contextual information in an AF, $\mathcal{S}$ can simply be empty. They might still accept the use of $w_{\mathcal{A}}$ for expressing some kind of 'intrinsic' strength of the arguments, or ignore $w_{\mathcal{A}}$ as well.

Note that, differently from all previous models, the relationship between arguments is implicit in the GAF model. This is because we consider a complete graph, where any pair of arguments has a weighted relationship. For practical purposes, weight 0 can be interpreted as the absence of any (attack or support)

---

[1] We are aware of other works about trust in argumentation, but since they are later than [14] and do not refer it, we assume there is no sufficient relationship to this work, which builds on [14].

[2] This allows us to embed in GAFs existing proposals in the literature.

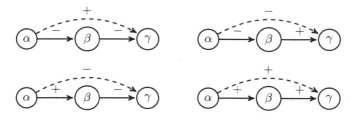

Fig. 1. Sign rule for attacks and supports

relationship, and ignored when drawing the argumentation graph. The bipolar relationship considered in BWAFs can be easily extracted as

$$\hat{\mathcal{R}} = \{(\alpha, \beta) \in \mathcal{A} \times \mathcal{A} \mid w_{\mathcal{R}}(\alpha, \beta) \neq 0\}$$

Not only using negative weights for attacks and positive weights for supports is quite intuitive (attacking an argument subtracts to its credibility, supporting it adds to its credibility) and comfortable (the kind of relationship can be immediately distinguished by its sign). Using negative weights for attacks also allows us to straighforwardly translate the traditional assumptions for the bipolar case:

1. attacking the attacker of an argument amounts to defending (i.e., somehow supporting) that argument (known as *reinstatement*);
2. attacking the supporter of an argument amounts to attacking that argument;
3. supporting the attacker of an argument amounts to attacking that argument;
4. supporting the supporter of an argument amounts to supporting that argument;

into mathematical computations, since they clearly correspond to the sign rule used in mathematics:

followed by	Support	Attack
Support	Support	Attack
Attack	Attack	Support

×	+	−
+	+	−
−	−	+

(see Fig. 1 for a graphical representation).

This rule also allows us to immediately turn the notions of indirect attacks and defenses into mathematical operations. Indeed, just like a path of relationships including an even number of attacks amounts to a defense, so the product of an even number of minus signs gets a plus sign; *vice versa*, just like a path of relationships including an odd number of attacks still amounts to an attack, so the product of an odd number of minus signs gets a minus sign. So, we can define:

Definition 7. *Given a GAF $F = \langle \mathcal{A}, \mathcal{S}, w_{\mathcal{A}}, w_{\mathcal{R}} \rangle$ and a sequence of arguments $\langle x_0, x_1, \ldots, x_n \rangle$ such that $\forall i = 0, \ldots, n : x_i \in \mathcal{A}$, we say that:*

- x_0 g-defends x_n *iff* $\prod_{i=1}^{n} w_{\mathcal{R}}(x_{i-1}, x_i) > 0$
- x_0 g-attacks x_n *iff* $\prod_{i=1}^{n} w_{\mathcal{R}}(x_{i-1}, x_i) < 0$

Note that we may consider any sequence of arguments, not only those for which a path actually exists in the graph. Indeed, when a sequence is not associated to a path, the missing links would have weight 0 and thus would bring the product at 0. So, the GAF formalization also provides a computational means to determine whether or not two arguments affect each other along a given path.

The formalization of GAFs also allow us to easily compute statistics on the direct attacks and supports for an argument, useful for defining some semantics:

Definition 8. *Given a GAF $F = \langle \mathcal{A}, \mathcal{S}, w_{\mathcal{A}}, w_{\mathcal{R}} \rangle$ and an argument $x_0 \in \mathcal{A}$, we can compute:*

- *the* number of attacks *received by x_0 as* $\sum_{x \in \mathcal{A}, w_{\mathcal{R}}(x, x_0) < 0} 1$
- *the* number of supports *received by x_0 as* $\sum_{x \in \mathcal{A}, w_{\mathcal{R}}(x, x_0) > 0} 1$
- *the* direct justification balance *of x_0 as* $\sum_{x \in \mathcal{A}} 1 \cdot \operatorname{sign}(w_{\mathcal{R}}(x, x_0))$
- *the* cumulative weighted attack *received by x_0 as* $\sum_{x \in \mathcal{A}, w_{\mathcal{R}}(x, x_0) < 0} -w_{\mathcal{R}}(x, x_0)$
- *the* cumulative weighted support *received by x_0 as* $\sum_{x \in \mathcal{A}, w_{\mathcal{R}}(x, x_0) > 0} w_{\mathcal{R}}(x, x_0)$
- *the* weighted direct justification balance *of x_0 as* $\sum_{x \in \mathcal{A}} w_{\mathcal{R}}(x, x_0)$

Compared to traditional weighted frameworks (WAFs), where the weight of an attack could be any number, bounding the absolute weights within fixed minimum and maximum values intuitively allows one to identify a level of strength at which the attacking argument 'fully' defeats the attacked one (or the supporting argument 'fully' supports the supported one). The specific $[0, 1]$ range also helps intuition due to its wide use in probability theory.

3.1 Mapping from Existing Frameworks

Since one stated objective of our proposal is that it should be able to encompass, combine and extend less expressive models, a basic requirement is that GAFs can at least simulate the established models in the literature, namely BWAFs, WAFs, BAFs, and AFs. The following proposition confirms that our generality hypothesis holds.

Proposition 1. *Given an argumentation framework in any of the less expressive models (BWAF, WAF, BAF, AF), a corresponding GAF $F = \langle \mathcal{A}, \mathcal{S}, w_{\mathcal{A}}, w_{\mathcal{R}} \rangle$ can be defined, including only the portion of information that they are able to express.*

Intuitively, the GAF can be defined by setting:

- $\mathcal{S} = \{\bot\}$, i.e., a single uninformative item;
- $w_{\mathcal{A}} = 1$, i.e., the constant function returning 1 for any argument, meaning full reliability

and $w_{\mathcal{R}}$ as follows for the different models:

BWAF $\langle \mathcal{A}, \hat{\mathcal{R}}, w_{\hat{\mathcal{R}}} \rangle$:

$$w_{\mathcal{R}}(\alpha, \beta) = \begin{cases} w_{\hat{\mathcal{R}}}(\alpha, \beta) & \text{if } (\alpha, \beta) \in \hat{\mathcal{R}} \\ 0 & \text{otherwise} \end{cases}$$

i.e., by adding a relationship with 0 weight for any pair of arguments not involved in an attack nor in a support.

WAF $\langle \mathcal{A}, \hat{\mathcal{R}}, w_{\hat{\mathcal{R}}} \rangle$:

$$w_{\mathcal{R}}(\alpha, \beta) = \begin{cases} -\frac{w_{\hat{\mathcal{R}}}(\alpha, \beta)}{\overline{w}} & \text{if } (\alpha, \beta) \in \hat{\mathcal{R}} \\ 0 & \text{otherwise} \end{cases}$$

where

$$\overline{w} = \max_{\alpha, \beta \in \mathcal{A}} w_{\hat{\mathcal{R}}}(\alpha, \beta)$$

i.e., by normalizing the attack weights into $[0, 1]$. Note that, since this kind of framework typically comes with a justification threshold θ used to determine what arguments survive the attacks, also θ must be normalized using the same parameter:

$$\theta_{\text{GAF}} = -\frac{\theta}{\overline{w}}$$

BAF $\langle \mathcal{A}, \hat{\mathcal{R}}_{att}, \hat{\mathcal{R}}_{sup} \rangle$:

$$w_{\mathcal{R}}(\alpha, \beta) = \begin{cases} -1 & \text{if } (\alpha, \beta) \in \hat{\mathcal{R}}_{att} \\ 1 & \text{if } (\alpha, \beta) \in \hat{\mathcal{R}}_{sup} \\ 0 & \text{otherwise} \end{cases}$$

i.e., by setting a full attack wherever the BAF sets an attack, and a full support wherever the BAF sets a support (and a relationship with 0 weight for all other pairs of arguments). Note that the computation of g-attacks and g-supports is compliant with this representation, since the product of values all equal to ± 1 is still equal to ± 1, i.e., a full attack or support (having the same strength as direct ones).

AF $\langle \mathcal{A}, \hat{\mathcal{R}} \rangle$:

$$w_{\mathcal{R}}(\alpha, \beta) = \begin{cases} -1 & \text{if } (\alpha, \beta) \in \hat{\mathcal{R}} \\ 0 & \text{otherwise} \end{cases}$$

i.e., by setting a full attack wherever the AF sets an attack, and a relationship with 0 weight for all other pairs of arguments. Again, note that the computation of indirect attacks and defenses is compliant with this representation, thanks to the sign rule.

3.2   Mapping to Existing Frameworks

Conversely, when the additional information provided by GAFs is not needed for the current purposes, one might be interested in working in one of the simpler models (e.g., for using existing argument evaluation strategies and tools). The following proposition shows how a GAF can be reduced to each those models, by stripping the information they cannot convey and keeping only the portion that they can express.

Proposition 2. *Given a GAF $F = \langle \mathcal{A}, \mathcal{S}, w_{\mathcal{A}}, w_{\mathcal{R}} \rangle$, corresponding frameworks can be defined for each of the less expressive models (BWAF, WAF, BAF, AF) by extracting from F only the portion of information that they are able to express.*

Indeed, the less expressive frameworks are extracted from GAFs as follows:

BWAF $\langle \mathcal{A}, \hat{\mathcal{R}}, w_{\hat{\mathcal{R}}} \rangle$ with
$\quad \hat{\mathcal{R}} = \{(\alpha, \beta) \in \mathcal{A} \times \mathcal{A} \mid w_{\mathcal{R}}(\alpha, \beta) \neq 0\} \subseteq \mathcal{A} \times \mathcal{A}$ and
$\quad w_{\hat{\mathcal{R}}} = w_{\mathcal{R}}|_{\hat{\mathcal{R}}}$
by just removing pairs of arguments with 0 weight, which simply do not exist in BWAFs.
WAF $\langle \mathcal{A}, \hat{\mathcal{R}}, w_{\hat{\mathcal{R}}} \rangle$ with
$\quad \hat{\mathcal{R}} = \{(\alpha, \beta) \in \mathcal{A} \times \mathcal{A} \mid w_{\mathcal{R}}(\alpha, \beta) < 0\} \subseteq \mathcal{A} \times \mathcal{A}$ and
$\quad w_{\hat{\mathcal{R}}} = -w_{\mathcal{R}}|_{\hat{\mathcal{R}}}$
by reporting in the WAF only the attacks, changing the sign of their weight so as to make it positive. The resulting weights are real numbers in $]0, 1]$, but can be easily translated into integers (if needed) as follows:
  1. determine the number n of decimal digits to consider as a satisfactory precision (this can be the maximum number of decimal digits among all weights, if no weights with infinite decimal digits are present);
  2. multiply all weights times 10^n and take the integer part of the result:

$$\forall(\alpha, \beta) \in \hat{\mathcal{R}} : w'_{\hat{\mathcal{R}}} = \lfloor w_{\hat{\mathcal{R}}} \cdot 10^n \rfloor$$

  3. apply the same transformation to the justification threshold associated with the framework, if any:

$$\theta' = \lfloor \theta \cdot 10^n \rfloor$$

BAF $\langle \mathcal{A}, \hat{\mathcal{R}}_{att}, \hat{\mathcal{R}}_{sup} \rangle$ with
$\quad \hat{\mathcal{R}}_{att} = \{(\alpha, \beta) \in \mathcal{A} \times \mathcal{A} \mid w_{\hat{\mathcal{R}}}(\alpha, \beta) < 0\}$ and
$\quad \hat{\mathcal{R}}_{sup} = \{(\alpha, \beta) \in \mathcal{A} \times \mathcal{A} \mid w_{\hat{\mathcal{R}}}(\alpha, \beta) > 0\}$
by reporting in the BAF all pairs of arguments related with negative weight as attacks, and all those related with positive weight as supports.
AF $\langle \mathcal{A}, \hat{\mathcal{R}} \rangle$ with
$\quad \hat{\mathcal{R}} = \{(\alpha, \beta) \in \mathcal{A} \times \mathcal{A} \mid w_{\hat{\mathcal{R}}}(\alpha, \beta) > 0\} \subseteq \mathcal{A} \times \mathcal{A}$
by reporting in the AF only the attacks associated to pairs of arguments related with negative weight.

4   Sample Extensions of GAFs

To fully exploit the extended expressive power of GAFs, the contextual component $\mathcal{S}$ and its role in determining $w_{\mathcal{A}}$ and $w_{\mathcal{R}}$ must be defined. In particular, $\mathcal{S}$ must be preliminarily defined, since it is also used in the definition of $w_{\mathcal{A}}$. While the knowledge engineer is totally free in defining such component, in the following we propose some definitions for contextual components that capture a selection of proposals available in the literature.

4.1   Adding User and Topic Information

It is sensible to expect the interrelations existing in the community in which the argumentation takes place, and the topic about which the claims are made, to almost always significantly affect the evaluation of arguments. In this line of thought, we propose here a way to express in $\mathcal{S}$ some fundamental features that would probably be relevant to most practical cases of argumentation: community and topics. Consistently with our aim for generality, our proposal will still be very general and abstract, so that different exploitations will be possible for it. To model these features, we define *Trust-aware GAFs* (T-GAFs for short), that introduce these first two components in $\mathcal{S}$:

$\mathcal{U}$ the finite set of members of the community, possibly including the entities who put forward the arguments, and

$\mathcal{T}$ a finite set of topics that may be involved in an argumentation.

For practical purposes, we propose to consider $\mathcal{T}$ as always including an additional dummy topic $\top$ associated to the general authority and trust of a user, independent of specific topics. So, formally, $\mathcal{T} = \overline{\mathcal{T}} \cup \{\top\}$, where $\overline{\mathcal{T}}$ is the set of specific topics that may be involved in an argumentation.

Now, based on $\mathcal{U}$ and $\mathcal{T}$, additional components to be used in $w_{\mathcal{A}}$ and $w_{\mathcal{R}}$ can be defined, as well. Possible features connected to the assessment of the reliability of arguments are:

1. the subjective *confidence* that the members of the community (including the entity which posits the argument) have in an argument; specifically, the confidence of the entity which posits the argument can be handled differently from the confidence that all other members of the community have in that argument;
2. the subjective *confidence* that the members of the community have in a relationship between two arguments;
3. the recognized *authority* degree of the entity putting forward an argument on the topic of the argument[3];
4. the *trust* that the community of entities involved in the argumentation have in the entity putting forward an argument, relative to the topic of the argument (indeed, not just the quality of evidence, but also the credibility of the entity positing it is important).

---

[3] E.g., the education or skill level of the user on that topic —opinions of experts in a topic are typically more convincing than those of novices or outsiders of the topic.

While (3) expresses the degree of expertise of an entity about a topic (e.g., medicine), (1) expresses the degree of confidence of entities in a community about a specific claim, (2) expresses the degree of confidence of entities in a community about a specific attack or support, and (4) the degree of confidence by which a community member's opinions about a topic are taken into consideration by other members.

Example 1. Suppose that Joe, a MD, posits the argument $\alpha =$ "I am *quite confident* that by fall 2021 at least 80% of European population will get vaccinated against COVID-19 disease", we may consider:

- via (1), a degree of uncertainty expressed by Joe himself about the validity of the argument, in the phrase "quite confident" (which might be translated into an entity's confidence degree on that argument of 0.7), and different degrees of confidence of the various members of the community with respect to that claim (some will more or less agree with Joe, some will more or less disagree);
- via (3), a degree of authority of Joe about medicine (let's say it's 0.8, since Joe is a MD); and
- via (4), a degree of trust of the community in Joe as a doctor (many people might consider him not a very good doctor).

Suppose also that argument $\beta =$ "40% of European population is skeptical about vaccines" is in the given framework. Clearly, β attacks α, and:

- via (2), we may express the degrees of confidence of the various members of the community with respect to this attack (some might partially disagree, considering that the possibility of alleviating the serious consequences of the disease will prevail over normal skepticism).

The 4 features above are formalized by the following functions:

1. $w_c : \mathcal{U} \times \mathcal{A} \mapsto [0,1]$ where 1 means certainty, according to the classical probabilistic interpretation.
2. $w_r : \mathcal{U} \times \mathcal{A} \times \mathcal{A} \mapsto [0,1]$ where 1 means certainty, according to the classical probabilistic interpretation.
3. $w_a : \mathcal{U} \times \mathcal{T} \mapsto [0,1]$ where 1 means maximum authority of the user in the topic, and 0 absolutely no authority.
4. $w_t : \mathcal{U} \times \mathcal{T} \mapsto [-1,1]$ where -1 means total distrust, 0 means no opinion, and 1 means full trust.

Functions 1, 2 and 3 might be defined extensionally, by directly associating a value to each input n-tuple based on the available information. E.g., features 1 and 2 are quite subjective, and their values might be obtained by asking the single members of the community; feature 3 might be assessed based on the formal certifications owned by the arguer about the given topic (e.g., BSc, MS, PhD, etc.). Feature 4 is more complex, because it must be based on a formal model of trust that might involve many direct and indirect trust evaluations between the members of the community. A possible graph-based formal model of trust, proposed in [14], is based on the following definition:

Definition 9 (Community Trust Graph). *Given community $\mathcal{U}$, a Community Trust Graph (or CTG) for $\mathcal{U}$ is a complete directed weighted graph $G = \langle \mathcal{U}, \mathcal{E}, w_\mathcal{E} \rangle$ where:*

- *$\mathcal{U}$ is the set of members in the community,*
- *$\mathcal{E} = \mathcal{U} \times \mathcal{U}$ is the complete set of edges,*
- *$w_\mathcal{E} : \mathcal{E} \mapsto [-1, +1]$ is a function that, given two members $u_1, u_2 \in \mathcal{U}$, expresses the trust $w_\mathcal{E}(u_1, u_2)$ that member u_1 has for member u_2 (where -1 means total distrust, 0 means no opinion, and 1 means full trust).*

Like for the GAF definition, we consider a complete graph for the sake of formalization simplicity and for allowing a more straightforward translation of the graph into matrix representation. Again, for practical purposes, edges having 0 weight can be ignored and removed from the graphical representation. Using a $[-1, +1]$ range for trust provides the same computational advantages as in the case of GAF. Indeed, the sign rule can again be leveraged to handle the fact that, if u distrusts v and in turn v distrusts s, then this might be taken as a hint that u might somehow trust s.

Given a community $\mathcal{U}$, and a CTG G for $\mathcal{U}$, the overall trust for each member of $\mathcal{U}$ according to G, possibly based on the direct and indirect trust information expressed by G, can be determined by evaluating a function, say $t(u, G)$. For compliance with $w_\mathcal{E}$, this function might range in $[-1, +1]$ as well.

So, a T-GAF includes a CTG for each topic $T \in \mathcal{T}$ (let us call it G^T), and assessing the trust of a user u for T corresponds to computing

$$w_t(u, T) = t(u, G_T) \in [-1, +1]$$

Example 2. Given the set $\mathcal{T}_\alpha$ of topics associated to an argument α posited by user u, the trust of the community in u positing α might be computed as the average trust of the community in u for the topics associated to α, plus the generic trust represented by the dummy topic $\top$:

$$w_t(u, \alpha) = \frac{1}{|\mathcal{T}_\alpha| + 1} \cdot \sum_{T \in \mathcal{T}_\alpha \cup \top} w_t(u, T) \in [-1, +1]$$

Finally, given specific definitions for functions w_c, w_r, w_a and w_t (for the various topics), they can be combined in $w_\mathcal{A}$ (to obtain an overall assessment of the 'intrinsic' reliability of an argument in the GAF) and in $w_\mathcal{R}$ (to determine the strength of attacks and supports as a result of contextual information).

Example 3. As a possible practical application of T-GAFs, let us show how they can express the T-BWAF proposed in [14]. Consider an argument α, posited by user u and concerning topic T. Then, we define

$$w_\mathcal{A}(\alpha) = \beta \cdot w_c(u, \alpha) \cdot \max(\min_{v \neq u} w_\mathcal{E}^T(v, u), w_a(u)) + (1 - \beta) \cdot ca(\alpha)$$

where $\beta \in [0, 1]$ and the following notational correspondence was applied:

- $w_c(u, \alpha)$, called the 'User Argument Confidence' in [14]
- $\max(\min_{v \neq u}\{w_{\mathcal{E}}^T(v, u)\}, w_a(u_\alpha))$, called the 'Authority Degree' in [14], and also based on the Trust Users Graph as in GAFs, where

$$t(u, G^T) = \min_{v \neq u}\{w_{\mathcal{E}}^T(v, u)\}$$

- $w_{\mathcal{A}}(\alpha)$, called the 'Argument Strength' in [14]
- $ca(\alpha)$, called the 'Crowd's Agreement' of the community in [14], is implemented, following [9], as the Simple Vote Aggregation function:

$$ca(\alpha) = \begin{cases} 0 & \text{if } V^+(\alpha) = V^-(\alpha) = 0 \\ \frac{V^+(\alpha)}{V^+(\alpha) + V^-(\alpha)} & \text{otherwise} \end{cases}$$

where $V^+(\alpha)$ and $V^-(\alpha)$ denote, respectively, the number of positive and negative votes for argument $\alpha \in \mathcal{A}$. In the T-GAF model, they can be expressed in terms of w_c as follows:

- $V^+(\alpha) = |\{u \in \mathcal{U} \mid w_c(u, \alpha) > 0\}|$
- $V^-(\alpha) = |\{u \in \mathcal{U} \mid w_c(u, \alpha) < 0\}|$

4.2 Expressing Evidence and Necessity

We now show how evidential and necessary support can be expressed in GAFs. Let us call these frameworks *Evidence-based GAFS* (E-GAFs for short) and *Necessity-based GAFS* (N-GAFs for short), respectively. Given an EAS $\langle \mathcal{A}, \hat{\mathcal{R}}, \hat{\mathcal{E}} \rangle$, (resp., an AFN $\langle \mathcal{A}, \hat{\mathcal{R}}, \hat{\mathcal{N}} \rangle$), we define the E-GAF (resp., N-GAF) $\langle \mathcal{A}, \mathcal{S}, w_{\mathcal{A}}, w_{\mathcal{R}} \rangle$ where

$$\forall \alpha, \beta \in \mathcal{A} : w_{\mathcal{R}}(\alpha, \beta) = \begin{cases} -1 \text{ if } & (\alpha, \beta) \in \hat{\mathcal{R}} \\ +1 \text{ if } & (\alpha, \beta) \in \hat{\mathcal{E}}(\text{resp., } \hat{\mathcal{N}}) \\ 0 & \text{otherwise} \end{cases}$$

and the context $\mathcal{S}$ includes a 'parallel' GAF $G = \langle \mathcal{A}, \{\bot\}, w'_{\mathcal{A}}, w'_{\mathcal{R}} \rangle$ where no contextual information is used, and:

$$\forall \alpha, \beta \in \mathcal{A} : w'_{\mathcal{R}}(\alpha, \beta) = \begin{cases} 1 \text{ if } w_{\mathcal{R}}(\alpha, \beta) > 0 \\ 0 \text{ otherwise} \end{cases}$$

I.e., G is the subgraph of the original framework including only supports, all with full weight.

Now, in the E-GAF, $w'_{\mathcal{A}} = \mathbb{1}$ assigns 1 to all arguments $\alpha \in \mathcal{A}$ (all arguments are in principle acceptable ones), and the tracing back of an argument $\alpha \in \mathcal{A}$ to η can be expressed as the requirement that there exist some path in G for which η g-supports α. Indeed, for any sequence of arguments (path in G) $\langle \eta, \ldots, \alpha \rangle$, the product of weights of arcs in the path will be 0 if it includes at least one arc with weight 0 in the E-GAF (i.e., a pair for which no attack nor support is set in the EAS) or one attack. Intuitively, these arcs would 'break' the sequence of supports tracing back α to η in the EAS. So, to be sure that there is at least one path of supports tracing back α to η, it suffices that the sum of all possible such paths is greater than 0. This can be formalized by defining function $e : \mathcal{A} \to \{0,1\}$ in the context as follows:

$$\forall \alpha \in \mathcal{A} : e(\alpha) = \sum_{\langle \eta = x_0, \ldots, x_n = \alpha \rangle \in \mathcal{P}_G(\eta, \alpha)} \prod_{i=1,\ldots,n} w'_{\mathcal{R}}(x_{i-1}, x_i)$$

where $\mathcal{P}_F(\alpha, \beta)$ is the set of all possible paths from α to β in the AF F. Note that for $\alpha = \eta$ (i.e., a singleton path with no arcs), the product would be empty and thus equal to 1 by definition, which would still satisfy the requirement.

As regards the N-GAF, we need to recognize arguments that do not receive any support. This can be obtained by defining function:

$$w'_{\mathcal{A}}(\alpha) = \begin{cases} 0 \text{ if } \sum_{x \in \mathcal{A}} w'_{\mathcal{R}}(x, \alpha) > 0 \\ 1 \text{ otherwise} \end{cases}$$

Indeed, for any $x \in \mathcal{A}$, its weight in G is 0 if it is not related to α or it attacks α, and 1 otherwise. So, the sum will be greater than zero only if there is at least one support to α. This information can be used in a formula, based on the notion of g-support just like for E-GAFs, to determine whether a path starts from a non-supported argument:

$$\forall \alpha \in \mathcal{A} : e(\alpha) = \sum_{\langle x_0, \ldots, x_n = \alpha \rangle \in \mathcal{P}_G(\eta, \alpha)} w'_{\mathcal{A}}(x_0) \cdot \prod_{i=1,\ldots,n} w'_{\mathcal{R}}(x_{i-1}, x_i)$$

In this way, each element of the summation will be non-0 only if the first element of the sequence is unsupported, in which case its weight $w'_{\mathcal{A}}$ will be 1.

We may now go back to the E-GAF (resp., N-GAF) and complete its definition by defining its last component, so that arguments not allowed by the original EAS (resp., AFN) are inhibited:

$$w_{\mathcal{A}}(\alpha) = \begin{cases} 1 \text{ if } e(\alpha) > 0 \\ 0 \text{ otherwise} \end{cases}$$

that will assign reliability 0 to all arguments that cannot be traced back to η (resp., to an unsupported argument) through a path of supports in the EAS (resp., in the AFN). Of course, the above formulations for $e(\alpha)$ are just theoretical definitions to show that EASs and AFNs can be expressed as GAFs; in practice, enumeration of all possible paths in the graph should be avoided.

5   Matrix Representation and Examples

As in [15], we propose a matrix representation for GAFs. Indeed, in addition to providing a comfortable representation that is also consistent with intuition, matrices also provide an efficient computational tool for supporting many argument evaluation-related tasks, and may even suggest new semantics, especially

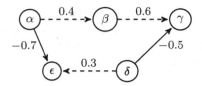

Fig. 2. Sample GAF G

in the extended framework where computations on argument and relationship weights are needed.

As regards the argument weights assigned by $w_{\mathcal{A}}$, they can be collected in a vector, indexed exactly like the argumentation matrix rows and columns, which allows their easy combination through standard matrix operators.

Definition 10. *Let* $F = \langle \mathcal{A}, \mathcal{S}, w_{\mathcal{A}}, w_{\mathcal{R}} \rangle$ *be a GAF with* $|\mathcal{A}| = n$. *Then, the* General Argumentation Matrix *of* F *is an* $n \times n$ *matrix* $\mathbf{M_F} = [m_{ij}]$ *such that*

$$\forall \alpha_i, \alpha_j \in \mathcal{A} : m_{ij} = w_{\mathcal{R}}(\alpha_i, \alpha_j)$$

The General Argumentation Vector *of* F *is a vector* $\mathbf{V_F} = [v_i]$ *of size* n *such that*

$$\forall \alpha_i \in \mathcal{A} : v_i = w_{\mathcal{A}}(\alpha_i)$$

Note that this representation for GAFs is even more straightforward than for BWAFs, since the 0 value for pairs of arguments having no relationship is explicit in the formalization of GAFs, while in BWAFs it must be handled as a default case.

Example 4. The GAF G in Fig. 2 has the following matrix representation:

$$
\mathbf{M_G} =
\begin{array}{c}
 \\
\alpha \\
\beta \\
\gamma \\
\delta \\
\epsilon
\end{array}
\begin{array}{c}
\begin{array}{ccccc}
\alpha & \beta & \gamma & \delta & \epsilon
\end{array} \\
\left[
\begin{array}{ccccc}
0 & 0.4 & 0 & 0 & -0.7 \\
0 & 0 & 0.6 & 0 & 0 \\
0 & 0 & 0 & 0 & 0 \\
0 & 0 & -0.5 & 0 & 0.3 \\
0 & 0 & 0 & 0 & 0
\end{array}
\right]
\end{array}
$$

In GAF G, the General Argumentation Vector would look like:

$$
\mathbf{V_G} =
\begin{array}{c}
\begin{array}{ccccc}
\alpha & \beta & \gamma & \delta & \epsilon
\end{array} \\
\left[
\begin{array}{ccccc}
w_\alpha & w_\beta & w_\gamma & w_\delta & w_\epsilon
\end{array}
\right]
\end{array}
$$

The GAF G is clearly also a BWAF. Ignoring the weights in G, we have a BAF B with the following GAF matrix representation:

$$
\mathbf{M_B} =
\begin{array}{c}
 \\
\alpha \\
\beta \\
\gamma \\
\delta \\
\epsilon
\end{array}
\begin{array}{c}
\begin{array}{ccccc}
\alpha & \beta & \gamma & \delta & \epsilon
\end{array} \\
\left[
\begin{array}{ccccc}
0 & 1 & 0 & 0 & -1 \\
0 & 0 & 1 & 0 & 0 \\
0 & 0 & 0 & 0 & 0 \\
0 & 0 & -1 & 0 & 1 \\
0 & 0 & 0 & 0 & 0
\end{array}
\right]
\end{array}
$$

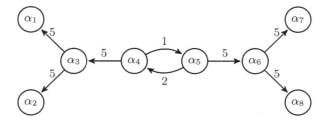

Fig. 3. Sample WAF W

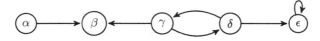

Fig. 4. Sample AF F

The GAF matrix representation for the WAF W in Fig. 3 is:

$$
M_W =
\begin{array}{c}
\\
\alpha_1 \\ \alpha_2 \\ \alpha_3 \\ \alpha_4 \\ \alpha_5 \\ \alpha_6 \\ \alpha_7 \\ \alpha_8
\end{array}
\begin{array}{cccccccc}
\alpha_1 & \alpha_2 & \alpha_3 & \alpha_4 & \alpha_5 & \alpha_6 & \alpha_7 & \alpha_8
\end{array}
\left[
\begin{array}{cccccccc}
0 & 0 & 0 & 0 & 0 & 0 & 0 & 0 \\
0 & 0 & 0 & 0 & 0 & 0 & 0 & 0 \\
-1 & -1 & 0 & 0 & 0 & 0 & 0 & 0 \\
0 & 0 & -1 & 0 & -0.2 & 0 & 0 & 0 \\
0 & 0 & 0 & -0.4 & 0 & -1 & 0 & 0 \\
0 & 0 & 0 & 0 & 0 & 0 & -1 & -1 \\
0 & 0 & 0 & 0 & 0 & 0 & 0 & 0 \\
0 & 0 & 0 & 0 & 0 & 0 & 0 & 0
\end{array}
\right]
$$

where weights were normalized with respect to $\max\limits_{\alpha,\beta \in \mathcal{A}} w_{\hat{\mathcal{R}}}(\alpha,\beta) = 5$.

Finally, the GAF matrix representation of the AF F in Fig. 4 is:

$$
M_F =
\begin{array}{c}
\\
\alpha \\ \beta \\ \gamma \\ \delta \\ \epsilon
\end{array}
\begin{array}{ccccc}
\alpha & \beta & \gamma & \delta & \epsilon
\end{array}
\left[
\begin{array}{ccccc}
0 & -1 & 0 & 0 & 0 \\
0 & 0 & 0 & 0 & 0 \\
0 & -1 & 0 & -1 & 0 \\
0 & 0 & -1 & 0 & -1 \\
0 & 0 & 0 & 0 & -1
\end{array}
\right]
$$

For the same reasons as for GAFs, we propose to use a similar matrix representation also for Community Trust Graphs:

Definition 11. *Let $G = \langle \mathcal{U}, \mathcal{E}, w_{\mathcal{E}} \rangle$ be a CTG with $|\mathcal{U}| = n$. Then, the Community Trust Matrix of G is an $n \times n$ matrix $M_G = [m_{ij}]$ such that*

$$
\forall u_i, u_j \in \mathcal{U} : m_{ij} = w_{\mathcal{E}}(u_i, u_j)
$$

Example 5. The graph for G in Fig. 2 can also be interpreted as a Community Trust Graph, where $\{\alpha, \beta, \gamma, \delta, \epsilon\}$ are the members in the community, solid edges denote negative trust between members, and dashed edges represent positive trust between members (and the weight represent the magnitude of the trust). Under this interpretation, matrix M_G in Example 4 would be the Community Trust Matrix.

6 Conclusion

The classical definition of Abstract Argumentation Frameworks considers only attacks between arguments, based on which different evaluation strategies ('semantics') have been proposed to identify the subsets of arguments that consistently support the same position in a dispute or debate ('extensions'), and possibly determine the winning position. However, in complex situations, additional information may be important to properly describe the debate and take better decisions. This led to the definition of extended frameworks, among which bipolar (considering also supports among arguments), and weighted ones (allowing to assign different importance to the attacks). Since most of these extended frameworks are disjoint, this paper proposed GAFs as a general model that encompasses all of them, and further extends them by allowing to express also contextual information. In particular, inspired by the literature, we have shown how contextual information concerning the argumentation community, and different requirements for supports, can be expressed in GAFs. We did not propose specific semantics for GAFs. However, since the previous models can be represented as GAFs, the semantics defined for the previous models can be also applied to GAFs. Moreover, new ones can be defined that exploit its extended expressiveness. Finally, we suggested that the definition of GAFs allows a straightforward matrix representation, that allows the use of matrix operations to improve efficiency in the evaluation of arguments, and perhaps to define new semantics.

In future work, we will investigate the definition of new semantics that can exploit the full expressive power of GAFs. We will also study the relationships of GAFs to other AFs proposed in the literature, and if and how they can be expressed as GAFs.

References

1. Amgoud, L., Ben-Naim, J.: Ranking-based semantics for argumentation frameworks. In: Liu, W., Subrahmanian, V.S., Wijsen, J. (eds.) SUM 2013. LNCS (LNAI), vol. 8078, pp. 134–147. Springer, Heidelberg (2013). https://doi.org/10.1007/978-3-642-40381-1_11
2. Amgoud, L., Ben-Naim, J.: Axiomatic foundations of acceptability semantics. In: Proceedings of the International Conference on Principles of Knowledge Representation and Reasoning, KR, vol. 16 (2016)

3. Amgoud, L., Cayrol, C.: A reasoning model based on the production of acceptable arguments. Ann. Math. Artif. Intell. **34**(1–3), 197–215 (2002). https://doi.org/10. 1023/A:1014490210693
4. Amgoud, L., Ben-Naim, J.: Weighted bipolar argumentation graphs: axioms and semantics. In: IJCAI 2018: Proceedings of the 27th International Joint Conference on Artificial Intelligence (2018)
5. Bench-Capon, T.J.M.: Persuasion in practical argument using value-based argumentation frameworks. J. Log. Comput. **13**(3), 429–448 (2003)
6. Cayrol, C., Lagasquie-Schiex, M.C.: On the acceptability of arguments in bipolar argumentation frameworks. In: Godo, L. (ed.) ECSQARU 2005. LNCS (LNAI), vol. 3571, pp. 378–389. Springer, Heidelberg (2005). https://doi.org/10.1007/ 11518655_33
7. Dung, P.M.: On the acceptability of arguments and its fundamental role in non-monotonic reasoning, logic programming and n-person games. Artif. Intell. **77**(2), 321–357 (1995)
8. Dunne, P.E., Hunter, A., McBurney, P., Parsons, S., Wooldridge, M.: Weighted argument systems: basic definitions, algorithms, and complexity results. Artif. Intell. **175**(2), 457–486 (2011)
9. Leite, J., Martins, J.: Social abstract argumentation. In: International Joint Conference on Artificial Intelligence, vol. 11, pp. 2287–2292 (2011)
10. Nouioua, F., Risch, V.: Argumentation frameworks with necessities. In: Benferhat, S., Grant, J. (eds.) SUM 2011. LNCS (LNAI), vol. 6929, pp. 163–176. Springer, Heidelberg (2011). https://doi.org/10.1007/978-3-642-23963-2_14
11. Oren, N., Norman, T.J.: Semantics for evidence-based argumentation. In: Computational Models of Argument, Frontiers in Artificial Intelligence and Applications, vol. 172, pp. 276–284 (2008)
12. Parsons, S., Tang, Y., Sklar, E., McBurney, P., Cai, K.: Argumentation-based reasoning in agents with varying degrees of trust. In: The 10th International Conference on Autonomous Agents and Multiagent Systems, vol. 2, pp. 879–886. International Foundation for Autonomous Agents and Multiagent Systems (2011)
13. Pazienza, A., Ferilli, S., Esposito, F.: Constructing and evaluating bipolar weighted argumentation frameworks for online debating systems. In: Proceedings of the 1st Workshop on Advances in Argumentation in Artificial Intelligence, AI^3 @ AI*IA 2017, pp. 111–125 (2017)
14. Pazienza, A., Ferilli, S., Esposito, F.: On the gradual acceptability of arguments in bipolar weighted argumentation frameworks with degrees of trust. In: Kryszkiewicz, M., Appice, A., Ślęzak, D., Rybinski, H., Skowron, A., Raś, Z.W. (eds.) ISMIS 2017. LNCS (LNAI), vol. 10352, pp. 195–204. Springer, Cham (2017). https://doi.org/10.1007/978-3-319-60438-1_20
15. Pazienza, A., Ferilli, S., Esposito, F.: Synthesis of argumentation graphs by matrix factorization. In: Proceedings of the 1st Workshop on Advances in Argumentation in Artificial Intelligence, AI^3 2017, pp. 1–6 (2017)
16. Polberg, S., Oren, N.: Revisiting support in abstract argumentation systems. In: Parsons, S., Oren, N., Reed, C., Cerutti, F. (eds.) Computational Models of Argument - Proceedings of the 5th International Conference on Computational Models of Argument (COMMA 2014). Frontiers in Artificial Intelligence and Applications, pp. 369–376. IOS Press (2014)
17. Toulmin, S.E.: The Uses of Argument. University Press (1958). https://books. google.it/books?id=WffWAAAAMAAJ

Towards an Implementation
of a Concurrent Language
for Argumentation

Stefano Bistarelli[1] and Carlo Taticchi[2(✉)]

[1] University of Perugia, Perugia, Italy
`stefano.bistarelli@unipg.it`
[2] Gran Sasso Science Institute, L'Aquila, Italy
`carlo.taticchi@gssi.it`

Abstract. While agent-based modelling languages naturally implement concurrency, the currently available languages for argumentation do not allow to explicitly model this type of interaction. In this paper we introduce a concurrent language for handling process arguing and communicating using a shared argumentation framework (reminding shared constraint store as in concurrent constraint). We introduce also basic expansions, contraction and revision procedures as main bricks for enforcement, debate, negotiation and persuasion.

Keywords: Argumentation Theory · Belief revision · Concurrency

1 Introduction

Many applications in the field of artificial intelligence aim to reproduce the human behaviour and reasoning in order to allow machines to think and act accordingly. One of the main challenges in this sense is to provide tools for expressing a certain kind of knowledge in a formal way so that the machines can use it for reasoning and infer new information. Argumentation Theory provides formal models for representing and evaluating arguments that interact with each other. Consider, for example, two people arguing about whether lowering taxes is good or not. The first person says that a) lowering taxes would increase productivity; the second person replies with b) a study showed that productivity decreases when taxes are lowered; then, the first person adds c) the study is not reliable since it uses data from unverified sources. The dialogue between the two people is conducted through three main arguments (a,b and c) whose internal structure can be represented through different formalisms [15,19], and for which we can identify the relations b attacks a and c attacks b. In this paper, we use

This work was developed within project "RACRA18 - Knowledge Representation and Automated Reasoning 2018", partially founded by Fondo Ricerca di Base 2018, University of Perugia, and project "Argumentation 360", partially founded by Fondo Ricerca di Base 2017, University of Perugia.

M. Baldoni and S. Bandini (Eds.): AIxIA 2020, LNAI 12414, pp. 154–171, 2021.
https://doi.org/10.1007/978-3-030-77091-4_10

the representation for Argumentation Frameworks introduced by Dung [11], in which arguments are abstract, that is their internal structure, as well as their origin, is left unspecified. Abstract Argumentation Frameworks (AFs), have been widely studied from the point of view of the acceptability of arguments and several authors have investigated the dynamics of AFs, taking into account both theoretical [6,17] and computational aspects (for example, a special track on dynamics appeared in the Third International Competition on Computational Models of Argumentation [4]).

Logical frameworks for argumentation, like the ones presented in [10,12], have been introduced to fulfil the operational tasks related to the study of dynamics in AFs, such as the description of AFs, the specification of modifications, and the search for sets of "good" arguments. Although some of these languages could be exploited to implement applications based on argumentation, for instance to model debates among political opponents, none of them consider the possibility of having concurrent interactions or agents arguing with each other. This lack represents a significant gap between the reasoning capacities of AFs and their possible use in real-life tools. As an example, consider the situation in which two debating agents share a knowledge base, represented by an AF, and both of them want to update it with new information, in such a way that the new beliefs are consistent with the previous ones. The agents can act independently and simultaneously. Similarly to what happens in concurrent programming, if no synchronization mechanism is taken into account, the result of update or revision can be unpredictable and can also lead to the introduction of inconsistencies.

Motivated by the above considerations, we introduce a concurrent language for argumentation (ConArg_Lang) that aims to be used also for modelling different types of interaction between agents (as negotiations, persuasion, deliberation and dialogues). In particular, our language allows for modelling concurrent processes, inspired by notions such as the *Ask-and-Tell constraint system* [18], and using AFs as centralised store. The language is thus endowed with primitives for the specification of interaction between agents through the fundamental operations of adding (or removing) and checking arguments and attacks. Besides specifying a logic for argument interaction, our language can model debating agents (e.g., chatbots) that take part in a conversation and provide arguments. Alchourrón, Gärdenfors, and Makinson (AGM) theory [1] gives operations (like expansion, contraction, revision) for updating and revising beliefs on a knowledge base. We propose a set of AGM-style operations that allow for modifying an AF (which constitutes the shared memory our agents access to communicate) and changing the status of its arguments so as to allow the implementation of more complex operations, like negotiation and the other forms of dialogues.

The rest of this paper, that extends [5], is structured as follows: in Sect. 2 we recall some notions from Argumentation Theory; in Sect. 3 we define a labelling semantics for AFs upon which the agents build their beliefs; in Sect. 4 we present the syntax and the operational semantics of our concurrent language, together with some high level operations that realize the interaction between agents; Sect. 5 describes how we implemented the language; in Sect. 6 we discuss existing formalisms from the literature that bring together argumentation and multiagent systems, highlighting the contact points and the differences with our work; Sect. 7 concludes the paper with final remarks and perspectives on future work.

2   Abstract Argumentation Frameworks

Argumentation is an interdisciplinary field that aims to understand and model the human natural fashion of reasoning. In Artificial Intelligence, argumentation theory allows one to deal with uncertainty in non-monotonic (defeasible) reasoning, and it is used to give a qualitative, logical evaluation to sets of interacting arguments, called extensions. In his seminal paper [11], Dung defines the building blocks of abstract argumentation: an Abstract Argumentation Framework is a pair $\langle Arg, R \rangle$ where $Arg \subseteq U$ is a set of arguments belonging to a "universe" U and R is a binary attack relation on Arg^1. AFs can be represented through directed graphs, that we depict using the standard conventions. For two arguments $a, b \in Arg$, $(a, b) \in R$ represents an attack directed from a against b. Moreover, we say that an argument b is *defended* by a set $B \subseteq Arg$ if and only if, for every argument $a \in Arg$, if $R(a, b)$ then there is some $c \in B$ such that $R(c, a)$.

The goal is to establish which are the acceptable arguments according to a certain semantics, namely a selection criterion. Non-accepted arguments are rejected. Different kinds of semantics have been introduced [2,11] that reflect qualities which are likely to be desirable for "good" subsets of arguments. In the rest of this paper, we will denote the extension-based semantics (also referred to as Dung semantics), namely admissible, complete, stable, preferred, and grounded, with their respective abbreviation *adm*, *com*, *stb*, *prf* and *gde*, and generically with σ. Besides enumerating the extensions for a certain semantics σ, one of the most common tasks performed on AFs is to decide whether an argument a is accepted in some extension of $S_\sigma(F)$ or in all extensions of $S_\sigma(F)$. In the former case, we say that a is *credulously* accepted with respect to σ; in the latter, a is instead *sceptically* accepted with respect to σ. The grounded semantics, in particular, coincides with the set of arguments sceptically accepted by the complete ones.

Many of the above-mentioned semantics (such as the admissible and the complete ones) exploit the notion of defence in order to decide whether an argument is part of an extension or not. The phenomenon for which an argument is accepted in some extension because it is defended by another argument belonging to that extension is known as *reinstatement* [7]. In that paper, Caminada also gives a definition for a reinstatement labelling, a total function that assigns a label to the arguments of an AF: an argument is labelled *in* if all its attackers are labelled *out*, and it is labelled *out* if at least an *in* node attacks it; in all

---

[1] We introduce both U and $Arg \subseteq U$ (not present in the original definition by Dung) for our convenience, since in the concurrent language that we will define in Sect. 4 we use an operator to dynamically add arguments from U to Arg.

other cases, the argument is labelled *undec*. A labelling-based semantics [2] associates with an AF a subset of all the possible labellings. Moreover, there exists a connection between reinstatement labellings and the Dung-style semantics: the set of *in* arguments in any reinstatement labelling constitutes a complete extension; then, if no argument is *undec*, the reinstatement labelling provides a stable extension; if the set of *in* arguments (or the set of *out* arguments) is maximal with respect to all the possible labellings, we obtain a preferred extension; finally the grounded extension is identified by labellings where either the set of *undec* arguments is maximal, or the set of *in* (respectively *out*) arguments is maximal.

3   A Four-State Labelling Semantics

When considering reinstatement labelling to inspect AFs, the information brought by the *undec* label can be misleading. The labelling by Caminada, indeed, does not allow to leave unlabelled arguments that we do not want to consider in computing acceptability, and forces all arguments that are neither *in* nor *out* to be labelled *undec*. Consequently, any reinstatement labelling corresponds to a complete extension and cannot identify conflict-free and admissible sets. This inconvenience can be solved using a four-state labelling which produces labellings as the one in Fig. 1, where the fact of *c* not being *in* or *undec* does not depend on the structure of the framework, but rather on the choice of just ignoring it.

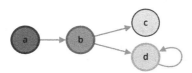

Fig. 1. Example of a four-state labelling where the label of argument *c* is $\emptyset$.

Even though the four-state labelling is more informative than the reinstatement labelling (that does not include an $\emptyset$ label), there is no direct connection between labellings and extensions of a certain semantics. To overcome this problem, we establish a mapping between the four-state labelling and the classical extension-based semantics (considering also admissible and conflict-free sets).

Definition 1 (Four-state labelling semantics). *Let U be a universe of arguments, $F = \langle Arg, R \rangle$ an AF with $Arg \subseteq U$ and $R \subseteq Arg \times Arg$ the arguments and attacks. L is a four-state labelling on F if and only if*

– $\forall a \in U \setminus Arg.L(a) = \emptyset$;
– $\forall a \in Arg$, *if $out \in L(a)$, then $\exists b \in Arg$ such that $(b,a) \in R$ and $in \in L(b)$;*
– $\forall a \in Arg$, *if $in \in L(a)$, then $\forall b \in Arg$ such that $(b,a) \in R$, $out \in L(b)$;*
– $\forall a \in Arg$, *if $in \in L(a)$, then $\forall c$ such that $(a,c) \in R$, $out \in L(c)$.*

Moreover,

- *L is a conflict-free labelling if and only if:*
  - $L(a) = \{in\} \implies \forall b \in Arg \mid (b,a) \in R.L(b) \neq \{in\}$ *and*
  - $L(a) = \{out\} \implies \exists b \in Arg \mid (b,a) \in R \wedge L(b) = \{in\}$
- *L is an admissible labelling if and only if:*
  - $L(a) = \{in\} \implies \forall b \in Arg \mid (b,a) \in R.L(b) = \{out\}$ *and*
  - $L(a) = \{out\} \implies \exists b \in Arg \mid (b,a) \in R \wedge L(b) = \{in\}$
- *L is a complete labelling if and only if:*
  - $L(a) = \{in\} \iff \forall b \in Arg \mid (b,a) \in R.L(b) = \{out\}$ *and*
  - $L(a) = \{out\} \iff \exists b \in Arg \mid (b,a) \in R \wedge L(b) = \{in\}$
- *L is a stable labelling if and only if:*
  - *L is a complete labelling and* $\nexists a \in Arg \mid L(a) = \{in, out\}$
- *L is a preferred labelling if and only if:*
  - *L is an admissible labelling and* $\{a \mid L(a) = \{in\}\}$ *is maximal among all the admissible labellings*
- *L is a grounded labelling if and only if:*
  - *L is a complete labelling and* $\{a \mid L(a) = \{in\}\}$ *is minimal among all the complete labellings*

Each different label can be traced to a particular meaning. $\emptyset$ stands for "don't care" [13] and identifies arguments that are not considered by the agents. For instance, arguments in $U \setminus Arg$, that are only part of the universe, but not of the shared AF, are labelled with $\emptyset$ since they are outside the interest of the agents. Accepted and rejected arguments (labelled as *in* and *out*, respectively), allow agents to discern true beliefs from the false ones. At last, *undec* arguments possess both *in* and *out* labels, meaning that agents cannot decide about the acceptability of a belief ("don't know", indeed).

We show that there is a correspondence between labellings satisfying the restrictions given in Definition 1 and the extensions of a certain semantics. We use the notation $L \in S_\sigma(F)$ to identify a labelling L corresponding to an extension of the semantics σ with respect to the AF F. An example is shown in Fig. 2.

Theorem 1. *A four-state labelling L of an AF $F = \langle Arg, R \rangle$ is a conflict-free (respectively admissible, complete, stable, preferred, grounded) labelling as in Definition 1 if and only if the set of arguments labelled in by L is a conflict-free (respectively admissible, complete, stable, preferred, grounded) extension of F.*

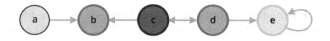

Fig. 2. Admissible labelling of an AF showed through colours. Argument c, highlighted in green, is the only *in*; red arguments b and d are *out*; the one in yellow, namely e, is *undec*; and the grey argument a are left with an empty label $\emptyset$. (Color figure online)

4   A Concurrent Argumentation Language

Agents/processes in a distributed/concurrent system can perform operations that affect the behaviour of other components. The indeterminacy in the execution order of the processes may lead to inconsistent results for the computation or even cause errors that prevent particular tasks from being completed. We refer to this kind of situation as a *race condition*. If not properly handled, race conditions can cause loss of information, resource starvation and deadlock. In order to understand the behaviour of agents and devise solutions that guarantee correct executions, many formalisms have been proposed for modelling concurrent systems. Concurrent Constraint Programming (CC) [18], in particular, relies on a constraint store of shared variables in which agents can read and write in accordance with some properties posed on the variables.

We replace the CC ask operation with three decisional operations: a syntactic *check* that verifies if a given set of arguments and attacks is contained in the knowledge base, and two semantic *test* operations that we use to retrieve information about the acceptability of arguments in an AF. The CC tell operation (that we call *add*) augments the store with additional arguments and attack relations. We can also remove parts of the knowledge base through a specifically designed removal operation. Finally, a guarded parallel composition $\|_G$ allows for executing all the operations that satisfy some given conditions, and a prioritised operator $+_P$ is used to implement if-then-else constructs. The syntax of our concurrent language for argumentation is presented in Table 1, while in Table 2 we give the definitions for the transition rules.

Table 1. CONARG_LANG syntax.

$$A ::= success \mid add(Arg, R) \rightarrow A \mid rmv(Arg, R) \rightarrow A \mid E \mid A\|A \mid \exists_x A$$
$$E ::= test_c(a, l, \sigma) \rightarrow A \mid test_s(a, l, \sigma) \rightarrow A \mid check(Arg, R) \rightarrow A \mid E + E \mid E +_P E \mid E\|_G E$$

Suppose to have an agent A whose knowledge base is represented by an AF $F = \langle Arg, R \rangle$. An $add(Arg', R')$ action performed by the agent results in the addition of a set of arguments $Arg' \subseteq U$ (where U is the universe) and a set of relations R' to the AF F. When performing an addition, (possibly) new arguments are taken from $U \setminus Arg$. We want to make clear that the tuple (Arg', R') is not an AF, indeed it is possible to have $Arg' = \emptyset$ and $R' \neq \emptyset$, which allows to perform an addition of only attack relations to the considered AF. It is as well possible to add only arguments to F, or both arguments and attacks. Intuitively, $rmv(Arg, R)$ allows to specify arguments and/or attacks to remove from the knowledge base. Removing an argument from an AF requires to also remove the attack relations involving that argument and trying to remove an argument (or an attack) which does not exist in F will have no consequences. The operation $check(Arg', R')$ is used to verify whether the specified arguments and attack

Table 2. CONARG_LANG operational semantics.

$$\langle add(Arg', R') \to A, \langle Arg, R \rangle \rangle \to \langle A, \langle Arg \cup Arg', R \cup R' \rangle \rangle \qquad \text{Addition}$$

$$\langle rmv(Arg', R') \to A, \langle Arg, R \rangle \rangle \to \langle A, \langle Arg \setminus Arg', R \setminus \{R' \cup R''\} \rangle \rangle$$
$$\text{where } R'' = \{(a, b) \in R \mid a \in Arg' \vee b \in Arg'\} \qquad \text{Removal}$$

$$\frac{Arg' \subseteq Arg \wedge R' \subseteq R}{\langle check(Arg', R') \to A, \langle Arg, R \rangle \rangle \to \langle A, \langle Arg, R \rangle \rangle} \qquad \text{Check}$$

$$\frac{\exists L \in S_\sigma(F) \mid l \in L(a)}{\langle test_c(a, l, \sigma) \to A, F \rangle \to \langle A, F \rangle} \qquad \frac{\forall L \in S_\sigma(F).l \in L(a)}{\langle test_s(a, l, \sigma) \to A, F \rangle \to \langle A, F \rangle} \qquad \begin{array}{c}\text{Credulous and} \\ \text{Sceptical Test}\end{array}$$

$$\frac{\langle A_1, F \rangle \to \langle A_1', F' \rangle}{\begin{array}{l}\langle A_1 \| A_2, F \rangle \to \langle A_1' \| A_2, F' \rangle \\ \langle A_2 \| A_1, F \rangle \to \langle A_2 \| A_1', F' \rangle\end{array}} \qquad \frac{\langle A_1, F \rangle \to \langle success, F' \rangle}{\begin{array}{l}\langle A_1 \| A_2, F \rangle \to \langle A_2, F' \rangle \\ \langle A_2 \| A_1, F \rangle \to \langle A_2, F' \rangle\end{array}} \qquad \text{Parallelism}$$

$$\frac{\langle E_1, F \rangle \to \langle A_1, F \rangle, \langle E_2, F \rangle \not\to}{\begin{array}{l}\langle E_1 \|_G E_2, F \rangle \to \langle A_1, F \rangle \\ \langle E_2 \|_G E_1, F \rangle \to \langle A_1, F \rangle\end{array}} \quad \frac{\langle E_1, F \rangle \to \langle A_1, F \rangle, \langle E_2, F \rangle \to \langle A_2, F \rangle}{\langle E_1 \|_G E_2, F \rangle \to \langle A_1 \| A_2, F \rangle} \qquad \begin{array}{c}\text{Guarded} \\ \text{Parallelism}\end{array}$$

$$\frac{\langle E_1, F \rangle \to \langle A_1, F \rangle}{\begin{array}{l}\langle E_1 + E_2, F \rangle \to \langle A_1, F \rangle \\ \langle E_2 + E_1, F \rangle \to \langle A_1, F \rangle\end{array}} \qquad \text{Nondeterminism}$$

$$\frac{\langle E_1, F \rangle \to \langle A_1, F \rangle}{\langle E_1 +_P E_2, F \rangle \to \langle E_1, F \rangle} \qquad \frac{\langle E_1, F \rangle \not\to, \langle E_2, F \rangle \to \langle A_2, F \rangle}{\langle E_1 +_P E_2, F \rangle \to \langle E_2, F \rangle} \qquad \text{If Then Else}$$

$$\frac{\langle A[y/x], F \rangle \to \langle A', F' \rangle}{\langle \exists_x A, F \rangle \to \langle A', F' \rangle} \text{ with } y \text{ fresh} \qquad \text{Hidden Variables}$$

relations are contained in the set of arguments and attacks of the knowledge base, without introducing any further change. If the check is positive, the operation succeeds, otherwise it suspends. We have two distinct test operations, both requiring the specification of an argument $a \in A$, a label $l \in \{in, out, undec, \emptyset\}$ and a semantics $\sigma \in \{adm, com, stb, prf, gde\}$. The credulous $test_c(a, l, \sigma)$ succeeds if there exists at least an extension of $S_\sigma(F)$ whose corresponding labelling L is such that $L(a) = l$; otherwise (in the case $L(a) \neq l$ in all labellings) it suspends. The sceptical $test_s(a, l, \sigma)$ succeeds[2] if a is labelled l in all possible labellings $L \in S_\sigma(F)$; otherwise (in the case $L(a) \neq L$ in some labellings) it suspends. The guarded parallelism $\|_G$ is designed to execute all the operations for which the guard in the inner expression is satisfied. More in detail, $E_1 \|_G E_2$ is successful when either E_1, E_2 or both are successful and all the operations that can be executed are executed. This behaviour is different both from classical

---

[2] Since the set of extensions $S_\sigma(F)$ is finite, $test_c(a, l, \sigma)$ and $test_s(a, l, \sigma)$ are decidable.

parallelism (for which all the agents have to terminate in order for the procedure to succeed) and from nondeterminism (that only selects one branch). The operator $+_P$ is left-associative and realises an if-then-else construct: if we have $E_1 +_P E_2$ and E_1 is successful, than E_1 will be always chosen over E_2, even if also E_2 is successful, so in order for E_2 to be selected, it has to be the only one that succeeds. Differently from nondeterminism, $+_P$ prioritises the execution of a branch when both E_1 and E_2 can be executed. Moreover, an if-then-else construct cannot be obtained starting from nondeterminism since of our language is not expressive enough to capture success or failure conditions of each branch.

The remaining operators are classical concurrency compositions: an agent in a parallel composition obtained through $\|$ succeeds if all the agents succeed; any agent composed through $+$ is chosen if its guards succeeds; the existential quantifier $\exists_x A$ behaves like agent A where variables in x are local to A. The parallel composition operator enables the specification of complex concurrent argumentation processes. For example, a debate involving many agents that asynchronously provide arguments can be modelled as a parallel composition of *add* operations performed on the knowledge base.

Example 1. Consider the AF in Fig. 3 (left), where the complete semantics is the set $\{\{a\}, \{a, e\}, \{a, d\}\}$ and the preferred coincides with $\{\{a, d\}, \{a, e\}\}$. An agent A in parallel with agent B wants to perform the following operation: if argument d is labelled *out* in all complete extensions, then remove the argument c from the knowledge base. At the same time, an agent B wants to add an argument f attacking d only if e is labelled *in* in some preferred extension. If A is the first agent to be executed, the sceptical test on argument d will suspend, since d belongs to the complete extension $\{a, d\}$. The credulous test performed by agent B, instead, is successful and so it can proceed to add an argument f that defeats d. Now d is sceptically rejected by the complete semantics and agent A can finally remove the argument c. After the execution of the program in Table 3, we obtain the AF of Fig. 3 (right).

Table 3. Example of a **ConArg_lang** program.

$$A : test_s(d, out, com) \rightarrow rmv(\{c\}, \{(a, c)\}) \rightarrow success$$
$$B : test_c(e, in, prf) \rightarrow add(\{f\}, \{(f, d)\}) \rightarrow success$$

4.1   Semantics of Failure

The language we presented in the previous section only allows two possible outcomes as result of an operation: it can either succeed, taking the execution to the next step, or suspend. Hence, it may happen that if the right conditions are not satisfied, some processes can get stuck in an endless wait. To solve the issue

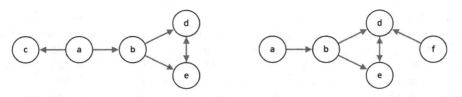

Fig. 3. The AF on the right is obtained from the one on the left trough the addition of an argument f attacking d and the removal of c together with the attack (a, c).

of termination, we introduce a distinction between the expressions that can be written using CONARG_LANG syntax: E^w represents an expression which suspends in the case the condition on its head is not satisfied; E^f can either succeed of fail, but never suspends. We then identify two further categories of operations for checking and testing the knowledge base, one allowing failure and the other which blocks the execution, namely $check^f(Arg', R')$, $test_c^f(Arg', R')$, $test_s^f(Arg', R')$ and $check^w(Arg', R')$, $test_c^w(Arg', R')$, $test_s^w(Arg', R')$, respectively. The revised syntax appears as shown below in Table 4.

Table 4. CONARG_LANG syntax for expressions with failure and wait.

$$E ::= E^w \mid E^f \mid E^f +_P E$$
$$E^w ::= test_c^w(a, l, \sigma) \rightarrow A \mid test_s^w(a, l, \sigma) \rightarrow A \mid check^w(Arg, R) \rightarrow A \mid E^w + E^w$$
$$E^f ::= test_c^f(a, l, \sigma) \rightarrow A \mid test_s^f(a, l, \sigma) \rightarrow A \mid check^f(Arg, R) \rightarrow A \mid E^f \|_G E^f \mid failure$$

We change the CONARG_LANG operational semantics accordingly (see Table 5), establishing the cases in which the expressions produce a failure or a suspension of the program (while the conditions for succeeding remains the same). Allowing expressions to fail, the program can continue the execution even if some of the operation does not succeeds. The $check^w(Arg, R)$ operation suspends when Arg and R are not part of the knowledge base, while $check^f(Arg, R)$ fails. When testing the acceptability of arguments, the $test_c^w(a, l, \sigma)$ and $test_s^w(a, l, \sigma)$ operations suspend in case of a negative response, while $test_c^f(a, l, \sigma)$ and $test_s^f(a, l, \sigma)$ fail. Parallelism and guarded parallelism are also affected by the introduction of failure. The parallel composition of two actions can result in three possible behaviours: it succeeds when both actions succeed, suspends when at least one action suspends and fail in the remaining case (i.e., when both actions fails). The guarded parallelism executes all branches which satisfy the given condition, and succeeds if at leas one expression succeeds. On the other hand, it fails if all the expressions fail. Since only the composition of expressions that can fail are allowed in a guarded parallelism, it cannot suspend under any circumstances. As we will see in the next session, we aim to use the operators of our language to model the behaviour of agents involved in particular argumentative processes (such as persuasion and negotiation). Note that the language is very permissive: there are no constraints on which arguments or attacks an agent can add/remove.

Table 5. CONARG_LANG operational semantics with failure and wait.

$$\frac{Arg' \subseteq Arg \wedge R' \subseteq R}{\langle check^*(Arg', R') \to A, \langle Arg, R\rangle\rangle \longrightarrow \langle A, \langle Arg, R\rangle\rangle} \qquad \text{Check (1)}$$

$$\frac{Arg' \not\subseteq Arg \vee R' \not\subseteq R}{\langle check^f(Arg', R') \to A, \langle Arg, R\rangle\rangle \longrightarrow failure} \qquad \text{Check (2)}$$

$$\frac{\exists L \in S_\sigma(F) \mid l \in L(a)}{\langle test_c^*(a, l, \sigma) \to A, F\rangle \longrightarrow \langle A, F\rangle} \quad \frac{\forall L \in S_\sigma(F). l \notin L(a)}{\langle test_c^f(a, l, \sigma) \to A, F\rangle \longrightarrow failure} \qquad \text{Credulous Test}$$

$$\frac{\forall L \in S_\sigma(F). l \in L(a)}{\langle test_s^*(a, l, \sigma) \to A, F\rangle \longrightarrow \langle A, F\rangle} \quad \frac{\exists L \in S_\sigma(F) \mid l \notin L(a)}{\langle test_s^f(a, l, \sigma) \to A, F\rangle \longrightarrow failure} \qquad \text{Sceptical Test}$$

$$\frac{\langle A_1, F\rangle \longrightarrow \langle A_1', F'\rangle}{\begin{array}{l}\langle A_1 \| A_2, F\rangle \longrightarrow \langle A_1' \| A_2, F'\rangle \\ \langle A_2 \| A_1, F\rangle \longrightarrow \langle A_2 \| A_1', F'\rangle\end{array}} \quad \frac{\langle A_1, F\rangle \longrightarrow \langle success, F'\rangle}{\begin{array}{l}\langle A_1 \| A_2, F\rangle \longrightarrow \langle A_2, F'\rangle \\ \langle A_2 \| A_1, F\rangle \longrightarrow \langle A_2, F'\rangle\end{array}} \qquad \text{Parallelism (1)}$$

$$\frac{\langle A_1, F\rangle \longrightarrow failure}{\begin{array}{l}\langle A_1 \| A_2, F\rangle \longrightarrow failure \\ \langle A_2 \| A_1, F\rangle \longrightarrow failure\end{array}} \qquad \text{Parallelism (2)}$$

$$\frac{\langle E_1, F\rangle \longrightarrow \langle A_1, F\rangle, \langle E_2, F\rangle \longrightarrow failure}{\begin{array}{l}\langle E_1 \|_G E_2, F\rangle \longrightarrow \langle A_1, F\rangle \\ \langle E_2 \|_G E_1, F\rangle \longrightarrow \langle A_1, F\rangle\end{array}} \qquad \text{Guarded Parallelism (1)}$$

$$\frac{\langle E_1, F\rangle \longrightarrow \langle A_1, F\rangle, \langle E_2, F\rangle \longrightarrow \langle A_2, F\rangle}{\langle E_1 \|_G E_2, F\rangle \longrightarrow \langle A_1 \| A_2, F\rangle} \qquad \text{Guarded Parallelism (2)}$$

$$\frac{\langle E_1, F\rangle \longrightarrow \langle A_1, F\rangle}{\langle E_1 +_P E_2, F\rangle \longrightarrow \langle E_1, F\rangle} \qquad \text{If Then Else (1)}$$

$$\frac{\langle E_1, F\rangle \longrightarrow failure, \langle E_2, F\rangle \longrightarrow \langle A_2, F\rangle}{\langle E_1 +_P E_2, F\rangle \longrightarrow \langle E_2, F\rangle} \qquad \text{If Then Else (2)}$$

4.2 Belief Revision and the AGM Framework

The AGM framework [1] provides an approach to the problem of revising knowledge bases by using theories (deductively closed sets of formulae) to represent the beliefs of the agents. A formula α in a given theory can have different statuses for an agent, according to its knowledge base K. If the agent can deduce α from its beliefs, then we say that α is *accepted* ($K \vdash \alpha$). Such a deduction corresponds with the entailment of α by the knowledge base. If the agent can deduce the negation of α, then we say that α is *rejected* $(K \vdash \neg\alpha)$. Otherwise, the agent cannot deduce anything and α is *undetermined*.

The correspondence between accepted/rejected beliefs and *in/out* arguments in a labelling (as depicted in Fig. 4) is straightforward. Since the undetermined status represents the absence of a piece of information (nothing can be deduced in favour of either accepting or rejecting a belief), it can be mapped into the empty label $\emptyset$. Finally, the *undec* label is assigned to arguments that are both *in* and *out*, boiling down to the notion of inconsistency in AGM. The empty label, in particular, plays a fundamental role in identifying new arguments that agents can bring to the debate to defend (or strengthen) their position. The status of a belief can be changed through some operations (namely expansion $\oplus$, contraction $\oslash$ and revision $\circledast$) on the knowledge base.

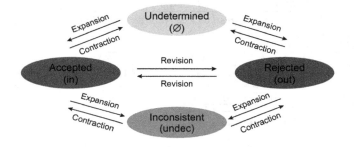

Fig. 4. Transitions between AGM beliefs states.

An expansion brings new pieces of information to the base, allowing for undetermined belief to become either accepted or refused. A contraction, on the contrary, reduces the information an agent can rely on in making its deduction, and an accepted (or refused) belief can become undetermined. A revision introduces conflicting information, making acceptable belief refused and vice-versa. Negotiation, that aims to solve conflicts arising from the interaction between two or more parties with different individual goals, could be implemented through expansion operations, modelling the behaviour of an agent presenting claims towards its counterparts, and contraction, representing the act of retracting a condition to successfully conclude the negotiation. Inconsistent beliefs in a debate can be made accepted through a contraction, while expansion can make beliefs which state is undetermined acceptable. Agents involved in persuasive dialogue games have to elaborate strategies for supporting their beliefs and defeating the adversaries. Again, revision operations on the knowledge base can change the status of the beliefs of a persuaded agent.

As for knowledge bases in belief revision, AFs can undergo changes that modify the structure of the framework itself, either integrating new information (and so increasing the arguments and the attacks in the AF) or discarding previously available knowledge. Agents using AFs as the mean for exchanging and inferring information have to rely on operations able to modify such AFs. Besides considering the mere structural changes, also modifications on the semantics level need to be addressed by the operations performed by the agents. In the following, we define three operators for AFs, namely *argument expansion, contraction* and *revision*, that comply with classical operators of AGM and that can be built as procedures in our language.

The argumentation frameworks $\langle Arg, R \rangle$ we use as the knowledge base for our concurrent agents are endowed with a universe of arguments U that are used to bring new information. Since arguments in $U \setminus Arg$ do not constitute an actual part of the knowledge base, they are always labelled $\emptyset$, until they are added into the framework and acquire an *in* and/or an *out* label. Notice also that changes to the knowledge base we are interested in modelling are restricted to a single argument at a time, miming the typical argument interaction in dynamic AF.

Definition 2 (Argument extension expansion, contraction, revision).
Let $F = \langle Arg, R \rangle$ be an AF on the universe U, $Arg \subseteq U$, $R \subseteq Arg \times Arg$, σ a semantics, $L \in S_\sigma(F)$ a given labelling, and $a \in U$ an argument.

- *An argument extension expansion $\oplus_{a,L}^{\sigma} : AF \to AF$ computes a new AF $F' = \oplus_{a,L}^{\sigma}(F)$ with semantics $S_\sigma(F')$ for which $\exists L' \in S_\sigma(F')$ such that $L'(a) \supseteq L(a)$ (if $L'(a) \supset L(a)$ the expansion is strict).*
- *An argument extension contraction $\oslash_{a,L}^{\sigma} : AF \to AF$ computes a new AF $F' = \oslash_{a,L}^{\sigma}(F)$ with semantics $S_\sigma(F')$ for which $\exists L' \in S_\sigma(F')$ such that $L(a) \supseteq L'(a)$ (if $L(a) \supset L'(a)$ the expansion is strict).*
- *An argument extension revision $\circledast_{a,L}^{\sigma} : AF \to AF$ computes a new AF $F' = \circledast_{a,L}^{\sigma}(F)$ with semantics $S_\sigma(F')$ for which $\exists L' \in S_\sigma(F')$ such that if $L(a) = in/out$, then $L'(a) = out/in$ and $\forall b \in Arg$ with $b \neq a$, $L'(b) = L(b) \lor L'(b) \neq undec$ (that is no inconsistencies are introduced).*

Moreover, we denote with $\oplus_{a,L}^{\sigma,l}(F)$, $\oslash_{a,L}^{\sigma,l}(F)$ and $\circledast_{a,L}^{\sigma,l}(F)$ an argument extension expansion, contraction and revision, respectively, that computes an AF F' with semantics $S_\sigma(F')$ for which $\exists L' \in S_\sigma(F')$ such that $L'(a) = l$.

The above Definition 2 can be extended by considering operations which only affect one labelling $L \in S_\sigma(F)$ and leave the rest unchanged. We call an operation of this kind *argument semantics expansion, contraction* or *revision*. Also note that the *add* operation may lead to a contraction, reducing the number of arguments with the labels *in* and/or *out*. Similarly, the removal of an argument may lead to an expansion.

AGM operators have already been studied from the point of view of their implementation in work as [3,9]. However, in the previous literature, realisability of extensions and not of single arguments is considered. The implementation of an argument expansion/contraction/revision operator changes according to the semantics we take into account. In the following, we consider the grounded semantics and show how the operators of Definitions 2 can be implemented. Notice that there exist many ways to obtain expansion, contraction and revision. We chose one that leverage between minimality with respect to the changes required in the framework and simplicity of implementation.

Proposition 1. *Let $F = \langle Arg, R \rangle$ be an AF on the universe U, $Arg \subseteq U$, $R \subseteq Arg \times Arg$, $a \in U$ an argument, and L the unique grounded labelling. A possible argument extension expansion $\oplus_{a,L}^{gde,l}(F)$ could act as:*

- *if $L(a) = \emptyset$ and $l = in$, add a to Arg*
- *if $L(a) = \emptyset$ and $l = out$,*
    - *if $\exists b \in Arg \mid L(b) = in$, add $\langle \{a\}, \{(b,a)\} \rangle$ to F*
    - *otherwise, add $\langle \{a,b\}, \{(b,a)\} \rangle$ to F*
- *if $L(a) = in$ and $l = undec$,*
    - *if $\exists b \in Arg \mid L(b) = undec$, add (b,a) to R*
    - *otherwise, add (a,a) to R*
- *if $L(a) = out$ and $l = undec$,*
    - *$\forall b \in Arg \mid L(b) = \{in\} \wedge (b,a) \in R$, add (a,b) to R*

Proposition 2. *Let $F = \langle Arg, R \rangle$ be an AF on the universe U, $Arg \subseteq U$, $R \subseteq Arg \times Arg$, $a \in U$ an argument, and L the unique grounded labelling. A possible argument extension contraction $\oslash_{a,L}^{gde,l}(F)$ could act as:*

- *if $L(a) = undec$ and $l = in$, $\forall b \in Arg \mid L(b) = undec$, remove (b,a) from R*
- *if $L(a) = undec$ and $l = out$,*
    - *if $\exists b \in Arg \mid L(b) = in$, add (b,a) to R*
    - *otherwise, add $\langle \{b\}, \{(b,a)\} \rangle$ to F*
- *if $L(a) = in$ and $l = \emptyset$, remove a (and all attacks involving a) from F*
- *if $L(a) = out$ and $l = \emptyset$, remove a (and all attacks involving a) from F*

Proposition 3. *Let $F = \langle Arg, R \rangle$ be an AF on the universe U, $Arg \subseteq U$, $R \subseteq Arg \times Arg$, $a \in U$ an argument, and L the unique grounded labelling. A possible argument extension revision $\circledast_{a,L}^{gde,l}(F)$ could act as:*

- *if $L(a) = in$,*
    - *if $\exists b \in Arg \mid L(b) = in$, add (b,a) to R*
    - *otherwise, add $\langle \{b\}, \{(b,a)\} \rangle$ to F*
    - *then $\forall c \in Arg \mid (a,c) \in R$, add (b,c) to R*
- *if $L(a) = out$, $\forall b \in Arg \mid L(b) \in \{in, undec\}$, remove (b,a) from R and then $\forall c \in Arg \mid (a,c) \in R \wedge L(c) \in \{in, undec\}$, remove (a,c) from R*

Note that the argument extension revision we propose for grounded semantics in Proposition 3 is more restrictive than necessary, since ensure that all the arguments different from a (that is the argument to be revised) maintain the exact same labels, while Definition 2 only forbids to change the label to *undec*. The three introduced operators can be implemented in our language.

Proposition 4. *The argument extension expansion, contraction and revision in Propositions 1, 2 and 3, respectively, can be implemented in* CONARG_LANG.

As an example, an expansion operator is shown in Table 6. In devising operations of Definitions 2, that allow agents for changing the labels of arguments in a shared knowledge base with respect to a given semantics, we reinterpret AGM operators for expansion, contraction and revision. Nonetheless, we maintain similarities with the AGM theory, to the point that we can highlight some similarities with the original postulates of [1] that characterise rational operators performing expansion, contraction and revision of beliefs in a knowledge base. Consider for instance an argument a of an AF F and a semantics σ. An argument semantics expansion $\oplus_a^\sigma$ produces as output an AF F' for which no labelling $L' \in S_\sigma(F')$ is such that a has less labels in L' than in any labelling L of F (i.e., the number of labels assigned to a either remains the same or increases after the expansion).

Table 6. Argument extension expansion operator (Proposition 1) in CONARG_LANG syntax where $test_c(a, S, \sigma) \to A$ is syntactic sugar for $\sum_{l \in S}(test_c(a, l, \sigma))$.

$$\oplus_{a,L}^{gde,in}(F) : add(\{a\}, \{\}) \to success$$
$$(L(a)=\emptyset)$$

$$\oplus_{a,L}^{gde,out}(F) : \sum_{b \in Arg}(test_c(b, in, gde) \to add(\{a\}, \{(b, a)\})) \to success$$
$$(L(a)=\emptyset)$$

$$+_P add(\{a, u\}, \{(u, a)\}) \to success$$

$$\oplus_{a,L}^{gde,undec}(F) : \sum_{b \in Arg}(test_c(b, undec, gde) \to add(\{\}, \{(b, a)\})) \to success$$
$$(L(a)=in)$$

$$+_P add(\{\}, \{(a, a)\}) \to success$$

$$\oplus_{a,L}^{gde,undec}(F) : \parallel_G (test_c(b, in, gde) \wedge check(\{\}, \{(b, a)\})$$
$$(L(a)=out) \quad b \in Arg$$

$$\to add(\{\}, \{(a, b)\})) \to success$$

5   Implementation

We develop a working implementation for our language using python and ANTLR, a parser generator for reading, processing, executing, and translating structured text. We define our grammar using the syntax given in Table 1. Starting from the grammar, ANTLR automatically generates all the components we will use for parsing the language, the most remarkable being the list of used tokens, the interpreter containing names for literal and rules and symbolic names for the tokens, a lexer which recognises input symbols from a character stream, the parser itself (endowed with all the necessary support code) and the visitor class. Then, we need to manually override the default methods provided in the visitor to customise the behaviour of the parser. The visit of the parse tree always starts with the execution of the function *visitPrg*, which recursively visits all its children. Below, we provide details on the implementation of visiting functions.

- *visitPrg*: calls the visit on its children, collects the results and, in case of termination, returns the output of the whole program.
- *visitPar*: starts two separated threads to execute (visit) two actions in parallel, returning true if both succeeds, false if at least one action fails, and suspends if an action is waiting for its guard to become true.
- *visitAdd* and *visitRmv*: modify the AF by either adding or removing part of the AF, respectively. Always succeeds and continues on the children. Note that *visitRmv* succeeds also if the specified arguments and/or attacks are not in the AF. In that case, the AF is left unchanged.
- *visitSuc* and *visitFlr*: correspond to visits to terminal nodes and return true (success) and false (failure), respectively.
- *visitNdt*: implements a concatenation of + operators, inspecting the guards of all its children and randomly selecting a branch to execute among the possible ones. A guard can be a waiting check or either of the waiting tests. If no guards are found with satisfiable conditions, *visitNdt* waits for changes in the AF until some child can be executed.
- *visitGpa*: implements a concatenation of $\|_G$ operators and execute all its children in separated threads. Contrary to *visitNdt*, *visitGpa* only works with expressions that can fail (and do not suspend), thus allowing for two possible outcomes, that is success if at least one expression succeeds, and failure if all expressions fail.
- *visitIte*: behaves like an if-then-else construct. The first child must be an expression with guaranteed termination (either success or failure). The children are executed in the same order in which they are specified and, as soon as a satisfiable guard is found, the corresponding branch is executed. Since some child can be a waiting expression, *visitIte* is not guaranteed to terminate.
- *visitCkw* and *visitCkf*: check if a given set of arguments and/or attacks is present in the knowledge base. In case of success, both nodes visit the consequent action. On the other hand, when the knowledge base does not contain the specified parts of AF, *visitCkw* waits for the condition to become true, while *visitCkf* immediately returns false and leads to branch failure.
- *visitTcw*, *visitTcf*, *visitTsw* and *visitTsf*: call a solver[3] to execute credulous and sceptical tests on the acceptability of a given set of arguments. As with the checks, the test functions are also available in two versions, one that always terminates (with either a success or a failure) and the other that possibly suspends and waits for the condition to become true.

In addition to the visiting functions, we have a set of core functions responsible for managing auxiliary tasks, like starting new threads when a parallel composition is detected, making changes to the shared AF and computing the semantics for the test operations. All the components are put together in the *Main* class, which takes in input and runs the user-defined program. First of

---

[3] ConArg website: http://www.dmi.unipg.it/conarg/.

all, the input stream is passed to the lexer, which extracts the tokens and sends them to the parser. Then, the parser uses the tokens to generate a tree ready to be traversed. Finally, the visitor walks the tree and executes the program.

6   Related Work

A formalism for expressing dynamics in AFs is defined in [17] as a *Dynamic Argumentation Framework* (DAF). The aim of that paper is to provide a method for instantiating Dung-style AFs by considering a universal set of arguments U. The introduced approach allows for generalising AFs, adding the possibility of modelling changes, but, contrary to our study, it does not consider how such modifications affect the semantics and does not allow to model the behaviour of concurrent agents.

The impact of modifications on an AF in terms of sets of extensions is studied in [8]. Different kinds of revision are introduced, in which a new argument interacts with an already existing one. All these revisions are obtained through the addition of a single argument, together with a single attack relation either towards or from the original AF, and can be implemented as procedures of our language. The review operator we define in the syntax of our language (as the other two operator for expansion and contraction), instead, does not consider whole extensions, but just an argument at a time, allowing communicating agents to modify their beliefs in a finer grain.

Focusing on syntactic expansion of an AF (the mere addition of arguments and attacks), [3] show under which conditions a set of arguments can be enforced (to become accepted) for a specific semantics. The notion of expansion we use in the presented work is very different from that in [3]. First of all, we take into account semantics when defining the expansion, making it more similar to an enforcement itself: we can increment the labels of an argument so to match a desired acceptance status. Then, our expansion results to be more general, being able to change the status of a certain argument not only to accepted, but also rejected, undecided or undetermined. This is useful, for instance, when we want to diminish the beliefs of an opponent agent.

7   Conclusion and Future Work

We introduced a concurrent language for argumentation, that can be used by (intelligent) agents to implement different forms of communications. The agents involved in the process share an abstract argumentation framework that serves as a knowledge base and where arguments represent the agreed beliefs. In order to take into account the justification status of such beliefs (which can be accepted, rejected, undetermined and inconsistent) we considered a four-state labelling semantics. Besides operations at a syntactic level, thus, we also defined semantic operations that verify the acceptability of the arguments in the store. Finally, to allow agents for realising more complex forms of communication (like negotiation and persuasion), we presented three AGM-style operators, namely of expansion, contraction and revision, that change the status of a belief to a desired one; we also showed how to implement them in our language.

For the future, we plan to extend this work in many directions. First of all, given the known issues of abstract argumentation [16], we want to consider structured AFs and provide an implementation for our expansion, contraction and revision operators, for which a different store (structured and not abstract, indeed) need to be considered. The concurrent primitives are already general enough and do not require substantial changes.

As a final consideration, whereas in real-life cases it is always clear which part involved in a debate is stating a particular argument, AFs do not hold any notion of "ownership" for arguments or attacks, that is, any bond with the one making the assertion is lost. To overcome this problem, we want to implement the possibility of attaching labels on (groups of) arguments and attacks of AFs, in order to preserve the information related to whom added a certain argument or attack, extending and taking into account the work in [14]. Consequently, we can also obtain a notion of locality (or scope) of the belief in the knowledge base: arguments owned by a given agents can be placed into a local store and used in the implementation of specific operators through hidden variables.

References

1. Alchourrón, C.E., Gärdenfors, P., Makinson, D.: On the logic of theory change: partial meet contraction and revision functions. J. Symbolic Logic **50**(02), 510–530 (1985)
2. Baroni, P., Caminada, M., Giacomin, M.: An introduction to argumentation semantics. Knowl. Eng. Rev. **26**(4), 365–410 (2011)
3. Baumann, R., Brewka, G.: Expanding argumentation frameworks: enforcing and monotonicity results. In: Baroni, P., Cerutti, F., Giacomin, M., Simari, G.R. (eds.) Computational Models of Argument: Proceedings of COMMA 2010, Desenzano del Garda, Italy, 8–10 September 2010. Frontiers in Artificial Intelligence and Applications, vol. 216, pp. 75–86. IOS Press (2010)
4. Bistarelli, S., Kotthoff, L., Santini, F., Taticchi, C.: A first overview of ICCMA'19. In: Fazzinga, B., Furfaro, F., Parisi, F. (eds.) Proceedings of the Workshop on Advances In Argumentation In Artificial Intelligence 2020 co-located with the 19th International Conference of the Italian Association for Artificial Intelligence (AIxIA 2020), Online, 25–26 November 2020. CEUR Workshop Proceedings, vol. 2777, pp. 90–102. CEUR-WS.org (2020)
5. Bistarelli, S., Taticchi, C.: A concurrent language for argumentation. In: Fazzinga, B., Furfaro, F., Parisi, F. (eds.) Proceedings of the Workshop on Advances In Argumentation In Artificial Intelligence 2020 co-located with the 19th International Conference of the Italian Association for Artificial Intelligence (AIxIA 2020), Online, 25–26 November 2020. CEUR Workshop Proceedings, vol. 2777, pp. 75–89. CEUR-WS.org (2020)
6. Boella, G., Kaci, S., van der Torre, L.: Dynamics in argumentation with single extensions: attack refinement and the grounded extension (extended version). In: McBurney, P., Rahwan, I., Parsons, S., Maudet, N. (eds.) ArgMAS 2009. LNCS (LNAI), vol. 6057, pp. 150–159. Springer, Heidelberg (2010). https://doi.org/10.1007/978-3-642-12805-9_9

7. Caminada, M.: On the issue of reinstatement in argumentation. In: Fisher, M., van der Hoek, W., Konev, B., Lisitsa, A. (eds.) JELIA 2006. LNCS (LNAI), vol. 4160, pp. 111–123. Springer, Heidelberg (2006). https://doi.org/10.1007/11853886_11

8. Cayrol, C., de Saint-Cyr, F.D., Lagasquie-Schiex, M.C.: Revision of an argumentation system. In: Principles of Knowledge Representation and Reasoning: Proceedings of the Eleventh International Conference, KR 2008, Sydney, Australia, 16–19 September 2008, pp. 124–134. AAAI Press (2008)

9. Coste-Marquis, S., Konieczny, S., Mailly, J., Marquis, P.: Extension enforcement in abstract argumentation as an optimization problem. In: Yang, Q., Wooldridge, M.J. (eds.) Proceedings of the Twenty-Fourth International Joint Conference on Artificial Intelligence, IJCAI 2015, Buenos Aires, Argentina, 25–31 July 2015, pp. 2876–2882. AAAI Press (2015)

10. Doutre, S., Herzig, A., Perrussel, L.: A dynamic logic framework for abstract argumentation. In: Principles of Knowledge Representation and Reasoning: Proceedings of the Fourteenth International Conference, KR 2014, Vienna, Austria, 20–24 July 2014 (2014)

11. Dung, P.M.: On the acceptability of arguments and its fundamental role in non-monotonic reasoning, logic programming and n-person games. Artif. Intell. **77**(2), 321–357 (1995)

12. Dupin de Saint-Cyr, F., Bisquert, P., Cayrol, C., Lagasquie-Schiex, M.C.: Argumentation update in YALLA (Yet Another Logic Language for Argumentation). Int. J. Approx. Reason. 75, 57–92 (2016)

13. Jakobovits, H., Vermeir, D.: Robust semantics for argumentation frameworks. J. Log. Comput. **9**(2), 215–261 (1999)

14. Maudet, N., Parsons, S., Rahwan, I.: Argumentation in multi-agent systems: context and recent developments. In: Maudet, N., Parsons, S., Rahwan, I. (eds.) ArgMAS 2006. LNCS (LNAI), vol. 4766, pp. 1–16. Springer, Heidelberg (2007). https://doi.org/10.1007/978-3-540-75526-5_1

15. Prakken, H.: An abstract framework for argumentation with structured arguments. Argument Comput. **1**(2), 93–124 (2010)

16. Prakken, H., Winter, M.D.: Abstraction in argumentation: necessary but dangerous. In: Modgil, S., Budzynska, K., Lawrence, J. (eds.) Computational Models of Argument - Proceedings of COMMA 2018, Warsaw, Poland, 12–14 September 2018. Frontiers in Artificial Intelligence and Applications, vol. 305, pp. 85–96. IOS Press (2018)

17. Rotstein, N.D., Moguillansky, M.O., Garcia, A.J., Simari, G.R.: An abstract argumentation framework for handling dynamics. In: Proceedings of the Argument, Dialogue and Decision Workshop in NMR 2008, Sydney, Australia, pp. 131–139 (2008)

18. Saraswat, V.A., Rinard, M.: Concurrent constraint programming. In: Proceedings of the 17th ACM SIGPLAN-SIGACT Symposium on Principles of Programming Languages - POPL 1990, San Francisco, California, USA, pp. 232–245. ACM Press (1990)

19. Toni, F.: A tutorial on assumption-based argumentation. Argument Comput. **5**(1), 89–117 (2014)

Planning and Scheduling

A Fault-Tolerant Automated Flight Path Planning System for an Ultralight Aircraft

Belén Santos León[1,2], Jane Jean Kiam[2(✉)], and Axel Schulte[2]

[1] Technical University of Munich, Munich, Germany
b.santos@tum.de
[2] Bundeswehr University Munich, Neubiberg, Germany
{jane.kiam,axel.schulte}@unibw.de

Abstract. The development and integration of fault-tolerant systems has considerably increased flight safety over the years. One of the research areas that has made this improvement possible is the development of more advanced flight guidance systems, that are able to compute feasible flight trajectories in an automated manner, even under non-nominal conditions. However, such highly automated systems are normally not available for low-cost ultralight aircraft, which are usually piloted by non-professional pilots, who may not react properly under adverse circumstances. In this paper, we propose a model-based flight path planning system that uses an automated AI planner. By leveraging the flexibility of the AI planner to adapt to different planning problem models, we integrate "fault-tolerant" capabilities into the planning system. Therefore, optimal control parameters learned for various non-nominal flight conditions can be considered too. Finally, extension tests were performed under a selected number of scenarios to validate the feasibility of the plans.

Keywords: Flight path planning · Model-based planning · Fault-tolerant planning · Automated guidance system · 3D flight trajectory generation · PDDL+

1 Introduction

Motivated by safety reasons, the development of automation in aviation started in the second half of the 20th century. With the integration of the first autonomous systems, a significant descent of aviation accidents has been achieved since then [4]. This trend has exponentially increased in the recent years, and is typically driven by the increasing number of unmanned aerial vehicles (UAVs), resulting in sophisticated automated flight systems capable of maneuvering autonomously the aircraft or assisting manned aviation in routine tasks or in emergency situations [20]. However, such systems are still uncommon in ultralight aviation, which is usually practised by non-professional pilots who

© Springer Nature Switzerland AG 2021
M. Baldoni and S. Bandini (Eds.): AIxIA 2020, LNAI 12414, pp. 175–190, 2021.
https://doi.org/10.1007/978-3-030-77091-4_11

are more prone to committing errors while flying, resulting in numerous accidents every year [6]. Hence, such an automated flight guidance system for an ultralight aircraft can be life-saving.

In this paper, an automated Flight Path Planning (FPP) system to be integrated into the flight guidance system of a single-pilot ultralight platform is designed, implemented and analysed. Typically, the automated FPP is capable of computing feasible flight trajectories even under non-nominal circumstances. The FPP uses a PDDL+ (Planning Domain Definition Language) planner coupled with a knowledge base of sets of control parameters that are optimal for flight under non-nominal conditions learned using k-means clustering [14]. The planning problem model encoded in PDDL+ can be adapted according to flight conditions using these parameters. Note that the PDDL+ planning model is adapted from [11], and extended to include three-dimensional flight paths. By coupling the FPP with an autopilot module based on Proportional-Integral-Derivative (PID) control loops [1] and optimized with Particle Swarm Optimization (PSO) [9], the planned flight paths are studied for selected emergency scenarios and tested with the X-Plane flight simulator of the Aerolite 103 [15], in order to validate the fault-tolerant capabilities of the FPP.

1.1   Related Work

Most flight path planning techniques are based on geometric calculations [13,17], without considering the current internal causal parameters, e.g. dynamics of the aircraft, and external causal parameters, e.g. weather conditions. The planned paths can be feasible, if the incompleteness of the planning model can be compensated by the flight control system. However, this is often not the case, especially when 1) the aircraft is faulty and the current dynamics are not considered, or 2) the actual environment differs too substantially from the simplified environment considered in the FPP, resulting thereby in iterative replanning during plan execution [5].

PDDL+ planners are designed for general AI planning [8], but as demonstrated for the first time in [11], PDDL+ can also model a flight path planning domain, which is itself, a kinodynamic path planning problem [7]. Being model-based by relying on the clean separation of the domain description and the problem instance, PDDL+ planners can be exploited to cope with different problem instances of the same system domain, which in our case is the flight path planning system domain for a fixed-wind aircraft, while each problem instance encodes the precise description of the current planning scenario, even under non-nominal or failure conditions if a faulty model of the aircraft is properly defined and encoded in the system, allowing therefore to adapt to different planning problem models, e.g. the modified dynamics of a faulty aircraft.

1.2   System Description

Figure 1 provides overview of the system in which the FPP system developed in this work is integrated. The FPP system is integrated within the flight guidance

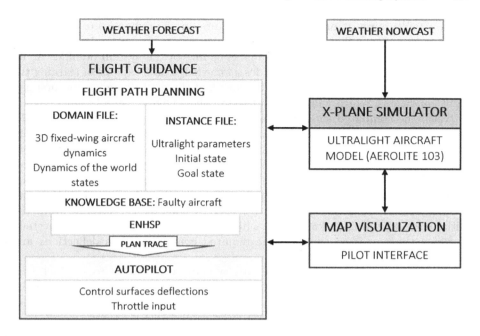

Fig. 1. System architecture

system, which receives weather forecast data, and interacts with the aircraft's model simulated using X-Plane, as well as with a visualization module acting as an interface between the flight guidance system and the pilot in the cockpit. Besides the FPP module, the flight guidance system also comprises an autopilot, which is designed hand-in-hand with the FPP module, so that the generated plans can be followed closely.

The FPP module is composed by a PDDL+ based domain-independent planner, namely Expressive Numeric Heuristic Search Planner (ENHSP) [19], which had been proven in several previous works [11,18] to be capable of coping with mixed discrete-continuous planning domains that include non-linear mathematical operations, such as trigonometric or exponential functions, necessary for describing the kinematics of the aircraft. The computed plan is a sequence of time-stamped actions $\pi = < (a_1, t_1), \cdots, (a_n, t_n) >$, where $a_i \in \mathcal{C}$ and $\mathcal{C}$ being the union of the sets of control parameters, i.e. $\mathcal{C}_{\dot{\chi}}$, $\mathcal{C}_{\dot{\theta}}$, and $\mathcal{C}_{\dot{v}}$, which denote respectively the set of discretized yaw rate, pitch rate and acceleration over the admissible ranges of each of these parameters.

Furthermore, planning problems with PDDL+ are modelled in two separate entities: the domain, which contains the innate properties of the system, and the problem instance, which contains the initialization of planning parameters, as well as the goals for the planning problem. This separation enables a model-based planning approach, which is exploited in this work for adapting the planning problem to different models of the aircraft, so that the modified dynamics of a faulty aircraft or the additional limits on the dynamics of the aircraft imposed by extreme flight conditions can be considered accordingly in the problem instance, while still using the same encoding of the system domain. As an extension of [18], this work also includes a knowledge base capable of learning the optimal parameters to describe the dynamics of the aircraft under non-nominal flight conditions, which will be considered in the PDDL+ formulation.

With the computed time-stamped actions in the plan, the kinematic model of the aircraft, as well as the given data on the environment (i.e. weather data such as wind field and cloud map), a plan trace, or rather a flight trajectory consisting of a sequence of waypoints $\pi_{WP} = < s_1, ..., s_P >$ can be computed, where s_p denotes the tuple containing a vector representing the position and attitude of the aircraft, a scalar representing the True Air Speed (TAS), and another representing the time instant, thereby guiding the aircraft from the initial state to the final state. π_{WP} will be processed by the autopilot system, of which the aim is to compute the required control surfaces deflections and throttle input to follow the plan.

Additionally, the system incorporates a map visualization tool, which acts as the interface between the flight guidance system and the pilot by displaying the aircraft's current position, the planned trajectory, weather data, as well as other relevant information such as system warnings, fuel level, etc.

2   Flight Path Planning System

The main goal of this work is to develop an FPP system capable of generating in an automated manner feasible flight trajectories for the targeted platform, i.e. an ultralight aircraft to operate under nominal, as well as non-nominal conditions. To cope with the latter, fault-tolerant capabilities are necessary. For feasibility, mixed discrete-continuous behaviour of the system, i.e. the internal, as well as the numerous external influence factors on the system performance, must be considered.

2.1   Flight Path Planning in PDDL+

We leverage the capabilities of PDDL+ to model the flight path planning problem. PDDL+ is an extension of PDDL, enabling additionally the modelling of hybrid domains, i.e. domains which include continuous and discrete behaviour [8]. In [18], the work presented in [11], and specifically the model of the planning problem on the generation of 2D trajectories for a High-Altitude Pseudo-Satellite (HAPS) was extended, to allow for the generation of 3D trajectories for an ultralight aircraft. Building on [18], this paper reports more in detail on the feasibility of the generated plans, as well as how the planning problem can be adapted using optimal sets of model parameters of the dynamics of the aircraft for planning under various non-nominal conditions, enabling thereby the FPP to be fault-tolerant.

As described in Sect. 1.2, a planning problem encoded in PDDL+ is separated into two files: the domain description and the problem instance description. The former describes the innate physical properties of the system, which in this case, is the flight kinematics of a fixed-wing aircraft. Under the assumption of spherical Earth and by considering the wind field, these can be expressed as follows:

$$\dot{\lambda}(t) = \frac{u_{\text{wind}}(t) + v_{\text{TAS}}(t) \cos \theta(t) \sin \chi(t)}{(R + h(t)) \cos \phi(t)}, \tag{1}$$

$$\dot{\phi}(t) = \frac{v_{\text{wind}}(t) + v_{\text{TAS}}(t) \cos \theta(t) \cos \chi(t)}{R + h(t)}, \tag{2}$$

$$\dot{h}(t) = w_{\text{wind}}(t) + v_{\text{TAS}}(t) \sin \theta(t), \tag{3}$$

where λ, ϕ, and h are the coordinates in WGS84 of the aircraft, namely the longitude, latitude and altitude, R is the Earth's mean radius, χ and θ are the yaw and pitch angles, v_{TAS} is the aircraft's True Air Speed, u_{wind}, v_{wind} are the wind components on the horizontal plane, i.e. the East and North components, and w_{wind} the vertical wind component directed perpendicularly upward formed by the East and North axes, using the right-hand rule. These first derivatives can be used, by performing stepwise integrations of Eqs. 1 to 3, to derive the position of the aircraft over time, which in PDDL+, are encoded as *processes*, as shown in Fig. 2a. Similarly, the TAS and attitude angles, yaw and pitch, are also updated by considering the stepwise integration of the control parameters $\dot{v}(t)$, $\dot{\chi}(t)$ and $\dot{\theta}(t)$, which are encoded as *actions* in PDDL+ (see Fig. 2b).

Furthermore, wind data is considered in the encoding of the kinematics of the aircraft and assigned with a discrete *event* according to the weather forecast (see Fig. 2c). Areas of high cloud coverage, which are considered no-go areas, are encoded as global constraints. Furthermore, global constraints can also be exploited to impose constraints on the numeric ranges admissible for the numeric model parameters of the aircraft (also known as "fluents"), as shown in Fig. 2d for the climb rate, acceleration and TAS.

2.2 Trajectory Planning Under Non-nominal Conditions

The instance file, on the other hand, defines the current model of 1) the dynamics of the aircraft, 2) the environment and 3) the desired goal state (see Fig. 3a) known at the initial time of the planning phase.

We exploit the capability of PDDL+ planners as a model-based planner. While the flight physics are encoded in the domain file, the type of fixed-wing aircraft is defined in the problem instance file. In this work, it can either be a fixed-wing ultralight aircraft operating under nominal conditions, or one operating under non-nominal conditions, requiring thereby a different set of parameters of the aircraft's dynamics to be encoded in the problem instance file. To this end, the control parameters (or actions in PDDL+) and other parameters are encoded to restrain the respective numeric ranges of the model parameters. An encoding example of this can be seen in Fig. 3b for the pitch and yaw rate, pitch angle,

```
(:process update_latitude
 :parameters (?aircraft -aircraft)
 :precondition ()
 :effect (and
         (increase (latitude ?aircraft)(* (/ (* #t (/ (+ (* (airspeed ?aircraft)
         (* (cos(pitch ?aircraft))(sin(yaw ?aircraft)))) (v_wind))(+ (R_earth)(altitude
         ?aircraft)))) 3.14159) 180.0))
))
```

(a) Process formulation to update the latitude of the ultralight aircraft

```
(:action increase_pitch_rate
 :parameters (?aircraft -aircraft)
 :precondition ()
 :effect (and
         (increase (pitch_rate ?aircraft) (delta_pitch_rate ?aircraft))
))
```

(b) Action formulation to increase the pitch rate of the ultralight aircraft

```
(:event assign_wind
 :parameters (?aircraft -aircraft ?wind_grid -wind_grid ?altitude_range -altitude_range)
 :precondition (and
               (>= (longitude ?aircraft) (long_west ?wind_grid))
               (< (longitude ?aircraft) (long_east ?wind_grid))
               (>= (latitude ?aircraft) (lat_south ?wind_grid))
               (< (latitude ?aircraft) (lat_north ?wind_grid))
               (>= (altitude ?aircraft) (alt_lower_bound ?altitude_range))
               (< (altitude ?aircraft) (alt_upper_bound ?altitude_range)))
 :effect (and
         (assign (u_wind) (u_wind ?wind_grid ?altitude_range))
         (assign (v_wind) (v_wind ?wind_grid ?altitude_range))
         (assign (w_wind) (w_wind ?wind_grid ?altitude_range))
))
```

(c) Event formulation to assign wind components at the current position of the ultralight aircraft

```
(:constraint speed_acceleration
 :parameters (?aircraft -aircraft)
 :condition (and
            (<= (climb_rate ?aircraft) (max_climb_rate ?aircraft))
            (>= (climb_rate ?aircraft) (min_climb_rate ?aircraft))
            (<= (acceleration ?aircraft) (max_acceleration ?aircraft))
            (>= (acceleration ?aircraft) (min_acceleration ?aircraft))
            (<= (airspeed ?aircraft) (max_airspeed ?aircraft))
            (>= (airspeed ?aircraft) (max_airspeed ?aircraft))
))
```

(d) Global constraint formulation to ensure that the climb rate, acceleration and TAS of the ultralight aircraft remain within the specified ranges

Fig. 2. Formulation in PDDL+ of the operators included in the domain file of the ultralight aircraft

TAS, acceleration and climb rate, which are then considered in the domain file as global constraints as shown in Fig. 2d.

In this work, we propose to exploit k-means clustering, a widely-use unsupervised learning method, to obtain the desired optimal numeric ranges of the model parameters. Algorithm 1 recapitulate and specify the steps we implemented for this purpose.

```
(:goal
    (and
        (>= (longitude aerolite) 11.75)
        (<= (longitude aerolite) 11.76)
        (>= (latitude aerolite) 48.88)
        (<= (latitude aerolite) 48.885)
        (>= (altitude aerolite) 1020)
        (<= (altitude aerolite) 1025)
        (>= (yaw aerolite) 0.31)
        (<= (yaw aerolite) 0.33)
    )
)
```

```
(:init
    ... ...
    (= (max_pitch_rate aerolite) 0.25)
    (= (min_pitch_rate aerolite) -0.25)
    (= (max_yaw_rate aerolite) 0.052)
    (= (min_yaw_rate aerolite) -0.052)
    (= (max_pitch aerolite) 0.35)
    (= (min_pitch aerolite) -0.35)
    (= (max_airspeed aerolite) 29)
    (= (min_airspeed aerolite) 13)
    (= (max_acceleration aerolite) 0.5)
    (= (min_acceleration aerolite) -0.5)
    (= (max_climb_rate aerolite) 3.3)
    (= (min_climb_rate aerolite) -2.0)
    ... ...
)
```

(a) Goal state definition in the instance file

(b) Assignment of admissible ranges for the variables in the instance file

Fig. 3. Snippets of the model encoding in the instance file formulation in PDDL+

The prerequisite is a set of training data stored in a matrix $\mathcal{R}$ of dimension $(I \times L)$, where each row x_i includes the data collected in a flight simulation and each column x_l denotes a feature relevant for the learning. Some of the features considered are time elapsed t_i, total distance covered d_i, fuel used $w_{\text{f},i}$, TAS $v_{\text{TAS},i}$, climb rate $\dot{h}_{\text{climb},i}$, wind speed $v_{\text{wind},i}$ or wind direction on the horizontal plane $\chi_{\text{wind},i}$, where i is the data collected from the i-th simulation. Since the measurements of these features are given in different units, it is necessary to scale them, so that they are equally weighted (see Line 3). This is computed using the mean m_{x_l} and the standard deviation σ_{x_l} of each feature x_l with the standard score formula suggested in [12].

Subsequently, from the features considered initially, the most relevant ones, i.e. features which collect more information about the data set, are extracted with Principal Component Analysis (PCA) (see Line 6), using the method described in [10]. PCA is a statistical method commonly used to transform data into a set of uncorrelated variables, namely principal components (PC). By projecting the data set into the new basis, the features with higher score on the PCs are extracted for clustering. Furthermore, since the correct number of clusters is pertinent to the quality of the clusters determined [22], we evaluate the Calinski Harabasz Criterion [3], as this criterion was empirically proven to be the most effective in determining the optimal number of clusters for our data set [21]. By maximizing the criterion (see Line 7), the optimal number of clusters k can be determined, i.e. $\text{argmax}_k = SS_B/SS_W \cdot (I - k)/(k - 1)$, where SS_B is the overall between-cluster variance, SS_W is the overall within-cluster variance. By maximizing the criterion, we ensure that the clusters be as dense (intra-cluster) and as separated (inter-cluster) as possible.

Finally, an improved version of the standard k-means algorithm [22] is implemented (see Lines 8 to 31). The algorithm is initiated with a random set of cluster centroids, i.e. $c_1, \cdots, c_k$ (see Line 9), followed by the assignment of each data point i to the closest centroid (see Line 15) to form the k clusters. Subsequently,

---

Algorithm 1. Preprocessing of training data and k-means clustering to learn optimal set of control parameters under non-nominal conditions

---

Require: Training data $\mathcal{R}$
1: **for all** $l \in L$ **do**
2:     **for all** $i \in I$ **do**
3:         scale the features with $\bar{x}_{i,l} = \frac{x_{i,l} - m_{x_l}}{\sigma_{x_l}}$
4:     **end for**
5: **end for**
6: determine $\tilde{\mathcal{R}}$, the training data with reduced dimensions using PCA
7: determine k, total number of clusters, using Calinski Harabasz Criterion
8: **for all** $r = 1$ to R **do**
9:     assign initial cluster centroids randomly $< c_1, \cdots, c_K > \in \tilde{\mathcal{R}}$
10:     $b_c = true$
11:     $iter = 1$
12:     **while** b_c **do**
13:         $< c_1, \cdots, c_K > = < c'_1, \cdots, c'_K >$
14:         **for all** $i \in I$ **do**
15:             assign the closest centroid to i-dataset $a_i = \arg\min_{c_k} \|(\bar{x}_i - c_k)\|_2$
16:         **end for**
17:         **for all** $k \in K$ **do**
18:             find v, the set of simulation index i where $a_i = k$
19:             $d_k = \Sigma_{i \in v}(\bar{x}_i - c_k)$
20:             $c'_k = d_k / |v|$
21:         **end for**
22:         $iter = iter + 1$
23:         **if** $< c'_1, \cdots, c'_K > == < c_1, \cdots, c_K >$ or $iter == max_{iter}$ **then**
24:             $b_c = false$
25:             $< c_{1,r}, \cdots, c_{K,r} > = < c'_1, \cdots, c'_K >$
26:             $< a_{1,r}, \cdots, a_{K,r} > = < a'_1, \cdots, a'_K >$
27:             $d_r = \Sigma_{k \in K}(d_k)$
28:         **end if**
29:     **end while**
30: **end for**
31: determine final centroids $c_k = c_{k,r_{best}}$ and dataset assignment $a_i = a_{i,r_{best}}$ with $r_{best} = \arg\min(d_r)$

---

the new centroid positions for each cluster are computed by evaluating the mean of the data points within the same cluster (see Lines 17 to 21). The assignment of data points and centroid calculation is repeated until termination conditions are met, i.e. maximum number of iterations achieved or centroids do not change with respect to the previous iteration (see Lines 23 to 28). Lines 9 to 29 are repeated R times with different initial assignment for the centroid positions. Finally, the best clustering is selected by evaluating the sum of the distances of each data point to its cluster centroid, and finding the replicate with the lowest total value (see Line 31).

With the clusters obtained, the optimal model parameters for various emergency situations, including faulty aircraft, can be derived. These model parameters will in return be considered in the problem instance definition similarly to the encoding shown in Fig. 3b.

3   System Validation and Results

In this section, the underlying fault-tolerant capabilities of the FPP are analysed for two scenarios conceptualized by considering possible non-nominal flight conditions. These are an emergency landing triggered by a critical fuel level and a flight with a broken wing. The computed trajectories and the performance of the flight guidance system are validated using X-Plane, which is a flight simulator that considers realistic flight physics. For the purpose of this work, we use specifically the Aerolite 103 ultralight simulator available in X-Plane.

Given the planning flexibility of PDDL+ planners, that is, the model of the aircraft can be adapted according to the detected anomalies, by considering different optimal model parameters learned using k-means clustering on the data sets collected for these non-nominal conditions, as described in Sect. 2.2. Although many PDDL+ planners are available, ENHSP is chosen; to the best of our knowledge, ENHSP is the only PDDL+ planner that supports non-linear operations, such as trigonometric and exponential operations necessary to describe flight kinematics. Furthermore, we set the greedy best-first search as search strategy, together with the Additive Interval-Based Relaxation (AIBR) heuristic, which are determined empirically to be the most efficient for our class of problem. Additionally, the search and validation time steps are both set to 1 s.

The obtained plan will be communicated to the autopilot (see Fig. 1), which commands, via a User Datagram Protocol (UDP) based communication link [2], the actuators of the aircraft simulated in X-Plane, e.g. throttle input, deflections of the control surfaces, etc. Note that the autopilot used in this work is PID-based [1], as the one previously reported in [18]. Improvements have been performed on the autopilot used in this work by optimizing the control gains using Particle Swarm Optimization (PSO) analysis, a population-based random-search algorithm [9], to achieve more robustness to cope with more challenging situations.

Additionally, historical weather data from the National Oceanic and Atmospheric Administration (NOAA) weather forecast [16] is used for the validation test. While weather forecast data is used in the FPP, nowcast data is used for the flight simulator, resulting thereby in some discrepancies with respect to the assumptions made on the weather situation at the planning phase and during the simulated flight.

3.1   Test Scenarios

As the FPP was already tested and validated under nominal flight conditions in [18], in this work, we focus on the validation test conducted under the consideration of non-nominal flights.

The first scenario (referred to as *Scenario 1* hereafter) entails an emergency landing triggered by low fuel level. The training data was generated by setting the fuel level of the aircraft prior to the emergency landing to 10% lower than the nominal necessary fuel consumption for landing. The landing is composed of two phases, first a horizontal flight to a goal position near the identified safe landing zone, followed by a descent to land (see Fig. 4a). In the initial set of training data, 20% of them ended up in a crash, exhibiting thereby the necessity of determining optimal model parameters on the aircraft dynamics for low-consumption manoeuvres, in order for the FPP to achieve a higher success rate in safe landing.

The second scenario (referred to as *Scenario 2* hereafter) entails flight with structural damage. In order to generate the training data, one of the wings of the ultralight was purposely set as a "broken wing" in the flight simulator. Furthermore, the topology of the scenario requires a horizontal and a climb phase be undertaken (to avoid an obstacle) before reaching a safe area to land (see Fig. 4b). Although the autopilot is able to cope with the flight plan (with a success rate of 97.5%), frequent oscillations were observed in the flight trajectories. It is intended in this scenario to validate the ability of the FPP in generating trajectories with less oscillations by using the learned optimal set of model parameters to describe the dynamics of the faulty aircraft (with a broken wing).

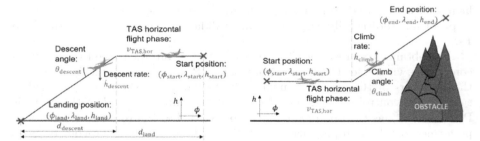

(a) Horizontal and descent phases of the emergency landing scenario   (b) Horizontal and climb phases of the broken wing scenario

Fig. 4. 2D illustration of the flight phases for the studied test scenarios

3.2   Test Results and Discussion

Scenario 1: Emergency Landing. The training data collected from 239 simulations for this scenario was processed according to Algorithm 1. Ten features were selected using PCA, these are time elapsed t, distance from the landing point to the desired landing position d_{land}, fuel used w_f, thrust T, lateral distance from landing position to start descent phase $d_{descent}$, descent rate $h_{descent}$, descent angle $\theta_{descent}$, TAS in horizontal flight $v_{TAS,hor}$, wind speed v_{wind} and wind direction χ_{wind}. Furthermore, the Calinski Harabasz Criterion indicated that six clusters are optimal for the k-means clustering.

Out of the six clusters obtained, three clusters of data sets have a higher overall success rates. Moreover, the wind direction features of these three clusters are distinct: tailwind, crosswind and headwind. Therefore, the numeric range of the optimal model parameters for less consuming landing manoeuvres, namely TAS for the horizontal phase $v_{TAS,hor}$, descent rate $\dot{h}_{descent}$ and descent angle $\theta_{descent}$ for the descent phase can be statistically devised from each of these three clusters, by considering the range $[\mu - \sigma; \mu + \sigma]$, where μ is the mean of the population of the cluster, and σ the standard deviation, as shown in Table 1.

Table 1. Optimal model parameters for a low-fuel landing

Wind direction	Horizontal TAS (m/s)	Descent rate (m/s)	Descent angle (rad)
Tailwind	[18.85, 20.66]	[−1.81, −3.08]	[−0.065, −0.104]
Crosswind	[19.6, 22.66]	[−1.24, −1.53]	[−0.055, −0.07]
Headwind	[21.06, 22.44]	[−1.05, −1.61]	[−0.061, −0.077]

The emergency landing is planned by calling ENHSP iteratively, once for planning for the horizontal flight leg to reach a position close to the landing zone within an admissible yaw angle, followed by the planning of the descent phase. While the range of the horizontal TAS is encoded in PDDL+ problem instance for the horizontal flight phase depending on the general wind situation (i.e. head-, tail-, or crosswind), the ranges for the descent rate and descent angle respectively are encoded for the descent phase. Note that there can be a discontinuity with respect to the descent rate between the plans generated for the horizontal flight and the decent phase. This can however be regulated by the flight control of the autopilot.

Using the learnt control parameters for the different flight phases leading to low-fuel landing, tests were performed to validate the feasibility of the plans generated by the FPP and evaluate the benefits of the approach. Figure 5 depicts the discrepancies between the planned trajectory and the simulated trajectory, by showing the lateral distance over time between the two trajectories, the difference in altitude over time, as well as the difference in TAS over time. It can be observed that the lateral distance between the planned and simulated trajectories tested under tailwind, crosswind and headwind (see Fig. 5a) remains insignificant and under 3 m for most part of the plan. At some instances, the lateral distance can exceed 10 m under tailwind, 8 m under crosswind and 5.5 m under headwind. However, this discrepancy is quickly compensated, therefore no behavior of divergence is observed. The discrepancy in altitude shown in Fig. 5b is minimal during horizontal flight and increases when the descent phase begins with the discrepancy being the most substantial under tailwind. This is expected since some delay is caused by the abrupt discontinuity in the control parameters at the transition from the plan generated for the horizontal flight to the plan generated for the descent phase. However, the discrepancy is again quickly regulated without further divergence. Relative to the airspeed of the aircraft, which is about 20 m/s, the discrepancy is considered minimal even in the worst scenario, which is with headwind and the maximum discrepancy is 0.5 m/s (see Fig. 5c). The analysis of the observed discrepancies between the planned and simulated trajectories show that the FPP system manages to generate plans that are feasible.

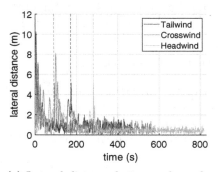 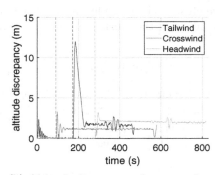

(a) Lateral distance between planned and simulated trajectories.

(b) Altitude discrepancy between planned and simulated trajectories.

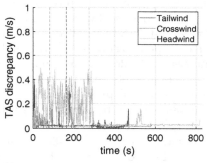

(c) TAS discrepancy between planner and simulated trajectories

Fig. 5. Discrepancies between the computed plans and the simulated results for the low-fuel landing scenario under the tailwind, crosswind and headwind.

Using a PDDL+ planner as a model-based planner to cope with different constraints on the aircraft model for low-consumption emergency landing has proven to be beneficial. Table 2 summarizes the success rate of safety landing without adapting the problem model and with the adaption of the problem model. By adapting to the problem model using the learned parameters in Table 1, the success rate increases significantly, especially for landing in the presence of crosswind and headwind. It is also interesting to observe that the success rate of safe landing in the presence of headwind is still significantly inferior to the case of tailwind and crosswind. This is expected since the fuel consumption for a landing in the presence of headwind is the highest in general, as the headwind reduces the ground speed of the aircraft, resulting in a longer duration for the overall trajectory.

Table 2. Success rate with and without optimal planning parameters

	Without optimal parameters	With optimal parameters	Increase
Tailwind	100%	100%	+0%
Crosswind	89%	98%	+9%
Headwind	63.5%	84%	+20.5%
Total	80.5%	93.5%	+13%

Based on the presented results, it is recommended to perform, if possible, a tailwind or crosswind landing in case of low fuel conditions, since these scenarios show higher success rate of the landing manoeuvre. However, landing with headwind is also feasible if proper landing variables, i.e. TAS in horizontal flight, descent angle and descent rate, are defined in the FPP as demonstrated in this section.

Scenario 2: Flight with a Broken Wing. Similar to Scenario 1, the training data collected from 499 simulations of a flight with a broken wing was processed using Algorithm 1. Nine features are extracted using PCA; these are time elapsed t, total distance covered d, fuel used w_f, thrust T, climb rate $\dot{h}_{climb}$, climb angle θ_{climb}, TAS in horizontal flight $v_{TAS,hor}$, wind speed v_{wind} and oscillation index σ_{osc}, defined as the standard deviation of the turn rate along the trajectory. The evaluation using Calinski Harabasz Criterion indicated that four clusters will provide the optimal clustering behavior.

From the clusters obtained using Algorithm 1, one exhibits a much lower oscillation index σ_{osc}. The optimal control parameters, i.e. TAS in horizontal flight $v_{TAS,hor}$, climb rate $\dot{h}_{climb}$ and climb angle θ_{climb}, are statistically devised by considering the same confidence interval as for Scenario 1, and are summarized in Table 3.

Table 3. Optimal model parameters for a flight with a broken wing

Horizontal Airspeed (m/s)	Climb rate (m/s)	Climb angle (rad)
[25.79, 27.92]	[1.45, 2.1]	[0.066, 0.098]

Flight plans generated for this scenario are also feasible, as evaluated from the discrepancies with respect to the parameters obtained from the planned and simulated trajectories. Furthermore, using the optimal control parameters derived from the clustering, the σ_{osc} was reduced. This is compared over a total flight time of 87 min, of which 44 min correspond to a horizontal flight phase and 43 min to climbing flight. It is observed that when executing plans generated by the FPP using optimal model parameters from Table 3, the desired oscillations are substantially decreased, i.e. by 17.4% in the horizontal flight, and by 18.8% during the climb, as shown in Table 4. An example of the oscillating behaviour observed while flying without optimal control parameters under broken wing conditions is depicted in Fig. 6 for a simple straight 2D trajectory.

Table 4. Comparison of the percentage of flight time with oscillation for two flight plans with and without optimal parameters

Flight phase	Without optimal parameters	With optimal parameters	Oscillation decrease
Horizontal	24%	6.6%	−17.4%
Climb	26.8%	8%	−18.8%

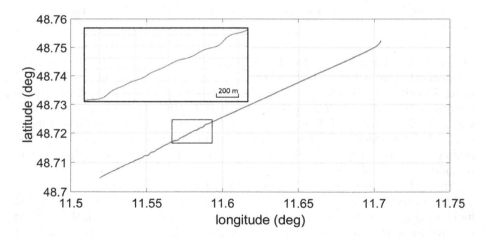

Fig. 6. 2D trajectory with a broken wing and zoom in on the oscillating behaviour

Again, the integration in the FPP of optimal control parameters for the studied scenario has enabled the generation of feasible and more adequate flight plans with respect to the computed ones without optimal parameters, proving thereby the success of the learning approach and the potential of a model-based FPP to generate feasible flight plans adapted to a damaged aircraft.

4   Conclusion and Future Work

In this work, we leverage the flexibility of a PDDL+ planner (i.e. ENHSP, given its ability to support non-linear operations) as a planner solver for the FPP system. Apart from providing more details (compared to [18]) on the extension from the 2D flight kinematics to 3D flight kinematics encoded in the PDDL+ domain and instance files, we also included additionally fault-tolerant capabilities in the FPP to cope with non-nominal flight conditions, by learning the model of the aircraft with respect to optimal numeric ranges of the model parameters, and by adapting the planning problem model encoded in the PDDL+ instance file.

The extension, specifically regarding the fault-tolerant capabilities, was tested under two non-nominal scenarios: emergency landing with low fuel level, and flight with a broken wing. Test results show that the autopilot developed for the ultralight, of which the control gains are optimized using PSO, can cope with the computed plans, validating thereby the feasibility of the plans generated by the FPP. Besides, the model-adaptive planning was also proven to be beneficial for increasing flight safety, i.e. increased success rate in emergency landing due to critical fuel level and reduced oscillations in flights with a broken wing.

However, more emergency scenarios can be studied in the future, such as an emergency landing triggered by an engine failure, flight with adverse weather conditions or flight with a blocked control surface. Besides, after having proven that learning from data can be efficient for devising multidimensional control parameters for increasing flight performance and flight safety, in the future, other more advanced learning algorithms can be explored, for example deep reinforcement learning, so that circumstantial control parameters can be devised and optimized for finer classification of environment, so that even dynamic local wind gust at the landing zone that is influenced by the topology of the surrounding, e.g. buildings and uneven terrains, can be coped with.

The focus of this work is the use of a PDDL+ planner as a model-based planner solver for the FPP. The flexibility of deployment and efficiency in planning were investigated; however, in order to ensure acceptance of the FPP, the aspect of transparency and explicability must also be studied in the future. This can be done by leveraging the validator function of ENHSP to explain the safety aspect and optimality of flight plans to the pilot. By doing so, a mixed-initiative flight path planning functionality can be envisaged, reducing thereby the pilot's over-reliance on automation.

References

1. Albaker, B., Rahim, N.: Flight path PID controller for propeller-driven fixed-wing unmanned aerial vehicles. Int. J. Phys. Sci. **6**(8), 1947–1964 (2011)
2. Bittar, A., Figuereido, H.V., Avelar Guimaraes, P., Correa Mendes, A.: Guidance software-in-the-loop simulation using x-plane and simulink for UAVs. In: 2014 International Conference on Unmanned Aircraft Systems (ICUAS), pp. 993–1002. IEEE (2014)

3. Caliński, T., Harabasz, J.: A dendrite method for cluster analysis. Commun. Stat.-Theory Methods **3**(1), 1–27 (1974)
4. Chialastri, A.: Automation in Aviation. INTECH Open Access Publisher (2012)
5. Chien, S.A., Knight, R., Stechert, A., Sherwood, R., Rabideau, G.: Using iterative repair to improve the responsiveness of planning and scheduling. In: AIPS, pp. 300–307 (2000)
6. De Voogt, A., Chaves, F., Harden, E., Silvestre, M., Gamboa, P.: Ultralight Accidents in the US, UK, and Portugal. Safety **4**(2), 23 (2018)
7. Donald, B., Xavier, P., Canny, J., Reif, J.: Kinodynamic motion planning. J. ACM **40**, 1048–1066 (1993)
8. Fox, M., Long, D.: Modelling mixed discrete-continuous domains for planning. J. Artif. Intell. Res. **27**, 235–297 (2006)
9. Giriraj Kumar, S., Jayaraj, D., Kishan, A.R.: PSO based tuning of a PID controller for a high performance drilling machine. Int. J. Comput. Appl. **1**(19), 12–18 (2010)
10. Jolliffe, I.T.: Principal Components Analysis. Springer Series in Statistics **29** (2002). https://doi.org/10.1007/b98835
11. Kiam, J.J., Scala, E., Ramirez Javega, M., Schulte, A.: An AI-based planning framework for HAPS in a time-varying environment. In: Proceedings of the International Conference on Automated Planning and Scheduling, vol. 30, pp. 412–420 (2020)
12. Kreyszig, E.: Advanced Engineering Mathematics, 10th edn. Wiley, Hoboken (2009)
13. Lekkas, A., Dahl, A.R., Breivik, M., Fossen, T.I.: Continuous-curvature path generation using fermat's spiral. J. Modeling Identification Control **34**(4), 183–198 (2013)
14. Lloyd, S.: Least squares quantization in PCM. IEEE Trans. Inf. Theory **28**(2), 129–137 (1982)
15. Meyer, A.: Laminar Research: X-Plane. https://www.x-plane.com/
16. Oceanic, U.N., Administration, A.: NOMADS-NOAA Operational Model Archive and Distribution System. https://nomads.ncep.noaa.gov/
17. Piprek, P.: Clothoid development for a trajectory system. Master's thesis, Technical University of Munich (2014)
18. Santos León, B., Kiam, J.J., Schulte, A.: Model-based automated flight path planner for an ultralight aircraft. In: CEUR Workshop Proceedings of the 8th Italian Workshop on Planning and Scheduling (IPS), vol. 2745 (2020)
19. Scala, E.: Expressive Numeric Heuristic Search Planner (ENHSP). https://gitlab.com/enricos83/ENHSP-Public/
20. Schatz, S.P., Holzapfel, F.: Modular trajectory/path following controller using nonlinear error dynamics. In: 2014 IEEE International Conference on Aerospace Electronics and Remote Sensing Technology, pp. 157–163. IEEE (2014)
21. Ünal, F., Ekici, S.: A new clustering approach for monthly electricity consumption data. In: International Applied Sciences Congress (2020)
22. Zhu, Q., Pei, J., Liu, X., Zhou, Z.: Analyzing commercial aircraft fuel consumption during descent: a case study using an improved k-means clustering algorithm. J. Clean. Prod. **223**, 869–882 (2019)

In Defence of Design Patterns for AI Planning Knowledge Models

Mauro Vallati$^{(\boxtimes)}$ (ID) and Thomas L. McCluskey (ID)

School of Computing and Engineering, University of Huddersfield, Queensgate,
Huddersfield HD1 3DH, UK
{m.vallati,lee}@hud.ac.uk

Abstract. Design patterns are widely used in various areas of computer science, the most notable example being software engineering. They have been introduced also for supporting the encoding of automated planning knowledge models, but up till now, with little success.

In this paper, we investigate the merits of design patterns, as an example of the broader class of reusable abstractions, in the automated planning context; particularly, we aim at drawing attention to their potential usefulness for the explainability of domain-independent planning systems. Further, we argue that to foster the use of design patterns, there is a need for a centralised repository, and we describe the functionalities that such repository should provide to support knowledge engineers.

Keywords: Automated planning · Knowledge engineering · Design patterns · Explainability

1 Introduction

Automated planning is a research discipline that addresses the problem of generating a totally- or partially-ordered sequence of actions that transform the environment from some initial state to a desired goal state [13]. Automated planning has been successfully applied in a range of challenging real-world domains, including drilling [10], transport [20], smart grid [34], UAV control [25], e-learning [12], machine tool calibration [23], and mining [16].

Undoubtedly, the intensive development of domain-independent planning techniques has contributed to the advancement of planning technology. In domain-independent planning there is a decoupling between the planning logic, that is embodied in the planning engine, and the domain knowledge, that comes under the form of knowledge models. As the two components rely on a well-defined interface language, they can be substituted by other approaches without any changes to the rest of the framework.

A critical aspect of domain-independent planning, is the application knowledge that must be added to the planner to create a complete planning application. This is made explicit in (i) a domain model, which is a formal representation

M. Baldoni and S. Bandini (Eds.): AIxIA 2020, LNAI 12414, pp. 191–203, 2021.
https://doi.org/10.1007/978-3-030-77091-4_12

of the persistent domain knowledge, and (ii) an associated problem instance, containing the details of the particular problem to be solved. Both these components are used by automated planning engines for reasoning, in order to synthesise a solution plan. The success of the exploitation of automated planning in a given domain, strongly depends on the quality of the provided domain knowledge: even minor modelling issues can result in an increased complexity of the problems to be solved [35].

Formulating knowledge for use in planning engines is currently something of an ad-hoc process, where the skills of knowledge engineers significantly influence the quality of the resulting planning application [5]. This is despite the pivotal role played by the application knowledge, and the fact that a well-engineered formulating process can support the assessment of the quality of some characteristics of the resulting models [38].

In this paper, we argue about the merits of reusable abstractions, in particular design patterns, in the automated planning context. By facilitating the reuse of good design practice, they can provide a useful means for supporting the encoding of planning knowledge, thus fostering the development of quality models. Further, we aim at drawing attention to the potential usefulness of design patterns for the explainability of domain-independent planning systems. They can be exploited as a structured framework for explaining and motivating design decisions, as well as valuable source of knowledge to support explanations on the behaviour of the planning system. To foster the use of design patterns, we highlight the need for a centralised repository that stores them, and we characterise its required functionalities.

The remainder of this paper is organised as follows. Section 2 gives a knowledge engineering perspective of the field of AI planning. Then, Sect. 3 describes how design patterns can play a major role in the field of explainability. Section 4 provides an example of a design pattern for planning, and Sect. 5 details the functionalities of a centralised repository for design patterns. Finally, Sect. 6 discusses the use of design patterns with multiple AI planning languages, and Sect. 7 gives the conclusions.

2   A Knowledge Engineering (Historical) Perspective

Studies on Knowledge Engineering for Planning and Scheduling (KEPS) have led to the creation of several tools and techniques to support the design of domain knowledge structures, and the use of planners for real-world problems [18,36]. KEPS has not yet reached the maturity of other traditional engineering areas (e.g., software engineering) in having an established standard design process. In KEPS, tools are still rarely used when experts have to engineer new knowledge models [5].[1] It may be due to the fact that experts have to adapt the encoding and refining processes according to the functionalities of a given tool. Further, the learning curve can be particularly steep for this kind of tools.

---

[1] For an overview of the available KEPS tools, the interested reader is referred to [27].

A different yet complementary approach relies on the notion of reusable abstractions (see, for instance, [22]): instead of encoding planning knowledge models directly in a low-level language[2] such as PDDL, this approach envisages the use of more abstract level descriptions, that foster the design and use of modular structures. This would support re-use of similar structures, and provide a mean for justifying some decisions made during the knowledge acquisition and encoding processes. One of such reusable abstraction techniques for planning was proposed in the early 2000s, and leveraged on the notion of design patterns [28]. Design patterns [1] facilitate reuse of good design practices, as they describe a recurrent problem and a well-tested solution. In their most common form, design patterns are represented as a document that includes the following components:

- (i) Intent – What does the pattern aims to achieve;
- (ii) Problem – The problem it solves;
- (iii) A discussion – Details of how it works;
- (iv) Structure – How it can be implemented;
- (v) An Example of its use.

Since their introduction, design patterns have been swiftly and successfully adopted in most areas of computer science, most notably software engineering, as a mean for fostering reusable and easy to generalise solutions [11].

The approach introduced by Simpson *et al.* [28] proposed a tool for organising and managing patterns, and a way for generating the corresponding solution either in OCL [17] or in PDDL, to be then incorporated in knowledge models that can be used by domain-independent planning engines. Examples of the patterns proposed include a general approach for moving elements, and to describe structures such as maps, sets, or sequences.

Design patterns, if used as in software engineering as library of off-the-shelf solutions to common problems, remove the mentioned issue of KEPS tools, particularly the need to learn to use a dedicated tool, and can actively support the widespread use of best practices in the field. This is also related to the availability of a range of benchmark instances and to events such as the International Planning Competition,[3] that can play a major role in identifying best practices for dealing with common (and uncommon) problems. GIPO [19] is the KEPS tool that introduced the notion of design patterns for planning, and provided a way for encoding and re-using them. itSIMPLE [39] is another tool that supports the use of design patterns: it allows to generate a UML-like to design planning models. Using the UML diagrams, it is then possible to identify reusable abstractions, and to exploit some of the design patterns introduced for software engineering purposes. In more recent times, rudimentary form of design patterns is implemented in the well-known online editor *planning.domains*,[4] as

---

[2] Low-level in the sense that the design of the language is much influenced by its use in plan generation engines, much as machine code is designed to align with the execution architecture of the machine that runs it.

[3] https://www.icaps-conference.org/competitions/.

[4] http://editor.planning.domains/.

the "Misc PDDL Generators" plugin. This plugin provides the PDDL code for representing some common structures, such as grids and maps. There is not, however, a description of the problem that such structures are aimed at solving, and there is no justification for the specific encoding that is suggested. Despite the mentioned limitations, the plugin is helpful in supporting the encoding of PDDL models, and in reducing the likeliness of bugs and errors in the encoded structures.

Unfortunately, design patterns are not widely used by the planning community. A reason for that may be the lack of a centralised repository for managing such design patterns and the lack of a commonly agreed way for encoding them. There is also the challenge of providing empirical evidence of the beneficial impact of design patterns; this is extremely hard to produce, as demonstrated by past works from the software engineering community [24]. The problem is not that design patterns may not be useful, but that designing experiments for quantitatively assessing their impact on the knowledge engineering process is very complicated. Finally, there is the fact that the encoding of planning knowledge models is still seen as a sort of ad-hoc artisan process, whose shortcomings can be dealt with by using high-performance planning engines rather than a proper engineering process.

3   Beyond Knowledge Encoding: Explainability

Here we would like to highlight the important role that reusable abstractions, and particularly design patterns, can play for AI planning knowledge models, beside the discussed support for knowledge encoding and acquisition.

An area of growing importance for the automated planning field, as well as for AI in general, is that of explainability. The idea being that an AI system should be able to explain, to some extent, its behaviour to stakeholders. Focusing on the narrower topic dubbed XAIP, as for EXplainable AI Planning, a number of recent works considered the problem of defining what "explainable" means for an automated planning system, explaining and describing generated plans, bridging the gap between machines and human stakeholders, and designing approaches to explain the behaviour of planning systems [3,4,8,9,30,33].

As noted in the previous sections, domain-independent planning systems are heavily dependent on the provided knowledge models; this is also true when explainability is concerned. The behaviour of a planning system can not transcend the knowledge model, and the importance of the planning knowledge model has been well-argued [21]. In fact, in the XAIP field, the knowledge model is more and more regarded as a source of knowledge that can explain the behaviour of the planning system [14,37]. This is also because, during the knowledge engineering process of encoding specifications into an appropriate and operational planning knowledge model, a number of design decisions have to be made. Some of those decisions are due to the experience of the encoder, while others are due to either common or specific knowledge about the application context. Clearly, other aspects of the knowledge model support explainability also: the fact that dynamic knowledge is stated with both a procedural and declarative interpretation means that parts of the knowledge can be used in isolation within an explanation. Even namings within the model can be used as an understandable unit of the explanation.

It should therefore come as no surprise that design patterns can play a significant role in the XAIP field. Design patterns can provide a valuable and well-defined mean for supporting explanations. This is because, when design patterns are implemented in a planning model, the design pattern description becomes a valuable source of additional knowledge, that is not encoded in the model. Further, there is not even the need for finding a way to "attach" such additional knowledge to the standard planning models. The management of additional knowledge is a potential issue for planning systems [37]. Instead, having a centralised repository for planning design patterns (something similar to what *Source Making*[5] does for software engineering, for instance) would allow planning models to be encoded and circulated as they are right now, and would support explanation engines in looking for patterns and descriptions in a structured manner. In fact, the XAIP field can provide new momentum to the use and management of design patterns for planning.

In a sense, the use of patterns becomes then an explicit way for providing explanations, that can of course be complemented by the line of work that devises techniques for identifying known substructures of planning models, and link them to an expected behaviour (see for instance [15]). It is naive to believe that a complex planning model can be composed only by design patterns, but at least the core elements are expected to be encoded using some form of patterns. Additional sources of domain-specific knowledge can then be sought via ontologies or similar structures [37].

4   Example: The Mobile Design Pattern

For exemplifying our vision for the use of design patterns for explainability, let us consider the `Mobile` design pattern introduced by Simpson *et al.* [28], and partly shown in Figs. 1 and 2. In particular, the figures provide an overview of the interface that Simpson *et al.* proposed for describing and configuring design patterns, that relies on the approach they used to encode the patterns and to make them available. Notably, this interface has then been implemented in GIPO [19], together with the below described functionalities and characteristics.

The Mobile pattern deals with the problem of encoding mobile elements (typically vehicles) in the models, that can be used to carry goods or people, and may require a driver to be moved. Mobile elements can move between adjacent or connected locations. As it is apparent, this pattern embodies an aspect of planning knowledge that is frequently faced by knowledge engineers, and that is included also in a variety of well-known benchmark planning models used in the International Planning Competition.

---

[5] https://sourcemaking.com/.

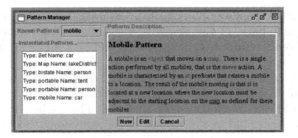

Fig. 1. The Mobile design pattern, described using a textual description (right), and the way in which its variable components has to be instantiated (left) using the tool introduced in [28].

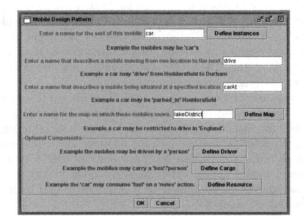

Fig. 2. The interface proposed in [28] to define the behaviour of the Mobile design pattern via its components.

The problem description, the use of appropriate naming convention, and the optional components can allow to deal with the classes of explanations that Vallati, McCluskey and Chrpa defined as *context-related* and *assumption-related* [22]. The former class refers to explanations that relate to contextual knowledge about the domains, the latter class requires information about assumptions and decisions made during the knowledge encoding process.

A context-related question that can be answered using knowledge that comes with the Mobile design pattern would be: *Why can the vehicle not move from location X to location Y?* The pattern description includes the answer to this question, by stating that the movement can be allowed between adjacent locations in a map. Similarly, taking into account the optional components, the use of the design pattern can help to answer questions like *Why did the vehicle not move immediately at the start of the plan?* Here the fact that a vehicle needs a driver to move can help in addressing this question. Assumptions-related questions can then relate to the maximum capacity of the vehicle, for instance, or to the fuel consumption of the vehicle. While the knowledge needed for generating explanations is part of the design pattern structure, it can come under the form of free text. For this reason, it is important to either empower XAIP systems with natural language understanding and natural language generation capabilities [6], or to investigate structured ways to encode the relevant knowledge that allows its reuse.

With regards to the considered Mobile pattern, but in general for any design pattern introduced for PDDL, it is easy to notice that many different versions of the pattern are needed. For instance, the vehicle represented via the Mobile pattern can allow to move goods or passengers, may need a key to get started, etc. All these aspects can be configured using the interfaces shown in Figs. 1 and 2, and this provides a valuable source of knowledge to address questions such as those indicated above. Further, this flexibility of the patterns can lead to a hierarchy, where the different versions are put in relations with each other. A possible hierarchy for the Mobile pattern is shown in Fig. 3. An important aspect of the hierarchy, is that it can also include other types that are needed by the pattern in object. For our example, the Mobile pattern allows a vehicle to move between locations, that can be specified via a map. It also can carry "portable" elements, that can be goods, passengers, or objects with a specific meaning for the vehicle, such as a key.

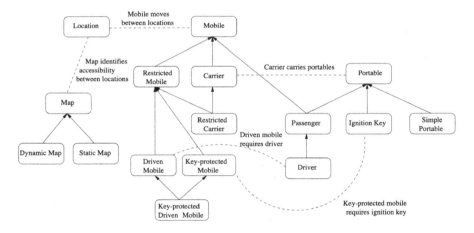

Fig. 3. The relations between different versions of the Mobile design pattern, and relevant generic types by [28] to define the behaviour of the Mobile design pattern via its components.

The hierarchy of a design pattern becomes a valuable source of knowledge for explaining the behaviour of the planning system, and can provide a solid ground for supporting processes such as the reconciliation between the model used by the planning agent, and a human stakeholder [32]. In a nutshell, model

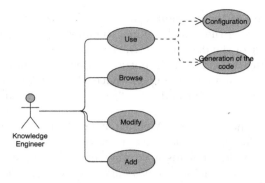

Fig. 4. The functionalities that a centralised repository for planning design pattern should implement.

reconciliation is the process where discrepancies in the models used by different agents can be identified and removed. The use of the hierarchy can support the reconciliation of issues related to different understandings of the characteristics of the vehicle, in the provided example of the Mobile pattern. In particular, it may also help in providing "suggestions" about potential features that the considered vehicle should have.

To exploit design patterns for supporting explainability, there is the need for structuring the way in which the corresponding problem description, optional components, hierarchy, etc. are encoded in a repository, and for dedicated approaches able to identify the most relevant knowledge with regards to a given query. On this regards, the planning community can take inspiration from the work done in other research areas, for instance Knowledge Engineering and Knowledge Management, that have decades of experience in addressing similar challenges. ConceptNet[6] [31], for instance, is a semantic network that relates different terms and notions in a machine- and human-readable formats, and can give useful insights into the challenges faced, and best practices, in building the kind of knowledge base that would be needed for a centralised repository of design patterns in planning.

5   Functionalities of the Centralised Repository

The centralised repository would play a pivotal role for the widespread use of design patterns. For this reason, it is worth specifying the kind of interactions with knowledge engineers, or more in general users interested in exploiting design patterns for encoding planning knowledge under the form of domain models, that it should support.

Figure 4 shows a UML use case diagram of the main interactions that a human user can have with the centralised repository. We describe them below.

---

[6] https://conceptnet.io/.

- **Browse**: A user should be allowed to browse and search the list of available design patterns, and of the corresponding information and hierarchy.
- **Modify** and **Add**: Perhaps less frequently than the browse mentioned above, it should be possible to update the design patterns. Updates can relate to the actual PDDL encoding, to the configurable options, or to the overall hierarchy of the pattern. Similarly, it should be possible to add new patterns, if necessary. Beside the addition of a new design pattern, it should also be possible to define the relations between the new pattern and the existing ones, if any. Further, it should be noted that there must be a well-defined process that is enforced to update and add patterns: for instance, there must be a process to demonstrate that the modifications are improving the pattern, and that a pattern to be added is not included, under any form, in the repository.
- **Use**: This is likely to be the most important use case of the repository. Knowledge engineers that have browsed the list of patterns and identified one that is suitable to be included in the model they are working on, should have a way for optimising the pattern, and obtaining the corresponding PDDL code.

It is worth noting that the browse functionality can serve two main aims: providing an overview of the available design patterns, and identifying the most suitable design pattern to use. The identification step can be supported by decision-making approaches, in order to ensure that the most suitable design pattern is selected also by inexperienced users. An example of a decision-making tool can be the Analytic Hierarchy Process (AHP) [26]. One of the main advantages of this method is the relative ease with which it handles multiple criteria, and that it can effectively handle both qualitative and quantitative data. The AHP approach has been employed in a range of application [7].

To ensure that design patterns incorporated in a knowledge model are correctly recognised by XAIP systems, there is the need to include some identifiers. This can be done in different ways, for instance by defining some identification code to be added under the form of comments, or by using some unique naming conventions.

The use case diagram shown in Fig. 4 is focused on the interaction between a human stakeholder and the centralised repository. There is another major actor for the repository, that is the XAIP system. With regards to the interactions with the repository, the XAIP systems are expected to be more limited than knowledge engineers. In its basic implementation, a XAIP system will need to be able to download (or explore online) the knowledge related to a given design pattern. Notably, beside design pattern itself and its characteristics, the relations with other patterns could also play an important role in helping the XAIP system generating explanations.

6   Discussion on Languages for Planning Knowledge Models

The seminal work by Simpson *et al.* [28], focused on the notion of design patterns for PDDL planning models. For this reason, in this paper we took a similar perspective, also considering that PDDL is the language exploited in the International Planning Competition,[7] and a sort of de-facto standard for benchmarking planning systems. It is worth noticing that design patterns and more in general reusable abstractions, can be constructively employed in the wide range of languages used to encode planning knowledge models. The example provided in the previous sections shed some light also on how design patterns can be exploited in languages that are based on PDDL, such as PDDL+ or MA-PDDL. It is clear that patterns in PDDL are composed by operators, predicates, and a corresponding hierarchy of types. They need therefore to be extended for different languages, according to the structures provided by the considered language. For instance, it is easy to get an intuition of how the presented Mobile pattern can be extended for PDDL+: it would include processes that measure the time spent travelling and the fuel consumption, and events that are triggered in case of failures. Such structures would need additional functions to be defined, to represent and store the required numeric values. However, design patterns can be exploited also for planning languages that are based on radically different perspectives, such as timeline-based planning (see, e.g., GHOST [2] and ANML [29]) or stochastic planning (RDDL).

Design patterns aimed at different languages are very different in nature. This is because the expressivity and the syntax of the language imposes some hard constraints on what can be represented, and on the possible ways in which a concept can be represented. Due to that, it is unlikely that a single centralised repository could work for multiple planning languages at the same time. Instead, it would be envisaged the use of different repositories for each language, or family of languages, so that all the nuances of the language can also be reflected in the structure of the repository and in the way in which patterns are stored. This also points to the fact that the processes for assessing the quality of the patterns, updating patterns, etc. should be tailored to the characteristics of the considered language.

7   Conclusion

Reusable abstractions, mostly under the form of design patterns, have been introduced for supporting the knowledge encoding and acquisition processes. However, they did not have great success in the KEPS field.

In this paper, we point to the fact that design patterns can play a significant role also for supporting the explainability of the behaviour of a planning system. The benefit for Knowledge engineers derived by using design patterns in planning models can therefore be twofold: (i) design patterns allow to deal with common problems by reusing best practices, and (ii) they directly support the explanaibility of the knowledge models and, indirectly, of the overall planning system.

In order to foster the use of design patterns in AI planning, a centralised repository, as it is currently done for benchmarks, is needed. In this paper, we

---

[7] https://www.icaps-conference.org/competitions/.

defined the functionalities that such a centralised repository should provide, and we highlighted some of the processes that would need to be implemented to populate, update, and make useful the repository. We also highlighted the need for an approach that support not experienced knowledge engineers in selecting the most suitable design pattern to use.

Future work is envisaged in identifying suitable way for storing and managing design patterns for automated planning, with focus given to the way in which the problem they address is described in an explainable-friendly manner, and to the planning languages that are supported. We are also interested in designing and developing the centralised repository.

References

1. Alexander, C.: A Pattern Language: Towns, Buildings, Construction. Oxford University Press (1977)
2. Bernardi, G., Cesta, A., Orlandini, A., Umbrico, A., Mayer, M.C.: A language for timeline-based planning. In: Proceedings of the 2nd Workshop on Artificial Intelligence and Formal Verification, Logic, Automata, and Synthesis, pp. 53–58 (2020)
3. Caminada, M.W., Kutlak, R., Oren, N., Vasconcelos, W.W.: Scrutable plan enactment via argumentation and natural language generation. In: Proceedings of the 2014 International Conference on Autonomous Agents and Multi-agent Systems, pp. 1625–1626 (2014)
4. Chakraborti, T., Kulkarni, A., Sreedharan, S., Smith, D.E., Kambhampati, S.: Explicability? Legibility? Predictability? Transparency? Privacy? Security? The emerging landscape of interpretable agent behavior. In: Proceedings of the Twenty-Ninth International Conference on Automated Planning and Scheduling, ICAPS, pp. 86–96 (2019)
5. Chrpa, L., McCluskey, T.L., Vallati, M., Vaquero, T.S.: The fifth international competition on knowledge engineering for planning and scheduling: summary and trends. AI Mag. **38**(1), 104–106 (2017)
6. Clark, A., Fox, C., Lappin, S.: The Handbook of Computational Linguistics and Natural Language Processing. Wiley, Hoboken (2013)
7. Durán, O.: Computer-aided maintenance management systems selection based on a fuzzy AHP approach. Adv. Eng. Softw. **42**(10), 821–829 (2011)
8. Eifler, R., Cashmore, M., Hoffmann, J., Magazzeni, D., Steinmetz, M.: A new approach to plan-space explanation: analyzing plan-property dependencies in oversubscription planning. In: The Thirty-Fourth AAAI Conference on Artificial Intelligence, AAAI, pp. 9818–9826 (2020)
9. Fox, M., Long, D., Magazzeni, D.: Explainable planning. CoRR abs/1709.10256 (2017)
10. Fox, M., Long, D., Tamboise, G., Isangulov, R.: Creating and executing a well construction/operation plan (2018). uS Patent App. 15/541,381
11. Gamma, E., Helm, R., Vlissides, J., Johnson, R.: Design Patterns Elements of Reusable Object-Oriented Software. Addison-Wesley (1997)
12. Garrido, A., Morales, L., Serina, I.: Using AI planning to enhance e-learning processes. In: Proceedings of the Twenty-Second International Conference on Automated Planning and Scheduling, ICAPS. AAAI (2012)

13. Ghallab, M., Nau, D., Traverso, P.: Automated Planning: Theory and Practice. Elsevier (2004)
14. Lindsay, A.: Towards exploiting generic problem structures in explanations for automated planning. In: Proceedings of the 10th International Conference on Knowledge Capture, K-CAP, pp. 235–238 (2019)
15. Lindsay, A.: Using generic subproblems for understanding and answering queries in XAIP. In: Proceedings of KEPS (2020)
16. Lipovetzky, N., Burt, C.N., Pearce, A.R., Stuckey, P.J.: Planning for mining operations with time and resource constraints. In: Proceedings of the International Conference on Automated Planning and Scheduling (2014)
17. Liu, D., McCluskey, T.: The OCL language manual. Technical report, Version 1.2. Technical report, Department of Computing and Mathematical (2000)
18. McCluskey, T.L., et al.: Knowledge Engineering for Planning Roadmap (2003). http://scom.hud.ac.uk/planet/home
19. McCluskey, T.L., Simpson, R.M.: Knowledge formulation for AI planning. In: Motta, E., Shadbolt, N.R., Stutt, A., Gibbins, N. (eds.) EKAW 2004. LNCS (LNAI), vol. 3257, pp. 449–465. Springer, Heidelberg (2004). https://doi.org/10.1007/978-3-540-30202-5_30
20. McCluskey, T.L., Vallati, M.: Embedding automated planning within urban traffic management operations. In: Proceedings of the International Conference on Automated Planning and Scheduling (2017)
21. McCluskey, T.L., Vaquero, T.S., Vallati, M.: Engineering knowledge for automated planning: towards a notion of quality. In: Proceedings of the Knowledge Capture Conference, K-CAP, pp. 14:1–14:8 (2017)
22. McCluskey, T., Simpson, R.: Towards an algebraic formulation of domain definitions using parameterised machines. In: Proceedings of the Annual UK PLANSIG Workshop (2005)
23. Parkinson, S., Longstaff, A.P.: Multi-objective optimisation of machine tool error mapping using automated planning. Expert Syst. Appl. **42**(6), 3005–3015 (2015)
24. Porras, G.C., Guéhéneuc, Y.G.: An empirical study on the efficiency of different design pattern representations in UML class diagrams. Empirical Softw. Eng. **15**(5), 493–522 (2010)
25. Ramírez, M., et al.: Integrated hybrid planning and programmed control for real time UAV maneuvering. In: Proceedings of the 17th International Conference on Autonomous Agents and MultiAgent Systems, AAMAS, pp. 1318–1326 (2018)
26. Saaty, T.L., Vargas, L.G.: Models, Methods, Concepts & Applications of the Analytic Hierarchy Process, vol. 175. Springer (2012). https://doi.org/10.1007/978-1-4614-3597-6
27. Silva, J.R., Silva, J.M., Vaquero, T.S.: Formal knowledge engineering for planning: pre and post-design analysis. In: Vallati, M., Kitchin, D. (eds.) Knowledge Engineering Tools and Techniques for AI Planning, pp. 47–65. Springer, Cham (2020). https://doi.org/10.1007/978-3-030-38561-3_3
28. Simpson, R., Mccluskey, T., Long, D., Fox, M.: Generic types as design patterns for planning domain specification. In: AIPS2002 Workshop on Knowledge Engineering Tools and Techniques for AI Planning (2002)
29. Smith, D., Frank, J., Cushing, W.: The ANML language. In: Workshop on Knowledge Engineering for Planning and Scheduling (KEPS) (2008)
30. Sohrabi, S., Baier, J.A., McIlraith, S.A.: Preferred explanations: theory and generation via planning. In: Twenty-Fifth AAAI Conference on Artificial Intelligence (2011)

31. Speer, R., Chin, J., Havasi, C.: Conceptnet 5.5: an open multilingual graph of general knowledge. In: AAAI Conference on Artificial Intelligence, pp. 4444–4451 (2017)
32. Sreedharan, S., Chakraborti, T., Kambhampati, S.: Handling model uncertainty and multiplicity in explanations via model reconciliation. In: Proceedings of the Twenty-Eighth International Conference on Automated Planning and Scheduling, ICAPS, pp. 518–526 (2018)
33. Sreedharan, S., Srivastava, S., Smith, D., Kambhampati, S.: Why can't you do that hal? explaining unsolvability of planning tasks. In: International Joint Conference on Artificial Intelligence (2019)
34. Thiébaux, S., Coffrin, C., Hijazi, H., Slaney, J.: Planning with MIP for supply restoration in power distribution systems. In: Proceedings of the International Joint Conference on Artificial Intelligence (2013)
35. Vallati, M., Chrpa, L.: On the robustness of domain-independent planning engines: the impact of poorly-engineered knowledge. In: Proceedings of the 10th International Conference on Knowledge Capture, K-CAP, pp. 197–204 (2019)
36. Vallati, M., Kitchin, D.E. (eds.): Knowledge Engineering Tools and Techniques for AI Planning. Springer, Heidelberg (2020). https://doi.org/10.1007/978-3-030-38561-3
37. Vallati, M., McCluskey, L., Chrpa, L.: Towards explanation-supportive knowledge engineering for planning. In: Proceedings of XAIP (2018)
38. Vallati, M., McCluskey, T.L.: A quality framework for automated planning knowledge models. In: Proceedings of the 13th International Conference on Agents and Artificial Intelligence (ICAART) (2021)
39. Vaquero, T.S., Romero, V., Tonidandel, F., Silva, J.R.: itSIMPLE 2.0: an integrated tool for designing planning domains. In: Proceedings of the International Conference on Automated Planning and Scheduling, ICAPS, pp. 336–343 (2007)

Solving Operating Room Scheduling Problems with Surgical Teams via Answer Set Programming

Carmine Dodaro[1], Giuseppe Galatà[2], Muhammad Kamran Khan[3],
Marco Maratea[3(✉)], and Ivan Porro[2]

[1] DEMACS, University of Calabria, Rende, Italy
dodaro@mat.unical.it
[2] SurgiQ srl, Genova, Italy
{giuseppe.galata,ivan.porro}@surgiq.com
[3] DIBRIS, University of Genova, Genova, Italy
muhammad.kamrankhan@edu.unige.it,marco.maratea@unige.it

Abstract. The optimization of daily operating room surgery schedule can be problematic because of many constraints, like to determine the starting time of different surgeries and allocating the required resources, including the availability of surgical teams for complete surgical procedures. Recently, Answer Set Programming (ASP) has been successfully employed for addressing and solving real-life scheduling and planning problems in the healthcare domain. In this paper we present an enhanced solution using ASP for scheduling operating rooms taking explicitly into consideration availability of surgical teams, that include a surgeon and an anesthetist in different specialties for the entire duration of the surgery. We tested our solution on different benchmarks with realistic parameters for schedule's length up to the target 5-days planning. The results of our experiments show that ASP is a suitable methodology for solving also such enhanced problem.

1 Introduction

Hospitals, whose production output is service, often come across issues of long waiting times, surgeries cancellation for patients and even worst resource overload occur frequently. Within every Hospital, Operating Rooms (ORs) are an important unit. As indicated in [30], the ORs account for approximately 33% of the total hospital budget because it includes high staff costs (e.g., surgeons, anaesthetists, nurses) and material cost. Nowadays, in most modern Hospitals, long surgical waiting lists are present because of inefficient planning. Therefore, it is extremely important to improve the efficiency of ORs to enhance the survival rate and satisfaction of patients, thereby improving the overall quality of healthcare system. The Operating Room Scheduling (ORS) [1,6,29,30] problem is the task of assigning patients to ORs by considering specialties, surgery durations, shift durations, beds availability and, most importantly the availability of

M. Baldoni and S. Bandini (Eds.): AIxIA 2020, LNAI 12414, pp. 204–220, 2021.
https://doi.org/10.1007/978-3-030-77091-4_13

surgical teams for the entire duration of the surgery. Further, the solution must prioritise patients based on health urgency. In recent years a solution based on Answer Set Programming (ASP) [8,21,22] was proposed and is used for solving such problem [14,15], together with other similar scheduling problems in this context, given its intuitive semantics [9] and the availability of efficient solvers put forward by ASP Competitions (see, e.g., [10,18,19]). We have recently enhanced the first solution by incorporating beds management [12]. However, the drawback with these solutions is that they do not consider availability of surgical teams which are an important part of the surgical process.

In this paper we improve our basic solution [14,15] following another direction, and present an enhanced encoding that takes into explicit account the availability of surgical teams for planning surgical procedures. The problem is expressed in ASP as modular additions to previous, more limited, encoding of ASP rules implementing the surgical teams, and then efficient solvers like CLINGO [17] are used to solve the resulting ASP encoding. Results for planning horizons up to the target 5-days planning, obtained on different benchmarks and scenario with realistic parameters for a small-medium-sized Hospital, are positive and inline with Hospital needs, and further confirm that ASP is a suitable methodology for solving scheduling problems in this context.

The paper is structured as follows. Section 2 presents needed preliminary about ASP. Then, Sect. 3 describes the target problem in an informal way and as a mathematical formulation, whose ASP encoding is presented in Sect. 4. Section 5 shows the results of our experiments. The paper ends in Sect. 6 and 7 by discussing related work, and by showing conclusions and possible topics for further research.

2   Answer Set Programming

Answer Set Programming (ASP) is a programming paradigm developed in the field of non monotonic reasoning and logic programming. It is a form of declarative programming oriented towards difficult primarily NP-hard search problems and is based on the stable model (answer set) semantics. This section presents in the first paragraph the syntax of the ASP language, for easy the readability of the encoding, and then a widely used shortcut in the second paragraph. The semantics is presented informally while describing the encoding, and details can be found in [9].

Syntax. The syntax of ASP is similar to the one of Prolog. Variables are strings starting with uppercase letter and constants are non-negative integers or strings starting with lowercase letters. A *term* is either a variable or a constant. A *standard atom* is an expression $p(t_1, \ldots, t_n)$, where p is a *predicate* of arity n and $t_1, \ldots, t_n$ are terms. An atom $p(t_1, \ldots, t_n)$ is ground if $t_1, \ldots, t_n$ are constants. A *ground set* is a set of pairs of the form $\langle consts : conj \rangle$, where *consts* is a list of constants and *conj* is a conjunction of ground standard atoms. A *symbolic set* is a set specified syntactically as $\{Terms_1 : Conj_1; \cdots ; Terms_t : Conj_t\}$, where

$t > 0$, and for all $i \in [1, t]$, each $Terms_i$ is a list of terms such that $|Terms_i| = k > 0$, and each $Conj_i$ is a conjunction of standard atoms. A *set term* is either a symbolic set or a ground set. Intuitively, a set term $\{X : a(X, c), p(X); Y : b(Y, m)\}$ stands for the union of two sets: the first one contains the X-values making the conjunction $a(X, c), p(X)$ true, and the second one contains the Y-values making the conjunction $b(Y, m)$ true. An *aggregate function* is of the form $f(S)$, where S is a set term, and f is an *aggregate function symbol*. Basically, aggregate functions map multisets of constants to a constant. The most common functions implemented in ASP systems are the following:

- #*count*, number of terms;
- #*sum*, sum of integers.

An *aggregate atom* is of the form $f(S) \prec T$, where $f(S)$ is an aggregate function, $\prec \in \{<, \leq, >, \geq, \neq, =\}$ is a comparison operator, and T is a term called guard. An aggregate atom $f(S) \prec T$ is ground if T is a constant and S is a ground set. An *atom* is either a standard atom or an aggregate atom. A *rule r* has the following form:

$$a_1 \vee \ldots \vee a_n :- b_1, \ldots, b_k, not\ b_{k+1}, \ldots, not\ b_m.$$

where $a_1, \ldots, a_n$ are standard atoms, $b_1, \ldots, b_k$ are atoms, $b_{k+1}, \ldots, b_m$ are standard atoms, and $n, k, m \geq 0$. A literal is either a standard atom a or its negation *not a*. The disjunction $a_1 \vee \ldots \vee a_n$ is the *head* of r, while the conjunction $b_1, \ldots, b_k, not\ b_{k+1}, \ldots, not\ b_m$ is its *body*. Rules with empty body are called *facts*. Rules with empty head are called *constraints*. A variable that appears uniquely in set terms of a rule r is said to be *local* in r, otherwise it is a *global* variable of r. An ASP program is a set of *safe* rules, where a rule r is *safe* if both the following conditions hold: *(i)* for each global variable X of r there is a positive standard atom ℓ in the body of r such that X appears in ℓ; and *(ii)* each local variable of r appearing in a symbolic set $\{Terms : Conj\}$ also appears in $Conj$.

A *weak constraint* ω is of the form:

$$:\sim b_1, \ldots, b_k, not\ b_{k+1}, \ldots, not\ b_m. \ [w@l]$$

where w and l are the weight and level of ω, respectively. (Intuitively, $[w@l]$ is read "as weight w at level l", where weight is the "cost" of violating the condition in the body of w, whereas levels can be specified for defining a priority among preference criteria). An ASP program P is a finite set of rules. An ASP program with weak constraints is $\Pi = \langle P, W \rangle$, where P is a program and W is a set of weak constraints.

A standard atom, a literal, a rule, a program or a weak constraint is *ground* if no variables appear in it.

Syntactic Shortcuts. We will also use *choice rules* of the form $\{p\}$, where p is an atom. Choice rules can be viewed as a syntactic shortcut for the rule $p \vee p'$, where p' is a fresh new standard atom not appearing elsewhere in the program.

3   Problem Description

This section provides the description and the requirements of our problem, both informally and as a mathematical formulation, in two separate subsections.

3.1   Informal Description

The elements of the waiting list are called registrations. Moreover, registrations are not all equal, as they can belong to different specialties and they can have different priorities and duration. All ORs are available for a specialty according to the Hospital Master Surgical Schedule (MSS), and for 5 consecutive hours (300 min) in a single shift, while a full day consists of two shifts. Of course, the assignments must guarantee that the sum of the predicted duration of surgeries assigned to a particular OR shift does not exceed the length of the shift itself. For each registration we consider three priority score P1, P2, and P3, where P1 is for high priority registrations or very urgent, P2 is for medium priority and P3 is for low priority. Since P1 gathers high priority registrations, they must be all assigned to an OR, followed by P2 registrations over the P3. Additionally, in each specialty (considered to be 5 as target in small-medium-sized Hospitals) surgical teams are allocated with number of surgeons and anaesthetists every day as shown in Table 1. Tables 2 and 3, instead, show how many surgeons/anesthetists are available in each shift and for each specialty. However, surgeons assigned to a shift in a day are different from the ones assigned for the other shift of the same day, while the same anesthetists cover both shifts of the same day. Every surgeon works specifically for a number of hours every day; also surgeons in each specialty are assigned only to a single shift in a day, i.e., they either work in the morning (represented as shift 1, 3, 5, 7 and 9) or in evening shift (represented as shift 2, 4, 6, 8 and 10) as shown in Table 2. The anaesthetists are also linked to specialty and they also work for a fixed number of hours every day, but they can work together with surgeons during any shift of the day as shown in Table 3. In our model, we also assume that once a surgery is started in an OR it cannot be interrupted. Further, surgeons cannot operate on more than one patient at the same time. The overall goal is to assign the maximum number of registrations to the ORs, respecting the priorities, and taking into account the availability of respective surgical teams in a particular specialty for the complete surgery duration.

3.2   Mathematical Formulation

In this subsection we proceed by expressing our ORS problem in a more rigorous mathematical formulation. The first step is to describe more rigorously the elements we are dealing with. Let

- R be a set of registrations,
- SP be a set of specialties,
- O be a set of operating rooms,

Table 1. Total number of surgeons and anaesthetists in each specialty.

Specialty	Number of surgeons	Number of anaesthetists
1	6	6
2	4	4
3	4	4
4	2	2
5	4	4
Total	20	20

Table 2. Surgeons availability for each specialty and in each day.

Days (D)	1		2		3		4		5	
Shifts (s)	1	2	3	4	5	6	7	8	9	10
Specialty (SP)	Surgeons									
1	3	3	3	3	3	3	3	3	3	3
2	2	2	2	2	2	2	2	2	2	2
3	2	2	2	2	2	2	2	2	2	2
4	1	1	1	1	1	1	1	1	1	1
5	2	2	2	2	2	2	2	2	2	2

- SU be a set of surgeons,
- A be a set of anaesthetists,
- SH be a set of shifts,
- D be the set of days in the planning period,
- $shift\_duration$ be a constant equal to 300 and representing the duration in minutes of each shift,
- $slot\_duration$ be a number in the set $\{10, 20, 40, 60\}$ representing the duration in minutes of each slot,
- $ST = \{0, 1, \ldots, shift\_duration \div slot\_duration\}$ be the set of time slots.

Table 3. Anaesthetists availability for each specialty and in each day.

Days (D)	1		2		3		4		5	
Shifts (s)	1	2	3	4	5	6	7	8	9	10
Specialty (SP)	Anaesthetists									
1	6	6	6	6	6	6	6	6	6	6
2	4	4	4	4	4	4	4	4	4	4
3	4	4	4	4	4	4	4	4	4	4
4	2	2	2	2	2	2	2	2	2	2
5	4	4	4	4	4	4	4	4	4	4

We are ready to define the functions that can help establish the relations between the elements of the ORS problem.

Definition 1. *(ORS problem) Let*

- *$p : R \mapsto \{1,2,3\}$ be a function associating each registration to a priority;*
- *$\delta : R \mapsto [1, shift\_duration]$ be a function associating each registration to a duration;*
- *$\sigma : R \mapsto SP$ be a function associating each registration to a specialty;*
- *$mss : O \times SH \times SP \times D \mapsto \{0,1\}$ be a function such that $mss(o, sh, sp, d) = 1$ if the OR o is reserved to the shift sh and the specialty sp during the day d, and 0 otherwise;*
- *$surg : SU \times SP \times SH \mapsto \{0,1\}$ be a function such that $surg(su, sp, sh) = 1$ if the surgeon su is associated to the specialty sp during the shift sh, and 0 otherwise;*
- *$an : A \times SP \times SH \mapsto \{0,1\}$ be a function such that $an(a, sp, sh) = 1$ if the anaesthetist a is associated to the specialty sp during the shift sh, and 0 otherwise;*
- *$surgWT : SU \times D \mapsto \mathbb{N}$ be a function associating each surgeon and day to a working time;*
- *$anWT : A \times D \mapsto \mathbb{N}$ be a function associating each anaesthetist and day to a working time.*

Let $x : R \times SU \times A \times O \times SH \times D \times ST \mapsto \{0,1\}$ be a function such that $x(r, su, a, o, sh, d, st) = 1$ if the registration r is assigned to the surgeon su, the anaesthetist a and the operating room o during the shift sh of the day d and the time slot st, and 0 otherwise. Moreover, for a scheduling x let $A_x = \{(r, su, a, o, sh, d, st) \mid r \in R, su \in SU, a \in A, o \in O, sh \in SH, d \in D, st \in ST, x(r, su, a, o, sh, d, st) = 1\}$ and $R_x^* = \{r \mid (r, su, a, o, sh, d, st) \in A_x\}$. Then, given sets $R, SP, O, SU, A, SH, D, ST$ and functions $p, \delta, \sigma, surg, an, surgWT, anWT$, and $shift\_duration = 300$ and $slot\_duration \in \{10, 20, 40, 60\}$, the ORS problem is defined as the problem of finding a schedule x, such that

(c1) $st \cdot slot\_duration + \delta(r) \leq shift\_duration \quad \forall(r, su, a, o, sh, d, st) \in A_x$;

(c2) $mss(o, sh, \sigma(r), d) \cdot surg(su, \sigma(r), sh) \cdot an(a, \sigma(r), sh) = 1 \quad \forall(r, su, a, o, sh, d, st) \in A_x$;

(c3) $|\{(su, a, o, sh, d, st) : (r, su, a, o, sh, d, st) \in A_x\}| \leq 1 \quad \forall r \in R$;

(c4) $x(r_1, su_1, a_1, o, sh, d, st) \cdot x(r_2, su_2, a_2, o, sh, d, st) = 0 \quad \forall r_1, r_2 \in R : r_1 \neq r_2$;

(c5) $|\{r : (r, su, a, o, sh, d, st) \in A_x, st \leq t < st + \delta(r) \div slot\_duration\}| \leq 1 \quad \forall o \in O, sh \in SH, t \in ST : mss(o, sh, sp, d) = 1$;

(c6) $|\{r : (r, su, a, o, sh, d, st) \in A_x\}| \leq 1 \quad \forall su \in SU : surg(su, sp, sh) = 1, sp \in SP$;

(c7) $|\{r : (r, su, a, o, sh, d, st) \in A_x, st \leq t < st + \delta(r) \div slot\_duration\}| \leq 1 \quad \forall su \in SU : surg(su, sp, sh) = 1, sp \in SP$;

(c8) $|\{r : (r, su, a, o, sh, d, st) \in A_x\}| \leq 1 \quad \forall a \in A : an(a, sp, sh) = 1, sp \in SP$;

(c9) $|\{r : (r, su, a, o, sh, d, st) \in A_x, st \leq t < st + \delta(r) \div slot\_duration\}| \leq 1 \quad \forall a \in A : an(a, sp, sh) = 1, sp \in SP$;

$(c10)$ $\sum_{(r,su,a,o,sh,d,st) \in A_x} \delta(r) \leq surgWT(su, d)$ $\forall su \in SU, d \in D;$

$(c11)$ $\sum_{(r,su,a,o,sh,d,st) \in A_x} \delta(r) \leq anWT(a, d)$ $\forall a \in A, d \in D;$

$(c12)$ (c_{12}) $\{r : r \in R, p(r) = 1\} \subseteq R_x^*;$

Condition $(c1)$ ensures that each registration is assigned to a time slot only if it does not exceed the shift duration.

Condition $(c2)$ ensures that each registration is assigned to an OR, surgeon and anaesthetist that are in the same specialty of the registration.

Condition $(c3)$ ensures that each registration is scheduled at most once.

Condition $(c4)$ ensures that two different registrations cannot be scheduled in the same OR, shift and time slot.

Condition $(c5)$ extends condition $(c4)$ to take into account the duration of each registration.

Condition $(c6)$ ensures that a surgeon cannot work at the same time slot and shift in different ORs.

Condition $(c7)$ extends condition $(c6)$ to take into account the duration of each registration.

Conditions $(c8)$ and $(c9)$ are similar to $(c6)$ and $(c7)$, respectively, by considering anaesthetists instead of surgeons.

Condition $(c10)$ (resp. $(c11)$) ensures that surgeons (resp. anaesthetists) do not exceed their daily number of working hours.

Finally, condition $(c12)$ imposes all priority 1 registrations to be assigned.

Definition 2. *(Solution) A solution ψ is a schedule x that satisfies all conditions from (c1) to (c12).*

Definition 3. *(Unassigned registrations) Given a solution ψ, let $R_\psi^{pr} = \{r \mid r \in R, p(r) = pr, r \notin R_\psi^*\}$. Intuitively, R_ψ^{pr} represents the set of registrations of priority pr that were not assigned to any OR.*

Definition 4. *(Minimal scheduling solution) A solution ψ is said to dominate solution ψ' if $|R_\psi^2| < |R_{\psi'}^2|$, or if $|R_\psi^2| = |R_{\psi'}^2|$ and $|R_\psi^3| < |R_{\psi'}^3|$. A solution is minimal, if it is not dominated by any other scheduling solutions.*

4   ASP Encoding for ORS with Surgical Teams

In this section we present the input predicates and our ASP encoding for representing data and our solution, in two different subsections.

4.1   Data Model

The input data to our model is specified by means of the following atoms:

– Instances of `time(S,ST)` show the time slots (`ST`) for each shift (`S`), i.e., each shift is divided it into a certain number of time slots, say n. In our case, we have exactly n instances of `time(S,ST)` for each shift, where ST ranges from 1 to n. Note that n is set to *shift_duration* $\div$ *slot_duration* as described in Sect. 3.

```
(r₁) {x(R,P,SR,AN,O,S,D,ST): (ST+SU) <= slots} :- registration(R,P,SU,SP),
        mss(O,S,SP,D), surgeon(SR,SP,S), an(AN,SP,S), time(S,ST).
(r₂) :- registration(R,_,_,_), #count{R,SR,AN,O,S,D,ST : x(R,P,SR,AN,O,S,D,ST)}>1.
(r₃) :- x(R1,_,_,_,_,O,S,D,ST), x(R2,_,_,_,_,O,S,D,ST), R1 != R2.
(r₄) :- #count{R:x(R,_,_,_,_,O,S,_,ST), registration(R,_,SU,_), T>=ST, T<ST+SU}>1,
        mss(O,S,_,_), time(S,T).
(r₅) :- #count{R:x(R,_,SR,_,_,S,_,ST)} > 1, surgeon(SR,_,S), time(S,ST).
(r₆) :- #count{R:x(R,_,SR,_,_,S,_,ST), registration(R,_,SU,_), T>=ST, T<ST+SU}>1,
        surgeon(SR,_,S), time(S,T).
(r₇) :- #count{R:x(R,_,_,AN,_,S,_,ST)} > 1, an(AN,_,S), time(S,ST).
(r₈) :- #count{R:x(R,_,_,AN,_,S,_,ST), registration(R,_,SU,_), T>=ST, T<ST+SU}>1,
        an(AN,_,S), time(S,T).
(r₉) :- #sum{SU,R:x(R,_,SR,_,_,_,D,_), registration(R,_,SU,_)} > SWT, surgWT(SWT,SR,D).
(r₁₀) :- #sum{SU,R:x(R,_,_,AN,_,_,D,_), registration(R,_,SU,_)} > AWT, anWT(AWT,AN,D).
(r₁₁) :- #count{R:x(R,1,_,_,_,_,_,_)} < totRegsP1.
(r₁₂) :~ M=#count{R:x(R,2,_,_,_,_,_,_)}, N=totRegsP2-M. [N@3]
(r₁₃) :~ M=#count{R:x(R,3,_,_,_,_,_,_)}, N=totRegsP3-M. [N@2]
```

Fig. 1. ASP encoding of the ORS problem with surgical teams.

- Instances of `registration(R,P,SU,SP)` represent the registrations, with an identifier (R), a priority score (P), the duration of the surgery expressed in terms of time slots (SU), and the id of the specialty it belongs to (SP).
- Instances of `mss(O,S,SP,D)` link each operating room (O) to a shift (S) for each specialty (SP) and planning day (D), as established by the MSS.
- Instances of `surgeon(SR,SP,S)` represent the surgeons with an id (SR) for each specialty (SP) and shift (S).
- Instances of `an(AN,SP,S)` show the anaesthetists with an id (AN) for each specialty (SP) and shift (S).
- Instances of `surgWT(SWT,SR,D)` represent the total work time (SWT) expressed in time slots for surgeons with id (SR) for each day (D).
- Instances of `anWT(AWT,AN,D)` represent the total work time (AWT) expressed in time slots for anaesthetists with id (AN) for each day (D).

The output is stored in an assignment to atom of the following form:

```
x(R,P,SR,AN,O,S,D,ST)
```

representing that the registration (R) with priority (P) is assigned with surgeon id (SR) and anaesthetist id (AN) to the operating room (O) during the shift (S) of the day (D) with a time slot (ST).

4.2 Encoding

The related ASP encoding is shown in Fig. 1, and is described in this subsection. The encoding is based on the Guess&Check programming methodology.

Rule (r_1) guesses an assignment for the registrations, surgeons and anaesthetists to an OR in a given day, shift and with a time slot among the ones permitted by the MSS for the particular specialty the registrations, surgeons and anaesthetists belongs to, such that the registrations assigned with a slot

Table 4. Total number of randomly generated registrations for each benchmark.

Specialty	Registrations				ORs
	5-day	3-day	2-day	1-day	
1	80	48	32	16	3
2	70	42	28	14	2
3	70	42	28	14	2
4	60	36	24	12	1
5	70	42	28	14	2
Total	350	210	140	70	10

time and surgery duration should be less than `slots` of OR, where `slots` represents the total number of slots in the shift. Note that (r_1) encodes conditions $(c1)$ and $(c2)$ thanks to the minimality property of the ASP semantics.

After guessing an assignment for the registrations, the encoding presents constraints from (r_2) to (r_{11}) to discard some unwanted assignments. Note that each constraint r_i $(i = 2..11)$ encodes condition (cN), $N = i+1$.

Finally, weak constraints (r_{12}) and (r_{13}) are used to give preference to registrations having priority 2 over those having priority 3, where `totRegsP2` and `totRegsP3` are constants representing the total number of registrations having priority 2 and 3, respectively.

5   Experimental Results

This section reports about the results of an empirical analysis of the ORS problem with surgical teams. In the first subsection we present the benchmarks we have employed, whose results coupled with our encoded are shown in the second subsection. The third subsection reports about a further analyses focused on anesthetists WT efficiency.

5.1   Benchmarks

For each scenario, the characteristics of the tests are as follows:

- 4 scenarios for testing the dimension of the slot interval: A, B, C, and D for slot interval of 10, 20, 30, and 60 min, respectively.
- 4 different benchmarks, with a planning period of 1, 2, 3 and 5 working days;
- For each benchmark the total number of randomly generated registrations are 350 for 5 days, 210 for 3 days, 140 for 2 days and 70 for 1 day, respectively;
- 5 specialties;
- 20 surgeons assigned to the 5 specialties;
- 20 anaesthetists assigned to the 5 specialties;
- 4 h of work time in a day for each surgeon;
- 6 h of work time in a day for each anaesthetist;

- 10 ORs distributed among the specialties;
- 5 h morning and afternoon shifts for each OR summing up to 500, 300, 200 and 100 h of OR available time for the four benchmarks, resp..

Table 4 shows the distribution of the total number of randomly generated registrations for each benchmark of 5, 3, 2 and 1 day, for each specialty, together with the distribution of ORs for each specialty.

5.2   Results

Experiments have been run on a HP 630 Notebook with Intel(R) Core(TM) i3 CPU M380@2.53GHz. The ASP system used is CLINGO [17]. Results of the experiments are reported for scenario A in Table 5, for scenario B in Table 6, for scenario C in Table 7 and for scenario D in Table 8, respectively.

Each benchmark was tested 10 times with different randomly generated inputs. A time limit of 300 s was set for each experiment. In each table averages for 10 instances for each benchmark are reported. The first three columns show the number of assigned registrations out of the generated ones for each priority P1, P2 and P3, the fourth column shows the cumulative assigned registrations, while the last three columns show a measure of the total time occupied by the assigned registrations as a percentage of the total OR time available (indicated as OR time Eff in the tables) and the total percentage of surgeons and anesthetists working time (indicated as Surg WT Eff and Anest WT Eff in the tables, respectively).

As we can see in scenario A (Table 5), with slot interval of 10 min, we obtain results only for schedules up to 3 days, while in the case of the 5-day benchmark the computation time exceeds our time limit on all instances. Scenario B (Table 6) details the scheduling results with slot interval of 20 min. It can be seen that OR efficiency is 75% while the Surgeons and Anesthetists WT efficiency remain greater than 90% and 60%, respectively, for all benchmarks in this scenario. In scenario C (Table 7) with a slot interval of 30 min, the OR efficiency is around 76% while the Surgeons and Anesthetists WT efficiency are enhanced up to 95% and 63% for all benchmarks, respectively. In scenario D (Table 8) with a slot interval of 60 min, OR efficiency is almost 79% while the Surgeons WT efficiency is further enhanced to more than 95%, and Anesthetists WT efficiency is up to 65%.

In all the evaluated benchmarks for different scenarios we observed that the OR efficiency and the anesthetists WT efficiency are limited by the fact that we reached the ceiling of the surgeons maximum working hours. Considering that in our setup we had one anesthetist for each surgeon, the ratio between anesthetist and surgeon efficiencies coincides to the ratio between their maximum working time of the surgeons and the anesthetists, i.e., 2/3. In a real application, this would be a useful information for the Hospital manager to quantify the excess of anesthetists and reorganize their numbers or their working times.

Overall, we obtained satisfying results but for the 5-day schedule length for the more fine-grained slot interval of Scenario A. In order to further investigate the issue, we moved on a different dimension and tested the Scenario A configuration with half the number of registrations (35 instead of 70 for each planning day), surgeons (10 instead of 20), anesthetists (10 instead of 20) and ORs (5 instead of 10). With these numbers we can reach acceptable solutions after 60 s of computation time (see Table 9) for every benchmark, including the 5-day one.

Table 5. Averages of the results for 5, 3, 2 and 1 day benchmarks for Scenario A.

Bench.	P1	P2	P3	Total	OR time Eff.	Surg WT Eff.	Anest WT Eff.
5 days	–	–	–	–	–	–	–
3 days	43.1/43.1	53.0/81.6	26.2/85.3	122.3/210.0	73.5%	91.8%	61.2%
2 days	29.9/29.9	37.0/54.7	17.7/55.4	84.6/140.0	74.7%	93.4%	62.3%
1 day	13.4/13.4	22.8/28.0	8.9/28.6	46.1/70.0	75.6%	94.5%	62.9%

Table 6. Averages of the results for 5, 3, 2 and 1 day benchmarks for Scenario B.

Bench.	P1	P2	P3	Total	OR time Eff.	Surg WT Eff.	Anest WT Eff.
5 days	71.2/71.2	99.4/140.1	38.3/138.7	208.9/350.0	75.1%	93.8%	62.5%
3 days	40.9/40.9	61.6/85.3	25.2/83.8	127.7/210.0	75.3%	94.1%	62.8%
2 days	28.2/28.2	41.1/56.1	14.9/55.7	84.2/140.0	75.0%	93.7%	62.5%
1 day	12.5/12.5	23.1/29.7	8.9/27.8	43.5/70.0	75.5%	94.4%	62.9%

5.3   Extended Analysis

In order to improve the anesthetists WT efficiency, we further analysed our solution considering the new setting introduced at the end of the previous analysis, and introducing 3 alternative scenarios wrt number of surgeons and anesthetists:

- Scenario 1: 10 surgeons and 8 anesthetists
- Scenario 2: 10 surgeons and 7 anesthetists
- Scenario 3: 10 surgeons and 5 anesthetists

Overall, for each new scenario, the characteristics of the tests performed that were modified wrt the analysis in the previous subsection are:

- For each benchmark the total number of randomly generated registrations were 175 for 5 days, 105 for 3 days, 70 for 2 days and 35 for 1 day;

Table 7. Averages of the results for 5, 3, 2 and 1 day benchmarks for Scenario C.

Bench.	P1	P2	P3	Total	OR time Eff.	Surg WT Eff.	Anest WT Eff.
5 days	71.9/71.9	99.0/139.8	44.1/138.3	215.0/350.0	76.0%	95.2%	63.3%
3 days	41.7/41.7	66.9/84.8	21.6/83.5	130.2/210.0	76.1%	95.1%	63.5%
2 days	27.9/27.9	42.7/53.8	16.9/58.3	87.5/140.0	76.2%	95.2%	63.5%
1 day	14.2/14.2	23.0/29.4	6.7/26.4	43.9/70.0	76.2%	95.1%	63.5%

Table 8. Averages of the results for 5, 3, 2 and 1 day benchmarks for Scenario D.

Bench.	P1	P2	P3	Total	OR time Eff.	Surg WT Eff.	Anest WT Eff.
5 days	68.7/68.7	109.6/143.8	46.9/137.5	224.8/350.0	79.0%	98.8%	65.8%
3 days	41.8/41.8	65.1/ 81.9	25.5/86.3	132.4/210.0	78.7%	98.4%	65.6%
2 days	27.5/27.5	46.5/ 54.5	14.6/58.0	87.7/140.0	79.2%	98.9%	65.9%
1 day	13.3/13.3	23.1/27.5	8.3/29.2	44.7/70.0	78.3%	97.8%	65.2%

- 10 surgeons assigned to the 5 specialties;
- 10 anaesthetists assigned to the 5 specialties;
- 5 ORs, unevenly distributed among the specialties;

Results of the extended analysis are reported in this section for Scenario 1 in Table 10, for Scenario 2 in Table 11 and for Scenario 3 in Table 12, respectively, organized as Tables 5, 6, 7 and 8. Each benchmark was tested 10 times with different randomly generated inputs with a time limit of 60 s set for each experiment, and averages over 10 instances.

As we can see, in Scenario 1 (Table 10) the OR efficiency is greater than 64% while the Surgeons and Anesthetists WT efficiency remain greater than 80% and 67%, respectively. In Scenario 2 (Table 11) OR efficiency is again between 64% and 68%, with the Surgeons WT efficiency of around 84% and improved Anesthetists WT efficiency up to 80%. Finally, on Scenario 3 (Table 12) the OR efficiency decreases around 50%, while the Surgeons WT efficiency is still from 64% to 67%, and Anesthetists WT efficiency is further enhanced up tp 90%.

6   Related Work

In this section we discuss some relevant works related to this research. Meskens et al. [30] considered the surgical teams in the computation of an OR schedule, and developed a model using Constraint Programming (CP) with multiple constraints such as availability, staff preferences and affinities among surgical teams. They optimize the use of ORs by minimizing makespan and maximizing affinities among surgical team members. The effectiveness of their proposed method for improving surgical cases was evaluated using real data from an Hospital. Hamid et al. [29] incorporated the decision-making styles (DMS) of the surgical team

Table 9. Averages of the results for 5, 3, 2 and 1 day benchmarks with slot interval 10 min and reduced number of registrations.

Bench.	P1	P2	P3	Total	OR time Eff.	Surg WT Eff.	Anest WT Eff.
5 days	35.5/35.5	52.3/68.3	17.0/71.2	104.8/175.0	74.4%	93.1%	62.0%
3 days	19.0/19.0	31.9/41.2	12.9/40.8	63.8/105.0	74.4%	93.0%	62.0%
2 days	14.2/14.2	20.8/28.6	6.9/26.3	40.9/70.0	73.0%	91.3%	60.8%
1 day	5.5/5.5	10.4/15.1	3.6/14.4	19.5/35.0	70.7%	89.5%	58.9%

Table 10. Averages of the results for 5, 3, 2 and 1 day benchmarks with 10 surgeons and 8 anesthetists for Scenario 1.

Bench.	P1	P2	P3	Total	OR time Eff.	Surg WT Eff.	Anest WT Eff.
5 days	35.5/35.5	47.0/68.3	13.5/71.2	93.0/175.0	67.6%	84.5%	70.2%
3 days	19.0/19.0	29.3/41.2	10.3/41.2	58.6/105.0	68.1%	85.1%	70.9%
2 days	13.9/13.9	18.8/28.2	5.3/26.9	38.0/70.0	66.8%	83.6%	69.7%
1 day	5.5/5.5	9.8/15.1	2.4/14.4	17.7/35.0	64.3%	80.4%	67.0%

Table 11. Averages of the results for 5, 3, 2 and 1 day benchmarks with 10 surgeons and 7 anesthetists for Scenario 2.

Bench.	P1	P2	P3	Total	OR time Eff.	Surg WT Eff.	Anest WT Eff.
5 days	35.5/35.5	45.2/68.3	14.8/71.2	95.5/175.0	67.3%	84.1%	80.2%
3 days	19.0/19.0	30.3/41.2	9.0/44.8	58.3/105.0	67.6%	84.5%	80.5%
2 days	13.9/13.9	19.1/28.2	4.8/26.9	37.9/70.0	67.2%	84.0%	80.0%
1 day	5.5/5.5	9.8/15.1	2.4/14.4	17.7/35.0	64.3%	80.4%	76.5%

Table 12. Averages of the results for 5, 3, 2 and 1 day benchmarks with 10 surgeons and 5 anesthetists for Scenario 3.

Bench.	P1	P2	P3	Total	OR time Eff.	Surg WT Eff.	Anest WT Eff.
5 days	35.5/35.5	35.3/68.3	9.4/71.2	80.2/175.0	53.6%	67.0%	89.4%
3 days	19.0/19.0	25.2/41.2	3.6/44.8	48.3/105.0	54.3%	67.8%	90.4%
2 days	13.9/13.9	14.6/28.2	2.8/26.9	31.0/70.0	53.4%	66.7%	88.0%
1 day	5.5/5.5	7.8/15.1	1.5/14.3	14.9/35.0	51.2%	64.0%	85.3%

to improve the compatibility level by considering constraints such as the availability of material resources, priorities of patients, and availability, skills, and competencies of the surgical team. They developed a multi-objective mathematical model to schedule surgeries. Two metaheuristics, namely Non-dominated Sorting Genetic Algorithm and Multi-Objective Particle Swarm Optimization, were developed to find pareto-optimal solutions. Xiang et al. [34] proposed an Ant Colony Optimization (ACO) approach to surgical scheduling taking into account all resources in the entire process of a surgery. The problem was represented as an extended multi-resource constrained flexible job shop scheduling problem, which was solved using a two-level hierarchical graph to integrate sequencing job and allocating resources. To evaluate the efficiency of ACO, a Discrete Event System (DES) model of an OR system was developed in the simulation platform SIMIO. Monteiro et al. [31] developed a comprehensive multiobjective mathematical model using epsilon-constraint method coupled to the CPLEX solver. Vijayakumar et al. [33] used Mixed Integer Programming (MIP) model for multi-day, multi-resource, patient-priority-based surgery scheduling. A First Fit Decreasing algorithm was developed. From a solution time perspective, their model took hours and in most cases was unable to optimally solve the problem. Belkhamsa et al. [7] proposed two meta heuristics, an Iterative Local Search (ILS) approach and Hybrid Genetic Algorithm (HGA) to solve a daily surgery scheduling problem. Zhou et al. [35] developed an Integer Programming model for optimal surgery schedule of assigning patients to different resources in any surgical stage. They used Lagrangian Relaxation algorithm and solved the subproblem by using branch and bound. They verified their model using real data instances from an Hospital. A common issue with all such solutions seem to be computation time and scalability.

About, instead, other scheduling problems in which ASP have been proficiently employed: Nurse Scheduling Problem [3, 4, 16], where the goal is to create a scheduling for nurses working in Hospitals; Team Building Problem [32], where the goal is to allocate the available personnel of a seaport for serving the incoming ships; the Conference Paper Assignment Problem [5], which deals with the problem of assigning reviewers in the PC to submitted conference papers; and scheduling production materials between storage locations and assembly station [20].

Finally, this is an extended and revised version of a paper appearing in [13], with the following main improvements: (i) the mathematical formulation (Sect. 3.2), (ii) the precise definition of the problem (still Sect. 3.2), and (iii) the extended experimental analysis (Sect. 5.3).

7   Conclusions

In this paper we employed ASP for solving ORS problems with surgical teams. The results of our experiments confirm that ASP is a suitable methodology for addressing planning and scheduling problems in healthcare system. We presented the results of an experimental analysis on several directions to check scalability of our solution in terms of efficiency, considering shift duration, surgeons and anesthetist working hours. This solution achieved satisfied ORs, surgeons' and anaesthetists' efficiency also for the planning length of 5 days. As a future work we would like first to analyze the performance of our solution on real data, that we only recently obtained. We also want to integrate the extension of the

ORS model with beds management with the one presented in this paper, in order to have a more complete unified solution. We also plan to compare to alternative methods, assuming this is possible (i.e., availability of alternative solutions), and viable (i.e., very same problem solved). Finally, through results are satisfying, we plan to work also on improving performance by both evaluating more solvers, e.g., WASP [2], other than Clingo actually used, and employing SAT techniques (e.g., [11,25–28]), given the strong existing relation between ASP and SAT [23,24].

References

1. Abedini, A., Ye, H., Li, W.: Operating room planning under surgery type and priority constraints. Proc. Manuf. **5**, 15–25 (2016)
2. Alviano, M., Amendola, G., Dodaro, C., Leone, N., Maratea, M., Ricca, F.: Evaluation of disjunctive programs in WASP. In: Balduccini, M., Lierler, Y., Woltran, S. (eds.) LPNMR 2019. LNCS, vol. 11481, pp. 241–255. Springer, Cham (2019). https://doi.org/10.1007/978-3-030-20528-7_18
3. Alviano, M., Dodaro, C., Maratea, M.: An advanced answer set programming encoding for nurse scheduling. In: Esposito, F., Basili, R., Ferilli, S., Lisi, F. (eds.) AI*IA 2017. LNCS, vol. 10640. Springer, Cham (2017). https://doi.org/10.1007/978-3-319-70169-1_35
4. Alviano, M., Dodaro, C., Maratea, M.: Nurse (re)scheduling via answer set programming. Intelligenza Artificiale **12**(2), 109–124 (2018)
5. Amendola, G., Dodaro, C., Leone, N., Ricca, F.: On the application of answer set programming to the conference paper assignment problem. In: Adorni, G., Cagnoni, S., Gori, M., Maratea, M. (eds.) AI*IA 2016. LNCS (LNAI), vol. 10037, pp. 164–178. Springer, Cham (2016). https://doi.org/10.1007/978-3-319-49130-1_13
6. Aringhieri, R., Landa, P., Soriano, P., Tànfani, E., Testi, A.: A two level metaheuristic for the operating room scheduling and assignment problem. Comput. Oper. Res. **54**, 21–34 (2015)
7. Belkhamsa, M., Jarboui, B., Masmoudi, M.: Two metaheuristics for solving no-wait operating room surgery scheduling problem under various resource constraints. Comput. Ind. Eng. **126**, 494–506 (2018)
8. Brewka, G., Eiter, T., Truszczynski, M.: Answer set programming at a glance. Commun. ACM **54**(12), 92–103 (2011)
9. Calimeri, F., et al.: ASP-Core-2 input language format. Theory Pract. Logic Program. **20**(2), 294–309 (2020)
10. Calimeri, F., Gebser, M., Maratea, M., Ricca, F.: The design of the fifth answer set programming competition. CoRR abs/1405.3710 (2014). http://arxiv.org/abs/1405.3710
11. Di Rosa, E., Giunchiglia, E., Maratea, M.: A new approach for solving satisfiability problems with qualitative preferences. In: Ghallab, M., Spyropoulos, C.D., Fakotakis, N., Avouris, N.M. (eds.) ECAI. Frontiers in Artificial Intelligence and Applications, vol. 178, pp. 510–514. IOS Press (2008)
12. Dodaro, C., Galatà, G., Khan, M.K., Maratea, M., Porro, I.: An ASP-based solution for operating room scheduling with beds management. In: Fodor, P., Montali, M., Calvanese, D., Roman, D. (eds.) RuleML+RR 2019. LNCS, vol. 11784, pp. 67–81. Springer, Cham (2019). https://doi.org/10.1007/978-3-030-31095-0_5

13. Dodaro, C., Galatà, G., Khan, M.K., Maratea, M., Porro, I.: An ASP based solution for operating room scheduling with surgical teams in hospital environments. In: Benedictis, R.D., et al. (eds.) Joint Proceedings of the 8th Italian Workshop on Planning and Scheduling and the 27th International Workshop on Experimental Evaluation of Algorithms for Solving Problems with Combinatorial Explosion. CEUR Workshop Proceedings, vol. 2745. CEUR-WS.org (2020)
14. Dodaro, C., Galatà, G., Maratea, M., Porro, I.: Operating room scheduling via answer set programming. In: Ghidini, C., Magnini, B., Passerini, A., Traverso, P. (eds.) AI*IA 2018. LNCS (LNAI), vol. 11298, pp. 445–459. Springer, Cham (2018). https://doi.org/10.1007/978-3-030-03840-3_33
15. Dodaro, C., Galatà, G., Maratea, M., Porro, I.: An ASP-based framework for operating room scheduling. Intelligenza Artificiale 13(1), 63–77 (2019)
16. Dodaro, C., Maratea, M.: Nurse scheduling via answer set programming. In: Balduccini, M., Janhunen, T. (eds.) LPNMR 2017. LNCS (LNAI), vol. 10377, pp. 301–307. Springer, Cham (2017). https://doi.org/10.1007/978-3-319-61660-5_27
17. Gebser, M., Kaminski, R., Kaufmann, B., Ostrowski, M., Schaub, T., Wanko, P.: Theory solving made easy with Clingo 5. In: ICLP (Technical Communications). OASICS, vol. 52, pp. 2:1–2:15. Schloss Dagstuhl - Leibniz-Zentrum fuer Informatik (2016)
18. Gebser, M., Maratea, M., Ricca, F.: The design of the seventh answer set programming competition. In: Balduccini, M., Janhunen, T. (eds.) LPNMR 2017. LNCS (LNAI), vol. 10377, pp. 3–9. Springer, Cham (2017). https://doi.org/10.1007/978-3-319-61660-5_1
19. Gebser, M., Maratea, M., Ricca, F.: The seventh answer set programming competition: design and results. Theory Pract. Log. Program. 20(2), 176–204 (2020)
20. Gebser, M., Obermeier, P., Schaub, T., Ratsch-Heitmann, M., Runge, M.: Routing driverless transport vehicles in car assembly with answer set programming. Theory Pract. Log. Program. 18(3–4), 520–534 (2018)
21. Gelfond, M., Lifschitz, V.: The stable model semantics for logic programming. In: Proceedings of the Fifth International Conference and Symposium, Seattle, Washington, 15–19 August 1988 (2 Volumes), pp. 1070–1080. MIT Press (1988)
22. Gelfond, M., Lifschitz, V.: Classical negation in logic programs and disjunctive databases. New Gener. Comput. 9(3/4), 365–386 (1991). https://doi.org/10.1007/BF03037169
23. Giunchiglia, E., Leone, N., Maratea, M.: On the relation among answer set solvers. Ann. Math. Artif. Intell. 53(1–4), 169–204 (2008). https://doi.org/10.1007/s10472-009-9113-1
24. Giunchiglia, E., Maratea, M.: On the relation between answer set and SAT procedures (or, between CMODELS and SMODELS). In: Gabbrielli, M., Gupta, G. (eds.) ICLP 2005. LNCS, vol. 3668, pp. 37–51. Springer, Heidelberg (2005). https://doi.org/10.1007/11562931_6
25. Giunchiglia, E., Maratea, M.: Solving optimization problems with DLL. In: Brewka, G., Coradeschi, S., Perini, A., Traverso, P. (eds.) ECAI. Frontiers in Artificial Intelligence and Applications, vol. 141, pp. 377–381. IOS Press (2006)
26. Giunchiglia, E., Maratea, M., Tacchella, A.: Dependent and independent variables in propositional satisfiability. In: Flesca, S., Greco, S., Ianni, G., Leone, N. (eds.) JELIA 2002. LNCS (LNAI), vol. 2424, pp. 296–307. Springer, Heidelberg (2002). https://doi.org/10.1007/3-540-45757-7_25
27. Giunchiglia, E., Maratea, M., Tacchella, A.: (In)Effectiveness of look-ahead techniques in a modern SAT solver. In: Rossi, F. (ed.) CP 2003. LNCS, vol. 2833, pp.

842–846. Springer, Heidelberg (2003). https://doi.org/10.1007/978-3-540-45193-8_64

28. Giunchiglia, E., Maratea, M., Tacchella, A., Zambonin, D.: Evaluating search heuristics and optimization techniques in propositional satisfiability. In: Goré, R., Leitsch, A., Nipkow, T. (eds.) IJCAR 2001. LNCS, vol. 2083, pp. 347–363. Springer, Heidelberg (2001). https://doi.org/10.1007/3-540-45744-5_26

29. Hamid, M., Nasiri, M.M., Werner, F., Sheikhahmadi, F., Zhalechian, M.: Operating room scheduling by considering the decision-making styles of surgical team members: a comprehensive approach. Comput. Oper. Res. **108**, 166–181 (2019)

30. Meskens, N., Duvivier, D., Hanset, A.: Multi-objective operating room scheduling considering desiderata of the surgical team. Decis. Support Syst. **55**(2), 650–659 (2013). https://doi.org/10.1016/j.dss.2012.10.019

31. Monteiro, T., Meskens, N., Wang, T.: Surgical scheduling with antagonistic human resource objectives. Int. J. Prod. Res. **53**(24), 7434–7449 (2015)

32. Ricca, F., et al.: Team-building with answer set programming in the Gioia-Tauro seaport. Theory Pract. Logic Program. **12**(3), 361–381 (2012)

33. Vijayakumar, B., Parikh, P.J., Scott, R., Barnes, A., Gallimore, J.: A dual bin-packing approach to scheduling surgical cases at a publicly-funded hospital. Eur. J. Oper. Res. **224**(3), 583–591 (2013)

34. Xiang, W., Yin, J., Lim, G.: An ant colony optimization approach for solving an operating room surgery scheduling problem. Comput. Ind. Eng. **85**, 335–345 (2015)

35. Zhou, B., Yin, M., Lu, Z.: An improved Lagrangian relaxation heuristic for the scheduling problem of operating theatres. Comput. Ind. Eng. **101**, 490–503 (2016)

Artificial Intelligence and Robotics

Optimal Control of Point-to-Point Navigation in Turbulent Time Dependent Flows Using Reinforcement Learning

Michele Buzzicotti[1], Luca Biferale[1]([✉]), Fabio Bonaccorso[1,2],
Patricio Clark di Leoni[3], and Kristian Gustavsson[4]

[1] Department of Physics and INFN, University of Rome Tor Vergata,
Via della Ricerca Scientifica 1, 00133 Rome, Italy
{michele.buzzicotti,biferale,fabio.bonaccorso}@roma2.infn.it
[2] Center for Life Nano Science@La Sapienza,
Istituto Italiano di Tecnologia, 00161 Rome, Italy
[3] Department of Mechanical Engineering,
Johns Hopkins University, Baltimore, MD 21218, USA
pato@jhu.edu
[4] Department of Physics, University of Gothenburg,
41296 Gothenburg, Sweden
kristian.gustafsson@physics.gu.se

Abstract. We present theoretical and numerical results concerning the problem to find the path that minimizes the time to navigate between two given points in a complex fluid under realistic navigation constraints. We contrast deterministic Optimal Navigation (ON) control with stochastic policies obtained by Reinforcement Learning (RL) algorithms. We show that Actor-Critic RL algorithms are able to find quasi-optimal solutions in the presence of either time-independent or chaotically evolving flow configurations. For our application, ON solutions develop unstable behavior within the typical duration of the navigation process, and are therefore not useful in practice. We first explore navigation of turbulent flow using a constant propulsion speed. Based on a discretized phase-space, the propulsion direction is adjusted with the aim to minimize the time spent to reach the target. Further, we explore a case where additional control is obtained by allowing the engine to power off. Exploiting advection of the underlying flow, allows the target to be reached with less energy consumption. In this case, we optimize a linear combination between the total navigation time and the total time the engine is switched off. Our approach can be generalized to other setups, for example, navigation under imperfect environmental forecast or with different models for the moving vessel.

1 Introduction

Controlling and planning paths of small autonomous marine vehicles [16] such as wave and current gliders [10], active drifters [13], buoyant underwater explorers, and small swimming drones is important for many geo-physical [11] and

© Springer Nature Switzerland AG 2021
M. Baldoni and S. Bandini (Eds.): AIxIA 2020, LNAI 12414, pp. 223–234, 2021.
https://doi.org/10.1007/978-3-030-77091-4_14

engineering [3] applications. In realistic open environments, these vessels are affected by disturbances like wind, waves and ocean currents, characterized by unpredictable (chaotic) trajectories. Furthermore, active control is also limited by engineering and budget aspects as for the important case of unmanned drifters for oceanic exploration [6,18]. The problem of (time) optimal point-to-point navigation in a flow, known as Zermelo's problem [24], is interesting *per se* in the framework of Optimal Control Theory [5]. In this paper, we extend some of the results from a recent theoretical and numerical study [4], tackling Zermelo's problem for navigation in a two-dimensional fully turbulent flow in the presence of an inverse energy cascade, i.e. with chaotic, multi-scale and rough velocity distributions [1], see Fig. 1 for a summary of the problem. In such a flow, even for time-independent configurations, trivial or naive navigation policies can be extremely inefficient and ineffective if the set of actions by the vessel are limited. We show that an approach based on semi-supervised AI algorithms using actor-critic Reinforcement Learning (RL) [21] is able to find robust quasi-optimal stochastic policies that accomplish the task. Furthermore, we compare RL with solutions from Optimal Navigation (ON) theory [17] and show that the latter is of almost no practical use for the case of navigation in turbulent flows due to strong sensitivity to the initial (and final) conditions, in contrast to what happens for simpler advecting flows [20]. RL has shown to have promising potential to similar problems, such as the training of smart inertial particles or swimming objects navigating intense vortex regions [7–9].

We present here results from navigating one static snapshot of 2D turbulence (for time-dependent flows see [4]). In Fig. 1 we show a sketch of the setup. Our goal is to find trajectories (if they exist) that join the region close to x_A with a target close to x_B in the shortest time, supposing that the vessels obey the following equations of motion:

$$\begin{cases} \dot{X}_t = u(X_t, t) + U^{ctrl}(X_t) \\ U^{ctrl}(X_t) = V_s n(X_t) \end{cases} \tag{1}$$

where $u(X_t, t)$ is the velocity of the underlying 2D advecting flow, and $U^{ctrl}(X_t) = V_s n(X_t)$ is the control slip velocity of the vessel with fixed intensity V_s and varying steering direction: $n(X_t) = (\cos[\theta_t], \sin[\theta_t])$, where the angle is evaluated along the trajectory, $\theta_t = \theta(X_t)$. We introduce a dimensionless slip velocity by normalizing with the maximum velocity u_{max} of the underlying flow: $\tilde{V}_s = V_s / u_{max}$. Zermelo's problem reduces to optimize the steering direction θ in order to reach the target [24]. For time independent flows, optimal navigation (ON) control theory gives a general solution [14,22]. Assuming that the angle θ is controlled continuously in time, the optimal steering angle must satisfy the following time-evolution:

$$\dot{\theta}_t = A_{21} \sin^2 \theta_t - A_{12} \cos^2 \theta_t + (A_{11} - A_{22}) \cos \theta_t \sin \theta_t, \tag{2}$$

where $A_{ij} = \partial_j u_i(X_t)$ is evaluated along the agent trajectory X_t obtained from Eq. (1). The set of equations (1–2) may lead to chaotic dynamics even for

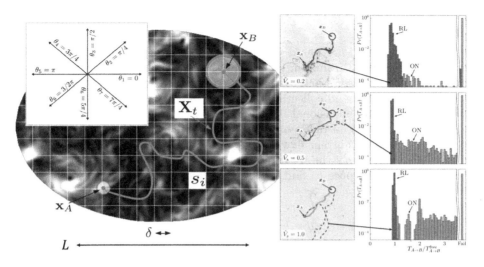

Fig. 1. Left: Image of one turbulent snapshot used as the advecting flow, with the starting, x_A, and ending point, x_B, of our problem. We also show an illustrative navigation trajectory X_t. The flow is obtained from a spatially periodic snapshot of a 2D turbulent configuration in the inverse energy cascade regime with a multi-scale power-law Fourier spectrum, $E(k) = \sum_{k<k<k+1} |u(k)|^2 \sim k^{-5/3}$. For RL optimization, the initial conditions are taken randomly inside a circle of radius d_A centered around x_A. Similarly, the final target is the circle of radius d_B centered around x_B. The flow area is covered by a grid-world with tiles s_i with $i = 1, \ldots, N_s$ and $N_s = 900$ of size $\delta \times \delta$ which identify the state-space for the RL protocol. The large-scale periodicity of the underlying flow is L, and we fixed $\delta = L/10$. Every time interval Δt, the unmanned vessel selects one of the 8 possible actions a_j with $j = 1 \ldots 8$ (the steering directions θ_j depicted in left top inset) according to a policy $\pi(a|s)$, where π is the probability distribution of the action a given the current state s of the agent at that time. The policy is optimized during the learning to maximize the total reward, r_{tot}, proportional to minus the navigation time, $r_{tot} \sim -T_{x_A \to x_B}$, so that the maximal reward corresponds to the fastest trajectory. For the policy to converge, the actor-critic method requires to accumulate experience over a number of the order of 1000 different trajectories, with small variations depending on the values of the slip velocity $\tilde{V}_s$ and the specific flow properties. In a second series of experiments we added an additional action, the possibility to switch off the power, i.e. to let $V_s = 0$. This allows the vessel to fully take advantage of the flow and save energy (see Sect. 3.2). Right: spatial concentrations of trajectories for three values of $\tilde{V}_s$. The flow region is color coded proportionally to the time the trajectories spend in each pixel area for both ON (red) and RL (blue). Light colors refer to low occupation and bright to high occupation. The green-dashed line shows the best ON out the 20000 trajectories. Right histograms: arrival time distribution for ON (red) and RL (blue). Probability of not reaching the target within the upper time limit is plotted in the *Fail* bar. (Color figure online)

time-independent flows in two spatial dimensions. Due to the sensitivity to small perturbations in chaotic systems the ON approach becomes useless for many practical applications.

2   Methods

RL applications [21] are based on the idea that an optimal solution can be obtained by learning from continuous interactions of an agent with its environment. The agent interacts with the environment by sampling its states s, performing actions a and collecting rewards r. In our case the vessel acts as the agent and the two-dimensional flow as the environment. In the approach used here, actions are chosen randomly with a probability that is given by the policy $\pi(a|s)$, given the current flow-state s. The goal is to find the optimal policy $\pi^*(a|s)$ that maximizes the total reward, $r_{\text{tot}} = \sum_t r_t$, accumulated along one episode. For the purpose to find the fastest trajectory we used r_t composed of three different terms;

$$r_t = -\Delta t + \frac{|\boldsymbol{x}_B - \boldsymbol{X}_{t-\Delta t}|}{V_s} - \frac{|\boldsymbol{x}_B - \boldsymbol{X}_t|}{V_s}. \tag{3}$$

The first term accumulates a large penalty if it takes long for the agent to reach the end point, while the second and third terms describe the change in free-flight time to the target, i.e. the difference in time it would take, if the flow is neglected, to reach the target from the locations at this and the previous state change [2]. It follows the the total reward is proportional to minus the actual time taken by the trajectory to reach the target,

$$r_{tot} \sim -T_{\boldsymbol{x}_A \rightarrow \boldsymbol{x}_B},$$

neglecting a constant term that does not depend on the training, see [4] and Fig. 1 for precise definition of flow-states and agent-actions. An episode is finalized when the trajectory reaches the circle of radius d_B around the target. In order to converge to robust policies each episode is started with a uniformly random position within a given radius, d_A, from the starting point. To estimate the expected total future reward we follow the one-step actor-critic method [21] based on a gradient ascent in the policy parametrization. In the second part of our work, we modify the navigation setup by allowing the unmanned vessel to turn off its 'engine', to allow it to navigate just following the flow without its own propulsion speed. In this framework, navigation can be optimal with respect to minimal energy consumption rather than time, or to a tradeoff between energy consumption and time. To repeat the training of the optimal policy taking into account of both aspects, energy and time, we modified our RL scheme as follows. First, we added the new action to turn off the vessel propulsion speed, i.e. letting $V_s = 0$, in addition to the eight possible navigation angles considered before. Second, we modified the reward function in order to weigh the relative importance of navigation time and energy consumption. This was obtained by adding a new term describing the time the vessel consumes energy, $-\lambda \Delta t_{pow}$, to the instantaneous reward in Eq. (3) as follows

$$r_t = -(\Delta t + \lambda \Delta t_{pow}) + \frac{|\boldsymbol{x}_B - \boldsymbol{X}_{t-\Delta t}|}{V_s} - \frac{|\boldsymbol{x}_B - \boldsymbol{X}_t|}{V_s}. \tag{4}$$

The total reward becomes proportional to minus the sum of the two time contributions,

$$r_{tot} \sim -\left(T_{\boldsymbol{x}_A \to \boldsymbol{x}_B} + \lambda T_{pow}\right). \tag{5}$$

The time Δt_{pow} counts the time the vessel navigates with self propulsion, giving a total time T_{pow} where energy is spent. The factor λ weighs the importance of energy consumption time and total navigation time in the optimisation. We have repeated the training of the RL optimal policy with the new time-energy combined goals in the time-independent flow shown in Fig. 1, as well as in a more realistic time-dependent 2D turbulent flow. The latter was obtained by solving the incompressible Navier-Stokes equations on a periodic square domain with side length $L = 2\pi$ and $N = 512^2$ number of collocation points, see [4] for more details about the flow.

3 Results (Time-Independent Flows)

3.1 Shortest Time, No Energy Constraints

In the right part of Fig. 1 we show the main results comparing RL and ON approaches [4]. The minimum time taken by the best trajectory to reach the target is of the same order for the two methods. The most important difference between RL and ON lies in their robustness as seen by plotting the spatial density of trajectories in the right part of Fig. 1 for the optimal policies of ON and RL with three values of $\tilde{V}_s$. We observe that the RL trajectories (blue coloured area) form a much more coherent cloud in space, while the ON trajectories (red coloured area) fill space almost uniformly. Moreover, for small navigation velocities, many trajectories in the ON system approach regular attractors, as visible by the high-concentration regions. The rightmost histograms in Fig. 1 show a comparison between the probability of arrival times for the trajectories illustrated in the two-dimensional domain, providing a quantitative estimation of the better robustness of RL compared to ON. Other RL algorithms, such as Q-learning[21], could also be implemented and compared with other path search algorithms such as A^* which is often used in computer science [12, 19].

3.2 Minimal Energy Consumption

In this section we present results on the simultaneous optimisation of minimal travel time and energy consumption. To begin with, we consider the same time-independent flow as in the previous section. In Fig. 2 we show three sets of trajectories following three policies obtained by optimising the reward (5) for $\lambda = 0$, 2 and 6. The trajectories are superposed on the flow velocity amplitude $|\boldsymbol{u}(\boldsymbol{X}_t, t)|$ (left panel) and the Okubo-Weiss parameter Δ_{OW} [15, 23] (right panel), defined as;

$$\Delta_{OW} = (A_{11} - A_{22})^2 + (A_{21} + A_{12})^2 - (A_{21} - A_{12})^2. \tag{6}$$

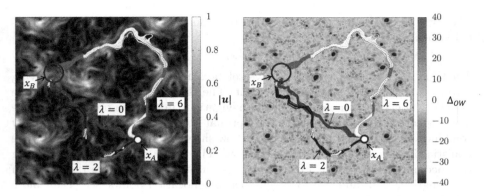

Fig. 2. Three sets of fifty trajectories going from point x_A to point x_B, following the optimal policies for three values of λ with propulsion speed either turned on, $\tilde{V}_s = 0.8$ (color), or turned off, $V_s = 0$ (white). (Left panel) The trajectories are plotted on top of the amplitude of the time-independent flow velocity, $|u|$. (Right panel) Same trajectories plotted over the Okubo-Weiss parameter, Δ_{OW}, see Eq. (6). (Color figure online)

Here A_{ij} is the fluid-gradient matrix as defined after Eq. (2). The decomposition in Eq. (6) is particularly useful to distinguish strain dominated ($\Delta_{OW} > 0$, orange-red colors) from vortex dominated ($\Delta_{OW} < 0$, green-blue colors) regions of the flow. Colored regions of the trajectories show where the action is to have the propulsion on and white regions show where the propulsion is off. When $\lambda = 0$, the energy consumption does not matter for the reward, and the only difference compared to the case in the previous section is that the policy can now choose one additional action: the zero self propulsion speed. However, as seen from Fig. 2, this action is rarely chosen when $\lambda = 0$, and the vessel navigates with a constant self-propelling velocity. On the other hand, when the energy-dependent reward is activated, as in the case of $\lambda = 2$, we observe a difference in the optimal path followed by the vessel. This is because it has to balance the penalties from the total navigation time and the time with self-propulsion. When λ becomes larger, this difference in the optimal path becomes more significant. For $\lambda = 6$ we observe trajectories that are much longer and dominated by passive navigation, just following the flow. To have a more accurate comparison of the arrival time to the target, $T_{x_A \to x_B}$, and the total active navigation time, T_{pow}, for the different values of λ, we show in Fig. 3 the evolution of these two terms as functions of the episode number during the training of the three different policies. The total reward (5) is a linear combination of these two terms, where T_{pow} is multiplied by the factor λ. We first observe that the training converges after around 10k episodes. Second, we see that for $\lambda = 0$, both $T_{x_A \to x_B}$ and T_{pow} lies close to each other for all episodes, suggesting that the optimal policy never found a state where it is better to navigate with zero propulsion to reach the target faster. For values of λ larger than zero, the found policies end up with T_{pow} below the value of the $\lambda = 0$ case, with the consequence of saving energy

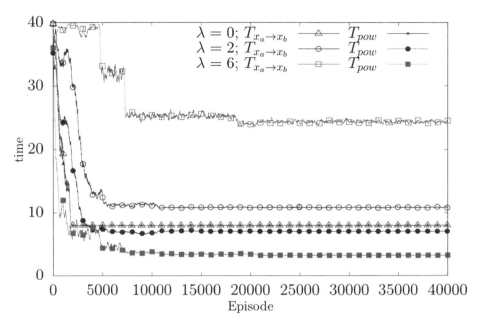

Fig. 3. Total navigation time, $T_{x_A \to x_B}$ (open symbols) and total power-on time, T_{pow} (full symbols), measured for different trajectories obtained during the training as a function of the episode number, and for three different values of λ.

even though the time to reach the target is longer. A final result for this case of time-independent flow is shown in Fig. 4, where we present the Probability Density Functions (PDFs) of the total navigation time, $T_{x_A \to x_B}$ (main panel) and of the power-on navigation time T_{pow} (inset). The distributions are sampled over 40k trajectories with initial conditions close to x_A that follows the optimal policies obtained for five values of λ. These PDFs show that for $\lambda = 0$, both times are of the order of $1.2\,T_{A \to B}^{free}$, where $T_{A \to B}^{free} = |x_B - x_A|/V_s \sim 6.4$ is the free-flight time to go from point A to point B with a fixed self propulsion speed V_s and without flow. For larger λ, the total navigation time increases while the power-on time decreases monotonically up to $\lambda = 6$. Increasing λ up to 10 we do not observe further reduction of T_{pow}, the PDF only becomes more peaked around the value $\approx 0.4\,T_{A \to B}^{free}$ as found for $\lambda = 6$. This result suggests that we have found the minimal amount of propulsion required for the vessel to be able to navigate to the target.

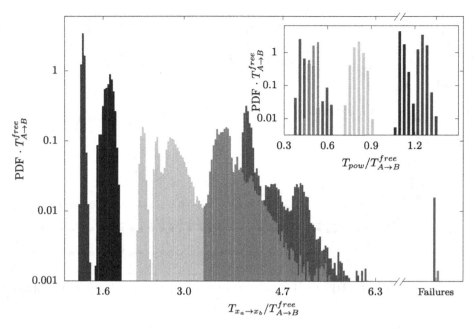

Fig. 4. (Main panel) PDFs of the arrival time, $T_{x_A \to x_B}$ normalized by the free-flight time $T_{A \to B}^{free}$, and measured over 40k different trajectories evolving on a time-independent flow. The different colors indicate different values of λ, from $\lambda = 0$ (no extra cost for using power-on, green color) up to $\lambda = 10$ (yellow color). The failures bars indicate the probability that a trajectory following a given policy does not reach the final target. (Inset) PDFs of the power-on time, T_{pow}, normalized by $T_{A \to B}^{free}$, measured along the same 40k trajectories shown in the main panel. (Color figure online)

4   Results (Time-Dependent Flow)

In this last section we consider the same optimal navigation problem as in the previous section, but with a more realistic time-dependent flow. For this case we adopted a small self-propulsion velocity, $\tilde{V}_s = 0.2$, i.e. only 20% of the maximal flow velocity amplitude. In Fig. 5 we present, as in the previous section, the PDFs of both $T_{x_A \to x_B}$ (solid lines full symbols) and T_{pow} (dashed lines empty symbols) obtained over 60k different trajectories following the converged optimal policies for $\lambda = 0$, and $\lambda = 2$. These results show that, as for the time-independent case, when $\lambda > 0$ RL finds a solution that spends less energy at the cost of a longer total navigation time compared to the solution when $\lambda = 0$. Let us stress that with a probability of the order of 1 in 1000 we observed trajectories that were not able to reach the final target, as indicated by the failure bars reported in Fig. 5. Finally, Fig. 6 shows six different snapshots at different times during the evolution of two different sets of trajectories that follows the optimal policies obtained for $\lambda = 0$ and $\lambda = 2$. The trajectories are superposed on the time-dependent flow velocity. Similar to Fig. 2, white regions on the trajectories show

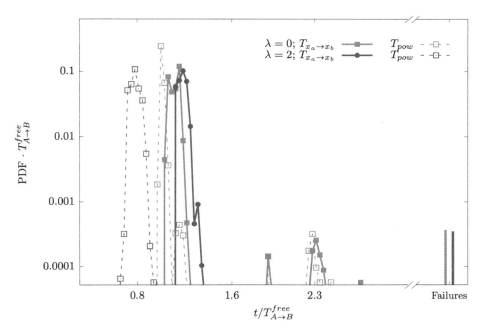

Fig. 5. PDFs of the arrival time, $T_{x_A \to x_B}$ (solid lines, full symbols) and of the power-on time, T_{pow} (dashed lines, open symbols) measured over 60k different trajectories following the optimal policy in a time-dependent flow, both normalized by the free-flight time $T_{A \to B}^{free}$. Colours distinguish the two values of λ used during the training. The navigation speed used along these trajectories is $\tilde{V}_s = 0.2$, hence, 20% of the maximum flow velocity amplitude. The failures bars indicate the probability of a trajectory to not reach the target after a long navigation time. (Color figure online)

where the vessel is navigating with zero self propulsion speed. We remark that even when $\lambda = 0$, the found optimal policy chooses the $V_s = 0$ action in the region close to the target. As a result, the PDFs of the total navigation time and the power-on time are not identical even for the case of $\lambda = 0$. This is a very nice example of the fact that the resulting policy in RL benefits from the added control when the set of allowed actions is enlarged and that, in our particular application, passively moving with the flow can be better than navigating when the flow blows you in the right direction, independently of the requirement to minimize energy.

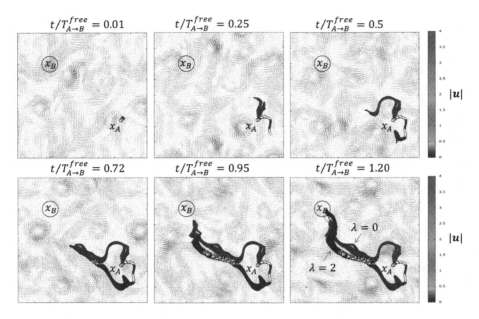

Fig. 6. Six snapshots at different times taken during the evolution of two sets of trajectories in a time-dependent flow, following the optimal policies for $\lambda = 0$ (green color) and $\lambda = 2$ (blue color). The six times are normalized to the free flight time. The flow streamlines are coloured proportionally to their amplitude, while the white points along the navigation trajectories indicate locations where the selected action was passive navigation, i.e. $V_S = 0$. (Color figure online)

5   Conclusions

We have first discussed a systematic investigation of Zermelo's time-optimal navigation problem in a realistic 2D turbulent flow, comparing both RL and ON approaches [4]. We showed that RL stochastic algorithms are key to bypass unavoidable instability given by the chaoticity of the environment and/or by the strong sensitivity of ON on the initial conditions in the presence of non-linear flow configurations. RL methods offer also a wider flexibility, being applicable to energy-minimization problems and in situations where the flow evolution is known only in a statistical sense as in partially observable Markov processes. Let us stress that, instead of starting from a completely random policy as we did here, it is also possible to implement RL to improve a-priori policies designed for a particular problem. For example, one can use an RL approach to optimize an initial *trivial policy*, where the navigation angle is selected as the action that points most directly toward the target. In the second part of this work, we further analyzed the more complex problem where the optimization of the total navigation time is balanced by the energy consumption required to reach the target. Also in this case, we found that RL is able to converge to non-trivial solutions where the vessel navigates most of the time as a passive object transported by the flow, with only a minimum number of corrections to its trajectory required to reach the final target.

Acknowledgments. This project has received partial funding from the European Research Council (ERC) under the European Union's Horizon 2020 research and innovation programme (grant agreement No 882340). K.G. acknowledges funding from the Knut and Alice Wallenberg Foundation, Grant No. KAW 2014.0048, and Vetenskapsrådet, Grant No. 2018-03974. F.B acknowledges funding from the European Research Council under the European Union's Horizon 2020 Framework Programme (No. FP/2014–2020) ERC Grant Agreement No. 739964 (COPMAT).

References

1. Alexakis, A., Biferale, L.: Cascades and transitions in turbulent flows. Phys. Rep. **767–769**, 1–101 (2018)
2. Andrew, Y.N., Harada, D., Russelt, S.: Policy invariance under reward transformations: theory and application to reward shaping. ICML **99**, 278 (1999)
3. Bechinger, C., Di Leonardo, R., Löwen, H., Reichhardt, C., Volpe, G., Volpe, G.: Active particles in complex and crowded environments. Rev. Mod. Phys. **88**(4), 045006 (2016)
4. Biferale, L., Bonaccorso, F., Buzzicotti, M., Clark Di Leoni, P., Gustavsson, K.: Zermelo's problem: optimal point-to-point navigation in 2D turbulent flows using reinforcement learning. Chaos: Interdisc. J. Nonlinear Sci. **29**(10), 103138 (2019)
5. Bryson, A.E., Ho, Y.: Applied Optimal Control: Optimization, Estimation and Control. Routledge, New York (1975)
6. Centurioni, L.R.: Drifter technology and impacts for sea surface temperature, sea-level pressure, and ocean circulation studies. In: Venkatesan, R., Tandon, A., D'Asaro, E., Atmanand, M.A. (eds.) Observing the Oceans in Real Time. SO, pp. 37–57. Springer, Cham (2018). https://doi.org/10.1007/978-3-319-66493-4_3
7. Colabrese, S., Gustavsson, K., Celani, A., Biferale, L.: Flow navigation by smart microswimmers via reinforcement learning. Phys. Rev. Lett. **118**(15), 158004 (2017)
8. Colabrese, S., Gustavsson, K., Celani, A., Biferale, L.: Smart inertial particles. Phys. Rev. Fluids **3**(8), 084301 (2018)
9. Gustavsson, K., Biferale, L., Celani, A., Colabrese, S.: Finding efficient swimming strategies in a three-dimensional chaotic flow by reinforcement learning. Eur. Phys. J. E **40**(12), 1–6 (2017). https://doi.org/10.1140/epje/i2017-11602-9
10. Kraus, N.D.: Wave glider dynamic modeling, parameter identification and simulation. Ph.D. thesis, University of Hawaii at Manoa, Honolulu, May 2012 (2012)
11. Lermusiaux, P.F., et al.: A future for intelligent autonomous ocean observing systems. J. Mar. Res. **75**(6), 765–813 (2017)
12. Lerner, J., Wagner, D., Zweig, K.: Algorithmics of Large and Complex Networks: Design, Analysis, and Simulation, vol. 5515. Springer, Heidelberg (2009). https://doi.org/10.1007/978-3-642-02094-0
13. Lumpkin, R., Pazos, M.: Measuring surface currents with surface velocity program drifters: the instrument, its data, and some recent results. In: Lagrangian Analysis and Prediction of Coastal and Ocean Dynamics, pp. 39–67 (2007)
14. Mannarini, G., Pinardi, N., Coppini, G., Oddo, P., Iafrati, A.: VISIR-I: small vessels-least-time nautical routes using wave forecasts. Geosci. Model Dev. **9**(4), 1597–1625 (2016)

15. Okubo, A.: Horizontal dispersion of floatable particles in the vicinity of velocity singularities such as convergences. In: Deep Sea Research and Oceanographic Abstracts, vol. 17, pp. 445–454. Elsevier (1970)
16. Petres, C., Pailhas, Y., Patron, P., Petillot, Y., Evans, J., Lane, D.: Path planning for autonomous underwater vehicles. IEEE Trans. Robot. **23**(2), 331–341 (2007)
17. Pontryagin, L.S.: Mathematical Theory of Optimal Processes. Routledge, London (2018)
18. Roemmich, D., et al.: The Argo program: observing the global ocean with profiling floats. Oceanography **22**(2), 34–43 (2009)
19. Russell, S., Norvig, P.: Artificial intelligence: a modern approach (2002)
20. Schneider, E., Stark, H.: Optimal steering of a smart active particle. arXiv preprint arXiv:1909.03243 (2019)
21. Sutton, R.S., Barto, A.G.: Reinforcement Learning: An Introduction. MIT Press, Cambridge (2018)
22. Techy, L.: Optimal navigation in planar time-varying flow: Zermelo's problem revisited. Intell. Serv. Robot. **4**(4), 271–283 (2011). https://doi.org/10.1007/s11370-011-0092-9
23. Weiss, J.: The dynamics of enstrophy transfer in two-dimensional hydrodynamics. Phys. D: Nonlinear Phenomena **48**(2–3), 273–294 (1991)
24. Zermelo, E.: Über das navigationsproblem bei ruhender oder veränderlicher windverteilung. ZAMM-J. Appl. Math. Mech./Zeitschrift für Angewandte Mathematik und Mechanik **11**(2), 114–124 (1931)

Brain-Driven Telepresence Robots: A Fusion of User's Commands with Robot's Intelligence

Gloria Beraldo[1,2(✉)] [ID], Luca Tonin[1] [ID], Amedeo Cesta[2] [ID],
and Emanuele Menegatti[1] [ID]

[1] Department of Information Engineering, University of Padova, Padua, Italy
{gloria.beraldo,luca.tonin,emg}@dei.unipd.it
[2] Institute of Cognitive Sciences and Technologies (ISTC), National Research
Council, ISTC-CNR, Rome, Italy
{gloria.beraldo,amedeo.cesta}@istc.cnr.it

Abstract. This paper presents different methodologies to enhance the human-robot interaction during the control of brain-machine interface (BMI) driven telepresence robots. To overcome the limitations of BMIs, namely the low bit rate and the intrinsic uncertainty as a control channel, we hypothesize that the fusion of the user's commands with the robot's intelligence is essential to achieve robust and natural systems. Compared to most current neurorobotics works, we exploit the robot as an intelligent agent that contributes at different levels to choose the final action to perform. Furthermore, we present the first implementation of a BMI system inside the Robot Operating System (ROS) designed to facilitate the combination between BMI and robotics.

Keywords: Neurorobotics · Brain-machine interface · Telerobotics
and teleoperation · Behavior-based systems

1 Introduction

Brain-Machine Interfaces (BMIs) are able to detect and translate electrical signals produced by brain activity into outputs for external devices [1–3]. These systems mainly target end-users suffering from severe motor impairments (e.g., amyotrophic lateral sclerosis, brainstem stroke, cerebral palsy, and spinal cord injury) [2,4]. Over the last decades, many robotic devices have been integrated with BMIs to improve the independence of the end-users such as prosthesis, exoskeletons, wheelchairs, telepresence robots [5–8]. In particular, BMI driven telepresence robots enable end-users to keep in contact and interact with relatives and friends located in different environments through a video streaming connection to the robot [9]. However, the human-robot interaction through BMIs suffers from noise due to the instability of the neurophysiological signals and low bit rate (i.e., the user can only send discrete and rare commands). Moreover,

© Springer Nature Switzerland AG 2021
M. Baldoni and S. Bandini (Eds.): AIxIA 2020, LNAI 12414, pp. 235–248, 2021.
https://doi.org/10.1007/978-3-030-77091-4_15

the control of the robot with BMIs requires a certain mental effort and concentration. In this context, one of the challenges is first to reduce the user's workload needed to control the robot. Secondly, given that in the last years, neurorobotics studies mainly focus on creating sophisticated methods to decode the user's input by providing only simple implementations of the robotic part, the next goal consists of augmenting the human-robot interaction in the perspective of using this technology in complex and unstructured environments. One solution to both the challenges might be to fuse the user's commands with the robot's intelligence to fully exploit the robot's functionalities and evaluate the user's commands according to the context. An illustrative representation of how the user's commands decoded by BMI are fused with the robot's intelligence is shown in Fig. 1.

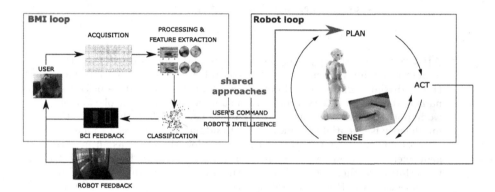

Fig. 1. Representation of the fusion between the user's commands and the robot's intelligence to mentally drive telepresence robots. The BMI commands are decoded by the BMI system (left). The user is required to perform a specific mental task (e.g., the imagination of the movements of the both hands vs. both feet). The brain signals are acquired and processed to detect the features associated with the mental task. The probability distribution given in output by the classifier is converted into a command for the robot and then the related BMI feedback is provided to the user. In the meantime, the robot is involved in the canonical *plan-sense-act* architecture (right). In *shared* approaches, the robot receives the user's commands and contextualizes them according to its context awareness. Finally, the streaming video from the robot's camera is shown to the user.

The user has the role of choosing the high-level details of the task such as the selection of a destination or a specific behavior for the robot and the choice of the directional commands to drive the robot. The robot adapts its motion according to the surrounding environment. On the one side, the robot manages the low-level operations such as obstacle avoidance to reduce the user's mental workload. On the other, the robot can enhance the interaction achievable via BMI. Since the BMI's commands are translated into only a few robot's actions (e.g., turn left and turn right), the robot can implement other behaviors (e.g., the passage through the door) by recognizing elements in the environment without requiring the send of specific inputs from the user (e.g., the door is target, center the door, etc.).

These approaches that consider both the agents, the human and the robot, are called *shared* because the final robot's action is determined by evaluating the shared information between them (i.e., user's commands and robot's perception).

This paper aims at showing the advantages of fusing the user's commands with the robot's intelligence to mentally drive telepresence robots. For the sake of clarity, we first introduce a taxonomy characterizing *shared* approaches at different levels of abstraction according to the human-robot interaction (see Sect. 2). Then, we focus on presenting two main strategies to overcome the challenges in BMI driven robots mentioned above. From the robot side, we present different systems that reduce the user's effort by increasing the robot capabilities: (i) the robot performs pre-defined behaviors in autonomy under the user's supervision (ii) the user's and the robot's inputs are equally combined to determine the robot's behavior and hence the wrong user's commands are smoothed or avoided. From the BMI's side, we propose a modular implementation of the BMI loop inside the Robot Operating System (ROS) ecosystem, the worldwide standard de facto in robotics, to facilitate the development of brain-driven telepresence robots (see Sect. 5).

2   Taxonomy of Shared Approaches

In the literature, several terms are introduced to refer to *shared* approaches, but there is not a clear definition yet to distinguish them and/or to specify the most appropriate terminology to use. With this regard, we critically revisit the literature by also considering other contexts where the user is involved in demanding tasks and for which *shared* approaches are effective to reduce the user's workload. For instance, in the aviation field, the problem of fusing the human's and the robot's contributions was described in terms of the partition of the sub tasks performed by the human and those delegated to the robot, resulting in the level of automation (LOA) [10–12]. From this point of view, *traded control* [13] and *shared control* [14–16] are the most common terms to highlight that the robot influences the situations and changes some control variables (e.g., the motion's speed, the motion's direction). *Supervisory control* [17] and *shared autonomy* [18] are preferred to emphasize that the users can avoid controlling the robot all time, but they let it execute pre-defined operations autonomously under their supervisions. The level of autonomy of the robot can not be fixed a priori for which the term *adjustable autonomy* [19] was introduced for systems with a continuous and transparent change of robot's autonomy during the task [19]. In the multiagents community, the user and the robot in *shared* approaches are considered as a team where the two agents dynamically adapt their roles to best reach the common goal according to their skills [20]. In this perspective, the robot's contribution is defined in terms of the initiative the robot exerts and hence researchers typically opt for the terms *mixed-initiative interaction* [20] or *mixed initiative planning and execution* [21,22]. The initiative is negotiated and it might vary from low-level motion control of the robot to the seize of human's control such as in emergency situations [23].

The proposed taxonomy incorporates these aspects into three forms of interaction that we name *shared control, shared autonomy* and *shared intelligence* [24]. The choice of three typologies of human-robot interaction is inspired from the decision-making theory that categorizes the human choices into three levels [15,25]:

(i) operational to refer to detailed and short term decisions;
(ii) tactical including the settings and allocating resources over a medium planning horizon;
(iii) strategic namely all the strategies chosen to achieve high goals and with a longer validity than in the other two levels.

We assume that the fusion of the user's commands with the robot's intelligence reflects the kind of decisions taken by the user and by the robot and therefore the role of the two agents in determining the actions performed by the robot. Furthermore, we represent the three kinds of human-robot interaction in a pyramid model to recall the decision-making theory from the point of view of the level of details of the decisions taken by the user and by the robot (see Fig. 2):

(i) low level human-robot interaction indicates the execution of specific control signals that quickly expire;
(ii) medium level refers to procedures performed by the robot in autonomy in a medium time;
(iii) high level is associated with policies that strategically guides both human and robot's choices in reaching the common goal during the whole interaction.

Therefore, in *shared control* approaches, the user interacts at low-level (execution) by delivering steering/turning commands to the robot. The robot implements simple adjustments of the user's commands (e.g., change of the angle of rotation) to avoid collisions, but it cannot take high decisions. In emergency or in demanding situations, the robot stops until the user delivers a new command. In *shared autonomy* the robot autonomously implements determined behaviors according to routines or procedures established a priori. The main aim of *shared autonomy* approach is to reduce the effort required by the user by requiring him/her only to supervise the robot without specifying the low-level details even if he/she can intervene at any time. Finally, we also include the *shared intelligence* to characterise the interaction between human and robot in which also the robot's contribution is equally fused with the user's inputs. Hence, in *shared intelligence*, the robot could implement actions/motion that are different from the original user's commands.

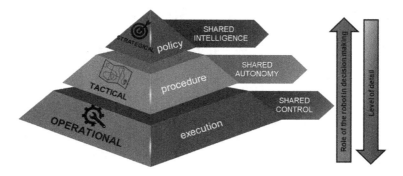

Fig. 2. The proposed taxonomy detects three main forms of interaction: *shared control*, *shared autonomy* and *shared intelligence*. The hierarchical representation recalls the *decision-making* theory from which the model is inspired. The three approaches differ in terms of role of the robot in the decision-making phase and the level of details of the choices taken by the user and by the robot.

3   Shared Autonomy Approaches Based on Pre-coded Behaviors

In this section, we face the challenges of explicitly designing advanced interactions between the user and the telepresence robot through *shared autonomy* approaches. We propose systems that increase the robot's perception and activate predetermined reactive behaviors to aid the user when the robot detects demanding situations. Specifically, we examine the three common scenarios in telepresence applications:

(i) The presence of landmarks in the environment (Fig. 3a): they represent points of interest. In particular, we focus on doors since they are one of the most characterizing landmarks of each indoor environment. Moreover, doors can influence the behavior of the robot according to their status (open enough or closed) with the possibility to activate *"the passage through the door"* procedure [26].

(ii) The presence of people (Fig. 3b): in the perspective of introducing robots to operate in everyday life and to communicate with other people in a populated environment, robots should behave acceptably by implementing "social behaviors" and respecting the social norms (e.g., personal space). Therefore, in that scenario, the robot behavior is driven by people that can be classified as targets or obstacles, but with the additional difficulty of being dynamic.

(iii) "Obstacle avoidance behaviors" (Fig. 3c): they are based on knowledge a priori of the environment (e.g., map) provided to the robot and robust localization techniques. Thanks to the detailed knowledge of the area where it is acting, the robot optimizes the motion from one position to another, simplifying the contextualization of the user's commands and limiting the number of collisions [9].

Shared autonomy approaches based on pre-coded behaviors

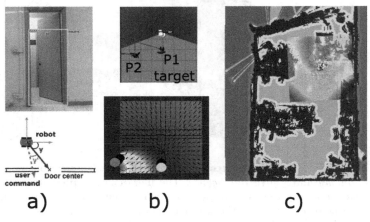

a)   b)   c)

Fig. 3. Representation of the shared autonomy approaches based on *behavior assistance.* (a) The perception of doors activates the *"passage through the door"* procedure coherently with the user commands and the status of the door (open/close). (b) "Social navigation" where people influence the robot's motion considering the social rules based on proxemics constraints. People are target (e.g., P1) when the user wants to interact with them or dynamic obstacles to avoid (e.g., P2). (c) "Obstacle avoidance behaviors": the user's commands are evaluated by matching the map in input with the data coming from the robot's sensors as well as its position in the environment.

To facilitate the control of the user and exploit the potentialities of the robot, we adapt the advances in the field of autonomous mobile robotics to the case of *human-in-the-loop* applications. In particular, we take inspiration from the *goal-oriented* navigation that assigns high-level goals to the robot and, in combination with a motion planner, determines the best trajectory for the robot towards the goal position [9,26]. The common strategy of the proposed *shared autonomy* approaches consists in defining a temporary destination called *subgoal* for the robot that is set according to the specific behaviors implemented by the robot:

(i) *Shared autonomy driven by a door detection module:* the *subgoal* is set beyond the door if coherent with the user's intention and the robot passes through the door without any user's input. Our system determines the *subgoal* positions by evaluating different attractive/repulsive effects of many components such as obstacles, the user's input and the doors. However, in contrast to systems based on potential field techniques [27–30], we avoid determining the speed of the robot from the resulting forces, but we combine them into a heuristic function only for the *subgoal* computation. The motivation is to reduce the local minima and the consequent interruption of the robot's motion. Please refer to [26] for further details about the implementation of the proposed system. Furthermore, our system detects and tracks doors by using the camera on board of the robot without any markers [31–33] or specialized sensor setups [34,35]. We introduce a robust detection module that also estimates online the aperture of the door to avoid the problems arisen in the previous systems: (i) the difficulty on centering the robot within the door using only sonars [30,36]; (ii) the definition of pre-programmed paths the robot follows [37] that make the system not easily exploitable in other environments as well as too dependent on the driving skill of the user.

(ii) *Shared autonomy driven by people:* the *subgoal* is set close to a target person or far if people are dynamic obstacles. When a person is selected as a target, the robot moves towards that person by considering also the presence of other people (both static and dynamic). We modeled the effect generated by humans into the robot using the behavioral potential field, an extended version of potential field that also evaluates the motion of the people namely their direction and speed [38]. However, we extend the original version proposed in [38] not only to teleoperate the telepresence robots but also to include the proxemics conventions introduced by Hall et al. [39] and previously evaluated with autonomous robots approaching people [40–42]. This aspect contributes to the transferring the application of *shared autonomy* to drive telepresence robots in dynamic environments. Previous works about *shared autonomy* are typically tested in static environment (e.g., without dynamic obstacles) except the work [43]. In comparison to [43], in our system we focus not only on increasing the collision avoidance algorithm but also to enable user to interact with others.

(iii) *Shared autonomy driven by a priori knowledge of the environment:* the *subgoal* is set to a free cell of a global map of the environment provided to the robot and on which the robot localizes. However, in comparison to autonomous mobile robotics, we simultaneously exploit two maps (one more detailed for navigation, one less detailed for localization), increasing the reliability of the system and showing an improvement of the navigation [9]. The user successfully controls the robot only by focusing on the final destination, while the robot handles the obstacle detection by implementing reliable "obstacle avoidance behaviors" as well as with the planning of the most suitable trajectory. Please refer to [9] for further details. Since the robot has the map of the environment available, in *emergency*, the robot activates in autonomy the *recovery procedure* without stopping the navigation when it is possible.

In all the presented systems, we assume that the user is the one who takes care of the global planning phase. This means that the user is involved in the loop and delivers high-level commands to the robot (e.g., the selection of targets, directional commands). The robot processes the user's commands as triggers to activate the available behaviors.

The introduction of *shared autonomy* strategies has reduced the number of commands than a manual teleoperation (taken as reference), suggesting also a reduction of the effort required to the user in all the three examined scenarios. Furthermore, the increment of time in *shared autonomy* was limited and not statistically significant due to the impossibility of the user in controlling any single detail of the motion [9,26].

4 Shared Intelligence Approach Based on Policies

Although the aforementioned *shared autonomy* approaches were effective in fostering the human-robot interaction and reducing the user's workload, they show some limitations:

(i) A setup phase is required before using it in other contexts because all the proposed *shared autonomy* approaches rely on specific information of the environment (e.g., the map and the constraints about the door shape).
(ii) The robot behaviors are defined a priori according to fixed triggers. This means that the available robot's behaviors are activated only if certain situations occur.

Therefore, the application of the approaches presented in Sect. 3 might be complex in everyday life scenarios where it is hard to define strict and constant constraints for regulating the robot's motion.

To overcome the highlighted drawbacks, we designed a more flexible system that is based on a *shared intelligence* strategy where the robot's behaviors are not established a priori. On the contrary, the most appropriate behavior is determined by the fusion of several *policies*. The *policies* are associated with the different sources of information that might influence the robot's motion. In the case of brain-driven telepresence robots, each *policy* returns a probability grid defined in the 2D area around the robot. The merging of all the *policies* gives in output the *subgoal* representing the position towards the robot moves. A scheme of our *shared intelligence* approach is presented in Fig. 4.

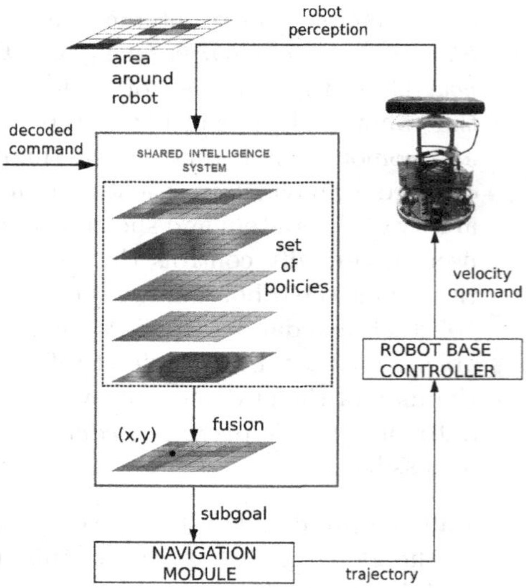

However, in contrast to *shared autonomy* methods, all the *policies*

Fig. 4. A representation of the proposed *shared intelligence* based on *policies*.

equally contribute determining the final robot's action. Hence, in agreement with the taxonomy presented in Sect. 2, the user's inputs have the same importance as the robot's perception in determining the navigation. This feature is novel in the context of brain-driven robot's where instead *shared control* systems are the most common: the role of the robot is only limited to reactive obstacle avoidance behaviors [7, 44, 45] in order to implement the user's commands safely. Herein, the "intelligence" of the robot always contributes to decide the next robot's movements by taking into account not only the obstacles and the user's inputs but also other aspects such as the natural direction of robot's motion.

We tested the system with 13 healthy people that drove a telepresence robot via 2-classes BMIs based on motor imagery. Our first experiments demonstrated the expected robot's behaviors in different situations (free space area, door passage, corridor, crossroad, area covered by obstacles)[1]. The robot behavior was perceived natural and in line with the user's intentions according to a questionnaire administered to participants. Furthermore, the robot's motion via BMI was coherent with the one derived from the continuous teleoperation. This last result highlights the potentiality of the presented *shared intelligence* approach. Although the user could deliver only two kinds of commands associated with the two BMI mental tasks, the users could maintain a robust control of the robot without specifying pre-conditions.

5 ROS-Neuro: A Common Framework for Developing Neurorobotics Applications

Herein, we facilitate the integration between BMIs and telepresence robots by providing a common framework for the implementation of BMI systems and robotic controllers that we called ROS-Neuro[2] [46, 47] (previously ROS-Health [48]). ROS-Neuro exploits the tools and the standard provided by Robot Operating System ecosystem (ROS) such as the real-time capabilities, the multiprocessing architecture and a robust communication infrastructure. Moreover, the modularity of ROS reflects the structure of each BMIs that is composed by several modules (see Fig. 1). Furthermore, ROS-Neuro will allow researchers to easily share the software and test the same BMIs for driving different robotic platforms without requiring the implementation of specific plugins [48]. Finally, we firmly believe that ROS-Neuro will enable to take full advantage from the robot because the brain signals' data are processed in the same manner of the robot's sensors information facilitating the implementation of own *shared approach* or by exploiting the algorithms already available inside ROS. An illustrative representation of the ROS-Neuro structure is shown in Fig. 5:

(i) *rosneuro_acquisition:* the package acquires the brain signals from different commercial amplifier systems. The data are available through *NeuroFrame* messages[3].

(ii) *rosneuro_recorder:* the package stores the acquired data in common formats and the related events are published in the form of *NeuroEvent* messages[4].

---

[1] https://aixia2020.di.unito.it/awards/premio-pietro-torasso.
[2] https://github.com/rosneuro.
[3] *NeuroFrame* is a custom message defined according to the ROS's standard.
[4] *NeuroEvent* is a custom message defined according to the ROS's standard.

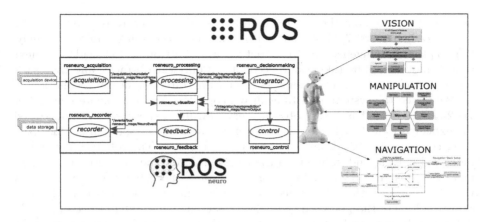

Fig. 5. ROS-Neuro is designed to be a common open-source framework for BMI and robotics research and applications. ROS-Neuro is developed inside the Robot Operating System (ROS) ecosystem [49]. The different modules of the BMI systems are implemented in the form of ROS packages containing nodes (in green) that exchange custom messages through topics (in blue). The key advantage of ROS-Neuro is the possibility to process the neural data real-time and easily used them as input to drive robots with the possibility of exploiting the already available state-of-the-art algorithms in robotics. (Color figure online)

(iii) *rosneuro_processing:* the package filters the data and it applies common machine learning techniques to extract features and finally returns the raw posterior probability distribution over the classes through *NeuroOutput* messages[5].

(iv) *rosneuro_decisionmaking:* the packages further elaborates the output of the processing to decode the BMI commands.

 (v) *rosneuro_control:* the packages provides functionalities to translate the output from ROS-Neuro to an external devices such as an interface or a robot.

(vi) *rosneuro_feedback:* the packages implements the graphical interface to achieve the BMI protocols.

In our tests during the Cybathlon 2020 competition[6], ROS-Neuro has demonstrated stability and reliability. The delays among the different ROS packages were negligible and the predictions returned in output were coherent with the expected values [47].

6   Conclusion

Given the need to boost the interaction between the human and the robot in neurorobotics applications, we show the benefits of introducing classical robotics

---

[5] *NeuroOutput* is a custom message defined according to the ROS's standard.

[6] https://cybathlon.ethz.ch/en.

and the artificial intelligence techniques to develop innovative brain-driven telepresence robots. After introducing the literature about *shared approaches*, we propose different *shared autonomy* and *shared intelligence* systems able to reduce the user's workload by relying on the robot's capabilities. In both systems, the robot plays an active role namely it is an intelligent agent that is involved in the *plan-sense-act* paradigm. Hence, in light of the results, the robot achieves a symbiotic interaction with the user because it guides him/her by recognizing targets and implementing the expected behaviors and/or contribute to the decision-making process.

Finally, from the BMIs side, we promote ROS-Neuro as framework to implement BMI loops inside the same robotic ecosystem in order to easily support the exchange of the information between BMI and robot and hence the introduction of *shared* approaches.

Acknowledgments. This research was partially supported by Fondazione Ing. Aldo Gini, by MIUR (Italian Minister for Education) under the initiative "Departments of Excellence" (Law 232/2016) and by SI Robotics project (Invecchiamento sano e attivo attraverso SocIal ROBOTICS) project – PON 12 Aree Call 2017.

References

1. Wolpaw, J.R., Birbaumer, N., McFarland, D.J., Pfurtscheller, G., Vaughan, T.M.: Brain-computer interfaces for communication and control. Clin. Neurophysiol. **113**(6), 767–791 (2002)
2. del Millán, J.R., et al.: Combining brain-computer interfaces and assistive technologies: state-of-the-art and challenges. Front. Neurosci. **4**, 161 (2010)
3. Chaudhary, U., Birbaumer, N., Ramos-Murguialday, A.: Brain-computer interfaces for communication and rehabilitation. Nat. Rev. Neurol. **12**(9), 513–525 (2016)
4. Birbaumer, N., et al.: A spelling device for the paralysed. Nature **398**(6725), 297–298 (1999)
5. Lee, K., Liu, D., Perroud, L., Chavarriaga, R., del Millán, J.R.: A brain-controlled exoskeleton with cascaded event-related desynchronization classifiers. Robot. Auton. Syst. **90**, 15–23 (2017)
6. He, Y., Eguren, D., Azorín, J.M., Grossman, R.G., Luu, T.P., Contreras-Vidal, J.L.: Brain-machine interfaces for controlling lower-limb powered robotic systems. J. Neural Eng. **15**(2), 1–16 (2018)
7. Tonin, L., Leeb, R., Tavella, M., Perdikis, S., del Millán, J.R.: The role of shared-control in BCI-based telepresence. In: 2010 IEEE International Conference on Systems, Man and Cybernetics, pp. 1462–1466. IEEE (2010)
8. Iturrate, I., Antelis, J.M., Kubler, A., Minguez, J.: A noninvasive brain-actuated wheelchair based on a P300 neurophysiological protocol and automated navigation. IEEE Trans. Robot. **25**(3), 614–627 (2009)
9. Beraldo, G., Antonello, M., Cimolato, A., Menegatti, E., Tonin, L.: Brain-Computer Interface meets ROS: a robotic approach to mentally drive telepresence robots. In: Proceedings of the 2018 IEEE International Conference on Robotics and Automation (ICRA), pp. 1–6. IEEE (2018)
10. Endsley, M.R.: Level of automation: integrating humans and automated systems. In: Proceedings of the Human Factors and Ergonomics Society Annual Meeting, Volume 41, SAGE Publications, Sage CA, Los Angeles, CA (1997)

11. Kaber, D.B., Endsley, M.R.: Out-of-the-loop performance problems and the use of intermediate levels of automation for improved control system functioning and safety. Process Saf. Progr. **16**(3), 126–131 (1997)
12. Murphy, R.R.: Introduction to AI Robotics (2000)
13. Sheridan, T.B.: Telerobotics. Automatica **25**(4), 487–507 (1989)
14. Goodrich, K., Schutte, P., Flemisch, F., Williams, R.: Application of the H-mode, a design and interaction concept for highly automated vehicles, to aircraft. In: Proceedings of the 25th IEEE Digital Avionics Systems Conference, pp. 1–13 (2006)
15. Flemisch, F., Abbink, D., Itoh, M., Pacaux-Lemoine, M.P., Weßel, G.: Shared control is the sharp end of cooperation: towards a common framework of joint action, shared control and human machine cooperation. IFAC-PapersOnLine **49**(19), 72–77 (2016)
16. Abbink, D.A., et al.: A topology of shared control systems-finding common ground in diversity. IEEE Trans. Hum.-Mach. Syst. **48**(5), 509–525 (2018)
17. Ferrell, W.R., Sheridan, T.B.: Supervisory control of remote manipulation. IEEE Spectr. **4**(10), 81–88 (1967)
18. Schilling, M., et al.: Towards a multidimensional perspective on shared autonomy. In: Proceedings of the AAAI Fall Symposium Series 2016, Stanford (USA) (2016)
19. Bradshaw, J.M., Feltovich, P.J., Jung, H., Kulkarni, S., Taysom, W., Uszok, A.: Dimensions of adjustable autonomy and mixed-initiative interaction. In: Nickles, M., Rovatsos, M., Weiss, G. (eds.) AUTONOMY 2003. LNCS (LNAI), vol. 2969, pp. 17–39. Springer, Heidelberg (2004). https://doi.org/10.1007/978-3-540-25928-2_3
20. Allen, J., Guinn, C.I., Horvtz, E.: Mixed-initiative interaction. IEEE Intell. Syst. Appl. **14**(5), 14–23 (1999)
21. Finzi, A., Orlandini, A.: Human-robot interaction through mixed-initiative planning for rescue and search rovers. In: Bandini, S., Manzoni, S. (eds.) AI*IA 2005. LNCS (LNAI), vol. 3673, pp. 483–494. Springer, Heidelberg (2005). https://doi.org/10.1007/11558590_49
22. Bevacqua, G., Cacace, J., Finzi, A., Lippiello, V.: Mixed-initiative planning and execution for multiple drones in search and rescue missions. In: Proceedings of the International Conference on Automated Planning and Scheduling, vol. 25 (2015)
23. Horvitz, E.: Principles of mixed-initiative user interfaces. In: Proceedings of the SIGCHI Conference on Human Factors in Computing Systems, pp. 159–166 (1999)
24. Beraldo, G., Tonin, L., Cesta, A., Menegatti, E.: Shared-control, shared-autonomy and shared-intelligence in assistive technologies: three forms of cooperation between user and robot. In: Proceedings of the IEEE International Workshop Adaptive Behavioral Models of Robotic Models of Robotic Systems Based on Brain-Inspired AI Cognitive Architectures (APHRODITE). IEEE (2020)
25. Donges, E.: Aspekte der aktiven sicherheit bei der führung von personenkraftwagen. Automob-Ind **27**(2) (1982)
26. Beraldo, G., Termine, E., Menegatti, E.: Shared-autonomy navigation for mobile robots driven by a door detection module. In: Alviano, M., Greco, G., Scarcello, F. (eds.) AI*IA 2019. LNCS (LNAI), vol. 11946, pp. 511–527. Springer, Cham (2019). https://doi.org/10.1007/978-3-030-35166-3_36
27. Khatib, O.: Real-time obstacle avoidance for manipulators and mobile robots. In: Cox, I.J., Wilfong, G.T. (eds.) Autonomous Robot Vehicles, pp. 396–404. Springer, New York (1986). https://doi.org/10.1007/978-1-4613-8997-2_29
28. Koren, Y., Borenstein, J.: Potential field methods and their inherent limitations for mobile robot navigation. In: Proceedings of the 1991 IEEE International Conference on Robotics and Automation, pp. 1398–1404. IEEE (1991)

29. Aigner, P., McCarragher, B.: Human integration into robot control utilising potential fields. In: Proceedings of the International Conference on Robotics and Automation, vol. 1, pp. 291–296. IEEE (1997)

30. Simpson, R.C., Levine, S.P., Bell, D.A., Jaros, L.A., Koren, Y., Borenstein, J.: NavChair: an assistive wheelchair navigation system with automatic adaptation. In: Mittal, V.O., Yanco, H.A., Aronis, J., Simpson, R. (eds.) Assistive Technology and Artificial Intelligence. LNCS, vol. 1458, pp. 235–255. Springer, Heidelberg (1998). https://doi.org/10.1007/BFb0055982

31. Kim, B.K., Tanaka, H., Sumi, Y.: Robotic wheelchair using a high accuracy visual marker Lentibar and its application to door crossing navigation. In: Proceedings of the 2015 IEEE International Conference on Robotics and Automation (ICRA), pp. 4478–4483. IEEE (2015)

32. Winiarski, T., Banachowicz, K., Seredyński, D.: Multi-sensory feedback control in door approaching and opening. In: Filev, D., et al. (eds.) Intelligent Systems 2014. AISC, vol. 323, pp. 57–70. Springer, Cham (2015). https://doi.org/10.1007/978-3-319-11310-4_6

33. Carlson, T., Demiris, Y.: Human-wheelchair collaboration through prediction of intention and adaptive assistance. In: Proceedings of the 2008 IEEE International Conference on Robotics and Automation, pp. 3926–3931. IEEE (2008)

34. Barber, R., Salichs, M.: Mobile robot navigation based on event maps. In: Proceedings of the Field and Service Robotics, pp. 61–66 (2001)

35. Joo, K., Lee, T.K., Baek, S., Oh, S.Y.: Generating topological map from occupancy grid-map using virtual door detection. In: Proceedings of the IEEE Congress on Evolutionary Computation, pp. 1–6. IEEE (2010)

36. Levine, S.P., Bell, D.A., Jaros, L.A., Simpson, R.C., Koren, Y., Borenstein, J.: The NavChair assistive wheelchair navigation system. IEEE Trans. Rehabil. Eng. **7**(4), 443–451 (1999)

37. Zeng, Q., Burdet, E., Rebsamen, B., Teo, C.L.: Evaluation of the collaborative wheelchair assistant system. In: Proceedings of the 2007 IEEE 10th International Conference on Rehabilitation Robotics, pp. 601–608. IEEE (2007)

38. Hoshino, S., Maki, K.: Safe and efficient motion planning of multiple mobile robots based on artificial potential for human behavior and robot congestion. Adv. Robot. **29**(17), 1095–1109 (2015)

39. Hall, E.T.: The Hidden Dimension, vol. 609. Doubleday, Garden City (1910)

40. Mead, R., Matarić, M.J.: Autonomous human-robot proxemics: socially aware navigation based on interaction potential. Auton. Robots **41**(5), 1189–1201 (2017). https://doi.org/10.1007/s10514-016-9572-2

41. Rios-Martinez, J., Spalanzani, A., Laugier, C.: From proxemics theory to socially-aware navigation: a survey. Int. J. Soc. Robot. **7**(2), 137–153 (2015)

42. Scandolo, L., Fraichard, T.: An anthropomorphic navigation scheme for dynamic scenarios. In: 2011 IEEE International Conference on Robotics and Automation, pp. 809–814. IEEE (2011)

43. Zhang, B., Holloway, C., Carlson, T.: A hierarchical design for shared-control wheelchair navigation in dynamic environments. In: Proceedings of the IEEE International Conference on Systems, Man, and Cybernetics (SMC) (2020)

44. Philips, J., et al.: Adaptive shared control of a brain-actuated simulated wheelchair. In: 2007 IEEE 10th International Conference on Rehabilitation Robotics, pp. 408–414. IEEE (2007)

45. Lopes, A.C., Pires, G., Vaz, L., Nunes, U.: Wheelchair navigation assisted by Human-Machine shared-control and a P300-based Brain Computer Interface. In:

Proceedings of the 2011 IEEE/RSJ International Conference on Intelligent Robots and Systems, pp. 2438–2444. IEEE (2011)

46. Tonin, L., Beraldo, G., Tortora, S., Tagliapietra, L., del Millán, J.R., Menegatti, E.: ROS-Neuro: a common middleware for BMI and robotics. The acquisition and recorder packages. In: Proceedings of the 2019 IEEE International Conference on Systems, Man and Cybernetics (SMC), pp. 2767–2772. IEEE (2019)

47. Beraldo, G., Tortora, S., Menegatti, E., Tonin, L.: ROS-Neuro: implementation of a closed-loop BMI based on motor imagery. In: Proceedings of the 2020 IEEE International Conference on Systems, Man and Cybernetics (SMC). IEEE (2020)

48. Beraldo, G., et al.: ROS-Health: an open-source framework for neurorobotics. In: Proceedings of the 2018 IEEE International Conference on Simulation, Modeling, and Programming for Autonomous Robots (SIMPAR), pp. 174–179. IEEE (2018)

49. Quigley, M., et al.: ROS: an open-source robot operating system (2009)

Knowledge-Driven Conversation for Social Robots: Exploring Crowdsourcing Mechanisms for Improving the System Capabilities

Lucrezia Grassi(✉)📧, Carmine T. Recchiuto📧, and Antonio Sgorbissa📧

DIBRIS, Università di Genova, via all'Opera pia 13, 16145 Genova, Italy
lucrezia.grassi@edu.unige.it

Abstract. Social robots and artificial agents should be able to interact with the user in the most natural way possible. This work describes the basic principles of a conversation system designed for social robots and artificial agents, which relies on knowledge encoded in the form of an Ontology. Given the knowledge-driven approach, the possibility of expanding the Ontology in run-time, during the verbal interaction with the users is of the utmost importance: this paper also deals with the implementation of a system for the run-time expansion of the knowledge base, thanks to a crowdsourcing approach.

Keywords: Social robots · Autonomous conversation · Ontology · Knowledge-driven conversation · NLP · Crowdsourcing

1 Introduction

Achieving a natural interaction between a human and a robot is a very complex task. A list of ten desired features that a conversational robot should have is presented in [1]: among the most relevant aspects, the capability of *breaking the "simple commands only" barrier*, and having *multiple speech acts* should be pointed out.

The recent EU-Japan project CARESSES has dealt with some of these aspects [2]. In the context of the project, whose main focus was the development of *culturally-competent* robots, i.e., robots able to adapt verbal and non-verbal interaction to the user's cultural background, a framework for autonomous conversation has been developed [3,4]. The framework was able to achieve mixed-initiative dialogues by exploiting the hierarchical structure of an Ontology, thus implementing rich, knowledge-grounded conversations [5].

However, although significant progress has been achieved during the last years, assistive robots and chatbots still have many limitations. Some of the most common limitations are (i) failing to answer, (ii) not understanding the local language of the user, (iii) not giving the proper answer if there is some

© Springer Nature Switzerland AG 2021
M. Baldoni and S. Bandini (Eds.): AIxIA 2020, LNAI 12414, pp. 249–259, 2021.
https://doi.org/10.1007/978-3-030-77091-4_16

spelling mistake or some slang, (iv) having a limited knowledge, which can result in a repetitive conversation, and (v) not being coherent when answering to what the user says [6].

The work proposes an approach that mainly deals with (iv), relying on the framework for autonomous conversation developed within the CARESSES project, but suggesting a *crowdsourcing approach* for adding knowledge as a consequence of the interaction with the users.

2   Knowledge-Driven Conversation

Usually, knowledge-grounded conversation frameworks generate appropriate responses that reflect the acquired knowledge by relying on data-driven conversation models [7], or considering contextual information based on previous utterances [8]. In the proposed approach, the nucleus of the conversational framework is a Description Logic Ontology [9].

The Dialogue Tree is built starting from the Ontology structure, and the relation between topics is borrowed from the structure of the Ontology: specifically, Object Properties, Data Properties, and the hierarchical relationships among instances, are analyzed to define the branches of the Dialogue Tree. Based on the Dialogue Tree, the policies for knowledge-driven conversation can be briefly summarized as follows [10]. Each time a user sentence is acquired:

1. A keyword-based Language Processing algorithm is applied to check if the sentence may trigger one of the topics in the tree;
2. If no topics are triggered, the conversation follows one of the branches of the tree, depending on the probabilities of each node (probabilities are encoded in the Ontology, and they depend on the user-specific preferences and on the user's cultural background);
3. Whatever node has been chosen, the system:
   (a) proposes some of the corresponding sentences (encoded in the Ontology as Class restrictions and Data Properties);
   (b) acquires the user's feedback that can be used to update the Ontology and/or determine the next node to move to.

3   Crowdsourcing Mechanisms for the Run-Time Expansion of the Knowledge Base

The possibility of acquiring knowledge systematically by relying on networked interactions with human users has been recently explored in different domains. For example, some museum collections have used a "social tagging" approach to enhance curatorial documentation [11], allowing users to assign tags to museum objects displayed on a website, while the New York Public Library has launched a web-based crowdsourcing project, asking people to transcribe menus from its historical menu collection [12]. Crowdsourcing mechanisms have also been investigated for collaborative Ontology construction projects: [13] proposed a two-phase methodology for allowing non-expert users to concurrently build an Ontology about dietary approaches, while a method to verify if automated techniques for building biomedical Ontology hierarchies are reliable, based on a Bayesian inference model, has been developed in [14].

This work proposes the usage of crowdsourcing mechanisms for a run-time expansion of the knowledge base used for building the Dialogue Tree. A three-step approach has been implemented:

1. Recognition of relevant concepts in the user's sentence;
2. Insertion of the concepts in the Ontology;
3. Validation of the concepts.

During the conversation, the user is spurred to talk: he/she will mention concepts that will be recognized (1) and inserted into the Ontology (2) through one of the developed insertion procedures. Eventually, the newly added concepts will be subjected to a validation procedure (3).

Step 1 is discussed in detail in Sect. 4.

Regarding 2, different techniques for the insertion of new concepts (and related sentences) in the right place of the Ontology have been implemented. Such techniques involve the usage of NLP tools for detecting the category of the user's sentence and the type of the recognized entity, and they are currently under evaluation. Finally, a procedure for validating the concepts inserted in run-time has also been developed (3). Such procedure is based on a revision process that indirectly asks users to independently revise others' information, to reach a consensual version. This *peer-review* approach, complemented by an external moderation, is also being evaluated.

The insertion (2) and validation (3) procedures will not be covered in detail in this discussion: they will be addressed in papers being published.

4   Recognition of Relevant Concepts

To recognize relevant concepts in the user's sentence, Dialogflow [15] turned out to be the most suitable tool.

4.1   Dialogflow: Agents and Intents

Dialogflow is a web service allowing to manage functionalities for autonomous conversation. A Dialogflow Agent is a natural language understanding module that understands the nuances of human language. The Agents are characterized by *Intents*, which categorize end-user's intention for one conversation turn, and *Parameters*, which are values extracted from the sentence depending on the training of the Agent. Dialogflow offers a wide variety of pre-trained Agents able to manage the most common functionalities for which it is used, such as reminders, weather forecasts, alarm, etc., however, if it is used for unprecedented purposes, as in our case, the Agent needs to be trained from scratch. The purpose of the training is to make the Agent able to correctly match the Intent of the sentence provided as input, and return a response containing the name of the Intent and the recognized parameter(s).

Creating different Intents, related to different contexts to which the sentence may belong, allows to deliver a more appropriate response. For this reason, after creating the Agent, rather than having only one Intent to manage all possible types of input sentence, the choice fell on creating different Intents for different kinds of inputs. In particular, four Intents have been defined: (i) preferences, (ii) memories-past, (iii) norms, and (iv) beliefs. Such Intents, according to the CARESSES guidelines, drawn up by experts in the field of Transcultural Nursing [16], reflect the most relevant themes during a conversation when taking into account cultural aspects, and they correspond to conversation topics already present in the starting Ontology.

When the end-user sentence is sent to Dialogflow, it is matched to the best Intent in the Agent: matching an Intent is also known as *Intent classification*.

4.2   Dialogflow Agent Training

All intents have been trained with example phrases for what end-users might say, which include some manually tagged parameters.

To collect appropriate training phrases for each Intent, in such a way that Dialogflow could correctly perform the *Intent matching*, a vocal questionnaire has been created, where participants were required to answer, using their microphone, to 20 questions subdivided into four sections (5 questions for each Intent); in each one, we chose the questions to make sure that the answers had a similar syntactic structure:

Preferences:

1. How do you like to spend time with your friends?
2. What are your favourite foods?
3. Please tell me about your favourite songs.
4. I would love to know about the movies you like and your favourite actors.
5. What is your favourite animal?

Memories-past:

1. How have things changed compared to when you were young?
2. Please tell me about your childhood.
3. Please tell me about your childhood friends.
4. What games did you use to play when you were a child?
5. Please tell me about the school you went to.

Norms:

1. Please tell me how to celebrate the birthday of a loved one.
2. As your robot assistant, how should I behave with your friends?
3. Please tell me about the good manners that matter to you.

4. What are the things people shouldn't do in the presence of others?
5. Are there any foods or drinks people should avoid?

Beliefs:

1. What do you think about life?
2. I would like to know what you think about religion.
3. I would like to know what you think about marriage.
4. Do you think family relationships are important? Please tell me your thoughts.
5. People say: "healthy body in a healthy mind". I would be happy to know what you think about this.

To create the questionnaire we used JotForm[1], which is an online form building company. For our purposes, JotForm proved to be more suitable than Google Forms, as it allows to easily gather vocal answers: this point is crucial, as the whole system is designed primarily to work as a robot assistant and not as a chatbot.

As it can be seen in Fig. 1, the *preferences* Intent contains training phrases such as "*I love <tagged parameter>*": whenever the user says "*I love <concept>*", this sentence is matched to the *preferences* Intent and whatever the value of *concept* is, it is returned as a response.

Fig. 1. Sample of training phrases for the *preferences* Intent

Figure 2 shows some training phrases used for the *memories-past* Intent. These sentences regard the period of childhood. Thanks to the kind of sentences used to train this Intent, if someone says "*I used to play <concept>*", the system will match the sentence to the *memories-past* Intent and it will return the played game as response.

Figure 3 reports a sample of the training phrases used for the *norms* Intent. Such sentences are extracted from the answers given to questions regarding how

---

[1] https://www.jotform.com.

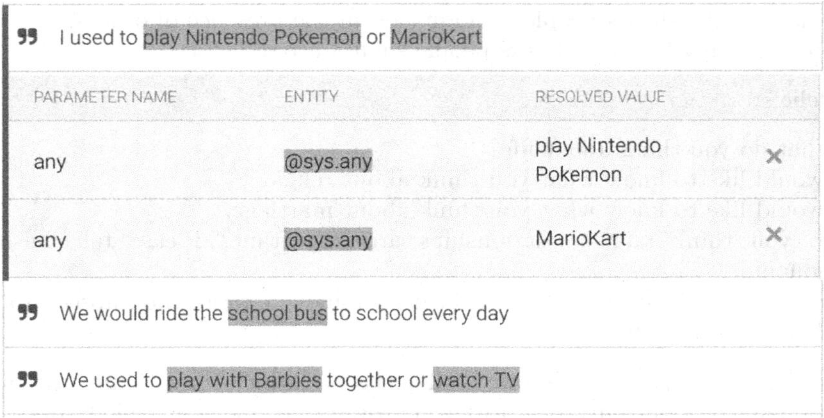

Fig. 2. Sample of training phrases for the *memories-past* Intent

people think one should behave in certain situations: if the user says "*You should <concept>*", this sentence will be matched with the *norms* Intent, and the norm is returned as response.

Fig. 3. Sample of training phrases for the *norms* Intent

Figure 4 shows a sample of the training phrases used for the *beliefs* Intent, that has the aim of extracting parameters related to what people believe or think. As an example, if the user says "*I think that <concept> is ...*", the sentence will be matched to the *beliefs* Intent and the *concept* is recognized as the relevant parameter.

Fig. 4. Sample of training phrases for the *beliefs* Intent

5   Experiment and Discussion

This section presents the experiments carried on to assess the performances of the first step of the process, i.e., the recognition of relevant concepts in the user's sentence, and discusses the results.

A total of 30 participants have been recruited for the experiments: 20 questionnaires have been used to train the Agent, while the answers of the remaining 10 questionnaires have been set aside to use them to test the Agent. To validate the approach, two independent *taggers* have tagged the 20 questionnaires of the training set, while a different person has tagged the evaluation set. It is worth to mention that the Agent has been trained with pieces of the sentences (split by "and"). For this reason, to assess the performances of the Agent, the test answers have been split according to the same rules used for the training answers. The splitting also increases the probability of extracting at least one meaningful concept in the whole answer, which is what matters to expand the knowledge base.

Each piece of the test answers has been classified as:

- True Positive (TP): if Dialogflow correctly recognized the concept that was manually tagged;
- False Positive (FP): if Dialogflow recognized something that was not tagged;
- True Negative (TN): if Dialogflow did not recognize anything and nothing was tagged;
- False Negative (FN): if Dialogflow did not recognize anything but something was tagged.

The results of the classification of the pieces of each answer are summarized in the Confusion Matrix shown in Fig. 5.a. By looking at the tables, it is immediately clear that almost every time Dialogflow recognized something it was a tagged concept. However, in many cases, it did not recognize what had been tagged: as it will be clear in the following, this is not an issue if we reason in terms of answers and not in terms of pieces of answers. Starting from the Confusion Matrix, the most common parameters for a binary classifier have been computed and reported in Fig. 5.b. The same analysis has been carried out (Fig. 6) considering the sentence as a whole, and by using this rationale, which allows to analyze if at least one concept has been correctly extracted from the whole sentence:

	PREDICTED YES	PREDICTED NO	Total
ACTUAL YES	203	119	322
ACTUAL NO	45	91	136
Total	248	210	458

(a) Confusion Matrix

Parameter	Formula	Value
Accuracy	$\dfrac{TP + TN}{TP + TN + FP + FN}$	0.64
Sensitivity (Recall)	$\dfrac{TP}{TP + FN}$	0.63
Specificity (SP)	$\dfrac{TN}{TN + FP}$	0.67
Precision	$\dfrac{TP}{TP + FP}$	0.82

(b) Parameters table

Fig. 5. Confusion Matrix containing the classifications of the answers' pieces (a) and related parameters of the classifier (b).

- If the answer contains at least one sentence classified as TP, the answer is considered as TP;
- If the answer does not contain any sentence classified as TP but it contains at least a sentence classified as FP, the whole answer is labelled as FP;

- If the answer does not contain any sentence classified as TP or FP, but it contains at least a sentence classified as FN, the whole answer is labelled as FN;
- If the answer does not contain any sentence classified as TP, FP or FN, but it contains at least a sentence classified as TN, the whole answer is labelled as TN.

	PREDICTED YES	PREDICTED NO	Total
ACTUAL YES	151	31	182
ACTUAL NO	17	1	18
Total	168	32	200

(a) Confusion Matrix

Parameter	Formula	Value
Accuracy	$\dfrac{TP + TN}{TP + TN + FP + FN}$	0.82
Sensitivity (Recall)	$\dfrac{TP}{TP + FN}$	0.83
Specificity (SP)	$\dfrac{TN}{TN + FP}$	0.06
Precision	$\dfrac{TP}{TP + FP}$	0.90

(b) Parameters table

Fig. 6. Confusion Matrix containing the classifications of the answers (a) and related parameters of the classifier (b).

From the analysis of the collected data, it may be observed that, working on the pieces of each answer, the system achieves a high Precision, which means that almost every recognized concept would have also been tagged manually. On the other side, the Accuracy (how often is the classifier correct?), the Sensitivity (when something is tagged, how often does it recognizes it?), and the Specificity (when something is not tagged, how often does it not recognize anything?) may be improved. However, when considering the whole answers to assess the capability of the system to extract at least one meaningful concept in each of them, all performance indicators are greater than 0.8, except the Specificity, due to a high number of FP.

6   Conclusions

This work describes the implementation of a crowdsourcing approach aimed at expanding, in run-time, the knowledge base of an autonomous conversational system. The proposed method tries to recognize relevant concepts in the user's sentence by relying on Dialogflow web service, and has already been integrated into the CARESSES framework (additional details about this integration will be the subject of future publications).

Preliminary tests have been carried out to assess the system performance when dealing with concept recognition, and they gave positive insights about the reliability of the proposed approach.

References

1. Mavridis, N.: A review of verbal and non-verbal human-robot interactive communication. Robot. Auton. Syst. **63**, 22–35 (2015)
2. Khaliq, A.A., et al.: Culturally aware planning and execution of robot actions. In: IEEE/RSJ International Conference on Intelligent Robots and Systems (IROS), pp. 326–332. IEEE (2018)
3. Sgorbissa, A., Papadopoulos, I., Bruno, B., Koulouglioti, C., Recchiuto, C.T.: Encoding guidelines for a culturally competent robot for elderly care. In: IEEE/RSJ International Conference on Intelligent Robots and Systems (IROS), pp. 1988–1995. IEEE (2018)
4. Bruno, B., et al.: Knowledge representation for culturally competent personal robots: requirements, design principles, implementation, and assessment. Int. J. Soc. Robot. **11**(3), 515–538 (2019). https://doi.org/10.1007/s12369-019-00519-w
5. Recchiuto, C.T., et al.: Cloud services for culture aware conversation: socially assistive robots and virtual assistants. In: 17th International Conference on Ubiquitous Robots (UR), pp. 270–277. IEEE (2020)
6. Raval, H.: Limitations of existing chatbot with analytical survey to enhance the functionality using emerging technology. Int. J. Res. Anal. Rev. (IJRAR) **7**(2) (2020)
7. Ghazvininejad, M., et al.: A knowledge-grounded neural conversation model. arXiv preprint arXiv:1702.01932 (2017)
8. Kim, S., Kwon, O.-W., Kim, H.: Knowledge-grounded chatbot based on dual Wasserstein generative adversarial networks with effective attention mechanisms. Appl. Sci. **10**(9), 3335 (2020)
9. Guarino, N., Oberle, D., Staab, S.: What is an ontology? In: Staab, S., Studer, R. (eds.) Handbook on Ontologies. IHIS, pp. 1–17. Springer, Heidelberg (2009). https://doi.org/10.1007/978-3-540-92673-3_0
10. Recchiuto, C.T., Sgorbissa, A.: A feasibility study of culture-aware cloud services for conversational robots. IEEE Robot. Autom. Lett. **5**(4), 6559–6566 (2020)

11. Trant, J.: Tagging, folksonomy and art museums: early experiments and ongoing research (2009)
12. Lascarides, M., Vershbow, B.: What's on the menu? Crowdsourcing at the New York public library. In: Crowdsourcing Our Cultural Heritage, pp. 113–1137. Ashgate Publishing Limited Farnham (2014)
13. Zhitomirsky-Geffet, M., Erez, E.S., Judit, B.-I.: Toward multiviewpoint ontology construction by collaboration of non-experts and crowdsourcing: the case of the effect of diet on health. J. Assoc. Inf. Sci. Technol. **68**(3), 681–694 (2017)
14. Mortensen, J.M., Musen, M.A., Noy, N.F.: Crowdsourcing the verification of relationships in biomedical ontologies. In: AMIA Annual Symposium Proceedings, vol. 2013, pp. 1020–1029. American Medical Informatics Association (2013)
15. DialogFlow Documentation. https://cloud.google.com/dialogflow/docs. Accessed 7 Oct 2020
16. Leininger, M., McFarland, M.R.: Transcultural Nursing. McGraw-Hill, New York (1987)

Natural Language for Artificial Intelligence

Grounding Dialogue History: Strengths and Weaknesses of Pre-trained Transformers

Claudio Greco[1]($\boxtimes$), Alberto Testoni[2], and Raffaella Bernardi[1,2]

[1] CIMeC - Center for Mind/Brain Sciences, University of Trento, Rovereto, Italy
{claudio.greco,raffaella.bernardi}@unitn.it
[2] DISI - Department of Information Engineering and Computer Science,
University of Trento, Rovereto, Italy
alberto.testoni@unitn.it

Abstract. We focus on visually grounded dialogue history encoding. We show that GuessWhat?! can be used as a "diagnostic" dataset to understand whether State-of-the-Art encoders manage to capture salient information in the dialogue history. We compare models across several dimensions: the architecture (Recurrent Neural Networks vs. Transformers), the input modalities (only language vs. language and vision), and the model background knowledge (trained from scratch vs. pre-trained and then fine-tuned on the downstream task). We show that pre-trained Transformers, RoBERTa and LXMERT, are able to identify the most salient information independently of the order in which the dialogue history is processed. Moreover, we find that RoBERTa handles the dialogue structure to some extent; instead LXMERT can effectively ground short dialogues, but it fails in processing longer dialogues having a more complex structure.

Keywords: Visual Dialogue · Language and vision · History encoding

1 Introduction

Visual Dialogue tasks have a long tradition (e.g. [1]). Recently, several dialogue tasks have been proposed as referential guessing games in which an agent asks questions about an image to another agent and the referent they have been speaking about has to be guessed at the end of the game [4, 7, 8, 10, 31, 33]. Among these games, GuessWhat?! and GuessWhich [4, 33] are asymmetrical – the roles are fixed: one player asks questions (the Questioner) and the other (the Oracle) answers. The game is considered successful if the Guesser, which can be the Questioner itself or a third player, selects the correct target.

C. Greco and A. Testoni—Equal contribution. The first two authors are reported in alphabetic order.

© Springer Nature Switzerland AG 2021
M. Baldoni and S. Bandini (Eds.): AIxIA 2020, LNAI 12414, pp. 263–279, 2021.
https://doi.org/10.1007/978-3-030-77091-4_17

Questioner	Oracle
1. Is it on a wooden surface?	Yes
2. Is it red?	No
3. Is it white?	No
4. Is it a scissor?	Yes
5. Is it the scissor on the left of the picture?	Yes

Fig. 1. GuessWhat?! human dialogues are short and with a clear division of roles between players; most of the last questions are answered positively, are long, and contain details suitable to guess the target object.

Most Visual Dialogue systems proposed in the literature share the encoder-decoder architecture [29] and are evaluated using the task-success of the Guesser. By using this metric, multiple components are evaluated at once: the ability of the Questioner to ask informative questions, of the Oracle to answer them, of the Encoder to produce a visually grounded representation of the dialogue history and of the Guesser to select the most probable target object given the image and the dialogue history.

In this paper, we disentangle the compressed task-success evaluation and focus on the ability of the Encoder to produce a dialogue hidden state representation that encodes the information necessary for the Guesser to select the target object. Hence, we use the dialogue history generated by humans playing the referential game so to be sure of the quality of the questions and of the answers. We run our analysis on GuessWhat?! since, as illustrated in Fig. 1, its dialogues are quite simple: a sequence of short questions answered by Yes or No containing on average 30.1 (±17.6) tokens per dialogue. The simplicity of the dialogue structure makes the dataset suitable to be used as a diagnostic dataset.

In [23], the authors have shown that neural models are not sensitive to the order of turns in dialogues and conclude they do not use the history effectively. In GuessWhat?! dialogues the order in which questions have been asked is not crucial: we would be able to guess the target object even if the question-answer pairs in Fig. 1 were provided in the reversed order. Indeed, we are able to use salient information independently of the turns where it occurs. We wonder whether the same holds for neural models trained to solve the GuessWhat?! task. As the example in the figure shows, the last question humans ask is usually quite rich in detail about the target object and is answered positively. We exploit these features of the dataset to run our in-depth analysis.

We compare encoders with respect to the architecture (Recurrent Neural Networks vs. Transformers), the input modalities (only language vs. language and vision), and the model background knowledge (trained from scratch vs. pretrained and then fine-tuned on the downstream task). Our analysis shows that:

- the GuessWhat?! dataset can be used as a diagnostic dataset to scrutinize models' performance: dialogue length mirrors the level of difficulty of the game; most questions in the last turn are answered positively and are longer than earlier ones;
- Trasformers are less sensitive than Recurrent Neural Network based models to ther order in which QA pairs are provided;
- pre-trained Transformers, RoBERTa and LXMERT, detect salient information, within the dialogue history, independently of the position in which it is provided;
- LXMERT outperforms RoBERTa on shorter dialogues, but it struggles in processing longer ones where the dialogue structure plays a major role.

2   Related Work

Scrutinizing Visual Dialogues Encoding. Interesting exploratory analysis has been carried out to understand Visual Question Answering (VQA) systems and highlight their weaknesses and strengths, e.g. [11,12,25,28]. Less is known about how well grounded conversational models encode the dialogue history.

In [23], the authors study how neural dialogue models encode the dialogue history when generating the next utterance. They show that neither recurrent nor transformer based architectures are sensitive to perturbations in the dialogue history and that Transformers are less sensitive than recurrent models to perturbations that scramble the conversational structure; furthermore, their findings suggest that models enhanced with attention mechanisms use more information from the dialogue history than their vanilla counterpart. We take inspiration from this study to understand how State-Of-The-Art (SOTA) models encode the visually grounded dialogues generated by humans while playing the Guess-What?! game.

In [13], the authors show that in many reading comprehension datasets, that presumably require the combination of both questions and passages to predict the correct answer, models can achieve quite a good accuracy by using only part of the information provided. We investigate the role of each turn in GuessWhat?! human dialogues and to what extent models encode the strategy seen during training.

SOTA LSTM Based Models on GuessWhat?! After the introduction of the supervised baseline model [33], several models have been proposed to play the GuessWhat?! game. They exploit either some form of reinforcement learning [6,21,22,34–37] or cooperative learning [21,26]; in both cases, the model is first trained with the supervised learning regime and then the new paradigm is applied. This two-step process has been shown to reach higher task success than the supervised approach when the Questioner and Oracle models are put to play together. Since our focus is on the Guesser and we are evaluating it on human dialogues, we will compare models that have undergone only the supervised training step. We compare these recurrent models (based on LSTMs [24]) against models based on Transformers [32].

Transformer Based Models. [32] showed the power of the attention mechanisms at the core of Transformers. The last years have seen an increasing popularity of these models trained on several tasks to reach task-agnostic multimodal representations [2,14,17,20,27,30]. ViLBERT [17] has been recently extended by means of multi-task training involving 12 datasets which include GuessWhat?! [18] and has been fine-tuned to play the Answerer of VisDial [19]. Among these universal multimodal models, we choose LXMERT [30]. [3] propose methods for directly analyzing the attention heads aiming to understand whether they specialize in some specific foundational aspect (like syntactic relations) functional to the overall success of the model. We take inspiration from their work to shed light on how Transformers, that we adapt to play GuessWhat?!, encode the dialogues.

3   Dataset

The GuessWhat?! dataset was collected via Amazon Mechanical Turk by [33]. It is an asymmetric game involving two human participants who see a real-world image taken from the MS-COCO dataset [15]. One of the participants (the Oracle) is assigned a target object in the image and the other participant (the Questioner) has to guess it by asking Yes/No questions to the Oracle. There are no time constraints to play the game.

The dataset contains 155K English dialogues about approximately 66K different images. The answers are respectively 52.2% No, 45.6% Yes, and 2.2% N/A (not applicable); the training set contains 108K datapoints and the validation and test sets 23K each. Dialogues contain on average 5.1 ($\pm$3.3) question-answer (QA) pairs and the vocabulary consists of around 4900 words; each game has at least 3 and at most 20 candidates. We evaluate models using human dialogues, selecting only the games on which humans have succeed finding the target and contain at most 10 turns (total number of dialogues used: 90K in training and around 18K both in validation and testing).

We run a careful analysis of the dataset aiming to find features useful to better understand the performance of models. Although the overall number of Yes/No answers is balanced, the shorter the dialogues, the higher the percentage of Yes answers is: it goes from the 75% in dialogues with 2 turns to the 50% in the 5 turn cluster to the 35% in the 10 turn cluster. Interestingly, most of the questions in the last turns obtain a positive answer and these questions are on average longer than earlier ones (see Fig. 1 for an example). A model that encodes these questions well has almost all the information to guess the target object without actually using the full dialogue history. Not all games are equally difficult: in shorter dialogues the area of the target object is bigger than the one of target objects in longer dialogues, and their target object is quite often a "person" – the most common target in the dataset; moreover, the number of distractors in longer dialogues is much higher. Hence, the length of a dialogue is a good proxy of the level of difficulty of the game. Figure 2 reports the statistics of the training set; similar ones characterize the validation and the test sets.

The length of the dialogue is a good proxy of the level of difficulty of the game. Figure 3 shows that longer dialogues contain more distractors and in particular

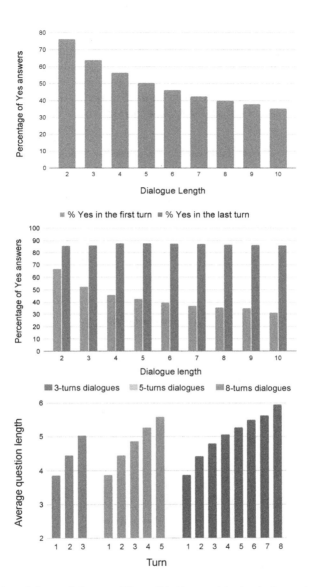

Fig. 2. Statistics of the training set (the validation and test sets have similar distributions). Dialogue length refers to the number of turns. **Up:** The distribution of Yes/No questions is very unbalanced across the clusters of games (the percentage of Yes answers is much higher in shorter dialogues); **Middle** In the large majority of games, the last question is answered positively; **Bottom:** The last questions are always longer (length of questions per turn for the clusters with dialogues having 3, 5, and 8 turns).

more distractors of the same category of the target object; the latter are supposed to be especially challenging for the models, because the usual architecture of the Guesser receives the category and the coordinates of each candidate object. Moreover, the area occupied by target objects is smaller in longer dialogues and the most representative category among target objects ("person") is less frequent. Finally, longer dialogues contain more words which occur rarely in the training set (i.e., words appearing less than 15 times in the training set). We will exploit these features of the dataset to scrutinize the behaviour of models.

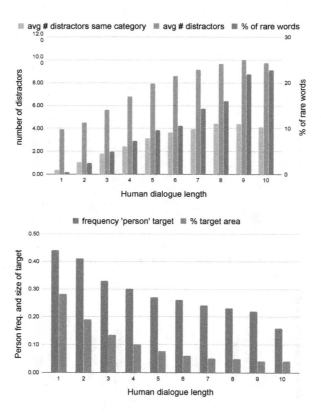

Fig. 3. Up: longer human dialogues contain more distractors and more distractors of the same category of the target object, and more rare words; **Down**: The distribution of target objects is unbalanced, since "person" is the most frequent target.

4   Models

All the evaluated models share the skeleton as illustrated in Fig. 4: an encoder paired with a Guesser. For the latter, all models use the module proposed in [33].

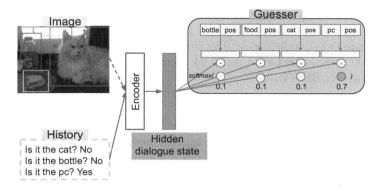

Fig. 4. Shared Encoder-Guesser skeleton. The Guesser receives the category labels (e.g., "bottle") and the spatial coordinates (pos) of each candidate object. Multimodal encoders receive both the image and the dialogue history, whereas blind models receive only the latter.

Candidate objects are represented by the embeddings obtained via a Multi-Layer Perceptron (MLP) starting from the category and spatial coordinates of each candidate object. The representations so obtained are used to compute dot products with the hidden dialogue state produced by an encoder. The scores of each candidate object are given to a softmax classifier to choose the object with the highest probability. The Guesser is trained in a supervised learning paradigm, receiving the complete human dialogue history at once. The models we compare differ in how the hidden dialogue state is computed. We compare LSTM vs. Transformers when receiving only the language input (henceforth, Blind models) or both the language and the visual input (henceforth, Multimodal models).

4.1 Language-Only Encoders

LSTM. As in [33], the representations of the candidates are fused with the last hidden state obtained by an LSTM which processes only the dialogue history.

RoBERTa. In the architecture of the model described above, we replace the LSTM with the robustly-optimized version of BERT [5], RoBERTa, a SOTA universal transformer based encoder introduced in [16].[1] We use RoBERTa$_{BASE}$ which has been pre-trained on 16GB of English text trained for 500K steps to perform masked language modeling. It has 12 self-attention layers with 12 heads each. It uses three special tokens, namely CLS, which is taken to be the representation of the given sequence, SEP, which separates sequences, and EOS, which denotes the end of the input. We give the output corresponding to the CLS

---

[1] We have also tried BERT, but we obtained higher accuracy with RoBERTa.

token to a linear layer and a *tanh* activation function to obtain the hidden state which is given to the Guesser. To study the impact of the pre-training phase, we have compared the publicly available pre-trained model, which we fine-tuned on GuessWhat?! (**RoBERTa**), against its counterpart trained from scratch only on the game (**RoBERTa-S**).

4.2 Multimodal Encoders

V-LSTM. We enhance the LSTM model described above with the visual modality by concatenating the linguistic and visual representation and scaling its result with an MLP; the result is passed through a linear layer and a *tanh* activation function to obtain the hidden state which is used as input for the Guesser modules. We use a frozen ResNet-152 pre-trained on ImageNet [9] to extract the visual vectors.

LXMERT. To evaluate the performance of a universal multimodal encoder, we employ LXMERT (Learning Cross-Modality Encoder Representations from Transformers) [30]. It represents an image by the set of position-aware object embeddings for the 36 most salient regions detected by a Faster R-CNN and it processes the text input by position-aware randomly-initialized word embeddings. Both the visual and linguistic representations are processed by a specialized transformer encoder based on self-attention layers; their outputs are then processed by a cross-modality encoder that through a cross-attention mechanism generates representations of the single modality (language and visual output) enhanced with the other modality as well as their joint representation (cross-modality output). As RoBERTa, LXMERT uses the special tokens CLS and SEP. Differently from RoBERTa, LXMERT uses the special token SEP both to separate sequences and to denote the end of the textual input. LXMERT has been pre-trained on five tasks.[2] It has 19 attention layers: 9 and 5 self-attention layers in the language and visual encoders, respectively and 5 cross-attention layers. We process the output corresponding to the CLS token as in RoBERTa. Similarly, we consider both the pre-trained version (**LXMERT**) and the one trained from scratch (**LXMERT-S**).

5 Experiments

We compare the models described above using human dialogues aiming to shed lights on how the encoders capture the information that is salient to guess the target object.

---

[2] Masked cross-modality language modeling, masked object prediction via RoI-feature regression, masked object prediction via detected-label classification, cross-modality matching, and image question answering.

5.1 Task Success

As we can see in Table 1, the pre-trained Transformers LXMERT and RoBERTa obtain the highest results, with the multimodal model scoring slightly higher (69.2 vs. 67.9).[3] The high accuracy obtained by RoBERTa shows that the dialogue history per se is quite informative to select the right target object. If we go back to the example in Fig. 1, we realize it is possible to succeed in that game if we are given the dialogue only and are asked to select the target object (the scissor on the left) among candidates for which we are told the category and the coordinates – as it is the case for the Guesser.

The comparison between the pre-trained version of these models with their from-scratch counterparts highligths the role of the pre-training in language understanding (RoBERTa vs. RoBERTa-S) and in language grounding (LXMERT vs. LXMERT-S). To better understand the difference between the models, Table 1 reports also the accuracy by clusters of games based on the dialogue length. Quite interesting LXMERT performes very well on short dialogues: it reaches 80.5% accuracy on 3-turn dialogues, but it has a rather big drop when dialogues get longer. The difference between LXMERT and LXMERT-S is minimal for the 8-turn cluster. Instead, RoBERTa is less affected by the length of the dialogues. This difference between the two pre-trained transformers suggests that LXMERT is good in exploiting language grounding when the dialogue (and maybe also the image) is not too complex, while RoBERTa can handle the dialogue structure to some extent.

Table 1. Model comparison on the accuracy results for all games, and for those of 3/5/8 dialogue length.

	LSTM	RoBERTa-S	RoBERTa	V-LSTM	LXMERT-S	LXMERT
All	64.7	64.2	**67.9**	64.5	64.4	**69.2**
3	72.5	72.7	75.3	71.9	72.7	**80.5**
5	59.3	58.3	60.1	59.3	58.9	**63.1**
8	47.3	45.1	**51.0**	47.2	46.1	45.0

In the following, we are running an in-depth analysis to understand whether models are able to identify salient information indipendently of the position in which they occur.

5.2 Are Models Sensitive to the Strategy Seen During Training?

In Sect. 3, we have seen that human dialogues tend to share a specific strategy, i.e. questions that are asked in first turns are rather short whereas those in

---

[3] The model proposed in [18] based on ViLBERT obtains an accuracy on GuessWhat?! with human dialogues of 65.04% when trained together with the other 11 tasks and 62.81% when trained only on it.

the last turns provide relevant details about the most probable target object. We wonder whether the models under analysis become sensitive to the above-mentioned strategy and learn to focus on some turns more than others rather than on the actual salient QA pair.

Inspired by [23], we perturb the dialogue history in the test set by reversing the order of turns from the last to the first one. Differently from them, given the nature of the GuessWhat?! dialogue history, we value positively models that are robust to this change in the dialogue history order. In the following, we refer to the dialogues provided in the order asked by humans as Ground Truth (GT) and to the dialogues provided in the reverse order as Reversed.

Our experiment (Table 2) shows that Transformers are less sensitive than LSTMs to the order in which QA pairs are provided. Interestingly, the pre-training phase seems to mitigate the effect of the change of the order even more. Indeed, RoBERTa has a drop of just −1.4, whereas the accuracy of its from-scratch counterpart drops of −6.4. The difference is even more noticeable in the case of LXMERT: while LXMERT has a drop of 4.1, the accuracy of its from-scratch counterpart drops of −6.6. In other words, **(pre-trained) Transformers seem to be able to identify salient information independently of the position in which it is provided within the dialogue history**.

Table 2. Accuracy obtained on the test set containing dialogues in the Ground Truth order (GT) vs. the reversed order (Reversed).

		GT	Reversed
BLIND	LSTM	64.7	56.0
	RoBERTa-S	64.2	57.8
	RoBERTa	**67.9**	**66.5**
MM	V-LSTM	64.5	51.3
	LXMERT-S	64.4	57.8
	LXMERT	**69.2**	**65.1**

5.3   The Role of the Last Question

Table 3 reports the results of the models when receiving all the turns of the dialogue history, when receiving the dialogue history without the last turn, and when receiving only the last turn. As we can see all models undergo a rather big drop in accuracy when removing the last question. It is worth noting that RoBERTa outperforms other models when removing the last turn, confirming that RoBERTa is able to better encode the full dialogue history and not only parts of it. This holds for different dialogue lengths as shown in the Table. Interestingly, LXMERT performs quite well in short dialogues also when given only the last question: it reaches already 68.6% in the 3-turn cluster, namely +7.6

than RoBERTa. Instead, with longer dialogues it does not manage to exploit the last question so well reaching an accuracy closer to RoBERTa's (32.3 vs. 30.1). By comparing the accuracy of each model when receiving only the last turn and when receiving all turns except the last one, we can notice an interesting pattern: whereas in short dialogues models obtain a rather high accuracy when receiving either only the last question or only the previous turns, they are able to profit of the last turn much less in longer dialogues. This could be due to the fact that in short dialogues the last question describes the target object without relying on too many information stated far away on previous turns.

Table 3. Accuracy of the models when receiving all turns of the dialogue history and when removing the last turn (W/o last) or receiving only the last turn (Last) for dialogues with 3, 5, and 8 turns.

Model	3-Q			5-Q			8-Q		
	All	W/o last	Last	All	W/o last	Last	All	W/o last	Last
LSTM	72.5	53.4	56.9	59.3	46.8	39.3	47.3	38.4	26.7
RoBERTa-S	72.7	55.4	55.3	58.3	44.9	37.4	45.0	38.9	27.6
RoBERTa	75.3	**58.2**	61.0	60.1	49.3	39.4	51.0	42.0	30.1
V-LSTM	71.9	53.8	53.0	59.3	43.7	34.0	47.2	36.5	21.9
LXMERT-S	72.7	55.4	56.7	58.9	46.9	38.7	46.1	39.7	28.8
LXMERT	80.5	56.8	**68.6**	63.1	47.7	46.0	45.0	37.7	32.3

5.4   How Attention Is Distributed Across Turns

So far we have seen that the last turn is usually answered positively (Sect. 3 and that it is quite informative to detect the target object (Sect. 5.1). We wonder whether this is reflected on how models distribute their attention across turns within a dialogue. To this end, we analyze how much each turn contributes to the overall self-attention within a dialogue by summing the attention of each token within a turn. We run this analysis for LXMERT and RoBERTa in their various versions: **all models put more attention on the last turn** when the GT order of turns is given.

In Table 2, we have seen that Transformers are more robust than the other models when the dialogue history is presented in the reversed order (the first QA pair of the GT is presented as the last turn and the last QA pair is presented as first turn). Our analysis of the attention heads of RoBERTa and LXMERT shows that these models, both in their from scratch and pre-trained version, focus more on the question *asked* last **also in the reversed test set** where it is *presented* in the first position. This shows they are still able to identify the most salient information. In Fig. 5, we report the attention per turn of LXMERT-S when receiving the GT and the reversed test set in 5-turn dialogues.

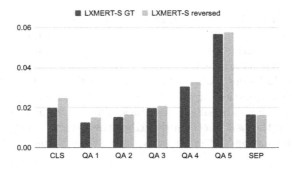

Fig. 5. Attention assigned by LXMERT-S to each turn in a dialogue when the dialogue history is given in the GT order (from QA1 to QA5) or in the reversed order (from QA5 to QA1).

5.5 Qualitative Evaluation

The quantitative analysis reported so far shows that the pre-trained transformers, LXMERT and RoBERTa, overall have a similar performance, but that LXMERT is much better in exploiting the last question in short dialogues and fails encoding the information provided by long dialogues. RoBERTas instead is affected less by the dialogue length and takes less adventage of the informative question asked in the last turn by humans. In order to gain a deeper understanding about the differences between these two models, we analyzed games which are solved successfully by RoBERTa and not by LXMERT and vice-versa. Dialogues solved by RoBERTa and not by LXMERT have a mean length of 5.5 (±2.3), whereas dialogues belonging to the opposite case have a mean length of 4.5 (±2.0). This confirms the hypothesis that RoBERTa encodes longer dialogues better than LXMERT. The qualitative analysis shows that LXMERT has an advantage when dealing with shorter dialogues that require to rely on vision.

In Fig. 6, we show two examples of dialogues one which has been solved by LXMERT and not by RoBERTa (left) and on solved by RoBERTa but not by LXMERT (right). In the dialogue on the left, the model needs to ground the question "Is he wearing blue?" in the image to properly process it. LXMERT succeeds in this game. This suggests that though the Guesser does not see the candidate visual representation it manages to profit of the language grounding ability of the encoder. In the dialogue on the right, the model needs to properly solve the anaphora in the last question "Is it in the back?" connecting the pronoun to the "car" mentioned in the second turn. LXMERT fails establishing such connection whereas RoBERTa seems to succeed in solving the anaphora.

5.6 Details for Reproducibility

In our experiments, we used the GuessWhat?! dataset (http://guesswhat.ai/download). The dataset contains 155000 English dialogues about approximately

Questioner	Oracle
1. Is it a sign?	No
2. Is it a car?	Yes
3. Is it white?	No
4. Is it in the middle?	No
5. Is it in the back?	Yes

Questioner	Oracle
1. Is it a person?	Yes
2. Is he in the foreground?	No
3. Is he wearing blue?	Yes

Fig. 6. A game solved successfully by LXMERT and not by RoBERTa (left) and a game solved by RoBERTa and not by LXMERT (right). (Color figure online)

66000 different images. The training split contains 108000 datapoints, the validation split 23000 datapoints, and the test split 23000 datapoints. We considered only the dialogues corresponding to the games succeeded by humans and having less or equal than 10 turns.

For training LSTM based models we adapted the source codes available at https://github.com/shekharRavi/Beyond-Task-Success-NAACL2019 and at https://github.com/GuessWhatGame/guesswhat/. For training transformer based models we adapted the source code available at https://github.com/huggingface/transformers. The scripts for all the experiments and the modified models will be made available upon acceptance. For all models, we used the same hyperparameters of the original works. When adapting Transformers to the GuessWhat?! task, we scaled the representation of the CLS token from 768 to 512. We used PyTorch 1.0.1 for all models except for LSTM, for which we have used Tensorflow 1.3. All models are trained with Adam optimizer. For transformer based models we used a batch size equal to 16, a weight decay equal to 0.01, gradient clipping equal to 5, and a learning rate which is warmed up over the first 10% iterations to a peak value of 0.00001 and then linearly decayed.

Regarding the infrastructure, we used 1 Titan V GPU. LSTM based models took about 15 h for completing 100 training epochs. Transformer based models took about 4 days for completing 25 training epochs. Each experiment took about 10 min to evaluate the best trained models.

Details on the best epoch, the validation accuracy, and the number of parameters of each model are reported in Table 4.

Table 4. Epoch, validation accuracy, and number of parameters for best models.

Model	Best epoch	Validation accuracy	Parameters
LSTM	19	65.6	5,030,144
RoBERTa	7	68.7	125,460,992
RoBERTa-S	14	64.7	125,460,992
V-LSTM	9	65.2	10,952,818
LXMERT-S	16	65.2	208,900,978
LXMERT	12	70.0	208,900,978

6   Conclusion

Our detailed analysis of the GuessWhat?! dataset has revealed features of its games that we have exploited to run a diagnostic analysis of SOTA models.

Our comparative analysis has shown that Trasformers are less sensitive than LSTMs to the order in which QA pairs are provided and that their pre-trained versions are even stronger in detecting salient information, within the dialogue history, independently of the position in which it is provided.

We also shown that RoBERTa is the encoder providing the Guesser with the most informative representation of the dialogue history. Its advantage is particularly strong in longer dialogues. On the other hand, LXMERT greatly outperforms all the other models on 3-turn dialogues: indeed, it succeeds in providing the Guesser with a grounded representation of the dialogue history when the latter consists of a few turns while it fails in doing so for longer dialogues. All our models currently rely on categories to represent candidate objects in the Guesser. It would be interesting to see how models would perform when they have to rely on visual information rather than categories.

Acknowledgments. We kindly acknowledge the support of NVIDIA Corporation with the donation of the GPUs used in our research at the University of Trento. We acknowledge SAP for sponsoring the work and thank the reviewers of the NLP4AI workshop for their valuable comments on a previous version of this paper.

References

1. Anderson, A.H., et al.: The HCRC map task corpus. Lang. Speech **34**, 351–366 (1991)
2. Chen, Y.C., et al.: UNITER: learning universal image-text representations (2019). arXiv:1909.11740
3. Clark, K., Khandelwal, U., Levy, O., Manning, C.D.: What does BERT look at? An analysis of BERT's attention. In: Proceedings of the 2019 ACL Workshop BlackboxNLP: Analyzing and Interpreting Neural Networks for NLP, pp. 276–286 (2019)

4. Das, A., Kottur, S., Moura, J.M., Lee, S., Batra, D.: Learning cooperative visual dialog agents with deep reinforcement learning. In: 2017 IEEE International Conference on Computer Vision, pp. 2951–2960 (2017)
5. Devlin, J., Chang, M.W., Lee, K., Toutanova, K.: BERT: pre-training of deep bidirectional transformers for language understanding. In: Proceedings of the 2019 Conference of the North American Chapter of the Association for Computational Linguistics: Human Language Technologies, (Long and Short Papers), vol. 1, pp. 4171–4186. Association for Computational Linguistics, Minneapolis, Minnesota, June 2019. https://doi.org/10.18653/v1/N19-1423. https://www.aclweb.org/anthology/N19-1423
6. Gan, Z., Cheng, Y., Kholy, A.E., Li, L., Liu, J., Gao, J.: Multi-step reasoning via recurrent dual attention for visual dialog. In: Proceedings of the 57th Annual Meeting of the Association for Computational Linguistics, pp. 6463–6474 (2019)
7. Haber, J., Baumgärtner, T., Takmaz, E., Gelderloos, L., Bruni, E., Fernández, R.: The PhotoBook dataset: building common ground through visually-grounded dialogue. In: Proceedings of the 57th Annual Meeting of the Association for Computational Linguistics, pp. 1895–1910, July 2019. https://doi.org/10.18653/v1/P19-1184. https://www.aclweb.org/anthology/P19-1184
8. He, H., Balakrishnan, A., Eric, M., Liang, P.: Learning symmetric collaborative dialogue agents with dynamic knowledge graph embeddings. In: Proceedings of the 55th Annual Meeting of the Association for Computational Linguistics, pp. 1766–1776 (2017)
9. He, K., Zhang, X., Ren, S., Sun, J.: Deep residual learning for image recognition. In: Proceedings of the IEEE Conference on Computer Vision and Pattern Recognition, pp. 770–778 (2016)
10. Ilinykh, N., Zarrieß, S., Schlangen, D.: Tell me more: a dataset of visual scene description sequences. In: Proceedings of the 12th International Conference on Natural Language Generation, pp. 152–157 (2019). https://www.aclweb.org/anthology/W19-8621
11. Johnson, J., Hariharan, B., van der Maaten, L., Fei-Fei, L., Zitnick, C.L., Girshick, R.B.: CLEVR: a diagnostic dataset for compositional language and elementary visual reasoning. In: IEEE Conference on Computer Vision and Pattern Recognition, vol. abs/1612.06890 (2017)
12. Kafle, K., Kanan, C.: An analysis of visual question answering algorithms. In: Proceedings of the IEEE International Conference on Computer Vision, pp. 1965–1973 (2017)
13. Kaushik, D., Lipton, Z.C.: How much reading does reading comprehension require? A critical investigation of popular benchmarks. In: Proceedings of the 2018 Conference on Empirical Methods in Natural Language Processing, pp. 5010–5015 (2018)
14. Li, L.H., Yatskar, M., Yin, D., Hsieh, C.J., Chang, K.W.: VisualBERT: a simple and performant baseline for vision and language (2019). arXiv:1908.03557
15. Lin, T.-Y., et al.: Microsoft COCO: common objects in context. In: Fleet, D., Pajdla, T., Schiele, B., Tuytelaars, T. (eds.) ECCV 2014. LNCS, vol. 8693, pp. 740–755. Springer, Cham (2014). https://doi.org/10.1007/978-3-319-10602-1_48
16. Liu, Y., et al.: RoERTa: a robustly optimized bert pretraining approach (2019). arXiv:1907.11692
17. Lu, J., Batra, D., Parikh, D., Lee, S.: ViLBERT: pretraining task-agnostic visiolinguistic representations for vision-and-language tasks. In: Advances in Neural Information Processing Systems, pp. 13–23 (2019)
18. Lu, J., Goswami, V., Rohrbach, M., Parikh, D., Lee, S.: 12-in-1: multi-task vision and language representation learning. In: Proceedings of CVPR (2020)

19. Murahari, V., Batra, D., Parikh, D., Das, A.: Large-scale pretraining for visual dialog: a simple state-of-the-art baseline. arXiv preprint arXiv:1912.02379 (2019)
20. amd Nan Duan, G.L., Fang, Y., Gong, M., Jiang, D., Zhou, M.: Unicoder-VL: a universal encoder for vision and language by cross-modal pre-training. In: Proceedings of AAAI (2020)
21. Pang, W., Wang, X.: Visual dialogue state tracking for question generation. In: Proceedings of 34th AAAI Conference on Artificial Intelligence (2020)
22. Sang-Woo, L., Tong, G., Sohee, Y., Jaejun, Y., Jung-Woo, H.: Large-scale answerer in questioner's mind for visual dialog question generation. In: Proceedings of International Conference on Learning Representations, ICLR (2019)
23. Sankar, C., Subramanian, S., Pal, C., Chandar, S., Bengio, Y.: Do neural dialog systems use the conversation history effectively? An empirical study. In: Proceedings of the 57th Annual Meeting of the Association for Computational Linguistics, pp. 32–37 (2019). https://www.aclweb.org/anthology/P19-1004
24. Schmidhuber, J., Hochreiter, S.: Long short-term memory. Neural Comput. $9(8)$, 1735–1780 (1997)
25. Shekhar, R., et al.: FOIL it! Find one mismatch between image and language caption. In: Proceedings of the 55th Annual Meeting of the Association for Computational Linguistics (Long Papers), vol. 1, pp. 255–265 (2017)
26. Shekhar, R., et al.: Beyond task success: a closer look at jointly learning to see, ask, and GuessWhat. In: Proceedings of the 2019 Conference of the North American Chapter of the Association for Computational Linguistics: Human Language Technologies, (Long and Short Papers), vol. 1, pp. 2578–2587 (2019). https://doi.org/10.18653/v1/N19-1265. https://www.aclweb.org/anthology/N19-1265
27. Su, W., et al.: VL-BERT: pre-training of generic visual-linguistic representations. In: ICLR (2020)
28. Suhr, A., Lewis, M., Yeh, J., Artzi, Y.: A corpus of natural language for visual reasoning. In: Proceedings of the Annual Meeting of the Association for Computational Linguistics, Vancouver, Canada, pp. 217–223. Association for Computational Linguistics, July 2017. http://aclweb.org/anthology/P17-2034
29. Sutskever, I., Vinyals, O., Le, Q.V.: Sequence to sequence learning with neural networks. In: Advances in Neural Information Processing Systems. pp. 3104–3112 (2014)
30. Tan, H., Bansal, M.: LXMERT: learning cross-modality encoder representations from transformers. In: Proceedings of the 2019 Conference on Empirical Methods in Natural Language Processing and the 9th International Joint Conference on Natural Language Processing (EMNLP-IJCNLP), pp. 5103–5114 (2019)
31. Udagawa, T., Aizawa, A.: A natural language corpus of common grounding under continuous and partially-observable context. In: Proceedings of the AAAI Conference on Artificial Intelligence, vol. 33, pp. 7120–7127 (2019)
32. Vaswani, A., et al.: Attention is all you need. In: Advances in Neural Information Processing Systems, pp. 5998–6008 (2017)
33. de Vries, H., Strub, F., Chandar, S., Pietquin, O., Larochelle, H., Courville, A.C.: GuessWhat?! Visual object discovery through multi-modal dialogue. In: 2017 IEEE Conference on Computer Vision and Pattern Recognition, pp. 5503–5512 (2017)
34. Yang, T., Zha, Z.J., Zhang, H.: Making history matter: history-advantage sequence training for visual dialog. In: Proceedings of the International Conference on Computer Vision (ICCV) (2019)
35. Zhang, J., Zhao, T., Yu, Z.: Multimodal hierarchical reinforcement learning policy for task-oriented visual dialog. In: Proceedings of the 19th Annual SIGdial

Meeting on Discourse and Dialogue, pp. 140–150 (2018). https://www.aclweb.org/anthology/W18-5015

36. Zhang, J., Wu, Q., Shen, C., Zhang, J., Lu, J., van den Hengel, A.: Goal-oriented visual question generation via intermediate rewards. In: Ferrari, V., Hebert, M., Sminchisescu, C., Weiss, Y. (eds.) ECCV 2018. LNCS, vol. 11209, pp. 189–204. Springer, Cham (2018). https://doi.org/10.1007/978-3-030-01228-1_12

37. Zhao, R., Tresp, V.: Improving goal-oriented visual dialog agents via advanced recurrent nets with tempered policy gradient. In: Proceedings of IJCAI (2018)

Breaking Down High-Level Robot Path-Finding Abstractions in Natural Language Programming

Yue Zhan$^{(\boxtimes)}$ and Michael S. Hsiao

Bradley Department of Electrical and Computer Engineering, Virginia Tech,
Blacksburg, VA 24060, USA
{zyue91,hsiao}@vt.edu

Abstract. Natural language programming (NLPr) allows people to program in natural language (NL) for specific domains. It poses great potential since it gives non-experts the ability to develop projects without exhaustive training. However, complex descriptions can sometimes have multiple interpretations, making program synthesis difficult. Thus, if the high-level abstractions can be broken down into a sequence of precise low-level steps, existing natural language processing (NLP) and NLPr techniques could be adaptable to handle the tasks. In this paper, we present an algorithm for converting high-level task descriptions into low-level specifications by parsing the sentences into sentence frames and using generated low-level NL instructions to generate executable programs for pathfinding tasks in a LEGO Mindstorms EV3 robot. Our analysis shows that breaking down the high-level pathfinding abstractions into a sequence of low-level NL instructions is effective for the majority of collected sentences, and the generated NL texts are detailed, readable, and can easily be processed by the existing NLPr system.

Keywords: Natural language processing · Natural language programming · Program synthesis · LEGO Mindstorms EV3

1 Introduction

The field of robotics has made significant strides because of the growth of market demands in recent years. However, despite the growing interest in educational robots, the time-consuming learning process and the steep learning curve of programming robots still challenge young robotics enthusiasts. Natural language programming (NLPr) offers a potential way to lower the bar of entry by allowing the users to "program" the robot using natural language (NL). The readability and expressive nature of natural language make it an ideal way to simplify the learning process. Though promising for this use case, NLPr has several challenges of its own. First, NL texts used to give instructions are typically low-level (LL) specifications to ensure precision and completeness. For example, the movement specifications used in the NLPr system for LEGO Mindstorms EV3 robot in

© Springer Nature Switzerland AG 2021
M. Baldoni and S. Bandini (Eds.): AIxIA 2020, LNAI 12414, pp. 280–297, 2021.
https://doi.org/10.1007/978-3-030-77091-4_18

the work [24] are categorized as a controlled natural language (CNL) [7]. The movement sentences used in the system are object-oriented sentences like *"The robot goes forward/backward/left/right ..."*. The requirement to use such low-level specifications makes the process of directing the robot more difficult for novice users, as they would rather give a high-level instruction such as *"The robot moves from point A to point B"* than to list out every individual step the robot must take. Unconstrained NL texts are highly flexible and expressive but can sometimes be ambiguous. Designing a language model for NLPr to cover all of the language structures in NL is extremely difficult, if not impossible [2]. As such, it would be a huge benefit for NLPr tasks if the information in a higher-level abstraction can be effectively extracted and used to generate a sequence of precise, unambiguous lower-level sentences that explain the intention and plans the proper actions. Suppose the information related to the robot tasks can be extracted. In that case, the language structures that need to be covered in the domain-specific function library and lexicon can be simplified, and the existing NLPr system can be directly adapted with fewer necessary modifications to handle the high-level (HL) NL abstractions, as shown in Fig. 1.

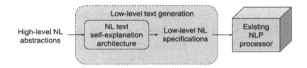

Fig. 1. High-level NL to low-level NL transformation

The key challenge addressed in this paper is effectively extracting semantic information from high-level sentences to synthesize low-level pathfinding NL instructions. In order to demonstrate our proposed low-level text generation process, we use a robot pathfinding task, in which a robot must find an optimal path between two points while avoiding obstacles along the way. To succeed at this task, our system must generate a sequence of low-level instructions that take the robot to its goal while minimizing the time cost and the number of actions taken by the robot. Once our system identifies a path based on the high-level input, it outputs a sequence of low-level NL to an existing NLPr system [24], which then generates the executable program for the LEGO Mindstorms EV3 robot.

2   Previous Work

Due to its promise of better ease of use and improved human-computer interaction, the foundations of NL based programming for robotics have been well established. In [8,13], an NLPr system that navigates a vision-based robot with an instruction-based learning method is presented. In these systems, robot-understandable procedures are generated from command-like NL instructions based on a set of pre-programmed sensory-motor action primitives and routes in a miniature city map. Users can give instructions based on available primitives to the robot when facing an unknown route with a human-robot interaction interface. In the work [23], a Vision-language robot navigation (VLN) system that combines the vision information and descriptive NL commands reasoning using a data-based model is proposed for in-home environments. When the NL instructions are given, a sequence of actions is generated by the reasoning navigator. Gathering sufficient data on various environments for model training purposes could be costly. In the work [15], a probabilistic combinatory categorial grammar (PCCG) based parser is used to translate procedural NL commands into logic-based Robot Control Language (RCL) for robot navigation. In [24], a grammar-based Object-Oriented Programming Controlled Natural Language (OOP-CNL) model is used to translate NL sentences into executable code for LEGO robots. In this work, the NLPr program synthesis system utilizes contextual and grammatical information to derive desired robot functionalities with a domain-specific function library and lexicon. While the language model used here can process more complex sentence structures, such as conditional statements, the sentences used for navigating the robot are still at a lower level.

There has been a significant amount of work done in the field of NLPr program synthesis, and most of this work has been focused on solving domain-specific problems. The work in [3] emphasizes the importance of NLP techniques in analyzing textual contents in software programs. The authors propose a system called Toradocu, which they developed using Stanford parser and a pattern and lexical similarity matching that coverts Javadoc comments into assertions, and a system called Tellina, which is trained with an RNN [10] to generate bash commands and use these systems to illustrate the potential of program synthesis with NL texts. The Metafor platform [11,18] is a descriptive NLPr system that can convert NL components into class descriptions with associated objects and methods. This work takes advantage of the NL parsing toolkit MontyLingua, mixed-initiative dialog, and programming by example techniques. The authors state that modern parsing techniques and the integration of common sense knowledge can help developers link humans' narrative capacities with traditional programming languages. However, the programs generated by Metafor are not directly executable. Another work, DeepCoder [1] extends the programming by example framework *Learning Inductive Program Synthesis* (LIPS)[17] into a big data problem. DeepCoder generates a sequence of SQL-like function calls for given integer input-output examples by training a neural network to predict possible mathematical properties. However, the generated function calls are basic and low-level. In work [5], an NLPr video game design system translates object-oriented English sentences into JavaScript game code. A hybrid context and grammar analysis is used. Conditional statements also can be handled in this system.

Text generation is a topic of interest in NLP research, and it is also receiving attention in the domain of robotics. A number of systems have worked towards explaining robot behavior, including verbalizing the robot's navigation decisions

[19,21] and explaining robot policies by generating behavioral explanations in NL [4]. The idea of generating low-level robot NL specifications based on robot paths presented in this paper is similar to these works: breaking down abstracted robot missions into sequential steps describing robot behaviors. However, instead of being used to explain the navigation to humans, the generated low-level NL texts are used for NLPr program synthesis.

3   Problem Formulation and System Design

3.1   High-Level to Low-Level (HL2LL) System Overview

Parsing and understanding the semantic meanings of high-level abstractions have been a significant challenge in NLP and NLPr research due to their complex linguistic nature. Just like explaining a complex concept to a child, one needs to break the concept down to a sequence of discrete, straightforward, and actionable steps for machines to understand. In this work, particularly, the HL2LL mechanism is built upon a domain-specific library; in this case, the LEGO robot functions. The OOP-CNL language model L [24] is used to extract the function information from NL inputs and to match a suitable combination of robot functions in this work. In a nutshell, when the function information extracted from the high-level abstraction contains motion language features that cannot be translated into individual functions in the function library $\mathcal{F}$, the system would further search for identifying high-level abstractions, like color line tracking or moving to specific mission regions. The high-level abstractions can be explained using a set of low-level specifications. For example, *"The robot moves forward 10 in."* is an example of a low-level specification, while *"The robot walks to M4 from M1."* is considered a high-level abstraction since it can be described using a set of low-level instructions. The transformation process, shown in Fig. 2, consists of four steps:

1. Parse the high-level abstraction: Identify the task details from given input sentences.
2. High-level abstraction to path: Find a qualified path from the *source* to the *target* based on the given high-level abstraction using the algorithm in Sect. 3.3.
3. Path to low-level NL specifications: Generate a set of low-level NL specifications that describe the actions needed for the robot to follow the qualified path.
4. Low-level NL specifications to code: Translate low-level NL specifications into executable codes using the NLPr system.

3.2   Map Representation

We model our robot's task after the First LEGO League (FLL)[1] competition, with an $88'' \times 44''$ *Mission Map* based on the FLL 2018/2019 official competition

---

[1] https://www.firstlegoleague.org/.

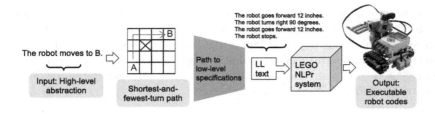

Fig. 2. System overview

arena serving as our robot's environment, shown in Fig. 3a. The arena contains eight mission regions, denoted using red blocks and several thick black lines on the map, which can be recognized using the robot's color sensor. The *Base* located at the bottom left is the required starting point for each run. In this paper, we focus on the task of planning a path for the robot between specified mission regions. Some other actions involving motor and sensor usages can be performed in addition to navigation, as described in the LEGO NLPr system [24].

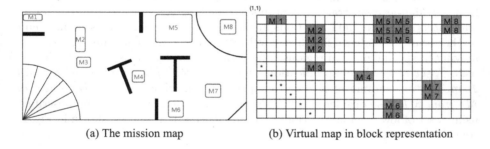

(a) The mission map   (b) Virtual map in block representation

Fig. 3. Virtual game maps

In order to simplify pathfinding, we break the *Mission Map* into grid squares, as shown in Fig. 3b. We denote this grid representation the *Virtual Map*. In the *Virtual Map* asterisks denote the edge of the start region and mission regions are represented by mission blocks. Mission blocks are shaded cells of the form M_n where the n represents the mission index. Each grid block corresponds to a block with size of $4'' \times 4''$. The top left corner of the map is initialized with coordinate $(1, 1)$. If the mission regions are treated as block-like obstacles, and the robot is restricted to movement in the cardinal directions, the task of pathfinding in the *Virtual Map* can be treated as a 2D Manhattan pathfinding problem.

3.3 Lee's Algorithm and Its Adaption

Lee's Algorithm [9] is one of the most effective breadth-first search (BFS) based single-layer routing methods for finding the shortest paths in a Manhattan graph.

Lee's Algorithm searches for the target from the source using a wave-like propagation. With a source block S and a target set of adjacent blocks T, there are two main phases in Lee's Algorithm:

1. **Search**: Begin by labelling block S as k, where $k = 0$. Fill the valid neighbors of blocks labeled k (not already filled and not outside of the map) with label $k + 1$. Proceed to step $k + 1$, repeating the previous process until either the destination T is reached or there are no more valid neighbors.
2. **Retrace**: Once T has been reached, trace backward to build the path from T to S by following the descend of k from k to 0. It is possible that multiple equal-length paths exist between S and T.

Lee's Algorithm can be modified to break ties between equal-length paths in favor of the path with the fewest turns, as shown in Algorithm 1 [16]. By minimizing the number of turns that the robot makes, we reduce the number of NL sentences our system must generate and the accumulation of navigation errors that occur as the robot turns. In the **Search** process, the direction and coordinates are recorded for the **Retrace** phase's reference. An alternative method approach would be to rank paths first by the number of turns taken and only then consider the overall path length, effectively trading off reduced turning time for potentially longer paths [25]. However, FLL players need to finish as many tasks as possible within a given time limit, and as such, we prefer to rank by path length first. Figure 4 shows an example of a grid's state after Algorithm 1 has been executed. Although there are multiple equal-length paths in the grid, the path highlighted in green is chosen by the adapted Lee's Algorithm because it has the fewest turns among the eligible shortest paths.

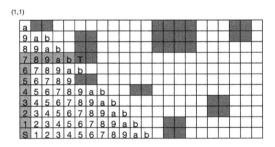

Fig. 4. Finding a path from the Base to M_2

3.4 Path Information Extraction for NLPr

Information extraction (IE) [6] in NLP is the process of converting raw text into a form that can be easily processed by machines. A task-driven domain-specific function library $\mathcal{F}$ is used to narrow down the space of function matching for program synthesis in this study. The function library $\mathcal{F}$ includes actions that a LEGO robot can perform with the supported sensors and motors. The key to

---

Algorithm 1 Shortest-and-fewest-turn path: Search and Retrace

---

1: **procedure** SEARCH(*current_point, target_point*)
2:     *queue.push*([*source_point*, 0])
3:     **while** *queue* **do**
4:         *current_point, counter* ← *queue.popleft*()
5:         *i, j* ← *current_point.i, current_point.j*
6:         *emap*[*i*][*j*] ← *counter*   ▷ label the current point
7:         *queue.push*(*neighborsOf*(*i, j*), *counter* + 1) if valid
8:         **if** any neighbor reaches the *target_point* **then**
9:             *goal_point* ← (*i, j*), break   ▷ path found
10:     **if** *goal_point* = *source_point* **then**
11:         return   ▷ no such path exists
12:     **else**
13:         save *current_dir*

1: **procedure** RETRACE(*current_point, source_point*)
2:     *get_dir* ← *current_dir*
3:     **while** *current_point* ≠ *source_point* **do**
4:         *i, j, id* ← *current_point.i, current_point.j, emap*[*i*][*j*]
5:         *L_id, R_id, U_id, D_id* ← *neighbors*(*emap*[*i*][*j*]) if exists
6:         **if** *get_dir* ∈ [*L, R, U, D*] and (*X_id* = *id* − 1) **then**   ▷ X: dir as id↓ along
    get_dir
7:             update *i, j*
8:         **else**
9:             compare to neighbors in different dirs
10:             update *i, j, get_dir*
11:         *current_point* ← (*i, j*)
12:         *path.push*(*current_point*)

---

parsing a sentence's semantic meaning is to split the sentence into sentence frame components and identify the dependency relations in and between each frame. A grammar-based OOP-CNL model $\mathcal{L}$ [24] is used to construct an intermediate representation for pathfinding based on part-of-speech (POS) tags [22] and parse information using NLTK toolkits [12], defined as:

$$\mathcal{L} = (O, A, P, R) \tag{1}$$

where O stands for the objects in the arena, A represents the robot actions, P indicates the adjectives or adverbs affiliated with the objects and actions, and R represents the requirements or conditions for the objects or the actions.

In order to provide sufficient information for program synthesis for the task-driven robot NLPr system, the following sentence components must first be identified: the object O, the action A, their corresponding properties P, and the conditional rules R, if any exist. After an initial preprocessing step based on lemmatization and tokenization, keywords from the lexicon, such as sensor names, sensor and motor port numbers, and mission region names are identified. Then the sentence tokens are categorized based on grammatical tags and dependency relations. For example, in the input sentence *"A happy robot goes to M2.*" O is the `robot`; A is `go to M2`; P is a Boolean state `happy`, and the R is that the expression `happy==True` must evaluate to true in order for the object to perform the action, as shown in Fig. 5. In an ideal world, the combination of $OAPR$ extracted from a sentence would correspond to exactly one function in the function library $\mathcal{F}$. However, due to the ambiguous nature of NL, there exist sentences for which $OAPR$ either cannot be mapped to any function in the library and there exist sentences for which $OAPR$ can map to multiple functions. These sentences pose a problem because if they are passed to the downstream NLPr system, the system could generate a program that does not perform the action the user intended. One way to prevent passing these sentences downstream is to use a formal validation step, which can provide early detection of such ambiguous sentences. The validation of input sentences is done with a formal analysis engine powered by a context-sensitive hierarchical finite-state machine (HFSM), which will be introduced in Sect. 3.7.

In a robot path finding task, when mission regions are detected in the sentence, an error-checking step is invoked to detect any underlying errors in the text, as described in Algorithm 2. The object and action pairs identified in this step continue to a function matching process in the function library $\mathcal{F}$. The object `robot` and action `go` match the pathfinding function `find_path(start,target)` instead of the function `move(dir,num,unit)` because of the presence of the target `M2` in this example.

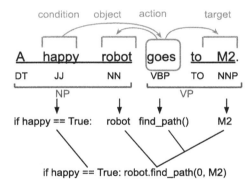

Fig. 5. Parsing a sentence and constructing the intermediate representation.

For our robot application, the number of object and action combinations is finite. For sentences with no ambiguity or errors, each $\mathcal{L}$ should have only one valid match in the finite function library $\mathcal{F}$. If the system fails to identify such a 1:1 match in the function library, the system will generate an error message with diagnostic information to help users to debug their input. When multiple objects, actions, or interpretations exist, the pre-defined higher priority functions will be chosen to ensure a sample program can be generated. For example, the sentence "*The robot goes straight to M3.*" maps to function `move(forward,0,0)` and function `find_path(0,M3)`. As such, the system cannot determine the user's intention. The system responds to this situation by generating a warning message, notifying users that "straight" is ignored for this conflict. Rather than not produce any low-level output at all, the system produces an output based on the `find_path` function, as it is a higher priority action.

When multiple mission regions are present, the pathfinding process needs to be split into steps. Each input sentence describing robot navigation may contain one midpoint and one avoid-point. For example, in the sentence *"If the robot sees an obstacle in 20 in., it goes to M7 through M3 but avoids M4"*, the path is parsed into two steps with the midpoint (through (M3)), the target (to (M7)), and the avoid-point (avoids (M4)), under the condition (if `ultrasound_sensor()<20 inches`).

Algorithm 2 Check for errors in the pathfinding sentence

1: **procedure** CHECK_ERRORS(*tokens*)
2:     *tokens, unknowns = tokens.validate(lexicon)*
3:     **if** *unknowns* **then**
4:         Warning: Skipping detected unknown tokens.
5:     *obj, act ← tokens.intersection(obj_dict, act_dict)*
6:     **if** *obj ≠ robot* or *act ≠ find_path* **then**   ▷ mismatch
7:         Error: not valid combination
8:     *missions ← tokens.intersection(emap)*   ▷ get all mission regions in the sentence
9:     **if** *len(missions) ≥ 4* **then**
10:         Error: too many mission regions in one sentence. Consider re-write.
11:     *source, target, mid_point ← dependency(tokens)*
12:     **if** *!target* or any *mission ∈ missions* unsigned **then**
13:         Error: no valid target or dangling tokens
14:     **else**
15:         return [*robot.find_path(source, mid_point, target)*]

Multi-conditional statements can be handled in such a language model $\mathcal{L}$ by processing each condition as a Boolean statement and each action separately. For the example shown in Fig. 6, the sentence is processed into an *if* statement with 2 conditions: condition 1 (NP (`color sensor`) VP (`see black`)), condition 2 (NP (`robot`) VP (`is happy`)), and action (NP (`it`) VP (`move to M2`)). The reference relation between `it` and `robot` is done by contextual analysis on current and previous contents combined with function library restrictions. e.g. `robot` is chosen because of it matches with the action `move` behavior both contextually and functionally.

While an action might have several interpretations, the functions implied in a sentence are limited by the task-driven domain-specific function library. For example, in the sentence *"When the robot sees red at M1, it will speed up and go through M2 to reach M3."*, the `color` subject indicates a color sensor is needed.

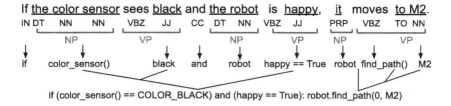

Fig. 6. Complex sentence example

Similarly, "see a wall" indicates the ultrasound sensor usage and "touch a wall" indicates the touch sensor usage.

3.5   Path to Low-Level Sentence

Once a path between S and T is identified, a sequence of low-level NL sentences describing the corresponding step-by-step actions needed to navigate the LEGO robot is generated. A grammar-based formalization method is used to construct the object-oriented low-level NL sentences. The generated NL texts will be fed to an NLPr system for further translation, as opposed to being intended for humans to read. Our proposed method does not require a large dataset for training and can be adapted to other high-level abstractions when a suitable function library is available.

Fig. 7. The robot moves from A to B.

If the robot starts off facing North/up, path 1 in Fig. 7 is described in low-level NL specifications as:

Path 1: $[4, 1] \to ... \to [1, 1] \to ... \to [1, 4] \Rightarrow$ The robot goes forward 12 inches. The robot turns right 90 degrees. The robot goes forward 12 inches.

The pseudocode in Algorithm 3 illustrates the above path-to-sentence conversion. First, every two neighboring coordinates in the path array are compared to detect turns and step numbers in each turn. The function `compare((pre_row, pre_col), (row, col))` returns `state` that determines if the robot needs to turn. If not, it means the robot still follows the previous direction `pre_state`. The counter records the number of steps in the current direction. Once a turn occurs, a set of NL sentences is generated based on the number of steps, recorded direction, and previous state, i.e., the function `path2NL(pre_state, dir, count)` generates the NL sentences for each turn. We then update the direction and reset the counter for the next steps.

Algorithm 3 Path to NL Generation

1: **procedure** NL TEXT GENERATION(*path, direct*)
2:    $total\_step, (pre\_row, pre\_col) \leftarrow len(path), path[0]$ ▷ total number of steps
3:    $counter, state, pre\_state \leftarrow 0, 0, 0$
4:    **for** i in range(*1, total_step*) **do**
5:       $row, col \leftarrow path[i]$
6:       $state \leftarrow$ compare$((pre\_row, pre\_col), (row, col))$
7:       **if** $state = pre\_state$ **then**
8:          $counter += 1$
9:       **if** $state \neq pre\_state$ or $i = total\_step - 1$ **then**
10:          $NL\_text \leftarrow$ path2NL$(pre\_state, dir, counter)$
11:          update$(dir), counter \leftarrow 1$
12:          NL2Code(NL_text) ▷ NL texts to code
13:       $pre\_state, pre\_row, pre\_col \leftarrow state, row, col$

3.6 Generating Code from NL Specifications Using the NLPr System

The LEGO NLPr program synthesis system [24] generates executable text-based programs directly from the NL input instead of the graph-based programs typical of LEGO robots. The input English Code (EC) is processed into intermediate representations using NLP techniques like, lemmatization, tokenization, categorization, and a function matching procedure. Such intermediate representations contain information extracted from the input that indicate the desired functions that need to be translated into formal program snippets. These intermediate representations are used for program synthesis and producing feedback or error information for users. The NL-to-code program synthesis system, NL2Code(NL_text) in Algorithm 3, calls the functions that handle the conversion of generated low-level NL specifications into executable programs. A set of robot motion functions in $\mathcal{F}$ are combined to synthesize the output program based on the intermediate representations. For example, the sentence *"The robot goes forward for 12 in."* can be represented by robot.move(forward,12,inch). This representation is translated into 28 lines of code.

3.7 Formal Validation Using HFSM

Finite-state machines (FSMs) are a powerful formal validation technique widely used in NLP applications such as IE and natural language parsing [14]. An FSM is an automaton with a finite number of transition states and terminal states. The transitions from one state to another are triggered with a predetermined

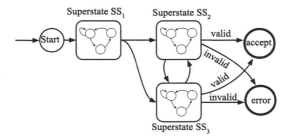

Fig. 8. Example HFSM

set of coded instructions [20]. At each state, the relevant FSM path to the next state is determined by the next input token in the sequence. Accurate translations are critical for NL-based robot program synthesis as misunderstanding the input's intention might lead to physical damage to the robot. The deterministic properties of FSMs help generate more trustworthy intermediate semantic representations and also help detect errors in the input, both of which contribute to less error-prone results for the NLPr system. In our LEGO NLPr system, the validation process in Algorithm 2, is powered by a *context-sensitive* hierarchical FSM based formal validation engine. This formal validation engine helps us to both validate input sentences and generate error messages whenever an error state is reach.

The FSM's hierarchical structure reduces the complexity of the system and allows us to specify the system more in detail by breaking the state machine into several *superstates*, denoted as SS_i, where $SS_i \in \mathbb{SS}, 1 \leq i \leq m$, as shown in Fig. 8. A *superstate* represents a cluster of one or more substates, as shown in Fig. 8. As mentioned above, the LEGO NLPr system is capable of handling conditional statements. To avoid mistranslation, the parsing process is split into two separate HFSMs with one for the condition and one for the action in a sentence. Take Boolean variable checking as an example: the conditional statement if "the robot is happy" refers to an expression that checks to see if the variable *happy* is True, while the action statement "the robot is happy" refers to a variable assignment that assigns *True* to happy.

For the robot pathfinding task we focused on in this paper, the transition from the robot *superstate* SS_1 to the pathfinding *superstate* SS_5 is triggered when a valid mission region name M_x is identified, as shown in Fig. 9. Within the pathfinding *superstate* SS_5, the target, source, midpoint, and avoid-point are identified. The formal validation within the *superstate* will check if any errors exist, such as illegal mission region names that are not registered on the mission map or having two target regions.

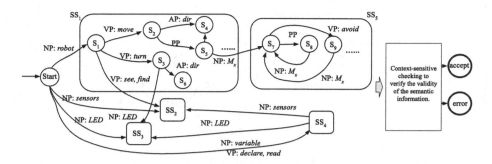

Fig. 9. Simplified robot action HFSM with some states omitted.

In order to guarantee the validity of the information extracted by the HFSM, we include a context-sensitive semantic checking based case analysis prior to transitioning to any terminal state, a step not present in conventional FSMs. For example, the case analysis would report errors and leads to the *error* terminal state if there are any conflicts between the target, source, midpoint, and avoid-point.

4   Experimental Results

We evaluate our system's performance on a set of 162 robot pathfinding related descriptions. These descriptions were collected manually by the authors, and they collectively describe movements between all eight mission regions. Each description consists of one or more sentences.

Our system successfully translates all 36 descriptions with 2 or fewer mission regions, resulting in programs that navigate the robot on the shortest path with the fewest turns between the source and the target. Of the 56 descriptions that navigate between three mission regions, 91.1% of the generated programs are correct. Our system performs worse on descriptions with more complicated structures, namely those involving more than three mission regions, with only 68.6% of the 70 such descriptions being translated into programs that conform to the original semantic meaning of the descriptions. Overall, our system correctly translated 135 (83.3%) of the 162 collected descriptions. Some example descriptions and their corresponding number of lines of code generated are shown in Table 1.

These results show that our proposed high-level abstractions to low-level NL instructions transformation system can successfully translate the large majority of the collected high-level robot navigation task sentences into low-level instructions for producing executable programs. This supports our hypothesis that with the POS tagging and a domain-specific function library and lexicon, the objects, actions, and targets in $\mathcal{L}$ can be effectively identified and useful intermediate representations for further program synthesis can then be generated.

However, despite our system's strengths, it still struggles with more complicated sentence structures due to the ambiguous and expressive nature of NL. One such description that poses a challenge for our system is "*The robot wanders through M1 M2 and M3.*" This description cannot be translated properly because there is no clear indication of the robot's source and target. As this description would be difficult for a human to convert to low-level instructions, it is understandable that the system fails to translate it correctly.

High-level robot navigation abstractions are translated into varying numbers of lines of code depending on the complexity of the NL instructions. When an NL description includes information that the system cannot handle, a best-guess program skeleton and accompanying debugging feedback are generated.

Table 1. English code examples with corresponding number of lines of code generated

Eg#	English Code Examples	# of lines
1	The robot goes from M5 to M3	99
2	The robot starts with facing to the right	109
	The robot goes to M8 from M1 but avoids M2	
3	The robot goes to M1 without going through M2 via M3	81
4	If the robot is happy, it goes to M2	67
5	When robot does not see the red line, it goes straight to M3	105
	Otherwise, it follows the red line	
6	If the robot sees an obstacle in 20 in., it goes to M7 through M3	108
	but avoids M4	
7	If the ultrasound sensor sees a ball in 5 in., the robot is happy	112
	A happy robot goes to M7 though M3 but avoids M4	

4.1 Case Study

Example 1. 109 lines of code are generated for Example description #2 in Table 1 for navigating from M5 to M3, shown in Fig. 10a.

Generated path $[1, 2] \rightarrow \cdots \rightarrow [7, 2] \rightarrow \cdots \rightarrow [7, 8] \rightarrow [6, 8] \rightarrow \cdots \rightarrow [6, 17] \rightarrow [5, 17] \cdots \rightarrow [2, 17] \cdots \rightarrow [2, 19]$

Generated low-level instructions "The robot turns right 90 degrees. The robot goes forward 24 in. The robot stops. The robot turns left 90 degrees. The robot goes forward 24 in. The robot stops. The robot turns left 90 degrees. The robot goes forward 4 in. The robot stops. The robot turns right 90 degrees. The robot goes forward 36 in. The robot stops. The robot turns left 90 degrees. The robot goes forward 16 in. The robot stops. The robot turns right 90 degrees. The robot goes forward 8 in. The robot stops."

Example 2. Paths for sample #7 in Table 1 are shown in Figs. 10b and 10c. Sample #7 in Table 1 is a multiple-phase pathfinding task, and as such our system must compute two paths. Note that when the robot reaches mission region #3, the robot is pointing to the East/right. Therefore, the second path starts with turning to the right only 90 degrees rather than turning 180 degrees. The second sentence's robot movements would only be performed when the state happy is true from the last sentence.

Generated path 1 $[11, 1] \rightarrow \cdots \rightarrow [6, 1] \rightarrow \cdots \rightarrow [6, 6]$
Generated path 2 $[6, 6] \rightarrow \cdots \rightarrow [9, 6] \rightarrow \cdots \rightarrow [9, 17]$
Generated low-level instructions "The robot goes forward 20 in. The robot
stops. The robot turns right 90 degrees. The robot goes forward 20 in. The
robot stops. The robot turns right 90 degrees. The robot goes forward 12 in.
The robot stops. The robot turns left 90 degrees. The robot goes forward
44 in. The robot stops."

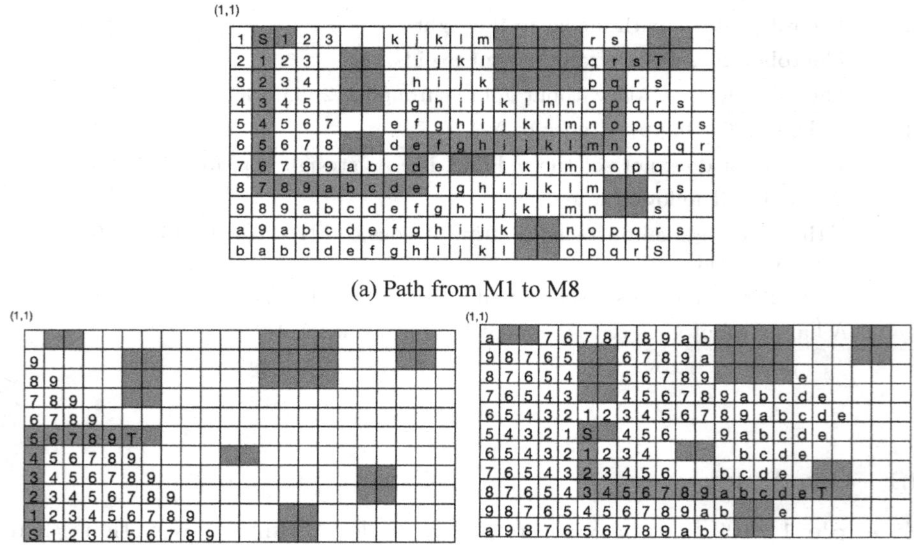

(a) Path from M1 to M8

(b) Path to M3

(c) Path from M3 to M7

Fig. 10. Case study tasks

5   Future Work

There are two main directions in which we intend to extend this work. First, we found that some input sentences may be invalid as they contain unclear or unknown information, meaning that they cannot be translated into robot functions even by a human, e.g. *"The robot hates moving forward"*. In order to make the system more robust to invalid inputs, it will be necessary to validate inputs with domain-specific formal reasoning and analysis. This will ensure the correctness of the system's understanding of the users' intentions and the correctness of the generated programs. Second, the function space contains several basic robot motions. As such, we intend to expand the function space with more low-level and even middle-level NL texts to develop the high-level abstraction self-explaining architecture further.

6 Conclusion

This work investigates the interdisciplinary NLP and robot path navigation task of breaking down complex high-level robot pathfinding abstractions into low-level NL instructions that can be processed directly by a LEGO NLPr system. The system we propose utilizes an efficient information extraction method with a OOP-CNL language model that analyzes and validates the sentence components' semantic meanings and relations. The system also contains an error-checking component that evaluates the input sentences' validity, and can also serve as a starting point for developing formal analysis methods for NLPr. We demonstrated how robot pathfinding problems for 2D Manhattan graphs could be handled by transforming the complicated high-level robot abstractions into a sequence of low-level NL instructions using NLP techniques and the domain-specific function library. The experimental results show that existing NLPr systems can be adapted to produce executable code using generated low-level NL specifications due to the simplicity, concreteness, and precise nature of the generated low-level sentences.

Although the study in this paper is limited in scope to pathfinding for LEGO Mindstorms EV3 robots, it lays a foundation for the task-driven HL2LL NL text self-explaining mechanism based on a domain-specific library. As complicated robot procedures can be explained using detailed sequential steps in natural language, we believe such a self-explaining mechanism could be a highly promising avenue for future NLP research.

References

1. Balog, M., Gaunt, A.L., Brockschmidt, M., Nowozin, S., Tarlow, D.: Deepcoder: learning to write programs. CoRR abs/1611.01989 (2016)
2. Dijkstra, E.W.: On the foolishness of "natural language programming". In: Bauer, F.L., et al. (eds.) Program Construction. LNCS, vol. 69, pp. 51–53. Springer, Heidelberg (1979). https://doi.org/10.1007/BFb0014656
3. Ernst, M.D.: Natural language is a programming language: applying natural language processing to software development. In: The 2nd Summit on Advances in Programming Languages, SNAPL 2017, CA, USA, pp. 4:1–4:14. Asilomar, May 2017

4. Hayes, B., Shah, J.A.: Improving robot controller transparency through autonomous policy explanation. In: Proceedings of the 2017 ACM/IEEE International Conference on Human-Robot Interaction, HRI 2017, New York, NY, USA, pp. 303–312. Association for Computing Machinery (2017)
5. Hsiao, M.S.: Automated program synthesis from object-oriented natural language for computer games. In: Controlled Natural Language - Proceedings of the Sixth International Workshop, CNL 2018, Maynooth, Co., Kildare, Ireland, 27–28, August 2018, pp. 71–74 (2018)
6. Jurafsky, D., Martin, J.H.: Speech and Language Processing, 2nd edn. Prentice-Hall Inc., Hoboken (2009)
7. Kuhn, T.: A survey and classification of controlled natural languages. Comput. Linguist. **40**(1), 121–170 (2014)
8. Lauria, S., Bugmann, G., Kyriacou, T., Klein, E.: Mobile robot programming using natural language. Robot. Auton. Syst. **38**(3), 171–181 (2002). Advances in Robot Skill Learning
9. Lee, C.Y.: An algorithm for path connections and its applications. IRE Trans. Electron. Comput. **EC-10**(3), 346–365 (1961)
10. Lin, X.V., Wang, C., Pang, D., Vu, K., Zettlemoyer, L., Ernst, M.D.: Program synthesis from natural language using recurrent neural networks. Technical report, UW-CSE-17-03-01, University of Washington Department of Computer Science and Engineering, Seattle, WA, USA, Mar 2017
11. Liu, H.: Metafor: visualizing stories as code. In: 10th International Conference on Intelligent User Interfaces, pp. 305–307. ACM Press (2005)
12. Loper, E., Bird, S.: NLTK: the natural language toolkit. In: Proceedings of the ACL-02 Workshop on Effective Tools and Methodologies for Teaching Natural Language Processing and Computational Linguistics, ETMTNLP 2002, USA, vol. 1, pp. 63–70. Association for Computational Linguistics (2002)
13. Lopes, L.S., Teixeira, A.: Human-robot interaction through spoken language dialogue. In: Proceedings of the 2000 IEEE/RSJ International Conference on Intelligent Robots and Systems (IROS 2000) (Cat. No. 00CH37113), vol. 1, pp. 528–534 (2000)
14. Manning, C.D., Schütze, H.: Foundations of Statistical Natural Language Processing. MIT Press, Cambridge (1999)
15. Matuszek, C., Herbst, E., Zettlemoyer, L., Fox, D.: Learning to parse natural language commands to a robot control system. In: Desai, J., Dudek, G., Khatib, O., Kumar, V. (eds.) Experimental Robotics, pp. 403–415. Springer, Heidelberg (2013). https://doi.org/10.1007/978-3-319-00065-7_28
16. Maxemchuk, N.: Routing in the Manhattan street network. IEEE Trans. Commun. **35**(5), 503–512 (1987)
17. Menon, A.K., Tamuz, O., Gulwani, S., Lampson, B., Kalai, A.T.: A machine learning framework for programming by example. In: Proceedings of the 30th International Conference on International Conference on Machine Learning, ICML 2013, vol. 28, pp. I-187–I-195. JMLR.org (2013)
18. Mihalcea, R., Liu, H., Lieberman, H.: NLP (Natural Language Processing) for NLP (Natural Language Programming). In: Gelbukh, A. (ed.) CICLing 2006. LNCS, vol. 3878, pp. 319–330. Springer, Heidelberg (2006). https://doi.org/10.1007/11671299_34
19. Perera, V., Selveraj, S.P., Rosenthal, S., Veloso, M.: Dynamic generation and refinement of robot verbalization. In: 2016 25th IEEE International Symposium on Robot and Human Interactive Communication (RO-MAN), pp. 212–218, August 2016

20. Rangra, R., Madhusudan: Natural language parsing: using finite state automata. In: 2016 3rd International Conference on Computing for Sustainable Global Development (INDIACom), pp. 456–463 (2016)
21. Rosenthal, S., Selvaraj, S.P., Veloso, M.: Verbalization: narration of autonomous robot experience. In: Proceedings of the Twenty-Fifth International Joint Conference on Artificial Intelligence, IJCAI 2016, pp. 862–868. AAAI Press (2016). http://dl.acm.org/citation.cfm?id=3060621.3060741
22. Toutanova, K., Klein, D., Manning, C.D., Singer, Y.: Feature-rich part-of-speech tagging with a cyclic dependency network. In: Proceedings of the 2003 Human Language Technology Conference of the North American Chapter of the Association for Computational Linguistics, pp. 252–259 (2003). https://www.aclweb.org/anthology/N03-1033
23. Wang, X., et al.: Reinforced cross-modal matching and self-supervised imitation learning for vision-language navigation. CoRR abs/1811.10092 (2018)
24. Zhan, Y., Hsiao, M.S.: A natural language programming application for Lego Mindstorms EV3. In: 2018 IEEE International Conference on Artificial Intelligence and Virtual Reality (AIVR), pp. 27–34, December 2018
25. Zhou, Y., Wang, W., He, D., Wang, Z.: A fewest-turn-and-shortest path algorithm based on breadth-first search. Geo-spatial Inf. Sci. **17**(4), 201–207 (2014)

Experimental Evaluation of Algorithms for Solving Problems with Combinatorial Explosion

Interleaving Levels of Consistency Enforcement for Singleton Arc Consistency in CSPs, with a New Best (N)SAC Algorithm

Richard J. Wallace[✉]

Insight Centre for Data Analytics, Department of Computer Science,
University College Cork, Cork, Ireland
richard.wallace@insight-centre.org

Abstract. A basic technique used in algorithms for constraint satisfaction problems (CSPs) is removing values that are locally inconsistent, since they cannot form part of a globally consistent solution. The best-known algorithms of this type establish arc consistency (AC), where every value has support in neighbouring domains. Here, we consider algorithms that use AC repeatedly under severe local assumptions to achieve higher overall levels of consistency. These algorithms establish (neighbourhood) singleton arc consistency ((N)SAC). Most of these use simple AC interleaved with the basic (N)SAC procedure. To date, however, this strategy of interleaving weaker and stronger forms of reasoning has not received much attention in and of itself. Moreover, one of the best (N)SAC algorithms (called (N)SACQ) does not use this method. This paper investigates the effects of interleaving and presents new methods based on this idea. We show that different kinds of problems vary greatly in their amenability to AC interleaving; while in most cases it is beneficial, with some algorithms and problem types it can be harmful. More significantly, when this feature is added to (N)SACQ algorithms, the latter's superiority to other (N)SAC algorithms becomes more consistent and decisive. We also consider an AC-4 based approach to interleaving as well as interleaving with stronger methods than AC.

1 Introduction

The constraint satisfaction problem is a basic form of representation for many important AI problems such as configuration, planning, and scheduling. It has also led to new approaches to solving problems in the field of combinatorial optimisation. The key idea is to discard elements in the search space that cannot be part of a solution by showing that they lead to inconsistencies within small parts of the problem. Often this can be done in polynomial time.

The simplest and best-known methods establish *arc consistency* (AC), that roughly means consistency with one's neighbours in the network of constraints. However, in recent years, considerable attention has been paid to specialized

© Springer Nature Switzerland AG 2021
M. Baldoni and S. Bandini (Eds.): AIxIA 2020, LNAI 12414, pp. 301–317, 2021.
https://doi.org/10.1007/978-3-030-77091-4_19

methods for ensuring stronger forms of consistency. The most important methods use either AC reasoning based on strongly reduced domains, e.g. singleton arc consistency (SAC) and neighbourhood SAC (NSAC) [2,3,11], or reduced forms of path consistency [9]. In the present paper only the former methods are discussed.

In some algorithms, stronger forms of consistency reasoning are interleaved with weaker forms. This includes those (N)SAC algorithms where each SAC- or NSAC-based value deletion is followed by an AC step to make the entire problem arc consistent before proceeding to the next (N)SAC-based step.

Until now, such interleaving has not been the focus of research in this area. Yet its properties make it a strategy of considerable interest. The most important property is that interleaving as it is normally used does not affect the level of consistency eventually achieved, even though this level is greater than that obtained by the interleaved algorithm. This means that overall efficiency can be improved without any decrement in effectiveness, where the latter refers to values deleted and more generally to the degree of problem simplification.

However, the degree to which such interleaving actually improves performance is not known. Since both SAC and NSAC dominate AC, interleaving is not necessary. Moreover, there are algorithms that do not use interleaving, in particular SACQ and NSACQ, that often perform as well or better than those that do. Given such results, it is important to learn more about interleaving, to determine the conditions under which it speeds up processing, and, conversely, whether there are conditions (problem features) where it should be avoided. In particular, at this time it is not known whether SACQ and NSACQ would be even more efficient if AC interleaving was added.

Interleaving in (N)SAC algorithms is a special case of using multiple propagators in constraint programming [4,8]. It also has some relation to adaptive propagation [1,7], although the latter uses heuristic methods to find a best level of consistency to apply to a problem or constraint rather than mixing propagators to achieve a given level of consistency more efficiently. In addition, previous work has involved only a limited amount of empirical investigation. In particular, we would like to know not only whether to use such methods, but where one should use them.

The present paper subjects this form of multiple propagation in the (N)SAC setting to closer examination. We find that AC interleaving is generally beneficial, although there are conditions where it is detrimental. We show that there is a simple measure that can be used to determine whether a given problem type will be amenable to such methods. We also show that interleaving enhances (N)SACQ algorithms, which in their original form do not use this method; with this improvement, SACQ clearly becomes the best SAC algorithm, while the dominance of NSACQ over other NSAC algorithms is made more decisive. We also consider other approaches to interleaving, specifically a procedure based on the AC-4 algorithm, and interleaving with higher forms of consistency.

2 Background

2.1 General Concepts

A constraint satisfaction problem (CSP) is defined as a tuple, (X, D, C) where X are variables, D are domains (of values) such that D_i is associated with X_i, and C are constraints that place restrictions on the values that can be assigned to their respective variables. A *solution* to a CSP is an assignment or mapping from variables to values that includes all variables and does not violate any constraint in C.

CSPs can be represented as (hyper)graphs, where nodes are the variables and (hyper)edges are constraints. This representation highlights the importance of graph parameters such as *density*, based on the number of contraints, and *tightness* of individual constraints, i.e. the number of possibilities not allowed. For example, in a constraint between two variables whose domains have ten values, a tightness of 0.9 means that ninety of the 100 possible value pairings are not consistent.

CSPs have an important monotonicity property in that inconsistency with respect to even one constraint implies inconsistency with respect to the entire problem. This has given rise to algorithms for filtering out values that cannot participate in a solution, based on local inconsistencies, i.e. inconsistencies with respect to subsets of constraints. By doing this, these algorithms can establish well-defined forms of local consistency in a problem. The most widely used methods establish arc consistency, as noted earlier. In problems with binary constraints, AC refers to the property that for every value a in the domain of variable X_i and for every constraint C_{ij} with X_i in its scope, there is at least one value b in the domain of X_j such that (a,b) satisfies that constraint. For non-binary or n-ary constraints, generalized arc consistency refers to the property that for every value a in the domain of variable X_i and for every constraint C_j with X_i in its scope, there is a tuple of values that includes a that satisfies that constraint.

Singleton arc consistency, or SAC, is a particular form of AC in which the just-mentioned value a, for example, is considered the sole value in the domain of X_i. If AC cannot be established in the reduced problem, then there can be no solution with value a assigned to X_i, since AC is a necessary condition for the existence of such a solution. So a can be discarded. If this condition can be established for all values in problem P, then the problem is singleton arc consistent. (Obviously, SAC implies AC, but not vice versa.)

Neighbourhood SAC establishes SAC with respect to the neighbourhood of the variable whose domain is a singleton.

Definition 1. The *neighbourhood* of a variable X_i is the set $X_N \subseteq X$ of all variables in all constraints whose scope includes X_i, excluding X_i itself. Variables belonging to X_N are called the neighbours of X_i.

Definition 2. A problem P is neighbourhood singleton arc consistent with respect to value v in the domain of X_i, if when D_i (the domain of X_i) is restricted to v, the problem $P_N = (X_N \cup X_i, C_N)$ is arc consistent, where X_N is the neighbourhood of X_i and C_N is the set of all constraints whose scope is a subset of $X_N \cup X_i$.

In this definition, note that C_N includes constraints among variables other than X_i, provided these do not include variables outside the neighbourhood of X_i. Problem P is neighbourhood singleton arc consistent if each value in each of its domains is neighbourhood singleton arc consistent.

2.2 (N)SAC Algorithms

Since the initial description of SAC-1 [3], several different SAC and NSAC algorithms have been described. This paper will restrict itself to the three SAC algorithms and two NSAC algorithms that are the most efficient in practice [10,11]. The SAC algorithms are SAC-1, SAC-3, and SACQ. The NSAC algorithms are NSAC-1 and NSACQ.

All SAC algorithms proceed by setting a domain to a single value and then establishing arc consistency under that condition. This is done for every value in every domain; hence AC is performed repeatedly until no more values can be removed in this manner. SAC-1 accomplishes this by using a repeat loop and going through the entire set of current domains again and again until nothing is deleted.

SAC-3 [2,5] also uses a repeat loop for the same purpose. However, instead of testing each domain value without reference to the others, values in different domains are tested using the problem reduced by earlier tests. This continues until a failure occurs; however, only when the failure occurs at the beginning of such a sequence (called a "branch") can the value be discarded. Savings in time occurs because values subsequent to the first on a branch are tested with a reduced problem. (If arc consistency can be established under these more restrictive conditions, then it will hold in the unreduced problem.) In practice, this can result in considerable speedup.

Instead of a repeat loop, SACQ [11] uses a queue of variables to be tested, consisting of the entire variable set. If a domain value is discarded, then any variable not on the queue is put back. Unlike the other SAC algorithms, which perform AC on the full problem after each SAC-based deletion, SACQ eschews this step, relying only on the basic SAC strategy to remove values.

NSAC-1 and NSACQ are identical to SAC-1 and SACQ, respectively, except that following the reduction of a domain to a singleton, AC is only performed on the neighbourhood subgraph. They, therefore, establish the more restricted form of singleton arc consistency called neighbourhood SAC.

To make all this more concrete, consider the pseudocode in Fig. 5 below, for a type of NSAC algorithm. Line 8 shows the NSAC-based consistency step, which is carried out for each domain value. (The domain reduction step precedes this on line 7.) Line 12 shows the AC step, which is *interleaved* between repeated NSAC steps. Note that this action only occurs if the NSAC step fails (produces a wipeout). SAC algorithms interleave AC in the same way, but in this case SAC is established at each step (line 8) instead of NSAC.

3   To Interleave or Not: Some (N)SAC Variants

The main purpose of the present paper is to evaluate the usefulness of the AC step that typically follows a singleton-based deletion in (N)SAC algorithms. Since both SAC and NSAC dominate AC, it is possible to eliminate AC interleaving in SAC-1 and SAC-3 as well as NSAC-1. In this paper, these will be called SAC-1noac, SAC-3noac, and NSAC-1noac.

While it is possible to add an AC step to SACQ or NSACQ, there are some complications. Since these algorithms use a queue rather than a repeat loop, if AC is done in addition, then after every AC-based deletion, the algorithm must ensure that all neighbouring variables are on the queue in order to be equivalent to the other (N)SAC-based algorithms. For this reason, these algorithms will be called SACQacn and NSACQacn. (Note. In some tables acn is shortened to ac and noac to no.)

Proposition 1. Both SACQacn and NSACQacn achieve the same unique fix-points as SAC-1 and NSAC-1, respectively.

Proof. We begin with the fact that the basic versions of (N)SACQ achieve the same fixpoint as the corresponding (N)SAC-1 algorithms [11]. By this token, if the basic (N)SACQ procedure is followed, then the same dependencies between discarded values will be discovered as in the NSAC phase of (N)SAC-1. Since in addition we perform AC after each (N)SAC-based deletion, this reduces the problem in the same way as in the (N)SAC-1 case. Finally, by the Neighbourhood Lemma [11], the only way that an AC-based deletion of a value in the domain of variable X_j can affect the singleton arc consistency of any value in the remaining problem is via neighbours of X_j. So if these are put back on the queue after every AC- as well as (N)SAC-based deletion, such dependencies will always be discovered.   □

4   (N)SAC with and Without AC: Initial Experiments

Algorithms were implemented in Common Lisp, and experiments were run in the Xlispstat environment with a Unix OS on a Dell Poweredge 4600 machine (1.8 GHz). Cross-checks were made for all problems tested to confirm that each type of (N)SAC algorithm deleted the same number of values for problems not proven unsatisfiable, and that the same unsatisfiable problems were proven unsatisfiable by equivalent algorithms (i.e. by all SAC and all NSAC algorithms, respectively). In these experiments, variables and values were always chosen according to the lexical order of these elements.

In this section we will only consider random (binary) problems where the probabilities of a constraint between two variables as well as a given tuple belonging to a constraint relation are the same throughout the problem. This will allow us to make initial comparisons among algorithms and to analyze why a given variant is better under a given condition. (As we will see, different parameter classes do give different patterns of results.)

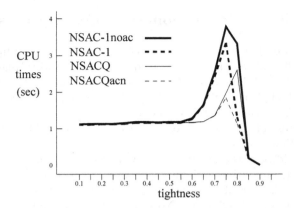

Fig. 1. Runtimes for four NSAC algorithms on random problems, <100, 20, .05, t> series. Note. In this and all other figures and tables, CPU times, ("runtimes") are for consistency (i.e. preprocessing) algorithms only. (Search times of course depend only on the level of consistency established, not the algorithm used to achieve this.)

We first look at a problem series that has been examined in the past [5, 11]. These problems have 100 variables, domain size 20, and graph density 0.05. Constraint tightness is varied in steps of 0.05 from 0.1 to 0.9 inclusive; at each step 50 problems were tested. Another series of random problems was also tested. These had the same parameters as the first series except that the density was 0.25.

Figure 1 shows average runtimes for NSAC variants based on the first series, Fig. 2 for the second series. The first thing to note is that in the first series, both versions with AC interleaved outperform their simpler counterpart in some regions of the parameter space. On the other hand, for the second series, in the one range where the variants differ in performance (tightness 0.55 to 0.70), the non-interleaved versions outperform the corresponding versions with AC interleaving.

To understand these differences, first it should be noted that in the first series AC alone is sufficient to prove that problems at the two highest tightnesses are unsatisfiable, and for the second series this is true for the three highest tightnesses and almost true for the fourth (0.75, 47/50 proven unsatisfiable by AC). Hence, these cases are irrelevant for our purposes, since problems are proven unsatisfiable by the initial AC.

In the first series, NSAC can prove most problems unsatisfiable for tightness 0.8. For this tightness, AC interleaving reduces runtimes by a factor of 2, and this is the only case where this procedure makes a large difference. In this case, the interleaved AC sometimes deletes numerous values following an NSAC deletion, so many that in a number of cases wipeout occurs during the AC phase. Figure 3 shows NSAC and AC deletions for a problem that was not proved unsatisfiable during preprocessing. It illustrates how a single NSAC deletion can lead to numerous values deleted during the subsequent bout of AC. For lower tight-

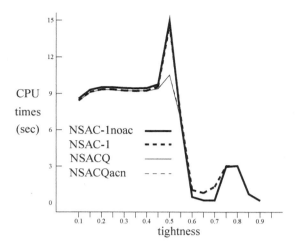

Fig. 2. Runtimes for four NSAC algorithms on random problems. <100, 20, .25, t> series

nesses, beginning with 0.75, very few values are deleted during the AC phase; here, runtimes are similar with or without interleaving.

In the second series (0.25 density), NSAC preprocessing proves all problems unsatisfiable over the range from 0.55 to 0.70, where a difference between NSAC variants is found. As with the first series, the interleaved AC deletes many values, but in this case NSAC reasoning alone produces a domain wipe-out with the first or second variable tested. Hence, while interleaved AC does lead to a wipe-out, sometimes after fewer singleton values have been tested, the process is slower, usually by a factor of 7–8, than with NSAC alone. Fortunately, the conditions under which this occurs seem to preclude long runtimes with or without interleaving, so this isn't a major drawback in itself.

Since for the most part the curves occlude each other, the significant portion of the data for SAC variants is shown in Tables 1 and 2. For the sparser problem series (Table 1), the only place where there are clear differences is for tightness = 0.75. For this tightness, all problems are proven unsatisfiable by SAC. With interleaved AC, during the AC phase very few values are deleted initially. But after several variables have been tested, there is an upsurge of AC-based deletions leading to wipe-out. Note, however, that runtime differences were only found for SAC-1 and SACQ.

For the denser problem series (Table 2), interleaving with SAC-1 or SACQ outperforms non-interleaving at two and possibly three tightness values (0.55 and 0.60 and possibly 0.50). In the first two cases, all problems are proven unsatisfiable by SAC, and, again, with interleaving the same eventual upsurge in AC-based deletions is found as in the first series. (For tightness 0.50, no problem was proven unsatisfiable by SAC.) It should also be noted that with SAC, differences due to interleaving are proportionally much smaller than with NSAC.

Table 1. Times for different forms of SAC on random problems at 5 tightness levels (<100, 20, .05, t> Series)

t	SACQ	SACQac	SAC-1	SAC-1no	SAC-3	SAC-3no
0.60	6.7	6.5	7.0	7.0	8.6	8.6
0.65	12.2	11.8	14.3	14.3	20.3	20.4
0.70	42.8	41.3	49.6	49.7	89.2	89.2
0.75	15.0	12.4	13.0	15.1	24.2	25.0
0.80	1.3	1.3	1.3	1.3	2.1	1.7

Means of 50 probs. Times in sec. "t" tightness.

With SAC-3, interleaving actually slows down the algorithm at one tightness value. (A possible reason for this will be discussed in a later section where tests with structured problems give similar results.)

What these results show is that for problems of this sort, interleaving only improves efficiency over a small part of the range of tightness values. The basic rule of thumb is that, if constraints are tight enough, then AC alone is likely to remove some values. This is observed in the initial AC. Afterwards, if NSAC removes more values, this increases the tightness in the neighbourhood of these values, and AC can again be effective.

Table 2. Times for different forms of SAC on random problems at 5 tightness levels (<100, 20, .25, t> Series)

t	SACQ	SACQac	SAC-1	SAC-1no	SAC-3	SAC-3no
0.50	131.5	128.5	159.4	160.2	893.1	906.3
0.55	162.5	156.5	154.0	163.0	252.9	225.0
0.60	20.9	17.1	16.9	20.9	18.7	22.4
0.65	8.0	8.3	8.2	8.1	9.7	8.6
0.70	3.9	4.6	4.5	4.0	6.4	4.2

See Table 1 for notes.

For random problems like these, this rule of thumb can be expressed in a simple formula, *expected support · p(support)* < 1, where "expected support" is the number of supporting values for the value in question (i.e. those consistent with it) across a given constraint, and probability of support refers to the likelihood that those values are supported by some value across some other constraint. The basic idea is that interleaving will work when there are few supporting values, and the latter themselves do not have much support.

A simple statistic has proven useful for predicting the effectiveness of interleaving. This is the number of AC deletions per bout, where the number of bouts is equal to the number of (N)SAC deletions. For example, in the first problem series, at tightness 0.8 the average ratio of AC to NSAC deletions (here called the "bout ratio") was 1.58 for the seven problems not proven unsatisfiable, while for tightness 0.75, where there was only a slight difference in favour of interleaving, the ratio was 0.19, and for lower tightnesses the ratio was 0.

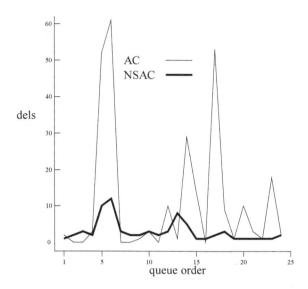

Fig. 3. Number of deletions for successive variables in queue. Problem from <100, 20, .05, 0.80> set, where interleaving lowers runtimes appreciably (Bout ratio for problem = 3.79. Points in graph represent one to several bouts, depending on how many values of the variable being tested were deleted by NSAC.)

For problems like these, we can also infer whether AC interleaving is likely to be effective from the results of the initial AC: if numerous values are deleted at this time, then interleaving AC with NSAC or SAC is likely to be effective as well. To determine if this rule has general application, we must look at a variety of problem classes.

5   (N)SAC with and Without AC: More Extended Tests

More extended tests were done using various problem types including randomly generated structured problems, benchmarks, and benchmarks with added global constraints. All problems used in these tests had solutions; hence, both AC and NSAC always ran to completion without generating a wipeout. In addition, problems were chosen where (N)SAC deleted a large number of values on top of the initial AC.

The following problem classes were used:

- Relop problems had 150 variables, domain size 20, with constraint graph density of 0.30. Half the constraints were of the form $X_i \geq X_j$ and half were inequality constraints.

- Distance problems had 150 variables, domain size 12, and constraint graph density = 0.0307. Constraints were of the form $|X_i - X_j| \otimes k$, where $\otimes$ was either $<>$ (60%), $\geq$ (30%), or $=$ (10%). The value for k varied from 1 to 8, with a mean value of 4.

- RLFAP-graph problems were benchmarks, with 200 or 400 variables; these problems also have distance constraints where $\otimes$ is either $=$ or $>$ (for the former k is always 128; for the latter it varies widely). (It may be noted that these were drawn from an original set of 7, where four had solutions, two of which did not give deletions with any form of SAC-based preprocessing.)

- Driverlog problems were benchmarks, which are CSP representations of a well-known transportation problem. All but the smallest problem were used. The number of variables varies from 272 to 408. For the smallest problem, domain sizes range from two to eight; for the largest the range is 2–11. Constraints are binary table constraints, many very loose.

- Open shop problems were from the Taillard series. The ones used here are the Taillard-4-100 set. Constraints are disjunctive of the form $X_i + k_i \leq X_j \bigvee X_j + k_j \leq X_i$.

- The RLFAP-occurrence problems were based on the RLFAP-graph3 benchmark. In this case ten percent of the k values of $>$ distance constraints were altered (by randomly incrementing or decrementing them) to make the base problem more difficult. Then various forms of occurrence constraints were added: three atmost, three atleast, and three among. In addition, one disjoint constraint was also included. For occurrence constraints, arity varied between four and six; the disjoint constraint always had arity 10 based on two mutually exclusive sets of five variables. Each occurrence constraint could affect a maximum of 75% of the variables in its scope. The among constraints could involve up to 50% of the possible values. There was no overlap in the scopes of constraints of the same type; between types up to 50% of the scope could overlap.

- Configuration problems were derived from an original benchmark refrigerator configuration problem ("esvs") composed of table constraints with arities ranging from two to five. To make these problems, some constraints were tightened, and in some cases the problem was doubled in size by duplicating the constraint patterns.

- Golomb ruler problems were benchmarks obtained from a website formerly maintained at the Université Artois. Constraints had arities 2 or 3. Since NSAC only deleted a few more values than AC, tests were restricted to SAC for these problems.

Results are shown in Table 3 for NSAC and Table 4 for SAC. In addition to number of values deleted by AC and by NSAC following AC and overall runtimes, Table 3 shows the proportional changes in runtime, when interleaving is used versus no interleaving based on the formula:

$$reduct = \frac{basic - interleave}{basic}$$

(In Table 4, only the proportional changes in runtimeare shown.) Results for the algorithm whose best variant also gave the best performance overall are shown in boldface. Changes that resulted in runtime differences that were statistically significant at the 0.01 level (paired comparison t-test, two-tailed) are underlined.

As Table 3 indicates, the effectiveness of interleaving with neighbourhood SAC algorithms varied significantly for different problem types. The data for bout ratios show that this was because problems varied widely in their amenability to AC interleaving.

As in earlier work, it was found that NSACQ (in either form) was usually the more efficient algorithm. In cases where interleaving was effective, both NSAC algorithms showed improvement; as a result NSACQ maintained its superiority, and in some cases the difference became even greater. The one exception to this pattern was the RLFAP-occurrence problem set, where the basic NSACQ algorithm was markedly inferior to NSAC-1 (205 versus 102 sec per problem). However, with interleaving it became the most efficient overall (84 sec). Another finding was that the intermittent deletion of larger numbers of values, as shown in Fig. 3, occurred with all types of problems in which interleaving was effective.

With full SAC algorithms, the pattern of effectiveness of interleaving across problem types was similar to NSAC (Table 4). With these more powerful consistency algorithms all problem classes showed some amenability to interleaved AC in terms of values deleted. However, as with NSAC, very small bout ratios were associated with increases in runtime when interleaving was used.

Table 3. Effect of interleaving NSAC and AC for various problem classes

probs	n	removals		NSAC-1			NSACQ			btratio
		iAC	NSAC	rt-no	rt-yes	reduct	rt-no	rt-yes	reduct	
Relop	41	0	1702	231.4	183.1	21	194.9	161.7	**17**	1.12
Distance	33	215	23	6.4	4.3	28	2.7	2.4	**9**	2.58
RLFAP-graph	2	558	997	1166.6	944.6	16	552.1	496.8	**6**	1.25
Driverlog	5	55	51	163.0	167.0	−2	93.9	97.0	**−3**	0
Open shop	10	117	862	73.0	83.6	−14	65.6	71.8	**−9**	0
RLFAP-occur	50	346	5452	269.5	101.9	62	204.9	84.2	**59**	3.81
Configuration	9	46	28	0.1	0.1	−3	0.1	0.1	**−18**	0.04

n is number of problems in group. removals is values deleted. iAC is initial AC. NSAC is NSAC after iAC. rt-no and rt-yes are runtimes without and with inter-leaving. Reduct is percent time reduction due to interleaving. btratio is bout ratio. All values except those under n are group means.

Some anomalous results were found with SAC-3. For this algorithm interleaving sometimes had untoward effects with respect to runtime that were greater than for the other two algorithms, and in one case (RLFAP-occ) this occurred in spite of the large bout ratio. Presumably there are interactions between inter-leaving and the branch strategy, perhaps because the latter entails a different order of value testing (since only one value per domain can appear on a branch). (Configuration problems were not tested with this algorithm because it wasn't clear how to combine branch-building with simple table reduction.)

Table 4. Effect of interleaving SAC and AC for various problem classes

probs	n	removals		SAC1	SAC3	SACQ	btratio
		iAC	SAC	Reduct	Reduct	Reduct	
Relop	41	0	2204	<u>30</u>	**37**	<u>26</u>	0.91
Distance	33	215	139	<u>10</u>	9	**<u>10</u>**	1.36
RLFAP-grph	2	558	1517	−1	−1	**4**	1.16
Driverlog	5	55	437	10	1	**3**	0.64
Open shop	10	117	1549	−9	−32	**−3**	0.14
RLFAP-occ	50	346	6042	**<u>31</u>**	−27	**27**	5.04
Configurat	9	46	58	−5	*	−11	0.18
Golomb-3	10	221	473	3	1	**4**	0.55

* denotes combination not tested. See Table 3 for further notes.

Turning to specific problem classes, for the relop problems AC by itself does not delete any values. However, since these constraints are highly structured, one cannot infer from this that interleaving will be ineffective. (This shows that the initial AC rule suggested earlier does not hold in all cases.) In fact, for $>$ or $\geq$ constraints the amount of support for a given value ranges from d or $d-1$ down to 1 or 0. Hence, there are always values with little or no support. Moreover, this type of constraint has a 'progressive' property in that, if values with the least amount of support are deleted, then the values with minimal extra support become as poorly supported as the values that were deleted. Because of these features interleaving was in fact beneficial; as the bout ratios show, slightly more values were deleted by interleaved AC when NSAC was used, and slightly less with SAC. For problems of this type, the variability of this ratio across individual problems was quite small (range $\approx$0.3).

In contrast to most problem classes, bout patterns for distance problems were quite variable. For 17 of the original 50 problems, NSAC did not delete any more values than AC; hence, these were not included in the table. For the remaining 33 problems, the bout ratio varied from 0 to 13.0. Overall, however, interleaving was effective, more so for NSAC than for SAC.

For RLFAPs, all SAC- or NSAC-based deletions were followed by at least one AC-based deletion. (This is due to the equality constraints that affect successive pairs of variables.) Only a very few times in the series did interleaving lead to a large number of deletions. For RLFAP-occurrence problems, the singleton deletion pattern naturally also occurred; in addition, there were more bouts where large numbers of deletions occurred in the AC phase.

Golomb ruler problems showed a different pattern of AC deletions. In each case, AC deletions only occurred within the first 7-17 SAC deletions depending on the problem (out of a total of 44-339). In each case the first AC deletion occurred after the second SAC-based deletion, after which there was a pattern in which the greatest number of AC deletions occurred after the third SAC deletion, the second greatest after the fifth, and so forth, the pattern becoming clearer with larger problems where the series was longer.

Together, these results show that having "structure" does not in itself alter basic propagation effects, in particular the intermittency of large numbers of deletions, or the deductions that can be made regarding relative efficiency derived on this basis (reflected in the bout ratios).

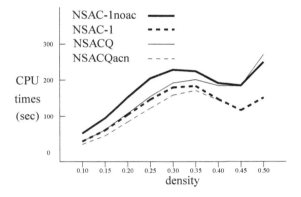

Fig. 4. Runtimes for four NSAC algorithms on random relop problems of varying density.

For randomly generated problems, one can vary problem parameters systematically in order to compare performance across the problem space. This was done with relop problems in an experiment where density was varied from 0.10 to 0.50 in steps of 0.05. (Fifty problems were tested at each density. Those for density 0.3 include the problems used in Table 3.) Results are shown in Fig. 4. At densities >0.3 all problems were unsatisfiable, while <0.3 all were satisfiable. At density 0.35, NSAC proved one problem unsatisfiable; at density 0.4, NSAC proved 32 problems unsatisfiable; at higher densities all 50 problems could be proven unsatisfiable.

Figure 4 shows that carrying out NSAC is fairly expensive. However, for some of these problem sets NSAC can reduce search times by a much larger amount. It also shows that interleaving is always more efficient and that for some problems, it can reduce runtimes by about 100 s per problem (a reduction of about 40%).

6   Comparisons with an AC4-Style Interleaving Algorithm

As we have seen, by testing a few problems in a class, it is sometimes possible to determine whether AC interleaving is likely to have benefits. In addition, it was thought that it might be possible to finesse the problem to a degree by using a more efficient form of interleaving. To this end, an algorithm based on AC-4 data structures was devised. (Here, we will only consider the binary form of this algorithm.)

To understand the algorithm, the reader should recall that AC-4 has two phases. In phase 1, all value combinations are checked, and data structures representing support sets are set up; these include lists of values supported by each value for each constraint (support sets), counters that tally the number of supports for a value across each constraint, and an array of binary values to indicate whether a value in a given domain is still viable. Phase 2 begins with the values found to have no support across some constraint (the "badlist") and uses these to decrement counters for each member of the support set associated with each bad value. This continues, with new values being added to the badlist if one of their counters goes to zero, until the badlist is empty or a wipeout has occurred. (See [6] for details.)

```
      Procedure NSAC-1AC4
1        OK ← AC4(P)
3        Repeat                    /* if OK */
4           Changed ← false
5           Foreach X_i ∈ X
6              Foreach v_j ∈ dom(X_i)
7                 dom'(X_i) ← {v_j}
8                 If AC3(X_i+neighbours(X_i)) leads to wipeout
9                    dom(X_i) ← dom(X_i)/v_j
10                   Set entry for v_j in mark array to false
11                      and set badlist to ((X_i, v_j))
12                   OK ← AC4phase2(P)
13                   Changed ← true
14       Until Changed == false or not OK
```

Fig. 5. Pseudocode for NSAC-1 incorporating AC-4.

When combined with NSAC, AC-4 is used for the initial AC pass. During subsequent (N)SAC processing, the support count system continues to be used whenever SAC-based processing proves that a value can be discarded. Hence, the phase 1 set up is done only once. In devising this procedure, the assumption was that the main cost of AC-4 involves the setting up of data structures in phase 1. For SAC or NSAC algorithms, the original cost may therefore be amortized through repeated use of the efficient phase 2 procedure.

The present algorithm uses AC-3 for (N)SAC-based reasoning, and uses phase 2 only for AC interleaving. Figure 5 gives pseudocode for the algorithm when used with NSAC-1.

Proposition 2. The NSAC-AC4 algorithm given in Fig. 5 is correct, complete and terminates.

Proof Sketch. Since the algorithm has only been coded in its binary form, we will restrict our arguments to this class of problems. Here, we assume the soundness of the basic (N)SAC procedures. Since AC-4 establishes complete sets of supports, then for each value that is found to be (N)SAC-inconsistent, all counters associated with adjacent values will be decremented properly. The same is true for variables adjacent to the latter, etc.; this follows from the correctness of the AC-4 procedure. Hence, by the correctness and completeness of AC-4, after an (N)SAC-based deletion all values deleted will have become arc-inconsistent and all arc-inconsistent values will be deleted. Hence, after each instance of (N)SAC-based deletion, the network will be made arc consistent as required. $\square$

Unfortunately, the assumption about the efficiency of AC-4 phase 2 turned out to be false, at least for the present implementation. In practice, the present algorithm typically runs an order of magnitude slower than the algorithms based on AC-3. In fact, this is likely to be a general problem since constantly updating a large number of entries is bound to take time, but this is required for the correctness of the algorithm.

7   Other Kinds of Interleaving

Interleaving using NSAC was also tested, where SAC is the basic algorithm. The simplest combination is to use NSAC initially and then run the SAC algorithm. With the SACQacn algorithm, this has resulted in improvements of up to 30% (e.g. with RLFAPs), although in one case it led to a 10% decrement (with driver-log problems). The key factor seems to be the effectiveness of NSAC relative to SAC; if the former algorithm is almost as effective, then a noticeable speedup can be obtained. (For example, for the graph3 RLFAP included in Tables 3 and 4, NSAC deletes 1064 values, SAC 1274, so that after an initial NSAC run, there are only 210 values left to delete.) But if SAC is much more effective than NSAC, then interleaving with the latter can increase overall runtime.

Note that in the present implementation AC is run first as before, then NSAC, then SAC. Thus, a cascade of consistency maintenance algorithms is applied, beginning with the weakest.

To date, no pattern of actually interleaving with NSAC has yielded further benefits. Further experiments showed that with the same problems, the earlier that interleaving with NSAC was done, the more effective it was. When two interleavings are allowed with the same problems (after one- and two-thirds of the SAC deletions), the runtime increases to about what it is with SAC alone, and with more interleavings performance is worse.

Another strategy that was tried is based on observation of the pattern of deletions by (N)SAC and AC. It was noted that in most cases large numbers of values were deleted by AC following a series of SAC-based deletions from the same domain. However, to date, interleaving with NSAC under these circumstances did not confer any further benefit.

8   Conclusions

This paper explores a little studied topic in the field of constraint satisfaction. Although the basic method has been used for many years (with SAC algorithms other than SACQ), heretofore it has not been the subject of analysis in its own right. One purpose of the present paper is to call attention to what may be a significant topic for further research.

By employing interleaving in a somewhat novel context, in combination with the queue-based strategy used in SACQ and NSACQ, it has been possible to produce the best algorithms proposed to date for SAC and neighbourhood SAC. Since arc consistency can be extended to generalized arc consistency in a straightforward way, these algorithms can be used with constraints of any arity; to date, the improvements demonstrated here apply to n-ary problems as much as to problems with only binary constraints. This work also serves to confirm the general superiority of AC-3 to AC-4 techniques.

Since for all problem classes interleaving AC was only intermittently effective, this suggests that this procedure could be used only intermittently to achieve even better performance. However, in this case one runs the risk of using SAC or NSAC to delete a value that could have been deleted with AC. Since some problem types are not amenable to AC interleaving, a better strategy may be to make such interleaving optional, using it only for problems where one can expect it to be effective.

From the present experiments, it appears that interleaving with more powerful algorithms than AC only works when the interleaved algorithm is itself effective on the same problem and when it is used early in the SAC process, e.g. when it is used before running SAC. However, this field is still wide open. In addition, there are many interesting tradeoffs that should be explored further, such as those related to the costs of the interleaved and base algorithm, and to their relative effectiveness.

Acknowledgements. I thank the anonymous reviewers for their close reading and apposite comments, which definitely improved the quality of the paper. This work was done using facilities supported by Science Foundation Ireland.

References

1. Balafrej, A., Bessière, C., Bouyakhf, E., Trombettoni, G.: Adaptive singleton-based consistencies. In: Twenty-Eighth AAAI Conference on Artificial Intelligence - AAAI 2014, pp. 2601–2607. AAAI (2014)

2. Bessière, C., Cardon, S., Debruyne, R., Lecoutre, C.: Efficient algorithms for singleton arc consistency. Constraints **16**, 25–53 (2011)
3. Debruyne, R., Bessière, C.: Some practicable filtering techniques for the constraint satisfaction problem. In: Fifteenth International Joint Conference on Artifcial Intelligence - IJCAI 1997, vol. 1. pp. 412–417. Morgan Kaufmann (1997)
4. Granvilliers, L., Monfroy, E.: Implementing constraint propagation by composition of reductions. In: Proceedings Nineteenth International Conference on Logic Programming. LNCS No. 2916. pp. 300–314. Springer (2003)
5. Lecoutre, C., Cardon, S.: A greedy approach to establish singleton arc consistency. In: Fourteenth International Joint Conference on Artificial Intelligence - IJCAI 2005, pp. 199–204. Professional Book Center (2005)
6. Mohr, R., Henderson, T.C.: Arc and path consistency revisited. Artif. Intell. **28**, 225–233 (1986)
7. Paparrizou, A., Stergiou, K.: Evaluating simple fully automated heuristics for adaptive constraint propagation. In: Twenty-Fourth International Conference on Tools with Artificial Intelligence - ICTAI 2012, pp. 880–885 (2012)
8. Schulte, C., Stuckey, P.J.: Efficient constraint propagation engines. ACM Trans. Program. Lang. Syst. **31**(1), 1–43 (2008)
9. Stergiou, K.: Restricted path consistency revisited. In: Pesant, G. (ed.) CP 2015. LNCS, vol. 9255, pp. 419–428. Springer, Cham (2015). https://doi.org/10.1007/978-3-319-23219-5_30
10. Wallace, R.J.: Light-weight versus heavy-weight algorithms for SAC and neighbourhood SAC. In: Russell, I., Eberle, W. (eds.) Twenty-Eighth International Florida Artificial Intelligence Research Society Conference - FLAIRS-28, pp. 91–96. AAAI Press (2015)
11. Wallace, R.J.: SAC and neighbourhood SAC. AI Commun. **28**, 345–364 (2015)

Improving the Efficiency of Euclidean TSP Solving in Constraint Programming by Predicting Effective Nocrossing Constraints

Elena Bellodi[ID], Alessandro Bertagnon[ID], Marco Gavanelli[(✉)][ID],
and Riccardo Zese[ID]

Department of Engineering, University of Ferrara,
Via G. Saragat 1, 44122 Ferrara, Italy
{elena.bellodi,alessandro.bertagnon,marco.gavanelli,
riccardo.zese}@unife.it

Abstract. The Traveling Salesperson Problem (TSP) is a well-known problem addressed in the literature through various techniques, including Integer Linear Programming, Constraint Programming (CP) and Local Search. Many real life instances belong to the subclass of Euclidean TSPs, in which the nodes to be visited are points in the Euclidean plane, and the distance between them is the Euclidean distance. A well-known property of the Euclidean TSP is that no crossings can exist in an optimal solution. In a previous publication, we exploited this property to speed-up the solution of Euclidean instances in CP, by imposing a quadratic number of so-called no-overlapping constraints. In this work, we observe that not all the no-overlapping constraints are equally useful: by experimental analysis, some of them provide a speed-up, while others only introduce overhead. Thus, it is important to define a way to classify useful constraints. To do so, we use machine learning approaches with the objective to impose only those no-overlapping constraints that have been classified as effective. We compare two classifiers based on Random Forest and Neural Networks, which show to be effective, with a slight prevalence for Random Forest.

Keywords: Constraint programming · Euclidean TSP · Supervised machine learning · Random forest · Neural networks · Redundant constraints

1 Introduction

The Traveling Salesperson Problem (TSP) is one of the best-known problems in computer science; given a graph with non-negative weights on the edges (interpreted as traveling costs), the objective is to find a circuit visiting each node

---

This paper is a revised and extended version of the paper [7]. This work is partially supported by GNCS-INdAM.

M. Baldoni and S. Bandini (Eds.): AIxIA 2020, LNAI 12414, pp. 318–334, 2021.
https://doi.org/10.1007/978-3-030-77091-4_20

exactly once and with minimal total cost. The TSP is notoriously NP-hard, and was approached through various techniques. The current state of the art is the Concorde solver [4], that employs various techniques including Integer Linear Programming, local search, and branch-and-cut. Concorde, however, cannot address problems in which additional constraints exist, such as the SET-TSP (in which not all nodes are visited), or the Vehicle Routing Problem (in which more than one vehicle exists). The TSP was also addressed in Constraint Programming (CP), that offers more flexibility and lets one add the so-called side constraints [8, 13, 15, 17, 18, 30].

One interesting case of TSP is the Euclidean TSP, in which the nodes are associated with points in the Euclidean plane, and the cost is the Euclidean distance. The Euclidean TSP is NP-Hard [23], and, although it admits Polynomial Time Approximation Schemes [5, 38], the usual way to address it is to convert it into a TSP by computing the distance matrix between each pair of nodes, and then use a TSP solver (e.g., Concorde) to find the optimal solution. This method completely disregards the additional information intrinsic in the Euclidean TSP formulation, such as the coordinates in the plane of the nodes.

In CP, two methods exploit the information about the problem coordinates to speed up the solution process of the Euclidean TSP. Deudon *et al.* [15] train a Deep Neural Network with the point coordinates in order to learn efficient heuristics to explore the search space. In the other [9], instead, we proposed the first approach in which the information about the point coordinates was used to prune the search space of the constraint programming formulation. The work started from the well-known observation that in an optimal Euclidean TSP two edges cannot cross each other, otherwise there exists another circuit with shorter length. We proposed a constraint `nocrossing` that imposes that the edges exiting from two given nodes do not cross each other. This constraint is imposed for each of the $\frac{n(n-1)}{2}$ pairs of nodes. Experimental results show the effectiveness of the approach.

As all constraints, each of them must be present in memory, can be awaken (activated) if suitable conditions occur (typically, the removal of an element from one domain), possibly performs some pruning and then becomes dormant again. When the solver wakes up a constraint, some computation time is spent in awaking, scheduling the constraint and performing the checks required by its logic. Nevertheless, the experimental results in [9] show that the additional pruning widely compensates the introduced overhead, globally.

However, although globally the set of constraints is worth imposing, it still might be the case that some of the $\frac{n(n-1)}{2}$ constraints never perform any pruning, and only introduce overhead. Stated otherwise, one wonders whether all these $\frac{n(n-1)}{2}$ constraints equally contribute to the effectiveness of the method, or whether some of these constraints perform strong pruning, while others perform little or no pruning. If one were able to guess a priori which constraints will perform pruning and which, instead, will only provide overhead, she/he could avoid imposing the useless ones, reducing the overhead associated with the set of `nocrossing` constraints, while retaining all (or, almost all) their pruning.

This paper is a revised and extended version of the workshop publication [7], where we studied how much pruning is performed by each of the $\frac{n(n-1)}{2}$ constraints. We labelled each constraint as *useful* or *useless* considering the number of times the constraint is woken and the amount of pruning it performs and learned a random forest (binary) classifier to predict which of the constraints in a new instance would have been useful and which useless. We showed that the approach was effective with respect to a model imposing the `nocrossing` constraints for *all* pairs of nodes. In this paper, we extended the experimental tests by:

1. enlarging the dataset considering also another type of instances (*morphed*), beside the *uniform* and *clustered*; this could make the obtained results more robust;
2. improving the dataset including features concerning the whole TSP instance along those considering single `nocrossing` constraints;
3. re-training the random forest classifier and learning a neural network (binary) classifier, we decided to consider also this approach because of its ability to model complex interactions among features;
4. comparing the two classifiers to a baseline where pruning is performed by constraints randomly selected.

The rest of the paper is organized as follows: after some preliminaries in Sect. 2, we recap from [9] the basic idea of removing crossings and the declarative semantics of the `nocrossing` constraint in Sect. 3. Section 4 explains the data we collected running the Euclidean TSP solver on various instances. Section 5 is devoted to the Machine Learning approaches considered. In Sect. 6 we show the experimental results of the classifiers and the resulting Euclidean TSP solver exploiting their predictions. Finally, Sect. 7 discusses related work and Sect. 8 concludes the paper and provides insights into future work.

2 Preliminaries

Let $G = (V, E, w)$ be a weighted graph, where V is a set of nodes, E is a set of edges, and $w : E \mapsto \mathbb{R}^+$. A *path* is a sequence $p_{v_{s_0}\text{-}v_{s_k}} = v_{s_0} e_{s_0,s_1} v_{s_1} \cdots e_{s_{k-1},s_k} v_{s_k}$ such that *(i)* $v_{s_0}, \ldots, v_{s_k} \in V$ and are all distinct, and *(ii)* $e_{s_0,s_1}, \ldots, e_{s_{k-1},s_k} \in E$. To simplify the notation we will often write paths as sequences of nodes. The length of a path p is $L(p) = \sum_{i=0}^{k-1} w(e_{s_i,s_{i+1}})$. Given a path $p_{v_{s_0}\text{-}v_{s_k}}$, the sequence obtained by appending e_{s_k,s_0} to a path $p_{v_{s_0}\text{-}v_{s_k}}$ is called a *circuit c*.

A Euclidean TSP is a TSP on a complete graph in which the distance function is the Euclidean distance. Let $\mathcal{P} = \{P_1, \ldots, P_n\}$ be a set of points, The graph associated with $\mathcal{P}$ is $G^{\mathcal{P}} = (\mathcal{P}, E^{\mathcal{P}}, w^{\mathcal{P}})$, where $E^{\mathcal{P}} = \{e_{i,j} \equiv (P_i, P_j) \mid P_i, P_j \in \mathcal{P}, i \neq j\}$ and $w(P_i, P_j) = d(P_i, P_j)$, where d is the Euclidean distance.

CLP on Finite Domains (CLP(FD)) is a logic language that exploits a constraint solver to perform powerful inferences on variables ranging on finite domains. The most popular inference method, named constraint propagation, relies on a consistency algorithm, such as AC3 [36], in which each constraint is activated (or awaken), possibly deletes from the domains of the variables a number of values that cannot lead to a solution (usually achieving a level of consistency that depends on the employed constraint propagation algorithm) and finally suspends, waiting for some event (typically, the removal of values from one of the domains of the involved variables) to happen. When such event occurs, the constraint is again awaken and can possibly perform further pruning.

In the Constraint Programming literature, three main constraint models have been proposed to address the TSP: the *permutation* representation, the *successor* representation and the *set variable* representation [8].

In this paper we adopt the successor representation; it is defined with a set of n variables *Next*, each ranging on the set of available nodes. $Next_i = j$ means that the successor of node i is node j. The constraint model includes:

- an `alldifferent`(*Next*) constraint [42], that imposes that each node is the successor of exactly one other node,
- a `circuit`(*Next*) constraint [13] that excludes the creation of sub-circuits, i.e., circuits that do not involve the whole set of nodes,
- and an objective function aimed at minimizing the total length of the TSP.

3   Avoiding Crossings

The following is a well-known result in the literature.

Theorem 1. [19]. *Let c^* be an optimal tour of a Metric TSP. Then, for each $e_{i,j}, e_{k,l} \in c^*$ such that $\{i, j, k, l\}$ are all different, the segments $\overline{P_i P_j} \cap \overline{P_k P_l} = \emptyset$.*

In order to speed up the search, in [9], we proposed a constraint that avoids, during search, the solutions that include crossings. The `nocrossing` constraint

$$\texttt{nocrossing}(i, \mathit{Next}_i, j, \mathit{Next}_j)$$

imposes that the segment $\overline{P_i P_{Next_i}}$ and the segment $\overline{P_j P_{Next_j}}$ do not intersect, or intersect at most in one of the extremes P_i or P_j.

Clearly, this constraint should be imposed for each pair of nodes, i.e. a quadratic number of constraints. Notice that these constraints are aimed only at improving the efficiency of the solution, they are not necessary for its correctness; they are in fact redundant constraints. One question could be whether all these constraints perform effective pruning, reducing the search space, or whether only some of them are actually useful, while others do not perform any significant pruning while introducing overhead. In next section, we try to reply to this question.

4   The Collected Data

To evaluate the performance of each constraint we collected data while solving Euclidean TSP instances. In order to have a statistically significant number of instances, we used randomly-generated ones from multiple TSP generators.

We generate instances from 3 different classes. The first class, named *uniform*, is that of the random uniform Euclidean instances obtained by placing points uniformly distributed in a $10^6 \times 10^6$ square. We used the generator of the DIMACS challenge [29]. The second set of instances consists of *clustered* instances. Clustered instances have been generated through the R-package `netgen` and its function `generateClusteredNetwork`. The last type of generated instances is a combination of the two above. Morphed instances are in fact obtained by combining two TSP instances with the same number of nodes. Each *morphed* instance is generated by applying a convex combination to the coordinates of node pairs, we used a morphing factor $\alpha = 0.5$ (coefficient for convex combination). The morphed instances were also obtained using the R-package `netgen` and in particular the function `morphInstances`. We randomly generated 1532 instances from 18 to 32 nodes equally distributed in the three classes. For the clustered instances half were generated with the number of clusters $n_c = 2$ and the other half with $n_c = 5$.

For each `nocrossing` constraint, in each instance, we measured 3 indicators: the number of activations $N_{activations}$, the number of value deletions N_{pruned} from the domains of the variables, and the number of failures (and therefore backtracks) generated as a result of the deletion of values. The first two indicators were then combined to obtain a fourth one, denoted as `RTIO` and calculated as the ratio $\frac{N_{pruned}}{N_{activations}}$. A constraint with a low `RTIO` wakes up many times without being able to perform pruning so it produces an unwanted overhead, while a constraint with a high `RTIO` can perform a much stronger pruning compared to the number of activations and therefore it is worth imposing it.

First, we studied the problem by checking how many value deletions and failures each `nocrossing` constrain performs, the `RTIO` and checking which constraints did not perform any pruning as well to identify useful or the useless instances of `nocrossing` constraints; unluckily we were not able to observe any interesting pattern. So, we decided then to introduce a machine learning step.

Each constraint was labelled by means of the `RTIO`, interpreted as an indicator of the "goodness" of a constraint. While in a preliminary version [7] we arbitrarily chose to consider as useful all constraints in an instance $\mathcal{I}$ having `RTIO` superior to the average for their instance $\mu_{\mathcal{I}}^{\text{RTIO}}$, in this paper we adopt a threshold θ^{RTIO}, and postpone to the experimental evaluation the decision of its most suitable value. More precisely, given a threshold θ^{RTIO}, a constraint `nocrossing`$(i, Next_i, j, Next_j)$ is labeled as *useful* in an instance $\mathcal{I}$ if

$$\text{RTIO}_{\mathcal{I}}^{i,j} \geq \theta^{\text{RTIO}} \cdot \mu_{\mathcal{I}}^{\text{RTIO}}$$

and *useless* otherwise.

The relation we wish to learn could be seen as a function mapping each pair of points (in a generic Euclidean TSP instance) to the set {*useful*, *useless*}. In principle, each point could be identified solely by its coordinates, but this could be a too specific information: the effectiveness of a constraint should be independent from rigid transformations of the whole set of points, such as rotations, axial symmetries, or even scaling.

For this reason we computed a set of features trying to synthesize some further information that is invariant with respect to these transformations. As a guidance, we chose some features reflecting information exploited by effective TSP solving algorithms, in the hope that they could also serve as guidance for the effectiveness of the `nocrossing` constraints.

One effective algorithm for solving TSPs, by Held and Karp [26], is based on spanning trees. The minimum spanning tree of the set of nodes can be computed in polynomial time, and is a popular valid lower bound on the value of the optimal solution. One of the properties we chose for a pair of points is whether the segment connecting them belongs to a minimum spanning tree.

Another interesting property is the so-called necklace condition [16]. Suppose to find a set of discs, each centered on one of the points to be visited, such that the interiors of two discs do not intersect. Clearly, an optimal tour should enter and exit each of the discs, so a valid lower bound is twice the sum of the radii of the discs. From this observation, another interesting property could be the distance of each node to the closest other node.

Finally, in [9] we also introduced constraints that performed pruning based on the convex Hull of the set of points; that pruning was also extended to the case of *interior Hulls*, after (during search) some of the segments in the current path were already fixed.

Inspired by works in the literature that attempt to characterise TSP instances by calculating features [27,31,37,40,44], we decided to introduce features concerning the whole instance rather than the single `nocrossing` constraint. In particular, we focused on a subset of the features introduced by Hutter *et al.* [27] which in turn built on the set previously introduced by Smith-Miles *et al.* [44]. These features are indicated below with an asterisk.

Considering what has been introduced so far, we have identified the following 45 features for each `nocrossing`$(i, Next_i, j, Next_j)$ constraint in the dataset. For each instance, let N_i be the point corresponding to P_i with normalized coordinates, such that coordinates span in the $[0,100]$ interval.

- 1–3: **Cost Matrix Statistics***: Mean (c_{avg}), variation coefficient, skew;
- 4–5: **Distance**: Euclidean distance $d_{N_i N_j}$ between points N_i and N_j and normalized version $\frac{d_{N_i N_j}}{c_{avg}}$, where c_{avg} is the average distance in the cost matrix.
- 6: **Radius***: Mean distance from each node to the centroid;
- 7–10: **Centroid Distance**: Euclidean distance from the centroid C to the two extremes N_i ($d_{C N_i}$) and N_j ($d_{C N_j}$) respectively and their normalized versions $\frac{d_{C N_i}}{c_{avg}}$, $\frac{d_{C N_j}}{c_{avg}}$.
- 11–12: **Levels**: Level of points P_i and P_j. The idea is to distinguish the points on the perimeter of the convex hull from the internal ones, and have a numeric value suggesting how deep in the interior of the figure is each point. The level of a point P is defined inductively with respect to the set $\mathcal{P}$ of all the points: $lev(P) = lev_{\mathcal{P}}(P)$. The level of a point P with respect to a set $\mathcal{X}$ is 1 if P belongs to the *"exterior"* of $\mathcal{X}$ (precisely, the perimeter $Hull_{\mathcal{X}}$ of the convex

hull of $\mathcal{X}$) and is defined inductively as 1 plus the level of P on the *"interior"* set $\mathcal{X} \setminus Hull_\mathcal{X}$ otherwise;

- 13–15: **Cluster Distance Features***: Mean, variation coefficient, skew;
- 16–17: **Nearest Neighbour Distance***: Standard deviation and coefficient variation of the normalized nearest neighbour distance;
- 18–21: **Neighbours Distance**: Euclidean distance of the closest point $C(N_i)$ to N_i ($d_{C(N_i)N_i}$) and N_j ($d_{C(N_j)P_j}$) respectively, and normalized versions $\frac{d_{C(N_i)N_i}}{c_{avg}}, \frac{d_{C(N_j)N_j}}{c_{avg}}$;
- 22: **Neighbourhood size**: Number of points contained in the circle having as diameter the segment connecting points P_i and P_j;
- 23–26: **Minimum spanning tree cost statistics***: Sum, mean, variation coefficient, skew;
- 27–28: **Shortest Path in MST**: Cost of the shortest path p between N_i and N_j in a minimum spanning tree, and its normalized version
- 29–31: **Minimum spanning tree node degree statistics***: Mean, variation coefficient, skew;
- 32–33: **MST Degree**: Degree in the minimum spanning tree of P_i and P_j respectively;
- 34: **Segment in MST** (boolean value) Indicates whether the segment $\overline{P_iP_j}$ belongs to a minimum spanning tree.
- 34–35: **Segment crosses**: Number of segments crossing the segment $\overline{P_iP_j}$ and the version normalized, obtained dividing by the total number of arcs;
- 36–39: **Crossings**: Total number of crossings between edges exiting from P_i (resp. P_j) and other edges, and their normalized versions obtained dividing by the total number of arcs.
- 40–44: **Fraction of distinct distances***, with precision to $k \in \{1,2,3,4\}$ decimal digits. Each element of the distance matrix is rounded to k decimal digits, creating D^k, then the number of distinct values in such matrix is computed, and divided by the number of values in the matrix;
- 45: **Good**: (boolean value) label each constraint as useful (1) or useless (0).

5 Machine Learning the Goodness of Constraint Propagators

The dataset of labelled constraints is suitable for the application of supervised machine learning algorithms, with the goal of learning a model able to predict which of the constraints will be useful and which will be useless in a new unseen instance of the Euclidean TSP. As each constraint is labelled as useful or useless, a *binary* classifier can be learnt that discriminates between the negative class (*useless*, with label equal to 0) and the positive class (*useful*, with value 1 as label). Among the classification techniques, we consider two well-known and extensively used approaches: (1) Random Forest (RF), known for its good computational performance and scalability, and (2) Neural Networks (NN), which have proven to be very effective at modelling correlations among many features.

A random forest is a meta estimator that fits a number of decision tree classifiers on various sub-samples of the dataset and uses averaging to improve the predictive accuracy and control overfitting [12]. We used the implementation available in the WEKA [45] workbench for machine learning. Given a training set $\mathbf{X}$ of instances of Euclidean TSP, learning a random forest in WEKA involves the following steps [3]: (1) Bootstrap samples $\mathbf{B}_i$ for every tree t_i are drawn by randomly selecting pairs of points (the examples) with replacement from $\mathbf{X}$ until the sizes of $\mathbf{B}_i$ and $\mathbf{X}$ are equal; (2) a random subset of features (attributes) are selected for each $\mathbf{B}_i$ and used for the training of tree t_i in the forest; (3) an information gain metric is used to grow unpruned decision trees; and (4) the final classification result is the most popular of the individual tree predictions.

On the other hand, NN are able to identify and model complex interactions among the entities to be classified, in this case constraints. There are many types of NNs presenting different architectures. The simplest one is the Multi-Layer Perceptron (MLP), also called Fully Connected NN [2,25]. A MLP can be seen as a graph. It is divided in layers and each layer contains nodes, called neurons, where every neuron is connected to every neuron of the next layer. Every connection is associated with a trainable weight. The values of the weights are trained by means of an optimization algorithm, such as gradient descent, by computing the gradient of the output of the network with respect to each layer and updating the weights by moving along the gradient.

These two classifiers could then be independently used to predict if on new unseen pairs of points the `nocrossing` constraint should be imposed, at the same time indicating to avoid imposing constraints that have been assigned the negative class (useless). The whole proposed procedure is the following: 1. A training dataset of various Euclidean TSP instances, where each constraint has been labelled according to its own `RTIO`, is used to learn a RF or MLP classifier; 2. Given any new instance of the problem, for whose constraints the three indicators (and so the class) are unknown, apply the classifier to find pairs of points that are classified as *useful* for imposing the `nocrossing` constraint; 3. Run the instance together with the selected `nocrossing` constraints to solve the Euclidean TSP. With step 3, we try to eliminate the temporal overhead that might be introduced during the search for a solution by the constraints recognized as not effective (*useless*) by the random forest model. An advantage of this procedure is that, once the classifier has been learnt, it can be reused on any new instance of the problem, without re-performing the machine learning step, which is executed only once.

6 Experiments

6.1 Results of the Machine Learning Step

The machine learning task was carried out by training, independently, a RF classifier and a MLP classifier. For the former, WEKA version 3.8.5 [45] was used, for the latter we used Tensorflow[1] [1] version 2.0.0 of the framework with CUDA version 10.0.

The training phase of the RF classifier was controlled by the parameters:

- P 100: size of each bag, as a percentage of the training set size; the default value of 100 was kept;
- I 100: number of iterations (i.e., the number of trees in the random forest);
- num-slots 1: number of execution slots (thread) for constructing the ensemble. The default 1 means no parallelism;
- K 0: sets the number of randomly chosen attributes;
- M 1: the minimum number of instances per leaf;
- V 0.001: minimum numeric class variance proportion of train variance for split (it was kept the default value);
- S 1: seed for random number generator (it was kept the default value).

As for the MLP, we performed a random search to find the best combination for the number of layers, the number of neurons per layer, the optimizer among Adam and Stochastic Gradient Descent, the parameters for the optimizers, and the dropout rate. We trained among 300 configurations and we selected the MLP, that showed the best trade-of between classification performance and resource consumption in order to keep the entire resolution flow of the Euclidean TSP as efficient as possible. The resulting network has 13 layers: 2 layers × 128 neurons, 2 × 256, 4 × 1024, 2 × 256, 2 × 128, 1 × 1 neurons. All the layers, except the last one, use the ReLU activation function, while the last one uses the sigmoid function. Layers 2 to 11 apply batch normalization. Training was done by the Adam optimizer [32] and applying early stopping and learning rate decay.

Given a dataset of 434,352 nocrossing constraints - where 50% of them are labelled as *useful* and 50% as *useless* - collected from 1536 instances of Euclidean TSP, data were split into 66% for training and the remainder for test.

A performance summary over the test set is shown in Table 1 for both the RF and the MLP classifier. It is worth mentioning that the RF trained model occupies about 610 MBs of memory, while the MLP just about 45 MBs.

Recalling that each pair of points can be referred to as an 'example', the TP Rate is the fraction of true positives (TP) over the total positive examples, the FP Rate is the fraction of false positives (FP) over the total negative examples, Precision is $TP/(TP + FP)$, Recall corresponds to the TP Rate, F-measure is the harmonic mean of Precision and Recall, ROC and PR Areas represent the areas under the ROC and PR curves taking values in the range [0,1]. The ROC curve plots the TP Rate versus the FP Rate, the PR curve plots the Precision versus the Recall [14,41]. Accuracy is the number of correctly classified examples over all examples. The highest possible value for all metrics is 1, and, except for the FP Rate, the highest the value, the better the performance.

From the results shown in Table 1 it is clear that the RF is able to better recognize useful constraints than MLP, which achieves a higher score only for precision in classifying useless constraints (class 0), but needs ten times more memory.

---

[1] https://www.tensorflow.org/.

Table 1. Performance of the RF and MLP classifiers over the fraction of instances used for test. Class 0 corresponds to useless constraints.

Classifier	Class	Recall	FP Rate	Precision	F-Measure	ROC Area	PR Area	Accuracy
RF	0	0.760	0.155	0.830	0.793	0.883	0.894	
	1	0.845	0.240	0.779	0.811	0.883	0.862	
	W.Avg.	0.802	0.198	0.804	0.802	0.883	0.878	0.802
MLP	0	0.827	0.258	0.704	0.761	0.855	0.871	
	1	0.742	0.173	0.853	0.794	0.855	0.829	
	W.Avg.	0.785	0.215	0.779	0.777	0.855	0.850	0.779

6.2 Results of the Overall Euclidean TSP Solver

As already introduced in Sect. 4, we decided to empirically evaluate the best threshold value for $\theta^{\texttt{RTIO}}$ to label each constraint as *useful* or *useless*. We solved 192 instances of Euclidean TSP by varying the threshold value, in steps of 0.1, in the interval $[0.1, 2]$. The graph in Fig. 1 summarizes the results obtained, for each threshold value it shows the geometric mean of the solving time of all 192 instances. The curve shows a minimum at point $\theta^{\texttt{RTIO}} = 0.6$, which is the value we then used in creating the training dataset for the machine learning models.

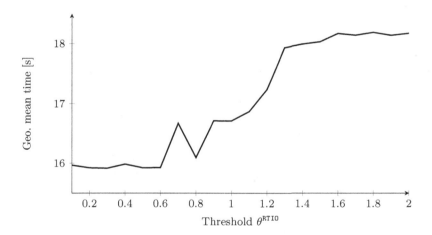

Fig. 1. Experimental evaluation of the $\theta^{\texttt{RTIO}}$ value.

In order to evaluate the improvements in solving time obtained thanks to the predictions made by in the machine learning step, we devised a series of experiments based on randomly-generated TSPs. The same techniques described in Sect. 4 were used to generate the TSPs used in the experiments. We generated a total of 480 test instances varying the size from 20 to 28 nodes, equally distributed in the three classes *uniform, clustered* and *morphed.*

We compared six constraint models based on the successor representation as introduced in Sect. 2:

- the basic constraint model described in the preliminaries (denoted as ECLP), including the `circuit` and `alldifferent` constraints required by the successor representation plus the objective function;
- the model imposing the `nocrossing` constraints for all pairs of nodes (denoted as ALL);
- the model imposing only the `nocrossing` constraints predicted as useful by the RF classifier (denoted as RF);
- the model imposing only the `nocrossing` constraints predicted as useful by the MLP classifier (denoted as MLP);
- moreover, in order to eliminate the hypothesis that a random removal of constraints could obtain the same speed-up, we also plot the timing results of two constraint models, in which, respectively, 70% of the `nocrossing` constraints were not imposed (denoted as RAND70) and half of these constraints were not imposed (denoted as RAND50).

All experiments use the *max regret* search strategy [13]. All algorithms are implemented in the ECL^{i}PS^e CLP language [43]. All tests were run on ECL^{i}PS^e v. 7.0, build #54, on Intel® Xeon® E5-2697 v4 CPUs running at 2.30 GHz, with one core and with 1 GB of reserved memory. The time limit was 3,600 s.

Figure 2 shows, for each constraint model, the number of instances that were solved within the timeout. We can see that the basic constraint model ECLP is the least effective, while adding `nocrossing` constraints can provide a significant speed-up. Removing constraints randomly is not effective, and it seems that as we increase the number of `nocrossing` constraints from 0 (ECLP) to 30% (RAND70), to 50% (RAND50), to 100% (ALL) we obtain increasing speed-ups.

The same does not hold if the constraints to be imposed are carefully selected: the two constraint models in which the `nocrossing` constraints imposed are those predicted through machine learning are the most effective, confirming the effectiveness of the machine learning - based approach proposed in this paper. MLP and RF performances are almost overlapping, with RF slightly more effective than the MLP, as expected from the results of Table 1, at the cost of higher memory needed: RF requires a memory amount larger one order of magnitude than MLP.

Figure 3 shows the running time when varying the size of the instance. It is worth noting that randomly selecting a set of `nocrossing` constraints to be removed does not pay off, and can even increase the running time with respect to adding no `nocrossing` constraints. In particular, in larger instances, the median value of the running time coincides with the timeout for the reference constraint model and for the random selection of constraints. Instead, the median value is significantly lower when selecting the constraints to be imposed with machine learning.

The selection of constraints also increased slightly the number of instances that could be solved: among the 480 tested instances, ECLP incurred in timeout

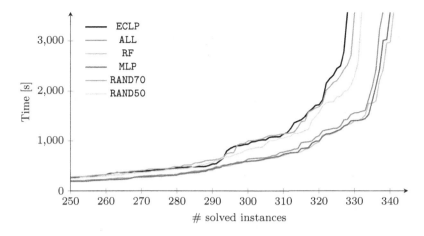

Fig. 2. Solving time as a function of the number of solved instances.

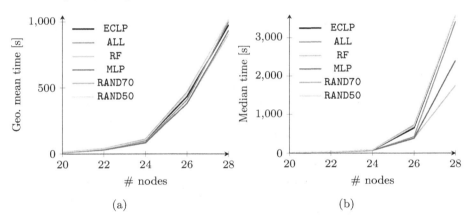

(a)   (b)

Fig. 3. (a) Geometric mean and (b) median of solving time of TSPs varying the size of the instances and constraint models.

on 153 instances, while `RAND70` on 151, `RAND50` on 149, `ALL` on 143, `RF` on 140 and `MLP` on 141.

Randomly-generated TSPs instances, collected runtime data and datasets are available online[2].

7 Related Work

There exists a wide literature on combinations of constraint programming with machine learning or data mining [11].

---

[2] https://github.com/abertagnon/ml-etsp.

One of the main ideas is portfolio selection (see, e.g., the survey [33] and references therein): given a set of algorithms (or solvers) that solve a same problem, select the best one for solving a given instance. The approach is based on obtaining data about the running time of the algorithms on a high number of instances. Also, for each instance a number of features are computed, hopefully synthesizing those characteristics that make it easy or hard to solve. After that, a classifier is learned trying to predict, given the set of features of a new unseen instance, which of the available solvers will be the fastest for that specific instance. Once a new instance is provided, the classifier chooses the best solver.

Our work could, in principle, be seen as an algorithm portfolio in which the classifier chooses among an exponential number of solving algorithms, each imposing a subset of the set of possible `nocrossing` constraints. However, we do not learn such a complex classifier (although in principle it could provide better results) because the number of possible solvers would be too large, but we try to predict which of the single `nocrossing` constraints will be effective.

Although less strictly related to this paper, we cite other approaches to combine Machine Learning and CP, including Empirical Model Learning [34,35], trying to learn some features of a physical system and including its input/output relation as a new constraint, or approaches that try to learn single constraints or a whole constraint model given examples from the user [6,10].

Various works in the CP literature address the TSP or some of its variants. Some of them propose implementations of the `circuit` constraint [13,17,22,30]: considering that the Hamiltonian Circuit Problem is NP-complete, obtaining Arc-Consistency for the `circuit` constraint would be NP-complete, so the works in the literature forego the idea of achieving Arc-Consistency, and propose instead different tradeoffs between computation time and pruning power.

Considering the objective function, various works exploit relaxations (as usually done in Integer Linear Programming) to quickly rule out non-promising solutions; the usual relaxations are the minimum spanning tree [20,21,39] and the assignment problem relaxations [20,21].

Starting with Benchimol et al. [8], various works propose to integrate the objective function into a constraint that ensures Hamiltonianicity of the graph [15,18,28] in order to achieve stronger pruning based on the current upper bound.

8   Conclusions and Future Work

In this paper, we proposed to predict and select the set of `nocrossing` constraints in Euclidean TSPs formulated in CP.

The experimental results are encouraging. Other possible new directions might be to consider to predict, instead of two classes, the actual ratio of pruning power versus activations $\frac{N_{pruned}}{N_{activations}}$, run experiments imposing only those `nocrossing` constraints whose ratio is predicted to be higher than a given threshold, and experimentally find the best possible value of the threshold. This changes the machine learning step from a classification to a regression task, which, on the other hand, may be more challenging. One could then move from supervised learning to reinforcement learning techniques and thus avoid collecting a training set.

Another possibility is to consider reinforcement learning approaches, but this needs a complete change in the definition of the machine learning problem both in terms of inputs, outputs, metrics to consider, and number of calls to the TSP solver, so, it is left for future work.

Some improvement could be obtained by expanding the dataset of experiments, i.e. by running experiments in more instances to widen the available data about number of activations and pruning of the nocrossing constraints. Also, in the current dataset only one search heuristic was employed, namely *max regret* [13]. Since max regret is a dynamic search heuristics, it might be the case that changing the set of nocrossing constraint, the search strategies change radically the exploration of the search tree, possibly shuffling the order in which nocrossing constraints are activated, and making effective some constraints that were not and vice-versa. So, a more precise classifier could be obtained by generating datasets with different search strategies.

Finally, instead of learning a classifier that chooses the set of nocrossing constraints that should be imposed a priori, one could use more dynamic strategies, like removing during search the nocrossing constraints that result less effective because they have not obtained significant pruning in the last activations. One source of inspiration could be the strategies used in SAT solvers to forget some of the nogoods [24].

References

1. Abadi, M., et al.: Tensorflow: Large-scale machine learning on heterogeneous distributed systems. arXiv preprint arXiv:1603.04467 (2016)
2. Aggarwal, C.: Neural Networks and Deep Learning - A Textbook. Springer, Heidelberg (2018). https://doi.org/10.1007/978-3-319-94463-0
3. Amrehn, M., Mualla, F., Angelopoulou, E., Steidl, S., Maier, A.: The random forest classifier in WEKA: discussion and new developments for imbalanced data (2019)
4. Applegate, D., Bixby, R., Chvátal, V., Cook, W.: TSP cuts which do not conform to the template paradigm. In: Jünger, M., Naddef, D. (eds.) Computational Combinatorial Optimization. LNCS, vol. 2241, pp. 261–303. Springer, Heidelberg (2001). https://doi.org/10.1007/3-540-45586-8_7
5. Arora, S.: Polynomial time approximation schemes for Euclidean TSP and other geometric problems. In: Proceedings of 37th Conference on Foundations of Computer Science, pp. 2–11, October 1996
6. Beldiceanu, N., Simonis, H.: ModelSeeker: extracting global constraint models from positive examples. In: Bessiere, C., De Raedt, L., Kotthoff, L., Nijssen, S., O'Sullivan, B., Pedreschi, D. (eds.) Data Mining and Constraint Programming. LNCS (LNAI), vol. 10101, pp. 77–95. Springer, Cham (2016). https://doi.org/10.1007/978-3-319-50137-6_4
7. Bellodi, E., Bertagnon, A., Gavanelli, M., Zese, R.: Improving the efficiency of euclidean TSP solving in constraint programming by predicting effective nocrossing constraints. In: Benedictis, R.D., et al. (eds.) Joint Proceedings of the 8th Italian Workshop on Planning and Scheduling and the 27th International Workshop

on Experimental Evaluation of Algorithms for Solving Problems with Combinatorial Explosion co-located with AIxIA 2020, Online Event, November 25–27, 2020. CEUR Workshop Proceedings, vol. 2745. CEUR-WS.org (2020). http://ceur-ws.org/Vol-2745/paper6.pdf

8. Benchimol, P., van Hoeve, W.J., Régin, J., Rousseau, L., Rueher, M.: Improved filtering for weighted circuit constraints. Constraints **17**(3), 205–233 (2012)

9. Bertagnon, A., Gavanelli, M.: Improved filtering for the Euclidean traveling salesperson problem in CLP(FD). In: The Thirty-Fourth AAAI Conference on Artificial Intelligence, AAAI 2020, The Thirty-Second Innovative Applications of Artificial Intelligence Conference, IAAI 2020, The Tenth AAAI Symposium on Educational Advances in Artificial Intelligence, EAAI 2020, New York, NY, USA, 7–12 February 2020, pp. 1412–1419. AAAI Press (2020). https://aaai.org/ojs/index.php/AAAI/article/view/5498

10. Bessiere, C., et al.: New approaches to constraint acquisition. In: Bessiere, C., De Raedt, L., Kotthoff, L., Nijssen, S., O'Sullivan, B., Pedreschi, D. (eds.) Data Mining and Constraint Programming. LNCS (LNAI), vol. 10101, pp. 51–76. Springer, Cham (2016). https://doi.org/10.1007/978-3-319-50137-6_3

11. Bessiere, C., et al. (eds.): Data Mining and Constraint Programming. LNCS (LNAI), vol. 10101. Springer, Cham (2016). https://doi.org/10.1007/978-3-319-50137-6

12. Breiman, L.: Random forests. Mach. Learn. **45**(1), 5–32 (2001)

13. Caseau, Y., Laburthe, F.: Solving small TSPs with constraints. In: Naish, L. (ed.) Logic Programming, Proceedings of the Fourteenth International Conference on Logic Programming, Leuven, Belgium, 8–11 July 1997, pp. 316–330. MIT Press (1997)

14. Davis, J., Goadrich, M.: The relationship between precision-recall and ROC curves. In: European Conference on Machine Learning (ECML 2006). ACM (2006)

15. Deudon, M., Cournut, P., Lacoste, A., Adulyasak, Y., Rousseau, L.-M.: Learning heuristics for the TSP by policy gradient. In: van Hoeve, W.-J. (ed.) CPAIOR 2018. LNCS, vol. 10848, pp. 170–181. Springer, Cham (2018). https://doi.org/10.1007/978-3-319-93031-2_12

16. Edelsbrunner, H., Rote, G., Welzl, E.: Testing the necklace condition for shortest tours and optimal factors in the plane. Theor. Comput. Sci. **66**(2), 157–180 (1989)

17. Fages, J., Lorca, X.: Improving the asymmetric TSP by considering graph structure. CoRR abs/1206.3437 (2012). http://arxiv.org/abs/1206.3437

18. Fages, J.-G., Lorca, X., Rousseau, L.-M.: The salesman and the tree: the importance of search in CP. Constraints **21**(2), 145–162 (2014). https://doi.org/10.1007/s10601-014-9178-2

19. Flood, M.M.: The traveling-salesman problem. Oper. Res. **4** (1956)

20. Focacci, F., Lodi, A., Milano, M.: Embedding relaxations in global constraints for solving TSP and TSPTW. Ann. Math. Artif. Intell. **34**(4), 291–311 (2002)

21. Focacci, F., Lodi, A., Milano, M.: A hybrid exact algorithm for the TSPTW. INFORMS J. Comput. **14**(4), 403–417 (2002)

22. Francis, K.G., Stuckey, P.J.: Explaining circuit propagation. Constraints **19**(1), 1–29 (2013). https://doi.org/10.1007/s10601-013-9148-0

23. Garey, M.R., Graham, R.L., Johnson, D.S.: Some NP-complete geometric problems. In: Proceedings of the Eighth Annual ACM Symposium on Theory of Computing, STOC 1976, pp. 10–22. ACM, New York (1976)

24. Gent, I.P., Miguel, I., Moore, N.C.A.: An empirical study of learning and forgetting constraints. AI Commun. **25**(2) (2012). https://doi.org/10.3233/AIC-2012-0524

25. Goodfellow, I., Bengio, Y., Courville, A.: Deep Learning. MIT Press (2016)
26. Held, M., Karp, R.M.: The traveling-salesman problem and minimum spanning trees. Oper. Res. **18**, 1138–1162 (1970)
27. Hutter, F., Xu, L., Hoos, H.H., Leyton-Brown, K.: Algorithm runtime prediction: methods & evaluation. Artif. Intell. **206**, 79–111 (2014)
28. Isoart, N., Régin, J.-C.: Integration of structural constraints into TSP models. In: Schiex, T., de Givry, S. (eds.) CP 2019. LNCS, vol. 11802, pp. 284–299. Springer, Cham (2019). https://doi.org/10.1007/978-3-030-30048-7_17
29. Johnson, D.S., McGeoch, L.A.: Experimental analysis of heuristics for the STSP. In: Gutin, G., Punnen, A.P. (eds.) The Traveling Salesman Problem and its Variations, pp. 369–443. Springer, Heidelberg (2007). https://doi.org/10.1007/0-306-48213-4_9
30. Kaya, L.G., Hooker, J.N.: A filter for the circuit constraint. In: Benhamou, F. (ed.) CP 2006. LNCS, vol. 4204, pp. 706–710. Springer, Heidelberg (2006). https://doi.org/10.1007/11889205_55
31. Kerschke, P., Kotthoff, L., Bossek, J., Hoos, H.H., Trautmann, H.: Leveraging TSP solver complementarity through machine learning. Evol. Comput. **26**(4), 597–620 (2018)
32. Kingma, D.P., Ba, J.: Adam: a method for stochastic optimization. In: Bengio, Y., LeCun, Y. (eds.) 3rd International Conference on Learning Representations, ICLR 2015, San Diego, CA, USA, 7–9 May 2015, Conference Track Proceedings (2015)
33. Kotthoff, L.: Algorithm selection for combinatorial search problems: a survey. In: Bessiere, C., De Raedt, L., Kotthoff, L., Nijssen, S., O'Sullivan, B., Pedreschi, D. (eds.) Data Mining and Constraint Programming. LNCS (LNAI), vol. 10101, pp. 149–190. Springer, Cham (2016). https://doi.org/10.1007/978-3-319-50137-6_7
34. Lombardi, M., Milano, M.: Boosting combinatorial problem modeling with machine learning. In: Lang, J. (ed.) Proceedings of the Twenty-Seventh International Joint Conference on Artificial Intelligence, IJCAI 2018, pp. 5472–5478. ijcai.org (2018)
35. Lombardi, M., Milano, M., Bartolini, A.: Empirical decision model learning. Artif. Intell. **244**, 343–367 (2017). https://doi.org/10.1016/j.artint.2016.01.005
36. Mackworth, A.K.: Consistency in networks of relations. Artif. Intell. **8**(1), 99–118 (1977). https://doi.org/10.1016/0004-3702(77)90007-8
37. Mersmann, O., Bischl, B., Trautmann, H., Wagner, M., Bossek, J., Neuman, F.: A novel feature-based approach to characterize algorithm performance for the traveling salesperson problem. Ann. Math. Artif. Intell. **69**(2), 151–182 (2013). https://doi.org/10.1007/s10472-013-9341-2
38. Mitchell, J.S.B.: Guillotine subdivisions approximate polygonal subdivisions: a simple polynomial-time approximation scheme for geometric TSP, k-MST, and related problems. SIAM J. Comput. **28**(4), 1298–1309 (1999)
39. Pesant, G., Gendreau, M., Potvin, J., Rousseau, J.: An exact constraint logic programming algorithm for the traveling salesman problem with time windows. Transp. Sci. **32**(1), 12–29 (1998)
40. Pihera, J., Musliu, N.: Application of machine learning to algorithm selection for TSP. In: 2014 IEEE 26th International Conference on Tools with Artificial Intelligence, pp. 47–54. IEEE (2014)
41. Provost, F.J., Fawcett, T.: Robust classification for imprecise environments. Mach. Learn. **42**(3), 203–231 (2001)
42. Régin, J.: A filtering algorithm for constraints of difference in CSPs. In: Hayes-Roth, B., Korf, R.E. (eds.) Proceedings of the 12th National Conference on Artificial Intelligence, Seattle, WA, USA, 31 July–4 August 1994, vol. 1, pp. 362–367. AAAI Press/The MIT Press (1994)

43. Schimpf, J., Shen, K.: Ecl^{i}ps^e - from LP to CLP. TPLP **12**(1–2), 127–156 (2012)
44. Smith-Miles, K., van Hemert, J., Lim, X.Y.: Understanding TSP difficulty by learning from evolved instances. In: Blum, C., Battiti, R. (eds.) LION 2010. LNCS, vol. 6073, pp. 266–280. Springer, Heidelberg (2010). https://doi.org/10.1007/978-3-642-13800-3_29
45. Witten, I.H., Frank, E., Hall, M.A.: Data Mining: Practical Machine Learning Tools and Techniques, 3rd edn. Morgan Kaufmann Series in Data Management Systems, Morgan Kaufmann (2011)

From Contrastive to Abductive Explanations and Back Again

Alexey Ignatiev[1] , Nina Narodytska[2(✉)] , Nicholas Asher[3] ,
and Joao Marques-Silva[3]

[1] Monash University, Melbourne, Australia
`alexey.ignatiev@monash.edu`
[2] VMware Research, Palo Alto, CA, USA
`nnarodytska@vmware.com`
[3] IRIT, CNRS, Toulouse, France
{`nicholas.asher,joao.marques-silva`}`@irit.fr`

Abstract. Explanations of Machine Learning (ML) models often address a 'Why?' question. Such explanations can be related with selecting feature-value pairs which are sufficient for the prediction. Recent work has investigated explanations that address a 'Why Not?' question, i.e. finding a change of feature values that guarantee a change of prediction. Given their goals, these two forms of explaining predictions of ML models appear to be mostly unrelated. However, this paper demonstrates otherwise, and establishes a rigorous formal relationship between 'Why?' and 'Why Not?' explanations. Concretely, the paper proves that, for any given instance, 'Why?' explanations are minimal hitting sets of 'Why Not?' explanations and vice-versa. Furthermore, the paper devises novel algorithms for extracting and enumerating both forms of explanations.

1 Introduction

The importance of devising mechanisms for computing explanations of Machine Learning (ML) models cannot be overstated, as illustrated by the fast-growing body of work in this area. A glimpse of the importance of explainable AI (XAI) is offered by a growing number of recent surveys and overviews [2,3,5,10,19,30–34,45,59–62,71,72,79].

Past work on computing explanations has mostly addressed *local* (or instance-dependent) explanations [15,16,38,51,69,70,75,76]. Exceptions include for example approaches that distill ML models, e.g. the case of NNs [26] among many others [69], or recent work on relating explanations with adversarial examples [39], both of which can be seen as seeking *global* (or instance-independent) explanations. Prior research has also mostly considered model-agnostic explanations [51,69,70]. Recent work on model-based explanations, e.g. [38,75], refers to local (or global) model-agnostic explanations as *heuristic*, given that these approaches offer no *formal* guarantees with respect to the underlying ML model. A taxonomy of ML model explanations is summarized in Table 1. Examples

© Springer Nature Switzerland AG 2021
M. Baldoni and S. Bandini (Eds.): AIxIA 2020, LNAI 12414, pp. 335–355, 2021.
https://doi.org/10.1007/978-3-030-77091-4_21

of heuristic approaches include [51,69,70], among many others[1]. In contrast, local (or global) model-based explanations are referred to as *rigorous*, since these offer the strongest formal guarantees with respect to the underlying ML model. Concrete examples of such rigorous approaches include [15,16,35,38–41,43,52,64,75–77].

Most work on computing explanations aims to answer a 'Why prediction π?' question. Some work proposes approximating the ML model's behavior with a linear model [51,69]. Most other work seeks to find a (often minimal) set of feature value pairs which is sufficient for the prediction, i.e. as long as those features take the specified values, the prediction does not change. For rigorous approaches, the answer to a 'Why prediction π?' question has been referred to as PI-explanations [75,76], abductive explanations [38], but also as (minimal) sufficient reasons [15,16]. (Hereinafter, we use the term *abductive explanation* because of the other forms of explanations studied in the paper.)

Another dimension of explanations, studied in recent work [60], is the difference between explanations for 'Why prediction π?' questions, e.g., 'Why did I get the loan?', and for 'Why prediction π and not δ?' questions, e.g., 'Why didn't I get the loan?'. Explanations for 'Why Not?' questions, labelled by [60] *contrastive* explanations, isolate a pragmatic component of explanations that *abductive explanations* lack. Concretely, an abductive explanation identifies a set of feature values which are sufficient for the model to make a prediction π and thus provides an answer to the question 'why π?' A contrastive explanation sets up a counterfactual link between what was a (possibly) *desired* outcome of a certain set of features and what was the observed outcome [1,13]. Thus, a contrastive explanation answers a 'Why π and not δ?' question [18,58,61].

In this paper we focus on the relationship between *local* abductive and contrastive explanations[2]. One of our contributions is to show how recent approaches for computing rigorous abductive explanations [15,16,38,75,76] can also be exploited for computing contrastive explanations. To our knowledge, this is new. In addition, we demonstrate that rigorous (model-based) local abductive and contrastive explanations are related by a minimal hitting set relationship[3], which builds on the seminal work of Reiter in the 80s [68]. Crucially, this novel hitting set relationship reveals a wealth of algorithms for computing and for enumerating contrastive and abductive explanations. We emphasize that it allows designing the first algorithm to *enumerate* abductive explanations. Finally, we demonstrate feasibility of our approach experimentally. Furthermore, our experiments show that there is a strong correlation between contrastive explanations and explanations produced by the commonly used SHAP explainer.

---

[1] There is also a recent XAI service offered by Google: https://cloud.google.com/explainable-ai/, inspired on similar ideas [28].

[2] In contrast with recent work [39], which studies the relationship between *global* model-based (abductive) explanations and adversarial examples.

[3] A local abductive (resp. contrastive) explanation is a minimal hitting set of the set of all local contrastive (resp. abductive) explanations.

Table 1. Taxonomy of ML model explanations used in the paper.

		Instance-		
		Dependent		*Independent*
ML model-	Agnostic	Heuristic *local* explanation for π Examples: SHAP, LIME, Anchor, etc.		Heuristic *global* explanation for π. Examples: SHAP, LIME (e.g. submodular pick)
	Based	Rigorous *local* explanation for π Examples:		Rigorous *global* explanation for π Examples: absolute/global AXps
		'Why π?'	'Why not $\neg\pi$?'	
		PI- (abductive) explanations (AXps)	contrastive (CXps) (our work)	

2   Preliminaries

Explainability in Machine Learning. The paper assumes an ML model $\mathbb{M}$, which is represented by a finite set of first-order logic (FOL) sentences $\mathcal{M}$. (When applicable, simpler alternative representations for $\mathcal{M}$ can be considered, e.g. (decidable) fragments of FOL, (mixed-)integer linear programming, constraint language(s), etc.)[4] A set of features $\mathcal{F} = \{f_1, \ldots, f_L\}$ is assumed. Each feature f_i is categorical (or ordinal), with values taken from some set D_i. An *instance* is an assignment of values to features. The space of instances, also referred to as *feature* (or *instance*) *space*, is defined by $\mathbb{F} = D_1 \times D_2 \times \ldots \times D_L$. For real-valued features, we require that a suitable interval discretization is applied first as a preprocessing step, e.g. if we consider an income feature for a person, we can split an interval of possible values into a set of intervals and treat each interval as a feature value. Therefore, our approach is applicable to any data that can be represented using a set of feature, e.g. tabular data, images, text, etc.

A (feature) literal λ_i is of the form $(f_i = v_i)$, with $v_i \in D_i$. In what follows, a literal will be viewed as an atom, i.e. it can take value *true* or *false*. As a result, an instance can be viewed as a set of L literals, denoting the L distinct features, i.e. an instance contains a single occurrence of a literal defined on any given feature. A set of literals is consistent if it contains at most one literal defined on each feature. A consistent set of literals can be interpreted as a conjunction or as a disjunction of literals; this will be clear from the context. When interpreted as a conjunction, the set of literals denotes a *cube* in instance space, where the unspecified features can take any possible value of their domain. When interpreted as a disjunction, the set of literals denotes a *clause* in instance space. As before, the unspecified features can take any possible value of their domain.

The remainder of the paper assumes a classification problem with a set of classes $\mathbb{K} = \{\kappa_1, \ldots, \kappa_M\}$. A prediction $\pi \in \mathbb{K}$ is associated with each instance

---

[4] $\mathcal{M}$ is referred to as the (formal) model of the ML model $\mathbb{M}$. The use of FOL is not restrictive, with fragments of FOL being used in recent years for modeling ML models in different settings. These include NNs [38] and Bayesian Network Classifiers [76], among others.

$X \in \mathbb{F}$. Throughout this paper, an ML model $\mathbb{M}$ will be associated with some logical representation (or encoding), whose consistency depends on the (input) instance and (output) prediction. Thus, we define a predicate $\mathcal{M} \subseteq \mathbb{F} \times \mathbb{K}$, such that $\mathcal{M}(X, \pi)$ is true iff the input X is consistent with prediction π given the ML model $\mathbb{M}^5$. We further simplify the notation by using $\mathcal{M}_\pi(X)$ to denote a predicate $\mathcal{M}(X, \pi)$ for a concrete prediction π.

Moreover, we will compute *prime implicants* of $\mathcal{M}_\pi$. These predicates defined on $\mathbb{F}$ and represented as consistent conjunctions (or alternatively as sets) of feature literals. Concretely, a consistent conjunction of feature literals τ is an implicant of $\mathcal{M}_\pi$ if the following FOL statement is true:

$$\forall(X \in \mathbb{F}).\tau(X) \rightarrow \mathcal{M}(X, \pi) \qquad (1)$$

The notation $\tau \vDash \mathcal{M}_\pi$ is used to denote that τ an implicant of $\mathcal{M}_\pi$. Similarly, a consistent set of feature literals ν is the negation of an implicate of $\mathcal{M}_\pi$ if the following FOL statement is true:

$$\forall(X \in \mathbb{F}).\nu(X) \rightarrow (\vee_{\rho \neq \pi} \mathcal{M}(X, \rho)) \qquad (2)$$

$\mathcal{M}_\pi \vDash \neg\nu$, or alternatively $(\nu \vDash \neg\mathcal{M}_\pi) \equiv (\nu \vDash \vee_{\rho \neq \pi} \mathcal{M}_\rho)$. An implicant τ (resp. implicate ν) is called *prime* if none of its proper subsets $\tau' \subsetneq \tau$ (resp. $\nu' \subsetneq \nu$) is an implicant (resp. implicate).

Abductive explanations represent prime implicants of the decision function associated with some predicted class π^6.

Analysis of Inconsistent Formulas. Throughout the paper, we will be interested in formulas $\mathcal{F}$ that are *inconsistent* (or *unsatisfiable*), i.e. $\mathcal{F} \vDash \bot$, represented as conjunctions of clauses. Some clauses in $\mathcal{F}$ can be *relaxed* (i.e. allowed not to be satisfied) to restore consistency, whereas others cannot. Thus, we assume that $\mathcal{F}$ is partitioned into two first-order subformulas $\mathcal{F} = \mathcal{B} \cup \mathcal{R}$, where $\mathcal{R}$ contains the *relaxable* clauses, and $\mathcal{B}$ contains the *non-relaxable* clauses. $\mathcal{B}$ can be viewed as (consistent) background knowledge, which must always be satisfied.

Given an inconsistent formula $\mathcal{F}$, represented as a set of first-order clauses, we identify the clauses that are responsible for unsatisfiability among those that can be relaxed, as defined next[7].

Definition 1 (Minimal Unsatisfiable Subset (MUS)). *Let $\mathcal{F} = \mathcal{B} \cup \mathcal{R}$ denote an inconsistent set of clauses ($\mathcal{F} \vDash \bot$). $\mathcal{U} \subseteq \mathcal{R}$ is a* Minimal Unsatisfiable Subset *(MUS) iff $\mathcal{B} \cup \mathcal{U} \vDash \bot$ and $\forall_{\mathcal{U}' \subsetneq \mathcal{U}}, \mathcal{B} \cup \mathcal{U}' \nvDash \bot$.*

---

[5] This alternative notation is used for simplicity and clarity with respect to earlier work [38,39,75]. Furthermore, defining $\mathcal{M}$ as a predicate allows for multiple predictions for the same point in feature space. Nevertheless, such cases are not considered in this paper.

[6] By definition of prime implicant, abductive explanations are sufficient reasons for the prediction. Hence the names used in recent work: abductive explanations [38], PI-explanations [75,76] and sufficient reasons [15,16].

[7] The definitions in this section are often presented for the propositional case, but the extension to the first-order case is straightforward.

Informally, an MUS provides the minimal information that needs to be added to the background knowledge $\mathcal{B}$ to obtain an inconsistency; it explains the causes for this inconsistency. Alternatively, one might be interested in correcting the formula, removing some clauses in $\mathcal{R}$ to achieve consistency.

Definition 2 (Minimal Correction Subset (MCS)). *Let* $\mathcal{F} = \mathcal{B} \cup \mathcal{R}$ *denote an inconsistent set of clauses* $(\mathcal{F} \vDash \perp)$. $\mathcal{T} \subseteq \mathcal{R}$ *is a* Minimal Correction Subset *(MCS) iff* $\mathcal{B} \cup \mathcal{R} \setminus \mathcal{T} \nvDash \perp$ *and* $\forall_{\mathcal{T'} \subsetneq \mathcal{T}}, \mathcal{B} \cup \mathcal{R} \setminus \mathcal{T'} \vDash \perp$.

A fundamental result in reasoning about inconsistent clause sets is the minimal hitting set (MHS) duality relationship between MUSes and MCSes [11,68]: *MCSes are MHSes of MUSes and vice-versa.* This result has been extensively used in the development of algorithms for MUSes and MCSes [8,48,49], and also applied in a number of different settings. Recent years have witnessed the proposal of a large number of novel algorithms for the extraction and enumeration of MUSes and MCSes [7,9,29,48]. Although most work addresses propositional theories, these algorithms can easily be generalized to any other setting where entailment is monotonic, e.g. SMT [17].

Running Example. The following example will be used to illustrate the main ideas.

Example 1. We consider a textbook example [66] [Figure 7.1, page 289] addressing the classification of a user's preferences regarding whether to read or to skip a given book. For this dataset, the set of features is:

$$\{ \text{ A(uthor), T(hread), L(ength), W(hereRead) } \}$$

All features take one of two values, respectively $\{\text{known, unknown}\}$, $\{\text{new, followUp}\}$, $\{\text{long, short}\}$, and $\{\text{home, work}\}$. An example instance is: $\{(\text{A} = \text{known}), (\text{T} = \text{new}), (\text{L} = \text{long}), (\text{W} = \text{home})\}$. This instance is identified as e_1 [66] with prediction skips. Figure 1a shows a possible decision tree for this example [66][8]. The decision tree can be represented as a set of rules as shown in Fig. 1b[9].

Our goal is to reason about the ML model, i.e. to implement model-based reasoning, so we need to propose a logical representation for the ML model.

Example 2. For implementing model-based reasoning, we need to develop an encoding in some suitable fragment of FOL[10]. 0-place predicates[11] are used for

---

[8] The choice of a decision tree aims only at keeping the example(s) presented in the paper as simple as possible. The ideas proposed in the paper apply to *any* ML model that can be represented with FOL. This encompasses *any* existing ML model, with minor adaptations in case the ML model keeps state.

[9] The abbreviations used relate with the names in the decision tree, and serve for saving space.

[10] Depending on the ML problem, more expressive fragments of FOL logic could be considered [47]. Well-known examples include real, integer and integer-real arithmetic, but also nonlinear arithmetic [47].

[11] Which in this case are used as propositional variables.

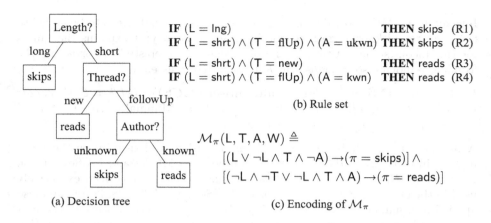

Fig. 1. Running example [66]

L, T, A and W, as follows. We will associate (L = long) with L and (L = short) with ¬L. Similarly, we associate (T = new) with ¬T, and (T = followUp) with T. We associate (A = known) with A and (A = unknown) with ¬A. Furthermore, we associate (W = home) with ¬W and (W = work) with W. An example encoding is shown in Fig. 1c. The explicit values of π are optional (i.e. propositional values could be used) and serve to illustrate how non-propositional valued could be modeled.

3   Contrastive vs. Abductive Explanations

Recent work [15,38,75,76] proposed to relate model-based explanations with prime implicants. All these approaches compute a set of feature values which, if unchanged, are sufficient for the prediction. Thus, one can view such explanations as answering a 'Why?' question: *the prediction is the one given, as long as some selected set of feature values is the one given.* In this paper, such explanations will be referred to as *abductive explanations*, motivated by one of the approaches used for their computation [38].

3.1   Defining Abductive Explanations (AXps)

As indicated earlier in the paper, we focus on *local model-based* explanations.

Definition 3 (Abductive Explanation [38]). *Given an instance τ, with a prediction π, and an ML model represented with a predicate $\mathcal{M}_\pi$, i.e. $\tau \vDash \mathcal{M}_\pi$, an* abductive explanation *is a minimal subset of literals of τ, $\sigma \subseteq \tau$, such that $\sigma \vDash \mathcal{M}_\pi$.*

Example 3. With respect to Example 1, let us consider the instance (A = known, T = new, L = short, W = work), which we represent instead as

$(A, \neg T, \neg L, W)$, corresponding to prediction $\pi = \mathsf{reads}$. By inspection of the decision tree (see Fig. 1a), a possible answer to the 'Why pred. reads?' question is: $\{\neg L, \neg T\}$. In this concrete case we can conclude that this is the only abductive explanation by inspection of the decision tree.

3.2 Defining Contrastive Explanations (CXps)

As [60] notes, contrastive explanations are,

> *"sought in response to particular counterfactual cases... That is, people do not ask why event P happened, but rather why event P happened instead of some event Q."*

As a result, we are interested in providing an answer to the question 'Why π and not δ?', where π is the prediction given some instance τ, and δ is some other (desired) prediction.

Example 4. We consider again Example 1, but with the instance specified in Example 3. A possible answer to the question 'Why pred. reads and not pred. skips??' is $\{L\}$. Indeed, given the input instance $(A, \neg T, \neg L, W)$, if the value of feature L changes from short to long, and the value of the other features remains unchanged, then the prediction will change from reads to skips.

The following definition of a (local model-based) contrastive explanation captures the intuitive notion of the contrastive explanation discussed in the example above.

Definition 4 (Contrastive Explanation). *Given an instance τ, with a prediction π, and an ML model represented by a predicate $\mathcal{M}_\pi$, i.e. $\tau \vDash \mathcal{M}_\pi$, a contrastive explanation is a minimal subset of literals of τ, $\rho \subseteq \tau$, such that $\tau \setminus \rho \nvDash \mathcal{M}_\pi$.*

This definition means that, there is an assignment to the features with literals in ρ, such that the prediction differs from π. Observe that a CXp is defined to answer the following (more specific) question 'Why (pred. π and) not $\neg\pi$?'. The more general case of answering the question 'Why (pred. π and) not δ?' will be analyzed later. Also, we point out a connection between notions of CXp and robustness defined in [74]. In [74], the local robustness for a given instance τ is defined as the minimum Hamming distance from τ to an perturbed input τ' s.t. $\tau' \vDash \neg\mathcal{M}_\pi$. Note that given such a perturbed sample τ', we can obtain a minimum size CXp. This CXp contains all perturbed features of τ. Furthermore, links between robustness and counterfactual explainability (and so contrastive explanations) have been studied in recent work [6].

3.3 Relating Abductive and Contrastive Explanations

The previous section proposed a rigorous, model-based, definition of contrastive explanation. Given this definition, one can think of developing dedicated algorithms that compute CXps using a decision procedure for the logic used for representing the ML model. Instead, we adopt a simpler approach. We build on a fundamental result from model-based diagnosis on the hitting set relationship between diagnoses and conflicts first investigated by Reiter [68] (and more generally for reasoning about inconsistency [8,11]) and demonstrate a similar relationship between AXps and CXps. In turn, this result reveals a variety of novel algorithms for computing CXps, but also offers ways for enumerating both CXps and AXps.

Local Abductive Explanations (AXps). Consider a set of feature values τ, s.t. the prediction is π, for which the notation $\tau \vDash \mathcal{M}_\pi$ is used. We will use the equivalent statement, $\tau \wedge \neg \mathcal{M}_\pi \vDash \bot$. Thus,

$$\tau \wedge \neg \mathcal{M}_\pi \tag{3}$$

is inconsistent, with the background knowledge being $\mathcal{B} \triangleq \neg \mathcal{M}_\pi$ and the relaxable clauses being $\mathcal{R} \triangleq \tau$. As proposed in [38,75], a (local abductive) explanation is a subset-minimal set σ of the literals in τ, such that, $\sigma \wedge \neg \mathcal{M}_\pi \vDash \bot$. Thus, σ denotes a subset of the example's input features which, no matter the other feature values, ensure that the ML model predicts π. Thus, any MUS of Eq. 3 is a (local abductive) explanation for $\mathbb{M}$ to predict π given τ.

Proposition 1. *Local model-based abductive explanations are MUSes of the pair* $(\mathcal{B}, \mathcal{R})$, $\tau \wedge \neg \mathcal{M}_\pi$, *where* $\mathcal{R} \triangleq \tau$ *and* $\mathcal{B} \triangleq \neg \mathcal{M}_\pi$.

Example 5. Consider the ML model from Example 1, the encoding from Example 2, and the instance $\{A, \neg T, L, \neg W\}$, with prediction $\pi = $ skips (wrt Fig. 1, we replace skips = skips with **true** and skips = reads with **false**). We can thus confirm that $\tau \vDash \mathcal{M}_\pi$. We observe that the following holds:

$$A \wedge \neg T \wedge L \wedge \neg W \vDash \begin{bmatrix} (L \vee \neg L \wedge T \wedge \neg A) \to \textbf{true} \\ \wedge \\ (\neg L \wedge \neg T \vee \neg L \wedge T \wedge A) \to \textbf{false} \end{bmatrix} \tag{4}$$

which can be rewritten as,

$$A \wedge \neg T \wedge L \wedge \neg W \wedge \begin{bmatrix} (L \vee \neg L \wedge T \wedge \neg A) \wedge \neg\textbf{true} \\ \vee \\ (\neg L \wedge \neg T \vee \neg L \wedge T \wedge A) \wedge \neg\textbf{false} \end{bmatrix} \tag{5}$$

It is easy to conclude that Eq. 5 is inconsistent. Moreover, $\sigma = (L)$ denotes an MUS of Eq. 5 and denotes one abductive explanation for why the prediction is skips for the instance τ.

Local Contrastive Explanations (CXps). Suppose we compute instead an MCS ρ of Eq. 3, with $\rho \subseteq \tau$. As a result, $\bigwedge_{l \in \tau \setminus \rho} (l) \wedge \neg \mathcal{M}_\pi \nvDash \bot$ holds. Hence, assigning feature values to the inputs of the ML model is consistent with a prediction that is *not* π, i.e. a prediction of some value other than π. Observe that ρ is a subset-minimal set of literals which causes $\tau \setminus \rho \wedge \neg \mathcal{M}_\pi$ to be satisfiable, with any satisfying assignment yielding a prediction that is not π.

Proposition 2. *Local model-based contrastive explanations are MCSes of the pair* $(\mathcal{B}, \mathcal{R})$, $\tau \wedge \neg \mathcal{M}_\pi$, *where* $\mathcal{R} \triangleq \tau$ *and* $\mathcal{B} \triangleq \neg \mathcal{M}_\pi$.

Example 6. From Eq. 3 and Eq. 5 we can also compute $\rho \subseteq \tau$ such that $\tau \setminus \rho \wedge \neg \mathcal{M}_\pi \nvDash \perp$. For example $\rho = (\mathsf{L})$ is an MCS of Eq. 5[12]. Thus, from $\{\mathsf{A}, \neg\mathsf{T}, \neg\mathsf{W}\}$ we can get a prediction other than skips, by considering feature value $\neg\mathsf{L}$.

Duality Among Explanations. Given the results above, and the hitting set duality between MUSes and MCSes [11,68], we have the following.

Theorem 1. *AXps are MHSes of CXps and vice-versa.*

Proof. Immediate from Definition 3, Definition 4, Proposition 1, Proposition 2, and Theorem 4.4 and Corollary 4.5 of [68].   □

Proposition 1, Proposition 2, and Theorem 1 can now serve to exploit the vast body of work on the analysis of inconsistent formulas for computing both contrastive and abductive explanations and, arguably more importantly, to enumerate explanations. Existing algorithms for the extraction and enumeration of MUSes and MCSes require minor modifications to be applied in the setting of AXps and CXps. The resulting algorithms are briefly summarized in Sect. 4. Interestingly, a consequence of the duality is that computing an abductive explanation is *harder* than computing a contrastive explanation in terms of the number of calls to a decision procedure Sect. 4.

Discussion. As observed above, the contrastive explanations we are computing answer the question: 'Why (π and) not $\neg\pi$?'. A more general contrastive explanation would be 'Why (π and) not δ, with $\pi \neq \delta$?' [60]. Note that, since the prediction π is given, we are only interested in changing the prediction to either $\neg\pi$ or δ. We refer to answering the first question as a *basic* contrastive explanation, whereas answering the second question will be referred to as a *targeted* contrastive explanation, and written as CXp$_\delta$. The duality result between AXps and CXps in Theorem 1 applies *only* to basic contrastive explanations. Nevertheless, the algorithms for MCS extraction for computing a basic CXp can also be adapted to computing targeted CXps, as follows. We want a pick of feature values such that the prediction is δ. We start by letting all features to take any value, and such that the resulting prediction is δ. We then iteratively attempt to fix feature values to those in the given instance, while the prediction remains δ. This way, the set of literals that change value are a subset-minimal set of feature-value pairs that is sufficient for predicting δ. Finally, there are crucial differences between the duality result established in this section, which targets local explanations, and a recent result [39], which targets *global* explanations. Earlier work established a relation between prime implicants and implicates as a way to relate global abductive explanations and so-called counterexamples.

---

[12] Although in general not the case, in Example 5 and Example 6 an MUS of size 1 is also an MCS of size 1.

Algorithm 1. Enumeration of CXps

Function CXpEnum($\mathcal{M}_\pi$,$\mathcal{C}$, π)
    Input: $\mathcal{M}_\pi$: ML model, $\mathcal{C}$: Input cube, π: Prediction
    Variables: $\mathcal{N}$ and $\mathcal{P}$ defined on the variables of $\mathcal{C}$

1 $\mathcal{I} \leftarrow \emptyset$;   // Block CXps
2 **while** true **do**
3     $\mu \leftarrow$ ExtractCXp($\mathcal{M}_\pi$,$\mathcal{C}$,π,$\mathcal{I}$)
4   **if** $\mu = \emptyset$ **then break**;
5   ReportCXp(μ)
6     $\mathcal{I} \leftarrow \mathcal{I} \cup$ NegateLiteralsOf(μ)

In contrast, we delved into the fundamentals of reasoning about inconsistency, concretely the duality between MCSes and MUSes, and established a relation between model-based *local* AXps and CXps.

4 Extracting and Enumerating Explanations

The results of Sect. 3.3 enable exploiting past work on extracting and enumerating MCSes and MUSes to the setting of contrastive and abductive explanations, respectively. Perhaps surprisingly, there is a stark difference between algorithms for extraction and enumeration of contrastive explanations and abductive explanations. Due to the association with MCSes, one contrastive explanation can be computed with a logarithmic number of calls to a decision procedure [49]. Moreover, there exist algorithms for the direct enumeration of contrastive explanations [49]. In contrast, abductive explanations are associated with MUSes. As a result, any known algorithm for extraction of one abductive explanation requires at best a linear number of calls to a decision procedure [42,44,54,55], in the worst-case. Moreover, there is no known algorithm for the direct enumeration of abductive explanations, and so enumeration can be achieved only through the enumeration of contrastive explanations [23,48,49,53,56,57].

We apply state-of-the-art algorithms for the enumeration of MUSes and MCSes [8,9,29,48,49] to find all the abductive and contrastive explanations. Note that, as in the case of enumeration of MCSes and MUSes, enumeration of CXps is comparatively easier than enumeration of AXps. Algorithm 1 shows our application of MCS enumeration algorithm to the enumeration of CXps [49]. Other alternatives [29] could be considered instead. Algorithm 1 finds a CXp, blocks it and finds the next one until no more exists. To extract a single CXp, we can use a standard algorithm, e.g. [8,53,56,57]. In principle, enumeration of AXps can be achieved by computing all CXps and then computing all the minimal hitting sets of all CXps, as proposed in the propositional setting [49]. However, there are more efficient alternatives that we can adapt here [8,9,48,63]. Algorithm 2 applies [48] to the case of computing both AXps and CXps. The algorithm simultaneously searches for AXps and CXps and is based on the hitting set duality defined above.

Algorithm 2. Enumeration of AXps (and CXps)

Function XPENUM($\mathcal{M}_\pi$,$\mathcal{C}$, π)
    Input: $\mathcal{M}_\pi$: ML model, $\mathcal{C}$: Input cube, π: Prediction
    Variables: $\mathcal{N}$ and $\mathcal{P}$ defined on the variables of $\mathcal{C}$

1   $\mathcal{K} = (\mathcal{N},\mathcal{P}) \leftarrow (\emptyset,\emptyset)$;   `// Block AXps & CXps`
2   **while** true **do**
3       $(st_\lambda, \lambda) \leftarrow$ FindMHS($\mathcal{P}$,$\mathcal{N}$) ;   `// MHS of` $\mathcal{P}$ `st` $\mathcal{N}$
4   **if** $\neg st_\lambda$ **then break**;
5       $(st_\rho, \rho) \leftarrow$ SAT($\lambda \wedge \neg \mathcal{M}_\pi$)
6   **if** $\neg st_\rho$ **then**   `// entailment holds`
7   ReportAXp(λ)
8           $\mathcal{N} \leftarrow \mathcal{N} \cup$ NegateLiteralsOf(λ)
9   **else**
10          $\mu \leftarrow$ ExtractCXp($\mathcal{M}_\pi, \rho, \pi$)
11   ReportCXp(μ)
12          $\mathcal{P} \leftarrow \mathcal{P} \cup$ UseLiteralsOf(μ)

---

5 Experimental Evaluation

This section details the experimental evaluation to assess the practical feasibility and efficiency of the enumeration of abductive and contrastive explanations for a few real-world datasets, studied in the context of explainability and algorithmic fairness. To evaluate, we use Algorithm 1 and Algorithm 2 in Sect. 4[13].

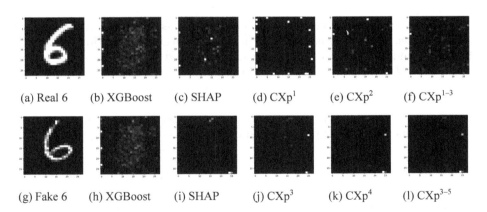

(a) Real 6   (b) XGBoost   (c) SHAP   (d) CXp^1 (e) CXp^2 (f) CXp$^{1-3}$

(g) Fake 6   (h) XGBoost   (i) SHAP   (j) CXp^3 (k) CXp^4 (l) CXp$^{3-5}$

Fig. 2. The 'real vs fake' images. The first row shows results for the real image 6; the second – results for the fake image 6. The first column shows examples of inputs; the second – heatmaps of XGBoost's important features; the third – heatmaps of SHAP's explanation. Last three columns show heatmaps of CXp of different cardinality. The brighter pixels are more influential features.

---

[13] The prototype and the experimental setup are available at https://github.com/alexeyignatiev/xdual.

5.1   Enumeration of CXps

Our experiments demonstrate a novel, unexpected practical use case of CXps enumeration algorithms. In particular, we show that our method gives a *new fine-grained view* on both global and local standard explanations extracted from ML models. The goal of these experiments is to *gain better understanding of existing explainers* rather than generate all CXps for a given input.

Setup. To perform enumeration of CXps in our first experiment, we use a constraint programming solver, ORtools [65]. To encode the enumeration problem with ORtools we converted scores of XGBoost models into integers keeping 5 digits precision. We enumerate contrastive explanations in the increasing order by their cardinality. This can be done by a simple modification of Algorithm 1 forcing it to return CXps in this order. So, we first obtain all minimum size contrastive explanations, and so on.

We conduct two sets of experiments. The first experiment, called "real vs fake", distinguishes real from fake images. A dataset contains two classes of images: (a) original MNIST digits and (b) fake MNIST digits produced by a standard DCGAN model [67] (see Fig. 2a and Fig. 2g for typical examples). The second experiment, called "3 vs 5 digits", uses a dataset that contains digits "3" and "5" from the standard MNIST dataset (these digits are similar in writing) and we distinguish "3" from "5" images.

Brief Overview of the SHAP Explainer. Given a classifier f and an explainer model g, SHAP aims to train g be similar to f in the neighborhood of some given point x. The objective function for SHAP is designed so that: (1) g approximates the behavior of the black box f accurately within the vicinity of x, and (2) g achieves lower complexity and is interpretable: $\xi(x) = \arg\min_{g \in G} L(\pi_x, g, f) + \Omega(g)$, where the loss function L is defined to minimize the distance between f and g in the neighborhood of x using a weight function π_x and $\Omega(g)$ quantifies the complexity of g; $\Omega(g)$ and π_x are defined based on game-theoretic notions [51]. We chose SHAP for our experiments due to its efficiency to generate an explanation (within seconds per input).

"Real vs Fake" Experiment. First, we discuss the results of the "real vs fake" experiment in details. We train an XGBoost model [14] with 100 trees of depth 6 (accuracy 0.85/0.80 on train/test sets). We quantized images so that each pixel takes a value between 0 and 15, image pixels are categorical features in the model.

Global and Local Explainers. We start by discussing our results on a few samples (Fig. 2a and Fig. 2g). First, we extract important features provided by XGBoost. As these features are *global* for the model, they are the same for all inputs (Fig. 2b and Fig. 2h are identical for real and fake images). Figure 2b shows that these important features are *no very informative* for this dataset as these pixels form a blob of pixels that cover an image. Then we compute an image-specific explanation using the standard explainer SHAP (see Fig. 2c for the real image and Fig. 2i for the fake image). SHAP explanations are more focused on specific parts of images compared to XGBoost. However, it is still not easy to gain insights about which areas of an image are more important as pixels all over the image participate in the explanations of SHAP and XGBoost. For example, both XGBoost and SHAP distinguish some edge and middle pixels as key pixels (the bright pixels are more important) but it is not clear why these are important pixels.

Enumeration. Our goal here is to investigate whether there is a connection between the important pixels that SHAP/XGBoost finds and CXps for a given image. The most surprising result is that, indeed, a connection exists and, for example, it reveals that the edge pixels of an image, highlighted by both SHAP and XGBoost as important pixels, are, reveal in fact, CXps of small cardinalities. For an image, we enumerate first 2000 CXps. Given all CXps of size k, we plot a heatmap of occurrences of each pixel in these CXps of size k. Let us focus on the first row with the real 6. Consider the heatmap CXp^1 at Fig. 2d that shows all CXps of size one for the real 6. It shows that most of important pixels of XGBoost and SHAP are actually CXps of size one. This means that *it is sufficient to change a single pixel value to some other value to obtain a different prediction.* Note that these results lead us to an interesting observation. DCGAN generates images with a few gray edges pixels (see Fig. 4. Indeed, some of them have several edge pixels in gray.) This 'defect' does not happen often for real MNIST images. Therefore, the classifier 'hooks' on this issue to classify an image as fake. Now, consider the heatmap CXp^2 at Fig. 2e of CXps of size two. It overlaps a lot with SHAP important pixels in the middle of the image explaining *why* these are important. Only a *pair* of these pixels can be changed to get a different prediction.

A Correlation Between CXps and SHAP's Important Features. To qualitatively measure our observations on correlation between key features of CXps and SHAP, we conducted the same experiment as above on 100 random images and measured the correlation between first CXps and SHAP features. First, we compute a set T of pixels that is the union of the first (top) 100 smallest size CXps. On average, we have 60 pixels in T. Note that the average 60 pixels represent a small fraction (7%) of the total number of pixels. Then we find a set S of $|T|$ SHAP pixels with highest absolute weights. Finally, we compute $corr = |S \cap T|/|S|$ as the correlation measure. Note that $corr = 0.4$ on average, i.e. our method hits 40% of best SHAP features. As the chances of two tools independently hitting the same pixel (out of 784) are quite low, the fact that 40% of $|S|$ are picked indicates a significant correlation.

"3 vs 5 Digits" Experiment. Consider our second the "3 vs 5 digits" experiment. We use a dataset that contains digits "3" (class 0) and "5" (class 1) from the standard MNIST (see Fig. 3a and Fig. 3g for representative samples).

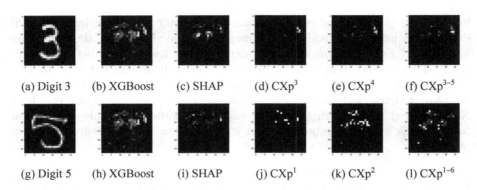

(a) Digit 3   (b) XGBoost   (c) SHAP   (d) CXp^3 (e) CXp^4 (f) CXp$^{3-5}$

(g) Digit 5   (h) XGBoost   (i) SHAP   (j) CXp^1 (k) CXp^2 (l) CXp$^{1-6}$

Fig. 3. Results of the 3 vs 5 digits experiments. The first row shows results for the image 3. The second row shows results for the image 5. The first column shows examples of inputs; the second column shows heatmaps of XGBoost's global important features; the third column shows heatmaps of SHAP's important features. Last three columns show heatmaps of CXp of different cardinality.

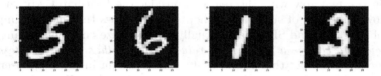

Fig. 4. Additional fake images. We reduced values of zero-valued pixels to highlight gray pixels on the edges for some fake images.

XGboost model has 50 trees of depth 3 with accuracy 0.98 (0.97) on train/test sets. We quantized images so that each pixel takes a value between 0 and 15. As before, each pixel corresponds to a feature. So, we have 784 features in our XGBoost model.

Global and Local Explainers. We start by discussing our results on few random samples (Fig. 3a and Fig. 3g). First, we obtain the important features from XGBoost. As these features are *global* for the model so they are the same for all inputs (Fig. 3b and Fig. 3h are identical for 3 and 5 images). Figure 2b shows that these important features. The important pixels highlight that the top parts of images are important, which is a plausible high-level explanation of the classifier behavior. Digits 3 and 5 are mostly differ in the top part of the image. However, some pixels are way more important than other and it is hard to understand why.

Next, we compute an image-specific explanation using the standard explainer SHAP (see Fig. 3c for the digit 3 and Fig. 3c for the digit 5). While SHAP explanations mimic XGBoost important features, they do provide additional insights for the user. Note that both XGBoost and SHAP mark a "belt" of pixels in the upper middle part that as important (bright pixels is the most important pixels).

Enumeration. We run our enumeration algorithm to produce CXps of increasing cardinality. For each image, we enumerate first 2000 CXps. Given all CXps of size k, we plot a heatmap of occurrences of each pixel in these CXps of size k. Let us focus on the second row with the digit 5. For example, CXp^2 (Fig. 3k) shows the heatmap of CXps of size two for the digit 5. As we mentioned above, both XGBoost and SHAP hint that the 'belt' of important pixels in the middle. Again, our method can explain *why* this is the case. Consider the heatmap CXp^1 at Fig. 3j. This picture shows all CXps of size one for the digit 5. It reveals that most of important pixels of XGBoost and SHAP are actually CXps of size one. We reiterate that it is sufficient to change a *single* pixel value to some other value to obtain a different prediction. Now, consider the heatmap CXp^{1-6} at Fig. 3l. This figure shows 2000 CXps (from size 1 to size 6). It overlaps a lot with SHAP important pixels in the middle of the image. So, these pixels occur in many small size CXps and changing their values leads to misclassification.

Correlation Between CXps and SHAP Features. To qualitatively measure our observations on correlation between key features of CXps and SHAP, we conducted the same experiment as above on 100 random images and measured the correlation between CXps and SHAP features. First, we compute a set T of pixels that is the union of the first (top) 100 smallest size CXps. On average, we have 38 pixels in T. Note that the average 38 pixels represent a small fraction (5%) of the total number of pixels. Then we find a set S of $|S|$ SHAP pixels with highest absolute weights. Finally, we compute $corr = |S \cap T|/|S|$ as the correlation measure. Note that $corr = 0.6$ on average, i.e. our method hits 60% of best SHAP features. As the chances of two tools independently hitting the same pixel (out of 784) are quite low, the fact that 60% of $|T|$ are picked indicates a significant correlation.

5.2   Enumeration of CXps and AXps

Datasets. Here, we aim at testing the *scalability* of explanation enumeration. The results are obtained on the six well-known and publicly available datasets. Three of them were previously studied in [70] in the context of heuristic explanation approaches, namely, Anchor [70] and LIME [69], including *Adult, Lending*, and *Recidivism*. These datasets were processed the same way as in [70]. The *Adult* dataset [46] is originally taken from the Census bureau and targets predicting whether or not a given adult person earns more than $50K a year depending on various attributes, e.g. education, hours of work, etc. The *Lending* dataset aims at predicting whether or not a loan on the Lending Club website will turn out bad. The *Recidivism* dataset was used to predict recidivism for individuals released from North Carolina prisons in 1978 and 1980 [73]. Two more datasets were additionally considered including *Compas* and *German* that were previously studied in the context of the FairML and Algorithmic Fairness projects [21,22,24,25], an area in which the need for explanations is doubtless. *Compas* is a popular dataset, known [4] for exhibiting racial bias of the COMPAS algorithm used for scoring criminal defendant's likelihood of reoffending.

Table 2. Results of the computational experiment on enumeration of AXps and CXps.

	Dataset					
	Adult	Lending	Recidivism	Compas	German	Spambase
# of instances	5579	4414	3696	778	1000	2344
Total time (sec.)	7666.9	443.8	3688.0	78.4	16943.2	6859.2
Minimal time (sec.)	0.1	0.0	0.1	0.0	0.2	0.1
Average time (sec.)	1.4	0.1	1.0	0.1	16.9	2.9
Maximal time (sec.)	13.1	0.8	8.9	0.5	193.0	23.1
Total oracle calls	492990	69653	581716	21227	748164	176354
Minimal oracle calls	14	11	17	13	23	12
Average oracle calls	88.4	15.8	157.4	27.3	748.2	75.2
Maximal oracle calls	581	73	1426	134	7829	353.
Total # of AXps	52137	8105	60688	1931.0	59222	18876
Average # of AXps	9.4	1.8	16.4	2.5	59.2	8.1
Average AXp size	5.3	1.9	6.4	3.8	7.5	4.6
Total # of CXps	66219	8663	77784	3558.0	66781	24774
Average # of CXps	11.9	2.0	21.1	4.6	66.8	10.6
Average CXp size	2.4	1.4	2.6	1.5	3.6	2.3

The latter dataset is a German credit data (e.g. see [22,25]), which given a list of people's attributes classifies them as good or bad credit risks. Finally, we consider the *Spambase* dataset from the UCI repository [20]. The main goal is to classify an email as spam or non-spam based on the words that occur in this email. Due to scalability constraints, we preprocessed the dataset to keep ten words per email that were identified as the most influential words by a random forest classifier.

Implementation and Setup. A prototype implementing Algorithm 2 targeting the enumeration of either (1) all abductive or (2) all contrastive explanations was created. In the experiment, the prototype implementation is instructed to enumerate all abductive explanations. (Note that, as was also mentioned before, no matter what kind of explanations Algorithm 2 aims for, all the dual explanations are to be computed as a side effect of the hitting set duality.) The prototype is able to deal with tree ensemble models trained with XGBoost [14]. For that purpose, a simple encoding of tree ensembles into satisfiability modulo theories (SMT) was developed. Concretely, the target formulas are in the theory of linear arithmetic over reals (RIA formulas). (Note that encodings of a decision tree into logic are known [12,50,78]. The final score summations used in tree ensembles can be encoded into RIA formulas.)

Due to the twofold nature of Algorithm 2, it has to deal with (1) implicit hitting set enumeration and (2) entailment queries with SMT. The former part is implemented using the award-winning maximum satisfiability solver RC2 [37] written on top of the PySAT toolkit [36]. SMT solvers are accessed through the

PySMT framework [27], which provides a unified interface to a variety of state-of-the-art SMT solvers. In the experiments, we use Z3 [17] as one of the best performing SMT solvers. The conducted experiment was performed in Debian Linux on an Intel Xeon E5-2630 2.60 GHz processor with 64GByte of memory. Given a dataset, we trained an XGBoost model containing 50 trees per class, each tree having depth 3. (Further increasing the number of trees per class and also increasing the maximum depth of a tree did not result in a significant increase of the models' accuracy on the training and test sets for the considered datasets.) All abductive explanations for every instance of each of the six datasets were exhaustively enumerated using the duality-based approach (Algorithm 2 in Algorithm 4). This resulted in the computation of all contrastive explanations as well).

Evaluation Results. Table 2 shows the results. There are several points to make. First, although it seems computationally expensive to enumerate all explanations for a data instance, it can still be achieved effectively for the medium-sized models trained for all the considered datasets. This may on average require from a few dozen to several hundred of oracle calls per data instance (in some cases, the number of calls gets up to a few thousand). Also observe that enumerating all explanations for an instance takes from a fraction of a second to a couple of seconds on average. These results demonstrate that our approach is practical.

Second, the total number of AXps is typically lower than the total number of their contrastive counterparts. The same holds for the average numbers of abductive and contrastive explanations per data instance. Third and finally, AXps for the studied datasets tend to be larger than contrastive explanations. The latter observations imply that contrastive explanations may be preferred from a user's perspective, as the smaller the explanation is the easier it is to interpret for a human decision maker. (Furthermore, although it is not shown in Table 2, we noticed that in many cases contrastive explanations tend to be of size 1, which makes them ideal to reason about the behaviour of an ML model.) On the other hand, exhaustive enumeration of contrastive explanations can be more time consuming because of their large number.

Summary of Results. We show that CXps enumeration gives us an insightful understanding of a classifier's behaviour. First, even in cases when we cannot enumerate all of CXps to compute AXps by duality, we can still draw some conclusions, e.g. CXps of size one are exactly features that occur in all AXps. Next, we clearly demonstrate the feasibility of the duality-based exhaustive enumeration of both AXps and CXps for a given data instance using a more powerful algorithm that performs enumeration of AXps and CXps.

6   Conclusions

This paper studies local model-based abductive and contrastive explanations. Abductive explanations answer 'Why?' questions, whereas contrastive explanations answer 'Why Not?' questions. Moreover, the paper relates explanations with the analysis of inconsistent theories, and shows that abductive explanations correspond to minimal unsatisfiable subsets, whereas contrastive explanations can be related with minimal correction subsets. As a consequence of this result, the paper exploits a well-known minimal hitting set relationship between MUSes and MCSes [11,68] to reveal the same relationship between abductive and contrastive explanations. In addition, the paper exploits known results on the analysis of inconsistent theories, to devise algorithms for extracting and enumerating abductive and contrastive explanations.

Acknowledgments. This work is supported by the AI Interdisciplinary Institute ANITI (Artificial and Natural Intelligence Toulouse Institute), funded by the French program "Investing for the Future – PIA3" under Grant agreement no ANR-19-PI3A-0004.

References

1. Achinstein, P.: The Nature of Explanation. Oxford University Press, Oxford (1980)
2. Adadi, A., Berrada, M.: Peeking inside the black-box: a survey on explainable artificial intelligence (XAI). IEEE Access **6**, 52138–52160 (2018)
3. Alonso, J.M., Castiello, C., Mencar, C.: A bibliometric analysis of the explainable artificial intelligence research field. In: Medina, J., et al. (eds.) IPMU 2018. CCIS, vol. 853, pp. 3–15. Springer, Cham (2018). https://doi.org/10.1007/978-3-319-91473-2_1
4. Angwin, J., Larson, J., Mattu, S., Kirchner, L.: Machine bias (2016). http://tiny.cc/dd7mjz
5. Anjomshoae, S., Najjar, A., Calvaresi, D., Främling, K.: Explainable agents and robots: results from a systematic literature review. In: AAMAS, pp. 1078–1088 (2019)
6. Asher, N., Paul, S., Russell, C.: Adequate and fair explanations. CoRR, abs/2001.07578 (2020)
7. Bacchus, F., Katsirelos, G.: Using minimal correction sets to more efficiently compute minimal unsatisfiable sets. In: Kroening, D., Păsăreanu, C.S. (eds.) CAV 2015. LNCS, vol. 9207, pp. 70–86. Springer, Cham (2015). https://doi.org/10.1007/978-3-319-21668-3_5
8. Bailey, J., Stuckey, P.J.: Discovery of minimal unsatisfiable subsets of constraints using hitting set dualization. In: Hermenegildo, M.V., Cabeza, D. (eds.) PADL 2005. LNCS, vol. 3350, pp. 174–186. Springer, Heidelberg (2005). https://doi.org/10.1007/978-3-540-30557-6_14
9. Bendík, J., Černá, I., Beneš, N.: Recursive online enumeration of all minimal unsatisfiable subsets. In: Lahiri, S.K., Wang, C. (eds.) ATVA 2018. LNCS, vol. 11138, pp. 143–159. Springer, Cham (2018). https://doi.org/10.1007/978-3-030-01090-4_9
10. Biran, O., Cotton, C.: Explanation and justification in machine learning: a survey. In: IJCAI-17 Workshop on Explainable AI (XAI), vol. 8, p. 1 (2017)
11. Birnbaum, E., Lozinskii, E.L.: Consistent subsets of inconsistent systems: structure and behaviour. J. Exp. Theoret. Artif. Intell. **15**(1), 25–46 (2003)
12. Bonfietti, A., Lombardi, M., Milano, M.: Embedding decision trees and random forests in constraint programming. In: Michel, L. (ed.) CPAIOR 2015. LNCS,

vol. 9075, pp. 74–90. Springer, Cham (2015). https://doi.org/10.1007/978-3-319-18008-3_6

13. Bromberger, S.: An approach to explanation. In: Butler, R. (ed.) Analytical Philsophy, pp. 72–105. Oxford University Press, Oxford (1962)
14. Chen, T., Guestrin, C.: XGBoost: a scalable tree boosting system. In: KDD, pp. 785–794. ACM (2016)
15. Darwiche, A.: Three modern roles for logic in AI. In: PODS, pp. 229–243 (2020)
16. Darwiche, A., Hirth, A.: On the reasons behind decisions. In: ECAI, pp. 712–720 (2020)
17. de Moura, L., Bjørner, N.: Z3: an efficient SMT solver. In: Ramakrishnan, C.R., Rehof, J. (eds.) TACAS 2008. LNCS, vol. 4963, pp. 337–340. Springer, Heidelberg (2008). https://doi.org/10.1007/978-3-540-78800-3_24
18. Dhurandhar, A., et al.: Explanations based on the missing: towards contrastive explanations with pertinent negatives. In: NIPS, pp. 590–601 (2018)
19. Dosilovic, F.K., Brcic, M., Hlupic, N.: Explainable artificial intelligence: a survey. In: MIPRO, pp. 210–215 (2018)
20. Dua, D., Graff, C.: UCI machine learning repository (2017)
21. Auditing black-box predictive models (2016). http://tiny.cc/6e7mjz
22. Feldman, M., Friedler, S.A., Moeller, J., Scheidegger, C., Venkatasubramanian, S.: Certifying and removing disparate impact. In: KDD, pp. 259–268. ACM (2015)
23. Felfernig, A., Schubert, M., Zehentner, C.: An efficient diagnosis algorithm for inconsistent constraint sets. Artif. Intell. Eng. Des. Anal. Manuf. **26**, 53–62 (2012)
24. Friedler, S., Scheidegger, C., Venkatasubramanian, S.: On algorithmic fairness, discrimination and disparate impact (2015)
25. Friedler, S.A., Scheidegger, C., Venkatasubramanian, S., Choudhary, S., Hamilton, E.P., Roth, D.: A comparative study of fairness-enhancing interventions in machine learning. In: FAT, pp. 329–338. ACM (2019)
26. Frosst, N., Hinton, G.E.: Distilling a neural network into a soft decision tree. In: CEx@AI*IA (2017)
27. Gario, M., Micheli, A.: PySMT: a solver-agnostic library for fast prototyping of SMT-based algorithms. In: SMT Workshop (2015)
28. Google. AI Explainability Whitepaper (2019). http://tiny.cc/tjz2hz
29. Grégoire, É., Izza, Y., Lagniez, J.: Boosting MCSes enumeration. In: IJCAI, pp. 1309–1315 (2018)
30. Guidotti, R., Monreale, A., Ruggieri, S., Turini, F., Giannotti, F., Pedreschi, D.: A survey of methods for explaining black box models. ACM Comput. Surv. **51**(5), 93:1–93:42 (2019)
31. Hoffman, R.R., Klein, G.: Explaining explanation, part 1: theoretical foundations. IEEE Intell. Syst. **32**(3), 68–73 (2017)
32. Hoffman, R.R., Miller, T., Mueller, S.T., Klein, G., Clancey, W.J.: Explaining explanation, part 4: a deep dive on deep nets. IEEE Intell. Syst. **33**(3), 87–95 (2018)
33. Hoffman, R.R., Mueller, S.T., Klein, G.: Explaining explanation, part 2: empirical foundations. IEEE Intell. Syst. **32**(4), 78–86 (2017)
34. Hoffman, R.R., Mueller, S.T., Klein, G., Litman, J.: Metrics for explainable AI: challenges and prospects. CoRR, abs/1812.04608 (2018)
35. Ignatiev, A.: Towards trustable explainable AI. In: IJCAI, pp. 5154–5158 (2020)
36. Ignatiev, A., Morgado, A., Marques-Silva, J.: PySAT: a Python toolkit for prototyping with SAT Oracles. In: Beyersdorff, O., Wintersteiger, C.M. (eds.) SAT 2018. LNCS, vol. 10929, pp. 428–437. Springer, Cham (2018). https://doi.org/10.1007/978-3-319-94144-8_26

37. Ignatiev, A., Morgado, A., Marques-Silva, J.: RC2: an efficient MaxSAT solver. J. Satisf. Boolean Model. Comput. **11**, 53–64 (2019)
38. Ignatiev, A., Narodytska, N., Marques-Silva, J.: Abduction-based explanations for machine learning models. In: AAAI, pp. 1511–1519 (2019)
39. Ignatiev, A., Narodytska, N., Marques-Silva, J.: On relating explanations and adversarial examples. In: NeurIPS, pp. 15857–15867 (2019)
40. Ignatiev, A., Narodytska, N., Marques-Silva, J.: On validating, repairing and refining heuristic ML explanations. CoRR, abs/1907.02509 (2019)
41. Izza, Y., Ignatiev, A., Marques-Silva, J.: On explaining decision trees. CoRR, abs/2010.11034 (2020)
42. Janota, M., Marques-Silva, J.: On the query complexity of selecting minimal sets for monotone predicates. Artif. Intell. **233**, 73–83 (2016)
43. Jha, S., Sahai, T., Raman, V., Pinto, A., Francis, M.: Explaining AI decisions using efficient methods for learning sparse Boolean formulae. J. Autom. Reasoning **63**(4), 1055–1075 (2019)
44. Junker, U.: QUICKXPLAIN: preferred explanations and relaxations for over-constrained problems. In: AAAI, pp. 167–172 (2004)
45. Klein, G.: Explaining explanation, part 3: the causal landscape. IEEE Intell. Syst. **33**(2), 83–88 (2018)
46. Kohavi, R.: Scaling up the accuracy of Naive-Bayes classifiers: a decision-tree hybrid. In: KDD, pp. 202–207 (1996)
47. Kroening, D., Strichman, O.: Decision Procedures - An Algorithmic Point of View. Texts in Theoretical Computer Science. An EATCS Series, 2nd edn. Springer, Heidelberg (2016). https://doi.org/10.1007/s10601-015-9183-0
48. Liffiton, M.H., Previti, A., Malik, A., Silva, J.M.: Fast, flexible MUS enumeration. Constraints **21**(2), 223–250 (2016). https://doi.org/10.1007/s10601-015-9183-0
49. Liffiton, M.H., Sakallah, K.A.: Algorithms for computing minimal unsatisfiable subsets of constraints. J. Autom. Reasoning **40**(1), 1–33 (2008). https://doi.org/10.1007/s10817-007-9084-z
50. Lombardi, M., Milano, M., Bartolini, A.: Empirical decision model learning. Artif. Intell. **244**, 343–367 (2017)
51. Lundberg, S.M., Lee, S.: A unified approach to interpreting model predictions. In: NIPS, pp. 4765–4774 (2017)
52. Marques-Silva, J., Gerspacher, T., Cooper, M.C., Ignatiev, A., Narodytska, N.: Explaining Naive Bayes and other linear classifiers with polynomial time and delay. In: NeurIPS (2020)
53. Marques-Silva, J., Heras, F., Janota, M., Previti, A., Belov, A.: On computing minimal correction subsets. In: IJCAI, pp. 615–622 (2013)
54. Marques-Silva, J., Janota, M., Belov, A.: Minimal sets over monotone predicates in Boolean formulae. In: Sharygina, N., Veith, H. (eds.) CAV 2013. LNCS, vol. 8044, pp. 592–607. Springer, Heidelberg (2013). https://doi.org/10.1007/978-3-642-39799-8_39
55. Marques-Silva, J., Janota, M., Mencía, C.: Minimal sets on propositional formulae. Problems and reductions. Artif. Intell. **252**, 22–50 (2017)
56. Mencía, C., Ignatiev, A., Previti, A., Marques-Silva, J.: MCS extraction with sublinear Oracle queries. In: Creignou, N., Le Berre, D. (eds.) SAT 2016. LNCS, vol. 9710, pp. 342–360. Springer, Cham (2016). https://doi.org/10.1007/978-3-319-40970-2_21
57. Mencía, C., Previti, A., Marques-Silva, J.: Literal-based MCS extraction. In: IJCAI, pp. 1973–1979 (2015)

58. Miller, T.: Contrastive explanation: a structural-model approach. CoRR, abs/1811.03163 (2018)
59. Miller, T.: "but why?" Understanding Explainable artificial intelligence. ACM Crossroads **25**(3), 20–25 (2019)
60. Miller, T.: Explanation in artificial intelligence: insights from the social sciences. Artif. Intell. **267**, 1–38 (2019)
61. Mittelstadt, B.D., Russell, C., Wachter, S.: Explaining explanations in AI. In: FAT, pp. 279–288 (2019)
62. Montavon, G., Samek, W., Müller, K.: Methods for interpreting and understanding deep neural networks. Digital Signal Process. **73**, 1–15 (2018)
63. Narodytska, N., Bjørner, N., Marinescu, M.V., Sagiv, M.: Core-guided minimal correction set and core enumeration. In: IJCAI, pp. 1353–1361 (2018)
64. Narodytska, N., Shrotri, A., Meel, K.S., Ignatiev, A., Marques-Silva, J.: Assessing heuristic machine learning explanations with model counting. In: Janota, M., Lynce, I. (eds.) SAT 2019. LNCS, vol. 11628, pp. 267–278. Springer, Cham (2019). https://doi.org/10.1007/978-3-030-24258-9_19
65. Perron, L., Furnon, V.: Or-tools
66. Poole, D., Mackworth, A.K.: Artificial Intelligence - Foundations of Computational Agents. Cambridge University Press, Cambridge (2010)
67. Radford, A., Metz, L., Chintala, S.: Unsupervised representation learning with deep convolutional generative adversarial networks. In: ICLR (2016)
68. Reiter, R.: A theory of diagnosis from first principles. Artif. Intell. **32**(1), 57–95 (1987)
69. Ribeiro, M.T., Singh, S., Guestrin, C.: "Why should I trust you?": explaining the predictions of any classifier. In: KDD, pp. 1135–1144 (2016)
70. Ribeiro, M.T., Singh, S., Guestrin, C.: Anchors: high-precision model-agnostic explanations. In: AAAI, pp. 1527–1535 (2018)
71. Samek, W., Montavon, G., Vedaldi, A., Hansen, L.K., Müller, K.-R. (eds.): Explainable AI: Interpreting, Explaining and Visualizing Deep Learning. LNCS (LNAI), vol. 11700. Springer, Cham (2019). https://doi.org/10.1007/978-3-030-28954-6
72. Samek, W., Müller, K.: Towards explainable artificial intelligence. In: Samek, et al. [71], pp. 5–22
73. Schmidt, P., Witte, A.D.: Predicting recidivism in North Carolina, 1978 and 1980. Inter-University Consortium for Political and Social Research (1988)
74. Shih, A., Choi, A., Darwiche, A.: Formal verification of Bayesian network classifiers. In: PGM, pp. 427–438 (2018)
75. Shih, A., Choi, A., Darwiche, A.: A symbolic approach to explaining Bayesian network classifiers. In: IJCAI, pp. 5103–5111 (2018)
76. Shih, A., Choi, A., Darwiche, A.: Compiling Bayesian network classifiers into decision graphs. In: AAAI, pp. 7966–7974 (2019)
77. Tran, S.N., d'Avila Garcez, A.S.: Deep logic networks: inserting and extracting knowledge from deep belief networks. IEEE Trans. Neural Netw. Learn. Syst. **29**(2), 246–258 (2018)
78. Verwer, S., Zhang, Y., Ye, Q.C.: Auction optimization using regression trees and linear models as integer programs. Artif. Intell. **244**, 368–395 (2017)
79. Xu, F., Uszkoreit, H., Du, Y., Fan, W., Zhao, D., Zhu, J.: Explainable AI: a brief survey on history, research areas, approaches and challenges. In: Tang, J., Kan, M.-Y., Zhao, D., Li, S., Zan, H. (eds.) NLPCC 2019. LNCS (LNAI), vol. 11839, pp. 563–574. Springer, Cham (2019). https://doi.org/10.1007/978-3-030-32236-6_51

Artificial Intelligence for an Ageing Society

Towards Positive Artificial Intelligence

Flavio S. Correa da Silva$^{(\boxtimes)}$

University of Sao Paulo, Rua do Matao 1010, Sao Paulo, SP, Brazil
fcs@usp.br

Abstract. *Positive Psychology* has been developed as a complement to traditional Psychology to cater for positive components of personality which can lead to sustainable satisfaction, happiness and well being. *Positive Technologies* have been developed to build technological tools to support Positive Psychology. *Artificial Intelligence* research has focused on the development of artefacts to relieve humans from undesired tasks, with lesser focus on artefacts to promote positive components towards well being and happiness. In this article, the concept of *Positive Artificial Intelligence* is proposed as a counterpart in Artificial Intelligence to the role Positive Psychology has played in Psychology.

Keywords: Positive technologies · AI for Good · Ageing society

1 Introduction

The works of Douglas Engelbart (1925–2013) and John McCarthy (1927–2011) were of fundamental importance for the development of computer technology. Engelbart was born in rural Oregon, northwestern US; McCarthy was born in industrialised Massachusets, northeastern US. Even though both developed most of their careers in California and their work seems, in retrospect, interconnected and interrelated, there are no historical indications that they ever worked together, despite being active at the same time and in the same region.

Engelbart decided in 1950 that he would design and engineer devices to augment human capabilities, so that humans could work collectively to solve complex problems and build a better world [28]. In 1957 he started to work at SRI International, where he started the *Augmentation Research Centre – ARC*, devoted to the development of methods, techniques and artefacts to broaden the spectrum of possibilities for human action and expression. Engelbart is considered one of the creators of the field of *Human-Machine Interaction*, and an advocate of computer technologies as means to promote human collaboration.

McCarthy organised the *Dartmouth Conference* in 1956, together with other scholars, as a two-months discussion aiming at the definition and structuring of the research area then coined *Artificial Intelligence*. In 1962, he became full

This work was developed with partial support from FAPESP *MCTIC/CGI – Future Internet for Smart Cities* and the INCT *InterSCity – Smart Cities*.

M. Baldoni and S. Bandini (Eds.): AIxIA 2020, LNAI 12414, pp. 359–371, 2021.
https://doi.org/10.1007/978-3-030-77091-4_22

professor at Stanford University, where he started the *Stanford AI Laboratory –
SAIL*. Artificial Intelligence has been since its inception a multifaceted endeav-
our. Several initiatives target the development of methods and techniques to
reconstruct intelligent behaviour in artefacts which could, ultimately, relieve
humans from unwanted activities which can be repetitive, strenuous and/or
potentially harmful.

This brief review of the work of founders of important areas in computer technology has the purpose of highlighting two complementary approaches to build
technologies that support human actions and interactions: a *positive* approach,
focusing on desired human capabilities to be enhanced *in* and *for the benefit
of humans*, and a *negative* approach, focusing on undesired human tasks and
traits to be *retracted from humans*, also *for the benefit of humans*. It resonates
with – and furthers – arguments presented by Winograd [44], suggesting that
the design of intelligent systems can be refined by accounting for both negative
and positive approaches.

The appropriateness of adoption of methodologies that encompass negative as well as positive approaches to design has been considered in different
domains. In *Positive Psychology*, similar arguments ground the proposition that
a *negative* approach – focusing on treatment of undesired psychological traits –
should be complemented by a *positive* approach – focusing on strengthening of
desired potentialities. *Positive Technologies* are an offspring of Positive Psychology towards the development of artefacts to support the flourishing of desired
potentialities.

In the present article the concept of *Positive Artificial Intelligence* is proposed as a complement to existing practices to design intelligent systems. The
article also brings forward the proposition that regulatory bodies concerned with
safety and ethical issues related to Artificial Intelligence should include strong
requirements related to Positive Artificial Intelligence in regulations, in order to
ensure that intelligent systems are not only harmless, but also useful. Section 2
contains a brief rendition of *Positive Psychology*. Section 3 contains a discussion
about *Positive Technologies*. Section 4 contains a brief presentation of intelligent
agents, highlighting how they could be enhanced by a positive approach to their
design. Section 5 brings forward the proposed concept of *Positive Artificial Intelligence*, including illustrative scenarios to characterise our proposition. Finally,
Sect. 6 contains some conclusions, discussion and proposed future work.

2   Positive Psychology

Positive Psychology has been developed since the 90s to contrast with "conventional psychology" – i.e. psychological methods based on psychoanalysis and
treatment of undesired hallmarks – by focusing on well being, happiness and
positivity [24]. It has been characterised as a branch of Psychology since the late
90s, with earlier roots in Humanistic Psychology [42], Logotherapy [15], Jungian
analysis and ancient Greek and Eastern philosophies [16,19,31].

Very briefly, Positive Psychology is grounded on the *PERMA* Theory proposed by Seligman [36] and the *Flow* Theory proposed by Csikszentmihalyi [9]:

- *PERMA* is an acronym for **P**ositive emotions, **E**ngagement, **R**elationships, **M**eaning and **A**chievement, which are identified as the five factors influencing the path towards a life of fulfilment and happiness.
- *Flow* is a state of awareness of inner and external events which leads to pleasure and satisfaction. A *state of Flow* is reached and sustained via the dynamic balance of perceived challenge and skills, which must be informed to the individual through feedback about inner and outer events and progress towards self determined goals.

Seligman and Csikszentmihalyi proposed a "Calculus of Well being" to clarify how "negative" and "positive" psychology could be balanced [37]. Resorting to a simplistic analogy with Newtonian mechanics, retraction of undesired psychological traits can neutralise acceleration of a patient towards an unwanted direction in life, but actual movement in a new direction can only be achieved by adding energy to potentialities that can overcome inertia and lead to a desired direction (Fig. 1).

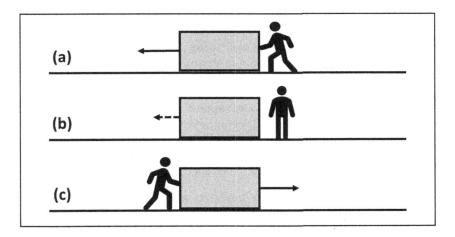

Fig. 1. Negative psychological traits move the individual (depicted as a block in this image) to one direction (a). In order to change direction of movement, it is necessary (1) to neutralise the negative traits (b), and also (2) to add enough energy to positive potentialities in order to overcome inertia and move to a new direction (c).

Seligman and Csikszentmihalyi, together with other scholars in Positive Psychology, also clarified the difference between *hedonic* and *eudaimonic* states, in order to highlight the importance of the latter over the former: hedonic forces – which relate to momentary pleasure, contentment and satisfaction – are not self sustained and require permanent extrinsic reinforcement, in contrast with eudaimonic forces – which relate to sensations of prosperity, blessedness and happiness, and are perennial or, at least, longlasting. Resorting to the same analogy with Newtonian mechanics, hedonic forces can change direction of movement of oneself but cannot alter friction that works to stop that movement in the long run, whereas eudaimonic forces change direction of movement *and* reduce friction towards zero.

A challenge to Positive Psychology has been the development of methods and techniques for effective interventions and assessment of results related to the strengthening of positive potentialities. *Positive Technologies* have been proposed as tools to enable controlled interventions and assessment methods.

3   Positive Technologies

Positive Technologies have been proposed to support Positive Psychology through artefact mediated, tangible and measurable actions and effects. In broad terms, Positive Technologies have addressed [18]:

- Mental health: promotion of Positive Psychology components in
  - patients in vulnerable situations;
  - patients presenting symptoms such as depression, eating disorders and other observable behaviours;
  - patients requiring emotion regulation.
- Neuro-rehabilitation: support to treatment of
  - patients with visuospatial partial disabilities;
  - patients in motor-cognitive neuro-rehabilitation;
  - patients with partial disabilities related to ageing.
- Empathy and pro-social behaviour: support to
  - patients with partial disabilities in development of empathy;
  - patients with partial learning disabilities;
  - scenarios in which cross-cultural integration is required.
- Self-transcendence: promotion of experiences that generate a state of *awe*.

Generally speaking, Positive Technologies must stand on three pillars:

1. Intervention: technology mediated construction of experiences that can induce states that promote Positive Psychology components.
2. Monitoring: (possibly quantified) assessment of effectiveness of intervention, through measurable surrogate markers such as
   - fluctuations in hemodynamic parameters [45],
   - occurrence and intensity of goosebumps [6,32],
   - monitoring and classification of micro-expressions, posture and gesture patterns [11].
3. Assessment: interpretation of monitored values and fluctuations based on theories grounded on Positive Psychology, often based on correlations between observations of values of markers and answers to standardised questionnaires such as Self-Regulation Questionnaires [5,25], Emotion-Regulation Questionnaires [21] and Technology-based Experience of Need Satisfaction Questionnaires [29].

An artefact whose design is based on these three pillars is capable of interventions which can be expected to help in the flourishing of Positive Psychology components, as validated by monitoring and empirical assessment.

If an artefact is comprised of technology to feature intelligent behaviour, it is called an *Intelligent Agent*. Intelligent Agents whose design is based on the three pillars of Positive Technology characterise Positive Artificial Intelligence. The following section contains a brief review of the concept of Intelligent Agents, as a final ingredient for the presentation of Positive Artificial Intelligence.

4   Intelligent Agents

Following the general literature about Artificial Intelligence [34,38], the field of Artificial Intelligence can be summarised as the scientific and technological development to build systems which can be organised according to two attributes:

1. *Structural/Imitative intelligence:*
   - Systems that are *inherently* intelligent by featuring structural organisation which aligns with explanatory theories of intelligence applicable to biological agents *versus*
   - Systems that are capable of *imitating* intelligent behaviour, regardless of their organisation; and
2. *Human/Mathematically defined rationality:*
   - Systems that adopt as reference for intelligence/intelligent behaviour human (or other biological) agents *versus*
   - Systems that adopt as reference some theory of rationality that characterises "optimal" intelligence in terms of efficiency in goal seeking.

The combination of possibilities builds four alternatives:

1. Systems that are approximately *intelligent as humans* (or other biological entities);
2. Systems that provide good approximate *imitations of intelligent behaviour* as observed in *humans* (or other biological entities);
3. Systems that are close to optimally aligned with *mathematical theories of rationality*; and
4. Systems that can generate outputs that are good approximations of what is determined by *mathematical theories of rationality*.

From an engineering standpoint, the focus in this article is on the second and fourth alternatives. Instead of considering them as a dichotomy, however, the consideration of a spectrum of possibilities is suggested, in which these attributes can be combined in different ways.

Mathematical theories of rationality are based on optimisation: how to optimally reach a (possibly multi-attribute) goal, maximising reward and minimising use of resources. When dealing with complex systems, it is frequently required to deal with incomplete mathematical models, in which equations and rules are not completely known or may not be analytically solvable. In such cases, surrogate systems must be developed, which are capable of *imitating* input-output behaviour of the complex systems being studied. Artificial Intelligence considering the fourth alternative above is about building such surrogate systems, which can be called *intelligent rational agents*.

Models of human behaviour are based on psychological theories and empirical data, which identify patterns in human behaviour and align these patterns with explanatory models. Artificial Intelligence considering the second alternative above is about building surrogate systems which are capable of *imitating* the behaviour of human agents when facing similar scenarios and stimuli. Such systems can be called *intelligent imitative agents*.

In general, these attributes are independent, and an intelligent agent can be better or worse as either an intelligent rational agent or an intelligent imitative agent. In some rare scenarios and problems, these attributes can be conflicting (e.g. when humans whose behaviour must be imitated show pathological self-destructive tendencies). In such cases, a choice must be made about giving priority to one of the attributes.

In both cases, another dimension for analysis and design of intelligent agents can be considered, which is coined here *degree of awareness of social interactions* and relates to the extent to which a designed agent includes consideration about relations with other agents – which can be other intelligent agents or humans (or other biological entities). In order to make the presentation clear, the spectrum of possibilities of awareness of social interactions is reduced to four values:

1. *Egocentric agents*, which only account for their own goals and resources and consider any other entity and event in the environment as either resources to be exploited or barriers to be overcome. Such agents correspond to what was considered during the pioneering development of Artificial Intelligence.
2. *Strategic agents*, which are aware of the existence of other agents, which also have goals and resources of their own, but still give full priority to management of their own resources to reach their own goals. These agents assume that the other agents will behave similarly, and build strategies which, in order to optimise their own goals and use of resources, may be mutually beneficial to other agents. Such agents correspond to what is considered in Classical Economics and Mathematical Game Theory [38].
3. *Social agents*, which take into account collective goals and resources and act to optimise them, considering long term goals that may outlive the agents themselves. Such agents consider the benefit of the collectivity and of future generations as well as their own.
4. *Empathic agents*, which are capable of "wearing other agents' shoes", balance the importance of their own goals with respect to those of other agents and decide for actions based on social emotions [22].

In this spectrum, each value adds to the previous one on refinement and, as a consequence, complexity of modelling of agent interactions: strategic agents are egocentric agents *plus* awareness of existence of other agents; social agents are strategic agents *plus* awareness of collective goals; and empathic agents are social agents *plus* awareness of (or "sensitivity" to) motivations based on social emotions.

Increased awareness of social interactions makes room for the design and development of intelligent agents capable of more effective human-agent interactions, which is fundamental to build intelligent agents as Positive Technologies – hence, *Positive Artificial Intelligence*.

5   Positive Artificial Intelligence

Ultimately, intelligent agents are designed and developed to serve human needs, hence – directly or indirectly – intelligent agents exist to interact with humans.

In some cases the interactions are more evident, e.g. when agents interact with humans as artefacts designed for end users. In all cases, consideration of the widest possible spectrum of consequences of interactions with intelligent agents is advised, and has become object of attention of scholars and regulatory agencies.

The ACM and the IEEE have prepared general Codes of Ethics for professionals in Computer Science and Engineering, catering specifically for autonomous and intelligent agents in specialised sections [1, 40], and specialised institutes and laboratories connected to well established universities have been structured to work on topics related to how to ensure that intelligent agents are used to promote well being following carefully crafted ethics guidelines[1].

Adopting a terminology suggested by Peters et al. [30], there has been an imbalance towards *"nonmaleficence"* over *beneficence* in the design of intelligent agents, i.e. codes and regulations have focused on what should be avoided to prevent harmful interactions, instead of what should be ensured to promote positive interactions (an important exception to this trend being the work of Peters et al. [29,30]).

Priority to "nonmaleficence" seems to be prevalent for certification and quality assurance, with regulations focusing on risk mitigation to avoid undesired behaviour of systems (see e.g. the preliminary proposal developed by the FDA – U.S. Food and Drugs Administration – to regulate *Artificial Intelligence and Machine Learning in Software as a Medical Device* [14]). This seems necessary, although not sufficient for interactive systems, and regulations must be complemented by requirements to ensure beneficence as well as "nonmaleficence".

The fundamental proposition in this article is precisely that, in order for intelligent agents that interact directly with end users to be certified by regulatory bodies, these agents should be required not only to ensure that all measures were taken to mitigate risks and avoid undesired issues, but also that interactions were designed following strict guidelines to ensure that positive outcomes are likely to result to users. As a common reference to characterise the practice of inclusion of attributes in intelligent agents to promote positive outcomes from

---

[1] see e.g. *Positive Computing* (http://www.positivecomputing.org/) and the *AI Now Institute* (https://ainowinstitute.org/).

interactions, the framework of *Blue Zones* is adopted [4,23]. Blue Zones are communities around the world which share empirically observable characteristics in their citizens: longevity, high sense of satisfaction with respect to life as a whole, good health and well being. Interestingly, these communities also share patterns in everyday habits, culture, family structure and social interactions, although disguised according to local culture and traditions. The first five Blue Zones that were studied are located in disparate locations such as Okinawa (Japan), Ogliastra (Sardinia, Italy), Ikaria (Greece), Loma Linda (Californa, US) and Nicoya (Costa Rica).

The common patterns in all Blue Zones produce observable hallmarks which can be assessed as markers of the "Blue Zone effect". These hallmarks can be summarised as:

- Having a physically active everyday life;
- Having frequent, small and well-balanced meals;
- Having a sense of community belonging such as what you get by surrounding yourself with friends, families and neighbours; and
- Finding a sense of purpose.

It is interesting to notice the correlation between these hallmarks and the *PERMA* Theory of Positive Psychology:

- A physically active life can bring a sense of **A**chievement, foster **P**ositive emotions and promote **E**ngagement;
- Similarly, carefully managed meals can leverage on a sense of **A**chievement, **E**ngagement and **P**ositive emotions;
- A sense of community belonging is directly related to **E**ngagement and **R**elationships;
- Finding a sense of purpose directly relates to finding **M**eaning, which in turn directly relates to **P**ositive emotions, **E**ngagement, **R**elationships and **A**chievement.

In the following paragraphs this proposition is illustrated with concrete scenarios, taking into account designed actions of intelligent agents which are potentially capable of leveraging these hallmarks.

5.1   Illustrative Scenario I: Improvements in Walking Experience for Elderly Pedestrians in Urban Roads

Two important trends can be observed globally: urbanisation and ageing[2]. Therefore, it is important to develop technologies to improve the quality of experience of elderly citizens as pedestrians in urban environments.

Several projects have been developed to study the behaviour of pedestrians in specific contexts [12,39], and several of these projects focus on the ageing

---

[2] see e.g. https://ourworldindata.org/ for up to date statistical data.

population [3,7,20]. Most projects focus on safety issues and how to improve safety through smart design and interactions with intelligent agents.

These are important issues, which nevertheless should be complemented with design practices and features in intelligent agents to cater for positive components [2,8,10,13,26]. Some aspects that can be considered, directly accounting for each of the *PERMA* factors, are:

- Route selection taking into account alternative routes which can include short detours along pleasant neighbourhoods.
- Insertion of game related features in route selection, to promote physical activity as well as socialisation through competition.
- Suggestion of routes that can increase probability of pleasant social encounters with friends, family members and acquaintances, to strengthen an awareness of existing relationships.
- Identification of opportunities for action that can bring utility to other individuals and the community as a whole while *en route*, this way strengthening a personal sense of purpose as well as community belonging.
- Suggestion of routes that visit "memorable spots" capable of arising reminiscences which indicate and acknowledge important achievements in life, such as schools, workplaces and locations devoted to cultural activities such as theatres and music halls.

Each of these aspects must be personalised, hence intelligent agents designed to account for *PERMA* must be prepared to adapt to individual taste and preferences. Personalisation, in this case, refers to psychological traits and values such as taste, preferences (which can be based on aesthetics, personal history, values, tradition etc.) and perceived capabilities, potentialities, scale of values and sense of community belonging. All these aspects are highly dynamic and directly related to the dynamics of interactions (1) between individuals, (2) between individuals and society, and (3) between individuals and artefacts comprising intelligent agents. Hence, contrasting with intelligent agents that are built considering only safety – which can be developed based on different possibilities in the spectrum of awareness of social interactions – the design of agents to interact with humans accounting for positive components *requires* empathy, which encompasses all other possibilities in the spectrum.

Design practices such as the ones sketched in the previous paragraphs, together with design patterns that can enable them, can be clearly characterised. Our strong claim in this article is that organisations devoted to the development of rules and regulations for certification of intelligent systems *should add* to their already existing norms specific design rules catering for positive components, and explicitly verify and require alignment with these rules for certification.

5.2 Illustrative Scenario II: Extended Interaction with Medical Devices for Treatment of Noncommunicable Diseases

Traditional medicine in China was centred around the *village doctors*, also referred to as *barefoot doctors*[3]. An interesting practice which is now withering away is to have village doctors remunerated by healthy villagers – citizens who fell sick would stop contributing to the remuneration of the doctor, and only start contributing again when they were again fit for work. This way, village doctors would focus on healthcare, instead of treatment, contrasting with Western practice.

In recent years, there has been growing interest in *Precision Medicine*, which has proven to be relevant particularly for patients who may be sensitive to the side effects of medications and treatments, e.g. older adults with cancer, who may need treatment based on radiotherapy and chemotherapy, which can cause longstanding, highly debilitating side effects and be aggressive to any patient, particularly to elderly individuals [17, 27].

This specific scenario illustrates a situation in which conventional Western medicine (which is *negative* in the sense of Positive Psychology) is obviously important but, also, clearly not sufficient. Novel technologies for Precision Medicine *should include, as a requirement from regulatory agencies,* functionalities to cater for *positive* components of well being for patients.

Two concrete examples which illustrate possibilities in this direction are:

1. An innovative medical device has been developed to treat specific types of cancer using electromagnetic fields to promote well being and decelerate the growth of tumours, which are calibrated for individual patients based on a database of previous treatments and Machine Learning techniques that classify patients by similarity with previous patients with respect to specific physiological response to stimuli [35]. Even though this initiative is still aligned with the perspective of Western medicine, the proposed measurement of success of treatment is based on a *Quality of Life Index*, instead of simplistic measurements such as growth ratio of tumours.
2. More directly to the point, studies have been developed to assess how technologies based on virtual reality, tele-presence and interaction with intelligent agents can be employed as Positive Technologies during treatment of patients with COVID-19 [33].

Possible convergence of these two initiatives could lead to enriched devices and treatment protocols which can complement therapies with decreased harmful side effects with immediate, medium and long term interventions such as:

– Incorporation of ludified and gamified experiences during treatment sessions, e.g. based on virtual reality that can promote *P*ositive emotions related to a sense of *A*chievement and *E*ngagement, as well as resources based on tele-presence that can promote *R*elationships and a sense of community belonging during treatments;

---

[3] see e.g. https://www.who.int/bulletin/volumes/86/12/08-021208/en/.

– Incorporation of followup experiences to manage diet, physical activities and long term outpatient treatment, which can also be ludified and gamified and promote *P*ositive emotions, *E*ngagement, *R*elationships, and a sense of *A*chievement;
– Incorporation of resources to promote participation in communities of support which can encourage proper management of treatment, reintroduction in social and professional activities – including support for self reinvention – and induction to transition from passive to active participation in such communities, therefore promoting a renovated sense of *M*eaning for recovered patients.

Functionalities to ensure positive components as the ones suggested in the previous paragraphs can be characterised based on design principles, which should be included by regulatory bodies as requirements for certification of novel devices and protocols for treatment of patients. This would bring Western medicine closer to a holistic and hence more effective approach to treatment, moving from *Precision Medicine* to *Precision Health and Care* [41,43].

6   Conclusion

In this article the concept of *Positive Artificial Intelligence* has been introduced, based on a particular view about the evolution of Artificial Intelligence and how the design of intelligent agents can be improved to include features that can promote well being.

This concept is illustrated with sketches of agent design which are *feasible, viable* and *desirable* [41]. The article brings forward the proposition that regulatory bodies in charge of certification of systems that embed intelligent agents should include explicit requirements catering for Positive Psychology components for certification.

Planned future work shall follow at least two lines:

1. Experimental design of intelligent agents focusing on Positive Psychology components, to build evidence of feasibility of what is proposed here; and
2. Development of concrete propositions of requirements that could be incorporated in existing standards and norms for certification of systems.

References

1. Anderson, R.E.: ACM code of ethics and professional conduct. Commun. ACM **35**(5), 94–99 (1992)
2. Avento, N.: Independent living in age-friendly cities: study on dyads of elderly pedestrians walking dynamics. Ph.D. thesis, Università degli Studi di Milano-Bicocca (2015)
3. Bandini, S., Crociani, L., Gorrini, A., Vizzari, G.: Crossing behaviour of the elderly: Road safety assessment through simulations. In: AIxAAL at AIxIA, pp. 4–16 (2017)
4. Buettner, D.: The secrets of long life. Natl. Geogr. **208**(5), 2–27 (2005)

5. Carey, K.B., Neal, D.J., Collins, S.E.: A psychometric analysis of the self-regulation questionnaire. Addict. Behav. **29**(2), 253–260 (2004)
6. Chirico, A., Ferrise, F., Cordella, L., Gaggioli, A.: Designing awe in virtual reality: an experimental study. Front. Psychol. **8**, 2351 (2018)
7. Choi, J., Tay, R., Kim, S., Jeong, S.: Behaviors of older pedestrians at crosswalks in south Korea. Accid. Anal. Prev. **127**, 231–235 (2019)
8. Costa, L.V., Veloso, A., Loizou, M., Arnab, S., Tomlins, R., Sukumar, A.P.: "What a mobility-limited world": design requirements of an age-friendly playable city. Preprints (2018)
9. Csikszentmihalyi, M., Abuhamdeh, S., Nakamura, J., et al.: Flow (1990)
10. Distefano, N., Pulvirenti, G., Leonardi, S.: Neighbourhood walkability: elderly's priorities. Res. Transp. Bus. Manag. 100547 (2020)
11. Ekman, P.: Emotions revealed. Bmj **328**(Suppl S5) (2004)
12. Feliciani, C., Gorrini, A., Crociani, L., Vizzari, G., Nishinari, K., Bandini, S.: Calibration and validation of a simulation model for predicting pedestrian fatalities at unsignalized crosswalks by means of statistical traffic data. J. Traffic Transp. Eng. (Engl. Ed.) **7**(1), 1–18 (2020)
13. Fietkau, J.: The case for including senior citizens in the playable city. In: Proceedings of the International Conference on Web Intelligence, pp. 1072–1075 (2017)
14. US Food and Drug Administration, et al.: Proposed regulatory framework for modifications to artificial intelligence. Machine Learning (AI/ML)-based Software as a Medical Device (SaMD) (2019). https://www.fda.gov/media/122535/download
15. Frankl, V.E.: Man's Search for Meaning. Simon and Schuster, New York (1985)
16. Froh, J.J.: The history of positive psychology: truth be told. NYS Psychol. **16**(3), 18–20 (2004)
17. Fumagalli, C., et al.: Molecular profile of advanced non-small cell lung cancers in octogenarians: the door to precision medicine in elderly patients. J. Clin. Med. **8**(1), 112 (2019)
18. Gaggioli, A., Villani, D., Serino, S., Banos, R., Botella, C.: Positive technology: designing e-experiences for positive change. Front. Psychol. **10**, 1571 (2019)
19. Gillham, J.E., Seligman, M.E.: Footsteps on the road to a positive psychology. Behav. Res. Ther. **37**(1), S163 (1999)
20. Gorrini, A., Vizzari, G., Bandini, S.: Age and group-driven pedestrian behaviour: from observations to simulations. Collective Dyn. **1**, 1–16 (2016)
21. Gullone, E., Taffe, J.: The emotion regulation questionnaire for children and adolescents (ERQ-CA): a psychometric evaluation. Psychol. Assess. **24**(2), 409 (2012)
22. Hareli, S., Parkinson, B.: What's social about social emotions? J. Theory Soc. Behav. **38**(2), 131–156 (2008)
23. Hitchcott, P.K., Fastame, M.C., Penna, M.P.: More to blue zones than long life: positive psychological characteristics. Health Risk Soc. **20**(3–4), 163–181 (2018)
24. Kitson, A., Prpa, M., Riecke, B.E.: Immersive interactive technologies for positive change: a scoping review and design considerations. Front. Psychol. **9**, 1354 (2018)
25. Levesque, C.S., Williams, G.C., Elliot, D., Pickering, M.A., Bodenhamer, B., Finley, P.J.: Validating the theoretical structure of the treatment self-regulation questionnaire (TSRQ) across three different health behaviors. Health Educ. Res. **22**(5), 691–702 (2007)
26. Musselwhite, C.: Creating a convivial public realm for an ageing population. Being a pedestrian and the built environment. In: Transport, Travel and Later Life, p. 129 (2017)
27. Novelli, G., Biancolella, M., Latini, A., Spallone, A., Borgiani, P., Papaluca, M.: Precision medicine in non-communicable diseases. High-throughput **9**(1), 3 (2020)

28. O'Brien, T.: Douglas Engelbart's lasting legacy. San Jose Mercury News (1999)
29. Peters, D., Calvo, R.A., Ryan, R.M.: Designing for motivation, engagement and wellbeing in digital experience. Front. Psychol. **9**, 797 (2018)
30. Peters, D., Vold, K., Robinson, D., Calvo, R.A.: Responsible AI–two frameworks for ethical design practice. IEEE Trans. Technol. Soc. **1**(1), 34–47 (2020)
31. Peterson, C., Park, N., et al.: Meaning and positive psychology. Int. J. Existent. Posit. Psychol. **5**(1), 7 (2014)
32. Quesnel, D., Riecke, B.E.: Are you awed yet? How virtual reality gives us awe and goose bumps. Front. Psychol. **9**, 2158 (2018)
33. Riva, G., Mantovani, F., Wiederhold, B.K.: Positive technology and COVID-19. Cyberpsychol. Behav. Soc. Netw. **23**, 581–587 (2020)
34. Russell, S.J., Norvig, P.: Artificial Intelligence: A Modern Approach, 4th edn. Pearson, London (2020)
35. Santana, E., et al.: 1604p exposure to low energy amplitude modulated radiofrequency electromagnetic fields (EMF) is associated with rapid improvement in quality of life (QoL) status in patients with advanced hepatocellular carcinoma (HCC), using various analyses of EORTC-C30. Ann. Oncol. **30**(Supplement_5), mdz261-006 (2019)
36. Seligman, M.E.: Flourish: A Visionary New Understanding of Happiness and Well-Being. Simon and Schuster, New York (2012)
37. Seligman, M.E., Csikszentmihalyi, M.: Positive psychology: an introduction. Am. Psychol. **55**(1), 5–14 (2000)
38. Shoham, Y., Leyton-Brown, K.: Multiagent Systems: Algorithmic, Game-Theoretic, and Logical Foundations. Cambridge University Press, Cambridge (2009)
39. Silva, J.C.C., Correa da Silva, F.S.: Contextual analysis of pedestrian mobility in transport terminals (2020, submitted)
40. Spiekermann, S.: Ieee p7000–the first global standard process for addressing ethical concerns in system design. In: Multidisciplinary Digital Publishing Institute Proceedings, vol. 1, no. 3, p. 159 (2017)
41. Starkweather, A., et al.: The use of technology to support precision health in nursing science. J. Nurs. Scholarsh. **51**(6), 614–623 (2019)
42. Taylor, E.: Positive psychology and humanistic psychology: a reply to Seligman. J. Humanist. Psychol. **41**(1), 13–29 (2001)
43. VanderWeele, T.J., McNeely, E., Koh, H.K.: Reimagining health–flourishing. JAMA **321**(17), 1667–1668 (2019)
44. Winograd, T.: Shifting viewpoints: artificial intelligence and human–computer interaction. Artif. Intell. **170**, 1256–1258 (2006)
45. Yamaguchi, D., Tezuka, Y., Suzuki, N.: The differences between winners and losers in competition: the relation of cognitive and emotional aspects during a competition to hemodynamic responses. Adapt. Hum. Behav. Physiol. **5**(1), 31–47 (2019). https://doi.org/10.1007/s40750-018-0104-5

Management at the Edge of Situation Awareness During Patient Telemonitoring

Carmelo Ardito[2] , Tommaso Di Noia[2] , Corrado Fasciano[1,2] ,
Domenico Lofù[1,2] , Nicola Macchiarulo[1,3] , Giulio Mallardi[1,2] ,
Andrea Pazienza[1(✉)] , and Felice Vitulano[1]

[1] Innovation Lab, Exprivia S.p.A., Via A. Olivetti 11, 70056 Molfetta, Italy
{corrado.fasciano,domenico.lofu,nicola.macchiarulo,
giulio.mallardi,andrea.pazienza,felice.vitulano}@exprivia.com
[2] Polytechnic University of Bari, Via E. Orabona 4, 70125 Bari, Italy
{carmelo.ardito,tommaso.dinoia,
corrado.fasciano,domenico.lofu,giulio.mallardi}@poliba.it
[3] University of Bari Aldo Moro, Via E. Orabona 4, 70125 Bari, Italy
nicola.macchiarulo@uniba.it

Abstract. The SARS-CoV-2 pandemic has brought unexpected new scenarios in patient-care journeys and has accelerated this innovative process in the healthcare sector, demonstrating the importance of a systemic rethinking of remote care, mostly when patients are discharged from the hospital and continue their therapies at home in autonomy. The possibility to remotely monitor patients at home by means of smart sensors and medical devices has a dramatic impact on the quality of health services. Situation awareness plays an essential role in the decision-making process about the users, patients in this case, and their behaviors. Leveraging an Edge Computing framework, with embedded Artificial Intelligence capabilities to process near real-time data gathered from connected smart devices, would provide automatic decision support, thus improving the physicians' course of action. In this paper we introduce, within an Edge AI framework, a dedicated module, called Clinical Pathway Adherence Checker (CPAC), which identifies the discrepancies between the modeled clinical pathway and the observed one by means of process mining techniques, and hence detecting early clinical deterioration of patient conditions. Also, further analyses are conducted in the anomaly detection at the Edge that may occur during the health data transmission process.

Keywords: Situation awareness · eHealth · Clinical pathway ·
Internet of medical things · Ambient assisted living · Edge computing ·
Process mining · SARS-CoV-2

1 Introduction

Situation Awareness (SA), already known as Situational Awareness, is an acclaimed decision process to maintain and understand what is happening in

© Springer Nature Switzerland AG 2021
M. Baldoni and S. Bandini (Eds.): AIxIA 2020, LNAI 12414, pp. 372–387, 2021.
https://doi.org/10.1007/978-3-030-77091-4_23

a certain situation and leverage this information to avoid or mitigate eventual risks. In the recent years, this trend is gaining strong interest in the eHealth sector [8,31], since several stakeholders, including domain experts, investors, and researchers, started to leverage awareness and clinical decision-making. One of the objectives of SA in eHealth is to personalize for every patient the therapeutic path, often referred as Clinical Pathway [13,15], including both the biological characteristics of the pathology, and the aspects of the clinical history, along with the characteristic elements, and the living environment. Despite the advantages given by its applicability, several studies relating to SA in eHealth, and in particular to the Clinical Pathway, offers several lines of research for still unsolved problems. The clinical path, in fact, is manifold and complex [29]: it is not limited only to the moment of the medical consultation or diagnostic examination, but it includes a series of tasks that can be carried out independently by the patient without being monitored by the healthcare staff.

Over the last year, the national health services of different countries have been affected by a substantial and dynamic downsizing of resources and, despite this, they have managed to withstand, albeit with difficulty, the impact of the health emergency related to SARS-CoV-2 [9]. In this scenario, Telemedicine –a particular sub-field of eHealth– arises as a necessary alternative form of care pathways management, allowing remote monitoring of the patient at home. In this perspective, individual patients are encouraged to handle their activities to be managed autonomously, that is, without the medical supervision until a follow-up, in the form of an in-hospital visit or a televisit, which determines an conceptual check-point. Considering the phase of medical-unsupervised clinical pathway management, we envision an autonomous supervision of the patient care to be delegated to an intelligent multi-agent system whose architecture can deal with the specific clinical sub-path for the discharged patient, also verifying its validation by a doctor or nurse, and ensuring compliance with the actual prescriptions. This proposal would bring numerous benefits not only to patients but also especially to caregivers, as telemonitoring-related activities deal with mitigating challenging problems in the Healthcare sector.

This challenging goal recalls the theme known as "domiciliary hospitalization", addressed with Ambient Assisted Living (AAL), a branch of Artificial Intelligence (AI), in which mobile technologies support patients at home with a continuous telemonitoring of their health conditions, addressing the case of clinical worsening which may require the backing of health personnel. Intelligent medical devices and sensors from the world of the Internet of Medical Things (IoMT), along with ambient and interactive devices with limited processing and storage capabilities, make it possible to say that each device connected to a smart home can transmit data that is useful for being aggregated, analyzed and processed. In this way, machine learning (ML) algorithms can be leveraged to provide predictive diagnostics that promote, adapt, and validate to the in-home patient's normal activities. Thus, the patient's tasks would be validated to her attached clinical path, that can be managed as a workflow in an evaluation phase of the Process Mining activity, such as [27]. Faced with this complex task, how-

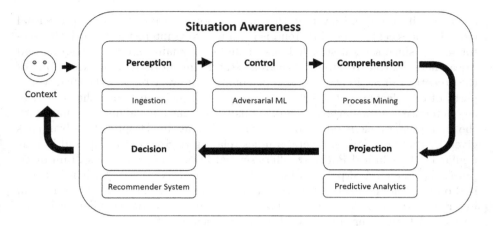

Fig. 1. An Overview of technical model of SA in eHealth.

ever, data security must not be overlooked. A reliable SA system in the eHealth and AAL scenario would be able to avoid the processing of false or inconsistent data, which could be life-threatening for a patient.

Therefore, in this paper, starting from the Edge Computing architecture, already proposed in [5], we extend the work presenting a new intelligent software module aimed at checking the adherence to the clinical pathway assigned to a patient at home being remotely monitored, which we call CPAC: Clinical Pathway Adherence Checker.

The remainder of the paper is structured as follows Sect. 2 provides an overview of related work and technologies which were investigated as background knowledge. Similarities, distinctions, and advancements of our approach in a comparison to them are briefly discussed. Section 3 recalls the Edge architecture which leverages on cloud, edge nodes and medical end-devices to perform AI tasks such as Process Mining and Machine Learning. Section 4 describes a possible scenario of a patient with SARS-CoV-2 symptoms that has to manage her clinical path in her home. Finally, Sect. 5 concludes the paper, with an outline of future work.

2   Background and Related Work

A desirable condition for providing digital support for strategic decisions during critical situations can be achieved through an SA approach. This is evidenced by the recent health crisis due to the COVID-19 pandemic [14]. Specifically, SA provides a series of techniques and tools to ensure a correct perception, in real time, of what happens in operational scenarios through the punctual analysis of information from a multitude of heterogeneous sources. In Fig. 1, we can see the chain of SA. In the clinical setting, the methods of intervention are always conditioned by the following parameters [6]:

1. *Perception* is related to data that comes from the context: in this sense, *Data Ingestion*, as a first step, collects data from all health information systems and standardizes it into a single formalism.
2. *Control* acts on the reliability of perceived data: *Adversarial Machine Learning* is an important area of Machine Learning that can help improve the reliability of systems and protect ingested data from fraudulent attacks in the healthcare sector where disinformation could endanger and compromise the health of patients [11].
3. *Comprehension* is related to the ability to understand the situation: this is why *Process Mining* for healthcare is an appropriate method to extract information from event logs that are scattered throughout the health system and to define (work-)flows to be analyzed.
4. *Projection* is the ability to prevent future events: for this reason *Predictive Analytics*, by means of Supervised Machine Learning techniques, is a good candidate to predict the flow trend in the system in order to monitor the growth likelihood of critical conditions.
5. *Decision* is the reasoned choice of one of the various possibilities of action or behavior in the face of a situation: *Recommender Systems* may help in personalizing the decision according to previous choices or any similar choices made by others, regardless that the choice is made by a human or an agent.

To achieve greater awareness, it is necessary to monitor the situation rigorously and continuously, through an evaluation process capable of detecting successes and possible bottlenecks of a system. Telemedicine, in this case, allows us to complete this task. On the other hand, data is only useful when analyzed. Therefore, the AI techniques, previously described at a high level, can help to perform an SA of the health system, returning an accurate overview. Process Mining techniques are particularly important in eHealth as they are particularly rich in sequential data, even if unexplored. It would become essential to root process management in the organization, accompanying the health facility towards real and in-depth knowledge of its operating mechanisms, through efficient techniques, with low economic impact, in rapid analysis times and guaranteeing the objectivity of the result. In general, workflows are used to support processes. To understand what it is, some brief notions are provided:

- A *process* is a sequence of elementary activities carried out by agents to achieve a goal.
- A *task* is a piece of work defined to be performed in many cases of the same type.
- An *activity* is the actual execution of tasks.
- A *workflow* (or process model) is therefore a formal specification of how a task sequence can be composed and can end in a valid process.
- A *case* is a specific execution of activities in a determined order, as described by a given workflow along an ordered set of steps (time points).
- *Case traces* are lists of events associated to steps (Fig. 2).

Health process records can be referred to both patient and healthcare facilities, can be extracted from different sources, and can have different types. For

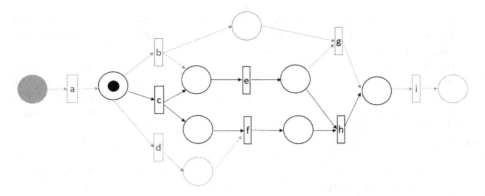

Fig. 2. Petri Net example describing a process that may occur in a Clinical Pathway.

example, the patient's vital parameters, the events associated with her (hospital-izations, rehabilitation, etc.) or even drug therapy, allow to define the treatment processes associated with the individual patient. To this information can be added data from administrative systems, clinical decision support systems, ERP or medical devices, which can be combined in different views: from patient to ward, up to the whole structure.

The term "compliance" is referred, in the medical field, to the behavioral rigor of a patient in following the prescriptions, defining the level at which the patient's actions (drug intake, adherence to diets, physical activity) are in line with the doctor's instructions. Failure to comply with best practice behavior could have repercussions on the quality of care and on the entire health system. For this reason, the Compliance Checking technique used in Process Mining would help discover the similarities and deviations between modeled behavior (the workflow) and detected behavior (the case traces).

In this regard, AAL systems should adapt to user needs and enable activities independently, using information derived from the context. In the operations of modeling human routines, particularly in the case of clinical pathways, it is necessary to understand the sequences of human activities. Therefore, routine depiction can be done using workflows. A workflow can be managed like a Petri net [1], an expressive formalism that can represent activities and their flow, and the competition between them. Workflows are important for describing human behavior, showing the chronological sequences of user activities. In smart contexts or intelligent environments, this allows us to understand events and build a series of services capable of responding to situations. Therefore, having identified the analogy between the workflow and the clinical path as the succession of events that are performed by a patient, this can be evaluated with process mining techniques to ensure adherence to the doctor's prescriptions and compliance with the clinical guidelines. To improve system performance, at this stage, the evaluation component of the process must be brought on board the Edge module.

The paper [18] discusses an example of eHealth process analysis. A solid basis for the management and improvement of processes within hospitals is provided. By combining event data and process mining techniques, it is possible to analyse fact-based processes within a hospital. In the paper [12], an ontological model is presented for auditing the clinical process to improve the quality of services and reduce hospital costs. Binti *et al.* [22] provide a methodology for the development of a clinical treatment pathway to facilitate the diagnosis and treatment of patients. This work is particularly contextualised in the treatment of patients with heart failure and makes use of machine learning techniques. Interestingly, the work in [20] is more focused on a well define condition like suffering from aftereffects of a stroke event, however, it does not account for monitoring the patient at home.

Aspland *et al.* [7] propose a literature review on taxonomies of problems related to clinical pathways. The authors explored the combination of this with Information Systems (IS), Operations Research (OR), and industrial engineering. The work [28] highlights in an AAL scenario, the context-awareness, and adaptability of a care pathway in the daily life of the patient. A review of process mining techniques used to manage clinical pathways is carried out in the papers [21,30]. Ardito *et al.* [2] provide a formalisation of the Clinical Pathway management method. Through the application of this, it is evident how patient monitoring is increasingly improved. Edge Computing is an architectural solution whereby the processing and storage of resource data are moved to the edge of the network. Thanks to the use of AI in the Edge, it is also possible to make a significant contribution to telemonitoring solutions in eHealth. Thanks to this combination, medical devices connected to the remote hospital information system (HIS) can be exploited even more efficiently. The combination of these has led to a massive deployment of smart and wearable devices and Internet of Things (IoT) communication technologies in the healthcare sector. The authors of the papers [24,26] highlight the potential of the IoT in integrating and harmonising the data produced by Cyber-Physical Systems (CPS) with those already present and generated by classical information systems. In this way, it is possible to unite people, processes, data, and things. The clinical domain is addressed in the work [23,25] in which the development of integrated solutions for seamless care is contextualised. AI and IoMT techniques at the Edge are used. The work emphasises a people-centered approach, which continuously adapts to the needs of caregivers and is embedded in their workflows.

Finally, Ardito *et al.* in [3] present an approach to bring together IoT technologies with End-User Development (EUD) tools and paradigms. This integration is aimed at identifying innovative scenarios in which end-users are directly involved in the creation and customisation of the AAL systems they use.

3 Edge Computing Cognitive Architecture

In this section we firstly present the Edge Computing architecture that permits to process data on devices (i.e. end-nodes) or gateways (i.e. Edge nodes). This

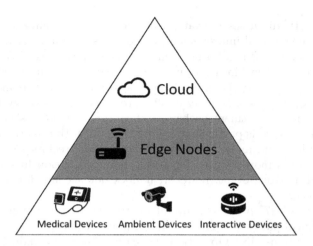

Fig. 3. Edge Computing Cognitive Architecture.

would reduce unnecessary processing latency and data traffic, which is a valuable benefit for applications like analyzing and monitoring critically ill patients. Afterwards, we show two intelligent modules that leverage data collected from sensors and devices connected to Edge nodes, and perform predictive analyzes preventing the worsening of the patient's clinical condition. In particular, the Clinical Pathway Adherence Checker (CPAC) module is introduced, aimed at verifying that the patient follows her therapeutic path correctly.

3.1 System Architecture

The system architecture is depicted in Fig. 3. The Edge architecture results quite general to be configured in an AAL typical scenario, specifically in the case of a Smart Home Environment. Here, we deal with an high number of heterogeneous devices which differ from one another in storage, computational, and communication capabilities. Therefore, the architecture, at the bottom of its pyramidal topology, presents three types of end-devices:

1. *Medical Devices*: any device adopted for medical purposes, such as the treatment, prevention, diagnosis, monitoring, alleviation or compensation of an illness.
2. *Ambient Devices*: any kind of consumer electronics that brings smartness to living environments, such as cameras, motion sensors, smoke sensors, smart appliances, etc.
3. *Interactive Devices*: any mobile or fixed hardware component which favors interaction between human users and an interactive application, such as wearable devices, smartphones, speech recognition devices, etc.

Above the end-devices, there is the Edge Layer, which is composed of one or more Edge nodes which can be an adjacent connectable device through a device-to-device (D2D) communication [10], a server attached to an access point (e.g. router, WiFi, base station), a network gateway or even a micro-datacenter available for neighboring devices. As shown in Fig. 3, Edge nodes can communicate with each other and exchange the results of a preliminary Edge processing phase. A typical Edge node adopted by the proposed architecture is a *Raspberry Pi 3 Model B* (RPi for short) with a 1.2 GHz quad-core 64-bit ARMv8 CPU and 1 GB of RAM. In order to implement a scalable, adaptable and general-purpose architecture, the maximum number of devices that can interact via Bluetooth Low Energy (BLE) connectivity simultaneously with RPi and the width of the time window in which the vital signs are collected have been set in a configuration file, parameterized as desired by the user. If, during the time window, the same information is updated several times, at the time of the final acquisition, the system considers the most updated value.

Lastly, the architecture presents a Cloud Layer in which collected raw data and processed data at the Edge are transmitted to enhance the general performances and supply a refinement of the clinical pathway just in case of patient's condition degradation. Consequently, the Cloud Layer would act as an intermediary, by receiving any alert and/or request sent by the Edge Layer after the collection of specific vital parameters, and by activating specific operating protocol with the hospital or the health personnel, hence supporting a remote adaptive and complex decision making process.

In this architecture, an Edge node can gather useful information from, ambient, interactive, and medical end-devices, and process them for a specific purpose. As shown in Fig. 4, a node in the Edge Layer is designed to run *Conformance Checking* on a predefined sub-process of the Clinical Pathway, another node would be exploited to be an *Anomaly Detection Module* which is able to address the security risks that may occur during the transmission process for the gathered data. Eventually, as already addressed in [23], a further node may be adopted as *Adaptive ML Module* for predicting the clinical risk of a patient, constantly monitored even where a limited number of vital parameters is readily measurable. Hence, introducing an Edge architecture to Healthcare would be beneficial to physician's workload by removing less critical tasks, such as collecting and managing patient data. Moreover, a major benefit would make healthcare more affordable and accessible, especially for remote areas where medical care is limited.

3.2 CPAC: The Clinical Pathway Adherence Checker Module

In this section, we introduce our approach to performing process mining tasks in eHealth domain. This would foster the intelligent software modules characterizing the Edge nodes in applying AI techniques to perform an automatic decision, and proactively support the patient at home. Within the clinical course, we can distinguish between the intervention made by health personnel, and the ones made by medical instruments. Considering the clinical pathway as a workflow, each activity is therefore represented as a node in the Petri Net. These nodes

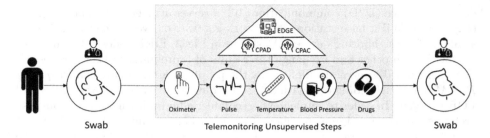

Fig. 4. Steps of a Clinical Pathway.

can, in turn, be sub-processes. Giving a formal notation, the following definition is formulated.

Definition 1. *The execution of a process σ is described as a sequence of actions $\sigma = \langle a_1, \ldots, a_n \rangle$, where $a_1, \ldots, a_n$ is the sequence of the single activities carried out by the user in a specific and strict order. We denote with $l_\sigma = n$ the length of σ.*

When the patient is discharged from the hospital and returned at home, she has the task of following the doctor's prescription, to maintain stable or improve the clinical situation. The prescription can be processed in a series of steps that make up the patient's clinical journey and must be performed by the patient at home without supervision. To manage this home monitoring, we introduce a new level of control that can replace medical personnel, as shown in the Fig. 4. Patients are endowed with one or more Edge devices that can process their activities at home aware of being constantly monitored. The part of the clinical pathway that has to be managed at home can be thought of as a specified subset of activities that the Edge node will be responsible for validation. In a formal way:

Definition 2. *Given an execution process σ, an execution of a sub-process τ, managed without supervision, is described as a sequence of actions $\tau = \langle b_1, \ldots, b_m \rangle$, with $l_\tau = m$, $\tau \subseteq \sigma$ and $l_\tau \leq l_\sigma$, and where $b_1, \ldots, b_m$ is the sequence of single activities, arbitrarily carried out by the user.*

A translation of these steps becomes a prescription to follow that cannot be verified except in the patient's level of rigor. Our idea is to introduce a control level, based on Edge computing, which can supervise and manage the phases of the Clinical Pathway that the patient must carry out independently at home to avert the worsening of the clinical picture and guide her towards a prompt healing.

As a first step, we have to perform a process model, to which an instance of patient activities must adhere. In this context, logs of general patient enrollment are fed into the process mining task to generate the process model. Once the reference model has been defined, the Edge component will be able to verify in real-time the correctness of the operations performed by the patient in the home concerning the clinical pathway. Thus, the Edge architecture will receive from the Cloud layer the process model to be stored. In particular, the Edge framework identifies the most suitable clinical path model for the type of patient by connecting to the cloud and downloading the portion of the clinical pathway as a validated process model. The development of the monitoring phase involves the activation of a series of medical devices that allow the collection of clinical data. These are collected by the Edge module which pre-processes them in log in a standard format (for example, eXtensible Event Stream, XES), with which the process model stored in our Edge node is represented. Logs analysis can be performed immediately for each individual step run (e.g. blood pressure measurement, medication intake, etc.) to verify model compliance. As a matter of choice, in less severe clinical pathways, it can be generated at the end of the period (e.g., a day), in order to appraise the discrepancy on individual activities or on the full pathway. Translating activities into formal notation is a first step to enable the use of algorithms that verify compliance and detect gaps from the process model.

Based on the deviation, it is possible to evaluate the discrepancy (e.g., missing to take pills) and also to define the corrective actions to bring back the executions towards the correct pathway model. In order to accomplish this task, we introduce a new module called Clinical Pathway Adherence Checker (CPAC). The strategy exploited in this module involves a Deep Learning approach. A Recurrent Neural Network would be able to suitably process sequences of observations to predict a probability of variation of the pathway. Therefore, a Long Short-Term Memory (LSTM) is the candidate deep architecture to perform the Conformance Checking task. The idea behind the approach is to consider the sequences of actions performed by a patient (stored in the logs) and analyze them as characterizing elements of a pattern. Each pattern can be compared with the ideal process model defined by the clinical staff and, through the use of the LSTM, it will be classified according to the level of compliance. Starting from event logs collected by the Edge node, we can give in input and infer the discrepancy from two different models: the first one for clinical pathway step prediction, and the second one for time prediction. A representation of this conceptual strategy is depicted in Fig. 5. At a later stage, in the event of non-compliance between the current execution and the model, the CPAC module autonomously discloses the specific incident to the medical personnel, sending reports to the Cloud layer of our Edge infrastructure.

3.3   CPAD: The Clinical Pathway Anomaly Detection Module

Supervised Machine Learning techniques can be used to predict when a clinical deterioration of vital parameters will occur. These techniques, which are also used in AAL scenarios, are able to understand whether the communication between the patient's devices in the care state is correct or compromised. Such methods, used to detect intrusions in the communication between devices (and

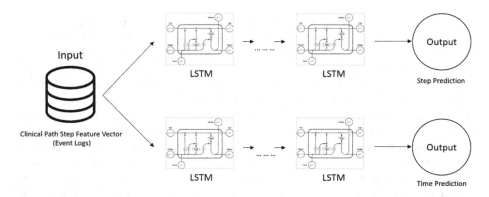

Fig. 5. Logs processing towards Conformance Checking predictions.

the related data exchange between these and the Edge node) have traditionally been developed under the assumption that the environment is not harmful.

In a hospital or home care context, it is reasonable to assume that there are no attackers who want to circumvent data monitoring systems. To avoid this issue, it is useful to equip the system with an anomaly detection module. We intend to define a system that is able to monitor several vital parameters of the patient (e.g. blood pressure, heart rate, and respiratory rate). Compromising the data collected by a sensor worn by the patient would risk compromising the clinical course, the doctor's diagnosis, and the patient's health. In order to verify the correct transmission of data and prevent the system from intrusions, the system is equipped with a module called Clinical Path Anomaly Detection (CPAD) [4].

Using Machine Learning techniques, the CPAD manages the security problems that may occur during the data transmission process, analysing them and, if necessary, notifying the anomalies detected. Using a Cognitive Security approach, thanks to advanced AI techniques, the system will be able to learn and analyse at each interaction any threats that are detected. By doing so, it will be able to provide the healthcare provider with an explanation of the intrusion, and thanks to this we will be able to correct the patient's clinical course immediately. In design terms, the data collected in the node can be viewed as a queue and organized into several sub-processes. Each sub-process represents the phase of detecting a vital parameter from a single device worn by the patient. Using a recurrent sequential autoencoder Long Short Term Memory (LSTM), the CPAD module analyzes the various sub-processes of the chain to perform anomaly detection on the steps of the chain [16,19]. In fact, the advantage of using sequential LSTM autoencoders is twofold: firstly, it takes advantage of the reduced dimensionality and extraction capabilities of the autoencoder to efficiently perform the data reconstruction process and then detect the anomaly, and secondly, it uses the networks to handle the sequential nature of the data detected by the sensors.

The anomaly could also result in an attack on the monitoring of the patient's clinical parameters. In doing so, it causes a dysfunction in the Clinical Pathway which in turn has a direct impact on the patient's health. The anomaly may represent a direct attack on the monitoring of vital parameters in order to modify the expected behaviour of the detection or to compromise it completely, with related tampering of the clinical pathway. Using intrusion detection techniques, the system is able to prevent attacks at various stages of the clinical pathway. It also provides intelligent information to the treating physician and allows domain experts (system IT administrators) to isolate the security breach and reschedule the clinical path together with the physician.

4 SARS-CoV-2 Patient Monitoring Scenario

We propose in this section a usage scenario for clinical pathway handling on Edge related to SARS-CoV-2 patients management. With the help of telemedicine, the traditional treatment scenarios have changed profoundly during the pandemic, bringing beyond its physical boundaries. Thanks to telemedicine, even patients who are distant and isolated can be reached, such as the ones undergoing quarantine measures as they test positive for SARS-CoV-2. In this context, the control setting provides the use of a monitoring and control kit, based on a telemedicine platform [17]. The patient's clinical pathway is downloaded on the Edge node from the aforementioned telemedicine platform, which acts as our Cloud layer, and enables the steps that must be activated at patient's home. The most suitable medical devices are involved, on the basis of the types of the activities to be performed by the patient, in order to detect and monitor the relevant vital parameters.

For example, a pill dispenser can be used to provide information on taking medications to follow the therapy, while the use of the blood pressure monitor can provide the clinical status of the patient. In the specific case of SARS-CoV-2, a subset of relevant vital parameters, such as heart rate, body temperature, and oxygen saturation, must be gathered several times in a day. With the interaction with the medical devices, Edge nodes can monitor the status related to Adherence and Anomalies with the CPAC and CPAD modules. If dangerous situations are detected, alerts can be sent in real-time to an operations center. Detecting simple vital signs can transform radically the lives of many people during a pandemic, while allowing them to monitor and contain the contagion. The crucial role of the health personnel was highlighted during the pandemic emergency. They need to perform their work in safety conditions. The usage of intelligent techniques at the Edge would help to ensure the required safety, thus making digitally viable the relationship between the hospital and the patients, and hence placing the whole monitoring process in a safer place. Providing continuously monitoring and information about the disease, possible complications, and the activities to be carried out can make patients feel more protected. The health personnel of the Medical Control Room, receive the monitoring data through the monitoring system, check the progress of the clinical path and evaluate any anomalies in the state of health that could require a change of therapy or a possible hospitalization. The Edge infrastructure ensure a high level of continuous surveillance and proactive collaboration, making the patient and his relatives more relaxed and making the experience discharge from the hospital more peacefully.

5   Concluding Remarks

The need for more healthcare choices for SA technologies is reflected in the pursue of established practices related to Telemedicine, allowing teleconsultations with specialists and a more flexible monitoring of the patients at home. In fact, SARS-CoV-2 has accelerated this innovative process in the healthcare sector, demonstrating the importance of a systemic rethinking of remote care.

Based on Edge Computing and AI techniques, this work presented a level of unmanned supervision which can somehow control the steps of the Clinical Pathway that the patient should follow autonomously in his/her living environment to deflect worsening of clinical conditions. The paper shed light on formal aspects of executing process mining tasks in an Edge infrastructure, in which activity logs are collected by data coming from medical, mobile, and interactive devices, in the spirit of IoMT perspective. The core proposal presented an intelligent module which is applied to check patient behavior by means of their adherence to their clinical pathway. This module, called CPAC (Clinical Pathway Adherence Checker) helps patients to follow medical prescriptions (i.e. therapies) and provides physicians actions to induce them to exclude a clinical deterioration. The present paper adds further conceptualization to the aim of designing and developing a full-Edge platform architecture, in which several AI modules cooperates towards a big conjunct goal or more little objectives related to the world of healthcare. The benefits are various: firstly by lightening the physician's workload by removing less critical tasks, secondly by making telemonitoring more affordable and accessible, especially for remote areas where medical care is limited, and lastly by stimulating the advancement of medical technology through Big Data. Definitively, Edge computing will make it easier to manage and classify data in a uniform, efficient, and secure way.

Aware of the intrinsic vulnerability of AI techniques, we detailed also the anomaly detection module, called CPAD (Clinical Pathway Anomaly Detection). Interestingly, the detection system may act as an Explainable Security module, which allows receiving an exhaustive explanation of the attack reports that can be easily interpreted even by non Machine Learning experts and therefore in this case by the physician and the user who is undergoing treatment. In fact, the Explainability of AI, which aims to make people understand how ML models work, is essential to promote trust and reliability in AI systems. It will also allow the patient in care to have an overview of the decision-making process of the system. Another scenario will involve this technology to explain other types of alarms that can emerge from the analysis of sensor data, providing explanations both to patients and, remotely, to physicians. Interestingly, one would think about the Petri Net representation to be exploited as an explanatory tool of the clinical pathway executed by the patients.

Future works will concern the many opportunities the Edge module could offer in healthcare. The research will continue in Robotic Process Automation (RPA) to automate the activities performed by physicians in interacting with patients (e.g. notification of therapy changes and acknowledgment). Also, we will investigate recommender systems to support physicians more directly in guiding the treatment path. In particular, we will focus on the fundamental aspects of data security at the Edge level: by combining the strengths of AI and human intelligence, it is possible to ensure a reliable level of privacy. Finally, while providing efficient and cost-effective monitoring action to gain situational awareness, the proposed study has laid the groundwork for improving the quality of action that can be taken by stakeholders with decision support systems. Equipping humans with the ability to make better decisions thanks to AI, and in particular AI on Edge, defines a process in which AI can be seen as a tool capable of strengthening and increasing human capabilities, thus approaching a Digital Twin model of the physician.

Acknowledgements. This work was partially funded by the Italian projects PROSIT (PON 2014–2020 FESR, project code F/080028/01-04/X35, from MISE – Ministero dello Sviluppo Economico).

References

1. Van der Aalst, W.M.: The application of petri nets to workflow management. J. Circuits Syst. Comput. **8**(01), 21–66 (1998)
2. Ardito, C., Bellifemine, F., Di Noia, T., Lofù, D., Mallardi, G.: A proposal of case-based approach to clinical pathway modeling support. In: IEEE International Conference on Evolving and Adaptive Intelligent Systems (EAIS), pp. 1–6. IEEE (2020)
3. Ardito, C., et al.: Enabling end users to define the behavior of smart objects in AAL environments. In: Leone, A., Caroppo, A., Rescio, G., Diraco, G., Siciliano, P. (eds.) ForItAAL 2018. LNEE, vol. 544, pp. 95–103. Springer, Cham (2019). https://doi.org/10.1007/978-3-030-05921-7_8
4. Ardito, C., et al.: Towards a trustworthy patient home-care thanks to an edge-node infrastructure. In: Bernhaupt, R., Ardito, C., Sauer, S. (eds.) HCSE 2020. LNCS, vol. 12481, pp. 181–189. Springer, Cham (2020). https://doi.org/10.1007/978-3-030-64266-2_11
5. Ardito, C., et al.: Towards a situation awareness for ehealth in ageing society. In: Proceedings of the Italian Workshop on Artificial Intelligence for an Ageing Society (AIxAS 2020), co-located with 19th International Conference of the Italian Association for Artificial Intelligence (AIxIA 2020), pp. 40–55 (2020)
6. Ardito, C., Di Noia, T., Lofù, D., Mallardi, G.: An adaptive architecture for healthcare situation awareness. In: Proceedings of i-CiTies 2020, 6th CINI Annual Conference on ICT for Smart Cities & Communities (2020)
7. Aspland, E., Gartner, D., Harper, P.: Clinical pathway modelling: a literature review. Health Syst. **10**(1), 1–23 (2019)

8. Casalino, G., Castellano, G., Consiglio, A., Liguori, M., Nuzziello, N., Primiceri, D.: A predictive model for MicroRNA expressions in pediatric multiple sclerosis detection. In: Torra, V., Narukawa, Y., Pasi, G., Viviani, M. (eds.) MDAI 2019. LNCS (LNAI), vol. 11676, pp. 177–188. Springer, Cham (2019). https://doi.org/10.1007/978-3-030-26773-5_16

9. Chamola, V., Hassija, V., Gupta, V., Guizani, M.: A comprehensive review of the COVID-19 pandemic and the role of IoT, drones, AI, blockchain, and 5G in managing its impact. IEEE Access **8**, 90225–90265 (2020)

10. Chen, X., Pu, L., Gao, L., Wu, W., Wu, D.: Exploiting massive D2D collaboration for energy-efficient mobile edge computing. IEEE Wirel. Commun. **24**(4), 64–71 (2017)

11. Finlayson, S., Bowers, J., Ito, J., Zittrain, J., Beam, A., Kohane, I.: Adversarial attacks on medical machine learning. Science **363**, 1287–1289 (2019). https://doi.org/10.1126/science.aaw4399

12. Fudholi, D.H., Mutawalli, L.: An ontology model for clinical pathway audit. In: 2018 4th International Conference on Science and Technology (ICST) (2018)

13. Graybeal, K.B., Gheen, M., McKenna, B.: Clinical pathway development: the overlake model. Nurs. Manag. **24**(4), 42 (1993)

14. Hollander, J.E., Carr, B.G.: Virtually perfect? Telemedicine for COVID-19. N. Engl. J. Med. **382**(18), 1679–1681 (2020)

15. Huang, Z., Lu, X., Duan, H.: On mining clinical pathway patterns from medical behaviors. Artif. Intell. Med. **56**(1), 35–50 (2012)

16. Leung, K., Leckie, C.: Unsupervised anomaly detection in network intrusion detection using clusters. Proceedings of the Twenty-eighth Australasian conference on Computer Science-Volume 38, pp. 333–342 (2005)

17. Mallardi, G., Mariani, A.M., Altomare, E., Maruccia, Y., Vitulano, F., Bellifemine, F.: Telemedicine solutions and services: a new challenge that supports active participation of patients. In: Proceedings of i-CiTies 2017, 3rd CINI Annual Conference on ICT for Smart Cities & Communities (2017)

18. Mans, R.S., van der Aalst, W.M.P., Vanwersch, R.J.B.: Process Mining in Healthcare. SBPM. Springer, Cham (2015). https://doi.org/10.1007/978-3-319-16071-9

19. Meidan, Y., et al.: N-BaIoT-network-based detection of IoT botnet attacks using deep autoencoders. IEEE Pervasive Comput. **17**, 12–22 (2018)

20. Mora, N., et al.: IoT-based home monitoring: supporting practitioners' assessment by behavioral analysis. Sensors **19**(14), 3238 (2019)

21. Quintano Neira, R.A., et al.: Analysis and optimization of a sepsis clinical pathway using process mining. In: Di Francescomarino, C., Dijkman, R., Zdun, U. (eds.) BPM 2019. LNBIP, vol. 362, pp. 459–470. Springer, Cham (2019). https://doi.org/10.1007/978-3-030-37453-2_37

22. Binti Omar, N., et al.: Personalized clinical pathway for heart failure management. In: 2018 International Conference on Applied Engineering (ICAE) (2018)

23. Pazienza, A., et al.: Adaptive critical care intervention in the internet of medical things. In: IEEE International Conference on Evolving and Adaptive Intelligent Systems (EAIS), pp. 1–8 (2020)

24. Pazienza, A., et al.: A novel integrated industrial approach with cobots in the age of industry 4.0 through conversational interaction and computer vision. In: Proceedings of the Sixth Italian Conference on Computational Linguistics (CLiC-it 2019) (2019)

25. Pazienza, A., Mallardi, G., Fasciano, C., Vitulano, F.: Artificial intelligence on edge computing: a healthcare scenario in ambient assisted living. In: Proceedings

of the 5th Italian Workshop on Artificial Intelligence for Ambient Assisted Living 2019, co-located with 18th International Conference of the Italian Association for Artificial Intelligence, AI*AAL@AI*IA 2019, pp. 22–37 (2019)

26. Pazienza, A., Polimeno, G., Vitulano, F., Maruccia, Y.: Towards a digital future: an innovative semantic IoT integrated platform for industry 4.0, healthcare, and territorial control. In: 2019 IEEE International Conference on Systems, Man and Cybernetics (SMC), pp. 587–592. IEEE (2019)

27. Rozinat, A., Van der Aalst, W.M.: Conformance checking of processes based on monitoring real behavior. Inf. Syst. **33**(1), 64–95 (2008)

28. Sánchez-Garzón, I., Milla-Millán, G., Fernández-Olivares, J.: Context-aware generation and adaptive execution of daily living care pathways. In: Bravo, J., Hervás, R., Rodríguez, M. (eds.) IWAAL 2012. LNCS, vol. 7657, pp. 362–370. Springer, Heidelberg (2012). https://doi.org/10.1007/978-3-642-35395-6_49

29. Schrijvers, G., van Hoorn, A., Huiskes, N.: The care pathway: concepts and theories: an introduction. Int. J. Integr. Care **12**(Special Edition Integrated Care Pathways), e192 (2012)

30. Scott, P., et al.: General system theory and the use of process mining to improve care pathways (chap. 11). In: Applied Interdisciplinary Theory in Health Informatics: A Knowledge Base for Practitioners, vol. 263 (2019)

31. Vessio, G.: Dynamic handwriting analysis for neurodegenerative disease assessment: a literary review. Appl. Sci. **9**(21), 4666 (2019)

A Community-Based Activity Center to Promote Social Engagement and Counteract Decline of Elders Living Independently

Matteo Luperto[1]([✉])[iD], Nicola Basilico[1][iD], Alessandro Vuono[1], Manuel Cid[2][iD],
Matteo Cesari[3][iD], Simona Ferrante[4][iD], and N. Alberto Borghese[1][iD]

[1] Dipartimento di Informatica, Università degli Studi di Milano, Milano, Italy
matteo.luperto@unimi.it
[2] SEPAD, Junta de Extremadura, Merida, Spain
[3] IRCCS Istituti Clinici Scientifici Maugeri, Università degli Studi di Milano,
Milan, Italy
[4] Dipartimento di Elettronica, Informatica e Bioingegneria, Politecnico di Milano,
Milano, Italy

Abstract. Global ageing of the population is deeply affecting the everyday lives of the frailest, by exposing them to increasing isolation and loneliness that, in turn, can cause or accelerate cognitive decline. The use of digital technologies and, in particular, social networks can be an effective tool to mitigate this phenomenon, by helping older age people to stay connected and be stimulated in the cognitive and physical sphere. In this work, we present a platform called Community-Based Activity Center (CBAC) a central tool developed within the scope of the European project MoveCare, an effort to leverage intelligent Ambient-Assisted Living technologies to promote active well-being for the elderly. CBAC conveys cross-domain stimulation in the cognitive, physical, and social scopes by providing a virtual community where different types of activities can be carried out alone or together with caregivers, members of the family, friends, and peers. We followed a modular approach, developing a flexible platform that be integrated with AI-based recommendations and that allows for transparent monitoring. The effectiveness of our platform has been extensively tested in a preliminary usability test and in a pilot experimental campaign that involved 25 selected seniors on a time span of 10 weeks.

Keywords: Community-Based Activity Center · AAL · Active ageing · ICT for ageing

---

Supported by the European Commission H2020 projects MoveCare, grant ICT-26-2016 – GA 732158, and Essence, grant SC1-PHE-CORONAVIRUS-2020-2B - GA 101016112.

© Springer Nature Switzerland AG 2021
M. Baldoni and S. Bandini (Eds.): AIxIA 2020, LNAI 12414, pp. 388–422, 2021.
https://doi.org/10.1007/978-3-030-77091-4_24

1   Introduction

Modern societies are rapidly ageing, and this is leading to changes and conse-quences in both healthcare and society at large [1], due to the constantly increas-ing proportion of elder population [2]. Moreover, because of looser family bonds, elders are left living alone more often than it has happened in the past [3]. As a result, this is leading to an increase in the number of *frail people* [4], who are people at risk of abrupt decline in health and function. Therefore, counteracting physical and cognitive decline is becoming one of the top priorities of Health and Social providers, such that the longer life that we are currently enjoying, can go hand in hand with a good life.

Three areas of intervention can be identified. They are monitoring (to early detect decline and to detect hazards and critical events), assistance (to let elders be at ease in their own houses), and stimulation (to promote an active lifestyle and counteract social isolation). In particular, *social isolation* is a key risk factor, as it is shown to be linked to a decrease in physical activity, depression, and, ultimately, to physical and cognitive decline [5,6]. Indeed, elders who have an extensive network of friends are shown to live longer and with a positive outcome in their life quality [7]. The recent pandemic, and the consequent change in the lifestyle, has substantially increased the risks connected to such factors [8].

In recent years ICT, with the development of social communities, has been proven particularly successful in providing tools to connect together people with shared needs by developing networks of social support [9–11]. Virtual commu-nities can create social support that positively affects stress levels and, in turn, improve the physical and psychological states [12]. Social networks and virtual communities increase social support by connecting together people who share a common condition, such as fighting a similar disease [13], allowing such people to find both emotional and informative support by sharing their experience and receiving feedback from people similar to them [14]. Within these frameworks, different forms of communication emerge [15]: on one side sharing past experi-ences allows users to identify with other members of the community and to be part of a group [16]. On the other side, this form of communication allows the cre-ation of interpersonal bonds with other members [16]. The trend of using social networks for such a purpose emerged particularly across homogeneous groups of people [17], as young people and adolescents, who were already active users of social networks and for whom was easy to form clusters of social communities related to social support and information sharing about a common condition by using technologies that they already know.

Although beneficial, the development of social communities tailored to elders' needs is difficult, since elders are often not comfortable in learning new func-tionalities and technologies [18]. Several works investigated the opportunity to facilitate elders in using existing social networks and communication tools (like Skype or Facebook). As an example, the work of [19] shows how the use of ICT-based social intervention based on Skype increased the number of social contacts and total communication time. Interestingly, a follow-up of such work allowed to discover that variation in the time spent in socializing through ICT is a valid indicator to unobtrusively detect mild cognitive impairment (MCI) [20]. However, these approaches suffer from a major limitation, namely that elders often do not find interesting social networks as a method of communication [21] per se and they do not find a motivation to engage in such online social network [22].

An alternative approach tries to improve motivation by developing new social communities around the elders' needs, similarly to what we propose in this work. In this approach the social community is designed and developed around activities and functionalities designed specifically to engage users and to stimulate them, thus leveraging on such motivation to foster socialization. As an example, the work of [23,24] shows how the development of digital activities specifically targeted to elders (as a digital card game) can be effectively used for such a purpose. The technology barrier is lowered by developing a simple and intuitive interface for a tablet and television. However, the framework proposed in these works is based on single activities, it was tested in controlled environments and in a preliminary controlled deployment. Moreover, no monitoring data are derived.

Another common limitation is that most approaches are aimed only to improve one of the three aforementioned target areas (monitoring, assistance, and stimulation) at once. Only a few of them offered a wider perspective on how to really improve later life quality by jointly addressing them [18]. However, these approaches are often limited as they are more designed as a social network to connect elders with their relatives while also sharing health-related monitoring data [25]. In this paper, we aim to tackle these limitations.

We propose an ICT framework to promote social engagement and an active lifestyle to pre-frail elders living alone. This is achieved through a Community-Based Activity Center (CBAC), a social engagement platform based on virtual rooms that provide a set of diverse physical or cognitive *activities* with the underlying goal of fostering socialization. Through the CBAC, the elder interacts with a virtual community of users directly from home and carries out social activities with the support of audio-video communication. At the same time, activities provide valuable quantitative monitoring data.

The platform was tested for a period of three-months on 11 elders living in Milan (Italy) and 14 living in Badajoz (Spain). All elders were living alone and were independent. The evaluation shows how, overall, people found the system easy to use, they felt confident and they would have liked to keep the system also after the pilot; moreover, the proposed platform allowed the user to develop new social connections, whom several of them maintained also after the end of the study.

This paper is an extended and revised version of the contribution presented at [26], which presented a preliminary version of the proposed framework. The proposed framework is integrated within a broader project, MoveCare [27,28], that had the goal to integrate several ICT components (as a service robot, smart objects, and an IoT network) to provide a heterogeneous, modular, and integrated AAL platform.

2   A Community-Based Activity Center

The design of an effective Community-Based Activity Center has to start from elders' needs. And we did follow this tenet [29]. Elders were actively involved in the development of the platform along with caregivers to suggest activities and scenarios; these were then prioritized according to their impact and implementation feasibility.

The final set of activities implemented comprehends several social games: Puzzle, Words, Draw & Guess (a drawing game), two card games (named Scopa and Briscola), and a set of physical activities. The choice of the particular card games was motivated by their diffusion in the south of Europe, where our system was evaluated. We have also developed gentle exercises to train body mobility and strength and an application to promote outdoor activities with peers.

Activities are the building blocks of the CBAC. Each activity has been designed following two desiderata, a) the activity should be engaging so that users are motivated in using the platform, and b) the tasks performed by the user during the activities should be useful to themselves by providing proper physical and cognitive stimulation. They were conceived to encourage socialization and are performed jointly by more than one user.

To this aim, the concept of **virtual room** has been introduced. In a virtual room, players can talk to each other while participating in the same activity, similarly to what would happen if they were all inside the same physical room, around a table. To achieve this, the interface of the activities has been conceived as split into two parts (See Fig. 1). The left side of the interface contains the **activity board**, where the activity takes place. (e.g., card deck, drawing board, a trainer for the exercise). Its content is synchronized in real-time for the different users who see at the same time the same content.

The right side of the interface contains the **social panel** that allows all the attendees to participate in the activity session and to communicate with each other using both audio and video. We limited the number of players participating together to the same virtual room to four so that each user can easily understand and communicate with all the others without the need of silencing their microphone or experiencing communication issues. The two modules are activated concurrently inside the same window. From the technological point of view, the activity board and the social panel are two modular web pages combined into a single one by means of HTML iframes (Fig. 1 depicts the obtained page) that is visualized as a single WEB page. The activity board exchanges commands and data with its activity server through a WebSocket connection. On the other side, the social panel provides real-time audio-video communication through a peer-to-peer network using a protocol based on the WebRTC standard. In particular, the social panel has been developed exploiting the EasyRTC[1] open-source toolkit.

This graphical design was the result of progressive refinement through two pre-pilot testing rounds which involved 16 end-users (see Sect. 3.1). The CBAC

---

[1] https://easyrtc.com/.

Fig. 1. Activities interface is split into two parts: an activity board on the left and a social panel on the right. In this particular case, the activity is a match of the card game Scopa.

does not provide only stimulation through activities, but it offers also monitoring capabilities. The CBAC collects both system usage statistics and the actions of the players that are evaluated and scored. These data could be used to infer a possible decline in cognitive and physical state. Its design is highly modular: each activity has its own activity server and clients that share the same communication mechanism, authentication mechanism, and interfaces. This makes it very easy to add new activities.

2.1   The CBAC Architecture

The CBAC has been designed according to a modular paradigm in which different applications, each responsible for a specific functionality, are designed and work together according to the controller model defined. Each functionality is implemented as a standalone application, which is part of a shared network that constitutes the backbone of the CBAC. To allow using the platform on different devices, the software has been developed as a web application using the SaaS (Software As A Service) model. It is largely based on Open standards (e.g. WebRTC for video-communication). The platform is configured as a classical client-server application of Web-applications, where the view of an activity is provided on the **client side** while the data model and the controller logic are deployed on the **server side**, following the Model View Controller architectural Paradigm (MVC), as illustrated in Fig. 2.

The entire platform software architecture is designed as federated architecture where activities can be independently deployed on the platform at any time. Substantially, an activity is designed as a real-time web application that provides on its front-end and interactive Graphical User Interface (GUI) for users to do things like playing a game, being guided during workouts, and socializing. Activities are devised as independent units, they contain arbitrary business logic enveloped in a container that must comply with specific interfacing requirements

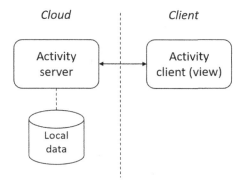

Fig. 2. The software achitecture of the CBAC server. Activities are constituted of an Activity Server and its client.

so that the platform can handle their instantiation and support interoperability as well as data-exchange functionalities.

The client and the server communicate either through HTTPS requests/ responses and by keeping a constant communication channel among them by using encrypted WebSockets. Websockets are also used to stream users' activity to the servers, who are responsible for storing usage data for monitoring purposes. The video communication is based on WebRTC[2] W3C standard, as it is supported by most popular browsers, and it supports multi-party real-time, synchronous, audio-video communication and data transmission.

2.2 The Client Side

The architecture above allows providing the user with simple and effective interfaces and interfacing modalities.

From the user's point of view, the CBAC appears as a single web application that can be accessed with any device that supports a web browser such as Google Chrome (Fig. 5). The client presents to the user the current view of an activity that is synchronized with the view of all other users who are carrying out that same activity. It has been realized as a standard web page served by the activity server. Such pages are configured according to the user state and device used. They have been realized through the Bootstrap framework[3], based on a graphical layout defined through style sheets (CSS). Modifications to the Document Object Model (DOM) implementing the logic activity, which ensures a dynamical behaviour, is implemented through client-side JavaScript. Each client traps user actions (e.g. dragging an icon, tapping, and so forth) and transmits this event to the server that, in turn, modifies the activity board accordingly for all users, by using WebSockets as a communication mechanism. At the same

---

[2] https://webrtc.org/.
[3] https://getbootstrap.com/.

time, JavaScript is used to log user activities and to transfer such data (through WebSockets) to the dedicated server for monitoring and analysis.

Interfaces are both responsive to the device used and to the user needs; moreover, DOM elements can be rearranged by the Artificial Intelligence (Sect. 2.3) according to elders' preferences. Card games have been implemented starting from an open-source available library specific for cards[4].

The CBAC has been embedded as an Android application. It has been released on Google Play Store (private link). This allows easy installation and maintenance to all clients: any time a new release is uploaded to the store, it is automatically downloaded to all clients (automatic updates).

2.3   The Server Side

The CBAC system logic and data management is resident on the server side, that is hosted in the cloud platform.

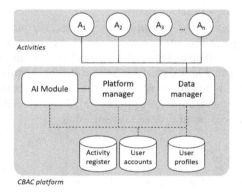

Fig. 3. The platform architecture.

Figure 3, depicts the general architecture formed by *activity units* (denoted as A_1, A_2, ..., A_n) and the CBAC platform that includes an application and a data layer. The application layer is composed of three modules that concur in gluing together a system that is more than the sum of its single parts. Indeed, the system is not merely composed of a list of independent activities but provides a number of user-centric cross features like providing access by means of user accounts, gathering data, and maintaining profiles to be used for suggestions and reminders, enabling socialization by allowing users to see who is online at the moment and to send them an invite to join an activity. In the following, we provide a short technical description of each module on the platform, by briefly discussing the services it provides.

---

[4] https://github.com/deck-of-cards/deck-of-cards.

Activity Units. Activities are implemented as independent **Activity units**. Each activity unit corresponds to a web application implemented according to a classical Model-View-Controller paradigm (see Fig. 2), as described in Sect. 2.1.

The activity server is the component responsible for providing the activity business logic as well as serving the view that allows the user to perform the activity from his client. The server also interacts with the aforementioned platform components, advertising its presence and entry point, as well as interacting with the data manager to collect data that users generated by doing the activity. Being implemented as web applications, activities provide a versatile client view that can be tailored for different types of user devices.

The main technologies adopted for the development of the whole platform and activity units are based on NodeJS and MongoDB.

The Platform Manager. The platform manager is the central actor covering the role of the orchestrator by keeping track of the activities deployed at the moment and ruling the users' accesses. It provides the following basic services.

Activity Management. Each time an activity module is loaded on the platform and starts, it announces itself to the platform manager who, from that moment on, keeps track of its status and maintains an updated list of available activities inside a DB called *activity register*. The activity register acts as a sort of "white-pages" service for activities and allows for smooth management of start/stop events for the activity units. If, for example, an activity stops due to a problem or is taken down for maintenance, the platform manager will update the activity register accordingly and will no longer present that activity in the user's choice menus. This service is achieved by means of HTTP REST internal APIs that allow activities to advertise their status to the platform manager, and the manager to query their status periodically.

Accounts and Accesses. User accesses to the platform must be granted in a centralized way. This is required for allowing users to provide their access credentials only once at the entry point, without having to re-post them each time they access a specific activity. For this reason, the platform manager acts as an authentication authority. A public web page is provided as the main entry point for the user. From such a web page, the user can register a new account on the platform and/or login into it. During account creation, the users are requested to provide, besides a username and a password to access the system, some personal information and some basic preferences over types of activities they might enjoy. These data will form the users' account containing theirs access credentials, personal data, and a profile (given by preferences collected during the registration phase) to be subsequently integrated and refined with usage data. The system login is performed by inserting the user name and password in the form provided by the entry page. Upon credentials validation, the platform manager creates a session for the user and releases a token to the client. Such a token shall be used by the client to access the activities without re-posting the credentials so that the user can be tracked and recognized in each activity.

Presence and Messages. Once users are logged into the system, they can choose an activity from the list of available ones and, upon selection, the user's client is redirected to the corresponding activity unit where the related web application is served. From the login moment on, the platform manager keeps track of the user presence on the system by assigning it a status:

- on-line and available: the user is logged into the system and has not initiated an activity yet;
- on-line and not available: the user is logged into the system and is conducting some specific activity;
- off-line: the user is not logged into the system at the moment.

By keeping track of user presence, the platform manager can maintain a list of online users. This list is key for enabling social interactions between users and multi-player activities. Moreover, the list of online users is also exploited by a message delivery system that the platform manager coordinates. User-to-user messages (for example, invitations for joining an activity) or system-to-user notifications (for example, reminders to play an activity) can be forwarded. Each message is qualified by a priority while a delivery policy establishes rules for deciding how messages should be displayed under a given level of priority and user presence status. For example, high priority messages can override the non-availability of on-line users, temporarily preempting an activity. Low priority messages, instead, will be placed in a queue and shown to the user as soon as he becomes available. Both presence tracking and message delivery are based on the WebSocket application protocol.

Administration. The platform manager also features an administration dashboard to provide monitoring and situation-awareness of the system. From such a panel, administrators can inspect the list of registered users and moderate accounts (enabling or disabling them). Also, a data visualization functionality provides a live interface where usage stats concerning activities and users can be analyzed.

The Data Manager. The data manager is the component responsible for collecting and maintaining the usage data generated by user activity. The bulk of data coming from a user defines his profile. During the execution of an activity and after its completion, usage and performance data will be pushed to the data manager that will store them inside a DB. The data manager also provides an access interface to the data to the other components of the platform. Some advanced functionalities have been developed to extract from such data performance indicators and statistics describing the users' behavior.

The AI Module. The AI module runs a reasoner that combines a set of predefined rules with the user profiles maintained by the data manager. By reasoning over those two sources of information, it generates recommendations tailored to each specific user. See Sect. 2.7 and [30] for further details.

2.4   The User Side

Our platform can be accessed through a multimodal interface through a *tablet*, a *TV set-top box*, or a *laptop* allowing technological equivalence - i.e., the possibility to deploy the platform on multiple (and simultaneous) devices adapting it to the user's behaviour and preferences. In this way, the users can choose to use the platform with the device they prefer.

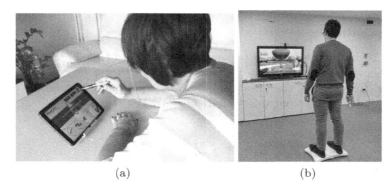

(a)   (b)

Fig. 4. On the left the Tablet setup with the support and the pen. On the right the TV set-top box setup: notice the webcam on the top of the TV screen.

The main device to access the CBAC is the tablet (Fig. 4a). In particular, for the tablet setup, we have chosen a Samsung Galaxy Tab A (Model 10.1, Wi-Fi, 32 GB) for its large screen size. It communicates with the Activity server through a WiFi connection. In our pre-pilot studies, the users reported that they were not comfortable in using the tablet flat on a table and that they felt that the tablet was too heavy to be held in one hand for several minutes, as it happens when the tablet is used. Consequently, following users' suggestions, we complemented the tablet with some accessories: a stand, a case, and a capacitive pen.

The second set-up is based on the home TV using a TV set-top box, a home station that provides a TV-based access through the main television of the user (Fig. 4b). In this setting, the CBAC is controlled with a remote wireless mouse (air mouse), similar to a remote controller. The TV set-top box is composed of a mobile computer connected to the television, a webcam placed on top of the television, and a remote controller. The TV is connected through its HMDI port to a NUC Intel® Core^{TM} i5-7260U minicomputer with Windows 10 in kiosk mode. A webcam is placed on top of the TV (Logitech C270 HD) for monitoring users when using the CBAC. This computational power and setting can easily be found inside Smart TV in the next future.

Besides this, we allow users to access the CBAC through a web application accessible from any computer equipped with a webcam. In this way, users who prefer to have a physical keyboard instead of a touch interface (as with the tablet) can use the platform.

The display of the three types of devices is characterized by different screen sizes and resolutions. Therefore to provide the same view of the interface on the different devices, the interface has been fully parameterized such that all interface elements can be scaled and positioned in the same relative position.

Besides providing the activities, the client can also receive notifications from other users even when the client is in stand-by mode.

2.5   Activities

The CBAC main interface is a personalized dashboard (Fig. 5) that is presented to the users each time they enter the platform. It shows some custom details for the users (for example, their avatar image, and a personalized welcome message) and showcases a set of buttons to start an activity.

Fig. 5. The CBAC home page.

Such a user interface has been designed considering elders as the primary target users. For this reason, it favors a minimal and regular organization of homogeneous buttons, each representing one particular activity that can be carried out in the CBAC. A limited color palette characterized by high contrast was chosen to obtain a neat display style and the number of buttons for side functionalities (like the profile and contact request) have been kept at the minimum to focus the interaction and to maximize the familiarization with the interface. The buttons on the dashboard are organized into three different groups, namely Play, Exercise and Utilities, and Socialize.

The main interface also features a dynamic behavior both in terms of graphical style and content organization. Specifically, to handle the difference between the various devices on which the interface could be displayed, the CBAC dashboard is dynamically reorganized: the size and position of the buttons are automatically rearranged depending on screen size and resolution. This behavior is obtained by exploiting the grid system of the Bootstrap framework used to develop the dashboard page. This provides different and modular grid classes that are associated to the type of device on which the GUI is currently displayed (e.g., tablet, TV set-top box, laptop).

Moreover, the CBAC's dashboard has been designed to accommodate dynamic content organization. For example, a particular activity can be promoted or one or more peers can be suggested as partners for an activity. When one of such directives is received, the CBAC rearranges the interface layout following the intent of the directive: the button of the suggested activity is shifted leftwards from the others and highlighted. Similarly, suggested peers can be put in the first spot of the user list suggested for that activity.

The CBAC dynamic behaviour also extends to the language spoken by the interface using a flexible internationalization functionality. Labels and messages provided by the interface are parametrized by a global variable indicating the current language. Each time a label or a message has to be displayed, the system automatically fetches the translation corresponding to the language indicated in such a parameter.

From this main window, all the activities can be accessed: by clicking on the associated button, the activity window is opened (Fig. 5).

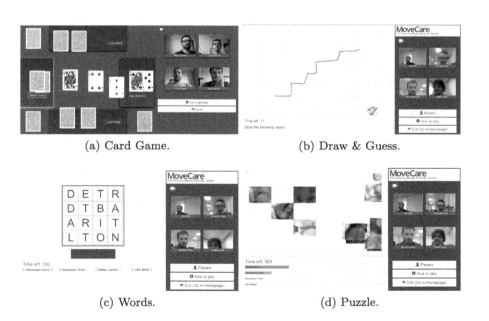

(a) Card Game.   (b) Draw & Guess.

(c) Words.   (d) Puzzle.

Fig. 6. An overview of the gaming activities of the CBAC.

The first line of the home interface contains games that can provide cognitively stimulating activities: a drawing game called Draw& Guess, Words, Puzzle and two cards games popular in South Europe, Scopa and Briscola (Escoba and Brisca in Spanish).

The **card** games can be played by two or four players simultaneously, according to the rules of each game, and they unfold in a sequence of matches within which players take turns. In each match, the allowed moves and the assigned scores are handled by the specific rules and mechanics of the game. An interactive card deck allows the user to drag and drop and rearrange cards on a virtual table resembling the movements that players would undertake with real cards, as can be seen in Fig. 6a. As both card games exist with different regional variants, so that those games are played with different rules in the two regions of Europe where this platform was tested, we implemented two slightly different versions of both card games (Scopa and Briscola for Italy, and Escoba and Brisca for Spain, respectively).

Draw and Guess is a turn-based drawing game inspired by the table game Pictionary. At each turn, one player has to draw on an interactive white-board a subject suggested by the game, as can be seen in Fig. 6b. Other players have to guess the subject by typing its name on a virtual keyboard. Scores are assigned proportionally to the number of corrected guesses a user managed to make.

In the other two games, called them **Words** and **Puzzle**, players do not follow a turn-based sequence of moves. Instead of turns, each player is presented with a game board to solve at the same time. The first game, Words, is inspired by the table game Boggle, while the second game is a puzzle game. In the case of Words, the board is a 4×4 matrix of letters where players must identify meaningful words by drawing sequences connecting adjacent cells. In the case of Puzzle, each player has to reconstruct a picture by properly positioning a set of shuffled square tiles on a grid. Each time players perform a correct move (forming a proper word in Words or placing a tile in the right spot in Puzzle) their score is increased. The objective in Words is to find as many words as possible while Puzzle requires solving it as fast as possible (a maximum timeout is imposed at the expiration of which the game ends). Actions are performed by drag and drop of items on the activity board (by selecting multiple letters in Words or by dragging tiles onto a grid in Puzzle). To boost competition during the games, each user can see the current score accrued by others in real-time. Figures 6c and 6d show example screenshots from these activities.

In the second line of the interface, activities that have a prevalent physical stimulation are reported. These activities combine physical and social stimulation: a Virtual Gym where to participate in gentle exercising sessions and a set of Outdoor Activities.

The **Virtual Gym** provides a set virtual rooms where users can follow together home-fitness sessions of gentle workouts. Figure 7a shows the activity's interface. Videos are kept synchronized between all the participants. An explanatory text is shown on the left side by side with the footage of a trainer guiding the workout. In this way, all users can do the exercises altogether. During

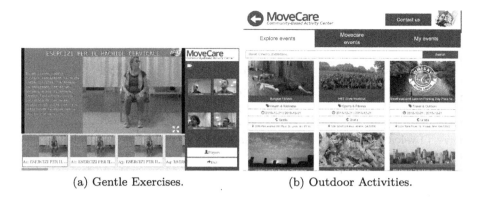

(a) Gentle Exercises.   (b) Outdoor Activities.

Fig. 7. An overview the physical activities of the CBAC.

the training session users can see each other in the social board, just like it happened in the games described above. Workouts are grouped into four different channels, each one containing a different set of exercises divided by type (e.g., exercises for the upper or lower limbs). During a session, users follow a predefined order as indicated by the domain experts who participated into the development of this activity and in the choice of the exercises. Videos were acquired with an actor performing the exercises and mounted together with a voice explaining the exercise and an explanatory text on the side. We rely on Youtube for hosting videos, while the streaming and synchronization among all users is embedded by our application by using Youtube APIs and websockets.

The second one, called **Outdoor Activities**, provides access to a geolocalized catalog of public events scheduled in the local area (see Fig. 7b). By accessing this activity, the user can read the description of the events, localize them on the map, and add them to a personal list of favorites. Participation in events can be advertised to the other members of the platform by means of a shared list. Users can also propose and agree on meeting points on the map to organize a rendezvous for attending a particular event. This activity encourages users to get out of their house and participate in social gatherings. Here, the social interaction carried out on the platform is not performed in real-time: participation in events is shared and advertised in an asynchronous way so that the users are supported in organizing real meetings to be enjoyed in the real world.

The last activity, **Video Chat**, is primarily focused on social interactions. It is a simple video-call application where users can spend time doing conversations together. A set of public rooms is always available for users to enter and exit at any time. Alternatively, users can invite people that are on-line on the platform and form private rooms with them.

Being the CBAC a social platform, a key functionality is the **invitation mechanism** through which each user can invite peers to join an activity. To this aim, the user can choose first an activity and then the users, or choose one or more users and then the activity. We rank users by putting first users with whom an activity was carried out recently. Offline users receive a notification that prompts them to answer the request.

2.6   Data Logged by the Platform

Besides providing the user with activities, the CBAC performs constant and transparent monitoring: events related to user activities are logged by the Data Collector and processed to derive **indicators** aimed to assess the cognitive/physical skills that the user is employing to play that particular physical or cognitive activity.

The Activity Server logs all the events (e.g., a card moved) and raw data (e.g., a sequence of position/velocity touch events on the tablet interface) of every single move in a game. At the end of each activity, such data are transformed into features that belong to two classes: **high-level features** that do not depend on the particular logic of the activity and **low-level** features that are activity-dependent.

High-level features include general usage statistics and apply to all activities: the *time of access* to a specific activity (a timestamp), the *duration* of the playing session, the *peers* (in case of multi-player activities) with whom the activity has been performed, and, for competitive games, the *score*. Clearly, this last indicator is present only for those activities where the concept of performance can be properly defined.

Low-level features are indicators whose meaning can only be interpreted within the scope of the particular activity they refer to. To provide a concrete example of low-level features, we provide here the list of those we computed from the raw logs of the cards game Scopa where each match of every single user was considered. Such low level features can be subdivided into **time indicators** and **performance indicators**.

Turn duration (T) is the total time taken by the user to complete a turn, from the moment the turn is assigned to when the action is performed.

The *Time to Action* (TTA) is the total time between the moment the turn is assigned and the moment the user "touches" any card on the deck; such a touch event can be interpreted as the beginning of the execution of a move. During this interval, the player is not physically interacting with the game board and it can be hypothesized that they are reasoning about the current state of the deck and about which card should they play. From those, we compute the *Plan-Act ratio*: the ratio between TTA and T.

Performance indicators describe how good to win the game is the action played. These indicators are related to the player's cognitive strength, by rewarding moves that yield strategic advantages and penalize those that advantage the opponents. For instance, in the word game performance indicators are the number of words identified and the score, in the drawing game the number of guesses, and so forth.

For card games that require a strategy to decide the play, performance indicators are based on *Action efficiency*: for each game board that the user faced during the match, we consider all the possible actions among which he had to undertake a selection and we rank them according to the immediate reward (in terms of score obtained) they would get in the current board; the action efficiency is then defined as the ratio between the reward obtained by the selected action and the reward of the best action. For each action played during the game, its efficiency is defined as the ratio between the score provided by that action and the score of the optimal action that the player could have selected. Computing the optimal action can be computationally expensive, since it requires, in principle, to search among an exponential space of possible game realizations. To ease this task, we compute the optimal action by solving a local *maxmin* problem where the solution is the action that would minimize the highest score of the opponent's next move under the assumption that this last one knows of all the cards that have not been played yet (worst-case assumption).

Low-level features like these can be used to perform a deep and detailed analysis of some performance trends that the user might have achieved in a particular activity. These indicators can be exploited to identify patterns of play or eventually they can be correlated with other validated measures like, for example, clinical cognitive assessments. However, due to their specificity, low-level features can hardly be adopted to improve the user experience at the general platform level. This task will be achieved by exploiting high-level features inside a key functionality provided by the platform: *intelligent recommendations*.

2.7   Recommendations

The CBAC Platform Manager and the AI module produce *Recommendations* to the users. Suggestions can be implemented as direct *reminders* and/or more indirect *interface adaptations* [30,31]. Recommendations represent the main approach of leveraging the data collected on the platform. Recommendations are computed after analyzing the user profile incrementally built from data and maintaining user-specific rankings over elements from two different domains: activities and users. For each user, elements are ranked by suggestion priority. Suggesting an activity means encouraging the user to play it. Similarly, suggesting a peer means encouraging the user to play together with him.

Reminders take the form of system-to-user notifications. For instance, the user can be remembered activities that were not carried out for a long time or new activities introduced in the platform

Interface adaptations apply an advertisement-like approach to the preference ranking over activities and users by changing the order in which these are displayed on the choice menus. Online users that have a high rank will be shown on top of their corresponding selection lists. Similarly, the activity buttons on the home page will be sorted according to their rank and the one that classifies first will be highlighted with a ribbon (see an example in Fig. 8).

The activity rank is used also to dynamically rearrange the buttons of the main CBAC interface and the one that classifies first will be highlighted with a ribbon.

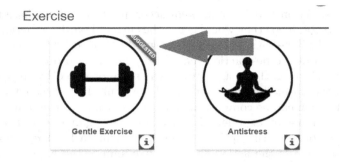

Fig. 8. A suggested activity.

2.8 Additional CBAC Functionalities

The CBAC provides additional functionalities that go beyond the aim of this paper

One additional functionality that we included in our platform is a suite of single-player *exergames* designed following the principles discussed in [32]. They are specifically tailored to exercise postural control with the aim of counteracting physical decline and can be tuned according to the user's current state thus providing a proper challenge level. Exergames are played by using a balance board positioned in front of the TV with the TV set-top box setup (see Fig. 4b) and require the user to control a virtual avatar/tool by moving his center of balance [33]. These need to be achieved by lateral or front-rear and left-right weight shifts performed while standing on the balance board (the exergames are called *Fruit Catcher,Bubbles, Hay Collect*), by sit-stand movements using a balance board and a chair (*Horse Runner*).

Finally, the CBAC is also used as a monitoring device, serving as a proxy for a set of digital cognitive tests we proposed in [34,35]. These tests can be scheduled by a clinician who, after their completion, can access their quantitative results.

3   Experimental Evaluation

The CBAC is part of a larger system that comprehends also a service robot, smart objects and an IoT subnetwork that was developed inside the H2020 MoveCare[5] project [27,28]. This had the goal to develop, integrate, and test a heterogeneous, modular, and integrated platform for the assistance of elders living independently and alone. We here describe in more detail the results of the CBAC. The CBAC has been tested in two pre-pilot rounds and a final pilot, which was also subdivided into two rounds.

---

[5] http://www.movecare-project.eu/.

3.1   Pre-pilot

Two preliminary experimental campaigns on sixteen independently living elders, eight for each round, have been carried out. The first round (1R) was conducted in May 2018; the second round (2R) in November 2018. During the two phases, we improved the system by implementing suggestions received at 1R, and by increasing the number of activities available to the users. Each pilot round, where the participants tested the CBAC, lasted three weeks.

During the first round only the first three activities implemented were used by the elderly, namely: Draw & Guess, Scopa, and Video-Chat. In the second round, the remaining activities were added to the initial three activities (which were improved following suggestions by users at the end of 1R). Moreover, the stand and the tablet pen were also provided.

In these two rounds of pre-pilot elders were tightly followed by two researchers: a computer scientist who participated in the implementation of the activities and a researcher in social sciences with previous research experience with elderly users. They explained in detail each activity and trained the elder to play several matches with them. Moreover, they were available throughout the pre-pilot period to answer questions, support elders, and collect feedback.

In the first round, one Tablet was delivered to each participant; in the second round, in addition to the Tablet, a tablet stylus/pen and a tablet stand were provided too, to ease the use of the tablet touch interface. The setup of the system (connectivity to the router and user registration) was performed by the researchers. When delivering the technological devices, the second researcher administered to the users the Mini-Mental State Examination (MMSE) [36], in order to evaluate their cognitive abilities. At the end of this period, the second researcher returned to the home of each participant to collect answers to a structured questionnaire for each activity and to collect opinions and comments regarding the usability and enjoyment of the games and activities performed. Moreover, 6 months after the first round all the participants (1R) were contacted by telephone for the administration of a follow-up questionnaire. This study was approved by the Ethics Committee of the University of Milan on May 25, 2018. All participants signed informed consent, containing clear and standardized information on the objectives and procedures of the research.

Sampling. The participants were recruited thanks to the help of ANTEAS (a local association in Milan) among older people aged 65 or older who lived in their home in the city of Milan and who had familiarity with one or more of the common technological devices, have a Wi-Fi internet at home, and were able to give their consent. First, we identified a set of 75 potential participants from which, according to their availability, 16 persons were then invited to take part in the study.

The first session of the study included 6 females (F) and 2 males (M). Their average age was 73.5 years (S.D: 4,47; Range: 66–80; Median: 74). The level of education of the participants was medium/high: 6 of them attended high school and 2 university. Regarding the housing situation, 5 lived with their partner,

2 with their own child, and 1 alone. Regarding their cognitive screening, the MMSE average score was 29.2/30 (S.D.: 0,83; Range: 28–30; Median: 29).

The second session of the study included 5 F and 3 M. Their average age was 75.1 years (S.D.: 3,72; Range: 71–82; Median: 74). The level of education of the participants was medium/high. Regarding the housing situation, 5 lived with their partner, 2 alone, and 1 with their own child. Their MMSE average score was 28,9/30 (S.D.: 0,83; Range: 27–30; Median: 29).

Data Collection. Structured questionnaires were used as data collection instruments for each game/activity of the CBAC. They were created ad hoc, starting from the System Usability Scale questionnaire, available in the literature [37], and for each questionnaire the content validation was made, according to [38]. For the content validity, which includes face validity, six experts were involved that evaluated the clarity (face validity) and relevance (content validity). Questions that did not met content validity were modified according to the indication provided by the experts' feedback. Questionnaires include single-choice closed questions (Likert scale from 1 = certainly no to 5 = certainly yes, plus the "not used" answer option), and open questions; the number of both types of questions changes on the basis of the game/activity. As users participating at 1R and to 2R experienced different setups of the system, data have been evaluated separately.

Data Analysis. A descriptive analysis of the data collected through the questionnaire was carried out. The results obtained through the open responses have been processed with methods of content analysis [39]. The results of the questionnaire were analyzed in order to gather information regarding the usability, clarity, and satisfaction of the CBAC. Moreover, we have investigated their level of confidence about the use of technology, as only two of them (1R) and one of them (2R) said they had a Tablet.

Overall, participants provided positive feedback regarding the proposed activities and the technology proposed to them. Users appreciated the tablet interface and the list of activities proposed, while also they enjoyed the social components embedded in each activity. However, despite this consideration, in 1R four users reported issues in understanding how to use the tablet touch interface and they felt some difficulties in performing some actions, like drawing, that they were used to do with a pen. For that reason, a tablet stylus/pen and a tablet stand were provided to the users.

From the answers to closed questions regarding the CBAC activities proposed to 1R, it emerged that overall the activities were perceived as simple, clear, and pleasing to the users. Interestingly, it emerged that Video Chat was used only by 5/8; a user that did not used the Video-Chat considered it as "superfluous" because during the two games there was a box in which to see and hear the other participants. From the answers to open questions emerged that the principal difficulty was the "use of the touch interface" and how to "moving the cards in the card game". Regarding the main positive aspects, it was signaled that users "like the video chat and (to) socialize while playing", while the negative aspects/critics concerned the "interruption of the video chat", that was due to internet issue related to the house set up.

In the 2R, more activities were made available to the user, who provided positive feedback similar to those reported in 1R. Activities were considered, overall, as simple, clear, and pleasing to the users. Six users (over 8) enjoyed the possibility to talk and Video-Chat while playing, indicating that this was a good method to "Feel in company" and to "Socialize (3/6)". Five users enjoyed also the possibility to turn on/off the video component of the chat to preserve privacy. However, the other three users reported that the possibility to turn-off/on the video chat while playing could be "unpleasant/rude" towards the other players. Overall, all users enjoyed the possibility to play with the tablet, while two users reported some issues in understanding the invitation mechanism used to start an activity.

The activity most appreciated in the Second round was Words. Words and Puzzle were the only games that were used by all participants, while no user used Video Chat; among all users, two participants considered it as "superfluous" as during the games there was the same possibility. The main positive aspect signaled was in the fact that the users liked to video chat while playing.

From the comparison between the two rounds (1R and 2R), it is possible to detect a homogeneity between the samples. Comparing the responses that emerged in the two rounds, the positive recurring aspect is in the fact that the users enjoyed the possibility to talk through a video chat while playing and, consequently to socialize. In 2R, compared to 1R, the main disagreement concerned the fact that no user has detected the difficulty in using the touch (reported, instead, from 50% in 1R). It is interesting to note that in the 2R a stylus and a tablet stand were provided.

A follow-up questionnaire administered to participants (1R) after 6 months from the experiment does not detect any significant variation in the use of technologies. However, this survey reported that 1 participant had remained in contact with two other participants (1R). The participant reported how he kept staying in touch periodically by phone and by occasional encounters in presence.

3.2   Final Pilot

In this Section, we present the main evaluation phase, where all the developed framework described in Sect. 2 was tested. The system was improved following the insights obtained through the preliminary assessment described in the previous section. This pilot study was performed in two rounds; half of the participants in the study were located in the city of Milan (Italy), while the other half of the participants were located in the city of Badajoz (Extremadura, Spain).

The CBAC was integrated within the MoveCare platform and the data collected by the IoT platform was provided, along with the data collected from the CBAC, to the AI module. The Giraff robot provided some assistive functionalities to the user, as searching for lost objects inside the house or establishing a teleoperation session with a caregiver in case of an emergency. The AI module could ask the robot to perform a reminder, that was used to suggest the user to do an activity (as, for example, to interact with the other components of the whole system). See [30,40] for more details. Only half of the users were provided with the robot. During the two rounds, the system was installed inside the house of elders living independently and freely available for 10 weeks.

The entire system was set up and configured by researchers (computer scientists who participated in the implementation of the platform). Each user was provided with a tablet, a home TV set-top box kit (with a webcam). The TV set-top box kit was connected to the main television in the house, usually in the living room or in the kitchen. Besides this, as part of the project, a set of IoT sensors were placed in every room and at the door entrance to detect the presence and activities performed by the user in the house. However, data recorded by IoT sensors were not used by the CBAC.

During the setup phase, a researcher with experience with elders provided instructions on the use of the tablet and the home TV set-top box and showed to the user all functionalities and activities. As the system was complex and involved several components, the training phase was divided into two sessions, lasting one to two hours, for each user. If needed, the users could request further training sessions with the researchers. During the selection phase of the user, the same researcher administered to the users the MMSE [36], to evaluate their cognitive abilities.

As the team that was available for the system's setup was one, and as each setup required one day, the duration of the pilot was slightly different across different users.

At the end of each pilot round, the researchers returned to the home of each participant to collect the devices left on loan for use and, on the same occasion, interviewed the user by administering a structured questionnaire, created ad hoc and validated. The questionnaire, focusing on each component of the system, collected opinions and comments regarding the usability and enjoyment of the games and activities performed (the content validation of the questionnaires was the same of the pre-pilot). As the system was composed of multiple functionalities, the questionnaires used for evaluation were less detailed and specific if compared with those used for a preliminary assessment, as they were developed to evaluate the entire framework. Nevertheless, they allowed a thorough evaluation of the CBAC.

Sampling. The elders enrolled in experiment were outside the frailty state. The participants have been chosen according to the following inclusion criteria

a) ≥ 65 years old;
b) living alone, receiving assistance in activity of daily living for no more than 1 h/day;
c) MMSE [36] ≥ 26;
d) maximum 1 or 2 points in Fried criteria [4] or robust people: 0 points in Fried criteria but with GDS (Geriatric Depression Scale) ≥ 9 or UCLA loneliness scale > 35 [41];

e) keen to use technology;

f) owning and using a smartphone;

g) Internet connection with at least 8 Mbps available at home.

Evaluation is performed by using standardized questionnaires administered to the user at the beginning and at the end of the participation to the pilot. Moreover, sensorial deficit (deafness, blindness) or motorial disability (paraplegia) that precludes the interaction with the system were considered as exclusion criteria.

A total of 25 different elders were recruited: 14 in Badajoz (Spain) and 11 in Milan (Italy). In Milan, 7 people were recruited among the local association of older volunteers and the patients afferent to the Day Hospital and the Ambulatory of the Geriatric Unit of Policlinico C Granda and 4 users among the residents of an Assisted Living (AL) facilities. The pilot was organized in two rounds of 15 elders each (first round September 2019-December 2019; second round: January 2020-March 2020). Five users of the first round (1R) decided to continue the experimentation in the second round (2R). During the study, only 1 participant from Spain dropped out during the pilot, because did not feel confident with the service robot included in the full system.

The two communities, in Italy and Spain, were separated (each participant could play games only with people in the same nation/community). The average age was 76.7 years (S.D:7.2; Range: 65–92; Median: 78.5). The participants in Italy were slightly older (average age 79.1 years) than the Spanish participants (average age 74.7 years). This is due to the fact that the users living in the AL facility were older than the other participants and lived in an independent apartment inside the facility (average age 84.8 years). Their MMSE average score was 28.75/30 (S.D:1.42; Range: 26–30; Median: 29). Users in the AL facility had a lower MMSE score (average of 27/30).

Participants were encouraged to promote the use of the CBAC among friends, caregivers, and members of their families, in order to increase their social network and the opportunities of play.

Data Collection. At the end of each pilot round, users were requested to evaluate their experience through the defined questionnaires. All the questionnaires analyzed here have been filled by the participants at the end of either the first round or the second round of the pilot, according to which one they have been part of. Participants who took part in both rounds filled the questionnaires at the end of the second round. Participants filled various questionnaires on the proposed system, its usability, and their satisfaction, the MoveCare components, the MoveCare high-level scenarios, and functionalities.

Questionnaires are divided into a series of topics. We administered a general satisfaction questionnaire, System Usability Questionnaires (SUS [37]), and a System Validation Questionnaire, where the entire system was evaluated. Moreover, we provided component-specific questionnaires where single functionalities and interfaces were evaluated independently. Questionnaires include single-choice closed questions (Likert scale from 1 = certainly no to 5 = certainly yes, plus the "not used" answer option), and open questions; the number of both types of questions changes on the base of the component evaluated.

The results discussed here are related to the CBAC, the detailed questionnaires with all their average responses can be found in Table 1.

As one of the 25 participants participant (from Spain) dropped out during the pilot, because did not feel confident with the system, a total of 24 participants completed the questionnaires.

As users participating in 1R and 2R experimented the same system setup, data acquired in both rounds are jointly evaluated. Moreover, we collected and analyzed the total usage time of the CBAC accrued by each pilot user in the two system installations (Italy and Spain), divided per activity. Finally, to evaluate socialization, we collected data about the interactions among users using the activities proposed by the CBAC.

Qualitative Analysis. Answers to the questionnaires were evaluated using descriptive analysis in order to organize and adequately summarize all the information collected on the different variables considered in the questionnaires. They are mostly ordinal qualitative variables in a 1 to 5 Likert scale using 1 for "strongly disagree" and 5 for "strongly agree". The median M and interquartile ranges IQ have been calculated for each variable. M and IQ of all questions are reported in Table 1.

Overall, participants enjoyed the use of the CBAC and found it stimulating. If we look to the question regarding the usability of the whole CBAC platform, users provided particularly positive remarks. The answer to the question if they found "the available games useful and stimulating" obtained $M = 4, IQ = 1.25$. Users stated that they "enjoyed being able to interact through video and voice with users during the activities" ($M = 4, IQ = 1$) and that they "would, if possible frequently use the cognitive games in the future" ($M = 4, IQ = 2.5$). The users appreciated fact that it was "easy to understand how to play each activity" ($M = 4, IQ = 2.25$).

Technological equivalence is also assessed. The users appreciated the fact that it was "easy to learn to use the platform to perform the required activities" both on the tablet interface ($M = 4, IQ = 1.5$) and for the TV set-top box ($M = 4, IQ = 1.5$). They provided similar answers when asked about the fact that the interface was "easy to interpret" ($M = 3, IQ = 2$ for both tablet and TV set-top box setup). However, they felt that the tablet interface was "more responsive to their inputs" when compared to the TV set-top box ($M = 4, IQ = 2.5$ and $M = 3.5, IQ = 2$, respectively).

On the negative side, the user signaled that the air mouse used to control the TV set-top box was difficult to be used and that sometimes it was not easy to recover the system if a wrong action was performed (both on the tablet and the TV set-top box). Overall, both setups were appreciated and equally used by the users.

When asked if the system was useful to socialize, users provided polarized answers; when asked if "using the CBAC [they] enjoyed the company of new friends online" and if they "hung out with new friends met on the CBAC" their answer was, respectively, $M = 1, IQ = 3$ and $M = 1, IQ = 3.75$. However, we remark here that the evaluation of the first question is the result of the computation of the median of two different sub-populations as shown by the large IQ range: 13 users answered 1, while 6 users answered 4 or 5. This clearly reflects the different attitude of the users as for some of them the CBAC turned out an effective mean to make new acquaintances. Similar observations apply to the answers to Question CBAC5 (see Table 1).

The analysis of how cognitive games have been received was done by administering 11 questions. Users reported how they "enjoyed playing the cognitive games" ($M = 4, IQ = 1.25$) that were also "easy to play" ($M = 4, IQ = 1.25$). The social component of the games was particularly appreciated: when asked if the users "enjoyed being able to interact while playing with peers" they replied with a high score ($M = 4, IQ = 1$).

The users particularly appreciated activities that addressed the physical domain. More precisely they stated that they "enjoyed practicing the gentle exercising" ($M = 4, IQ = 0.25$), found them "easy to use" ($M = 5, IQ = 2$) and that they would frequently play with them in the future ($M = 4, IQ = 2$).

Overall people found the system easy to use, they felt confident and they would have liked to keep the system also after the pilot, with an average score close to 4 over 5 on a Likert scale. The 72.7% of the participants rated positively the use of the system and 68.2% rated positively the satisfaction with the experience.

Quantitative Analysis. Figure 10 reports the total usage time of the CBAC accrued by each participant in the two system installations (Italy and Spain) in both rounds of the pilot experiment.

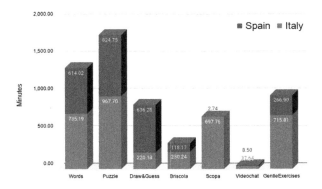

Fig. 9. The platform usage for each activity. (Color figure online)

For the Spanish pilot, the rate at which the line grows in the first round of pilot (before 15-12-2019) is roughly the same as that observed in the second round. In the case of Italy, the rate is slow at the beginning but then it grows faster in the second round due to the greater involvement of users and some improvements made to the system that have been suggested by users during the first round. The flat part of the curve reflects the Christmas break where the system was put in stand-by mode (CBAC was still active but no assistance was provided in that period).

Roughly around 8-3-2020, the local government in Northern Italy imposed a set of lockdown measures to face the COVID-19 health emergency. It can be seen in the plot how the increasing rate of the curve steepens in this period. This can be an indication of how the system was used as a way to face isolation even if the assistance provided by system administrators could be only from remote, and hence very limited, in this period.

Figure 9 reports a comparison of the usage time accrued by CBAC activities over the Italian (blue bars) and the Spanish (red bars) pilot rounds, divided for each activity.

In general, over both installations, it can be said that the co-existence of activities with social interactions showed a synergy: the activities that featured both those functionalities have received a fair amount of usage from the users. This holds especially true in the second round of the pilot where several improvements have been introduced from the feedback collected after the first round.

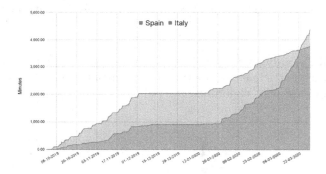

Fig. 10. Timeline of usage of the platform. (Color figure online)

4   Discussion

The CBAC integrates a highly heterogeneous set of activities targeted at cross-domain stimulation; physical, cognitive, and social. Differently from other platforms [23], the CBAC allows the combination of social engagement and physical and cognitive stimulation with monitoring capabilities that are used to provide better stimulation to the elder using engaging activities and leveraging on the concept of virtual rooms. This *transversal* approach, which combines monitoring

Table 1. Questionnaires about the use of the CBAC, divided per topic, used during the main experimental evaluation. M is Median, IQ is InterQuartile range, N is the number of pilot participants who answered to that question.

	Question	M	IQ	N
TI	Tablet Interface			
TI1	I can easily learn to use the interface to Perform the required tasks/games	4	1.5	23
TI2	Interacting with the tablet is easy	3	2	23
TI3	Functions related to buttons are clear	4	3	24
TI4	The tablet interface is responsive to my inputs	3	2	23
TI5	The tablet interface is easy to interpret	4	2.5	23
T16	Wrong actions can be easily recovered without any external help	2	2	23
TVI	Tv set-top box Interface			
TVI1	I can easily learn to use the interface to Perform the required tasks/games	4	1.5	24
TVI2	Interacting with the set-top-box through the airmouse is easy	2	2	24
TVI3	Functions related to buttons are clear	3.5	2.25	24
TVI4	The tv set-top-box interface is responsive to my inputs	3	2	24
TVI5	The tv set-top-box interface is easy to interpret	3.5	2	24
TVI6	Wrong actions can be easily recovered without any external help	2	2	23
TVI7	The media station interface is easier and more Comfortable to use than the Tablet's one	2.5	1.25	24
CBAC	Community-Based Activity Center			
CBAC1	The available games are useful and stimulating	4	1.25	24
CBAC2	I can easily interact with peers and other participants	2	1	23
CBAC3	I easily understand how to play each single game	4	2.25	24
CBAC4	Using the CBAC I enjoied the company of new friends online	1	3	20
CBAC5	I hung out with new friends met on the CBAC (or I plan to do so)	1	3.75	18
CG	Cognitive Games			
CG1	I enjoyed playing the cognitive games	4	1.25	24
CG2	I found the cognitive games easy to play	4	1.25	24
CG3	I found the cognitive games unnecessarily complex	2	2	24
CG4	I felt I needed the support of a technical person to be able to play the cognitive games	2.5	3	24
CG5	Inviting other users to join the cognitive games was easy	3	2	21
CG6	It was clear how to invite offline users to join the cognitive games	3	1.5	12
CG7	Accepting game requests from other users was easy	4	1	21
CG8	It was clear how to accept offline game requests from users	2	2	12
CG9	I enjoyed being able to interact (through video and voice) with other users during gameplay	4	1	16
CG10	If I have the possibility, I would frequently use the cognitive games in the future	4	2.5	23
CG11	I would imagine that most people of my age would learn how to play the cognitive games very quickly	3	2.25	24

(*continued*)

Table 1. (*continued*)

	Question	M	IQ	N
GE	Gentle Exercises			
GE1	I enjoyed practicing the gentle exercises	4	0.25	17
GE2	I found the gentle exercises easy to use	5	2	17
GE3	I found the gentle exercises unnecessarily complex	1	1	17
GE4	I felt I needed the support of a technical person to be able to use the gentle exercises	1	1.5	17
GE5	I enjoyed being able to interact (through video and voice) with other users during the gentle exercises	3	2.25	17
GE6	It was clear how to access the virtual room/channels to join the gentle exercises	2	2.5	17
GE7	The explanation of the gentle exercises was clear	4	1	17
GE8	I would imagine that most people of my age would learn how to use the gentle exercises very quickly	4	1	17
GE9	If I have the possibility, I would frequently use the gentle exercises in the future	4	2	17
EG	Outdoor Activities			
EG1	I enjoyed the Outdoor suggestions	3.5	1	6
EG2	I found the Outdoor suggestions easy to use	4	0	6
EG3	I found the Outdoor suggestions unnecessarily complex	2.5	1	6
EG4	I felt I needed the support of a technical person to be able to use the Outdoor suggestions	1.5	1.75	6
EG5	It was clear how to look for an event	4	1	6
EG6	It was clear how to choose to participate to an event	3	0	5
EG7	I would imagine that most people of my age would learn how to use the Outdoor suggestions very quickly	4	0	6
EG8	If I have the possibility, I would frequently use the Outdoor suggestions in the future	4	1	7

and simulation, allows mutual benefits across different domains. As an example, a user which is interested in activities that address the physical domain is encouraged through our platform to endow activities that also address the cognitive and, most importantly, the social one.

The CBAC is designed around the concept of virtual rooms inside which users can perform activities and socialize at the same time. Although the idea of a virtual room is not completely new [42,43], we provide here a generalization to generic activities on one side and the support of multi-party social interaction on the other. This is indeed what makes activities attractive to the elders: they do activities to know each other and would never start meeting people in a generic social community like Facebook [22].

The platform has been then developed around the concept of virtual room leading to a federated architecture where activities can be independently deployed on the platform at any time. Activities are devised as independent units, they contain arbitrary business logic enveloped in a container that must comply with specific interfacing requirements so that the platform can handle their instantiation and support interoperability, as well as data-exchange functionalities, [44]. This has allowed developing a very complex system in a relatively simple way. Moreover, this architecture enables several benefits such as

- can be easily extended with newly developed modules that provide new functionalities and new activities,
- allows the integration within the platform of external components that could provide new functionalities, such as sensorized objects/devices [45,46],
- allows technological equivalence - i.e. the possibility to deploy the platform on multiple (and simultaneous) devices adapting them to the user's behaviour and preferences,
- increases the robustness to faults of a single components/object – the system is able to cope with possible failure/errors of a component.

Among these benefits, the most important one is the plasticity of our proposed system with respect to multiple activities, devices, and the integration with external components. For instance, a newly developed module, which requires the use of an external sensor, could be easily added (or removed) from the CBAC by adding/removing it to the catalogue in the list of Activity Units server-side, thus enabling fast integration with new functionalities.

A good example of the modularity and of the capabilities of the proposed platform can be seen in its advanced functionalities (see Sect. 2.8). Different and heterogeneous activities can be added to the system easily, even if they require additional components. In particular, we added a set of exergames [33], played on the TV set-top-box and using a balance board as the main input device; exergames are used to provide physical stimulation as well as a set of activities that could be used for advanced monitoring purposes, as for an exergame called *Anti-stress*, that is played by means of a sensorized anti-stress ball and is focused on monitoring the grip force trends of the user (this is a particularly interesting indicator for detecting early signs of frailty). Further details can be found at [46]. Finally, we integrated within the platform the possibility to perform a set of neuropsychological tests (TMT-A/B and Bells) as additional Activity Units. See [35] for more details.

As an additional feature, data from the activities themselves are logged and then processed to compute a set of indicators that could, in principle, correlate with early physical and cognitive decline [4,47]. The same data is used to provide personalized suggestions by rearranging the layout of the buttons of the activities' main interface and ordering the list of peers available thus providing personalization. This is one of the key elements that is considered to increase user engagement [48,49].

A critical element that emerged in the pilot is the network connection. In most houses, this was through WiFi and was not always stable. This was especially critical for video communication. In general, elders had the impression that a need for technical personnel was required to overcome transient failures.

The CBAC has been largely evaluated on the field. This has been a continuous process that, especially in the initial stages, was tightly coupled with its development.

For some elders mastering the different functionalities of the CBAC was demanding and felt to need some training. As expected, younger participants enjoyed the games and used them more than the older participants [50]. Moreover, we observed by analyzing the answers by age that older subjects tended to rate the system more difficult to use, less friendly, and less compliant, while younger people were more enthusiastic and effective in using it. This is indeed a manifestation of a digital divide, that is expected to vanish in the next future where seniors will likely be more familiar with the technology.

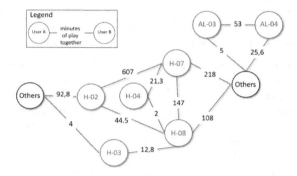

Fig. 11. The graph of how users interacted during the second round of Pilot in Milano, during the national COVID-19 lockdown. Users labeled with an H are those living in their houses, while users labeled AL are those living in the AL structure. Users H02-H07 did an activity together for a total of 607 min. A third user, H-08 did activities with both users, although for a more limited amount of time.

Usage data show a steep increase in the usage of the CBAC during the initial stage of the COVID-19 emergency (Fig. 10). Interestingly, looking at the social graph that shows the time spent in activities together, two users (H02–H07) did indeed a lot of activity together and, from the final questionnaire, it emerged that they have started to meet and go out together on a regular basis. From this point of view, the CBAC has shown its effectiveness. We remark that also two users of the second round of the pre-pilot met inside the CBAC and started to meet outside on a regular basis. If we compare the platform use between the first and second round, it can be hypothesized that the forced reclusion induced by the COVID-19 pandemic acted as an additional incentive for users to seek and find social interactions through the platform.

Overall two pairs of users, one in the pre-pilot and one in the pilot, met inside the CBAC and started meeting on a regular basis, becoming friends and

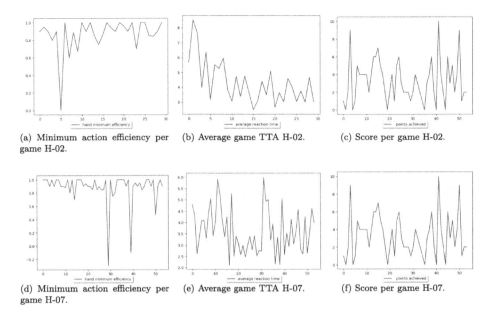

(a) Minimum action efficiency per game H-02.

(b) Average game TTA H-02.

(c) Score per game H-02.

(d) Minimum action efficiency per game H-07.

(e) Average game TTA H-07.

(f) Score per game H-07.

Fig. 12. Performance analysis playing the game Scoma for users H-02 and H-07. Time is in seconds. TTA is computed for each *hand* of the game - a turn of the user.

meeting also beyond the project-related occasions. A third elder of the pilot did a lot of activity with those two thus creating a triplet of people who started to meet virtually. The graph of how users have interacted with each other during the second Pilot phase can be seen in Fig. 11.

Data collected by users doing an activity can be used as an indicator about their performance and fed to the reasoning system [30]. Due to the limited duration of the pilot, we do not expect that data acquired could show any significant change into the cognitive abilities of the users. However, we envisage the fact that those data could provide significant insight into the user condition if used for a long time. Interestingly, we identified a mild correlation of the *Turn Duration* feature (see Sect. 2.6) with the age of the participants and we detected that the two users who played the most games are also the fastest ones. In Fig. 13 we report a preliminary analysis in this direction, where the monitoring data collected about the user performance in terms of minimum action efficiency (as described in Sect. 2.6) are shown.

As we gathered more data from the two most-active users, H-02 and H-07, we can make a more detailed analysis of their performances through the games (Fig. 12). This analysis, different from the one presented above, reports data obtained on each hand played by the user (while above we showed aggregated data from all players' games). On the x-axis of each graph is indicated the number of hands played.

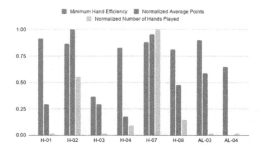

Fig. 13. An example of monitoring data that could be extracted from activities played in the CBAC. Here we report statistics about how users play at card games.

User H-02: We can see how all indicators show that H-02 has significantly improved especially in the first games becoming a faster player both in terms of TTA and T in the last games. This results also in a decrease, with each match, on the total duration of the match. Such improvement becomes stable in the last games performed. However, this trend is correlated with an increase in terms of performances, as overall the user efficiency is almost stable (besides some oscillations) in all games. The same consideration can be made when we consider the number of points obtained by the user. It can be seen how, despite the fact that the average minimum and average efficiency throughout all hands played by the user is consistent with respect to the average value obtained by the other players, in certain games, this player had a particularly low minimum hand efficiency (i.e., the user made a particularly bad move, as shown in the graph below there is one action with a minimum hand efficiency close to 0). This could be related to the fact that the user, who was an experienced player, has tried to perform a more risky move that could result either in a high revenue or in a high loss or simply that she made a mistake. This points out the fact that outliers can always occur and be considered in the evaluation through robust statistics. Less experienced users, with fewer hands played, show a lower average minimum and they have lower oscillations with respect to their minimum hand efficiency.

User H-07: We can see that the TTA of this user has been consistent for all games, so we are not observing a training effect. Similarly, T has not changed much during the pilot, with oscillations from game to game. Overall, the user seems not to have improved nor decreased his performance over the games.

5   Conclusion

This paper shows how Virtual Communities can be a powerful method to promote socialization when they are combined with activities of interest for the elders. Besides providing engagement and cross-domain stimulation, the platform can acquire activity data that can be valuable to early detect physical and cognitive decline. Such an approach has been further pursued by the H2020 Essence project[6]) aimed to support elders and children at home in the COVID-19 Pandemic in [51].

Acknowledgements. We gratefully acknowledge the European Commission H2020 project MoveCare grant ICT-26-2016b – GA 732158 and the European Commission H2020 project Essence grant SC1-PHE-CORONAVIRUS-2020-2B - GA 101016112 for financial partial support to the authors of this work.

References

1. Watkins, K.: Human development report 2005, Published for the United Nations Development Program (2005)
2. United Nations: World population ageing 1950–2050. United Nations, department of economic and social affairs, population division (2016)
3. Lutz, W., Sanderson, W., Scherbov, S.: The coming acceleration of global population ageing. Nature **451**(7179), 716–719 (2008)
4. Clegg, A., Young, J., Iliffe, S., Rikkert, M.O., Rockwood, K.: Frailty in elderly people. Lancet **381**(9868), 752–762 (2013)
5. Abrams, D., Russell, P.S., Vauclair, M., Swift, H.J.: Ageism in Europe: findings from the European social survey (2011)
6. Alaoui, M., Lewkowicz, M.: A livinglab approach to involve elderly in the design of smart TV applications offering communication services. In: Ozok, A.A., Zaphiris, P. (eds.) OCSC 2013. LNCS, vol. 8029, pp. 325–334. Springer, Heidelberg (2013). https://doi.org/10.1007/978-3-642-39371-6_37
7. Giles, L.C., Glonek, G.F., Luszcz, M.A., Andrews, G.R.: Effect of social networks on 10 year survival in very old Australians: the Australian longitudinal study of aging. J. Epidemiol. Commun. Health **59**(7), 574–579 (2005)
8. Di Santo, S.G., Franchini, F., Filiputti, B., Martone, A., Sannino, S.: The effects of COVID-19 and quarantine measures on the lifestyles and mental health of people over 60 at increased risk of dementia. Front. Psychiatr. **11** (20)
9. Rains, S.A., Wright, K.B.: Social support and computer-mediated communication: a state-of-the-art review and agenda for future research. Ann. Int. Commun. Assoc. **40**(1), 175–211 (2016)
10. Smith, K.P., Christakis, N.A.: Social networks and health. Ann. Rev. Sociol. **34**, 405–429 (2008)
11. Heaney, C.A., Israel, B.A.: Social networks and social support. Health Behav. Health Educ.: Theory Res. Pract. **4**, 189–210 (2008)
12. Nabi, R.L., Prestin, A., So, J.: Facebook friends with (health) benefits? Exploring social network site use and perceptions of social support, stress, and well-being. Cyberpsychol. Behav. Soc. Netw. **16**(10), 721–727 (2013)
13. Myrick, J.G., Holton, A.E., Himelboim, I., Love, B.: # stupidcancer: exploring a typology of social support and the role of emotional expression in a social media community. Health Commun. **31**(5), 596–605 (2016)
14. Frost, J., Massagli, M.: Social uses of personal health information within patients like me, an online patient community: what can happen when patients have access to one another's data. J. Med. Internet Res. **10**(3), e15 (2008)

---

[6] https://www.essence2020.eu/.

15. Gage-Bouchard, E.A., LaValley, S., Mollica, M., Beaupin, L.K.: Cancer communication on social media: examining how cancer caregivers use facebook for cancer-related communication. Cancer Nursing **40**(4), 332–338 (2017)
16. Zhu, Y., Stephens, K.K.: Online support group participation and social support: incorporating identification and interpersonal bonds. Small Group Res. **50**(5), 593–622 (2019)
17. Chou, W.-Y.S., Moskowitz, M.: Social media use in adolescent and young adult (AYA) cancer survivors. Curr. Opinion Psychol. **9**, 88–91 (2016)
18. Embarak, F., Ismail, N.A., Othman, S.: A systematic literature review: the role of assistive technology in supporting elderly social interaction with their online community. J. Ambient Intell. Hum. Comput. 1–14 (2020). https://doi.org/10.1007/s12652-020-02420-1
19. Jimison, H.B., Klein, K.A., Marcoe, J.L.: A socialization intervention in remote health coaching for older adults in the home. In: 35th Annual International Conference of the IEEE Engineering in Medicine and Biology Society (EMBC), 2013, pp. 7025–7028. IEEE (2013)
20. Kaye, J., et al.: Unobtrusive measurement of daily computer use to detect mild cognitive impairment. Alzheimer's Dementia **10**(1), 10–17 (2014)
21. Sundar, S.S., Oeldorf-Hirsch, A., Nussbaum, J., Behr, R.: Retirees on facebook: can online social networking enhance their health and wellness? In: CHI 2011 Extended Abstracts on Human Factors in Computing Systems, pp. 2287–2292 (2011)
22. Jung, E.H., Sundar, S.S.: Senior citizens on facebook: how do they interact and why? Comput. Hum. Behav. **61**, 27–35 (2016)
23. Doppler, J., Sommer, S., Gradl, C., Rottermanner, G.: BRELOMATE - a distributed, multi-device platform for online information, communication and gaming services among the elderly. In: Miesenberger, K., Bühler, C., Penaz, P. (eds.) ICCHP 2016. LNCS, vol. 9758, pp. 277–280. Springer, Cham (2016). https://doi.org/10.1007/978-3-319-41264-1_37
24. Doppler, J., Rottermanner, G., Sommer, S., Pflegerl, J., Judmaier, P.: Design and evaluation of a second screen communication and gaming platform to foster teleparticipation of the socially isolated elderly. In: Wichert, R., Klausing, H. (eds.) Ambient Assisted Living. ATSC, pp. 3–13. Springer, Cham (2016). https://doi.org/10.1007/978-3-319-26345-8_1
25. Miori, V., Russo, D.: Improving life quality for the elderly through the social Internet of Things (SIoT). In: 2017 Global Internet of Things Summit (GIoTS), pp. 1–6. IEEE (2017)
26. Borghese, N.A., Basilico, N., Luperto, M., Vuono, A.: Community based activity center to support independently living elders. In: Proceedings of the Workshop on Artificial Intelligence for an Ageing Society (AIxAS 2020) at the 19th International Conference of the Italian Association for Artificial Intelligence (AIxIA 2020) (2020)
27. Lunardini, F.: The movecare project: home-based monitoring of frailty. In: 2019 IEEE EMBS International Conference on Biomedical & Health Informatics (BHI), pp. 1–4. IEEE (2019)
28. Luperto, M.: A multi-actor framework centered around an assistive mobile robot for elderly people living alone. In: Robots for Assisted Living Workshop-International Conference on Intelligent Robots and Systems (IROS) (2018)
29. Daniele, K., Marcucci, M., Cattaneo, C., Borghese, N.A., Zannini, L.: How prefrail older people living alone perceive information and communications technology and what they would ask a robot for: qualitative study. J. Med. Internet Res. **21**(8), e13228 (2019)

30. Renoux, J., et al.: A virtual caregiver for assisted daily living of pre-frail users. In: Schmid, U., Klügl, F., Wolter, D. (eds.) KI 2020. LNCS (LNAI), vol. 12325, pp. 176–189. Springer, Cham (2020). https://doi.org/10.1007/978-3-030-58285-2_13

31. Vuono, A.: Seeking prevention of cognitive decline in elders via activity suggestion by a virtual caregiver. In: AAMAS, pp. 1835–1837 (2018)

32. Pirovano, M., Surer, E., Mainetti, R., Lanzi, P.L., Borghese, N.A.: Exergaming and rehabilitation: a methodology for the design of effective and safe therapeutic exergames. Entertainment Comput. **14**, 55–65 (2016)

33. Pezzera, M., Borghese, N.A.: Dynamic difficulty adjustment in exer-games for rehabilitation: a mixed approach. In: 2020 IEEE 8th International Conference on Serious Games and Applications for Health (SeGAH), pp. 1–7. IEEE (2020)

34. Lunardini, F., et al.: Supervised digital neuropsychological tests for cognitive decline in older adults: usability and clinical validity study. JMIR mHealth uHealth **8**(9), e17963 (2020)

35. Luperto, M., et al.: Evaluating the acceptability of assistive robots for early detection of mild cognitive impairment. In: IEEE/RSJ International Conference on Intelligent Robots and Systems, pp. 1–8 (2019)

36. Folstein, M.F., Folstein, S.E., McHugh, P.R.: "mini-mental state": a practical method for grading the cognitive state of patients for the clinician. J. Psychiatr. Res. **12**(3), 189–198 (1975)

37. Brooke, J.: Sus: a "quick and dirty"usability. In: Usability Evaluation in Industry, vol. 189 (1996)

38. Artino Jr., A.R., La Rochelle, J.S., Dezee, K.J., Gehlbach, H.: Developing questionnaires for educational research: AMEE guide no. 87. Med. Teach. **36**(6), 463–474 (2014)

39. Metastasio, R., Cini, F.: L'analisi del contenuto. Procedure di analisi dei dati con il programma SPAD, FrancoAngeli, Procedure di analisi dei dati con il programma SPAD (2009)

40. Luperto, M., et al.: Towards long-term deployment of a mobile robot for at-home ambient assisted living of the elderly. In: 2019 European Conference on Mobile Robots (ECMR), pp. 1–6. IEEE (2019)

41. Russell, D., Peplau, L.A., Cutrona, C.E.: The revised UCLA loneliness scale: concurrent and discriminant validity evidence. J. Pers. Soc. Psychol. **39**(3), 472 (1980)

42. Blaine, A.M.: Interaction and presence in the virtual classroom: an analysis of the perceptions of students and teachers in online and blended advanced placement courses. Comput. Educ. **132**, 31–43 (2019)

43. Pietroni, E., Adami, A.: Interacting with virtual reconstructions in museums: the etruscanning project. J. Comput. Cult. Heritage (JOCCH) **7**(2), 1–29 (2014)

44. Baldwin, C.Y., Clark, K.B.: Modularity in the design of complex engineering systems. In: Complex Engineered Systems, pp. 175–205. Springer (2006). https://doi.org/10.1007/3-540-32834-3_9

45. Lunardini, F., et al.: A smart ink pen for the ecological assessment of age-related changes in writing and tremor features. IEEE Trans. Instrument. Meas. **70**, 1–13 (2020)

46. Lunardini, F., Borghese, N.A., Piccini, L., Bernardelli, G., Cesari, M., Ferrante, S.: Validity and usability of a smart ball-driven serious game to monitor grip strength in independent elderlies. Health Inform. J. **26**, 1952–1968 (2020). 1460458219895381

47. Allan, C.L., Behrman, S., Ebmeier, K.P., Valkanova, V.: Diagnosing early cognitive decline–when, how and for whom? Maturitas **96**, 103–108 (2017)

48. Kocaballi, A.B.: The personalization of conversational agents in health care: systematic review. J. Med. Internet Res. **21**(11), e15360 (2019)
49. Kotler, M.J., Rey-Babarro, M., Friend, N.B., Kikin-Gil, E., Parker, C.W., Zaika, I.: Motivation of task completion and personalization of tasks and lists, uS Patent 10,192,176, 29 January 2019
50. Ramsetty, A., Adams, C.: Impact of the digital divide in the age of COVID-19. J. Am. Med. Inform. Assoc. **27**(7), 1147–1148 (2020)
51. Palumbo, F., et al.: "Hi This Is NESTORE, Your Personal Assistant": design of an integrated IoT system for a personalized coach for healthy aging. Front. Digit. Health **2**, 20 (2020)

Age-Related Walkability Assessment: A Preliminary Study Based on the EMG

Francesca Gasparini[1]($\boxtimes$) (iD), Alessandra Grossi[1] (iD), Katsuhiro Nishinari[2] (iD), and Stefania Bandini[1,2] (iD)

[1] Department of Computer Science, Systems and Communications,
University of Milano, Bicocca, Italy
{francesca.gasparini,stefania.bandini}@unimib.it,
a.grossi6@campus.unimib.it
[2] RCAST - Research Center for Advanced Science and Technology,
The University of Tokyo, Tokyo, Japan
tknishi@mail.ecc.u-tokyo.ac.jp

Abstract. Populations around the world are rapidly ageing as the population aged 65 and over is growing faster than all other age groups. Most of the daily life actions of active elderly are related to walking activities, thus guaranteeing walking environments that are elderly-friendly are nowadays a priority to ensure healthy aging. Measuring and recognizing the affective state of people during walking activities contribute to a better comprehension of their perception of the environment, and a better definition of walkable urban area. With the aim of paving the way for assessing walkability, introducing quantitative evaluation tools, this work proposes to compare physiological responses of subjects of different ages, in different walking conditions. To this end a proper experiment has been designed in a controlled environment, considering both young adults and elderly, and adopting wearable devices. In this paper the analysis of the leg muscles activity acquired with Electromyography is presented. The results of this preliminary study highlight age-related differences in subjects facing both forced speed walks and collision avoidance tasks.

Keywords: Physiological signals · Active ageing · Walkability · Affective state · Collision avoidance · Electromyography

1 Introduction

In recent years, an increase of longevity in developed countries has been observed [2,10,17]. Growth of social welfare, education, medical care are only few of the possible reasons for this increase [11]. In a world where the number of elderly people is expected to growth even more, the creation of an environment suitable for active aging people is becoming a first priority problem [17]. In this situation, particular attention should be paid to walking activity. In fact most of the daily life activities of the elderly, such as sports, consumer life and social interactions, take place in the neighborhood and are mainly realized through walking

© Springer Nature Switzerland AG 2021
M. Baldoni and S. Bandini (Eds.): AIxIA 2020, LNAI 12414, pp. 423–438, 2021.
https://doi.org/10.1007/978-3-030-77091-4_25

activities [10]. Some studies underline that physical activity plays an important role in aging people's health as its practice allows to avoid physical or mental illnesses [13]. A walking environment that is elderly-friendly is thus a priority while planning the design of the cities of the future as well as to improve the existing ones [5]. Measuring if and to which extent an environment is comfortable and walkable for ageing people is the first step towards this direction [12]. One way to obtain quantitative measures of walkability is to assess safety perception while moving within an urban environment, in particular while walking, crossing and in general trying to avoid collisions. The assessment of safety perception can be performed with experiments and observations both through the design of the experimental setting in a protected space (*in-vitro* experiments) and/or with data collections in the real world setups (*in-vivo* experiments), relying on physiological responses, through the introduction of what can be defined affective walkability [1]. Physiological responses, can be considered honest indicators of our emotions and mood, and are nowadays widely adopted to recognize affective states [3]. Thanks to the development of the technology, several sensors can be easily integrated into smartphones or wearable devices [18], making them more comfortable and usable even in case of elderly people. So these signals could be valid indicators to assess quantitatively the safety perception of the elderly while interacting with the surrounding environment.

To this end, an experiment has been carried out in an indoor and controlled environment. Two different populations have been involved in the experiment: young adults and elderly people, in order to compare different perception of safe walk, varying the age. Different walking conditions have been also investigated, including dynamic collision avoidance. Physiological signals such as Plethysmogram (PPG) and Galvanic Skin Response (GSR) have been acquired using a wearable device. PPG and GSR are well indicated to detect emotional arousal, related to sensory alertness, mobility, and readiness to respond, activated in the interaction between subjects and the environment as a defensive reaction to preserve safety. Moreover, dealing with a dynamic interaction, motion data both physiological, measuring the muscle activity with Electromyogram (EMG) and inertial (accelerometer and gyroscope data) have been acquired.

The study presented in this paper focuses only on the analysis of the EMG physiological signals in order to reveal differences in pace and leg movements between young adults and elderly, trying to detect patterns that characterize their walking attitude in different walking environments. In Sect. 2, the experiment in a controlled environment performed to assess walkability is introduced. EMG signal processing is described in Sect. 3, while the results of the analysis of different walking conditions and the comparison of the behaviour of the two populations are detailed in Sect. 4. Finally conclusions and future works are reported.

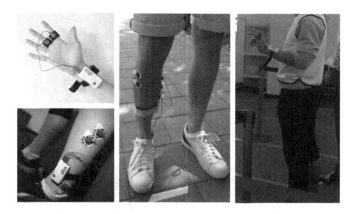

Fig. 1. Wearable devices adopted.

2 Experimental Setup for Data Collection

A controlled experiment in a real laboratory environment at the University of Tokyo has been performed to collect data for studying walkability. Three within subject conditions (collision avoidance, forced speed walk and free walk) have been administered in one experimental session, performed by two experimental groups: a population of young adults, composed of 14 Japanese master and PhD students, (average age = 24.7 years, standard deviation = 3.3, 4 women), and Japanese elderly people (retired), 20 subjects,(average age of 65.15, standard deviation = 2.7, 10 women). During the whole experiment, physiological signals have been collected using wearable sensors produced by Shimmer[1]. Five main signals have been acquired: i) Galvanic Skin Response (GSR), connected to sweating and perspiration on the skin, ii) Photoplethysmography (PPG), that measures the blood volume registered just under the skin, which can be used to obtain the heart rate of the subject; iii) Electromyography (EMG), which measures the muscle activity of the person by surface sensors. In particular, activities related to the medial gastrocnemius muscle and to the anterior tibial muscle have been acquired using the same device; and iv) inertial data, trough Accelerometer and Gyroscope sensors. The adopted sensors are shown in Fig. 1.

The experiment lasted about 30 min and it was set up to acquire data from the subjects in different walking environments. The protocol of the experiment includes two tasks:

- **Collision avoidance:** two subjects at the same time walk with their own pace along the path depicted in Fig. 2, top left, clockwise and counterclockwise respectively. At about half of the path, they reach the collision avoidance zone where they have to avoid the collisions with both the obstacles (swinging pendulum) and the other subject. Then they complete the U path, with their natural pace and go back in the opposite direction repeating the same actions.

---

[1] https://www.shimmersensing.com/.

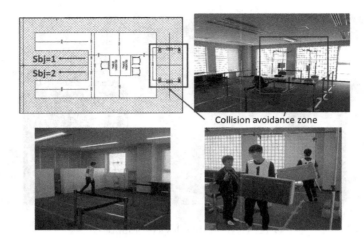

Fig. 2. Setting of the experiment. Top left: the plant of the indoor controlled environment, where a U path has been defined. The collision avoidance zone is identified by a red rectangle and depicted also in the image at the top right. The two obstacles are controlled by one of the experimenter and the two subjects have to avoid the collision (figure bottom right). During the rest of the U path, subjects walk with their own natural pace. (Color figure online)

- **Forced speed walk.** Participants walk with a forced speed based on the metronome ticking, along the same U path. Three speeds are considered: 70 bpm ($F1$), 85 bpm ($F2$) and 100 bpm ($F3$). This task lasts about 2 min. At the end, a questionnaire is provided to the participants to obtained information about the preferred walking frequency among those constrained by the metronome.

Only for the elderly there is a further task of **Free walk**, along the U path, back and forth, for about 40 s. In this task, participants can walk freely without obstacles or speed constraints.

All the tasks are separated by a period of resting time (**Baseline acquisition**) of about 1 min. The whole procedure is repeated three times.

GSR and PPG signals of all the subjects were collected, EMG signals were acquired only on a subset of participants. In particular, in the first experimental group EMG data were collected from 8 male subjects, while in the second group from 10 subjects including 3 females and 7 males.

3   EMG Data Analysis

The work here presented, focuses only on the analysis of the EMG signals. The two channel EMG have been acquired with a sampling frequency 512 Hz.

3.1   Subject Based Preprocessing

The two-channel EMG raw signals of each subject have been preprocessed by applying a denoising strategy based on the wavelet multi-resolution analysis

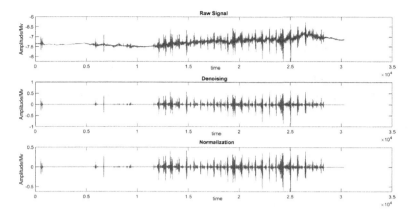

Fig. 3. Example of the applied preprocessing procedure on the EMG signal of a subject. Top image: the raw signal. Middle image: the results of the denoising procedure on the signal. Last image: Result of the normalization.

described in [16]. The signal is divided in frequency sub-bands using Maximal Overlap Discrete Transform (MODWT) with mother wavelet Daubeches-4 and with five levels of decomposition. To each sub-band, a Soft Thresholding is applied to the detail coefficients. The Universal Threshold calculated by the formula $t_k = \sqrt{2log(N_j))}$ was adopted, where N_j is the length of the j-th wavelet coefficient [4].

To compare signals of different individuals, permitting both inter and intra subjects analysis, the signals were normalized. Several different normalization strategies are reported in the literature, [6]. In this study each channel of the denoised EMG signals have been normalized dividing by the maximum peak activation level obtained from the signal under investigation. This value has been selected after an empirical study, because it has been observed to be able to decrease the variability between subjects. The normalization, as well as the denoising operation, have been applied to the whole signal of each subject, before segmenting the data into single tasks. An example of the preprocessing procedure on a subject's signal is showed in Fig. 3.

3.2 EMG Features Extraction

To compare different walking conditions and different behaviours of the two considered populations, two features have been extracted from the denoised and normalized EMG signals: walking frequency (known as Stride Frequency) and the mean power of the signal.

The first feature describes the number of steps performed by a subject per second and it is evaluated using a novel procedure described in this paper:

- **Task based pre-processing.** To further remove artifacts and noise, a task based denoising has been performed. This is a multi-resolution denoising approach, based on a Stationary Wavelet Transform with Haar mother wavelet, seven levels of decomposition and Universal Threshold.

- **Envelope calculation.** To preserve only the main structure of the signal, root-mean-square upper envelope has been calculated. For that purpose windows of 200 samples have been used.
- **Mean value removal.** The signal modified so far had only positive values. In order to make its mean equal to zero, a mean value removal has been applied.
- **Extract frequency sub-band.** Based on a priori knowledge [7,9], only envelope signal frequencies in the band [0.2, 1.4] Hz have been considered. It was observed that this range is the feasible interval for all possible stride frequencies while walking. To evaluate the envelope frequencies, a filter bank analysis using symlet wavelet with 13 levels of decomposition has been applied.
- **Periodogram computation and max peak evaluation.** The Periodogram of the envelope so filtered has been calculated and the three max peaks have been extracted.

The entire procedure is depicted in Fig. 4.

The second feature has been used to identify when subject slows down or stops. During these events the EMG signal power decreases and becomes near to zero when subject stops walking. The *Root Mean Square* of the signal has been used as feature representative of the signal power [15]:

$$RMS = \sqrt{\frac{1}{N} \sum_{n=1}^{N} x_n^2} \tag{1}$$

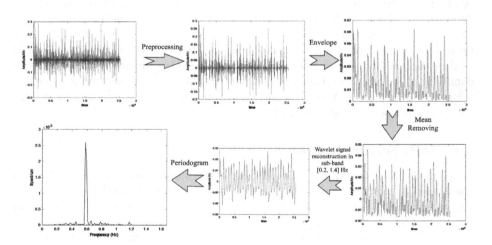

Fig. 4. Procedure applied to extract the Stride Frequency feature

4   Experimental Results

In this section the three different tasks of the experiment are analyzed using the EMG features described and a comparison between young and elderly people behavior is also performed.

Table 1. Accuracy reached by the Frequency Stride feature in evaluating the real pace of the subjects during forced speed walk tasks. The columns refer to the two EMG channels, while the two rows regard the two population groups analyzed.

	Gastrocnemius muscle	Tibial muscle
Elderly	98%	95%
Young adult	98%	98%

Table 2. Accordance in percentage between the computed Stride Frequencies and the metronome frequencies, evaluated with respect to the two muscle activities (columns) and the two considered populations (rows).

	Gastrocnemius muscle				Tibial muscle			
	F1	F2	F3	Total	F1	F2	F3	Total
Young adult	95%	90%	90%	**92%**	95%	90%	85%	**90%**
Elderly	57%	52%	89%	**66%**	68%	58%	92%	**72%**

4.1   Forced Speed Walk

The novel feature here proposed to estimate the Frequency Stride has been initially validated on EMG signals acquired during the forced speed task. During this task, participants were forced to walk at three specific speeds, dictated by a metronome. The subjects repeated these forced speed walks three times. Among all the processed signals, four of them related to the first channel and two related to the second channel have been removed due to low quality and absence of valuable information.

The three metronome speeds were $F1 = 70$, $F2 = 85$, and $F3 = 100$ bpm (beats/minute), and correspond to 1.167, 1.417 and 1.667 steps/second respectively, obtained dividing the metronome speed values by 60. Since the EMG sensor measures the muscle activity of one leg, these frequency values need to be halved to be compared with the values extracted by the proposed feature. The new frequencies used as ground truth become 0.583 steps/second for 70 bpm, 0.708 steps/second for 85 bpm and 0.833 steps/second for 100 bpm.

Firstly the accuracy of the proposed feature in evaluating the real pace of the subjects was assessed. It has been observed that hardly the subjects walked exactly at the speed dictated by the metronome. For this reason, in the evaluation of the performance of the proposed feature, we define the ground-truth following two steps: 1) the coherence between the activities of the two muscles; and 2) visual inspection. The overall accuracy of the measure is 98% considering both the experimental groups. In Table 1, the accuracy of the two population groups obtained analyzing the activity of the two muscles are reported.

As a second analysis, the computed Stride Frequencies were compared with the frequencies of the metronome, in order to compare the capability the two subject groups of following forced paces. In Table 2 the accordance between the subject paces and the three metronome frequencies has been reported, considering the two muscles, and comparing the two experimental groups of young adults and elderly people.

In the case of **young adults**, the percentage of accordance appears high. In details, considering all the metronome frequencies, 92% of accordance has been obtained from the medial gastrocnemius muscle activity, while 90% from the analysis of the tibial muscle one. In general, the forced frequency with the highest accordance was F1 (95% in both the channels) while the worst one was F3 (90% considering gastrocnemius muscle and 85% considering the tibial one).

Table 3. In this Table the mean and the standard deviation of the computed Frequency Stride for both subject groups are reported and compared with the metronome frequencies (F1, F2 and F3), considering both the EMG channels (gastrocnemius muscle and tibial muscle).

	Metronome frequency		Young adults		Elderly	
			Gastrocn.	Tibial	Gastrocn.	Tibial
F1	0.583	Mean	0.59	0.59	0.66	0.64
		Sd	0.02	0.02	0.10	0.09
F2	0.708	Mean	0.72	0.72	0.76	0.74
		Sd	0.02	0.01	0.06	0.10
F3	0.833	Mean	0.85	0.85	0.85	0.85
		Sd	0.02	0.02	0.03	0.02

A significantly lower accordance has been noticed in case of **elderly people**. The overall frequency accordance, evaluated on the first channel was 66%, while on the second one was 72%. The frequency more reproducible was F3, while the worst one was F2. Moreover, as reported in Table 3, the mean and the standard deviation of the Frequency Stride evaluated in case of elderly people appear higher than the ones observed in case of young adults and, in general, the ones dictated by metronome ticking. This may prove how the elderly struggle more than young adults to respect the metronome forced speeds, especially the two lower speeds F1 and F2, tending instead to walk at a faster cadence.

Finally a comparison between the values produced by the feature on the two channels has been performed. In many cases the values produced on the

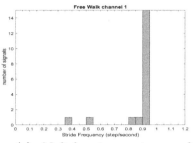
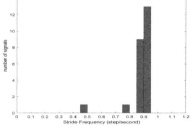

(a) *Medial gastrocnemius muscle*   (b) *Tibial muscle*

Fig. 5. Histograms of the Stride Frequencies computed for the free walk task, on the two muscles.

two signals appeared very similar even if, sometimes, not the same. A distance analysis, performed to compare the results quantitatively, showed that there is not a significant difference between them (root mean square distance = 0.002).

4.2 Free Walk

The same feature was applied to study the free walk task. For the sake of clarity, it is recalled that this task was performed only in the experiment with elderly. For young adults, further experiments will be performed in the future.

In Fig. 5 the histograms of the walking frequencies computed on the two channel signals in the free walk task are reported. Both the histograms highlight that in most of the cases the detected walking frequency is around 0.90 steps/second. This value agrees with the metronome frequency indicated by the participants as the most preferred one (F3) and with the normal pace speed reported in the literature (between 0.90 and 1 steps/second [9]). The lower frequencies in the histograms (0.35 and 0.54 steps/second) correspond to signals where noise and artifacts made difficult to identify the correct one. Usually in these cases a feasible value of human pace could be evaluated from the second or third peak extracted by the proposed feature. Moreover, it has been noted that the presence of other high peaks could be associated to changes in walking pace during the task. An example of a speed change during the free walk task is shown in Fig. 6, where the two different speeds are visible in both the EMG signal and in its Periodogram.

4.3 Collision Avoidance

To analyse changes in EMG signals during the walking task related to collision avoidance, the signal has been initially divided into five segments, using non-overlapping windows. Segments 1, 3, and 5 refer to the free walking phases that precede or follow the collision zone, while segments 2 and 4 refer to the effective pendulum avoidance zone (see Fig. 2). The procedure has been applied to signals

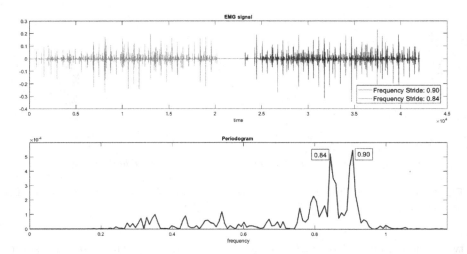

Fig. 6. Example of speed change of one subject during the free walk task. The two different speeds, as well as the two corresponding Frequency Strides, are visible in the EMG signal, (top row) where the two speeds are highlighted with two colors, and in the Periodogram (bottom row), where the two paces are visible as two distinct peaks with similar height. (Color figure online)

Table 4. Stride Frequencies in the five segments of the collision avoidance task, reported in steps/second, evaluated for one subject of the elderly group.

Free Walk	Obstacle	Free Walk	Obstacle	Free Walk
0.94	0.37	0.94	0.5	0.94

from both experimental groups and the Stride Frequency of every segments has been calculated. As an example, in Table 4 the Stride Frequencies (steps/second) calculated for one subject of the elderly group, for the five segments, are reported. The results of this analysis can be summarized as follow:

- For both experimental groups, during the free walking phases of the collision avoidance task (segments 1, 3 and 5), Stride Frequency values similar to those reported by the literature and, in case of elderly, also detected during the free walk task, have been observed. The values related to these segments were usually within the range [0.80–1] steps/second. To quantitatively evaluate the similarity of the walking speeds between: i) the task of pure free walk and ii) the segments of free walk in the collision avoidance task, a statistical similarity analysis using Kruskal Wallis test has been performed. It is important to recall that this analysis can be done only for the elderly, because the young adults did not performed the free walk task. The Kruskal Wallis test on the two distributions produces p-values greater than the significance level of 5% (p-value: 0.263 for Gastrocnemius Muscle and 0.349 for Tibial muscle), indicating that the two distributions can not be distinguished. These results seem to confirm that the pace of walking is not significantly influenced by the presence of an obstacle within the whole path.

- Analysing the values of the Stride Frequency during the free walk phases, before and after the collision avoidance one, it has also been noticed that subjects tend to change frequently their pace during the walking. Even if, in general, they appeared similar in values, the Frequency Strides computed during the walking, before and after passing the obstacle, present a greater variance compared to the one detected during the pure Free Walk task (Sd: 0.22 for Walking with obstacle vs 0.15 for pure Free Walk).

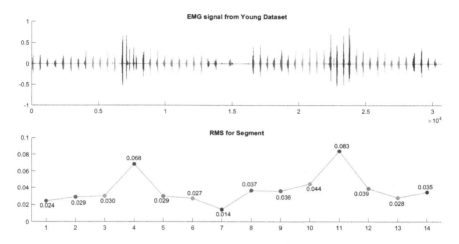

Fig. 7. Analysis on a trial of the collision avoidance task for one young subject. The signal has been divided into fourteen uniform windows (top row). Purple windows correspond to the collision avoidance events. Bottom row reports the trend of the energy values in different segments.

To better understand how does the walking pace change within the collision avoidance zone, an analysis based on signal energy has been performed. This study has been carried out with the idea of detecting stop points or deceleration patterns during this task. The feature chosen for this purpose is the Root Mean Square (RMS), described in Sect. 3.2. For this analysis, the EMG signal of each trial of the collision avoidance task has been now further segmented obtaining fourteen uniform windows.

The energy of the EMG signal has been evaluated for each window using the RMS feature. From the analysis of these RMS values, the following observations can be drawn:

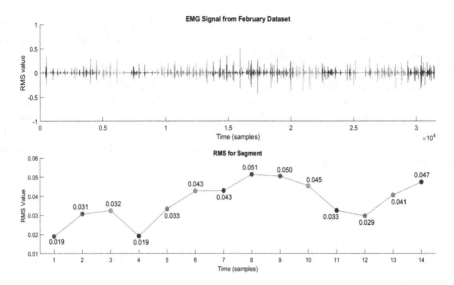

Fig. 8. Analysis on a trial of the collision avoidance task of one elderly subject. The signal has been divided into fourteen uniform windows (Top row). Purple windows correspond to the collision avoidance events. Bottom row reports the trend of the energy values in the different segments. (Color figure online)

- When **young adults** were involved, it has been noticed in general an increase of the signal power in correspondence to the collision avoiding events. Most of the time this growth seems due to a strong muscle activation, probably caused by the effort of the subject to accelerate and safely passing the obstacle, as can be seen in Fig. 7, where one trial of a young subject has been reported. Only in few cases (**5 out of 42**), participants decided to stop in front of the obstacle. Finally in only one case the subject seemed to be able to pass the obstacle without changing its speed. These results are coherent with what visually observed during the experiment, in which the young adults seemed less inclined to stop than the elderly.
- Analyzing the power of the EMG signals for the **elderly**, in many cases (**29 out of 37**), it has been observed a decreasing in signal power during collision avoiding events, (see Fig. 8 as an example for one elderly subject). These decreases are related to the observed evidence that, as already mentioned above, the participants decelerated or even stopped, waiting for the pendulum to pass, thus leading to a reduction in the electrical discharge produced by the muscle.

This analysis proves that elderly people are used to keep a more careful behavior than the young ones.

The different behaviour of young adults and elderly in facing up the obstacle has been also investigated using a statistical similarity analysis based on the Kruskal Wallis test, which has been already described in the previous chapter.

This test has been used to compare the two populations (young and elderly) evaluating the energy changes (increase or decrease in percentage) before and after crossing the collision avoidance zone. Two main analyses have been considered:

1. The analysis of the energy variation while crossing, which describes the change in the muscle energy between the free walk phase before the crossing and the crossing itself. The percentage of this variation has been calculated by the formula:

$$\frac{RMS_{crossing} - RMS_{beforeCrossing}}{RMS_{beforeCrossing}} \qquad (2)$$

The segment corresponding to the crossing ($RMS_{crossing}$) and the segment before it ($RMS_{beforeCrossing}$) are considered in this calculation.

2. The analysis of the energy variation after the crossing, which instead represents the change of muscle energy between the crossing and the free walk phase which follows it. The percentage of this variation has been calculated by the formula:

$$\frac{RMS_{afterCrossing} - RMS_{crossing}}{RMS_{crossing}} \qquad (3)$$

In this case, the two segments involved were the segment after the crossing ($RMS_{crossing}$) and the one relating to the crossing itself ($RMS_{beforeCrossing}$).

For both the two formulas, a positive percentage corresponds to an energy increment. On the other hand, a negative percentage refers to a decrease in energy. From these data the following analyses have been performed:

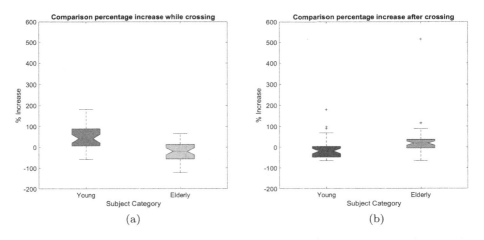

(a)   (b)

Fig. 9. Boxplots concerning the percentage increase of muscle energy detected in the two population analyzed (young adults and elderly) due to the crossing (Fig. 9a) and after that (Fig. 9b). A positive value corresponds to an increase in muscular energy, while a negative percentage represents a decrease in the energy value.

- **Energy variation while crossing**: the Kruskal Wallis test has been used to compare the two populations (young adults and elderly). A p-value lower than 0.001 has been obtained, thus the two distributions of energy variations are different. Moreover, as reported in the boxplot of Fig. 9a, in case of the elderly, the energy in general decreases, while in the case of young adults it increases, in agreement with what already described above, regarding the different behaviour between young adults and elderly.
- **Energy variation after crossing**: In this case, the elderly tend to increase their speed once passed the obstacle, unlike the young adults that tend to decelerate to come back to their previous speed. This different behaviour is once more visible from the comparison of the two populations applying the Kruskal Wallis test. Even in this case, in fact, the test generates a p-value very low (p-value < 0.001). The different values detected for the two populations are visible in Fig. 9b.

A final observation regards the differences between the signals of the two channels. The EMG signals acquired from the tibial muscle appeared in general more affected by noise that the ones recorded from the medial gastrocnemius muscle. Sometimes these artifacts negatively affected the power detected on the signals considered. For this reason the analysis presented in this section has been carried out considering only data collected from the first channel.

5   Conclusions

The analysis reported in this paper is part of an extensive study where physiological signals are adopted to assess walkability, especially in case of elderly. These studies are based on both *in-vitro* (i.e. in a controlled laboratory environment) and *in-vivo* (i.e. in a real uncontrolled scenario) experiments. In particular, the results obtained with the analysis of the EMG during different walking conditions confirm that physiological responses can give significant hints in studying pedestrian behaviour and their reactions and confidence within different environments. Moreover, this analysis permits to underline the different behaviour of the elderly with respect to young adults. In particular, the two population groups would need a more specific and in-depth analysis to create ad-hoc environments able to meet their needs. The results here reached, can be useful in different analysis, for instance, they may be used to better understand the age-related behaviour of subjects in real-world stressful urban environments like, for example, busy street or uncomfortable and crowded sidewalks. Besides, the novel methods of signal processing introduced in this paper (like, for example, the use of the periodogram to identify the walking speed) may be used in future works to analyse people gait in different situations or to predict the behaviour or subjects' status on the basis of their physiological responses. In future work the analysis on GSR and PPG as well as on inertial data will be performed and merged with the analysis on EMG data. There are, indeed, different works, in the state of art, that proves the goodness of these others signals in the research area of gait analysis. In particular, promising results have been reached using Inertial Motion Units (IMUs) [8,14] and the combination of them and the EMG signals [19]. In addiction, further experiments will be performed to collect more data that will permit classification of the tasks, based both on traditional machine learning techniques as well as deep learning approaches. In particular, the use of Neural Networks like the Long Short Term Memory LSTM, looks very promising [14] especially in distinguishing age-related differences in walking [8]. With respect to this topic, our near-future work will be mainly related to adopt pre-trained networks, fed with properly adapted data. For instance, converting monodimensional physiological signals into 2-D time-frequency data will permit to consider well-known CNNs.

Acknowledgment. This research is partially supported by Fondazione Cariplo, for the project LONGEVICITY - Social Inclusion for the Elderly through Walkability (Ref. 2017-0938) and by the Japan Society for the Promotion of Science (Ref. L19513). We want to give our thanks to Kenichiro Shimura and Daichi Yanagisawa, for their supporting work during the experimentation.

References

1. Bandini, S., Gasparini, F.: Towards affective walkability for healthy ageing in the future of the cities. In: Proceedings of the 5th Workshop on Artificial Intelligence for Ambient Assisted Living, AIxIA 2019, vol. 2559. CEUR-WS (2020)
2. U.S. Census Bureau: 2017 National Population Projections Datasets (2017)
3. Can, Y.S., Arnrich, B., Ersoy, C.: Stress detection in daily life scenarios using smart phones and wearable sensors: a survey. J. Biomed. Inform. **92**, 103139 (2019)
4. Donoho, D.L., Johnstone, J.M.: Ideal spatial adaptation by wavelet shrinkage. Biometrika **81**(3), 425–455 (1994)
5. Gaglione, F., Cottrill, C., Gargiulo, C.: Urban services, pedestrian networks and behaviors to measure elderly accessibility. Transp. Res. Part D: Transp. Environ. **90**, 102687 (2021)
6. Halaki, M., Ginn, K.: Normalization of EMG signals: to normalize or not to normalize and what to normalize to. In: Computational Intelligence in Electromyography Analysis-A Perspective on Current Applications and Future Challenges, pp. 175–194 (2012)
7. Hoeger, W.W., Bond, L., Ransdell, L., Shimon, J.M., Merugu, S.: One-mile step count at walking and running speeds. ACSM's Health Fitness J. **12**(1), 14–19 (2008)
8. Hu, B., Dixon, P., Jacobs, J., Dennerlein, J., Schiffman, J.: Machine learning algorithms based on signals from a single wearable inertial sensor can detect surface-and age-related differences in walking. J. Biomech. **71**, 37–42 (2018)
9. Ji, T., Pachi, A.: Frequency and velocity of people walking. Struct. Eng. **84**(3), 36–40 (2005)
10. Kim, H.: Wearable sensor data-driven walkability assessment for elderly people. Sustainability **12**(10), 4041 (2020)
11. King, A.C., et al.: Employing participatory citizen science methods to promote age-friendly environments worldwide. Int. J. Environ. Res. Public Health **17**(5), 1541 (2020)

12. Le, T.P.L., Leung, A., Kavalchuk, I., Nguyen, H.N.: Age-proofing a traffic saturated metropolis-evaluating the influences on walking behaviour in older adults in Ho Chi Minh City. Travel Behav. Soc. **23**, 1–12 (2021)
13. Lee, G., Choi, B., Jebelli, H., Ahn, C.R., Lee, S.: Wearable biosensor and collective sensing-based approach for detecting older adults' environmental barriers. J. Comput. Civ. Eng. **34**(2), 04020002 (2020)
14. Moon, S., et al.: Classification of Parkinson's disease and essential tremor based on balance and gait characteristics from wearable motion sensors via machine learning techniques: a data-driven approach. J. NeuroEng. Rehabil. **17**(1), 1–8 (2020)
15. Phinyomark, A., Limsakul, C., Phukpattaranont, P.: A novel feature extraction for robust EMG pattern recognition. arXiv preprint arXiv:0912.3973 (2009)
16. Wei, G., Tian, F., Tang, G., Wang, C.: A wavelet-based method to predict muscle forces from surface electromyography signals in weightlifting. J. Bionic Eng. **9**(1), 48–58 (2012)
17. Wren, M.A., et al.: Projections of demand for healthcare in Ireland, 2015–2030: first report from the Hippocrates model. ESRI Research Series Number 67 October 2017 (2017)
18. Yetisen, A.K., Martinez-Hurtado, J.L., Ünal, B., Khademhosseini, A., Butt, H.: Wearables in medicine. Adv. Mater. **30**(33), 1706910 (2018)
19. Zhang, X., Tang, X., Zhu, X., Gao, X., Chen, X., Chen, X.: A regression-based framework for quantitative assessment of muscle spasticity using combined EMG and inertial data from wearable sensors. Front. Neurosci. **13**, 398 (2019)

Discussion Papers

It's the End of the Gold Standard as We Know It
Leveraging Non-aggregated Data for Better Evaluation and Explanation of Subjective Tasks

Valerio Basile[(✉)]

University of Turin, Corso Svizzera 185, Turin, Italy
`valerio.basile@unito.it`

Abstract. Supervised machine learning, in particular in Natural Language Processing, is based on the creation of high-quality gold standard datasets for training and benchmarking. The de-facto standard annotation methodologies work well for traditionally relevant tasks in Computational Linguistics. However, critical issues are surfacing when applying old techniques to the study of highly subjective phenomena such as irony and sarcasm, or abusive and offensive language. This paper calls for a paradigm shift, away from monolithic, majority-aggregated gold standards, and towards an inclusive framework that preserves the personal opinions and culturally-driven perspectives of the annotators. New training sets and supervised machine learning techniques will have to be adapted in order to create fair, inclusive, and ultimately more informed models of subjective semantic and pragmatic phenomena. The arguments are backed by a synthetic experiment showing the lack of correlation between the difficulty of an annotation task, its degree of subjectivity, and the quality of the predictions of a supervised classifier trained on the resulting data. A further experiment on real data highlights the beneficial impact of the proposed methodologies in terms of explainability of perspective-aware hate speech detection.

Keywords: Linguistic annotation · Subjectivity · Inclusive machine learning

1 Introduction

Much of modern Natural Language Processing (NLP) and other areas of Artificial Intelligence (AI) are based on some form of supervised learning. In the past decades, models like Hidden Markov Models, Support Vector Machines, Convolutional and Recurrent Neural Networks, and more recently Transformers had represented the state of the art in many NLP tasks. However different the architectures may be, the common basis of supervised statistical models is data produced by humans by some process of *annotation*.

Linguistic annotation has always been a staple of the creation of language resources, which are employed as training material for supervised models as well

M. Baldoni and S. Bandini (Eds.): AIxIA 2020, LNAI 12414, pp. 441–453, 2021.
https://doi.org/10.1007/978-3-030-77091-4_26

as for benchmarking and to compare the performance of systems. The annotation for a language resource is a pretty standardized process. The techniques involved in the process come from the linguistic tradition and have been incorporated into the toolkit of the modern computational linguist. Such techniques include annotation by multiple subjects, measures of inter-annotator agreement, harmonization, aggregation by majority, and so on.

In parallel to the evolution of more and more technologically advanced statistical models, the focus of the attention of the NLP community has also shifted from more "low level" linguistic phenomena such as part-of-speech tagging and syntactic parsing, to more and more "high level"[1] tasks depending on extra-contextual cues and world knowledge. Seen from another angle, in recent years the attention has grown towards more and more **subjective** tasks such as sentiment analysis, irony detection, up to highly subjective tasks such as hate speech detection.

In this paper, I will highlight the main issues that arise when applying traditional language annotation methodologies to highly subjective phenomena. Starting with a brief reminder on the basic principles of standard annotation procedures, I will show how a paradigm shift is needed in order to fully model complex, multi-perspective language phenomena. I will then propose new directions to follow in order to foster the development of a new generation of inclusive supervised models, presenting the results of a simulated experiment, as well as evidence from recent literature, to support the claims.

2   A Quick Primer on Linguistic Annotation

To prepare the ground, let us introduce the basic principles of the process of manual annotating linguistic data. The main components of an annotation task are the following:

- A set of **instances** to annotate. These can be sentences, documents, words (in or out of context), or other linguistically meaningful units.
- A target **phenomenon**, described in detail by means of guidelines and examples.
- An annotation **scheme**, defining the possible values for the phenomenon to annotate, and additional rules, where applicable.
- A group of **annotators**, selected on the basis of expertise, availability, or a mix of the two.

The annotation process is an iterative process, where each **annotator** expresses their judgment about the target **phenomenon** on one **instance** at a time, in the modalities defined by the annotation **scheme**. The possible values may be categorical variables, real numbers, integers on a scale, and so on.

---

[1] The metaphor refers to the ideal spectrum often used in linguistics, where phenomena of natural language are organized on a scale roughly covering, in order: morphology, syntax, semantics, pragmatics.

The annotation is usually carried out by either experts and the crowd. Experts are a broad category comprising people considered competent on the phenomenon that is being annotated. However, this category has grown to include people that are not necessarily experts in certain phenomena by academic standards, but rather they present characteristics deemed relevant to a specific annotation, such as, for instance, victims of hate speech, or activists for social rights, in abusive language annotations [12]. Finally, experts are often simply the authors of the work involving the annotation, their associates, students, or friends. That is, expert annotation is often times a matter of availability of human resources to perform the annotation task.

Since the annotation of language data is notoriously costly, in the last decade scholars have turned more and more to crowdsourcing platforms, like Amazon Mechanical Turk[2] or Appen[3]. Through these online platforms, a large number of annotators are available for a reasonable price.[4] The trade-off, when using these services, is a lesser control on the identity of the annotators, although some filters based on geography and skill can be imposed. Moreover, as the number of annotators grows, the set of instances to annotate is divided among them unpredictably, and the participation of each individual to the annotation task is typically uneven. As a result, with crowdsourcing, the question-answer matrix is sparse, while it is in general complete with expert annotation.

Once a sufficient number of annotations on a sufficient number of instances is collected, they are compiled into a *gold standard* dataset that represents the truth against which comparing future predictions on the same set of instances, much like the gold standard in financial terms it gets its name from[5]. The most straightforward procedure to compile a gold standard from a set of annotations is to apply some form of instance-wise aggregation, such as by majority vote: for each instance, the choice indicated by the relative majority of the annotators is selected as the true value for the gold standard. Depending on a series of factors including the number of annotators, this phase can be more or less complicated, e.g., involving strategies to break the ties, or compute averages in the case of the annotation of numeric values on a scale. Sometimes, extra effort is put into resolving the disagreement. This is done by thoroughly discussing each disagreed-upon instance, going back to the annotation guidelines, or having an additional annotator make their judgment independently, or any combination of these methods. This phase takes the name of *harmonization*.

Quantitative measures of inter-annotator agreement are computed to track how much the annotators gave similar answers to the same questions. Among the most popular ones we find percent agreement (the ratio of the number of universally agreed-upon instances over the total number of instances), Cohen's Kappa (a metric that takes into account the probability of agreeing by chance), Fleiss' Kappa (a generalization of Cohen's Kappa to an arbitrary number of

---

[2] https://www.mturk.com/.
[3] https://appen.com/.
[4] Whether this price is fair has been debated for some years now [7].
[5] https://en.wikipedia.org/wiki/Gold_standard.

annotators), and Krippendorff's Alpha (a further generalization applicable to incomplete question-answer matrices). One of the purposes of computing inter-rater agreement is to provide a quantitative measure of how hard the task is for the human annotator. As such, the inter-annotator agreement is also interpreted as related to the upper bound of measurable computer performance on the same task. The inter-annotator agreement is typically computed before harmoniza-tion, sometimes both before and after, in order to measure the efficacy of the harmonization itself.

Lately, techniques from the Content Analysis community are being more and more integrated into the annotation process for machine learning purposes. Among these, it is not unusual that a small sample of instances are annotated by all the available annotators and the inter-annotator agreement metrics are computed on this set. The small sample is often called *test set*, which should not be confused with the meaning of the same term in machine learning lingo (a set of instances used to test the performance of a model. After the small sample is annotated, if the computed agreement is found satisfactory (e.g., above a predetermined threshold), the annotation continues by splitting the rest of the dataset among the annotators, who proceed independently from one another. While this methodology is capable of producing large amount of annotated data in shorter time, which is important especially in the era of deep learning, it does not solve the other issues which I raise in the rest of this paper.

3   The Annotation of Highly Subjective Phenomena

In this article, I am referring to a "subjective" task in the sense of a linguistic task for which the human judgment is inherently influenced by factors pertaining to the judges themselves, rather than the linguistic phenomenon. In contrast, human judgment on an "objective" task depends uniquely on the object to be judged. As a corollary, different judgments on an objective task should ideally always coincide, barring negligible amounts of measurement noise, while the same does not apply to subjective tasks.

One of the aims of this paper is to stimulate the discussion on the subjectivity of NLP tasks, how it affects their evaluation, and, ultimately, the development of systems capable of solving them. On an ideal scale from total objectivity to total subjectivity, traditional tasks in Computational Linguistics such as part-of-speech tagging sit towards the former end. During a POS-tag annotation, incon-sistencies can be found among the annotations coming from different judges. However, these are typically caused by a different interpretation of the rules, or genuine mistakes, rather than actual, heartfelt disagreement or divergence of opinions. On the contrary, while annotating a highly subjective tasks such as offensive language, different people could find different expressions offensive to very different extent. I argue that in such cases, **all the opinions** of the annotators **are correct**.

Proposition 1. *Disagreeing annotations that comes from diverging opinions should be equally considered in the construction of a gold standard dataset.*

Unfortunately, traditional annotation methodologies do not leave space to implement such proposition. The reason is that language annotation operates under the unwritten postulate that *there is exactly one truth*, i.e., the correct annotation towards which human judgments converge. Multiple annotations and aggregation by majority are the main tools to facilitate this convergence. However, **in the subjective task scenario, the one-truth assumption does not hold** anymore.

In standard linguistic annotation, agreement metrics are used to measure the difficulty of a task and the common understanding of the annotation guidelines by the annotators. Applied to a subjective task, agreement metrics inevitably capture divergence of opinions as well, mixing the signals into a single quantitative measure that therefore loses its meaning to a certain extent. To be fair, issues with current agreement metrics have been highlighted in recent literature [10]. Alternative metrics have been proposed that take disagreement into account [4], and frameworks to leverage the informative content of annotator disagreement have been implemented [3,11]. Some approaches address issues with the annotation methodology by tackling annotator reliability [8]. Perhaps the work that is most in line with the position expressed in the present paper is [9], which shows by statistical tests how "harmonization sometimes harms", and propose to use a weighting scheme based on individual annotations to improve the evaluation of NLP models for subjective tasks. In a recent paper, we propose a stronger version of such idea, in order to account for all the perspectives of a set of annotators, extracting the automatically and weighting them equally [2].

To address the issues described so far, we argue for two positions, complementary to each other. The first is a position **against the release of aggregated datasets** for benchmarking AI (and NLP in particular) models. The second is a position **for a new evaluation paradigm** for highly subjective NLP tasks, that takes multiple perspectives into account. These positions are detailed in the next sections.

4   The Power of Non-aggregated Data

In our own previous work, we have shown how leveraging the divergence of opinions of the human annotators of particularly subjective tasks can lead to an improvement of the quality of the annotated dataset for training purposes [1]. In that work, we defined a quantitative index to measure the *polarization* of the judgments on single instances as a distinct concept from inter-annotator agreement. Specifically, we employed the polarization index to filter out instances from hate speech detection benchmark datasets that showed a high degree of polarization, and give more weight to the less polarizing instances. The training set resulting from this transformation was found to induce a better model for the hate speech detection task, indicating that indeed the high subjectivity of the phenomenon tends to confuse the supervised classifier.

In a subsequent work [2], we took this approach one step further, by training separate classifiers to model different, automatically extracted perspectives of the annotators on the same instances. We trained an "inclusive" classifier that takes into account all of the extracted opinions, including the ones expressed by a minority of the annotators. Such inclusive classifier proved to work better than all the others in the highly subjective task of hate speech detection.

The common denominator of these works is that these approaches need access to the *non-aggregated* annotated data, i.e., every single annotation on the instances of the training dataset. The lesson learned is that the fine-grained information contained in the non-aggregated, complete annotation is extremely valuable in order to model different perspectives on a linguistic phenomenon, with particular importance towards subjective phenomena. Therefore, I put forward a call to action for every NLP researcher and developer of language resources:

Proposition 2. *Manually annotated language resources should always be published along with all their single annotations.*

5   Perspective-Aware Evaluation

The problem of modeling the personal point of view of the annotators is only partially solved by the approach presented so far. While a perspective-aware model can fare well on a standard benchmark, if the test set is constructed by means of aggregation (e.g., by majority voting on each instance) the evaluation will not be fair with respect to the multiple perspectives. In other words, a system capable of encoding multiple perspectives (by leveraging the information in a non-aggregated dataset) is difficult to evaluate if such perspectives are not represented also in the testing benchmark. The model would still be forced to produce one single label (or any other kind of single output) in order to match it with the gold standard test set. On the other hand, a benchmark where test sets are themselves in a non-aggregated state would enable a complete and fair evaluation with respect to all the perspective encoded in such test data. I therefore propose to radically change the way we test NLP systems, by taking into account the diverging opinions of the annotators throughout the entire evaluation pipeline:

Proposition 3. *Predictive models for subjective phenomena should be evaluated using non-aggregated benchmarks.*

The problem remains open of what kind of evaluation metrics one can use to carry out such perspective-aware evaluation. In the next section, I present an experiment with synthetic data, and showcase one possible methodology of evaluation, showing how it is effective, to a certain extent, at separating the quantitative measurement of the difficulty of a NLP task from its subjectivity.

6   An Experiment with Synthetic Data

In this section, an experiment is shown to further drive the points argued in the paper so far. The experiment is a simulation on synthetic data, presented in an attempt to exemplify the main arguments of this proposal with no additional real-world noise, rather than to show the practical effectiveness of a method implementing those principles.

The simulation involves an annotation task, with 10 annotators and 1,000 instances. The task is a binary classification, whereas the annotators are asked to mark each instance as either 0 or 1 (or true/false, black/white, or any other binary distinction). Each instance is encoded as a series of 100 binary features. The annotators have a "background", i.e., they are equally split into two groups.

Two parameters are set that influence the annotation, namely difficulty and subjectivity. A higher difficulty means that an annotators has a high chance of labeling an instance with the wrong label. Subjectivity is more subtle and interplays with the annotators' background. For each instance, there is a chance (depending on the value of the subjectivity parameter) to be a "subjective" instance. If that is the case, the label will depend on the background of the annotator, unless a wrong annotation is given because of the difficulty of the task.

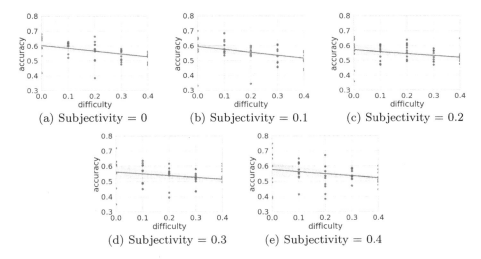

Fig. 1. Correlation between difficulty of the annotation task and the accuracy of a classifier trained on the resulting aggregated dataset in a cross-validation experiment.

Finally, the features are computed to correlate with the annotations, with 20% random noise artificially injected. The expected accuracy of a cross-validation experiment on this dataset, with zero difficulty and zero subjectivity in the annotation process, is around 80%.

The simulation is run ten times for each combination of the values of the two parameters in the range 0–0.4 in 0.1 steps, each run producing a full set of annotations, and a gold standard aggregated by majority voting. Each of these datasets is used in a 10-fold cross-validation supervised learning experiment, to

448   V. Basile

assess the quality of the annotation in a standard machine learning scenario. The classifier is a deep multi-layer perceptron with two 10-node hidden layers and a single output node. Nodes at the hidden and output level are equipped with a sigmoid activation function. For the purposes of this experiment, variation in the size of the network, activation function (e.g., sigmoid vs. linear), and hyperparameters were not critical, in that they did not change the conclusions in any significant way. The result of the cross-validation is a single figure for accuracy. We plot it, repeated for ten runs for each value of the hyperparameter space (difficulty and subjectivity of the annotation task) in multi-plots in Fig. 1.

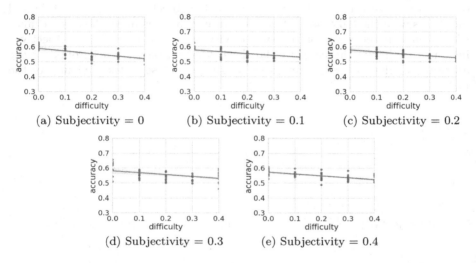

Fig. 2. Correlation between difficulty of the annotation task and the average accuracy scores of a set of classifiers trained on datasets representing individual annotations.

The plots show the expected negative correlation between accuracy and difficulty. It is not surprising that a difficult task will produce a dataset that is less informative to a supervised model, resulting in worse performance in cross validation. However, comparing the plots across increasing values for subjectivity, the correlation becomes less accentuated. The more a task is subjective, the less the evaluation is correlated with its difficulty alone. This is an indication that subjectivity and difficulty are indeed different phenomena, while standard evaluation methodology measures their respective signals at the same time.

The same experimental setting can also be used to test whether another evaluation framework is feasible, where aggregated data are avoided altogether. Here, the experiment is run exactly like in the previous iteration, except that separate classifiers are trained on each column of non-aggregated labels individually, and tested accordingly. The final accuracy score is simply the arithmetic mean of the ten annotator-specific accuracy scores. The results of this second experiment are shown in Fig. 2.

These plots, compared to the previous set, show an interesting pattern. The negative correlation between difficulty and accuracy is much clearer when the evaluation is done on non-aggregated data, as shown by the much narrower intervals where points lie on the y-axes. This is to be interpreted as evidence that indeed all the opinions from the annotators matter, not only in principle, but also towards a more fair evaluation for classifiers of subjective phenomena.

The evaluation methodology introduced in this section is straightforward when applied to "complete" annotated datasets, ones where every annotator annotated every instance. With some extra work, it can be adapted to the crowd-sourcing case—see the annotator-instance matrix transformation in the next section. The case of "parallel" annotation, where only a small set of instances are annotated by the entire set of available annotators, remains problematic for this kind of evaluation, although the difficulty/subjectivity distinction leads to think that such annotation procedure may be unfit for the annotation of subjective phenomena altogether.

7 Perspective-Aware Models and Impact on Explainability[6]

In the previous section, I have presented a simulated experiment to better drive the points made throughout this position paper. Here I present a further experiment, this time conducted on real data, with the aim of proving some of the potential benefits of adopting an anti-aggregation stance. In particular, I present a methodology that leverages the extra information provided by single annotations to create a perspective-aware supervised classifier, that is able to refrain from making a decision when an instance of a particular phenomenon is too subjective to personal interpretation. In such cases, the classifier does not output a value, but instead it provides examples showing how people with different perspectives would interpret that specific instance.

The method builds on [2], who defined an algorithm to automatically separate a set of human annotators in groups according to their perspective. Here I extended the method to cover the presence of "holes" in the annotation-instance matrix due, e.g., to crowdsourcing, and to work with multiclass problems rather than binary classification. Given a set of instances I, a set of labels L, and a set of annotators H, the annotation matrix is defined as $A = H \times I$, where the generic $A_{i,j} \in L \cap \{\lambda\}$ is the label given by the annotator i to the instance j (λ denotes the absence of annotation). From A we derive the matrix M such that: M is $|H| \times (|I| \cdot |L|)$, and

$$
M_{i,k \cdot |L| + w} = \begin{cases} 1 & if\ A_{i,j} = w \\ 0 & if\ A_{i,j} = \lambda \\ -1 & otherwise \end{cases}
$$

---

[6] A warning to the reader: this section contains strong language, in particular toward the end, merely employed for the sake of the exposition of experimental results.

where $1 \leq w \leq |L|$. The rows of A of length m are therefore converted into concatenations of m n-uples, with n equal to the number of possible labels. To make an example, a row vector representing the annotations of one annotator, e.g., $\{1, 3, 2, \lambda, ...\}$ with 3 possible labels $(1, 2, 3)$, is transformed into a row vector where for each original annotation there will be 3 values. Such values are 1 or -1 in correspondence of an instance actually annotated, and 0 in correspondence of empty annotations: $\{1, -1, -1, -1, -1, 1, -1, 1, -1, 0, 0, 0, ...\}$.

Given this vector representation of the annotators based on their annotation, we can compute a similarity metric between pairs of annotators simply by (the opposite of) cosine distance. Such metric is employed in a straightforward clustering algorithm such as K-means in order to obtain a partition of the original set of annotators into a fixed number of subsets, according to the similarity of their annotation, i.e., annotators that tend to give the same answer to the same questions will be clustered together. Note however that also annotators who answered to disjoint sets of questions can still be clustered together, e.g., if they are both similar to a third annotator.

I employed this method to automatically partition the annotators of a well-studied corpus of English tweets annotated with hate speech by crowdsourcing [5]. More precisely, each of the 24,786 instances is annotated with a label out of three possibilities: `hate`, `offensive`, and `neither`, by exactly three annotators. The dataset is randomly divided into 80% for training and 20% for testing. After clustering the annotators into two groups with the method described earlier, two additional training sets are created, by aggregating the annotations of each of the two annotator groups with a majority voting strategy. Since the number of annotations per instance is limited (3), in some cases there is not enough information to aggregate the annotations of an instance, e.g., if there are two discording annotations, or if there are none. In such cases, the gap is filled with the annotation from the original aggregated training set. The aim of this step is that of creating two parallel training sets encoding two different perspectives on the same phenomenon (hate speech) on the same data.

The training sets are used to train two perspective-aware supervised models for hate speech detection: models that encode not only knowledge about the phenomenon of hate speech in natural language, but also the particular perspective of each group of annotators as resulting from the automatically partitioning. The model is based on the Transformer neural network BERT [6], equipped with a standard language model of English (`uncased_L-12_H-768_A-12`) and trained for 10 epochs with a learning rate of 10^{-6} and a batch size of 128, implemented with the *keras-bert* Python library[7].

Running the trained models on the test set, the resulting predictions differ for about 7.2% of the instances. Focusing on the strong disagreement, that is, when one model predicts `hate` and the other predicts `neither`, the disagreement amounts to 15 instances in one direction and 86 in the other direction. Upon manual inspection, I found at least one strong signal in these two sets of instances. In one set, there are several occurrences of slurs typically used by

---

[7] https://github.com/CyberZHG/keras-bert.

black American speakers, including words like *cracker, honkies*, and *coon*. The other set, on the other hand, contains derogatory expressions that suggest their provenance as white Americans, such as *redneck, beaner, illegal aliens*, or *monkey*.

Obviously, this result should be interpreted carefully, since although the manual inspection was supported by generous native English speakers with diverse ethnicity and cultural background, it lacks a certain degree of systematicity and a significant statistical sample, and it is conducted only on English language from Twitter. Nevertheless, This experiment suggests that indeed a computational methodology for supervised learning that leverages fine-grained information at the individual annotation level is capable of modeling multiple perspectives.

This architecture can easily be adapted to support some kind of explanation by means of examples. It is possible to design a straightforward ensemble model that aggregates the predictions of any number of perspective-aware models, in a way similar to the "inclusive ensemble" of Akhtar et al. [2]. This new ensemble model, however, will not provide a label when the sub-models disagree, and instead outputs an explanation of the form: "this instance could be considered A by someone who would consider x_1, x_2, ... as A, B by someone who would consider y_1, y_2, ... as B, ..." and so on, where the A and B of the example are labels and x_i and y_j are instances selected among those where different subsets of annotators disagree.

8 Conclusion

In this paper, I argued for a paradigm shift regarding how language resources are created, published, and incorporated into experimental pipelines for benchmarking. I have shown how the methodology for manual annotation generally employed to create language resources, which comes from the linguistic tradition, suffers from a new set of issues when it is applied to NLP tasks that are becoming more prominent in recent times, focusing in particular on the problem of subjective tasks.

Following the development of recent literature, I formulated two recommendations, in an effort to stir the discussion about what I consider critical problems to solve for the next generation of NLP systems, and the future of a perspective-aware AI. To further drive the point across, I proposed an experiment with simulated data, to highlight *in vitro* what is the impact of my proposal on real world evaluation procedures.

To be fair, the international Natural Language Processing Community is starting to be sensitive to these ideas. An example is the shared task 12 organized at SemEval 2021 on Learning with Disagreements[8], where six datasets are proposed to the participants in their non-aggregated form.

As a conclusive remark, the thoughts expressed in this paper are, in a way, a formalization of a series of reflections coming from the author's experience and, to a great extent, feedback from and discussion with a number of scholars sensitive to the issues I raised here. As such, I believe the AI community is already

---

[8] https://sites.google.com/view/semeval2021-task12/home.

mature to accept the next step towards perspective-aware models and to recognize that more than one truth is possible when perception plays an important role in language-mediated communication. This work represents therefore just one possible way to implement such change.[9]

Acknowledgments. The author would like to express his gratitude to the anonymous reviewers of AIxIA, whose comments greatly contributed to improving this work for the final version. The author would also like to thank Thomas Davidson and his colleagues, for kindly and promptly provide the non-aggregated version of their corpus. This work is partially funded by the project "Be Positive!" (under the 2019 "Google.org Impact Challenge on Safety" call).[10]

References

1. Akhtar, S., Basile, V., Patti, V.: A new measure of polarization in the annotation of hate speech. In: Alviano, M., Greco, G., Scarcello, F. (eds.) AI*IA 2019. LNCS (LNAI), vol. 11946, pp. 588–603. Springer, Cham (2019). https://doi.org/10.1007/978-3-030-35166-3_41
2. Akhtar, S., Basile, V., Patti, V.: Modeling annotator perspective and polarized opinions to improve hate speech detection. In: Proceedings of the AAAI Conference on Human Computation and Crowdsourcing, vol. 8, no. 1, pp. 151–154, October 2020. https://ojs.aaai.org/index.php/HCOMP/article/view/7473
3. Aroyo, L., Welty, C.: Truth is a lie: crowd truth and the seven myths of human annotation. AI Mag. **36**(1), 15–24 (2015)
4. Checco, A., Roitero, K., Maddalena, E., Mizzaro, S., Demartini, G.: Let's agree to disagree: fixing agreement measures for crowdsourcing. In: Proceedings of the Fifth AAAI Conference on Human Computation and Crowdsourcing, HCOMP 2017, 23–26 October 2017, Québec City, Québec, Canada, pp. 11–20. AAAI Press (2017)
5. Davidson, T., Warmsley, D., Macy, M., Weber, I.: Automated hate speech detection and the problem of offensive language. In: Proceedings of the 11th International AAAI Conference on Web and Social Media, ICWSM 2017, pp. 512–515 (2017)
6. Devlin, J., Chang, M.W., Lee, K., Toutanova, K.: BERT: pre-training of deep bidirectional transformers for language understanding. In: Proceedings of the 2019 Conference of the North American Chapter of the Association for Computational Linguistics: Human Language Technologies, vol. 1 (Long and Short Papers), Minneapolis, MN, pp. 4171–4186. Association for Computational Linguistics (2019). https://doi.org/10.18653/v1/N19-1423. https://www.aclweb.org/anthology/N19-1423
7. Felstiner, A.: Working the crowd: employment and labor law in the crowdsourcing industry. Berkeley J. Employ. Lab. Law **32**, 143 (2011)
8. Hovy, D., Berg-Kirkpatrick, T., Vaswani, A., Hovy, E.: Learning whom to trust with MACE. In: Proceedings of the 2013 Conference of the North American

---

[9] The ideas presented in this position paper are also collected and organized around the online initiative **The Non-aggregation Manifesto**: https://valeriobasile.github.io/manifesto/.

[10] https://impactchallenge.withgoogle.com/safety2019.

Chapter of the Association for Computational Linguistics: Human Language Technologies, Atlanta, Georgia, pp. 1120–1130. Association for Computational Linguistics (2013). https://www.aclweb.org/anthology/N13-1132

9. Klenner, M., Göhring, A., Amsler, M.: Harmonization sometimes harms. In: Ebling, S., Tuggener, D., Hürlimann, M., Cieliebak, M., Volk, M. (eds.) Proceedings of the 5th Swiss Text Analytics Conference and the 16th Conference on Natural Language Processing, SwissText/KONVENS 2020, Zurich, Switzerland, 23–25 June 2020 [Online Only]. CEUR Workshop Proceedings, vol. 2624. CEUR-WS.org (2020). http://ceur-ws.org/Vol-2624/paper10.pdf

10. Powers, D.M.W.: The problem with kappa. In: Proceedings of the 13th Conference of the European Chapter of the Association for Computational Linguistics, Avignon, France, pp. 345–355. Association for Computational Linguistics, April 2012. https://www.aclweb.org/anthology/E12-1035

11. Uma, A., Fornaciari, T., Hovy, D., Paun, S., Plank, B., Poesio, M.: A case for soft loss functions. In: Proceedings of the AAAI Conference on Human Computation and Crowdsourcing, vol. 8, no. 1, pp. 173–177, October 2020. https://ojs.aaai.org/index.php/HCOMP/article/view/7478

12. Waseem, Z.: Are you a racist or am I seeing things? Annotator influence on hate speech detection on Twitter. In: Proceedings of the First Workshop on NLP and Computational Social Science, Austin, Texas, pp. 138–142. Association for Computational Linguistics, November 2016. https://doi.org/10.18653/v1/W16-5618. https://www.aclweb.org/anthology/W16-5618

Popularize Artificial Intelligence-"Pietro Torasso" Award

Shared Intelligence for User-Supervised Robots: From User's Commands to Robot's Actions

Gloria Beraldo[1,2]([✉]) [iD], Luca Tonin[1] [iD], and Emanuele Menegatti[1] [iD]

[1] Department of Information Engineering, University of Padova, Padua, Italy
{gloria.beraldo,luca.tonin,emg}@dei.unipd.it
[2] Institute of Cognitive Sciences and Technologies (ISTC), National Research
Council, ISTC-CNR, Rome, Italy

Abstract. This paper introduces a novel form of cooperation between
the humans and user-supervised robots that we name *shared intelligence*.
The fundamental principle at the base of *shared intelligence* is that the
user's commands are equally processed with the robot's perception in
order to create a successful interaction. We investigate a first *shared
intelligence* system to mentally teleoperate a mobile robot via brain-
machine interface. The preliminary results promote the introduction of
shared intelligence to augment the human-robot interaction without pre-
fixing specific constraints (environment-dependent) thanks to the coupling between the human and the robot.

Keywords: Neurorobotics · Brain-machine interface · Telerobotics
and teleoperation · Behavior-based systems

1 Introduction

Thanks to the continuous advancements in robotics and machine learning areas,
it has been possible to develop intelligent robots with increasing abilities. These
robots are considered intelligent because they abstract the biological intelligence
through the canonical paradigm *"plan, then sense-act"*. Hence, the robotic intelligence consists of four main functions: *reaction* to stimuli, *recognition* of symbols, *deliberation* and the *interaction* with the environment and the others. In
particular, in this paper we focus on the *interactive functionality* and we introduce the *shared intelligence* referring to a form of cooperation between the human
and robot that share a common goal [1]. This research can have an impact on
many human-in-the-loop applications where the user is actively involved in determining the actions performed by the robot such as in the case of robot-assisted
surgery, remote space exploration, assistive devices, and telepresence robots.
In all these scenarios, the user interacts with the robot by sending commands
through a particular interface. However, the main idea underlying the *shared
intelligence* provides that the robot is not passive during the human-robot interaction. On the contrary, the robot is able to lead the humans by interpreting

© Springer Nature Switzerland AG 2021
M. Baldoni and S. Bandini (Eds.): AIxIA 2020, LNAI 12414, pp. 457–465, 2021.
https://doi.org/10.1007/978-3-030-77091-4_27

their intentions and evaluating the inputs received according to the context. The robot contributes to the decision-making process by questioning the user's commands on the base of the information acquired through its sensors (e.g., laser rangefinder, camera) and with the possibility of taking the control over the human in case of emergency situations. It is worth highlighting that the user always supervises the robot and can interact at any time. This means that the user adjusts the next robot's action by delivering new commands if undesired robot's behaviors occur.

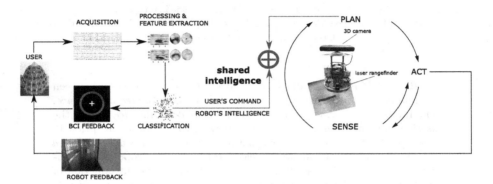

Fig. 1. *Shared intelligence* for controlling mobile robots via brain-computer interface. The user is required to perform a mental task to deliver new commands to the robot. The user's intention to interact with the robot is directly decoded from the acquired brain signals according to a subject-specific classifier. The decoded BCI commands are equally fused with the perception's of an intelligent robot. The robot is involved in the canonical *plan-sense-act* paradigm and contextualises the received user's commands in according to the context.

In this work, we address *shared intelligence* to the robot's teleoperation through an uncertain communication interface (see Fig. 1). Specifically, the user interacts via brain-computer interface (BCI) an interface that provides an alternative interaction channel that does not depend on the brain's normal output pathways of peripheral nerves and muscles [2,3]. Because of the non-muscular nature, BCIs is mainly introduced to allow people suffering from severe motor impairments to interact with external devices (e.g., interface, prosthesis, exoskeletons, wheelchairs, telepresence robots) directly according to their brain activity [2–8]. However, BCIs are characterised by low bit rate and noise due to the instability of the neurophysiological signals; which means the user can only interact with the robot by delivering sparse discrete commands. Moreover, the user's commands might be wrongly decoded in the BCIs system introducing the send of unintentional user's commands. These limitations motivate our hypothesis to rely on the robot's low-level intelligence to achieve an effective control thanks to the cooperation between the human and the robot.

2   Methods

In this section, we present the key characteristics of our *shared intelligence* approach to teleoperate a telepresence robot via BCI.

2.1   Brain-Computer Interface System to Detect the User's Commands

In our system, we exploit a 2-class BCI based on the sensorimotor rhythm (SMR) paradigm to detect the user's commands. In the neurorobotics field, SMR BCIs have been widely used to control external devices (e.g., in [7,9–11]) because contrariwise to exogenous approaches [8,12,13] enable users interact without the need of any external stimulation. The user learns how to voluntary modulate his/her brain rhythms. Specifically, to interact with the robot, the user is requested to perform specific mental tasks, namely the imagination of the movements of both hands and both feet, that activate the well-localized regions in the motor cortex area. We acquire the EEG signals from 16 channels placed on the sensorimotor cortex area (i.e., Fz, FC3, FC1, FCz, FC2, FC4, C3, C1, Cz, C2, C4, CP3, CP1, CPz, CP2, CP4 according to the international 10–20 system layout) and recorded through the g.USBamp, Guger Technologies, Graz, Austria amplifier 512 Hz sampling rate. The acquired signals are then processed to detect specific patterns associated with the mental tasks and correlated to the user cognitive states. In SMR BCI, according to the neuroscience findings, these patterns correspond to amplitude increment and decrement of the rhythmic activity during the imagination of both hands and feet movements that are called event-related desynchronization (ERD) and synchronization (ERS) [14]. We exploit ERD and ERS events to create subject-specific models (i.e., calibrated on the single person) using supervised machine learning techniques that optimize the discrimination between the two classes. In detail, we process the EEG signals by applying a laplacian spatial filter. The power spectral density (PSD) of the signal was continuously computed via Welch's algorithm in the μ (8–12 Hz) and β (16–30 Hz) bands activated during the required motor task. The selected features (channel-frequency pairs) are the basis of a Gaussian classifier trained with a set of samples acquired during a calibration phase to decode the user's intention of performing the specific mental tasks. Indeed, with this purpose, before controlling the robot, the user is instructed to perform the same two mental tasks but in specific windows of time in order to acquire the training dataset and the related labels of the two classes (see Fig. 2).

Finally, the posterior probabilities in output from the classifier are communicated to the user through a visual feedback (see Fig. 2). Furthermore, by comparing the posterior probabilities with respect to a threshold, new discrete commands are identified and given in input to the *shared intelligence* system, that congruently translates them into movements of the robot.

BMI feedback

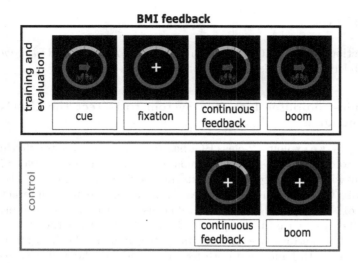

Fig. 2. SMR BCI feedback. In the *BCI calibration* and *evaluation* runs the users were instructed with a visual signal (cue) about the mental task to perform. During the *control*, no cue is provided because participants decided by their own the command to deliver. In both cases, they received a continuous feedback representing their mental state. When a new command was detected the wheel reached the extremity in the corresponding direction (boom).

2.2 The Fusion of the User's Commands with the Robot's Intelligence

In this work, we propose a first simple version of a *shared intelligence* system designed for the robot's navigation based on the information about obstacles, the natural direction of motion, the preferable ranges of the robot's step during the navigation, the user's inputs. Since the robot's intelligence depends on different factors influencing the robot's motion, we design the system in a modular and flexible way. Each factor determines a sort of behavioral guideline for the robot (i.e., the robot should move far from obstacles, the robot should reach the target, the robot should implement the user's commands if possible), that we represent in the form of *policy*. The choice of the *policy* is motivated by the fact that in *shared intelligence* system, the robot's behavior is not pre-coded according to procedures, but it results from the interaction between the user and the robot as agent au pair [1]. In other words, in contrast to other approaches in the literature, the robot does not select a single behavior implemented separately, namely we do not include any arbiter or mechanism that selects a single policy as in the "winner-takes-all" approach. On the contrary, all these *policies* equally contribute in determining the robot's motion and the final robot's behavior results only from their fusion.

Specifically, in our system, each *policy* is a function that encodes the situation around the robot according to the behavioral guideline conditioning the

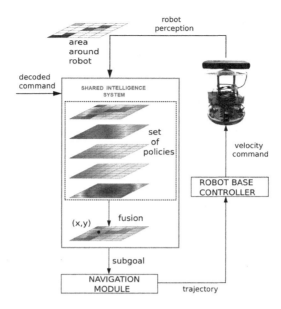

Fig. 3. An illustrative scheme of the proposed *shared intelligence*. The system is based on a set of *policies*. Each *policy* is associated with a factor that can influence the robot's motion: for instance in the case of the robot's teleoperation via BCI, we consider the distribution of obstacles, the user's inputs, the preferable direction of motion, the preferable ranges of the robot's step during the navigation. The *policies* compute probability grids in the local area of the robot. All the *policies* simultaneously determine the next robot's movements. Specifically, the fusion of all the *policies* outputs a position in the environment representing a target for the robot. Finally, the navigation module plans the best trajectory for the robot to move towards that position.

navigation and the related input (e.g., the distribution of obstacles, the user's commands, the current robot direction, the minimum/maximum admitted step). Let $\mathcal{A}$ be the area around the robot by size s (in our case $s = m \times n$) and I_t the input of the policy at time t, in our system, a *policy* p is defined as follows:

$$p : \{I_t \to [0,1]^s \mid \forall x, y \in \mathcal{A}, \ p(x,y) \in [0,1]\} \qquad (1)$$

namely a *policy* outputs a probability grid in the neighborhood of the robot starting from the given input and it assigns a value between 0 and 1 for each position of the probability grid. Then, all the probabilities grids returned by N *policies* are fused together

$$\Sigma_p = \prod_{k=1}^{N} p_k \qquad (2)$$

and the result is then normalised to obtain again a probability grid Σ_p', calculated on each position (x,y) in the area around the robot $\mathcal{A}$. From the fused probability grid Σ_p', we select one position (the most probable), called *subgoal*, that represents a temporary target for the robot. Finally, to avoid falling into local minima, a navigation module based on a motion planning optimizes the robot's motion towards that position determining the best trajectory for the robot, while the robot base controller is in charge to determine the velocity commands according to the trajectory calculated. An illustrative representation of the key principle underlying our system is shown in Fig. 3.

It is worth highlighting that in our system, we only exploit the information from the robot's perception in its local area in order to extract the distribution of obstacles. Indeed, the strength point of our approach is the independence from specific information of the environment (e.g., global map) nor procedures strictly linked to the kind of the landmarks inside (the passage through doors or the alignment with respect to the corridor) in contrast to [11,15–17]. This aspect simplifies its reproducibility in different everyday life contexts because any pre-setup phase is not required.

3   Experiments

The presented *shared intelligence* system was evaluated with 13 healthy subjects without any previous experience in a pilot experiment. All the participants signed a written informed consent in accordance with the principles of the Declaration of Helsinki. The study was approved by the Cantonal Committee of Vaud (Switzerland) for ethics in human research under the protocol number PB_2017-00295.

The participants were asked to mentally navigate the robot in an unmodified office environment with seven target positions in Fig. 4.

We compare the performance of the proposed *shared intelligence* system driven by brain-computer interface with respect to a manual teleoperation based on joystick that is taken as reference as best teleoperation interface (since the user can control any single movements of the robot at any time). Each participant repeats the navigation task via BCI four times. An illustrative video is available at https://aixia2020.di.unito.it/awards/premio-pietro-torasso.

4   Preliminary Results

The first tests were successful in demonstrating the flexibility of the presented *shared intelligence* in the typical circumstances of the indoor environment as in our setup (see Fig. 4): the free space area, door passage, corridor, crossroad, areas covered by obstacles. We evaluate the performance using the following quantitative metrics that are typically considered in the case of BCI driven mobile robots: the number of commands, the spent time and the path length in the two conditions (BCI vs. joystick). The results are shown in Fig. 5. We perform multiple two-sided Wilcoxon rank-sum to verify statistically significant difference between the two modalities.

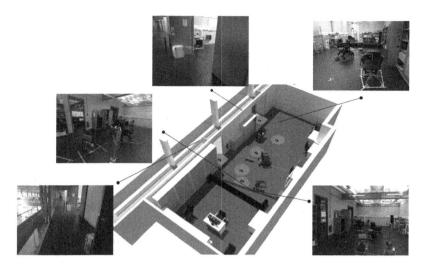

Fig. 4. Experimental setup. The participants control the robot in the represented unmodified environment with the seven target positions (in green). (Color figure online)

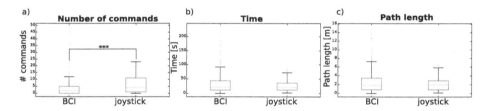

Fig. 5. Boxplots of the performances in terms of number of commands delivered (a), time spent (b) and path length per modality. The box edges signify the 75th (top) and 25(th) (bottom) percentiles and the horizontal line represents the median of the corresponding distribution. The whiskers extend to the largest and smallest non outlier values. Outliers are marked with red crosses. Statistically significant differences are shown with two-sided Wilcoxon rank-sum (***): $p < 0.001$. (Color figure online)

As expected, BCI users delivered a significant reduced number of commands with respect to the teleoperation through a joystick (BCI = 3.99 ± 6.66, joystick = 6.01 ± 6.25, p = 0.00093). The average time with BCI is slightly longer and the path length higher than joystick but any statistical difference was found (respectively BCI = 34.89 ± 38.74 s, joystick = 26.50 ± 22.3198 s for the time and BCI = 2.74 ± 2.94 m, joystick = 2.20 ± 1.86 m in terms of path length).

Finally, participants gave qualitative feedback through a questionnaire based on a 5-point Likert-type scale. They reported that the robot helped them to reach the target positions (3.38 ± 0.86) and the robot's behavior was expected through the BCI (3.153 ± 0.98).

5   Conclusion

In this paper, we introduce the concept of *shared intelligence* to combine the user's commands with the robot's perception to navigate a mobile robot via BCI. Despite the flourishing of many brain-actuated robots during the three decades of BCI research, in most of the state-of-the-art studies the interaction between human and robot is still rudimentary in which the robot implements the user's commands passively [11,18]. Herein, on the contrary, we promote the applications of artificial intelligence algorithms and robotic knowledge to create an effective and ecological system that enhances the role of the robot. In particular, we simultaneously fuse the different information relevant in the robot's navigation into a modular system based on *policies* that put on the same level the robot's inputs according to its perception with the user's commands. Since our system does not make any assumption about the kind of environment but rather it is based on the cooperation between the user and the robot, our approach might facilitate the transfer of BCI driven robots outside the laboratory. The preliminary results suggest performance comparable with a joystick teleoperation despite the limitation interaction derived from BCI. Furthermore, participants confirmed that the system supported them and that the robot's behavior was in line with their intentions. This aspect is a major point in developing user-centric solutions and in guaranteeing user's acceptance.

Acknowledgments. This research was partially supported by Fondazione Ing. Aldo Gini, by MIUR (Italian Minister for Education) under the initiative "Departments of Excellence" (Law 232/2016) and by SI Robotics project (Invecchiamento sano e attivo attraverso SocIal ROBOTICS).

References

1. Beraldo, G., Tonin, L., Cesta, A., Menegatti, E.: Shared-control, shared-autonomy and shared-intelligence in assistive technologies: three forms of cooperation between user and robot. In: Proceedings of the IEEE International Workshop Adaptive Behavioral Models of Robotic Systems Based on Brain-Inspired AI Cognitive Architectures (APHRODITE). IEEE (2020)
2. Wolpaw, J.R., Birbaumer, N., McFarland, D.J., Pfurtscheller, G., Vaughan, T.M.: Brain-computer interfaces for communication and control. Clin. Neurophysiol. **113**, 767–791 (2002)
3. Millán, J.R., et al.: Combining brain-computer interfaces and assistive technologies: state-of-the-art and challenges. Front. Neurosci. **4**, 161 (2010)
4. Chaudhary, U., Birbaumer, N., Ramos-Murguialday, A.: Brain-computer interfaces for communication and rehabilitation. Nat. Rev. Neurol. **12**(9), 513–525 (2016)
5. Lee, K., Liu, D., Perroud, L., Chavarriaga, R., Millán, J.R.: A brain-controlled exoskeleton with cascaded event-related desynchronization classifiers. Robot. Auton. Syst. **90**, 15–23 (2017)
6. He, J., Eguren, D., Azorín, J.M., Grossman, R.G., Luu, T.P.: Brain–machine interfaces for controlling lower-limb powered robotic systems. J. Neural Eng. **15**(2), 021004 (2018)

7. Tonin, L., Leeb, R., Tavella, M., Perdikis, S., Millán, J.R.: The role of shared-control in BCI-based telepresence. In: 2010 IEEE International Conference on Systems, Man and Cybernetics, pp. 1462–1466. IEEE (2010)
8. Iturrate, I., Antelis, J.M., Kubler, A., Minguez, J.: A noninvasive brain-actuated wheelchair based on a P300 neurophysiological protocol and automated navigation. IEEE Trans. Rob. **25**(3), 614–627 (2009)
9. Philips, J., et al.: Adaptive shared control of a brain-actuated simulated wheelchair. In: 2007 IEEE 10th International Conference on Rehabilitation Robotics, pp. 408–414. IEEE (2007)
10. Millán, J.R.: Brain-controlled robots. Technical report (2008)
11. Beraldo, G., Antonello, M., Cimolato, A., Menegatti, E., Tonin, L.: Brain-computer interface meets ROS: a robotic approach to mentally drive telepresence robots. In: Proceedings of the 2018 IEEE International Conference on Robotics and Automation (ICRA), pp. 1–6. IEEE (2018)
12. Lopes, A.C., Pires, G., Vaz, L., Nunes, U.: Wheelchair navigation assisted by human-machine shared-control and a P300-based brain computer interface. In: Proceedings of the 2011 IEEE/RSJ International Conference on Intelligent Robots and Systems, pp. 2438–2444. IEEE (2011)
13. Beraldo, G., Tortora, S., Menegatti, E.: Towards a brain-robot interface for children. In: 2019 IEEE International Conference on Systems, Man and Cybernetics (SMC), pp. 2799–2805. IEEE (2019)
14. Pfurtscheller, G.: EEG event-related desynchronization (ERD) and synchronization (ERS). Electroencephalogr. Clin. Neurophysiol. **1**(103), 26 (1997)
15. Levine, S.P., Bell, D.A., Jaros, L.A., Simpson, R.C., Koren, Y., Borenstein, J.: The NavChair assistive wheelchair navigation system. IEEE Trans. Rehabil. Eng. **7**(4), 443–451 (1999)
16. Simpson, R.C., Levine, S.P., Bell, D.A., Jaros, L.A., Koren, Y., Borenstein, J.: NavChair: an assistive wheelchair navigation system with automatic adaptation. In: Mittal, V.O., Yanco, H.A., Aronis, J., Simpson, R. (eds.) Assistive Technology and Artificial Intelligence. LNCS, vol. 1458, pp. 235–255. Springer, Heidelberg (1998). https://doi.org/10.1007/BFb0055982
17. Beraldo, G., Termine, E., Menegatti, E.: Shared-autonomy navigation for mobile robots driven by a door detection module. In: Alviano, M., Greco, G., Scarcello, F. (eds.) AI*IA 2019. LNCS (LNAI), vol. 11946, pp. 511–527. Springer, Cham (2019). https://doi.org/10.1007/978-3-030-35166-3_36
18. Beraldo, G., et al.: ROS-Health: an open-source framework for neurorobotics. In: Proceedings of the 2018 IEEE International Conference on Simulation, Modeling, and Programming for Autonomous Robots (SIMPAR), pp. 174–179. IEEE (2018)

Author Index

Printed in the United States
by Baker & Taylor Publisher Services